RAMBLES AND RECOLLECTIONS
OF AN
INDIAN OFFICIAL

By

W. H. SLEEMAN

Double 9
BOOKS

Rambles And Recollections Of An Indian Official

by **W. H. Sleeman**

ISBN: 978-93-59392-71-4

Published by

DOUBLE 9 BOOKS

2/13-B, Ansari Road, Daryaganj
New Delhi – 110002
info@double9books.com
www.double9books.com
Tel. 011-40042856

ABOUT THE AUTHOR

Sir William Henry Sleeman (1788-1856) was a British soldier and administrator in British India, known for his efforts to suppress the criminal organization known as Thuggee. He also made significant contributions to paleontology and discovered the holotype specimen of the sauropod dinosaur Titanosaurus indicus in Jabalpur in 1828. Sleeman joined the Bengal Army in 1809 and later served in the Nepal War. In 1820, he was selected for civil employment and held various administrative positions in different districts of India. He displayed linguistic prowess, becoming fluent in Hindi-Urdu and familiar with other regional languages. In addition to his administrative work, Sleeman made important contributions to the fields of paleontology and ethnography. He discovered dinosaur fossils in India and documented his findings. He also wrote about cases of wild children raised by wolves, which inspired Rudyard Kipling's character Mowgli in "The Jungle Book." Sleeman's most significant achievement was his work in suppressing the Thuggee criminal society. He captured key members and obtained evidence that led to the execution or transportation Thugs. Sleeman served as Resident at Gwalior and Lucknow, surviving multiple assassination attempts. He died at sea in 1856 and was buried near Ceylon. His legacy includes his contributions to Indian administration, paleontology, and the suppression of Thuggee.

CONTENTS

EDITOR'S PREFACE (1893)[1]

The *Rambles and Recollections of an Indian Official,* always a costly book, has been scarce and difficult to procure for many years past. Among the crowd of books descriptive of Indian scenery, manners, and customs, the sterling merits of Sir William Sleeman's work have secured it pre-eminence, and kept it in constant demand, notwithstanding the lapse of nearly fifty years since its publication. The high reputation of this work does not rest upon its strictly literary qualities. The author was a busy man, immersed all his life in the practical affairs of administration, and too full of his subject to be careful of strict correctness of style or minute accuracy of expression. Yet, so great is the intrinsic value of his observations, and so attractive are the sincerity and sympathy with which he discusses a vast range of topics, that the reader refuses to be offended by slight formal defects in expression or arrangement, and willingly yields to the charm of the author's genial and unstudied conversation.

It would be difficult to name any other book so full of instruction for the young Anglo-Indian administrator. When this work was published in 1844 the author had had thirty-five years' varied experience of Indian life, and had accumulated and assimilated an immense store of knowledge concerning the history, manners, and modes of thought of the complex population of India. He thoroughly understood the peculiarities of the various native races, and the characteristics which distinguish them from the nations of Europe; while his sympathetic insight into Indian life had not orientalized him, nor had it ever for one moment caused him to forget his position and heritage as an Englishman. This attitude of sane and discriminating sympathy is the right attitude for the Englishman in India.

To enumerate the topics on which wise and profitable observations will be found in this book would be superfluous. The wine is good, and needs no bush. So much may be said that the book is one to interest that nondescript person, the general reader in Europe or America, as well as the Anglo-Indian official. Besides good advice and sound teaching on matters of policy and administration, it contains many charming, though inartificial, descriptions of scenery and customs, many ingenious speculations, and some capital stories. The ethnologist, the antiquary, the geologist, the soldier, and the missionary will all find in it something to suit their several tastes.

In this edition the numerous misprints of the original edition have been all, and, for the most part, silently corrected. The extremely erratic punctuation has been freely modified, and the spelling of Indian words and names has been systematized. Two paragraphs, misplaced in the original edition at the end of Chapter 48 of Volume I, have been removed, and inserted in their proper place at the end of Chapter 47; and the supplementary notes printed at the end of the second volume of the original edition have been brought up to the positions which they were intended to occupy. Chapters 37 to 46 of the first volume, describing the contest for empire between the sons of Shāh Jahān, are in substance only a free version of Bernier's work entitled, *The Late Revolution of the Empire of the Great Mogol*. These chapters have not been reprinted because the history of that revolution can now be read much more satisfactorily in Mr. Constable's edition of Bernier's Travels. Except as above stated, the text of the present edition of the *Rambles and Recollections* is a faithful reprint of the Author's text.

In the spelling of names and other words of Oriental languages the Editor has 'endeavoured to strike a mean between popular usage and academic precision, preferring to incur the charge of looseness to that of pedantry'. Diacritical marks intended to distinguish between the various sibilants, dentals, nasals, and so forth, of the Arabic and Sanskrit alphabets, have been purposely omitted. Long vowels are marked by the sign ¯. Except in a few familiar words, such as Nerbudda and Hindoo, which are spelled in the traditional manner, vowels are to be pronounced as in Italian, or as in the following English examples, namely: *ā*, as in 'call'; *e*, or *ē*, as the medial vowel in 'cake'; *i*, as in 'kill'; *ī*, as the medial vowels in 'keel'; *u*, as in 'full'; *ū*, as the medial vowels in 'fool'; *o*, or *ō*, as in 'bone'; *ai*, or *āi*, as 'eye' or 'aye', respectively; and *au*, as the medial sound in 'fowl'. Short *a*, with stress, is pronounced like the *u* in 'but'; and if without stress, as an indistinct vowel, like the *A* in 'America'.

The Editor's notes, being designed merely to explain and illustrate the text, so as to render the book fully intelligible and helpful to readers of the present day, have been compressed into the narrowest possible limits. Even India changes, and observations and criticisms which were perfectly true when recorded can no longer be safely applied without explanation to the India of to-day. The Author's few notes are distinguished by his initials.

A copious analytical index has been compiled. The bibliography is as complete as careful inquiry could make it, but it is possible that some anonymous papers by the Author, published in periodicals, may have escaped notice.

The memoir of Sir William Sleeman is based on the slight sketch prefixed to the *Journey through the Kingdom of Oude*, supplemented by much additional matter derived from his published works and correspondence, as well as from his unpublished letters and other papers generously communicated by his only son, Captain Henry Sleeman. Ample materials exist for a full account of Sir William Sleeman's noble and interesting life, which well deserves to be recorded in detail; but the necessary limitations of these volumes preclude the Editor from making free use of the biographical matter at his command.

The reproduction of the twenty-four coloured plates of varying merit which enrich the original edition has not been considered desirable. The map shows clearly the route taken by the Author in the journey the description of which is the leading theme of the book.

Notes:

1. Certain small changes have been made.

MEMOIR OF MAJ.-GEN. SIR WILLIAM HENRY SLEEMAN, K.C.B.

The Sleemans, an ancient Cornish family, for several generations owned the estate of Pool Park in the parish of Saint Judy, in the county of Cornwall. Captain Philip Sleeman, who married Mary Spry, a member of a distinguished family in the same county, was stationed at Stratton, in Cornwall, on August 8, 1788, when his son William Henry was born.

In 1809, at the age of twenty-one, William Henry Sleeman was nominated, through the good offices of Lord De Dunstanville, to an Infantry Cadetship in the Bengal army. On the 24th of March, in the same year, he sailed from Gravesend in the ship Devonshire, and, having touched at Madeira and the Cape, reached India towards the close of the year. He arrived at the cantonment of Dinapore, near Patna, on the 20th December, and on Christmas Day began his military career as a cadet. He at once applied himself with exemplary diligence to the study of the Arabic and Persian languages, and of the religions and customs of India. Passing in due course through the ordinary early stages of military life, he was promoted to the rank of ensign on the 23rd September, 1810, and to that of lieutenant on the 16th December, 1814.

Lieutenant Sleeman served in the war with Nepal, which began in 1814 and terminated in 1816. During the campaign he narrowly escaped death from a violent epidemic fever, which nearly destroyed his regiment. 'Three hundred of my own regiment,' he observes, 'consisting of about seven hundred, were obliged to be sent to their homes on sick leave. The greater number of those who remained continued to suffer, and a great many died. Of about ten European officers present with my regiment, seven had the fever and five died of it, almost all in a state of delirium. I was myself one of the two who survived, and I was for many days delirious.[1]

The services of Lieutenant Sleeman during the war attracted attention, and accordingly, in 1816, he was selected to report on certain claims to prize-money. The report submitted by him in February, 1817, was accepted as 'able, impartial, and satisfactory'. After the termination of the war he served with his regiment at Allahabad, and in the neighbouring district of Partābgarh, where he laid the foundation of the intimate knowledge of Oudh affairs displayed in his later writings.

In 1820 he was selected for civil employ, and was appointed Junior Assistant to the Agent of the Governor-General, administering the Sāgar and Nerbudda territories. Those territories, which had been annexed from the Marāthās two years previously, are now included in the jurisdiction of the Chief Commissioner of the Central Provinces. In such a recently-conquered country, where the sale of all widows by auction for the benefit of the Treasury, and other strange customs still prevailed, the abilities of an able and zealous young officer had ample scope. Sleeman, after a brief apprenticeship, received, in 1822, the independent civil charge of the District of Narsinghpur, in the Nerbudda valley, and there, for more than two years, 'by far the most laborious of his life', his whole attention was engrossed in preventing and remedying the disorders of his District.

Sleeman, during the time that he was in charge of the Narsinghpur District, had no suspicion that it was a favourite resort of Thugs. A few years later, in or about 1830, he was astounded to learn that a gang of Thugs resided in the village of Kandēlī, not four hundred yards from his court-house, and that the extensive groves of Mandēsar on the Sāgar road, only one stage distant from his head-quarters, concealed one of the greatest *bhīls*, or places of murder, in all India. The arrest of Feringheea, one of the most influential Thug leaders, having given the key to the secret, his disclosures were followed up by Sleeman with consummate skill and untiring assiduity. In the years 1831 and 1832 the reports submitted by him and other officers at last opened the eyes of the superior authorities and forced them to recognize the fact that the murderous organization extended over every part of India. Adequate measures were then taken for the systematic suppression of the evil. 'Thuggee Sleeman' made it the main business of his life to hunt down the criminals and to extirpate their secret society. He recorded his experiences in the series of valuable publications described in the Bibliography. In this brief memoir it is impossible to narrate in detail the thrilling story of the suppression of Thuggee, and I must be content to pass on and give in bare outline the main facts of Sleeman's honourable career.[2]

While at Narsinghpur, Sleeman received on the 24th April, 1824, brevet rank as Captain. In 1825, he was transferred, and on the 23rd September of the following year, was gazetted Captain. In 1826, failure of health compelled him to take leave on medical certificate. In March, 1828, Captain Sleeman assumed civil and executive charge of the Jabalpur (Jubbulpore) District, from which he was transferred to Sāgar in January, 1831. While stationed at Jabalpur, he married, on the 21st June, 1829, Amélie Josephine, the daughter of Count Blondin de Fontenne, a French nobleman, who, at the sacrifice of a considerable property, had managed to escape from the Revolution. A lady informs the editor that she remembers Sleeman's fine house at Jabalpur. It stood in a large walled park, stocked with spotted deer. Both house and park were destroyed when the railway was carried through the site.

Mr. C. Eraser, on return from leave in January, 1832, resumed charge of the revenue and civil duties of the Sāgar district, leaving the magisterial duties to Captain Sleeman, who continued to discharge them till January, 1835. By the Resolution of Government dated 10th January, 1835, Captain Sleeman was directed to fix his head-quarters at Jabalpur, and was appointed General Superintendent of the operations for the Suppression of Thuggee, being relieved from every other charge. In 1835 his health again broke down, and he was obliged to take leave on medical certificate. Accompanied by his wife and little son, he went into camp in November, 1835, and marched through the Jabalpur, Damoh, and Sāgar districts of the Agency, and then through the Native States of Orchhā, Datiyā, and Gwālior, arriving at Agra on the 1st January, 1836. After a brief halt at Agra, he proceeded through the Bharatpur State to Delhi and Meerut, and thence on leave to Simla. During his march from Jabalpur to Meerut he amused himself by keeping the journal which forms the basis of the *Rambles and Recollections of an Indian Official*. The manuscript of this work (except the two supplementary chapters) was completed in 1839, though not given to the world till 1844. On the 1st of February, 1837, in the twenty- eighth year of his service, Sleeman was gazetted Major. During the same year he made a tour in the interior of the Himalayas, which he described at length in an unpublished journal. Later in the year he went down to Calcutta to see his boy started on the voyage home.

In February, 1839, he assumed charge of the office of Commissioner for the Suppression of Thuggee and Dacoity. Up to that date the office of Commissioner for the Suppression of Dacoity had been separate from that of General Superintendent of the measures for the Suppression of Thuggee, arịd had been filled by another officer, Mr. Hugh Eraser, of the Civil Service. During the next two years Sleeman passed much of his time in the North-Western Provinces, now the Agra Province in the United Provinces of Agra and Oudh, making Murādābād his head-quarters, and thoroughly investigating the secret criminal organizations of Upper India.

In 1841 he was offered the coveted and lucrative post of Resident at Lucknow, vacant by the resignation of Colonel Low; but that officer, immediately after his resignation, lost all his savings through the failure of his bankers, and Sleeman, moved by a generous impulse, wrote to Colonel Low, begging him to retain the appointment.

Sleeman was then deputed on special duty to Bundēlkhand to investigate the grave disorders in that province. While at Jhānsī in December, 1842, he narrowly escaped assassination by a dismissed Afghan sepoy, who poured the contents of a blunderbuss into a native officer in attendance.[3]

During the troubles with Sindhia which culminated in the battle of Mahārājpur, fought on the 29th December, 1843, Sleeman, who had become a Lieut.-Colonel, was Resident at Gwālior, and was actually in Sindhia's camp when the battle unexpectedly began. In 1848 the Residency at Lucknow again fell vacant, and Lord Dalhousie, by a letter dated 16th September, offered Sleeman the appointment in the following terms:

The high reputation you have earned, your experience of civil administration, your knowledge of the people, and the qualifications you possess as a public man, have led me to submit your name to the Council of India as an officer to whom I could commit this important charge with entire confidence that its duties would be well performed. I do myself, therefore, the honour of proposing to you to accept the office of Resident at Lucknow, with especial reference to the great changes which, in all probability, will take place. Retaining your superintendency of Thuggee affairs, it will be manifestly necessary that you should be relieved from the duty of the trials of Thugs usually condemned at Lucknow. In the hope that you will not withhold from the Government your services in the capacity I have named, and in the further hope of finding an opportunity of personally making your acquaintance,

I have the honour to be,
Dear Colonel Sleeman,
Very faithfully yours,
DALHOUSIE.[4]

The remainder of Sleeman's official life, from January, 1849, was spent in Oudh, and was chiefly devoted to ceaseless and hopeless endeavours to reform the King's administration and relieve the sufferings of his grievously oppressed subjects. On the 1st of December, 1849, the Resident began his memorable three months' tour through Oudh, so vividly described in the special work devoted to the purpose. The awful revelations of the *Journey through the Kingdom of Oude* largely influenced the Court of Directors and the Imperial Government in forming their decision to annex the kingdom, although that decision was directly opposed to the advice of Sleeman, who consistently advocated reform of the administration, while deprecating annexation. His views are stated with absolute precision in a letter written in 1854 or 1855, and published in *The Times* in November, 1857:

We have no right to annex or confiscate Oude; but we have a right, under the treaty of 1837, to take the management of it, but not to appropriate its revenues to ourselves. We can do this with honour to our Government and benefit to the people. To confiscate would be dishonest and dishonourable. To annex would be to give the people a government almost as bad as their own, if we put our screw upon them (*Journey*, ed. 1858, vol. i, Intro., p. xxi).

The earnest efforts of the Resident to suppress crime and improve the administration of Oudh aroused the bitter resentment of a corrupt court and exposed his life to constant danger. Three deliberate attempts to assassinate him at Lucknow are recorded.

The first, in December, 1851, is described in detail in a letter of Sleeman's dated the 16th of that month, and less fully by General Hervey, in *Some Records of Crime*, vol. ii, p. 479. The Resident's life was saved by a gallant orderly named Tīkarām, who was badly wounded. Inquiry proved that the crime was instigated by the King's moonshee.

The second attempt, on October 9, 1853, is fully narrated in an official letter to the Government of India (Bibliography, No. 15). Its failure may be reasonably ascribed to a special interposition of Providence. The Resident during all the years he had lived at Lucknow had been in the habit of sleeping in an upper chamber approached by a separate private staircase guarded by two sentries. On the night mentioned the sentries were drugged and two men stole up the stairs. They slashed at the bed with their swords, but found it empty, because on that one occasion General Sleeman had slept in another room.

The third attempt was not carried as far, and the exact date is not ascertainable, but the incident is well remembered by the family and occurred between 1853 and 1856. One day the Resident was crossing his study when, for some reason or another, he looked behind a curtain screening a recess. He then saw a man standing there with a large knife in his hand. General Sleeman, who was unarmed, challenged the man as being a Thug. He at once admitted that he was such, and under the spell of a master-spirit allowed himself to be disarmed without resistance. He had been employed at the Residency for some time, unsuspected.

Such personal risks produced no effect on the stout heart of Sleeman, who continued, unshaken and undismayed, his unselfish labours.

In 1854 the long strain of forty-five years' service broke down Sleeman's strong constitution. He tried to regain health by a visit to the hills, but this expedient proved ineffectual, and he was ordered home. On the 10th of

February, 1856, while on his way home on board the Monarch, he died off Ceylon, at the age of sixty-seven, and was buried at sea, just six days after he had been granted the dignity of K.C.B.

Lord Dalhousie's desire to meet his trusted officer was never gratified. The following correspondence between the Governor-General and Sleeman, now published for the first time, is equally creditable to both parties:

BARRACKPORE PARK,
January 9th, 1856.

MY DEAR GENERAL SLEEMAN,

I have heard to-day of your arrival in Calcutta, and have heard at the same time with sincere concern that you are still suffering in health. A desire to disturb you as little as possible induces me to have recourse to my pen, in order to convey to you a communication which I had hoped to be able to make in person. Some time since, when adjusting the details connected with my retirement from the Government of India, I solicited permission to recommend to Her Majesty's gracious consideration the names of some who seemed to me to be worthy of Her Majesty's favour. My request was moderate. I asked only to be allowed to submit the name of one officer from each Presidency. The name which is selected from the Bengal army was your own, and I ventured to express my hope that Her Majesty would be pleased to mark her sense of the long course of able, and honourable, and distinguished service through which you had passed, by conferring upon you the civil cross of a Knight Commander of the Bath. As yet no reply has been received to my letter. But as you have now arrived at the Presidency, I lose no time in making known to you what has been done; in the hope that you will receive it as a proof of the high estimation in which your services and character arc held, as well by myself as by the entire community of India.

I beg to remain,
My dear General,
Very truly yours,
DALHOUSIE.

Major-General Sleeman.

Reply to above. Dated 11th January, 1856.

MY LORD,

I was yesterday evening favoured with your Lordship's most kind and flattering letter of the 9th instant from Barrackpore.

I cannot adequately express how highly honoured I feel by the mention that you have been pleased to make of my services to Her Majesty the Queen, and how much gratified I am by this crowning act of kindness from your Lordship in addition to the many favours I have received at your hands during the last eight years; and whether it may, or may not, be my fate to live long enough to see the honourable rank actually conferred upon me, which you have been so considerate and generous as to ask for me, the letter now received from your Lordship will of itself be deemed by my family as a substantial honour, and it will so preserved, I trust, by my son, with feelings of honest pride, at the thought that his father had merited such a mark of distinction from so eminent a statesman as the Marquis of Dalhousie.

My right hand is so crippled by rheumatism that I am obliged to make use of an amanuensis to write this letter, and my bodily strength is so much reduced, that I cannot hope before embarking for England to pay my personal respects to your Lordship.

Under these unfortunate circumstances, I now beg to take my leave of your Lordship; to offer my unfeigned and anxious wishes for your Lordship's health and happiness, and with every sentiment of respect and gratitude, to subscribe myself,

Your Lordship's most faithful and
Obedient servant,
W. H. SLEEMAN,
Major-General.

To the Most Noble
  The Marquis of Dalhousie, K.T.,
    Governor- General, &c., &c.,
      Calcutta.

Sir William Sleeman was an accomplished Oriental linguist, well versed in Arabic, Persian, and Urdu, and also in possession of a good working knowledge of Latin, Greek, and French. His writings afford many proofs of his keen interest in the sciences of geology, agricultural chemistry, and political economy, and of his intelligent appreciation of the lessons taught by history. Nor was he insensible to the charms of art, especially those of poetry. His favourite authors among the poets seem to have been Shakespeare, Milton, Scott, Wordsworth, and Cowper. His knowledge of the customs and modes of thought of the natives of India, rarely equalled and never surpassed, was more than half the secret of his notable success as an administrator. The greatest achievement of his busy and unselfish life was the suppression of the system of organized murder known as Thuggee, and in the execution of that prolonged and onerous task he displayed the most delicate tact, the keenest sagacity, and the highest power of organization.

His own words are his best epitaph: 'I have gone on quietly,' he writes, '"through evil and through good report", doing, to the best of my ability, the duties which it has pleased the Government of India, from time to time, to confide to me in the manner which appeared to me most conformable to its wishes and its honour, satisfied and grateful for the trust and confidence which enabled me to do so much good for the people, and to secure so much of their attachment and gratitude to their rulers.' [5]

His grandson. Captain J. L. Sleeman, who, when stationed in India from 1903 to 1908, visited the scenes of his grandfather's labours, states that everywhere he found the memory of his respected ancestor revered, and was given the assurance that no Englishman had ever understood the native of India so well, or removed so many oppressive evils as General Sir W. H. Sleeman, and that his memory would endure for ever in the Empire to which he devoted his life's work.

This necessarily meagre account of a life which deserves more ample commemoration may be fitly closed by a few words concerning the relatives and descendants of Sir William Sleeman.

His sister and regular correspondent, to whom he dedicated the *Rambles and Recollections*, was married to Captain Furse, R.N.

His brother's son James came out to India in 1827, joined the 73rd Regiment of the Bengal Army, was selected for employment in the Political Department, and was thus enabled to give valuable aid in the campaign against Thuggee. In due course he was appointed to the office of General Superintendent of the Operations against Thuggee, which had been held by his uncle. He rose to the rank of Colonel, and after a long period of excellent service, lived to enjoy nearly thirty years of honourable retirement. He died at his residence near Ross in 1899 at the age of eighty-one.

In 1831 Sir William's only son, Henry Arthur, was gazetted to the 16th (Queen's) Lancers, and having retired early from the army, with the rank of Captain, died in 1905.

His elder son William Henry died while serving with the Mounted Infantry during the South African War. His younger son, James Lewis, a Captain in the Royal Sussex Regiment, who also saw active service during the war, and was mentioned in dispatches, has a distinguished African and Indian record, and recently received the honorary degree of M.A. from the Belfast University for good work done in establishing the first Officers' Training Corps in Ireland. The family of Captain James Lewis Sleeman consists of two sons and a daughter, namely, John Cuthbert, Richard Brian, and Ursula Mary. Captain Sleeman, as the head of his family, possesses the MSS. &c. of his distinguished grandfather. The two daughters of Sir William who survived their father married respectively Colonel Dunbar and Colonel Brooke.

Notes:

1. *Journey through the Kingdom of Oude*, vol. ii, p. 105.

2. The general reader may consult with advantage Meadows Taylor, *The Confessions of a Thug*, the first edition of which appeared in 1839; and the vivid account by Mark Twain in *More Tramps Abroad*, chapters 49,50.

3. The incident is described in detail in a letter dated December 18, 1842, from Sleeman to his sister Mrs. Furse. Captain J. L. Sleeman has kindly furnished me with a copy of the letter, which is too long for reproduction in this place.

4. This letter is printed in full in the *Journey through the Kingdom of Oude*, pp. xvii-xix.

5. Letter to Lord Hardinge, dated Jhansee, 4th March, 1848, printed in *Journey through the Kingdom of Oude*, vol. i, p. xxvii.

BIBLIOGRAPHY OF THE WRITINGS OF MAJOR-GENERAL SIR W. H. SLEEMAN, K.C.B.

I. – PRINTED

(1.) 1819 Pamphlet.
Letter addressed to Dr. Tytler, of Allahabad, by Lieut. W. H. Sleeman, August 20th, 1819.
Copied from the *Asiatic Mirror* of September the 1st, 1819.
[This letter describes a great pestilence at Lucknow in 1818, and discusses the theory that cholera may be caused by 'eating a certain kind of rice'.]

(2.) Calcutta, 1836, 1 vol. 8vo.
Ramaseeana, or a Vocabulary of the Peculiar Language used by the Thugs, with an Introduction and Appendix descriptive of the Calcutta system pursued by that fraternity, and of the measures which have been adopted by the Supreme Government of India for its suppression.
Calcutta, G. H. Huttmann, Military Orphan Press, 1836.
[No author's name on title-page, but most of the articles are signed by W. H. Sleeman.]
Appendices A to Z, and A.2, contain correspondence and copious details of particular crimes. Total pages (v,+270+515) 790.
A very roughly compiled and coarsely printed collection of valuable documents. [A copy in the Bodleian Library and two copies in the British Museum. One copy in India Office Library.]

(2a.) Philadelphia 1839, 1 vol. 8vo.
The work described as follows in the printed Catalogue of Printed Books in the British Museum appears to be a pirated edition of *Ramaseeana*:

TheThugsorPhansīgarsofIndia:comprisingahistoryoftheriseandprogressofthat extraordinaryfraternityofassassins;andadescriptionofthesystemwhichitpursues,&c. Carey and Hart. Philadelphia, 1839. 8vo.

A Hindustani MS. in the India Office Library seems to be the original of the vocabulary and is valuable as a guide to the spelling of the words.

(3.) (?)1836 or 1837, Pamphlet.
On the Admission of Documentary Evidence.
Extract.
[This reprint is an extract from *Ramaseeana*. The rules relating to the admission of evidence in criminal trials are discussed. 24 pages.]

(4.) 1837, Pamphlet.
Copy of a Letter
which appeared in the *Calcutta Courier* of the 29th March, 1837, under the signature of 'Hirtius', relative to the Intrigues of Jotha Ram.
[This letter deals with the intrigues and disturbances in the Jaipur (Jyepoor) State in 1835, and the murder of Mr. Blake, the Assistant to the Resident. (See post, chap, 67, end.) The reprint is a pamphlet of sixteen pages. At the beginning reference is made to a previous letter by the author on the same subject, which had been inserted in the *Calcutta Courier* in November, 1836.]

(5.) Journal of Asiatic Society of Bengal, vol. vi. (1837), p. 621.
History of the Gurha Mundala Rajas, by Captain W. H. Sleeman.
[An elaborate history of the Gond dynasty of Garhā Mandlā, 'which is believed to be founded principally on the chronicles of the Bājpai family, who were the hereditary prime ministers of the Gond princes.' (*Central Provinces Gazetteer*, 1870, p. 282, note.) The history is, therefore, subject to the doubts which necessarily attach to all Indian family traditions.]

(6.) W. H. Sleeman. *Analysis and Review of the Peculiar Doctrines of the Ricardo or New School of Political Economy.*
8vo, Serampore, 1837.
[A copy is entered in the printed catalogue of the library of the Asiatic Society of Bengal.]

(7.) Calcutta (Serampore), 1839, 8vo.
A REPORT on THE SYSTEM OF MEGPUNNAISM,
or
The Murder of Indigent Parents for their Young Children (who are sold as Slaves) as it prevails in the Delhi Territories, and the Native States of Rajpootana, Ulwar, and Bhurtpore.
By Major W. H. Sleeman.
— —
From the Serampore Press.
1839.
[Thin 8vo, pp. iv and 121.
A very curious and valuable account of a little-known variety of Thuggee, which possibly may still be practised. Copies exist in the British Museum and India Office Libraries, but the Bodleian has not a copy.]

(8.) Calcutta, 1840, 8vo.
REPORT ON THE DEPREDATIONS COMMITTED BY THE THUG
GANGS of UPPER AND CENTRAL INDIA,
From the Cold Season of 1836-7, down to their Gradual
Suppression, under the operation of the measures adopted
against them by the Supreme Government in the year 1839.

By Major Sleeman
Commissioner for the Suppression of Thuggee and Dacoitee.

Calcutta:
G. H. Huttmann, Bengal Military Orphan Press.
1840.
[Thick 8vo, pp. lviii, 549 and xxvi.
The information recorded is similar to that given in the
earlier *Ramaseeana* volume. Pages xxv-lviii, by Captain N.
Lowis, describe River Thuggee. Copies in the British Museum
and India Office, but none in the Bodleian. This is the only
work by Sleeman which has an alphabetical index.]

(9.) Calcutta 1841, 8vo.
On the SPIRIT OF MILITARY DISCIPLINE
in our
NATIVE INDIAN ARMY.

By Major N.[*sic*] H. Sleeman, Bengal Native Infantry.
'Europaeque saccubuit Asia.'
'The misfortune of all history is, that while the motives of a few princes
and leaders in their various projects of ambition are detailed with
accuracy, the motives which crowd their standards with military followers
are totally overlooked.'—*Malthus.*
Calcutta:
Bishop's College Press.

M.DCCC.XLI.

[Thin 8vo. Introduction, pp. i-xiii; On the Spirit of Military Discipline
in the Native Army of India, pp. 1-59; page 60 blank; Invalid Establishment,
pp. 61-84. The text of these two essays is reprinted as chapters 28 and 29
of vol. ii of *Rambles and Recollections* in the original edition, corresponding
to Chapters 21 and 22 of the edition of 1893 and Chapters 76, 77 of this
(1915) edition. Most of the observations in the Introduction are utilized
in various places in that work. The author's remark in the Introduction to
these essays—'They may never be published, but I cannot deny myself the
gratification of printing them'—indicates that, though printed, they were
never published in their separate form. The copy of the separately printed

tract which I have seen is that in the India Office Library. Another is in the British Museum. The pamphlet is not in the Bodleian.]

(10.) 1841 Pamphlet.
MAJOR SLEEMAN
on the
PUBLIC SPIRIT of THE HINDOOS.

From the Transactions of the Agricultural and Horticultural Society, vol. 8. Art. XXII, *Public Spirit among the Hindoo Race as indicated in the flourishing condition of the Jubbulpore District in former times, with a sketch of its present state: also on the great importance of attending to Tree Cultivation and suggestions for extending it. By Major Sleeman, late in charge of the Jubbulpore District.*

[Read at the Meeting of the Society on the 8th September, 1841.]

[This reprint is a pamphlet of eight pages. The text was again reprinted verbatim as Chapter 14 of vol. 2 of the *Rambles and Recollections* in the original edition, corresponding to Chapter 7 of the edition of 1893, and Chapter 62 of this (1915) edition. No contributions by the author of later date than the above to any periodical have been traced. In a letter dated Lucknow, 12th January, 1853 (*Journey*, vol. 2, p. 390) the author says-'I was asked by Dr. Duff, the editor of the *Calcutta Review*, before he went home, to write some articles for that journal to expose the fallacies, and to counteract the influences of this [*scil.* annexationist] school; but I have for many years ceased to contribute to the periodical papers, and have felt bound by my position not to write for them.']

(11.) London, 1844, 2 vols. large 8vo.
RAMBLES AND RECOLLECTIONS OF AN INDIAN OFFICIAL
by
Lieutenant-Colonel W. H. Sleeman, of the Bengal Army.
'The proper study of mankind is man.' — POPE.
In Two Volumes.
London:
J. Hatchard and Son, 187, Piccadilly.
1844.

[Vol. I, pp. v and 478. Frontispiece, in colours, a portrait of 'The late Emperor of Delhi', namely, Akbar II. At end of volume, six full- page coloured plates, numbered 25-30, viz. No. 25, 'Plant'; No. 26, 'Plant'; No. 27, 'Plant'; No. 28, 'Ornament'; No. 29, 'Ornament'; No. 30, 'Ornaments'.

Vol. 2, pp. vii and 459. Frontispiece, in colours, comprising five miniatures; and Plates numbered 1-24, irregularly inserted, and with several misprints in the titles.

The three notes printed at the close of the second volume were brought up to their proper places in the edition of 1893, and are there retained in this (1915) edition. The following paragraph is prefixed to these notes in the original edition: 'In consequence of this work not having had the advantage of the author's superintendence while passing through the press, and of the manuscript having reached England in insulated portions, some errors and omissions have unavoidably taken place, a few of which the following notes are intended to rectify or supply.' The edition of 1844 has been scarce for many years,]

(11a.) Lahore 1888, 2 vols. in one 8vo.
RAMBLES AND RECOLLECTIONS, &o.
(Title as in edition of 1844.)
Republished by A. C, Majumdar.
Lahore:
Printed at the Mufid-i-am Press.
1888.
[Vol. 1, pp. xi and 351. Vol. 2, pp. v and 339. A very roughly executed reprint, containing many misprints. No illustrations. This reprint is seldom met with.]

(11b.) Westminster, 1893, 2 vols. in 8vo.
RAMBLES AND RECOLLECTIONS, &c.
A New Edition, edited by Vincent Arthur Smith, I.C.S.; being vol. 5 of Constable's Oriental Miscellany. The book is now scarce.

(12.) Calcutta, 1849.
REPORT
On
BUDHUK
Alias
BAGREE DECOITS
and other
GANG ROBBERS BY HEREDITARY PROFESSION,
and on
The Measures adopted by the Government of India
for their Suppression.
By Lieut.-Col. W. H. Sleeman, Bengal Army.
Calcutta:
J. C. Sherriff, Bengal Military Orphan Press.
1849.

[Folio, pp. iv and 433. Map. Printed on blue paper. A valuable work. In their Dispatch No. 27, dated 18th September, 1850, the Honourable Court of Directors observe that 'This Report is as important and interesting as that of the same able officer on the Thugs'. Copies exist in the British Museum and India Office Libraries, but there is none in the Bodleian. The work was first prepared for press in 1842 (Journey, vol. 1, p, xxvi).]

(13.) 1852, Plymouth, Pamphlet.
AN ACCOUNT of WOLVES NURTURING CHILDREN IN THEIR DENS. By an Indian Official.
Plymouth:
Jenkin Thomas, Printer,
9, Cornwall Street.
1852.

[Octavo pamphlet. 15 pages. The cases cited are also described in the *Journey through the Kingdom of Oude*, and are discussed in V. Ball, *Jungle Life in India* (De la Rue, 1880). The only copy known to me is that in possession of the author's grandson.]

(14.)Lucknow, 1852.

Sir William Sleeman printed his *Diary of a Journey through Oude* privately at a press in the Residency. He had purchased a small press and type for the purpose of printing it at his own house, so that no one but himself and the compositor might see it. He intended, if he could find time, to give the history of the reigning family in a third volume, which was written, but has never been published. The title is: Diary of a Tour through Oude in December, 1849, and January and February, 1850.

By The Resident
Lieutenant-Colonel W. H. Sleeman.
Printed at Lucknow in a Parlour Press.
1852.

Two vols. large 8vo. with wide margins. Printed well on good paper. Vol. 1 has map of Oude, 305 pp. text, and at end a printed slip of errata. Vol. 2 has 302 pp. text, with a similar slip of errata. The brief Preface contains the following statements:
'I have had the Diary printed at my own expense in a small parlour press which I purchased, with type, for the purpose. . . . The Diary must for the present be considered as an official document, which may be perused, but cannot be published wholly or in part without the sanction of Government previously obtained.' [1]

Eighteen copies of the Diary were so printed and were coarsely bound by a local binder. Of these copies twelve were distributed as follows, one to each person or authority: Government, Calcutta; Court of Directors; Governor-General; Chairman of Court of Directors; Deputy Chairman; brother of author; five children of author, one each (5); Col. Sykes, Director E.I.C. A Memorandum of Errata was put up along with some of the copies distributed. (*Private Correspondence,* Journey, *vol. 2, pp.* 357, 393, *under dates 4 April, 1852, and 12 Jan., 1853.*) The Bodleian copy, purchased in June, 1891, was that belonging to Mrs, (Lady) Sleeman, and bears her signature 'A. J. Sleeman' on the fly-leaf of each volume. The book was handsomely bound in morocco or russia, with gilt edges, by Martin of Calcutta. The British Museum Catalogue does not include a copy of this issue. The India Office Library has a copy of vol. 1 only. Captain J. L. Sleeman has both volumes.

(15.) 1853, Pamphlet.
Reprint of letter No. 34 of 1853 from the author to J, P. Grant, Esq., Officiating Secretary to the Government of India, Foreign Department, Fort William. Dated Lucknow Residency, 12th October, 1853.
[Six pages. Describes another attempt to assassinate the author on the 9th October, 1853. See ante, p. xxvi.]

(16.) London 1858, 2 vols. 8vo.
A Journey through the Kingdom of Oude, in 1849-50, by direction of the Right Hon. the Earl of Dalhousie, Governor-General.
With Private Correspondence relative to the Annexation of Oude to British India, &c.
By Major-General Sir W. H. Sleeman, K.C.B.,
Resident at the Court of Lucknow.

In two Volumes.
London:
Richard Bentley, Publisher in Ordinary to Her Majesty. 1858.

[Small 8vo. Frontispiece of vol. 1 is a Map of the Kingdom of Oude. The contents of vol. 1 are: Title, preface, and contents, pp. i-x; Biographical Sketch of Major-General Sir W. H. Sleeman, K.C.B., pp. xi-xvi; Introduction, pp. xvii-xxii; Private Correspondence preceding the Journey through the Kingdom of Oude, pp. xxiii-lxxx; Diary of a Tour through Oude, chapters i-vi. The contents of vol. 2 are: Title and contents, pp. i-vi; Diary of a Tour through Oude, pp. 1-331; Private Correspondence relating to the Annexation of the Kingdom of Oude to British India, pp. 332-424. The letters printed in this volume were written between 5th Dec., 1849, and 11th Sept., 1854, during and after the Tour. The dates of the letters in the first volume extend from 20th Feb., 1848, to 11th Oct., 1849. The Tour began on 1st Dec., 1849, The book, though rather scarce, is to be found in most of the principal libraries, and may be obtained from time to time.]

II. – UNPUBLISHED MANUSCRIPTS

(1.) 1809.

Two books describing author's voyage to India round the Cape.

(2.) 1837.

Journal of a Trip from Simla to Gurgoohee.

[Referred to in unpublished letters dated 5th and 30th August, 1837.]

(3.) *Circa*1824.

Preliminary Observations and Notes on Mr. Molony's Report on Narsinghpur.

[Referred to in *Central Provinces Gazetteer*, Nāgpur, 2nd ed., 1870, pp. xcix, cii, &c. The papers seem to be preserved in the record room at Narsinghpur.]

(4.) 1841.

History of Byza Bae (Baiza Bāī).

[Not to be published till after author's death. See unpublished *letter dated Jhānsī,* Oct. 22nd, 1841.]

(5.)

History of the Reigning Family of Oude.

[Intended to form a third volume of the *Journey.* See Author's *Letter to Sir James Weir Hogg, Deputy Chairman, India House,* dated Lucknow, 4th April, 1852; printed in *Journey,* vol. 2, p. 358.]

The manuscripts Nos. 1, 2, 4, and 5, and the printed papers Nos. 1, 3, 4, 10, 13, and 15, are in the possession of Captain J, L. Sleeman, Royal Sussex Regiment, grandson of the author. The India Office Library possesses copies of the printed works Nos. 2, 7, 8, 9, 11a, 12, 14 (vol. 1 only) and 16.

Notes:

1. The book was written in 1851, and the Directors' permission to publish was given in December, 1852. (*Journey,* ii, pp. 358, 393, ed. 1858. The Preface to that ed. wrongly indicates December, 1851, as the date of that permission.)

ABBREVIATIONS

A.C.   After Christ.

Ann. Rep.   Annual Report.

A.S. Archaeological Survey.

A.S.R.   Archaeological Survey Reports, by Sir Alexander
               Cunningham and his assistants; 23 vols. 8vo, Simla and
               Calcutta, 1871-87, with General Index (vol. xxiv, 1887) by
               V. A. Smith.

A.S.W.I.   Archaeological Survey Reports, Western India.

Beale.   T. W. Beale, *Oriental Biographical Dictionary*, ed. Keene,
               1894.

C.P.   Central Provinces.

E.& D.   Sir H. M. Elliot and Professor J. Dowson, *The History of India
               as told by its own Historians, Muhammadan Period;* 8 vols. 8vo,
               London, 1867-77.

E.H.I.   V. A. Smith, *Early History of India,* 3rd ed., Oxford, 1914.

Ep. Ind.   Epigraphia Indica, Calcutta.

Fanshawe.   H. C. Fanshawe, *Delhi Past and Present*, Murray, London,
               1902.

H.F.A.   V. A. Smith, *A History of Fine Art in India and Ceylon,* 4to,
               Oxford, 1911.

I.G.   Imperial Gazetteer of India, Oxford, 1907, 1908.

Ind. Ant.   Indian Antiquary, Bombay.

J.A.S.B.   Journal of the Asiatic Society of *Bengal,*Calcutta.

J.R.A.S.   Journal of the Royal Asiatic Society, London.

N.I.N.&   Qu. North-Indian Notes and Queries, Allahabad, 1891-6

N.W.P.   North-Western Provinces.

Z.D.M.G.   Zeitschrift   der   deutschen   morgenländischen
               Gesellschaft, Leipzig.

CHAPTER 1

Annual Fairs held upon the Banks of Sacred Streams in India.

Before setting out on our journey towards the Himālaya we formed once more an agreeable party to visit the Marble Rocks of the Nerbudda at Bherāghāt.[1] It was the end of Kārtik,[2] when the Hindoos hold fairs on all their sacred streams at places consecrated by poetry or tradition as the scene of some divine work or manifestation. These fairs are at once festive and holy; every person who comes enjoying himself as much as he can, and at the same time seeking purification from all past transgressions by bathing and praying in the holy stream, and making laudable resolutions to be better for the future. The ceremonies last five days, and take place at the same time upon all the sacred rivers throughout India; and the greater part of the whole Hindoo population, from the summits of the Himālaya mountains to Cape Comōrin, will, I believe, during these five days, be found congregated at these fairs. In sailing down the Ganges one may pass in the course of a day half a dozen such fairs, each with a multitude equal to the population of a large city, and rendered beautifully picturesque by the magnificence and variety of the tent equipages of the great and wealthy. The preserver of the universe (*Bhagvān*) Vishnu is supposed, on the 26th of Asārh, to descend to the world below (*Pātāl*) to defend Rājā Bali from the attacks of Indra, to stay with him four months, and to come up again on the 26th Kārtik.[3] During his absence almost all kinds of worship and festivities are suspended; and they recommence at these fairs, where people assemble to hail his resurrection.

Our tents were pitched upon a green sward on one bank of a small stream running into the Nerbudda close by, while the multitude occupied the other bank. At night all the tents and booths are illuminated, and the scene is hardly less animated by night than by day; but what strikes a European most is the entire absence of all tumult and disorder at such places. He not only sees no disturbance, but feels assured that there will be none; and leaves his wife and children in the midst of a crowd of a hundred thousand persons all strangers to them, and all speaking a language and following a religion different from theirs, while he goes off the whole day, hunting and shooting in the distant jungles, without the slightest feeling of apprehension for their safety or comfort. It is a singular fact, which I know to be true, that during the great mutiny of our native troops at Barrackpore in 1824, the chief leaders bound themselves by a solemn oath not to suffer any European lady or child to be injured or molested, happen what might to them in the collision with their officers and the Government. My friend Captain Reid, one of the general staff, used to allow his children, five in number, to go into the lines and play with the soldiers of the mutinous regiments up to the very day when the artillery opened upon them; and, of above thirty European ladies then at the station, not one thought of leaving the place till they heard the guns.[4] Mrs. Colonel Faithful, with her daughter and another young lady, who had both just arrived from England, went lately all the way from Calcutta to Lūdiāna on the banks of the Hyphasis, a distance of more than twelve hundred miles, in their palankeens with relays of bearers, and without even a servant to attend them.[5] They were travelling night and day for fourteen days without the slightest apprehension of injury or of insult. Cases of ladies travelling in the same manner by *dāk* (stages) immediately after their arrival from England to all parts of the country occur every day, and I know of no instance of injury or insult sustained by them.[6] Does not this speak volumes for the character of our rule in India? Would men trust their wives and daughters in this manner unprotected among a people that disliked them and their rule? We have not a garrison, or walled cantonments, or fortified position of any kind for our residence from one end of our Eastern empire to the other, save at the three capitals of Calcutta, Madras, and Bombay.[7] We know and feel that the people everywhere look up to and respect us, in spite of all our faults, and we like to let them know and feel that we have confidence in them.

Sir Thomas Munro has justly observed, 'I do not exactly know what is meant by civilizing the people of India. In the theory and practice of good government they may be deficient; but, if a good system of agriculture, if unrivalled manufactures, if the establishment of schools for reading and writing, if the general practice of kindness and hospitality, and, above all, if a scrupulous respect and delicacy towards the female sex are amongst the points that denote a civilized people; then the Hindoos are not inferior in civilization to the people of Europe'.[8]

Bishop Heber writes in the same favourable terms of the Hindoos in the narrative of his journey through India; and where shall we find a mind more capable of judging of the merits and demerits of a people than his?[9]

The concourse of people at this fair was, as usual, immense; but a great many who could not afford to provide tents for the accommodation of their families were driven away before their time by some heavy showers of, to them, unseasonable rains. On this and similar occasions the people bathe in the Nerbudda without the aid of priests, but a number of poor Brahmans attend at these festivals to receive charity, though not to assist at the ceremonies. Those who could afford it gave a trifle to these men as they came out of the sacred stream, but in no case was it demanded, or even solicited with any appearance of importunity, as it commonly is at fairs and holy places on the Ganges. The first day, the people bathe below the rapid over which the river falls after it emerges from its peaceful abode among the marble rocks; on the second day, just above this rapid; and on the third day, two miles further up at the cascade, when the whole body of the limpid stream of the Nerbudda, confined to a narrow channel of only a few yards wide, falls tumultuously down in a beautiful cascade into a deep chasm of marble rocks. This fall of their sacred stream the people call the 'Dhuāndhār', or 'the smoky fall', from the thick vapour which is always seen rising from it in the morning. From below, the river glides quietly and imperceptibly for a mile and a half along a deep, and, according to popular belief, a fathomless channel of from ten to fifty yards wide, with snow-white marble rocks rising perpendicularly on either side from a hundred to a hundred and fifty feet high, and in some parts fearfully overhanging. Suspended in recesses of these white rocks are numerous large black nests of hornets ready to descend upon any unlucky wight who may venture to disturb their repose;[10] and, as the boats of the curious European visitors pass up and down to the sound of music, clouds of wild pigeons rise from each side, and seem sometimes to fill the air above them. Here, according to native legends, repose the Pāndavas, the heroes of their great Homeric poem, the Mahābhārata, whose names they have transferred to the valley of the Nerbudda. Every fantastic appearance of the rocks, caused by those great convulsions of nature which have so much disturbed the crust of the globe, or by the slow and silent working of the, waters, is attributed to the god-like power of those great heroes of Indian romance, and is associated with the recollection of scenes in which they are supposed to have figured. [11]

The strata of the Kaimūr range of sandstone hills, which runs diagonally across the valley of the Nerbudda, are thrown up almost perpendicularly, in some places many hundred feet above the level of the plain, while in others for many miles together their tops are only visible above the surface. These are so many strings of the oxen which the arrows of Arjun, one of the five brothers, converted into stone; and many a stream which now waters the valley first sprang from the surface of the earth at the touch of his lance, as his troops wanted water. The image of the gods of a former day, which now lie scattered among the ruins of old cities, buried in the depth of the forest, are nothing less than the bodies of the kings of the earth turned into stone for their temerity in contending with these demigods in battle. Ponds among the rocks of the Nerbudda, where all the great fairs are held, still bear the names of the five brothers, who are the heroes of this great poem;[12] and they are every year visited by hundreds of thousands who implicitly believe that their waters once received upon their bosoms the wearied limbs of those whose names they bear. What is life without the charms of fiction, and without the leisure and recreations which these sacred imaginings tend to give to the great mass of those who have nothing but the labour of their hands to depend upon for their subsistence! Let no such fictions be believed, and the holidays and pastimes of the lower orders in every country would soon cease, for they have almost everywhere owed their origin and support to some religious dream which has commanded the faith and influenced the conduct of great masses of mankind, and prevented one man from presuming to work on the day that another wished to rest from his labours. The people were of opinion, they told me, that the Ganges, as a sacred stream, could last only sixty years more, when the Nerbudda would take its place. The waters of the Nerbudda are, they say already so much more sacred than those of the Ganges that to see them is sufficient to cleanse men from their sins, whereas the Ganges must be touched before it can have that effect.[13]

At the temple built on the top of a conical hill at Bherāghāt, overlooking the river, is a statue of a bull carrying Siva, the god of destruction, and his wife Pārvatī seated behind him; they have both snakes in their hands, and Siva has a large one round his loins as a waistband. There are several demons in human shape lying prostrate under the belly of the bull, and the whole are well cut out of one large slab of hard basalt from a dyke in the marble rock beneath. They call the whole group 'Gaurī Sankar', and I found in the fair, exposed for sale, a brass model of a similar one from Jeypore (Jaipur), but not so well shaped and proportioned. On noticing this we were told that 'such difference was to be expected, since the brass must have been made by man, whereas the "Gaurī Sankar" of the temple above was a real Pākhān, or a conversion of living beings into stone by the gods;[14] they were therefore the exact resemblance of living beings, while the others could only be rude imitations'. 'Gaurī', or the Fair, is the name of Pārvatī, or Dēvī, when she appears with her husband Siva. On such occasions she is always fair and beautiful. Sankar is another name of Siva, or Mahādēo, or Rudra. On looking into the temple at the statue, a lady expressed her surprise at the entireness as well as the excellence of the figures, while all round had been so much mutilated by the Muhammadans. 'They are quite a different thing from the others', said a respectable old landholder; 'they are a conversion of real flesh and blood into stone, and no human hands can either imitate or hurt them.' She smiled incredulously, while he looked very grave, and appealed to the whole crowd of spectators assembled, who all testified to the truth of what he had said; and added that 'at no distant day the figures would be all restored to life again, the deities would all come back without doubt and reanimate their old bodies again'.

All the people who come to bathe at the fair bring chaplets of yellow jasmine, and hang them as offerings round the necks of the god and his consort; and at the same time they make some small offerings of rice to each of the many images that stand within the same apartment, and also to those which, under a stone roof supported upon stone pillars, line the inside of the wall that surrounds the circular area, in the centre of which the temple stands. The images inside the temple are those of the three great gods, Brahma, Vishnu, and Siva, with their primaeval consorts;[15] but those that occupy the piazza outside are the representations of the consorts of the different incarnations of these three gods, and these consorts are themselves the incarnations of the primaeval wives, who followed their husbands in all their earthly ramblings. They have all the female form, and are about the size of ordinary women, and extremely well cut out of fine white and green sandstone; but their heads are those of the animals in which their respective husbands became incarnate, such as the lion, the elephant, &c., or those of the *'vāhans'*, or animals on which they rode, such as the bull, the swan, the eagle, &c. But these, I presume, are mere *capricios* of the founder of the temple. The figures are sixty- four in number, all mounted upon their respective *'vāhans'*, but have been sadly mutilated by the pious Muhammadans.[16]

The old 'Mahant', or high priest, told us that Mahādēo and his wife were in reality our Adam and Eve; 'they came here together', said he, 'on a visit to the mountain Kailās,[17] and being earnestly solicited to leave some memorial of their visit, got themselves turned into stone'. The popular belief is that some very holy man, who had been occupied on the top of this little conical hill, where the temple now stands, in austere devotions for some few thousand years, was at last honoured with a visit from Siva and his consort, who asked him what they could do for him. He begged them to wait till he should bring some flowers from the woods to make them a suitable offering. They promised to do so, and he ran down, plunged into the Nerbudda and drowned himself, in order that these august persons might for ever remain and do honour to his residence and his name. They, however, left only their 'mortal coil', but will one day return and resume it. I know not whether I am singular in the notion or not, but I think Mahādēo and his consort are really our Adam and Eve, and that the people have converted them into the god and goddess of destruction, from some vague idea of their original sin, which involved all their race in destruction. The snakes, which form the only dress of Mahādēo, would seem to confirm this notion.[18]

Notes:

1. The Nerbudda (Narbadā, or Narmadā) river is the boundary between Hindustan, or Northern India, and the Deccan (Dakhin), or Southern India. The beautiful gorge of the Marble Rocks, near Jubbulpore (Jabalpur), is familiar to modern tourists (see *I.G.*, 1908, s.v. 'Marble Rocks'). The remarkable antiquities at Bherāghāt are described and illustrated in *A.S.R.*, vol. ix, pp. 60-76, pl. xii-xvi. Additions and corrections to Cunningham's account will be found in *A.S.W.I Progr. Rep.*, 1893-4, p. 5; and *A.S. Ann. Rep., E. Circle*, 1907-8, pp. 14-18.

2. The eighth month of the Hindoo luni-solar year, corresponding to part of October and part of November. In Northern India the year begins with the month Chait, in March. The most commonly used names of the months are: (1) Chait; (2) Baisākh; (3) Jēth; (4) Asārh; (5) Sāwan; (6) Bhādon; (7) Kuār; (8) Kārtik; (9) Aghan; (10) Pūs; (II) Māgh; and (12) Phālgun.

3. *Bhagvān* is often used as equivalent for the word God in its most general sense, but is specially applicable to the Deity as manifested in Vishnu the Preserver. *Asārh* corresponds to June-July, *Pātāl* is the Hindoo Hades. Rājā Bali is a demon, and Indra is the lord of the heavens. The fairs take place at the time of full moon.

4. Barrackpore, fifteen miles north of Calcutta, is still a cantonment. The Governor General has a country house there. The mutiny of the native troops stationed there occurred on Nov. 1, 1824, and was due to the discontent caused by orders moving the 47th Native Infantry to Rangoon to take part in the Burmese War. The outbreak was promptly suppressed. Captain Pogson published a *Memoir of the Mutiny at Barrackpore* (8vo, Serampore, 1833).

5. Lūdiāna, the capital of the district of the same name, now under the Punjab Government. Hyphasis is the Greek name of the Biās river, one of the five rivers of the Punjāb.

6. Railways have rendered almost obsolete the mode of travelling described in the text. In Northern India palankeens (pālkīs) are now seldom used, even by Indians, except for purposes of ceremony.

7. This statement is no longer quite accurate, though fortified positions are still very few.

8. The editor cannot find the exact passage quoted, but remarks to the same effect will be found in *The Life of Sir Thomas Munro*, by the Rev. G. R. Gleig, in two volumes, a new edition (London, 1831), vol. ii, p. 175.

9. *Narrative of a Journey through the Upper Provinces of India, from Calcutta to Bombay, 1834-5, and a Journey to the Southern Provinces in 1826* (2nd edition, 3 vols. 8vo, London, 1828.)

10. The bees at the Marble Rocks are the *Apis dorsata*. An Englishman named Biddington, when trying to escape from them, was drowned, and they stung to death one of Captain Forsyth's baggage ponies (Balfour, *Cyclopaedia of India*, 3rd ed., 1885, s.v. Bee').

11. The vast epic poem, or collection of poems known as the Mahābhārata, consists of over 100,000 Sanskrit verses. The main subject is the war between the five Pāndavas, or sons of Pāndū, and their cousins the Kauravas, sons of Dhritarāshtra. Many poems of various origins and dates are interwoven with the main work. The best known of the episodes is that of *Nala and Damayantī*, which was well translated by Dean Milman, See Macdonell, *A History of Sanskrit Literature* (Heinemann, 1900).

12. The five Pāndava brothers were Yudhishthira, Bhīmia, Arjuna, Nakula, and Sahadeva, the children of Pāndū, by his wives Kuntī, or Prithā, and Madrī.

13. 'The Narbadā has its special admirers, who exalt it oven above the Ganges, . . . The sanctity of the Ganges will, they say, cease in 1895, whereas that of the Narbadā will continue for ever' (Monier Williams, *Religious Thought and Life in India*, London, 1883, p. 348), See *post*, Chapter 27.

14. Sleeman wrote 'Py-Khan', a corrupt spelling of pākhān, the Sanskrit pāshāna or pāsāna, 'a stone'. The compound pāshāna- mūrti is commonly used in the sense of 'stone image'. The sibilant *sh* or *s* usually is pronounced as *kh* in Northern India (Grierson, *J.R.A.S.*, 1903, p. 363).

15. Sarasvatī, consort of Brahma; Dēvī (Pārvatī, Durgā, &c.), consort of Siva; and Lakshmī, consort of Vishnu. All Hindoo deities have many names.

16. The author's explanation is partly erroneous. The temple, which is a very remarkable one, is dedicated to the sixty-four Joginīs. Only five temples in India are known to be dedicated to these demons. For details see Cunningham, *A.S.R.*, vol. ix, pp. 61-74, pl. xii-xvi; vol. ii, p. 416; and vol. xxi, p. 57. The word *vāhana* means 'vehicle'. Each deity has his peculiar vehicle.

17. The heaven of Siva, as distinguished from Vaikuntha, the heaven of Vishnu. It is supposed to be somewhere in the Himālaya mountains. The wonderful excavated rock temple at Ellora is believed to be a model of Kailās.

18. This 'notion' of the author's is not likely to find acceptance at the present day.

CHAPTER 2

Hindoo System of Religion.

The Hindoo system is this. A great divine spirit or essence, 'Brahma', pervades the whole universe; and the soul of every human being is a drop from this great ocean, to which, when it becomes perfectly purified, it is reunited. The reunion is the eternal beatitude to which all look forward with hope; and the soul of the Brahman is nearest to it. If he has been a good man, his soul becomes absorbed in the 'Brahma'; and, if a bad man, it goes to 'Narak', hell; and after the expiration of its period there of *limited imprisonment*, it returns to earth, and occupies the body of some other animal. It again advances by degrees to the body of the Brahman; and thence, when fitted for it, into the great 'Brahma'.[1]

From this great eternal essence emanate Brahma, the Creator, whose consort is Sarasvatī;[2] Vishnu, the Preserver, whose consort is Lakshmī; and Siva, *alias* Māhadēo, the Destroyer, whose consort is Pārvatī. According to popular belief Jamrāj (Yamarāja) is the judicial deity who has been appointed by the greater powers to pass the final judgement on the tenor of men's lives, according to proceedings drawn up by his secretary Chitragupta. If men's actions have been good, their souls are, as the next stage, advanced a step towards the great essence, Brahma; and, if bad, they are thrown back, and obliged to occupy the bodies of brutes or of people of inferior caste, as the balance against them may be great or small. There is an intermediate stage, a 'Narak', or hell, for bad men, and a 'Baikunth', or paradise, for the good, in which they find their felicity in serving that god of the three to which they have specially devoted themselves while on earth. But from this stage, after the period of their sentence is expired, men go back to their pilgrimage on earth again.

There are numerous Dēos (Devas), or good spirits, of whom Indra is the chief; [3] and Daityas, or bad spirits; and there have also been a great number of incarnations from the three great gods, and their consorts, who have made their appearance upon the earth when required for particular purposes. All these incarnations are called 'Avatārs', or descents. Vishnu has been eleven times on the globe in different shapes, and Siva seven times.[4] The avatārs of Vishnu are celebrated in many popular poems, such as the Rāmāyana, or history of the Rape of Sitā, the wife of Rāma, the seventh incarnation;[5] the Mahābhārata, and the Bhāgavata [Purāna], which describe the wars and amours of this god in his last human shape.[6] All these books are believed to have been written either by the hand or by the inspiration of the god himself thousands of years before the events they describe actually took place. 'It was', they say, 'as easy for the deity to write or dictate a battle, an amour, or any other important event ten thousand years before as the day after it took place'; and I believe nine-tenths, perhaps ninety-nine in a hundred, of the Hindoo population believe implicitly that these accounts were also written. It is now pretty clear that all these works are of comparatively recent date, that the great poem of the Mahābhārata could not have been written before the year 786 of the Christian era, and was probably written so late as A.D. 1157; that Krishna, *if born at all*, must have been born on the 7th of August, A.D. 600, but was most likely a mere creation of the imagination to serve the purpose of the Brahmans of Ujain, in whom the fiction originated; that the other incarnations were invented about the same time, and for the same object, though the other persons described as incarnations were real princes, Parasu Rāma, before Christ 1176, and Rāma, born before Christ 961. In the Mahābhārata Krishna is described as fighting in the same army with Yudhishthira and his four brothers. Yudhishthira was a real person, who ascended the throne at Delhi 575 B.C., or 1175 years before the birth of Krishna.[7] Bentley supposes that the incarnations, particularly that of Krishna, were invented by the Brahmans of Ujain with a view to check the progress of Christianity in that part of the world (see his historical view of the Hindoo astronomy). That we find in no history any account of the alarming progress of Christianity about the time these fables were written is no proof that Bentley was wrong.[8]

When Monsieur Thevenot was at Agra [in] 1666, the Christian population was roughly estimated at twenty-five thousand families. They had all passed away before it became one of our civil and military stations in the beginning of the present century, and we might search history in vain for any mention of them (see his *Travels in India*, Part III). One single prince, well disposed to give Christians encouragement and employment, might, in a few years, get the same number around his capital; and it is probable that the early Christians in India occasionally found such princes, and gave just cause of alarm to the Brahman priests, who were then in the infancy of their despotic power.[9]

During the war with Nepal, in 1814 and 1815,[10] the division with which I served came upon an extremely interesting colony of about two thousand Christian families at Betiyā in the Tirhūt District, on the borders of the Tarāi forest. This colony had been created by one man, the Bishop, a Venetian by birth, under the protection of a small Hindoo prince, the Rājā, of Betiyā.[11] This holy man had been some fifty years among these people, with little or no support from Europe or from any other quarter. The only aid he got from the Rājā was a pledge that no member of his Church should be subject to the *Purveyance system*, under which the people everywhere suffered so much,[12] and this pledge the Rājā, though a Hindoo, had never suffered to be violated. There were men of all trades among them, and they formed one very large street remarkable for the superior style of its buildings and the sober industry of its inhabitants. The masons, carpenters, and blacksmiths of this little colony were working in our camp every day, while we remained in the vicinity, and better workmen I have never seen in India; but they would all insist upon going to divine service at the prescribed hours. They had built a splendid *pucka*[13] dwelling-house for their bishop, and a still more splendid church, and formed for him the finest garden I have seen in India, surrounded with a good wall, and provided with admirable pucka wells. The native Christian servants who attended at the old bishop's table, taught by himself, spoke Latin to him; but he was become very feeble, and spoke himself a mixture of Latin, Italian, his native tongue, and Hindustānī. We used to have him at our messes, and take as much care of him as of an infant, for he was become almost as frail as one. The joy and the excitement of being once more among Europeans, and treated by them with so much reverence in the midst of his flock, were perhaps too much for him, for he sickened and died soon after.

The Rājā died soon after him, and in all probability the flock has disappeared. No Europeans except a few indigo planters of the neighbourhood had ever before known or heard of this colony; and they seemed to consider them only as a set of great scoundrels, who had better carts and bullocks than anybody else in the country, which they refused to let out at the same rate as the others, and which they (the indigo lords) were not permitted to seize and employ at discretion. Roman Catholics have a greater facility in making converts in India than Protestants, from having so much more in their form of worship to win the affections through the medium of the imagination.[14]

Notes:

1. Men are occasionally exempted from the necessity of becoming a Brahman first. Men of low caste, if they die at particular places, where it is the interest of the Brahmans to invite rich men to die, are promised absorption into the great 'Brahma' at once. Immense numbers of wealthy men go every year from the most distant parts of India to die at Benares, where they spend large sums of money among the Brahmans. It is by their

means that this, the second city in India, is supported. [W. H. S.] Bombay is now the second city in India, so far as population is concerned.

2. Brahma, with the short vowel, is the eternal Essence or Spirit; Brahmā, with the long vowel, is 'the primaeval male god, the first personal product of the purely spiritual Brahma, when overspread by Maya, or illusory creative force', according to the Vedanta system (Monier Williams, *Religious Thought and Life in India*, p. 44).

3. Indra was originally, in the Vedas, the Rain-god. The statement in the text refers to modern Hinduism.

4. The incarnations of Vishnu are ordinarily reckoned as ten, namely, (1) Fish, (2) Tortoise, (3) Boar, (4) Man-lion, (5) Dwarf, (6) Rāma with the axe, (7) Rāma Chandra, (8) Krishna, (9) Buddha, (10) Kalkī, or Kalkin, who is yet to come. I do not know any authority for eleven incarnations of Vishnu. The number is stated in some Purānas as twenty-two, twenty-four, or even twenty-eight. Seven incarnations of Siva are not generally recognized (see Monier Williams, *Religious Thought and Life in India*, pp. 78-86, and 107-16). For the theory and mystical meaning of *avatārs*, see Grierson, *J.R.A.S.*, 1909. The word avatār means 'descent', *scil.* of the Deity to earth, and covers more than the term 'incarnation'.

5. Sitā was an incarnation of Lakshmī. She became incarnate again, many centuries afterwards, as the wife of Krishna, another incarnation of Vishnu [W. H. S.]. Reckoning by centuries is, of course, inapplicable to pure myth. The author believed in Bentley's baseless chronology.

6. For the Mahābhārata, see *ante*, note 11, Chapter 1. The Bhāgavata Purāna is the most popular of the Purānas, The Hindi version of the tenth book (*skandha*) is known as the 'Prem Sāgar'. The date of the composition of the Purānas is uncertain.

7. The dates given in this passage are purely imaginary. Parts of the Mahābhārata are very ancient. Yudhishthira is no more an historical personage than Achilles or Romulus. It is improbable that a 'throne of Delhi' existed in 575 B.C., and hardly anything is known about the state of India at that date.

8. It is hardly necessary to observe that this grotesque theory is utterly at variance with the facts, as now known.

9. The existing settlements of native Christians at Agra are mostly of modern origin. Very ancient Christian communities exist near Madras, and on the Malabar coast. The travels of Jean de Thevenot were published in 1684, under the title of *Voyage, contenant la Relation de l'Indostan*. The English version, by A. Lovell (London, 1687), is entitled *The Travels of Monsieur de Thevenot into the Levant, in three Parts*. Part III deals with the East Indies,

The passage referred to is: 'Some affirm that there are twenty-five thousand Christian Families in Agra, but all do not agree in that' (Part III, p. 35). Thevonot's statement about the Christians of Agra is further discussed post in Chapter 52.

10. The war with Nepal began in October, 1814, and was not concluded till 1816. During its progress the British arms suffered several reverses.

11. The Betiyā (Bettiah of *I. G.*, 1908) Rāj is a great estate with an area of 1,824 square miles in the northern part of the Champāran District of Bihār, in the Province of Bihār and Orissa. A great portion of the estate is held (1908) on permanent leases by European indigo-planters.

12. For discussion of this system see post, Chapter 7.

13. 'Pucka' (*pakkā*) here means 'masonry', as opposed to 'Kutcha' (*kachchā*), meaning 'earthen'.

14. Native Christians, according to the census of 1872, number 1,214 persons, who are principally found in Bettiā thāna [police-circle]. There are two Missions, one at Bettiā, and the other at the village of Chuhārī, both supported by the Roman Catholic Church. The former was founded in 1746 by a certain Father Joseph, from Garingano in Italy, who went to Bettiā on the invitation of the Mahārāja. The present number of converts is about 1,000 persons. Being principally descendants of Brahmans, they hold a fair social position; but some of them are extremely poor. About one-fourth are carpenters, one- tenth blacksmiths, one-tenth servants, the remainder carters. The Chuhārī Mission was founded in 1770 by three Catholic priests, who had been expelled from Nepal [after the Gōrkha conquest in 1768]. There are now 283 converts, mostly descendants of Nepālis. They are all agriculturists, and very poor (Article 'Champāran District' in *Statistical Account of Bengal*, 1877).

The statement in *I.G.* 1908, s.v. Bettiah, differs slightly, as follows:

'A Roman Catholic Mission was established about 1740 by Father Joseph Mary, an Italian missionary of the Capuchin Order, who was passing near Bettiah on his way to Nepāl, when he was summoned by Rājā Dhruva Shah to attend his daughter, who was dangerously ill. He succeeded in curing her, and the grateful Raja invited him to stay at Bettiah and gave him a house and ninety acres of land.' The Bettiah Mission still exists and maintains the Catholic Mission Press, where publications illustrating the history of the Capuchin Missions have been printed. Father Felix, O.C., is at work on the subject.

CHAPTER 3

Legend of the Nerbudda River.

The legend is that the Nerbudda, which flows west into the Gulf of Cambay, was wooed and won in the usual way by the Sōn river, which rises from the same tableland of Amarkantak, and flows east into the Ganges and Bay of Bengal.[1] All the previous ceremonies having been performed, the Sōn [2] came with 'due pomp and circumstance' to fetch his bride in the procession called the 'Barāt', up to which time the bride and bridegroom are supposed never to have seen each other, unless perchance they have met in infancy. Her Majesty the Nerbudda became exceedingly impatient to know what sort of a personage her destinies were to be linked to, while his Majesty the Sōn advanced at a slow and stately pace. At last the Queen sent Johilā, the daughter of the barber, to take a close view of him, and to return and make a faithful and particular report of his person. His Majesty was captivated with the little Johilā, the barber's daughter, at first sight; and she, 'nothing loath', yielded to his caresses. Some say that she actually pretended to be Queen herself; and that his Majesty was no further in fault than in mistaking the humble handmaid for her noble mistress; but, be that as it may, her Majesty no sooner heard of the good understanding between them, than she rushed forward, and with one foot sent the Sōn rolling back to the east whence he came, and with the other kicked little Johilā sprawling after him; for, said the high priest, who told us the story, 'You see what a towering passion she was likely to have been in under such indignities from the furious manner in which she cuts her way through the marble rocks beneath us, and casts huge masses right and left as she goes along, as if they were really so many coco-nuts'. 'And was she', asked I, 'to have flown eastward with him, or was he to have flown westward with her?' 'She was to have accompanied him eastward', said the high priest, 'but her Majesty, after this indignity, declared that she would not go a single pace in the same direction with such wretches, and would flow west, though all the other rivers in India might flow east; and west she flows accordingly, a virgin queen.' I asked some of the Hindoos about us why they called her 'Mother Nerbudda', if she was really never married. 'Her Majesty', said they with great respect, 'would really never consent to be married after the indignity she suffered from her affianced bridegroom the Sōn; and we call her Mother because she blesses us all, and we are anxious to accost her by the name which we consider to be at once the most respectful and endearing.'

Any Englishman can easily conceive a poet in his highest 'calenture of the brain' addressing the ocean as 'a steed that knows his rider', and patting the crested billow as his flowing mane; but he must come to India to understand how every individual of a whole community of many millions can address a fine river as a living being, a sovereign princess, who hears and understands all they say, and exercises a kind of local superintendence over their affairs, without a single temple in which her image is worshipped, or a single priest to profit by the delusion. As in the case of the Ganges, it is the river itself to whom they address themselves, and not to any deity residing in it, or presiding over it: the stream itself is the deity which fills their imaginations, and receives their homage.

Among the Romans and ancient Persians rivers were propitiated by sacrifices. When Vitellius crossed the Euphrates with the Roman legions to put Tiridates on the throne of Armenia, they propitiated the river according to the rites of their country by the *suovetaurilia*, the sacrifice of the hog, the ram, and the bull. Tiridates did the same by the sacrifice of a horse. Tacitus does not mention the river *god*, but the river *itself*, as propitiated (see [*Annals*,] book vi, chap. 37).[3] Plato makes Socrates condemn Homer for making Achilles behave disrespectfully towards the river Xanthus, though acknowledged to be a divinity, in offering to fight him,[4] and towards the river Sperchius, another acknowledged god, in presenting to the dead body of Patroclus the locks of his hair which he had promised to that river.[5]

The Sōn river, which rises near the source of the Nerbudda on the tableland of Amarkantak, takes a westerly course for some miles, and then turns off suddenly to the east, and is joined by the little stream of the Johilā before it descends the great cascade; and hence the poets have created this fiction, which the mass of the population receive as divine revelation. The statue of little Johilā, the barber's daughter, in stone, stands in the temple of the goddess Nerbudda at Amarkantak, bound in chains.[6] It may here be remarked that the first overtures in India must always be made through the medium of the barber, whether they be from the prince or the peasant.[7] If a sovereign prince sends proposals to a sovereign princess, they must be conveyed through the medium of the barber, or they will never be considered as done in due form, as likely to prove propitious. The prince will, of course, send some relation or high functionary with him; but in all the credentials the barber must be named as the principal functionary. Hence it was that Her Majesty was supposed to have sent a barber's daughter to meet her husband.

The 'Mahātam' (greatness or holiness) of the Ganges is said, as I have already stated, to be on the wane, and not likely to endure sixty years longer; while that of the Nerbudda is on the increase, and in sixty years is entirely to supersede the sanctity of her sister. If the valley of the Nerbudda should continue for sixty years longer under such a government as it has enjoyed since we took possession of it in 1817,[8] it may become infinitely more rich, more populous, and more beautiful than that of the Nile ever was; and, if the Hindoos there continue, as I hope they will, to acquire wealth and honour under a rule to which they are so much attached, the prophecy may be realized in as far as the increase of honour paid to the Nerbudda is concerned. But I know no ground to expect that the reverence[9] paid to the Ganges will diminish, unless education and the concentration of capital in manufactures should work an important change in the religious feelings and opinions of the people along the course of that river; although this, it must be admitted, is a consummation which may be looked for more speedily on the banks of the Ganges than on those of a stream like the Nerbudda, which is neither navigable at present nor, in my opinion, capable of being rendered so. Commerce and manufactures, and the concentration of capital in the maintenance of the new communities employed in them, will, I think, be the great media through which this change will be chiefly effected; and they are always more likely to follow the course of rivers that are navigable than that of rivers which are not.[10]

Notes:

1. Amarkantak, formerly in the Sohāgpur pargana of the Bilāspur District of the Central Provinces, is situated on a high tableland, and is a famous place of pilgrimage. The temples are described by Beglar in *A.S.R.*, vol. vii, pp. 227-34, pl. xx, xxi. The hill has been transferred to the Rīwā State (*Central Provinces Gazetteer* (1870), and *I.G.* (1908), s.v. Amarkantak).

2. The name is misspelled Sohan in the author's text. The Sōn rises at Sōn Mundā, about twenty miles from Amarkantak (*A.S.R.*, vol. vii, 236).

3. 'Sacrificantibus, cum hic more Romano suovetaurilia daret, ille equum placando amni adornasset.'

4.　　　　　μέγας ποταμὸς βαθυδίνης,
δυ Ξάνθον καλέουσι θεοί, ἄνδρες δὲ Σκάμανδρον. — *Iliad* xx, 73.

5. *Iliad* xxiii. 140-153.

6. Mr. Crooke observes that the binding was intended to prevent the object of worship from deserting her shrine or possibly doing mischief elsewhere, and refers to his article, 'The Binding of a God, a Study of the Basis of Idolatry', in *Folklore*, vol. viii (1897), p.134. The name is spelt Johillā in *I.G.* (1908), s.v. Sōn River.

7. Monier Williams denies the barber's monopoly of match-making. 'In some parts of Northern India the match-maker for some castes is the family barber; but for the higher castes he is more generally a Brahman, who goes about from one house to another till he discovers a baby-girl of suitable rank' (*Religious Thought and Life in India*, p. 377). So far as the editor knows, the barber is ordinarily employed in Northern India.

8. During the operations against the Pindhārī freebooters. Many treaties were negotiated with the Peshwa and other native powers in the years 1817 and 1818.

9. The word in the text is 'revenue'.

10. Concerning the prophecy that the sanctity of the Ganges will cease in 1895, see note to Chapter 1, *ante*, [13]. The prophecy was much talked of some years ago, but the reverence for the Ganges continues undiminished, while the development of commerce and manufactures has not affected, the religious feelings and opinions of the people. Railways, in fact, facilitate pilgrimages and increase their popularity. The course of commerce now follows the line of rail, not the navigable rivers. The author, when writing this book, evidently never contemplated the possibility of railway construction in India. Later in life, in 1852, he fully appreciated the value of the new means of communication (*Journey*, ii, 370, &c.).

CHAPTER 4

A Suttee[1] on the Nerbudda.

We took a ride one evening to Gopālpur, a small village situated on the same bank of the Nerbudda, about three miles up from Bherāghāt. On our way we met a party of women and girls coming to the fair. Their legs were uncovered half-way up the thigh; but, as we passed, they all carefully covered up their faces. 'Good God!' exclaimed one of the ladies, 'how can these people be so very indecent?' They thought it, no doubt, equally extraordinary that she should have her face uncovered, while she so carefully concealed her legs; for they were really all modest peasantry, going from the village to bathe in the holy stream.[2]

Here there are some very pretty temples, built for the most part to the memory of widows who have burned themselves with the remains of their husbands, and upon the very spot where they committed themselves to the flames. There was one which had been recently raised over the ashes of one of the most extraordinary old ladies that I have ever seen, who burned herself in my presence in 1829. I prohibited the building of any temple upon the spot, but my successor in the civil charge of the district, Major Low, was never, I believe, made acquainted with the prohibition nor with the progress of the work; which therefore went on to completion in my absence. As suttees are now prohibited in our dominions[3] and cannot be often seen or described by Europeans, I shall here relate the circumstances of this as they were recorded by me at the time, and the reader may rely upon the truth of the whole tale.

On the 29th November, 1829, this old woman, then about sixty-five years of age, here mixed her ashes with those of her husband, who had been burned alone four days before. On receiving civil charge of the district (Jubbulpore) in March, 1828, I issued a proclamation prohibiting any one from aiding or assisting in suttee, and distinctly stating that to bring one ounce of wood for the purpose would be considered as so doing. If the woman burned herself with the body of her husband, any one who brought wood for the purpose of burning him would become liable to punishment; consequently, the body of the husband must be first consumed, and the widow must bring a fresh supply for herself. On Tuesday, 24th November, 1829, I had an application from the heads of the most respectable and most extensive family of Brahmans in the district to suffer this old woman to burn herself with the remains of her husband, Ummēd Singh Upadhya, who had that morning died upon the banks of the Nerbudda.[4] I threatened to enforce my order, and punish severely any man who assisted; and placed a police guard for the purpose of seeing that no one did so. She remained sitting by the edge of the water without eating or drinking. The next day the body of her husband was burned to ashes in a small pit of about eight feet square, and three or four feet deep, before several thousand spectators who had assembled to see the suttee. All strangers dispersed before evening, as there seemed to be no prospect of my yielding to the urgent solicitations of her family, who dared not touch food till she had burned herself, or declared herself willing to return to them. Her sons, grandsons, and some other relations remained with her, while the rest surrounded my house, the one urging me to allow her to burn, and the other urging her to desist. She remained sitting on a bare rock in the bed of the Nerbudda, refusing every kind of sustenance, and exposed to the intense heat of the sun by day, and the severe cold of the night, with only a thin sheet thrown over her shoulders. On Thursday, to cut off all hope of her being moved from her purpose, she put on the dhajā, or coarse red turban, and broke her bracelets in pieces, by which she became dead in law, and for ever excluded from caste. Should she choose to live after this, she could never return to her family. Her children and grandchildren were still with her, but all their entreaties were unavailing; and I became satisfied that she would starve herself to death, if not allowed to burn, by which the family would be disgraced, her miseries prolonged, and I myself rendered liable to be charged with a wanton abuse of authority, for no prohibition of the kind I had issued had as yet received the formal sanction of the Government.

On Saturday, the 28th, in the morning, I rode out ten miles to the spot, and found the poor old widow sitting with the dhajā round her head, a brass plate before her with undressed rice and flowers, and a coco-nut in each hand. She talked very collectedly, telling me that 'she had determined to mix her ashes with those of her departed husband, and should patiently wait my permission to do so, assured that God would enable her to sustain life till that was given, though she dared not eat or drink'. Looking at the sun, then rising before her over a long and beautiful reach of the Nerbudda river, she said calmly, 'My soul has been for five days with my husband's near that sun, nothing but my earthly frame is left; and this, I know, you will in time suffer to be mixed with the ashes of his in yonder pit, because it is not in your nature or usage wantonly to prolong the miseries of a poor old woman'.

'Indeed, it is not,—my object and duty is to save and preserve them [sic]; and I am come to dissuade you from this idle purpose, to urge you to live, and to keep your family from the disgrace of being thought your murderers.'

'I am not afraid of their ever being so thought: they have all, like good children, done everything in their power to induce me to live among them; and, if I had done so, I know they would have loved and honoured me; but my duties to them have now ended. I commit them all to your care, and I go to attend my husband, *Ummēd Singh Upadhya*, with whose ashes on the funeral pile mine have been already three times mixed.'[5]

This was the first time in her long life that she had ever pronounced the name of her husband, for in India no woman, high or low, ever pronounces the name of her husband,—she would consider it disrespectful towards him to do so; and it is often amusing to see their embarrassment when asked the question by any European gentleman. They look right and left for some one to relieve them from the dilemma of appearing disrespectful either to the querist or to their absent husbands—they perceive that he is unacquainted with their duties on this point, and are afraid he will attribute their silence to disrespect. They know that few European gentlemen are acquainted with them; and when women go into our courts of justice, or other places where they are liable to be asked the names of their husbands, they commonly take one of their children or some other relation with them to pronounce the words in their stead. When the old lady named her husband, as she did with strong emphasis, and in a very deliberate manner, every one present was satisfied that she had resolved to die. 'I have', she continued, 'tasted largely of the bounty of Government, having been maintained by it with all my large family in ease and comfort upon our rent-free lands; and I feel assured that my children will not be suffered to want; but with them I have nothing more to do, our intercourse and communion here end. My soul (*prān*) is with *Ummēd Singh Upadhya*: and my ashes must here mix with his.'

Again looking to the sun—'I see them together', said she, with a tone and countenance that affected me a good deal, 'under the bridal canopy!'—alluding to the ceremonies of marriage; and I am satisfied that she at that moment really believed that she saw her own spirit and that of her husband under the bridal canopy in paradise.

I tried to work upon her pride and her fears. I told her that it was probable that the rent-free lands by which her family had been so long supported might be resumed by the Government, as a mark of its displeasure against the children for not dissuading her from the sacrifice; that the temples over her ancestors upon the bank might be levelled with the ground, in order to prevent their operating to induce others to make similar sacrifices; and lastly, that not one single brick or stone should ever mark the place where she died if she persisted in her resolution. But, if she consented to live, a splendid habitation should be built for her among these temples, a handsome provision assigned for her support out of these rent-free lands, her children should come daily to visit her, and I should frequently do the same. She smiled, but held out her arm and said, 'My pulse has long ceased to beat, my spirit has departed, and I have nothing left but a little *earth*, that I wish to mix with the ashes of my husband. I shall suffer nothing in burning; and, if you wish proof, order some fire, and you shall see this arm consumed without giving me any pain'. I did not attempt to feel her pulse, but some of my people did, and declared that it had ceased to be perceptible. At this time every native present believed that she was incapable of suffering pain; and her end confirmed them in their opinion.

Satisfied myself that it would be unavailing to attempt to save her life, I sent for all the principal members of the family, and consented that she should be suffered to burn herself if they would enter into engagements that no other member of their family should ever do the same. This they all agreed to, and the papers having been drawn out in due form about midday, I sent down notice to the old lady, who seemed extremely pleased and thankful. The ceremonies of bathing were gone through before three [o'clock], while the wood and other combustible materials for a strong fire were collected and put into the pit. After bathing, she called for a 'pan' (betel leaf) and ate it, then rose up, and with one arm on the shoulder of her eldest son, and the other on that of her nephew, approached the fire. I had sentries placed all round, and no other person was allowed to approach within five paces. As she rose up fire was set to the pile, and it was instantly in a blaze. The distance was about 150 yards. She came on with a calm and cheerful countenance, stopped once, and, casting her eyes upward, said, 'Why have they kept me five days from thee, my husband?' On coming to the sentries her supporters stopped; she walked once round the pit, paused a moment, and, while muttering a prayer, threw some flowers into the fire. She then walked up deliberately and steadily to the brink, stepped into the centre of the flame, sat down, and leaning back in the midst as if reposing upon a couch, was consumed without uttering a shriek or betraying one sign of agony.

A few instruments of music had been provided, and they played, as usual, as she approached the fire, not, as is commonly supposed, in order to drown screams, but to prevent the last words of the victim from being heard, as these are supposed to be prophetic, and might become sources of pain or strife to the living.[6] It was not expected that I should yield, and but few people had assembled to witness the sacrifice, so that there was little or nothing in the circumstances immediately around to stimulate her to any extraordinary exertions; and I am persuaded that it was the desire of again being united to her husband in the next world, and the entire confidence that she would be so if she now burned herself, that alone sustained her. From the morning he died (Tuesday) till Wednesday evening she ate 'pans' or betel leaves, but nothing else; and from Wednesday evening she ceased eating them. She drank no water from Tuesday. She went into the fire with the same cloth about her that she had worn in the bed of the river; but it was made wet from a persuasion that even the shadow of any impure thing falling upon her from going to the pile contaminates the woman unless counteracted by the sheet moistened in the holy stream.

I must do the family the justice to say that they all exerted themselves to dissuade the widow from her purpose, and had she lived she would assuredly have been cherished and honoured as the first female member of the whole house. There is no people in the world among whom parents are more loved, honoured, and obeyed than among the Hindoos; and the grandmother is always more honoured than the mother. No queen upon her throne could ever have been approached with more reverence by her subjects than was this old lady by all the members of her family as she sat upon a naked rock in the bed of the river, with only a red rag upon her head and a single-white sheet over her shoulders.

Soon after the battle of Trafalgar I heard a young lady exclaim, 'I could really wish to have had a brother killed in that action'. There is no doubt that a family in which a suttee takes place feels a good deal exalted in its own esteem and that of the community by the sacrifice. The sister of the Rājā of Rīwā was one of four or five wives who burned themselves with the remains of the Rājā of Udaipur; and nothing in the course of his life will ever be recollected by her brother with so much of pride and pleasure, since the Udaipur Rājā is the head of the Rājpūt tribes.[7]

I asked the old lady when she had first resolved upon becoming a suttee, and she told me that about thirteen years before, while bathing in the river Nerbudda, near the spot where she then sat, with many other females of the family, the resolution had fixed itself in her mind as she looked at the splendid temples on the bank of the river erected by the different branches of the family over the ashes of her female relations who had at different times become suttees. Two, I think, were over her aunts, and one over the mother of her husband. They were very beautiful buildings, and had been erected at great cost and kept in good repair. She told me that she had never mentioned this her resolution to any one from that time, nor breathed a syllable on the subject till she called out 'Sat, sat, sat',[8] when her husband breathed his last with his head in her lap on the bank of the Nerbudda, to which he had been taken when no hopes remained of his surviving the fever of which he died.

Charles Harding, of the Bengal Civil Service, as magistrate of Benares, in 1806 prevented the widow of a Brahman from being burned. Twelve months after her husband's death she had been goaded by her family into the expression of a wish to burn with some relic of her husband, preserved for the purpose. The pile was raised to her at Rāmnagar,[9] some two miles above Benares, on the opposite side of the river Ganges. She was not well secured upon the pile, and as soon as she felt the fire she jumped off and plunged into the river. The people all ran after her along the bank, but the current drove her towards Benares, whence a police boat put off and took her in.

She was almost dead with the fright and the water, in which she had been kept afloat by her clothes. She was taken to Harding; but the whole city of Benares was in an uproar, at the rescue of a Brahman's widow from the funeral pile, for such it had been considered, though the man had been a year dead. Thousands surrounded his house, and his court was filled with the principal men of the city, imploring him to surrender the woman; and among the rest was the poor woman's father, who declared that he could not support his daughter; and that she had, therefore, better be burned, as her husband's family would no longer receive her. The uproar was quite alarming to a young man, who felt all the responsibility upon himself in such a city as[10] Benares, with a population of three hundred thousand people,[11] so prone to popular insurrections, or risings en masse very like them. He long argued the point of the time that had elapsed, and the unwillingness of the woman, but in vain; until at last the thought struck him suddenly, and he said that 'The sacrifice was manifestly unacceptable to their God — that the sacred river, as such, had rejected her; she had, without being able to swim, floated down two miles upon its bosom, in the face of an immense multitude; and it was clear that she had been rejected. Had she been an acceptable sacrifice, after the fire had touched her, the river would have received her'. This satisfied the whole crowd. The father said that, after this unanswerable argument, he would receive his daughter; and the whole crowd dispersed satisfied.[12]

The following conversation took place one morning between me and a native gentleman at Jubbulpore soon after suttees had been prohibited by Government:—

'What are the castes among whom women are not permitted to remarry after the death of their husbands?'

'They are, sir, Brahmans, Rājpūts, Baniyās (shopkeepers), Kāyaths (writers).'

'Why not permit them to marry, now that they are no longer permitted to burn themselves with the dead bodies of their husbands?'

'The knowledge that they cannot unite themselves to a second husband without degradation from caste, tends strongly to secure their fidelity to the first, sir. Besides, if all widows were permitted to marry again, what distinction would remain between us and people of lower caste? We should all soon sink to a level with the lowest.'

'And so you are content to keep up your caste at the expense of the poor widows?'

'No; they are themselves as proud of the distinction as their husbands are.'

'And would they, do you think, like to hear the good old custom of burning themselves restored?'

'Some of them would, no doubt.'

'Why?'

'Because they become reunited to their husbands in paradise, and are there happy, free from all the troubles of this life.'

'But you should not let them have any troubles as widows.'

'If they behave well, they are the most honoured members of their deceased husbands' families; nothing in such families is ever done without consulting them, because all are proud to have the memory of their lost fathers, sons, and brothers so honoured by their widows.[13] But women feel that they are frail, and would often rather burn themselves than be exposed all their lives to temptation and suspicion.'

'And why do not the men burn themselves to avoid the troubles of life?'

'Because they are not called to it from Heaven, as the women are.'

'And you think that the women were really called to be burned by the Deity?'

'No doubt; we all believe that they were called and supported by the Deity; and that no tender beings like women could otherwise voluntarily undergo such tortures—they become inspired with supernatural powers of courage and fortitude. When Dulī Sukul, the Sihōrā[14] banker's father, died, the wife of a Lodhī cultivator of the town declared, all at once, that she had been a suttee with him six times before; and that she would now go into paradise with him a seventh time. Nothing could persuade her from burning herself. She was between fifty and sixty years of age, and had grandchildren, and all her family tried to persuade her that it must be a mistake, but all in vain. She became a suttee, and was burnt the day after the body of the banker.'

'Did not Dulī Sukul's family, who were Brahmans, try to dissuade her from it, she being a Lodhī, a very low caste?'

'They did; but they said all things were possible with God; and it was generally believed that this was a call from Heaven.'

'And what became of the banker's widow?'

'She said that she felt no divine call to the flames. This was thirty years ago; and the banker was about thirty years of age when he died.'

'Then he will have rather an old wife in paradise?'

'No, sir; after they pass through the flames upon earth, both become young in paradise.'

'Sometimes women used to burn themselves with any relic of a husband, who had died far from home, did they not?'

'Yes, sir, I remember a fisherman, about twenty years ago, who went on some business to Benares from Jubbulpore, and who was to have been back in two months. Six months passed away without any news of him; and at last the wife dreamed that he had died on the road, and began forthwith, in the middle of the night, to call out "Sat, sat, sat!" Nothing could dissuade her from burning; and in the morning a pile was raised for her, on the north bank of the large tank of Hanumān,[15] where you have planted an avenue of trees. There I saw her burned with her husband's turban in her arms, and in ten days after her husband came back.'

'Now the burning has been prohibited, a man cannot get rid of a bad wife so easily?'

'But she was a good wife, sir, and bad ones do not often become suttees.'

'Who made the pile for her?'

'Some of her family, but I forget who. They thought it must have been a call from Heaven, when, in reality, it was only a dream.'

'You are a Rājpūt?'

'Yes.'

'Do Rājpūts in this part of India now destroy their female infants?'

'Never; that practice has ceased everywhere in these parts; and is growing into disuse in Bundēlkhand, where the Rājās, at the request of the British Government, have prohibited it among their subjects. This was a measure of real good. You see girls now at play in villages, where the face of one was never seen before, nor the voice of one heard.'

'But still those who have them grumble, and say that the Government which caused them to be preserved should undertake to provide for their marriage. Is it not so?'

'At first they grumbled a little, sir; but as the infants grew on their affections, they thought no more about it.'[16]

Gurcharan Baboo, the Principal of the little Jubbulpore College,[17] called upon me one forenoon, soon after this conversation. He was educated in the Calcutta College; speaks and writes English exceedingly well; is tolerably well read in English literature, and is decidedly a *thinking man*. After talking over the matter which caused his visit, I told him of the Lodhī woman's burning herself with the Brahman banker at Sihōrā, and asked him what he thought of it. He said that 'In all probability this woman had really been the wife of the Brahman in some former birth — of which transposition a singular case had occurred in his own family.

'His great-grandfather had three wives, who all burnt themselves with his body. While they were burning, a large serpent came up, and, ascending the pile, was burnt with them. Soon after another came up, and did the same. They were seen by the whole multitude, who were satisfied that they had been the wives of his great-grandfather in a former birth, and would become so again after this sacrifice. When the "srāddh", or funeral obsequies, were performed after the prescribed intervals,[18] the offerings and prayers were regularly made for *six souls* instead of four; and, to this day, every member of his family, and every Hindoo who had heard the story, believed that these two serpents had a just right to be considered among his ancestors, and to be prayed for accordingly in all "srāddh".'

A few days after this conversation with the Principal of the Jubbulpore College, I had a visit from Bholī Sukul, the present head of the Sihōrā banker's family, and youngest brother of the Brahman with whose ashes the Lodhī woman burned herself. I requested him to tell me all that he recollected about this singular suttee, and he did so as follows:

'When my eldest brother, the father of the late Dulī Sukul, who was so long a native collector under you in this district, died about twenty years ago at Sihōrā, a Lodhī woman, who resided two miles distant in the village of Khitolī, which has been held by our family for several generations, declared that she would burn herself with him on the funeral pile; that she had been his wife in three different births, had already burnt herself with him three times, and had to burn with him four times more. She was then sixty years of age, and had a husband living [of] about the same age. We were all astounded when she came forward with this story, and told her that it must be a mistake, as we were Brahmans, while she was a Lodhī. She said that there was no mistake in the matter; that she, in the last birth, resided with my brother in the sacred city of Benares, and one day gave a holy man who came to ask charity salt, by mistake, instead of sugar, with his food. That, in consequence, he told her she should, in the next birth, be separated from her husband, and be of inferior caste; but that, if she did her duty well in that state, she should be reunited to him in the following birth. We told her that all this must be a dream, and the widow of my brother insisted that, if she were not allowed to burn herself, the other should not be allowed to take her place. We prevented the widow from ascending the pile, and she died at a good old age only two years ago at Sihōrā. My brother's body was burned at Sihōrā, and the poor Lodhī woman came and stole one handful of the ashes, which she placed in her bosom, and took back with her to Khitolī. There she prevailed upon her husband and her brother to assist her in her return to her former husband and caste as a Brahman. No soul else would assist them, as we got the then native chief to prohibit it; and these three persons brought on their own heads the pile, on which she seated herself, with the ashes in her bosom. The husband and his brother set fire to the pile, and she was burned.'[19]

'And what is now your opinion, after a lapse of twenty years?'

'Why, that she had really been the wife of my brother; for at the pile she prophesied that my nephew Dulī should be, what his grandfather had been, high in the service of the Government, and, as you know, he soon after became so.'

'And what did your father think?'

'He was so satisfied that she had been the wife of his eldest son in a former birth, that he defrayed all the expenses of her funeral ceremonies, and had them all observed with as much magnificence as those of any member of the family. Her tomb is still to be seen at Khitolī, and that of my brother at Sihōrā.'

I went to look at these tombs with Bholī Sukul himself some short time after this conversation, and found that all the people of the town of Sihōrā and village of Khitolī really believed that the old Lodhī woman had been his brother's wife in a former birth, and had now burned herself as his widow for the fourth time. Her tomb is at Khitolī, and his at Sihōrā.

Notes:

1. *Satī*, a virtuous woman, especially one who burns herself with her husband. The word, in common usage, is transferred to the sacrifice of the woman.

2. The women of Bundēlkhand wear the same costume, a full loin-cloth, as those of the Jubbulpore district. North of the Jumna an ordinary petticoat is generally worn.

3. Suttee was prohibited during the administration of Lord William Bentinck by the Bengal Regulation xvii, dated 4th December, 1829, extended in 1830 to Madras and Bombay. The advocates of the practice unsuccessfully appealed to the Privy Council. Several European officers defended the custom. A well-written account of the suttee legislation is given in Mr. D. Boulger's work on Lord William Bentinck in the 'Rulers of India' series.

4. Whenever it is practicable, Hindoos are placed on the banks of sacred rivers to die, especially in Bengal.

5. For explanation of this phrase, see the following story of the Lodhī woman, following note [14], in this chapter. The name is abnormal. *Upadhya* is a Brahman title meaning 'spiritual preceptor'. Brahmans serving in the army sometimes take the title Singh, which is more properly assumed by Rājpūts or Sikhs.

6. An instance of such a prophecy, of a favourable kind, will be found at the end of this chapter; and another, disastrously fulfilled, in Chapter 21, *post*.

7. Rīwā (Rewah) is a considerable principality lying south of Allahabad and Mirzapore and north of Sāgar. The chiefs are Baghēl Rājpūts. The proper title of the Udaipur, or Mēwār, chief is Rānā, not Raja. See 'Annals of Mewar', chapters 1-18, pp. 173-401, in the Popular Edition of Tod's *Annals and Antiquities of Rajasthan* (Routledge, 1914), an excellent and cheap reprint. The original quarto edition is almost unobtainable.

8. The masculine form of the word satī (suttee).

9. Well known to tourists as the seat of the Mahārāja of Benares.

10. 'of' in text.

11. In the author's time no regular census had been taken. His rough estimate was excessive. The census figures, including the cantonments, are: 1872, 175,188; 1901, 209,331; 1911, 203,804.

12. This Benares story, accidentally omitted from the author's text, was printed as a note at the end of the second volume. It has now been inserted in the place which seems most suitable. Interesting and well-told narratives of several suttees will be found in Bernier, *Travels in the Mogul Empire*, pp.

306-14, ed. Constable. See also Dubois, *Hindu Manners*, &c., 3rd ed. (1906), chapter 19.

13. Widows are not always so well treated. Their life in Lower Bengal, especially, is not a pleasant one,

14. Sihōrā, on the road from Jubbulpore to Mirzāpur, twenty-seven miles from the former, is a town with a population of more than 5,000. A smaller town with the same name exists in the Bhandāra district of the Central Provinces.

15. The monkey-god. His shrines are very numerous in the Central Provinces and Bundēlkhand.

16. Within the last hundred years more than one officer has believed that infanticide had been suppressed by his efforts, and yet the practice is by no means extinct. In the Agra Province the severely inquisitorial measures adopted in 1870, and rigorously enforced, have no doubt done much to break the custom, but, in the neighbouring province of Oudh, the practice continued to be common for many years later. A clear case in the Rāi Barelī District came before me in 1889, though no one was punished, for lack of judicial proof against any individual. The author discusses infanticide as practised in Oudh in many passages of his *Journey through the Kingdom of Oudh* (Bentley, 1858), It is possible that female infanticide may be still prevalent in many Native States. Mr. Willoughby in the years preceding A.D. 1849 made great progress in stamping it out among the Jharejas of the Kathiāwār States in the Bombay Presidency. There is reason to hope that the crime will gradually disappear from all parts of India, but it is difficult to say how far it still prevails, though the general opinion is that it is now comparatively rare (*Census Report, India*, 1911, p. 217).

17. A college of more pretensions now exists at Jabalpur (Jubbulpore), and is affiliated in Arts and Law to the University of Allahabad established in 1887. The small college alluded to in the text was abolished in 1850.

18. For description of the tedious and complicated 'srāddh' ceremonies see chapter 11 of Monier Williams's *Religious Thought and Life in India*.

19. This version of the story differs in some minute particulars from the version given *ante*, [14].

CHAPTER 5

Marriages of Trees — The Tank and the Plantain — Meteors — Rainbows.

Before quitting Jubbulpore, to which place I thought it very unlikely that I should ever return, I went to visit the groves in the vicinity, which, at the time I held the civil charge of the district in 1828, had been planted by different native gentlemen upon lands assigned to them rent-free for the purpose, on condition that the holder should bind himself to plant trees at the rate of twenty-five to the acre, and keep them up at that rate; and that for each grove, however small, he should build and keep in repair a well, lined with masonry, for watering the trees, and for the benefit of travellers.[1]

Some of these groves had already begun to yield fruit, and all had been *married*. Among the Hindoos, neither the man who plants a grove, nor his wife, can taste of the fruit till he has *married* one of the mango-trees to some other tree (commonly the tamarind-tree) that grows near it in the same grove. The proprietor of one of these groves that stands between the cantonment and the town, old Barjōr Singh, had spent so much in planting and watering the grove, and building walls and wells of *pucka*[2] masonry, that he could not afford to defray the expense of the marriage ceremonies till one of the trees, which was older than the rest when planted, began to bear fruit in 1833, and poor old Barjōr Singh and his wife were in great distress that they dared not taste of the fruit whose flavour was so much prized by their children. They began to think that they had neglected a serious duty, and might, in consequence, be taken off before another season could come round. They therefore sold all their silver and gold ornaments, and borrowed all they could; and before the next season the grove was married with all due pomp and ceremony, to the great delight of the old pair, who tasted of the fruit in June 1834.

The larger the number of the Brahmans that are fed on the occasion of the marriage, the greater the glory of the proprietor of the grove; and when I asked old Barjōr Singh, during my visit to his grove, how many he had feasted, he said, with a heavy sigh, that he had been able to feast only one hundred and fifty. He showed me the mango-tree which had acted the part of the bridegroom on the occasion, but the bride had disappeared from his side. 'And where is the bride, the tamarind?' 'The only tamarind I had in the grove died', said the old man, 'before we could bring about the wedding; and I was obliged to get a jasmine for a wife for my mango. I planted it here, so that we might, as required, cover both bride and bridegroom under one canopy during the ceremonies; but, after the marriage was over, the gardener neglected her, and she pined away and died.'

'And what made you prefer the jasmine to all other trees after the tamarind?'

'Because it is the most celebrated of all trees, save the rose.'

'And why not have chosen the rose for a wife?'

'Because no one ever heard of marriage between the rose and the mango; while they [sic] take place every day between the mango and the chambēlī (jasmine).'[3]

After returning from the groves, I had a visit after breakfast from a learned Muhammadan, now guardian to the young Rājā of Uchahara,[4] who resides part of his time at Jubbulpore. I mentioned my visit to the groves and the curious notion of the Hindoos regarding the necessity of marrying them; and he told me that, among Hindoos, the man who went to the expense of making a tank dared not drink of its waters till he had married his tank to some banana-tree, planted on the bank for the purpose. [5]

'But what', said he with a smile, 'could you expect from men who believe that Indra is the god who rules the heavens immediately over the earth, that he sleeps during eight months in the year, and during the other four his time is divided between his duties of sending down rain upon the earth, and repelling with his arrows Rājā Bali, who by his austere devotions (tapasya) has received from the higher gods a promise of the reversion of his dominions? The lightning which we see', said the learned Maulavī, 'they believe to be nothing more than the glittering of these arrows, as they are shot from the bow of Indra upon his foe Rājā Bali '.[6]

'But, my good friend Maulavī Sāhib, there are many good Muhammadans who believe that the meteors, which we call shooting stars, are in reality stars which the guardian angels of men snatch from the spheres, and throw at the devil as they see him passing through the air, or hiding himself under one or other of the constellations. Is it not so?'

'Yes, it is; but we have the authority of the holy prophet for this, as delivered down to us by his companions in the sacred traditions, and we are bound to believe it. When our holy prophet came upon the earth, he found it to be infested with a host of magicians, who, by their abominable rites and incantations, get into their interest certain devils, or demons, whom they used to send up to heaven to listen to the orders which the angels received from God regarding men and the world below. On hearing these orders, they came off and reported them to the magicians, who were thereby enabled to foretell the events which the angels were ordered to bring about. In this manner they often overheard the orders which the angel Gabriel received from God, and communicated them to the magicians as soon as he could deliver them to our holy prophet. Exulting in the knowledge obtained in this diabolical manner, these wretches tried to turn his prophecies into ridicule; and, seeing the evil effects of such practices among men, he prayed God to put a stop to them. From that time guardian angels have been stationed in different parts of the heavens, to keep off the devils; and as soon as one of them sees a devil sneaking too near the heaven of heavens, he snatches the nearest star, and flings it at him.'[7] This, he added, was what all true Muhammadans believed regarding the shooting of stars. He had read nothing about them in the works of Plato, Aristotle, Hippocrates, or Galen, all of which he had carefully studied, and should be glad to learn from me what modern philosophers in Europe thought about them.

I explained to him the supposed distance and bulk of the fixed stars visible to the naked eye; their being radiant with unborrowed light, and probably every one of them, like our own sun, the great centre of a solar system of its own; embracing the vast orbits of numerous planets, revolving around it with their attendant satellites; the stars visible to the naked eye being but a very small portion of the whole which the telescope had now made distinctly visible to us; and those distinctly visible being one cluster among many thousand with which the genius of Galileo, Newton, the Herschells, and many other modern philosophers had discovered the heavens to be studded. I remarked that the notion that these mighty suns, the centres of planetary systems, should be made merely to be thrown at devils and demons, appeared to us just as unaccountable as those of the Hindoos regarding Indra's arrows.

'But', said he, 'these foolish Hindoos believe still greater absurdities. They believe that the rainbow is nothing but the fume of a large snake, concealed under the ground; that he vomits forth this fume from a hole in the surface of the earth, without being himself seen; and, when you ask them why, in that case, the rainbow should be in the west while the sun is in the east, and in the east while the sun is in the west, they know not what to say.'[8]

'The truth is, my friend Maulavī Sahib, the Hindoos, like a very great part of every other nation, are very much disposed to attribute to supernatural influences effects that the wiser portion of our species know to rise from natural causes.'

The Maulavī was right. In the *Mishkāt-ul- Masābih*,[9] the authentic traditions of their prophet,[10] it is stated that Ayesha, the widow of Muhammad, said, 'I heard His Majesty say, "The angels come down to the region next the world, and mention the works that have been pre-ordained in heaven; and the devils, who descend to the lowest region, listen to what the angels say, and hear the orders predestined in heaven, and carry them to fortune-tellers; therefore, they tell a hundred lies with it from themselves "'[11]

'Ibn Abbās said, "A man of His Majesty's friends informed me, that whilst His Majesty's friends were sitting with him one night, a very bright star shot; and His Highness said, "What did you say in the days of ignorance when a star shot like this?" They said, "God and His messenger know best; we used to say, a great man was born to-night, and a great man died."[12] Then His Majesty said, "You mistook, because the shootings of these stars are neither for the life nor death of any person; but when our cherisher orders a work, the bearers of the imperial throne sing hallelujahs; and the inhabitants of the regions who are near the bearers repeat it, till it reaches the lowest regions. After the angels which are near the bearers of the imperial throne say, "What did your cherisher order?" Then they are informed; and so it is handed from one region to another, till the information reaches the people of the lowest region. Then the devils steal it, and carry it to their friends, (that is) magicians; and these stars are thrown at these devils; not for the birth or death of any person. Then the things which the magicians tell, having heard from the devils, are true, but these magicians tell lies, and exaggerate in what they hear".'

Kutādah said, 'God has created stars for three uses; one of them, as a cause of ornament of the regions; the second, to stone the devil with; the third, to direct people going through forests and on the sea. Therefore, whoever shall explain them otherwise, does wrong, and loses his time, and speaks from his own invention and embellishes'.[13]

Ibn Abbās. ['The prophet said,] "Whoever attains to the knowledge of astrology for any other explanation than the three aforementioned, then verily he has attained to a branch of magic. An astrologer is a magician, and a magician is a necromancer, and a necromancer is an infidel."'[14]

This work contains the precepts and sayings of Muhammad, as declared by his companions, who themselves heard them, or by those who heard them immediately from those companions; and they are considered to be binding upon the faith and conduct of Musalmans, though not all delivered from inspiration.

Everything that is written in the Korān itself is supposed to have been brought direct from God by the angel Gabriel.[15]

Notes:

1. In planting mango groves, it is a rule that they shall be as far from each other as not to admit of their branches ever meeting. 'Plant trees, but let them not touch' ('*Ām lagao, nis lageñ nahīñ*') is the maxim. [W. H. S.]

2. *Pakkā*; the word here means 'cemented with lime mortar', and not only with mud (*kachchā*).

3. The *chambēlī* is known in science as the *Jasminum grandiflorum*, and the mango-tree as *Mangifera Indica*.

4. A small principality west of Rīwā, and 110 miles north-west of Jubbulpore. It is also known as Nāgaudh, or Nāgod.

5. Compare the account of the marriage of the *tulasī* shrub (*Ocymum sanctum*) with the sālagrām stone, or fossil ammonite, in Chapter 19, *post*.

6. There is a sublime passage in the Psalms of David, where the lightning is said to be the arrows of God. Psalm lxxvii:

17, 'The clouds poured out water: the skies sent out a sound: thine arrows also went abroad.

18. The voice of thy thunder was in the heaven; the lightnings lightened the world: the earth trembled and shook.' [W. H. S.]
The passage is quoted from the Authorized Bible
version; the Prayer Book version is finer.

7. 'We guard them from every devil driven away with stones; except him who listeneth by stealth, at whom a visible flame is darted.' Korān, chapter 15, Sale's translation. See *post*, end of this chapter.

8. Nine Hindoos out of ten, or perhaps ninety-nine in a hundred, throughout India, believe the rainbow to arise from the breath of the snake, thrown up from the surface of the earth, as water is thrown up by whales from the surface of the ocean. [W. H. S,]

9. '*Mishkāt* is a hole in a wall in which a lamp is placed, and *Masābih* the plural of "a lamp", because traditions are compared to lamps, and this book is like that which containeth a lamp. Another reason is, that *Masābih* is the name of a book, and this book comprehends its contents' (Matthews's translation, vol. i, p. v, note).

10. The full title is *Mishkāt-ul-Masābih, or a Collection of the most Authentic Traditions regarding the Actions and Sayings of Muhammed; exhibiting the Origin of the Manners and Customs; the Civil, Religious, and Military Policy of the*

Muslemāns. Translated from the original Arabic by Captain A. N. Matthews, Bengal Artillery. Two vols. 4to; Calcutta, 1809-10, This valuable work, published by subscription, is now very scarce. A fine copy is in the India Office Library.

11. Book xxi, chapter 3, part i; vol. ii, p. 384. The quotations as given by the author are inexact. The editor has substituted correct extracts from Matthews's text. Matthews spells the name of the prophet's widow as Aáyeshah.

12. In Sparta, the Ephoroi, once every nine years, watched the sky during a whole cloudless, moonless night, in profound silence; and, if they saw a shooting star, it was understood to indicate that the kings of Sparta had disobeyed the gods, and their authority was, in consequence, suspended till they had been purified by an oracle from Delphi or Olympia. [W. H. S.] This statement rests on the authority of Plutarch, *Agis,* 11.

13. *Mishkāt.* Part iii of same chapter; vol. ii, p. 386.

14. Ibid. p. 386.

15. But the prying character of these devils is described in the Korān itself. According to Muhammadans, they had access to all the seven heavens till the time of Moses, who got them excluded from three. Christ got them excluded from three more; and Muhammad managed to get them excluded from the seventh and last. 'We have placed the twelve signs in the heavens, and have set them out in various figures for the observation of spectators, and we guard them from every devil driven away with stones; except him who listeneth by stealth, at whom a visible flame is darted' (Chapter 15).

'We have adorned the lower heaven with the ornament of stars, and we have placed therein a guard against every rebellious devil, that they may not listen to the discourse of exalted princes, for they are darted at from every side, to repel them, and a lasting torment is prepared for them; except him who catcheth a word by stealth, and is pursued by a shining flame' (Chapter 37). [W. H. 8.] Passages of this kind should he remembered by persons who expect orthodox Muhammadans to accept the results of modern science.

CHAPTER 6

Hindoo Marriages.

Certain it is that no Hindoo will have a marriage in his family during the four months of the rainy season; for among eighty millions of souls[1] not one doubts that the Great Preserver of the universe is, during these four months, down on a visit to Rājā Bali, and, consequently, unable to bless the contract with his presence.[2]

Marriage is a sacred duty among Hindoos, a duty which every parent must perform for his children, otherwise they owe him no reverence. A family with a daughter unmarried after the age of puberty is considered to labour under the displeasure of the gods; and no member of the other sex considers himself *respectable* after the age of puberty till he is married. It is the duty of his parent or elder brothers to have him suitably married; and, if they do not do so, he reproaches them with his *degraded condition*. The same feeling, in a degree, pervades all the Muhammadan community; and nothing appears so strange to them as the apparent indifference of old bachelors among us to their *sad condition*.

Marriage, with all its ceremonies, its rights, and its duties, fills their imagination from infancy to age; and I do not believe there is a country upon earth in which a larger portion of the wealth of the community is spent in the ceremonies, or where the rights are better secured, or the duties better enforced, notwithstanding all the disadvantages of the laws of polygamy. Not one man in ten can afford to maintain more than one wife, and not one in ten of those who can afford it will venture upon 'a sea of troubles' in taking a second, if he has a child by the first. One of the evils which press most upon Indian society is the necessity which long usage has established of squandering large sums in marriage ceremonies. Instead of giving what they can to their children to establish them, and enable them to provide for their families and rise in the world, parents everywhere feel bound to squander all they can borrow in the festivities of their marriage. Men in India could never feel secure of being permitted freely to enjoy their property under despotic and unsettled governments, the only kind of governments they knew or hoped for; and much of the means that would otherwise have been laid out in forming substantial works, with a view to a return in income of some sort or another, for the remainder of their own lives and of those of their children, were expended in tombs, temples, sarāis, tanks, groves, and other works – useful and ornamental, no doubt, but from which neither they nor their children could ever hope to derive income of any kind. The same feeling of insecurity gave birth, no doubt, to this preposterous usage, which tends so much to keep down the great mass of the people of India to that grade in which they were born, and in which they have nothing but their manual labour to depend upon for their subsistence. Every man feels himself bound to waste all his stock and capital, and exhaust all his credit, in feeding idlers during the ceremonies which attend the marriage of his children, because his ancestors squandered similar sums, and he would sink in the estimation of society if he were to allow his children to be married with less.

But it could not have been solely because men could not invest their means in profitable works, with any chance of being long permitted to enjoy the profits under such despotic and unsettled governments, that they squandered them in feeding idle people in marriage ceremonies; since temples, tanks, and groves secured esteem in this life, and promised some advantage in the next, and an outlay in such works might therefore have been preferred. But under such governments a man's title even to the exclusive possession of his wife might not be considered as altogether secure under the mere sanction of religion; and the outlay in feeding the family, tribe, and neighbourhood during the marriage ceremony seems to have been considered as a kind of value in exchange given for her to society. There is nothing that she and her husband recollect through life with so much pride and pleasure as the cost of their marriage, if it happen to be large for their condition of life; it is their *amoka*, their title of nobility;[3] and their parents consider it their duty to make it as large as they can. A man would hardly feel secure of the sympathy of his family, tribe, circle of society, or rulers, for the loss of 'his ox, or his ass, or anything that is his', if it should happen to have cost him nothing; and, till he could feel secure of their sympathy for the loss, he would not feel very secure in the possession. He, therefore, or those who are interested in his welfare, strengthen his security by an outlay which invests his wife with a tangible value in cost, well understood by his circle and rulers. His family, tribe, and circle have received the purchase money, and feel bound to secure to him the commodity purchased; and, as they are in all such matters commonly much stronger than the rulers themselves, the money spent among them is more efficacious in securing the exclusive enjoyment of the wife than if it had been paid in taxes or fees to them for a marriage licence.[4] The pride of families and tribes, and the desire of the multitude to participate in the enjoyment of such ceremonies, tend to keep up this usage after the cause in which it originated may have ceased to operate; but it will, it is to be hoped, gradually decline with the increased feeling of security to person, property, and character under our rule. Nothing is now more common than to see an individual in the humblest rank spending all that he has, or can borrow, in the marriage of one of many daughters, and trusting to Providence for the means of marrying the others; nor in the higher, to find a young man, whose estates have, during a long minority, under the careful management of Government officers, been freed from very heavy debts, with which an improvident father had left them encumbered, the moment he attains his majority and enters upon the management, borrowing three times their annual rent, at an exorbitant interest, to marry a couple of sisters, at the same rate of outlay in feasts and fireworks that his grandmother was married with.[5]

Notes:

1. The author's figure of 'eighty millions' was a mere guess, and probably, even in his time, was much below the mark. The figures of the census of 1911 are:

Total population of India, excluding
Burma 301,432,623
Hindus 217,197,213
The proportions in different provinces vary enormously.

2. See *ante*. Chapter 1, note 3.

3. The word *amoka* is corrupt, and even Sir George Grierson cannot suggest a plausible explanation. Can it be a misprint for *anka*, in the sense of 'stamp'?

4. Akbar levied a tax on marriages, ranging from a single copper coin (*dām* = 1/40th of rupee) for poor people to 10 gold mohurs, or about 150 rupees, for high officials. Abūl Fazl declares that 'the payment of this tax is looked upon as auspicious', a statement open to doubt (Blochmann, transl. *Aīn*, vol. i, p. 278). In 1772 Warren Hastings abolished the marriage fees levied up to that time in Bengal by the Muhammadan law-officers. But I am disposed to think that a modern finance minister might reconsider the propriety of imposing a moderate tax, carefully graduated.

5. Extravagance in marriage expenses is still one of the principal curses of Indian society. Considerable efforts to secure reform have been made by various castes during recent years, but, as yet, small results only have been attained. The editor has seen numerous painful examples of the wreck of fine estates by young proprietors assuming the management after a long term of the careful stewardship of the Court of Wards.

CHAPTER 7

The Purveyance System,

We left Jubbulpore on the morning of the 20th November, 1835, and came on ten miles to Baghaurī. Several of our friends of the 29th Native Infantry accompanied us this first stage, where they had a good day's shooting. In 1830 I established here some venders in wood to save the people from the miseries of the purveyance system; but I now found that a native collector, soon after I had resigned the civil charge of the district, and gone to Sāgar,[1] in order to ingratiate himself with the officers and get from them favourable testimonials, gave two regiments, as they marched over this road, free permission to help themselves gratis out of the store- rooms of these poor men, whom I had set up with a loan from the public treasury, declaring that it must be the wish and intention of Government to supply their public officers free of cost; and consequently that no excuses could be attended to. From that time shops and shopkeepers have disappeared. Wood for all public officers and establishments passing this road has ever since, as in former times, been collected from the surrounding villages gratis, under the purveyance system, in which all native public officers delight, and which, I am afraid, is encouraged by European officers, either from their ignorance or their indolence. They do not like the trouble of seeing the men paid either for their wood or their labour; and their head servants of the kitchen or the wardrobe weary and worry them out of their best resolutions on the subject. They make the poor men sit aloof by telling them that their master is a tiger before breakfast, and will eat them if they approach; and they tell their masters that there is no hope of getting the poor men to come for their money till they have bathed or taken their breakfast. The latter wait in hopes that the gentleman will come out or send for them as soon as he has been tamed by his breakfast; but this meal has put him in good humour with all the world, and he is now no longer unwilling to trust the payment of the poor men to his butler, or his *valet de chambre*. They keep the poor wretches waiting, declaring that they have as yet received no orders to pay them, till, hungry and weary, in the afternoon they all walk back to their homes in utter despair of getting anything.

If, in the meantime, the gentleman comes out, and finds the men, his servants pacify him by declaring either that they have not yet had time to carry his orders into effect, that they could not get copper change for silver rupees, or that they were anxious to collect all the people together before they paid any, lest they might pay some of them twice over. It is seldom, however, that he comes among them at all; he takes it for granted that the people have all been paid; and passes the charge in the account of his servants, who all get what these porters ought to have received. Or, perhaps the gentleman may persuade himself that, if he pays his valet or butler, these functionaries will never pay the poor men, and think that he had better sit quiet and keep the money in his own pocket. The native police or revenue officer is directed by his superior to have wood collected for the camp of a regiment or great civil officers, and he sends out his myrmidons to employ the people around in felling trees, and cutting up wood enough to supply not only the camp, but his own cook-rooms and those of his friends for the next six months. The men so employed commonly get nothing; but the native officer receives credit for all manner of superlatively good qualities, which are enumerated in a certificate. Many a fine tree, dear to the affections of families and village communities, has been cut down in spite, or redeemed from the axe by a handsome present to this officer or his myrmidons. Lambs, kids, fowls, milk, vegetables, all come flowing in for the great man's table from poor people, who are too hopeless to seek for payment, or who are represented as too proud and wealthy to receive it. Such always have been and such always will be some of the evils of the purveyance system. If a police officer receives an order from the magistrate to provide a regiment, detachment, or individual with boats, carts, bullocks, or porters, he has all that can be found within his jurisdiction forthwith seized—releases all those whose proprietors are able and willing to pay what he demands, and furnishes the rest, which are generally the worst, to the persons who require them. Police officers derive so much profit from these applications that they are always anxious they should be made; and will privately defeat all attempts of private individuals to provide themselves by dissuading or intimidating the proprietors of vehicles from voluntarily furnishing them. The gentleman's servant who is sent to procure them returns and tells his master that there are plenty of vehicles, but that their proprietors dare not send them without orders from the police; and that the police tell him they dare not give such orders without the special sanction of the magistrate. The magistrate is written to, but declares that his police have been prohibited from interfering in such matters without special orders, since the proprietors ought to be permitted to send their vehicles to whom they choose, except on occasions of great public emergency; and, as the present cannot be considered as one of these occasions, he does not feel authorized to issue such orders. On the Ganges, many men have made large fortunes by pretending a general authority to seize boats for the use of the commissariat, or for other Government purposes, on the ground of having been once or twice employed on that duty; and what they get is but a small portion of that which the public lose. One of these self-constituted functionaries has a boat seized on its way down or up the river; and the crew, who are merely hired for the occasion, and have a month's wages in advance, seeing no prospect of getting soon out of the hands of this pretended Government servant, desert, and leave the boat on the sands; while the owner, if he ever learns the real state of the case, thinks it better to put up with his loss than to seek redress through expensive courts, and distant local authorities. If the boat happens to be loaded and to have a supercargo, who will not or cannot bribe high enough, he is abandoned on the sands by his crew; in his search for aid from the neighbourhood, his helplessness becomes known—he is perhaps murdered, or runs away in the apprehension of being so—the boat is plundered and made a wreck. Still the dread of the delays and costs of our courts, and the utter hopelessness of ever recovering the lost property, prevent the proprietors from seeking redress, and our Government authorities know nothing of the circumstances.

We remained at Baghauri the 21st to enable our people to prepare for the long march they had before them, and to see a little more of our Jubbulpore friends, who were to have another day's shooting, as black partridges[2] and quail had been found abundant in the neighbourhood of our camp.[3]

Notes:

1. Or Saugor, the head-quarters of the district of that name in the Central Provinces. The town is 109 miles north-west of Jabalpur. The author took charge of the Sāgar district in January 1831.

2. *Francolinus vulgaris.*

3. The purveyance system (Persian *rasad rasānī*) above described is one of the necessary evils of Oriental life. It will be observed that the author, though so keenly sensitive to the abuses attending the system, proposes no substitute for it, and confesses that the small attempt he made to check abuse was a failure. From time immemorial it has been the custom for Government officials in India to be supplied with necessaries by the people of the country through which their camps pass. Under native Governments no officials ever dream of paying for anything. In British territory requisitions are limited, and in well ordered civil camps nothing is taken without payment except wood, coarse earthen vessels, and grass. The hereditary village potter supplies the pots, and this duty is fully recognized as one attaching to his office. The landholders supply the wood and grass. None of these things

are ordinarily procurable by private purchase in sufficient quantity, and in most cases could not be bought at all. Officers commanding troops send in advance requisitions specifying the quantities of each article needed, and the indent is met by the civil authorities. Everything so indented for, including wood and grass, is supposed to be paid for, but in practice it is often impossible, with the agency available, to ensure actual payment to the persons entitled. Troops and the people in civil camps must live, and all that can be done is to check abuse, so far as possible, by vigilant administration. The obligation of landholders to supply necessaries for troops and officials on the march is so well established that it forms one of the conditions of the contract with Government under which proprietors in the permanently settled province of Benares hold their lands. The extreme abuses of which the system is capable under a lax and corrupt native Government are abundantly illustrated in the author's *Journey through the Kingdom of Oudh.* 'The System of Purveyance and Forced Labour' is the subject of article xxv in the Hon. F, J, Shore's curious book, *Notes on Indian Affairs* (London, 1837, 2 vols. 8vo). Many of the abuses denounced by Mr. Shore have been suppressed, but some, unhappily, still exist, and are likely to continue for many years.

CHAPTER 8

Religious Sects—Self-government of the Castes—Chimney- sweepers—
Washerwomen[1]—Elephant Drivers.

Mīr Salāmat Alī, the head native collector of the district, a venerable
old Musalmān and most valuable public servant, who has been labouring in
the same vineyard with me for the last fifteen years with great zeal, ability,
and integrity, came to visit me after breakfast with two very pretty and
interesting young sons. While we were sitting together my wife's under-
woman[2] said to some one who was talking with her outside the tent-
door, 'If that were really the case, should I not be degraded?' 'You see,
Mīr Sāhib',[3] said I, 'that the very lowest members of society among these
Hindoos still feel the pride of caste, and dread exclusion from their own,
however low.'[4]

'Yes', said the Mīr, 'they are a very strange kind of people, and I
question whether they ever had a real prophet among them.'

'I question, Mīr Sahib, whether they really ever had such a person.
They of course think the incarnations of their three great divinities were
beings infinitely superior to prophets, being in all their attributes and
prerogatives equal to the divinities themselves.[5] But we are disposed to
think that these incarnations were nothing more than great men whom
their flatterers and poets have exalted into gods—this was the way in which
men made their gods in ancient Greece and Egypt. These great men were
generally conquerors whose glory consisted in the destruction of their
fellow creatures; and this is the glory which their flatterers are most prone
to extol. All that the poets have sung of the actions of men is now received
as revelation from heaven; though nothing can be more monstrous than the
actions attributed to the best incarnation, Krishna, of the best of their gods,
Vishnu.[6]

'No doubt', said Salāmat Ali; 'and had they ever had a real prophet
among them he would have revealed better things to them. Strange people!
when their women go on pilgrimages to Gayā, they have their heads shaved

before the image of their god; and the offering of the hair is equivalent to the offer of their heads;[7] for heads, thank God, they dare no longer offer within the Company's territories.'

'Do you. Mīr Sahib, think that they continue to offer up human sacrifices anywhere?'

'Certainly I do. There is a Rājā at Ratanpur, or somewhere between Mandlā and Sambalpur, who has a man offered up to Dēvī every year, and that man must be a Brahman. If he can get a Brahman traveller, well and good; if not, he and his priests offer one of his own subjects. Every Brahman that has to pass through this territory goes in disguise.[8] With what energy did our emperor Aurangzēb apply himself to put down iniquities like this in the Rājputāna states, but all in vain. If a Rājā died, all his numerous wives burnt themselves with his body—even their servants, male and female, were obliged to do the same; for, said his friends, what is he to do in the next world without attendants? The pile was enormous. On the top sat the queen with the body of the prince; the servants, male and female, according to their degree, below; and a large army stood all round to drive into the fire again or kill all who should attempt to escape.'[9]

'This is all very true, Mīr Sāhib, but you must admit that, though there is a great deal of absurdity in their customs and opinions, there is, on the other hand, much that we might all take an example from. The Hindoo believes that Christians and Musalmāns may be as good men in all relations of life as himself, and in as fair a way to heaven as he is; for he believes that my Bible and your Korān are as much revelations framed by the Deity for our guidance, as the Shāstras are for his. He doubts not that our Christ was the Son of God, nor that Muhammad was the prophet of God; and all that he asks from us is to allow him freely to believe in his own gods, and to worship in his own way. Nor does one caste or sect of Hindoos ever believe itself to be alone in the right way, or detest any other for not following in the same path, as they have as much of toleration for each other as they have for us.[10]

'True,' exclaimed Salāmat Alī, 'too true! we have ruined each other; we have cut each other's throats; we have lost the empire, and we deserve to lose it. You won it, and you preserved it by your *union*—ten men with one heart are equal to a hundred men with different hearts. A Hindoo may feel himself authorized to take in a Musalmān, and might even think it *meritorious* to do so; but he would never think it meritorious to take in one of his own religion. There are no less than seventy- two sects of Muhammadans; and every one of these sects would not only take in the followers of every other religion on earth, but every member of every one of the other seventy-one sects; and the nearer that sect is to its own, the greater the merit in taking in its members.'[11]

'Something has happened of late to annoy you, I fear, Mīr Sāhib?'

'Something happens to annoy us every day, sir, where we are more than one sect of us together; and wherever you find Musalmāns you will find them divided into sects.'

It is not, perhaps, known to many of my countrymen in India that in every city and town in the country the right of sweeping the houses and streets is one of the most intolerable of monopolies, supported entirely by the pride of caste among the scavengers, who are all of the lowest class. The right of sweeping within a certain range is recognized by the caste to belong to a certain member; and, if any other member presumes to sweep within that range, he is excommunicated — no other member will smoke out of his pipe, or drink out of his jug; and he can get restored to caste only by a feast to the whole body of sweepers. If any housekeeper within a particular circle happens to offend the sweeper of that range, none of his filth will be removed till he pacifies him, because no other sweeper will dare to touch it; and the people of a town are often more tyrannized over by these people than by any other.[12]

It is worthy of remark that in India the spirit of combination is always in the inverse ratio to the rank of the class; weakest in the highest, and strongest in the lowest class. All infringements upon the rules of the class are punished by fines. Every fine furnishes a feast at which every member sits and enjoys himself. Payment is enforced by excommunication — no one of the caste will eat, drink, or smoke with the convicted till the fine is paid; and, as every one shares in the fine, every one does his best to enforce payment. The fines are imposed by the elders, who know the circumstances of the culprit, and fix the amount accordingly. Washermen will often at a large station combine to prevent the washermen of one gentleman from washing the clothes of the servants of any other gentleman, or the servants of one gentleman from getting their clothes washed by any other person than their own master's washerman. This enables them sometimes to raise the rate of washing to double the fair or ordinary rate; and at such places the washermen are always drunk with one continued routine of feasts from the fines levied.[13] The cost of these fees falls ultimately upon the poor servants or their masters. This combination, however, is not always for bad or selfish purposes. I was once on the staff of an officer commanding a brigade on service, whose elephant driver exercised an influence over him that was often mischievous and sometimes dangerous;[14] for in marching and choosing his ground, this man was more often consulted than the quarter-master-general. His bearing was most insolent, and became intolerable, as well to the European gentlemen as to the people of his caste. [15] He at last committed himself by saying that he would spit in the face of another gentleman's elephant driver with whom he was disputing. All the elephant drivers in our large camp were immediately assembled, and it was determined in council to refer the matter to the decision of the Rājā of Darbhanga's driver, who was acknowledged the head of the class. We were all breakfasting with the brigadier after muster when the reply came—the distance to Darbhanga from Nāthpur on the Kūsī river, where we then were, must have been a hundred and fifty miles.[16] We saw men running in all directions through the camp, without knowing why, till at last one came and summoned the brigadier's driver. With a face of terror he came and implored the protection of the brigadier; who got angry, and fumed a good deal, but seeing no expression of sympathy on the faces of his officers, he told the man to go and hear his sentence. He was escorted to a circle formed by all the drivers in camp, who were seated on the grass. The offender was taken into the middle of the circle and commanded to stand on one leg[17] while the Raja's driver's letter was read. He did so, and the letter directed him to apologize to the offended party, pay a heavy fine for a feast, and pledge himself to the offended drivers never to offend again. All the officers in camp were delighted, and some, who went to hear the sentence explained, declared that in no court in the world could the thing have been done with more solemnity and effect. The man's character was quite altered by it, and he became the most docile of drivers. On the same principle here stated of enlisting the community in the punishment of offenders, the New Zealanders, and other savage tribes who have been fond of human flesh, have generally been found to confine the feast to the body of those who were put to death for offences against the state or the individual. I and all the officers of my regiment were at one time in the habit of making every servant who required punishment or admonition to bring immediately, and give to the first religious mendicant we could pick up, the fine we thought just. All the religionists in the neighbourhood declared that justice had never been so well administered in any other regiment; no servant got any sympathy from them—they were all told that their masters were far too lenient.

We crossed the Hiran river[18] about ten miles from our last ground on the 22nd,[19] and came on two miles to our tents in a mango grove close to the town of Katangī,[20] and under the Vindhya range of sandstone hills, which rise almost perpendicular to the height of some eight hundred feet over the town. This range from Katangī skirts the Nerbudda valley to the north, as the Sātpura range skirts it to the south; and both are of the same sandstone formation capped with basalt upon which here and there are found masses of laterite, or iron clay. Nothing has ever yet been found reposing upon this iron clay.[21] The strata of this range have a gentle and almost imperceptible dip to the north, at right angles to its face which overlooks the valley, and this face has everywhere the appearance of a range of gigantic round bastions projecting into what was perhaps a lake, and is now a well-peopled, well-cultivated, and very happy valley, about twenty miles wide. The river crosses and recrosses it diagonally. Near Jubbulpore it flows along for some distance close under the Sātpura range to the south; and crossing over the valley from Bheraghāt, it reaches the Vindhya range to the north, at the point where it reaches the Hiran river, forty miles below.

Notes:

1. This is a slip, probably due to the printer's reader. There are no chimney-sweepers in India. The word should be 'sweepers'. The members of this caste and a few other degraded communities, such as the Doms, do all the sweeping, scavenging, and conservancy work in India. 'Washerwomen' is another slip: read 'Washermen'.

2. The 'under-woman', or 'second ayah', was a member of the sweeper caste.

3. The title Mīr Sāhib implies that Salāmat Alī was a Sayyid, claiming descent from Alī, the cousin, son-in-law, and pupil of Muhammad, who became Khalīf in A.D. 656.

4. The sweeper castes stand outside the Hindoo pale, and often incline to Muhammadan practices. They worship a special form of the Deity, under the names of Lāl Beg, Lāl Guru, &c.

5. No *avatār* or incarnation of Brahma is known to most Hindoos, and incarnations of Siva are rarely mentioned. The only *avatārs* ordinarily recognized are those of Vishnu, as enumerated ante. Chapter 2, note 4.

6. This theory is a very inadequate explanation of the doctrine of *avatārs*.

7. 'Women . . . are most careful to preserve their hair intact. They pride themselves on its length and weight. For a woman to have to part with her hair is one of the greatest of degradations, and the most terrible of all trials. It is the mark of widowhood. Yet in some sacred places, especially at the confluence of rivers, the cutting off and offering of a few locks of hair (*Venī-dānam*) by a virtuous wife is considered a highly meritorious act' (Monier Williams, *Religious Thought and Life in India*, p, 375). Gayā in Bihār, fifty-five miles south of Patna, is much frequented by pilgrims devoted to Vishnu.

8. All the places named are in the Central Provinces. Ratanpur, in the Bilāspur District, is a place of much antiquarian interest, full of ruins; Mandlā, in the Mandlā District, was the capital of the later Gond chiefs of Garhā Mandlā; and Sambalpur is the capital of the Sambalpur District. If the

story is true, the selection of a Brahman for sacrifice is remarkable, though not without precedent. Human sacrifice has prevailed largely in India, and is not yet quite extinct. In 1891 some Jāts in the Muzaffarnagar District of the United Provinces sacrificed a boy in a very painful manner for some unascertained magical purpose. It was supposed that the object was to induce the gods to grant offspring to a childless woman. Other similar cases have occurred in recent years. One occurred close to Calcutta in 1892. In the hill tracts of Orissa bordering on the Central Provinces the rite of human sacrifice was practised by the Khonds on an awful scale, and with horrid cruelty, It was suppressed by the special efforts of Macpherson, Campbell, MacViccar, and other officers, between the years 1837 and 1854. Daring that period the British officers rescued 1,506 victims intended for sacrifice (*Narrative of Major-General John Campbell, C.B., of his Operations in the Hill Tracts of Orissa for the Suppression of Human Sacrifices and Female Infanticide*. Printed for private circulation. London: Hurst and Blackett, 1861). The rite, when practised by Hindoos, may have been borrowed from some of the aboriginal races. The practice, however, has been so general throughout the world that few peoples can claim the honour of freedom from the stain of adopting it at one time or another, Much curious information on the subject, and many modern instances of human sacrifices in India, are collected in the article 'Sacrifice' in Balfour, *Cyclopaedia of India*, 3rd edition, 1885. Major S. C. Macpherson, *Memorials of Service in India* (1865), and Frazer, *Golden Bough*, 3rd edition, Part V, vol. i (1912), pp. 236 seq., may also be consulted.

9. Bernier vividly describes an 'infernal tragedy' of this kind which he witnessed, in or about the year 1659, during Aurangzēb's reign, in Rājputāna. On that occasion five female slaves burnt themselves with their mistress (*Travels*, ed. Constable and V. A. Smith (1914), p. 309).

10. Hinduism is a social system, not a creed, A Hindoo may believe, or disbelieve, what speculative doctrine he chooses, but he must not eat, drink, or marry, save in accordance with the custom of his caste. Compare Asoka on toleration; 'The sects of other people all deserve reverence for one reason or another' (Rock Edict xii; V. A. Smith, *Asoka*, 2nd edition (1909), p. 170).

11. Mīr Salāmat Alī is a stanch Sunnī, the sect of Osmān; and they are always at daggers drawn with the Shīas, or the sect of Alī. He alludes to the Shīas when he says that one of the seventy-two sects is always ready to take in the whole of the other seventy-one. Muhammad, according to the traditions, was one day heard to say, 'The time will come when my followers will he divided into seventy-three sects; all of them will assuredly go to hell save one.' Every one of the seventy-three sects believes itself to be the one happily excepted by their prophet, and predestined to paradise. I am sometimes disposed to think Muhammad was self-deluded, however

difficult it might be to account for so much 'method in his madness'. It is difficult to conceive a man placed in such circumstances with more amiable dispositions or with juster views of the rights and duties of men in all their relations with each other, than are exhibited by him on almost all occasions, save where the question of *faith* in his divine mission was concerned.

A very interesting and useful book might be made out of the history of those men, more or less mad, by whom multitudes of mankind have been led and perhaps governed; and a philosophical analysis of the points on which they were really mad and really sane, would show many of them to have been fit subjects for a madhouse during the whole career of their glory. [W. H. S.]

For an account of Muhammadan sects, see section viii of the Preliminary Dissertation in Sale's Korān, entitled, 'Of the Principal Sects among the Muhammadans; and of those who have pretended to Prophecy among the Arabs, in or since the Time of Muhammad'; and T. P. Hughes, *Dictionary of Islam* (1885). The chief sects of the Sunnīs, or Traditionists, are four in number. 'The principal sects of the Shīas are five, which are subdivided into an almost innumerable number.' The court of the kings of Oudh was Shīa. In most parts of India the Sunnī faith prevails.

The relation between genius and insanity is well expressed by Dryden (*Absalom and Achitopfel*):

Great wits are sure to madness near allied,
And thin partitions do their bounds divide.

The treatise of Professor Cesare Lombroso, entitled *The Man of Genius* (London edition, 1891), is devoted to proof and illustration of the proposition that genius is 'a special morbid condition'. He deals briefly with the case of Muhammad at pages 31, 39, and 325, maintaining that the prophet, like Saint Paul, Julius Caesar, and many other men of genius, was subject to epileptic fits. The Professor's book seems to be exactly what Sir W. H. Sleeman desired to see.

12. In the author's time, when municipal conservancy and sanitation were almost unknown in India, the tyranny of the sweepers' guild was chiefly felt as a private inconvenience. It is now one of the principal of the many difficulties, little understood in Europe, which bar the progress of Indian sanitary reform. The sweepers cannot be readily coerced because no Hindoo or Musalmān would do their work to save his life, nor will he pollute himself even by beating the refractory scavenger. A strike of sweepers on the occasion of a great fair, or of a cholera epidemic, is a most dangerous calamity. The vested rights described in the text are so fully recognized in practice that they are frequently the subject of sale or mortgage.

13. The low-caste Hindoos are generally fond of drink, when they can get it, but seldom commit crime under its influence.

14. An elephant driver, by reason of his position on the animal, has opportunities for private conversation with his master.

15. Elephant drivers (*mahouts*) are Muhammadans, who should have no caste, but Indian Musalmāns have become Hinduized, and fallen under the dominion of caste.

16. Darbhanga is in Tirhūt, seventy miles NE. of Dinapore. The Kūsī (Kōsī or Koosee) river rises in the mountains of Nepāl, and falls into the Ganges after a course of about 325 miles. Nāthpur, in the Puraniya (Purneah) District, is a mart for the trade with Nepal.

17. The customary attitude of a suppliant.

18. A small river which falls into the Nerbudda on the right-hand side, at Sānkal. Its general course is south-west.

19. November, 1835.

20. Described in the *Gazetteer* (1870) as 'a large but decaying village in the Jabalpur district, situated at the foot of the Bhānrer hills, twenty-two miles to the north-west of Jabalpur, on the north side of the Hiran, and on the road to Sāgar'.

21. The convenient restriction of the name Vindhya to the hills north, and of Sātpura to the hills south of the Nerbudda is of modern origin (*Manual of the Geology of India*, 1st ed., Part I, p. iv). The Sātpura range, thus defined, separates the valley of the Nerbudda from the valleys of the Taptī flowing west, and the Mahānadī flowing east. The Vindhyan sandstones certainly are a formation of immense antiquity, perhaps pre-Silurian. They are azoic, or devoid of fossils; and it is consequently impossible to determine exactly their geological age, or 'horizon' (ibid. p. xxiii). The cappings of basalt, in some cases with laterite superimposed, suggest many difficult problems, which will be briefly discussed in the notes to Chapters 14 and 17.

CHAPTER 9

The Great Iconoclast — Troops routed by Hornets —
The Rānī of Garhā — Hornets' Nests in India.

On the 23rd,[1] we came on nine miles to Sangrāmpur, and, on the 24th, nine more to the valley of Jabērā,[2] situated on the western extremity of the bed of a large lake, which is now covered by twenty-four villages. The waters were kept in by a large wall that united two hills about four miles south of Jabērā. This wall was built of great cut freestone blocks from the two hills of the Vindhiya range, which it united. It was about half a mile long, one hundred feet broad at the base, and about one hundred feet high. The stones, though cut, were never, apparently, cemented; and the wall has long given way in the centre, through which now falls a small stream that passes from east to west of what was once the bottom of the lake, and now is the site of so many industrious and happy little village communities.[3] The proprietor of the village of Jabērā, in whose mango grove our tents were pitched, conducted me to the ruins of the wall; and told me that it had been broken down by the order of the Emperor Aurangzēb.[4] History to these people is all a fairy tale; and this emperor is the great destroyer of everything that the Muhammadans in their fanaticism have demolished of the Hindoo sculpture or architecture; and yet, singular as it may appear, they never mention his name with any feelings of indignation or hatred. With every scene of his supposed outrage against their gods or their temples, there is always associated the recollection of some instance of his piety, and the Hindoos' glory — of some idol, for instance, or column, preserved from his fury by a miracle, whose divine origin he is supposed at once to have recognized with all due reverence.

At Bherāgarh,[5] the high priest of the temple told us that Aurangzēb and his soldiers knocked off the heads, arms, and noses of all the idols, saying that 'if they had really any of the godhead in them, they would assuredly now show it, and save themselves'. But when they came to the door of Gaurī Sankar's apartments, they were attacked by a nest of hornets, that put the whole of the emperor's army to the rout; and his imperial majesty called out: 'Here we have really something like a god, and we shall not suffer him to be molested; if all your gods could give us proof like this of their divinity, not a nose of them would ever be touched'.

The popular belief, however, is that after Aurangzēb's army had struck off all the prominent features of the other gods, one of the soldiers entered the temple, and struck off the ear of one of the prostrate images underneath their vehicle, the Bull. 'My dear', said Gaurī, 'do you see what these saucy men are about?' Her consort turned round his head;[6] and, seeing the soldiers around him, brought all the hornets up from the marble rocks below, where there are still so many nests of them, and the whole army fled before them to Teorī, five miles.[7] It is very likely that some body of troops by whom the rest of the images had been mutilated, may have been driven off by a nest of hornets from within the temple where this statue stands. I have seen six companies of infantry, with a train of artillery and a squadron of horse, all put to the rout by a single nest of hornets, and driven off some miles with all their horses and bullocks. The officers generally save themselves by keeping within their tents, and creeping under their bed-clothes, or their carpets; and servants often escape by covering themselves up in their blankets, and lying perfectly still. Horses are often stung to a state of madness, in which they throw themselves over precipices and break their limbs, or kill themselves. The grooms, in trying to save their horses, are generally the people who suffer most in a camp attacked by such an enemy. I have seen some so stung as to recover with difficulty; and I believe there have been instances of people not recovering at all. In such a frightful scene I have seen a bullock sitting and chewing the cud as calmly as if the whole thing had been got up for his amusement. The hornets seldom touch any animal that remains perfectly still.

On the bank of the Bīnā river at Eran, in the Sāgar district, is a beautiful pillar of a single freestone, more than fifty feet high, surmounted by a figure of Krishna, with the glory round his head.[8] Some few of the rays of this glory have been struck off by lightning; but the people declare that this was done by a shot fired at it from a cannon by order of Aurangzēb, as his army was marching by on its way to the Deccan. Before the scattered fragments, however, could reach the ground, the air was filled, they say, by a swarm of hornets, that put the whole army to flight; and the emperor ordered his gunners to desist, declaring that he was 'satisfied of the presence of the god'. There is hardly any part of India in which, according to popular belief, similar miracles were not worked to convince the emperor of the peculiar merits or sanctity of particular idols or temples, according to the traditions of the people, derived, of course, from the inventions of priests. I should mention that these hornets suspend their nests to the branches of the highest trees, under rocks, or in old deserted temples. Native travellers, soldiers, and camp followers, cook and eat their food under such trees; but they always avoid one in which there is a nest of hornets, particularly on a still day. Sometimes they do not discover the nest till it is too late. The unlucky wight goes on feeding his fire, and delighting in the prospect of the feast before him, as the smoke ascends in curling eddies to the nest of the hornets. The moment it touches them they sally forth and descend, and sting like mad creatures every living thing they find in motion. Three companies of my regiment were escorting treasure in boats from Allahabad to Cawnpore for the army under the Marquis of Hastings, in 1817.[9] The soldiers all took their dinners on shore every day; and one still afternoon a sipāhī (sepoy), by cooking his dinner under one of those nests without seeing it, sent the infuriated swarm among the whole of his comrades, who were cooking in the same grove, and undressed, as they always are on such occasions. Treasure, food, and all were immediately deserted, and the whole of the party, save the European officers, were up to their noses in the river Ganges. The hornets hovered over them; and it was amusing to see them bobbing their heads under as the insects tried to pounce upon them. The officers covered themselves up in the carpets of their boats; and, as the day was a hot one, their situation was still more uncomfortable than that of the men. Darkness alone put an end to the conflict.

I should mention that the poor old Rānī, or Queen of Garhā, Lachhmī Kuar, came out as far as Katangī with us to take leave of my wife, to whom she has always been attached. She had been in the habit of spending a day with her at my house once a week; and being the only European lady from whom she had ever received any attention, or indeed ever been on terms of any intimacy with, she feels the more sensible of the little offices of kindness and courtesy she has received from her.[10] Her husband, Narhar Sā, was the last of the long line of sixty-two sovereigns who reigned over these territories from the year A.D. 358 to the Sāgar conquest, A.D. 1781. [11] He died a prisoner in the fortress of Kūrai, in the Sāgar district, in A. D. 1789, leaving two widows.[12] One burnt herself upon the funeral pile, and the other was prevented from doing so, merely because she was thought too young, as she was not then fifteen years of age. She received a small pension from the Sāgar Government, which was still further reduced under the Nāgpur Government which succeeded it in the Jubbulpore district in which the pension had been assigned; and it was not thought necessary to increase the amount of this pension when the territory came under our dominion,[13] so that she has had barely enough to subsist upon, about one hundred rupees a month. She is now about sixty years of age, and still a very good- looking woman. In her youth she must have been beautiful. She does not object to appear unveiled before gentlemen on any particular occasion;

and, when Lord W. Bentinck was at Jubbulpore in 1833, I introduced, the old queen to him. He seemed much interested, and ordered the old lady a pair of shawls. None but very coarse ones were found in the store-rooms of the Governor-General's representative, and his lordship said these were not such as a Governor-General could present, or a queen, however poor, receive; and as his own 'toshakhāna' (wardrobe) had gone on,[14] he desired that a pair of the finest kind should be purchased and presented to her in his name. The orders were given in her presence and mine. I was obliged to return to Sāgar before they could be carried into effect; and, when I returned in 1835,[15] I found that the *rejected* shawls had been presented to her, and were such coarse things that she was ashamed to wear them, as much, I really believe, on account of the exalted person who had given them, as her own. She never mentioned the subject till I asked her to let me see the shawls, which she did reluctantly, and she was too proud to complain. How the good intentions of the Governor-General had been frustrated in this case I have never learned. The native officer in charge of the store was dead, and the Governor-General's representative had left the place. Better could not, I suppose, be got at this time, and he did not like to defer giving them.

Notes:

1. November, 1835.

2. Sangrāmpur is in the Jabalpur District, thirty miles north-west of Jabalpur, or the road to Sāgar, The village of Jabērā is thirty-nine miles from Jabalpur.

3. Similar lakes, formed by means of huge dams thrown across valleys, are numerous in the Central Provinces and Bundēlkhand. The embankments of some of these lakes are maintained by the Indian Government, and the water is distributed for irrigation. Many of the lakes are extremely beautiful, and the ruins of grand temples and palaces are often found on their banks. Several of the embankments are known to have been built by the Chandēl princes between A.D. 800 and 1200, and some are believed to be the work of an earlier Parihār dynasty.

4. A.D. 1658−1707. Aurangzēb, though possibly credited with more destruction than he accomplished, did really destroy many hundreds of Hindoo temples. A historian mentions the demolition of 262 at three places in Rājputāna in a single year (A.D. 1679-80) (E. and D. vii, 188).

5. This name is used as a synonym for Bheraghāt, *ante*, Chapter 1, paragraph 1. It is written Beragur in the author's text. The author, in *Ramaseeana*, Introduction, p. 77, note, describes the Gaurī-Sankar sculpture as being 'at Beragur on the Nerbudda river'.

6. Gaurī is one of the many names of Pārvatī, or Dēvī, the consort of the god Siva, Sankar, or Māhadēo, who rides upon the bull Nandī.

7. This village seems to be the same as Tewar, the ancient Tripura, 'six miles to the west of Jabalpur; and on the south side of the Bombay road' (*A. S. R.*, vol. ix, p. 57). The adjacent ruins are known by the name of Karanbēl.

8. The pillar bears an inscription showing that it was erected during the reign of Budha Gupta, in the year 165 of the Gupta era, corresponding to A.D. 484-5. This, and the other important remains of antiquity at Eran, are fully described in *A. S. R.*, vol. vii, p. 88; vol. x, pp. 76-90, pl. xxiii-xxx; and vol. xiv, p. 149, pl. xxxi; also in Fleet, *Gupta Inscriptions* (Calcutta, 1888). The material of the pillar is red sandstone. According to Cunningham the total height is 43 feet. The peculiar double-faced, two-armed image on the summit does not seem to be intended for Krishna, but I cannot say what the meaning is (H. F. A., p. 174, fig. 121).

9. During the wars with the Marāthās and Pindhārīs, which ended in 1819.

10. After we left Jubbulpore, the old Rānī used to receive much kind and considerate attention from the Hon. Mrs. Shore, a very amiable woman, the wife of the Governor-General's representative, the Hon. Mr. Shore, a very worthy and able member of the Bengal Civil Service. [W. H. S.] For notice of Mr. Shore, see note at end of Chapter 13.

11. See the author's paper entitled '*History of the Gurha Mundala Rajas*', in *J. A. S. B.*, vol. vi (1837), p. 621, and the article 'Mandla' in *C. P. Gazetteer* (1870).

12. Kūrai is on the route from Sāgar to Nasīrābād, thirty-one miles WNW. of the former.

13. The 'Sāgar and Nerbudda Territories', comprising the Sāgar, Jabalpur, Hoshangābād, Seonī, Damoh, Narsinghpur, and Baitūl Mandlā Districts, are now under the Local Administration of the Chief Commissioner of the Central Provinces, established in 1861 by Lord Canning, who appointed Sir Richard Temple Chief Commissioner. These territories were at first administered by a semi-political agency, but were afterwards, in 1852, placed under the Lieutenant-Governor of the North-Western Provinces (now the Agra Province in the United Provinces of Agra and Oudh), to whom they remained subject until 1861. They had been ceded by the Marāthās to the British in 1818, and the cession was confirmed by the treaty of 1826.

14. All official presents given by native chiefs to the Governor- General are credited to the 'toshakhāna', from which also are taken the official gifts bestowed in return.

15. By resolution of Government, dated January 10, 1836, the author was appointed General Superintendent of the Operations against Thuggee, with his head-quarters at Jubbulpore.

CHAPTER 10

The Peasantry and the Land Settlement.

The officers of the 29th had found game so plentiful, and the weather so fine, that they came on with us as far as Jaberā, where we had the pleasure of their society on the evening of the 24th, and left them on the morning of the 25th.[1] A great many of my native friends, from among the native landholders and merchants of the country, flocked to our camp at every stage to pay their respects, and bid me farewell, for they never expected to see me back among them again. They generally came out a mile or two to meet and escort us to our tents; and much do I fear that my poor boy will never again, in any part of the world, have the blessings of Heaven so fervently invoked upon him by so many worthy and respectable men as met us at every stage on our way from Jubbulpore. I am much attached to the agricultural classes of India generally, and I have found among them some of the best men I have ever known. The peasantry in India have generally very good manners, and are exceedingly intelligent, from having so much more leisure and unreserved and easy intercourse with those above them. The constant habit of meeting and discussing subjects connected with their own interests, in their own fields, and 'under their own fig-trees', with their landlords and Government functionaries of all kinds and degrees, prevents their ever feeling or appearing impudent or obtrusive; though it certainly tends to give them stentorian voices, that often startle us when they come into our houses to discuss the same points with us.

Nine-tenths of the immediate cultivators of the soil in India are little farmers, who hold a lease for one or more years, as the case may be, of their lands, which they cultivate with their own stock. One of these cultivators, with a good plough and bullocks, and a good character, can always get good land on moderate terms from holders of villages.[2] Those cultivators are, I think, the best, who learn to depend upon their stock and character for favourable terms, hold themselves free to change their holdings when their leases expire, and pretend not to any hereditary right in the soil. The lands are, I think, best cultivated, and the society best constituted in India, where the holders of estates of villages have a feeling of permanent interest in them, an assurance of an hereditary right of property which is liable only to the payment of a moderate Government demand, descends undivided by the law of primogeniture, and is unaffected by the common law, which prescribes the equal subdivision among children of landed as well as other private property, among the Hindoos and Muhammadans; and where the immediate cultivators hold the lands they till by no other law than that of common specific contract.

When I speak of holders of villages, I mean the holders of lands that belong to villages. The whole face of India is parcelled out into estates of villages.[3] The village communities are composed of those who hold and cultivate the land, the established village servants, priest, blacksmith, carpenter, accountant, washerman, basket-maker (whose wife is ex officio the midwife of the little village community), potter, watchman, barber, shoemaker, &c., &c.[4] To these may be added the little banker, or agricultural capitalist, the shopkeeper, the brazier, the confectioner, the ironmonger, the weaver, the dyer, the astronomer or astrologer, who points out to the people the lucky day for every earthly undertaking, and the prescribed times for all religious ceremonies and observances. In some villages the whole of the lands are parcelled out among cultivating proprietors, and are liable to eternal subdivisions by the law of inheritance, which gives to each son the same share. In others, the whole of the lands are parcelled out among cultivators, who hold them on a specific lease for limited periods from a proprietor who holds the whole collectively under Government, at a rate of rent fixed either permanently or for limited periods. These are the two extremes. There are but few villages in which all the cultivators are considered as proprietors—at least but few in our Nerbudda territories; and these will almost invariably be found of a caste of Brahmans or a caste of Rājpūts, descended from a common ancestor, to whom the estate was originally given in rent-free tenure, or at a quit-rent, by the existing Government for his prayers as a priest, or his services as a soldier. Subsequent Governments, which resumed unceremoniously the estates of others, were deterred from resuming these by a dread of the curses of the one and the swords of the other.[5] Such communities of cultivating proprietors are of two kinds: those among whom the lands are parcelled out, each member holding his share as a distinct estate, and being individually responsible for the payment of the share of the Government demand assessed upon it; and those among whom the lands are not parcelled out, but the profits divided as among copartners of an estate held jointly. They, in either case, nominate one of their members to collect and pay the Government demand; or Government appoints a man for this duty, either as a salaried servant or a lessee, with authority to levy from the cultivating proprietors a certain sum over and above what is demandable from him.

The communities in which the cultivators are considered merely as leaseholders are far more numerous; indeed, the greater part of the village communities in this part of India are of this description; and, where the communities are of a mixed character, the cultivating proprietors are considered to have merely a right of occupancy, and are liable to have their lands assessed at the same rate as those held on a mere lease tenure. In all parts of India the cultivating proprietors in such mixed communities are similarly situated; they are liable to be assessed at the same rate as others holding the same sort of lands, and often pay a higher rate, with which others are not encumbered. But this is not general; it is as much the interest of the proprietor to have good cultivating tenants as it is that of the tenants to have good proprietors; and it is felt to be the interest of both to adjust their terms amicably among themselves, without a reference to a third and superior party, which is always costly and commonly ruinous.[6]

It is a question of very great importance, no less morally and politically than fiscally, which of these systems deserves most encouragement—that in which the Government considers the immediate cultivators to be the hereditary proprietors, and, through its own public officers, parcels out the lands among them, and adjusts the rates of rent demandable from every minute partition, as the lands become more and more subdivided by the Hindoo and Muhammadan law of inheritance; or that in which the Government considers him who holds the area of a whole village or estate collectively as the hereditary proprietor, and the immediate cultivators as his lease-tenants—leaving the rates of rent to be adjusted among the parties without the aid of public officers, or interposing only to enforce the fulfilment of their mutual contracts. In the latter of these two systems the land will supply more and better members to the middle and higher classes of the society, and create and preserve a better feeling between them and the peasantry, or immediate cultivators of the soil; and it will occasion the re- investment upon the soil, in works of ornament and utility, of a greater portion of the annual returns of rent and profit, and a less expenditure in the costs of litigation in our civil courts, and bribery to our public officers.

Those who advocate the other system, which makes the immediate cultivators the proprietors, will, for the most part, be found to reason upon false premises—upon the assumption that the rates of rent demandable from the immediate cultivators of the soil *were everywhere limited and established by immemorial usage, in a certain sum of money per acre, or a certain share of the crop produced from it*; and that 'these rates were not only so limited and fixed, but everywhere *well known to the people'*, and might, consequently, have become well known to the Government, and recorded in public registers. Now every practical man in India, who has had opportunities of becoming well acquainted with the matter, knows that *the reverse is the case*; that the rate of rent demandable from these cultivators *never was the same upon any two estates at the same time: nor even the same upon any one estate at different limes, or for any consecutive number of years*.[7] The rates vary every year on every estate, according to the varying circumstances that influence them—such as greater or less exhaustion of the soil, greater or less facilities of irrigation, manure, transit to market, drainage—or from fortuitous advantages on one hand, or calamities of season on the other; or many other circumstances which affect the value of the land, and the abilities of the cultivators to pay. It is not so much the proprietors of the estate or the Government as the cultivators themselves who demand every year a readjustment of the rate demandable upon their different holdings. This readjustment must take place; and, if there is no landlord to effect it, Government must effect it through its own officers. Every holding becomes subdivided when the cultivating proprietor dies and leaves more than one child; and, as the whole face of the country is open and without hedges, the division is easily and speedily made. Thus the field-map which represents an estate one year will never represent it fairly five years after; in fact, we might almost as well attempt to map the waves of the ocean as field-map the face of any considerable area in any part of India.[8]

If there be any truth in my conclusions, our Government has acted unwisely in going, as it has generally done, into [one or other of] the two extremes, in its settlement of the land revenue.

In the Zamīndārī settlement of Bengal, it conferred the hereditary right of property over areas larger than English counties on individuals, and left the immediate cultivators mere tenants-at-will.[9] These individuals felt no interest in promoting the comfort and welfare of the village communities, or conciliating the affections of the cultivators, whom they never saw or wished to see; and they let out the village, or other subdivision of their estates, to second parties quite as little interested, who again let them out to others, so that the system of rack-renting went on over the whole area of the immense possession. This was a system 'more honoured in the breach than in the observance'; for, as the great landholders became involved in the ruin of their cultivators, their estates were sold for arrears of revenue due to Government, and thus the proprietary right of one individual has become divided among many, who will have the feelings which the larger holders wanted, and so remedy the evil. In the other extreme, Government has constituted the immediate cultivators the proprietors; thereby preventing any one who is supported upon the rent of land, or the profits of agricultural stock, from rising above the grade of a peasant, and so depriving society of one of its best and most essential elements. The remedy of both is in village settlements, in which the estate shall be of moderate size, and the hereditary property of the holder, descending on the principle of a principality, by the right of primogeniture, unaffected by the common law. This is the system which has been adopted in the Nerbudda territory, and which, I trust, will be always adhered to.

When we enter upon the government of any new territorial acquisition in India, we do not require or pretend to change the civil laws of the people; because their civil laws and their religion are in reality one and the same, and are contained in one and the same code, as certainly among the Hindoos, the Muhammadans, and the Parsees, as they were among the Israelites. By these codes, and the established usages everywhere well understood by the people, are their rights and duties in marriage, inheritance, succession, caste, contract, and all the other civil relations of life, ascertained; and when we displace another Government we do not pretend to alter such rights and duties in relation to each other, we merely change the machinery and mode of procedure by which these rights are secured and these duties enforced.[10]

Of criminal law no system was ever either regularly established or administered in any state in India, by any Government to which we have succeeded; and the people always consider the existing Government free to adopt that which may seem best calculated to effect the one great object, which criminal law has everywhere in view — *the security of life, property, and character, and the enjoyment of all their advantages*. The actions by which these are affected and endangered, the evidence by which such actions require to be proved, and the penalties with which they require to be visited, in order to prevent their recurrence, are, or ought to be, so much the same in every society, that the people never think us bound to search for what Muhammad and his companions thought in the wilds of Arabia, or the Sanskrit poets sang about them in courts and cloisters. They would be just as well pleased everywhere to find us searching for these things in the writings of Confucius and Zoroaster, as in those of Muhammad and Manu: and much more so, to see us consulting our own common-sense, and forming a penal code of our own, suitable to the wants of such a mixed community.[11]

The fiscal laws which define the rights and duties of the landed interests and the agricultural classes in relation to each other and to the ruling powers were also everywhere exceedingly simple and well understood by the people. What in England is now a mere fiction of law is still in India an essential principle. All lands are held directly or indirectly of the sovereign: to this rule there is no exception.[12] The reigning sovereign is essentially the proprietor of the whole of the lands in every part of India, where he has not voluntarily alienated them; and he holds these lands for the payment of those public establishments which are maintained for the public good, and are supported by the rents of the lands either directly under assignment, or indirectly through the sovereign proprietor. When a Muhammadan or Hindoo sovereign assigned lands rent-free in *perpetuity*, it was always understood, both by the donor and receiver, to be with the *small reservation* of a right in his successor to resume them for the public good, if he should think fit.[13] Hindoo sovereigns, or their priests for them, often tried to bar this right by *invoking curses* on the head of that successor who should exercise it.[14] It is a proverb among the people of these territories, and, I believe, among the people of India generally, that the lands which pay no rent to Government have no 'barkat', blessing from above—that the man who holds them is not blessed in their returns like the man who pays rent to Government and thereby contributes his aid to the protection of the community. The fact is that every family that holds rent-free lands must, in a few generations, become miserable from the minute subdivision of the property, and the litigation in our civil courts which it entails upon the holders.[15] It is certainly the general opinion of the people of India that no land should be held without paying rent to Government, or providing for people employed in the service of Government, for the benefit of the people in its defensive, religious, judicial, educational, and other establishments. Nine- tenths of the land in these Nerbudda territories are held in lease immediately under Government by the heads of villages, whose leases have been renewable every five years; but they are now to have a settlement for twenty.[l6] The other tenth is held by these heads of villages intermediately under some chief, who holds several portions of land immediately under Government at a quit-rent, or for service performed, or to be performed, for Government, and lets them out to farmers. These are, for the most part, situated in the more hilly and less cultivated parts.

Notes:

1. November, 1835.

2. This observation does not hold good in densely populated tracts, which are now numerous.

3. These 'estates of villages' are known by the Persian name of 'mauza'. The topographical division of the country into 'mauzas', which may be also translated by the terms 'townlands' or 'townships', has developed spontaneously. Some 'mauzas' are uninhabited, and are cultivated by the residents of neighbouring villages.

4. In some parts of Central and Southern India, the 'Gārpagrī', who charms away hail-storms from the crops, and 'Bhūmkā', who charms away tigers from the people and their cattle, are added to the number of village servants, [W. H .S.] 'In many parts of Berār and Mālwa every village has its

"bhūmkā", whose office it is to charm the tigers; and its "gārpagrī", whose duty it is to keep off the hail-storms. They are part of the village servants, and paid by the village community, After a severe hail-storm took place in the district of Narsinghpur, of which I had the civil charge in 1823, the office of "gārpagrī" was restored to several villages in which it had ceased for several generations. They are all Brahmans, and take advantage of such calamities to impress the people with an opinion of their usefulness. The "bhūmkās" are all Gōnds, or people of the woods, who worship their own Lares and Penates' (*Ramaseeana*, Introduction, p. 13. note).

5. Very often the Government of the country know nothing of these tenures; the local authorities allowed them to continue as a perquisite of their own. The holders were willing to pay them a good share of the rent, assured that they would be resumed if reported by the local authorities to the Government. These authorities consented to take a moderate share of the rent, assured that they should get little or nothing if the lands were resumed. [W. H. S.] 'Rent' here means 'land-revenue'. Of course, under modern British administration the particulars of all tenures are known and recorded in great detail,

6. Since the author wrote these remarks the legal position of cultivating proprietors and tenants has been largely modified by the pressure of population and a long course of legislation. The Rent Acts, which began with Act x of 1859, are now numerous, and have been accompanied by a series of Land Revenue Acts, and many collateral enactments. All the problems of the Irish land question are familiar topics to the Anglo-Indian courts and legislatures.

7. This proposition no doubt was true for the 'Sāgar and Nerbudda Territories' in 1835, but it cannot be predicated of the thickly populated and settled districts in the Gangetic valley without considerable qualification. Examples of long-established, unchanged, well-known rent-rates are not uncommon.

8. In recent years this task of 'mapping the waves of the ocean' has been attempted. Every periodical settlement of the land revenue in Northern India since 1833 has been accompanied by the preparation of detailed village maps, showing each field, even the tiniest, a few yards square, with a separate number. In many cases these maps were roughly constructed under non-professional supervision, but in many districts they have been prepared by the cadastral branch of the Survey Department. The difficulty mentioned by the author has been severely felt, and it constantly happens that beautiful maps become useless in four or five years. Efforts are made to insert annual corrections in copies of the maps through the agency of the village accountants, and the 'kānūngos', or officers who supervise them, but

the task is an enormous one, and only partial success is attained. In addition to the maps, records of great bulk are annually prepared which give the most minute details about every holding and each field.

9. The Permanent Settlement of Bengal, effected under the orders of Lord Cornwallis in 1793, was soon afterwards extended to the province of Benares, now included in the United Provinces of Agra and Oudh. Illusory provisions were made to protect the rights of tenants, but nothing at all effectual was done till the passing of Act x of 1859, which has been largely modified by later legislation.

10. The general principle here stated of respect for personal substantive law in civil matters is still the guide of the Indian Legislature, but the accumulation of Privy Council and High Court rulings, combined with the action of codes, has effected considerable gradual change. Direct legislation has anglicized the law of contract, and has modified, though not so largely, the law of marriage, inheritance, and succession.

11. In the author's time the courts of the East India Company still followed the Muhammadan criminal law, as modified by the Regulations. The Indian Penal Code of 1869 placed the substantive criminal law on a thoroughly scientific basis. This code was framed with such masterly skill that to this day it has needed little material amendment. The first Criminal Procedure Code, passed in 1861, has been twice recast. The law of evidence was codified by Sir James FitzJames Stephen in the Indian Evidence Act of 1870.

12. This proposition, in the editor's opinion, truly states the theory of land tenures in India, and it was a generally accurate statement of actual fact in the author's time. Since then the long continuance of settled government, by fostering the growth of private rights, has tended to obscure the idea of state ownership. The modern revenue codes, instead of postulating the ownership of the state, enact that the claims of the state—that is to say, the land- revenue—are the first charge on the land and its produce. The Malabar coast offers an exception to the general Hindu role of state ownership of land. The Nairs, Coorgs, and Tulus enjoyed full proprietary rights (Dubois, *Hindu Manners, &c.,* 3rd edition (1906), p. 57).

13. Amīr Khān, the Nawāb of Tonk, assigned to his physician, who had cured him of an intermittent fever, lands yielding one thousand rupees a year, in rent-free tenure, and gave him a deed signed by himself and his heir-apparent, declaring expressly that it should descend to him and his heir for ever. He died lately, and his son and successor, who had signed the deed, resumed the estate without ceremony. On being remonstrated with, he said that 'his father, while living, was, of course, master, and could make

him sign what he pleased, and give land rent-free to whom he pleased; but his successor must now be considered the best judge whether they could be spared or not; that if lands were to be alienated in perpetuity by every reigning Nawāb for every dose of medicine or dose of prayers that he or the members of his family required, none would soon be left for the payment of the soldiers, or other necessary public servants of any description'. This was told me by the son of the old physician, who was the person to whom the speech was made, his father having died before Amīr Khān. [W. H. S.] Amīr Khān was the famous Pindhārī leader. H. T. Prinsep translated his Memoirs from the Persian of Busawun Lāl (Calcutta, 1832).

14. The ancient deeds of grant, engraved on copper, of which so many have been published within the last hundred years, almost invariably conclude with fearful curses on the head of any rash mortal who may dare to revoke the grant. Usually the pious hope is expressed that, if he should be guilty of such wickedness, he may rot in filth, and be reborn a worm.

15. Revenue officers commonly observe that revenue-free grants, which the author calls rent-free, are often ill cultivated. The simple reason is that the stimulus of the collector's demand is wanting to make the owner exert himself.

16. These leases now carry with them a right of ownership, involving the power of alienation, subject to the lien of the land revenue as a first charge. Conversely, the modern codes lay down the principle that the revenue settlement must be made with the proprietor. The author's rule of agricultural succession by primogeniture in the Nerbudda territories has survived only in certain districts (see *post*, Chapter 47). The land-revenue law and the law concerning the relations between landlords and tenants have now been more or less successfully codified in each province. Mr. B. H. Baden-Powell's encyclopaedic work *The Land Systems of British India* (3 volumes: Oxford, Clarendon Press, 1892) gives very full information concerning Indian tenures as now existing, and the law applicable to them at the date of publication.

CHAPTER 11

Witchcraft.

On leaving Jabērā,[1] I saw an old acquaintance from the eastern part of the Jubbulpore district, Kehrī Singh.

'I understand, Kehrī Singh', said I, 'that certain men among the Gonds of the jungle, towards the source of the Nerbudda, eat human flesh. Is it so?'

'No, sir; the men never eat people, but the Gond women do.'

'Where?'

'Everywhere, sir; there is not a parish, nay, a village, among the Gonds, in which you will not find one or more such women.'

'And how do they eat people?'

'They eat their livers, sir.'

'Oh, I understand; you mean witches?'

'Of course! Who ever heard of other people eating human beings?'

'And you really still think, in spite of all that we have done and said, that there are such things as witches?'

'Of course we do—do not we find instances of it every day? European gentlemen are too apt to believe that things like this are not to be found here, because they are not to be found in their own country. Major Wardlow, when in charge of the Seonī district, denied the existence of witchcraft for a long time, but he was at last convinced.'

'How?'

'One of his troopers, one morning after a long march, took some milk for his master's breakfast from an old woman without paying for it. Before the major had got over his breakfast the poor trooper was down upon his back, screaming from the agony of internal pains. We all knew immediately that he had been bewitched, and recommended the major to send for some one learned in these matters to find out the witch. He did so, and, after hearing from the trooper the story about the milk, this person at once declared that the woman from whom he got it was the criminal. She was searched for, found, and brought to the trooper, and commanded to cure him. She flatly denied that she had herself conjured him; but admitted that her household gods might, unknown to her, have punished him for his wickedness. This, however, would not do. She was commanded to cure the man, and she set about collecting materials for the "pūjā" (worship); and before she could get quite through the ceremonies, all his pains had left him. Had we not been resolute with her, the man must have died before evening, so violent were his torments.'

'Did not a similar case occur to Mr. Fraser at Jubbulpore?'

'A "chaprāsī"[2] of his, while he had charge of the Jubbulpore district, was sent out to Mandlā[3] with a message of some kind or other. He took a cock from an old Gond woman without paying for it, and, being hungry after a long journey, ate the whole of it in a curry. He heard the woman mutter something, but being a raw, unsuspecting young man, he thought nothing of it, ate his cock, and went to sleep. He had not been asleep three hours before he was seized with internal pains, and the old cock was actually heard crowing in his belly. He made the best of his way back to Jubbulpore, several stages, and all the most skilful men were employed to charm away the effect of the old woman's spell, but in vain. He died, and the cock never ceased crowing at intervals up to the hour of his death.'

'And was Mr. Fraser convinced?'

'I never heard, but suppose he must have been.'

'Who ate the livers of the victims? The witches themselves, or the evil spirits with whom they had dealings?'

'The evil spirits ate the livers; but they are set on to do so by the witches, who get them into their power by such accursed sacrifices and offerings. They will often dig up young children from their graves, bring them to life, and allow these devils to feed upon their livers, as falconers allow their hawks to feed on the breasts of pigeons. You "sāhib lōg" (European gentlemen) will not believe all this, but it is, nevertheless, all very true.'[4]

The belief in sorcery among these people owes its origin, in a great measure, to the diseases of the liver and spleen to which the natives, and particularly the children, are much subject in the jungly parts of Central India. From these affections children pine away and die, without showing any external marks of disease. Their death is attributed to witchcraft, and any querulous old woman, who has been in the habit of murmuring at slights and ill treatment in the neighbourhood, is immediately set down as the cause. Men who practise medicine among them are very commonly supposed to be at the same time wizards. Seeking to inspire confidence in their prescriptions by repeating prayers and incantations over the patient, or over the medicine they give him, they make him believe that they derive aid from supernatural power; and the patient concludes that those who can command these powers to cure can, if they will, command them to destroy. He and his friends believe that the man who can command these powers to cure one individual can command them to cure any other; and, if he does not do so, they believe that it arises from a desire to destroy the patient. I have, in these territories, known a great many instances of medical practitioners having been put to death for not curing young people for whom they were required to prescribe. Several cases have come before me as a magistrate in which the father has stood over the doctor with a drawn sword by the side of the bed of his child, and cut him down and killed him the moment the child died, as he had sworn to do when he found the patient sinking under his prescriptions.[5]

The town of Jubbulpore contains a population of twenty thousand souls,[6] and they all believed in this story of the cock. I one day asked a most respectable merchant in the town, Nādū Chaudhrī, how the people could believe in such things, when he replied that he had no doubt witches were to be found in every part of India, though they abounded most, no doubt, in the central parts of it, and that we ought to consider ourselves very fortunate in having no such things in England. 'But', added he, 'of all countries that between Mandlā and Katāk (Cuttack)[7] is the worst for witches. I had once occasion to go to the city of Ratanpur[8] on business, and was one day, about noon, walking in the market-place and eating a very fine piece of sugar-cane. In the crowd I happened, by accident, to jostle an old woman as she passed me. I looked back, intending to apologize for the accident, and heard her muttering indistinctly as she passed on. Knowing the propensities of these old ladies, I became somewhat uneasy, and on turning round to my cane I found, to my great terror, that the juice had been all *turned to blood*. Not a minute had elapsed, such were the fearful powers of this old woman. I collected my followers, and, leaving my agents there to settle my accounts, was beyond the boundaries of the old wretch's influence before dark; had I remained, nothing could have saved me. I should certainly have been a dead man before morning. It is well known', said the old gentleman, 'that their spells and curses can only reach a certain distance, ten or twelve miles; and, if you offend one of them, the sooner you place that distance between you the better.'

Jangbār Khān, the representative of the Shāhgarh Rājā,[9] as grave and reverend an old gentleman as ever sat in the senate of Venice, told me one day that he was himself an eye-witness of the powers of the women of Khilautī. He was with a great concourse of people at a fair held at the town of Rāipur,[10] and, while sauntering with many other strangers in the fair, one of them began bargaining with two women of middle age for some very fine sugar-canes. They asked double the fair price for their canes. The man got angry, and took up one of them, when the women seized the other end, and a struggle ensued. The purchaser offered a fair price, seller demanded double. The crowd looked on, and a good deal of abuse of the female relations on both sides took place. At last a sepoy of the governor came up, armed to the teeth, and called out to the man, in a very imperious tone, to let go his hold of the cane. He refused, saying that 'when people came to the fair to sell, they should be made to sell at reasonable prices, or be turned out'. 'I', said Jangbār Khān, 'thought the man right, and told the sepoy that, if he took the part of this woman, we should take that of the other, and see fair play. Without further ceremony the functionary drew his sword, and cut the cane in two in the middle; and, pointing to both pieces, 'There', said he, 'you see the cause of my interference'. We looked down, and actually saw blood running from both pieces, and forming a little pool on the ground. The fact was that the woman was a sorceress of the very worst kind, and was actually drawing the blood from the man through the cane, to feed the abominable devil from whom she derived her detestable powers. But for the timely interference of the sepoy he would have been dead in another minute; for he no sooner saw the real state of the case than he fainted. He had hardly any blood left in him, and I was afterwards told that he was not able to walk for ten days. We all went to the governor to demand justice, declaring that, unless the women were made an example of at once, the fair would be deserted, for no stranger's life would be safe. He consented, and they were both sewn up in sacks and thrown into the river; but they had conjured the water and would not sink. They ought to have been put to death, but the governor was himself afraid of this kind of people, and let them off. There is not', continued Jangbār, 'a village, or a single family, without its witch in that part of the country; indeed, no man will give his daughter in marriage to a family without one, saying, "If my daughter has children, what will become of them without a witch to protect them from the witches of other families in the neighbourhood?" It is a fearful country, though the cheapest and most fertile in India.'

We can easily understand how a man, impressed with the idea that his blood had all been drawn from him by a sorceress, should become faint, and remain many days in a languid state; but how the people around should believe that they saw the blood flowing from both parts of the cane at the place cut through, it is not so easy to conceive.

I am satisfied that old Jangbār believed the whole story to be true, and that at the time he thought the juice of the cane red; but the little pool of blood grew, no doubt, by degrees, as years rolled on and he related this tale of the fearful powers of the Khilautī witches.

Notes:

1. *Ante*, Chapter 9.

2. An orderly, or official messenger, who wears a 'chaprās', or badge of office.

3. On the Nerbudda, fifty miles south-east of Jubbulpore.

4. Of the supposed powers and dispositions of witches among the Romans we have horrible pictures in the 5th Ode of the 6th Book of Horace, and in the 6th Book of Lucan's *Pharsalia*. [W. H. S.] The reference to Horace should be to the 5th Epode. The passage in the *Pharsalia*, Book VI, lines 420-830, describes the proceedings of Thessalian witches.

5. Such awkward incidents of medical practice are not heard of nowadays.

6. The population of Jabalpur (including cantonments) has increased steadily, and in 1911 was 100,651, as compared with 84,556 in 1891, and 76,023 in 1881.

7. Katāk, or Cuttack, a district, with town of same name, in Orissa.

8. In the Bilāspur district of the Central Provinces. The distance in a direct line between Mandlā and Katāk is about 400 miles.

9. Shāhgarh was formerly a petty native state, with town of same name. The chief joined the rebels in 1857, with the result that his dominions were confiscated, and distributed between the districts of Sāgar and Damoh in the Central Provinces, and Jhānsī (formerly Lalitpur) in the United Provinces of Agra and Oudh. The town of Shāhgarh is in the Sāgar district.

10. Rāipur is the chief town of the district of the same name in the Central Provinces, which was not finally annexed to the British dominions until 1854, when the Nāgpur State lapsed.

CHAPTER 12

The Silver Tree, or 'Kalpa Briksha' — The Singhāra or *Trapa bispinosa*, and the Guinea-Worm.

Poor old Salāmat Alī wept bitterly at the last meeting in my tent, and his two nice boys, without exactly knowing why, began to do the same; and my little son Henry[1] caught the infection, and wept louder than any of them. I was obliged to hurry over the interview lest I should feel disposed to do the same. The poor old Rānī,[2] too, suffered a good deal in parting from my wife, whom, she says, she can never hope to see again. Her fine large eyes shed many a tear as she was getting into her palankeen to return.

Between Jaberā and Harduā, the next stage, we find a great many of those large forest trees called 'kalap', or 'Kalpa Briksha' (the same which in the paradise of Indra grants what is desired), with a soft, silvery bark, and scarcely any leaves. We are told that the name of the god Rām (Rāma) and his consort Sītā will be found written by the hand of God upon all.[3]

I had the curiosity to examine a good many in the forest on both sides of the road, and found the name of this incarnation of Vishnu written on everyone in Sanskrit characters, apparently by some supernatural hand; that is, there was a softness in the impression, as if the finger of some supernatural being had traced the characters. Nathū, one of our belted attendants[4] told me that we might search as deeply as we would in the forest, but we should certainly find the name of God upon every one; 'for', said he, 'it is God himself who writes it'. I tried to argue him out of this notion; but, unfortunately, could find no tree without these characters — some high up, and some lower down in the trunk — some large and others small — but still to be found on every tree. I was almost in despair when we came to a part of the wood where we found one of these trees down in a hollow, under the road, and another upon the precipice above. I was ready to stake my credit upon the probability that no traveller would take the trouble to go up to the tree above, or down to the tree below, merely to write the name of the god upon them; and at once pledged myself to Nathū that he should find neither the god's name nor that of his wife. I sent one man up, and another man down, and they found no letters on the trees; but this did not alter their opinion on the point. 'God', said one, 'had no doubt put his name on these trees, but they had somehow or other got rubbed off. He would in good time renew them, that men's eyes might be blessed with the sight of His holy name, even in the deepest forest, and on the most leafless tree.'[5] 'But', said Nathū, 'he might not have thought it worth while to write his name upon those trees which no travellers go to see.' 'Cannot you see', said I, 'that these letters have been engraved by man? Are they not all to be found on the trunk within reach of a man's hand?' 'Of course they are', replied he, 'because people would not be able conveniently to distinguish them if God were to write them higher up.'

Shaikh Sādī has a very pretty couplet, 'Every leaf of the foliage of a green tree is, in the eye of a wise man, a library to teach him the wisdom of his Creator.'[6] I may remark that, where an Englishman would write his own name, a Hindoo would write that of his god, his parent, or his benefactor. This difference is traceable, of course, to the difference in their governments and institutions. If a Hindoo built a town, he called it after his local governor; if a local governor built it, he called it after the favourite son of the Emperor. In well regulated Hindoo families, one cannot ask a younger brother after his children in presence of the elder brother who happens to be the head of the family; it would be disrespectful for him even to speak of his children as his own in such presence—the elder brother relieves his embarrassment by answering for him.

On the 27th[7] we reached Damoh,[8] where our friends, the Browns, were to leave us on their return to Jubbulpore. Damoh is a pretty place. The town contains some five or six thousand people, and has some very handsome Hindoo temples. On a hill immediately above it is the shrine of a Muhammadan saint, which has a very picturesque appearance.

There are no manufactures at Damoh, except such as supply the wants of the immediate neighbourhood; and the town is supported by the residence of a few merchants, a few landholders, and agricultural capitalists, and the establishment of a native collector. The people here suffer much from the guinea-worm, and consider it to arise from drinking the water of the old tank, which is now very dirty and full of weeds. I have no doubt that it is occasioned either by drinking the water of this tank, or by wading in it: for I have known European gentlemen get the worm in their legs from wading in similar lakes or swamps after snipes, and the servants who followed them with their ammunition experience the same effect.[9] Here, as in most other parts of India, the tanks get spoiled by the water-chestnut, 'singhāra' (*Trapa bispinosa*), which is everywhere as regularly planted and cultivated *in fields* under a large surface of water, as wheat or barley is on the dry plains. It is cultivated by a class of men called Dhīmars, who are everywhere fishermen and palankeen bearers; and they keep boats for the planting, weeding, and gathering the 'singhāra'.[10] The holdings or tenements of each cultivator are marked out carefully on the surface of the water by long bamboos stuck up in it; and they pay so much the acre for the portion they till. The long straws of the plants reach up to the surface of the waters, upon which float their green leaves; and their pure white flowers expand beautifully among them in the latter part of the afternoon. The nut grows under the water after the flowers decay, and is of a triangular shape, and covered with a tough brown integument adhering strongly to the kernel, which is white, esculent, and of a fine cartilaginous texture. The people are very fond of these nuts, and they are carried often upon bullocks' backs two or three hundred miles to market. They ripen in the latter end of the rains, or in September, and are eatable till the end of November. The rent paid for an ordinary tank by the cultivator is about one hundred rupees a year. I have known two hundred rupees to be paid for a very large one, and even three hundred, or thirty pounds a year.[11] But the mud increases so rapidly from this cultivation that it soon destroys all reservoirs in which it is permitted; and, where it is thought desirable to keep up the tank for the sake of the water, it should be carefully prohibited. This is done by stipulating with the renter of the village, at the renewal of the lease, that no 'singhāra' shall be planted in the tank; otherwise, he will never forgo the advantage to himself of the rent for the sake of the convenience, and that only prospective, of the village community in general.

Notes:

1. Afterwards Captain H. A. Sleeman, He died in 1905.

2. Of Garhā, see *ante*, Chapter 9, prior to note 10.

3. The real 'kalpa', which now stands in the garden of the god Indra in the first heaven, was one of the fourteen varieties found at the churning of the ocean by the gods and demons. It fell to the share of Indra. [W. H. S.] The tree referred to in the text perhaps may be the *Erythrina arborescens*, or coral-tree, which sheds its leaves after the hot weather.

4. That is to say, orderlies, or 'chaprāsīs'.

5. Every Hindoo is thoroughly convinced that the names of Rām and his consort Sītā are written on this tree by the hand of God, and nine-tenths of the Musalmāns believe the same.

Happy the man who sees a God employed
In all the good and ill that chequer life,
Resolving all events, with their effects
And manifold results, into the will
And arbitration wise of the Supreme.
COWPER. [W. H. S.]

The quotation is from *The Task*, Book II, line 161.

6. Sādī (Sa'dī) is the poetic name, or *nom de plume*, of the celebrated Persian poet, whose proper name is said to have been Shaikh Maslah-ud-dīn, or, according to other authorities, Sharf-ud-dīn Mislah. He was born about A.D. 1194, and is supposed to have lived for more than a hundred years. Some writers say that he died in A.D. 1292. His best known works are the *Gulistān* and *Būstān*. The editor has failed to trace in either of these works the couplet quoted. Sādī says in the *Gulistān*, ii. 26, 'That heart which has an ear is full of the divine mystery. It is not the nightingale that alone serenades his rose; for every thorn on the rose-bush is a tongue in his or God's praise' (Ross's translation).

7. November, 1835.

8. Spelled Dhamow in the author's text. The town, the head- quarters of the district of the same name, is forty-five miles east of Sāgar, and fifty-five miles north-west of Jabalpur. The *C. P. Gazetteer* (1870) states the population to be 8,563. In 1901 it had grown to 13,335; and the town is still increasing in importance (*I. G.*, 1908). Inscriptions of the fourteenth and fifteenth centuries at Damoh are noticed in *A. S. R.*, vol. xxi, p. 168.

9. The guinea-worm (*Filaria medinensis*) is a very troublesome parasite, which sometimes grows to a length of three feet. It occurs in Africa, Arabia, Persia, and Turkistan, as well as in India.

10. The Dhīmars (Sanskrit *dhīvara*, 'fisherman') are the same caste as the Kahārs, or 'bearers'. The boats used by them are commonly 'dugout' canoes, exactly like those used in prehistoric Europe, and now treasured in museums.

11. In the author's time the rupee was worth two shillings, or more, that is to say, the ninth or tenth part of a sovereign. After 1873 the gold value of the rupee fell, so that at times it was worth little more than a shilling. Since 1899 special legislation has succeeded in keeping the rupee practically steady at 1s. 4d. In other words, fifteen rupees are the legal equivalent of a sovereign, and a hundred rupees are worth £6 13s. 4d.

CHAPTER 13

Thugs and Poisoners.

Lieutenant Brown had come on to Damoh chiefly with a view to investigate a case of murder, which had taken place at the village of Sujaina, about ten miles from Damoh, on the road to Hattā.[1] A gang of two hundred Thugs were encamped in the grove at Hindoria in the cold season of 1814, when, early in the morning, seven men well armed with svords and matchlocks passed them, bearing treasure from the bank of Motī Kochia at Jubbulpore to their correspondents at Bānda,[2] to the value of four thousand five hundred rupees.[3] The value of their burden was immediately perceived by these *keen-eyed* sportsmen, and Kosarī, Drigpāl, and Faringia, three of the leaders, with forty of their fleetest and stoutest followers, were immediately selected for the pursuit. They followed seven miles unperceived; and, coming up with the treasure- bearers in a watercourse half a mile from the village of Sujaina, they rushed in upon them and put them all to death with their swords.[4] While they were doing so a tanner from Sujaina approached with his buffalo, and to prevent him giving the alarm they put him to death also, and made off with the treasure, leaving the bodies unburied. A heavy shower of rain fell, and none of the village people came to the place till the next morning early; when some females, passing it on their way to Hattā, saw the bodies, and returning to Sujaina, reported the circumstance to their friends. The whole village thereupon flocked to the spot, and the body of the tanner was burned by his relations with the usual ceremonies, while all the rest were left to be eaten by jackals, dogs and vultures, who make short work of such things in India. [5]

We had occasion to examine a very respectable old gentleman at Damoh upon the case, Gobind Dās, a revenue officer under the former Government,[6] and now about seventy years of age. He told us that he had no knowledge whatever of the murder of the eight men at Sujaina; but he well remembered another which took place seven years before the time we mentioned at Abhāna, a stage or two back, on the road to Jubbulpore. Seventeen treasure-bearers lodged in the grove near that town on their way from Jubbulpore to Sāgar. At night they were set upon by a large gang of

Thugs, and sixteen of them strangled; but the seventeenth laid hold of the noose before it could be brought to bear upon his throat, pulled down the villain who held it, and made his way good to the town. The Rājā, Dharak Singh, went to the spot with all the followers he could collect; but he found there nothing but the sixteen naked bodies lying in the grove, with their eyes apparently starting out of their sockets. The Thugs had all gone off with the treasure and their clothes, and the Rājā searched for them in vain.

A native commissioned officer of a regiment of native infantry one day told me that, while he was on duty over some Thugs at Lucknow, one of them related with great seeming pleasure the following case, which seemed to him one of the most remarkable that he had heard them speak of during the time they were under his charge.

'A stout Mogul[7] officer of noble bearing and singularly handsome countenance, on his way from the Punjab to Oudh, crossed the Ganges at Garhmuktesar Ghāt, near Meerut, to pass through Murādābād and Bareilly.[8] He was mounted on a fine Tūrkī horse, and attended by his "khidmatgār" (butler) and groom. Soon after crossing the river, he fell in with a small party of well-dressed and modest- looking men going the same road. They accosted him in a respectful manner, and attempted to enter into conversation with him. He had heard of Thugs, and told them to be off. They smiled at his idle suspicions, and tried to remove them, but in vain. The Mogul was determined; they saw his nostrils swelling with indignation, took their leave, and followed slowly. The next morning he overtook the same number of men, but of a different appearance, all Musalmāns. They accosted him in the same respectful manner; talked of the danger of the road, and the necessity of their keeping together, and taking advantage of the protection of any mounted gentleman that happened to be going the same way. The Mogul officer said not a word in reply, resolved to have no companions on the road. They persisted—his nostrils began again to swell, and putting his hand to his sword, he bid them all be off, or he would have their heads from their shoulders. He had a bow and quiver full of arrows over his shoulders,[9] a brace of loaded pistols in his waist-belt, and a sword by his side, and was altogether a very formidable-looking cavalier. In the evening another party that lodged in the same "sarāi"[10] became very intimate with the butler and groom. They were going the same road; and, as the Mogul overtook them in the morning, they made their bows respectfully, and began to enter into conversation with their two friends, the groom and butler, who were coming up behind. The Mogul's nostrils began again to swell, and he bid the strangers be off. The groom and butler interceded, for their master was a grave, sedate man, and they wanted companions. All would not do, and the strangers fell in the rear. The next day, when they had got to the middle of an extensive and uninhabited plain, the Mogul in advance, and his two servants a few hundred yards behind, he came up to a party of six poor Musalmāns, sitting weeping by the side of a dead companion. They were soldiers from Lahore,[11] on their way to Lucknow, worn down by fatigue in their anxiety to see their wives and children once more, after a long and painful service. Their companion, the hope and prop of his family, had sunk under the fatigue, and they had made a grave for him; but they were poor unlettered men, and unable to repeat the funeral service from the holy Koran-would his Highness but perform this last office for them, he would, no doubt, find his reward in this world and the next. The Mogul dismounted—the body had been placed in its proper position, with its head towards Mecca. A carpet was spread—the Mogul took off his bow and quiver, then his pistols and sword, and placed them on the ground near the body—called for water, and washed his feet, hands, and face, that he might not pronounce the holy words in an unclean state. He then knelt down and began to repeat the funeral service, in a clear, loud voice. Two of the poor soldiers knelt by him, one on each side in silence. The other four went off a few paces to beg that the butler and groom would not come so near as to interrupt the good Samaritan at his devotions.

'All being ready, one of the four, in a low undertone, gave the "jhirnī" (signal),[12] the handkerchiefs were thrown over their necks, and in a few minutes all three—the Mogul and his servants—were dead, and lying in the grave in the usual manner, the head of one at the feet of the one below him. All the parties they had met on the road belonged to a gang of Jamāldehī Thugs, of the kingdom of Oudh.[13] In despair of being able to win the Mogul's confidence in the usual way, and determined to have the money and jewels, which they knew he carried with him, they had adopted this plan of disarming him; dug the grave by the side of the road, in the open plain, and made a handsome young Musalmān of the party the dead soldier. The Mogul, being a very stout man, died almost without a struggle, as is usually the case with such; and his two servants made no resistance.'

People of great sensibility, with hearts overcharged with sorrow, often appear cold and callous to those who seem to them to feel no interest in their afflictions. An instance of this kind I will here mention; it is one of thousands that I have met with in my Indian rambles. It was mentioned to me one day that an old 'fakīr',[14] who lived in a small hut close by a little shrine on the side of the road near the town of Morādābād, had lately lost his son, poisoned by a party of 'daturiās', or professional poisoners,[15] that now infest every road throughout India. I sent for him, and requested him to tell me his story, as I might perhaps be able to trace the murderers. He did so, and a Persian writer took it down while I listened with all the coldness of a magistrate who wanted merely to learn facts and have nothing whatever to do with feelings. This is his story literally:

'I reside in my hut by the side of the road a mile and [a] half from the town, and live upon the bounty of travellers, and the people of the surrounding villages. About six weeks ago, I was sitting by the side of my shrine after saying prayers, with my only son, about ten years of age, when a man came up with his wife, his son, and his daughter, the one a little older, and the other a little younger than my boy. They baked and ate their bread near my shrine, and gave me flour enough to make two cakes. This I prepared and baked. My boy was hungry, and ate one cake and a half. I ate only half a one, for I was not hungry. I had a few days before purchased a new blanket for my boy, and it was hanging in a branch of the tree that shaded the shrine, when these people came. My son and I soon became stupefied. I saw him fall asleep, and I soon followed. I awoke again in the evening, and found myself in a pool of water. I had sense enough to crawl towards my boy. I found him still breathing, and I sat by him with his head in my lap, where he soon died. It was now evening, and I got up, and wandered about all night picking straws—I know not why. I was not yet quite sensible. During the night the wolves ate my poor boy. I heard this from travellers, and went and gathered up his bones and buried them in the shrine. I did not quite recover till the third day, when I found that some washerwomen had put me into the pool, and left me there with my head out, in hopes that this would revive me; but they had no hope of my son. I was then taken to the police of the town; but the landholders had begged me to say nothing about the poisoners, lest it might get them and their village community into trouble. The man was tall and fair, and about thirty- five; the woman short, stout, and fair, and about thirty; two of her teeth projected a good deal; the boy's eyelids were much diseased.'

All this he told me without the slightest appearance of emotion, for he had not seen any appearance of it in me, or my Persian writer; and a casual European observer would perhaps have exclaimed, 'What brutes these natives are! This fellow feels no more for the loss of his only son than he would for that of a goat'. But I knew the feeling was there. The Persian writer put up his paper, and closed his inkstand, and the following dialogue, word for word, took place between me and the old man:

Question.—What made you conceal the real cause of your boy's death, and tell the police that he had been killed, as well as eaten, by wolves?

Answer.—The landholders told me that they could never bring back my boy to life, and the whole village would be worried to death by them if I made any mention of the poison.

Question. — And if they were to be punished for this they would annoy you?

Answer. — Certainly. But I believed they advised me for my own good as well as their own.

Question. — And if they should turn you away from that place, could you not make another?

Answer.-Are not the bones of my poor boy there, and the trees that he and I planted and watched together for ten years?

Question.-Have you no other relations? What became of your boy's mother?

Answer.-She died at that place when my boy was only three months old. I have brought him up myself from that age; he was my only child, and he has been poisoned for the sake of the blanket! (Here the poor old man sobbed as if his heartstrings would break; and I was obliged to make him sit down on the floor while I walked up and down the room.)

Question. — Had you any children before?

Answer. — Yes, sir, we had several, but they all died before their mother. We had been reduced to beggary by misfortunes, and I had become too weak and ill to work. I buried my poor wife's bones by the side of the road where she died; raised the little shrine over them, planted the trees, and there have I sat ever since by her side, with our poor boy in my bosom. It is a sad place for wolves, and we used often to hear them howling outside; but my poor boy was never afraid of them when he knew I was near him. God preserved him to me, till the sight of the new blanket, for I had nothing else in the world, made these people poison us. I bought it for him only a few days before, when the rains were coming on, out of my savings-it was all I had. (The poor old man sobbed again, and sat down while I paced the room, lest I should sob also; my heart was becoming a little too large for its apartment.) 'I will never', continued he, 'quit the bones of my wife and child, and the tree that he and I watered for so many years. I have not many years to live; there I will spend them, whatever the landholders may do — they advised me for my own good, and will never turn me out.'

I found all the poor man stated to be true; the man and his wife had mixed poison with the flour to destroy the poor old man and his son for the sake of the new blanket which they saw hanging in the branch of the tree, and carried away with them. The poison used on such occasions is commonly the datura, and it is sometimes given in the hookah to be smoked, and at others in food. When they require to poison children as well as grown-up people, or women who do not smoke, they mix up the poison in food. The intention is almost always to destroy life, as 'dead men tell no tales'; but the poisoned people sometimes recover, as in the present case, and lead to the detection of the poisoners. The cases in which they recover are, however, rare, and of those who recover few are ever able to trace the poisoners; and, of those who recover and trace them, very few will ever undertake to prosecute them through the several courts of the magistrate, the sessions, and that of last instance in a distant district, to which the proceedings must be sent for final orders.

The impunity with which this crime is everywhere perpetrated, and its consequent increase in every part of India, are among the greatest evils with which the country is at this time affected. These poisoners are spread all over India, and are as numerous over the Bombay and Madras Presidencies as over that of Bengal. There is no road free from them, and throughout India there must be many hundreds who gain their subsistence by this trade alone. They put on all manner of disguises to suit their purpose; and, as they prey chiefly upon the poorer sort of travellers, they require to destroy the greater number of lives to make up their incomes. A party of two or three poisoners have very often succeeded in destroying another of eight or ten travellers with whom they have journeyed for some days, by pretending to give them a feast on the celebration of the anniversary of some family event. Sometimes an old woman or man will manage the thing alone, by gaining the confidence of travellers, and getting near the cooking-pots while they go aside; or when employed to bring the flour for the meal from the bazaar. The poison is put into the flour or the pot, as opportunity offers.

People of all castes and callings take to this trade, some casually, others for life, and others derive it from their parents or teachers. They assume all manner of disguises to suit their purposes; and the habits of cooking, eating, and sleeping on the side of the road, and smoking with strangers of seemingly the same caste, greatly facilitate their designs upon travellers. The small parties are unconnected with each other, and two parties never unite in the same cruise. The members of one party may be sometimes convicted and punished, but their conviction is accidental, for the system which has enabled us to put down the Thug associations cannot be applied, with any fair prospect of success, to the suppression of these pests to society.[16]

The Thugs went on their adventures in large gangs, and two or more were commonly united in the course of an expedition in the perpetration of many murders. Every man shared in the booty according to the rank he held in the gang, or the part he took in the murders; and the rank of every man and the part he took generally, or in any particular murder, were generally well known to all. From among these gangs, when arrested, we found the evidence we required for their conviction—or the means of tracing it— among the families and friends of their victims, or with persons to whom the property taken had been disposed of, and in the graves to which the victims had been consigned.

To give an idea of the system by which the Government of India has been enabled to effect so great a good for the people as the suppression of these associations, I will suppose that two sporting gentlemen, A at Delhi, and B in Calcutta, had both described the killing of a tiger in an island in the Ganges, near Hardwār[17] and mentioned the names of the persons engaged with them. Among the persons thus named were C, who had since returned to America, D, who had retired to New South Wales, E to England, and F to Scotland. There were four other persons named who were still in India, but they are deeply interested in A and B's story not being believed. A says that B got the skin of the tiger, and B states that he gave it to C, who cut out two of the claws. Application is made to C, D, E, and F, and without the possibility of any collusion, or even communication between them, their statements correspond precisely with those of A and B, as to the time, place, circumstances, and persons engaged. Their statements are sworn to before magistrates in presence of witnesses, and duly attested. C states that he got the skin from B, and gave it to the Nawāb of Rāmpur[18] for a hookah carpet, but that he took from the left forefoot two of the claws, and gave them to the minister of the King of Oudh for a charm for his sick child.

The Nawāb of Rāmpur, being applied to, states that he received the skin from C, at the time and place mentioned, and that he still smokes his hookah upon it; and that it had lost the two claws upon the left forefoot. The minister of the King of Oudh states that he received the two claws nicely set in gold; that they had cured his boy, who still wore them round his neck to guard him from the evil eye. The goldsmith states that he set the two claws in gold for C, who paid him handsomely for his work. The peasantry, whose cattle graze on the island, declare that certain gentlemen did kill a tiger there about the time mentioned, and that they saw the body after the skin had been taken off, and the vultures had begun to descend upon it.

To prove that what A and B had stated could not possibly be true, the other party appeal to some of their townsmen, who are said to be well acquainted with their characters. They state that they really know nothing about the matter in dispute; that their friends, who are opposed to A and B, are much liked by their townspeople and neighbours, as they have plenty of money, which they spend freely, but that they are certainly very much addicted to field-sports, and generally absent in pursuit of wild beasts for three or four months every year; but whether they were or were not present at the killing of the great Garhmuktesar tiger, they could not say.

Most persons would, after examining this evidence, be tolerably well satisfied that the said tiger had really been killed at the time and place, and by the persons mentioned by A and B; but, to establish the fact judicially, it would be necessary to bring A, B, C, D, E, and F, the Nawāb of Rāmpur, the minister of the King of Oudh, and the goldsmith to the criminal court at Meerut, to be confronted with the person whose interest it was that A and B should not be believed. They would all, perhaps, come to the said court from the different quarters of the world in which they had thought themselves snugly settled; but the thing would annoy them so much, and be so much talked of, that sporting gentlemen, nawābs, ministers, and goldsmiths would in future take good care to have 'forgotten' everything connected with the matter in dispute, should another similar reference be made to them, and so A and B would never again have any chance.

Thug approvers, whose evidence we required, were employed in all parts of India, under the officers appointed to put down these associations; and it was difficult to bring all whose evidence was necessary at the trials to the court of the district in which the particular murder was perpetrated. The victims were, for the most part, money-carriers, whose masters and families resided hundreds of miles from the place where they were murdered, or people on their way to their distant homes from foreign service. There was no chance of recovering any of the property taken from the victims, as Thugs were known to spend what they got freely, and never to have money by them; and the friends of the victims, and the bankers whose money they carried, were everywhere found exceedingly averse to take share in the prosecution.

To obviate all these difficulties separate courts were formed, with permission to receive whatever evidence they might think likely to prove valuable, attaching to each portion, whether documentary or oral, whatever weight it might seem to deserve. Such courts were formed at Hyderabad, Mysore, Indore, Lucknow, Gwālior, and were presided over by our highest diplomatic functionaries, in concurrence with the princes at whose courts they were accredited; and who at Jubbulpore, were under the direction of the representative of the Governor-General of India.[19] By this means we had a most valuable species of unpaid agency; and I believe there is no part of their public life on which these high functionaries look back with more pride than that spent in presiding over such courts, and assisting the supreme Government in relieving the people of India from this fearful evil.[20]

Notes:

1. A town on the Allahabad and Sāgar road, sixty-one miles north-east of Sāgar. It was the head-quarters of the Damoh district from 1818 to 1835.

2. The chief town of the district of the same name in Bundēlkhand, situated on the Kēn river, ninety-five miles south-west from Allahabad.

3. Worth at that time £450 sterling, or a little more.

4. An unusual mode of procedure for professed Thugs to adopt, who usually strangled their victims with a cloth. Faringia (Feringheea) Brahman was one of the most noted Thug leaders. He is frequently mentioned in the author's *Report on the Depredations committed by the Thug Gangs* (1840), and the story of the Sujaina crime is fully told in the Introduction to that volume. Faringia became a valuable approver.

5. Lieutenant Brown was suddenly called back to Jubbulpore, and could not himself go to Sujaina. He sent, however, an intelligent native officer to the place, but no man could be induced to acknowledge that he had ever seen the bodies or heard of the affair, though Faringia pointed out to them exactly where they all lay. They said it must be quite a mistake — that such a thing could not have taken place and they know nothing of it. Lieutenant Brown was aware that all this affected ignorance arose entirely from the dread these people have of being summoned to give evidence to any of our district courts of justice; and wrote to the officer in the civil charge of the district to request that he would assure them that their presence would not be required. Mr. Doolan, the assistant magistrate, happened to be going through Sujaina from Sāgar on deputation at the time; and, sending for all the respectable old men of the place, he requested that they would be under no apprehension, but tell him the real truth, as he would pledge himself that not one of them should ever be summoned to any district court to give evidence. They then took him to the spot and pointed out to him where the bodies had been found, and mentioned that the body of the tanner had been burned by his friends. The banker, whose treasure they had been carrying, had an equal dislike to be summoned to court to give evidence, now that he could no longer hope to recover any portion of his lost money; and it was not till after Lieutenant Brown had given him a similar assurance, that he would consent to have his books examined. The loss of the four thousand five hundred rupees was then found entered, with the names of the men who had been killed at Sujaina in carrying it. These are specimens of some of the minor difficulties we had to contend with in our efforts to put down the most dreadful of all crimes. All the prisoners accused of these murders had just been tried for others, or Lieutenant Brown would not have been able to give the pledge he did. [W. H. S.] Difficulties of the same kind beset the administration of criminal justice in India to this day.

6. Of the Marāthās. The district was ceded in 1818.

7. More correctly written Mughal. The term is properly applied to Muhammadans of Turk (Mongol) descent. Such persons commonly affix the title Beg to their names, and often prefix the Persian title Mīrzā.

8. Meerut, the well-known cantonment, in the district of the same name. The name is written Meeruth by the author, and may be also written Mīrath. Ghāt (ghaut) means a ferry, or crossing- place. Murādābād and Bareilly (Barelī) are in Rohilkhand. The latter has a considerable garrison. Both places are large cities, and the head-quarter of districts.

9. The bow and quiver are now rarely seen, except, possibly, in remote parts of Rājputāna. A body of archers helped to hold the Shāh Najaf building at Lucknow against Sir Colin Campbell in 1858. Even in 1903-4 some of the Tibetans who resisted the British advance were armed with bows and arrows.

10. An inn of the Oriental pattern, often called caravanserai in books of travel.

11. Then the capital of Ranjit Singh, the great Sikh chief.

12. 'This is commonly given either by the leader of the gang or the *belhā*, who has chosen the place for the murder.' It was usually some commonplace order, such as 'Bring the tobacco' (*Ramaseeana*, p.99, &c.). See also Meadows Taylor, *Confessions of a Thug*.

13. The Jamāldehī Thugs resided 'in Oude and some other parts east of the Ganges. They are considered very clever and expert, and more stanch to their oath of secrecy than most other classes' (ibid. p. 97). At the time referred to Oudh was a separate kingdom, which lasted as such until 1856. A map included in the printed Thuggee papers reveals the appalling fact that the Thugs had 274 fixed burying-places for their victims in the area of the small kingdom, about half the size of Ireland.

14. Fakīr (fakeer), a religious mendicant. The word properly applies to Muhammadans only, but is often laxly used to include Hindoo ascetics.

15. So called because the poison they use is made of the seeds of the 'datura' plant (*Datura alba*), and other species of the same genus. It is a powerful narcotic.

16. The crime of poisoning travellers is still prevalent, and its detection is still attended by the difficulties described in the text. In some cases the criminals have been proved to belong to families of Thug stranglers. The poisoning of cattle by arsenic, for the sake of their hides, was very prevalent forty years ago, especially in the districts near Benares, but is now believed to be less practised. It was checked under the ordinary law by numerous convictions and severe sentences.

17. In the Sahāranpur district, where the Ganges issues from the hills.

18. A small principality in Rohilkhand, between Murādābād and Bareilly (Barēlī).

19. The special laws on the subject, namely: Acts xxx of 1836, xviii of 1837, xix of 1837, xviii of 1839, xviii of 1843, xxiv of 1843, xiv of 1844, v of 1847, x of 1847, iii of 1848, and xi of 1848, are printed in pp. 353-7 of the author's *Report on Budhuk alias Bagree Decoits, &c.* (1849). See Bibliography, *ante.* No. 12.

20. I may here mention the names of a few diplomatic officers of distinction who have aided in the good cause. *Of the Civil Service* — Mr. F. C. Smith, Mr. Martin, Mr. George Stockwell, Mr. Charles Fraser, the Hon. Mr. Wellesley, the Hon. Mr. Shore, the Hon. Mr. Cavendish, Mr. George Clerk, Mr. L. Wilkinson, Mr, Bax; *Majors-General* — Cubbon and Fraser; *Colonels* — Low, Stewart, Alves, Spiers, Caulfield, Sutherland, and Wade; Major Wilkinson; and, among the foremost, Major Borthwick and Captain Paton. [W. H. S.]

The author's characteristic modesty has prevented him from dwelling upon his own services, which were greater than those of any other officer. Some idea of them may be gathered from the collection of papers entitled *Ramaseeana,* the contents of which are enumerated in the Bibliography, *ante.* No. 2. Colonel Meadows Taylor has given a more popular account of the measures taken for the suppression of Thuggee (thagī) in his *Confessions of a Thug,* written in 1837 (1st ed. 1839). The Thug organization dated from ancient times, but attracted little notice from the East India Company's Government until the author, then Captain Sleeman, submitted his reports on the subject while employed in the Sāgar and Nerbudda Territories, where he had been posted in 1820. He proved that the Thug crimes were committed by a numerous and highly organized fraternity operating in all parts of India. In consequence of his reports, Mr. F. C. Smith, Agent to the Governor- General in the Sāgar and Nerbudda Territories, was invested, in the year 1829, with special powers, and the author, then Major Sleeman, was employed, in addition to his district duties, as Mr, Smith's coadjutor and assistant. In 1835 the author was relieved from district work, and appointed General Superintendent of the operations for the suppression of the Thug gangs. He went on leave to the hills in 1836, and on resuming duty in February, 1839, was appointed Commissioner for the suppression of Thuggee and Dacoity, which office he continued to hold in addition to his other appointments.

Between 1826 and 1835, 1,562 prisoners were tried for the crime of Thuggee, of whom 1,404 were either hanged or transported for life. Some individuals are said to have confessed to over 200 murders, and one confessed to 719. The Thug approvers, whose lives were spared, were detained in a special prison at Jubbulpore, where the remnant of them, with their families, were kept under surveillance. They were employed in a tent and carpet factory, known as the School of Industry, founded in 1838 by the author and Captain Charles Brown. If released, they would certainly have resumed their hereditary occupation, which exercised an awful fascination over its votaries. Most of the Thug gangs had been broken up by 1860, but cases of Thuggee have occurred occasionally since that date. A gang of Kahārs (palanquin bearers) committed a series of Thug murders in, I think, 1877, at Etāwa, in the United Provinces of Agra and Oudh. The office of Superintendent of Thuggee and Dacoity was kept up until 1904, but the officer in charge was more concerned with Dacoity (that is to say, organized gang-robbery with violence) in the Native States than with the secret crime of Thuggee. Secret crime is now watched by the Central Criminal Intelligence Department under the direct control of the Government of India, and has to deal with novel forms of evil-doing. In India it is never safe to assume that any ancient practice has been suppressed, and I have little doubt that, if administrative pressure were relaxed, the old form of Thuggee would again be heard of. The occasional discovery of murdered beggars, who could not have been killed for the sake of their property, leads me to suppose that the Megpunnia variety of Thuggee, that is to say, murder of poor persons in order to kidnap and sell their children, is still sometimes practised.

Among the officers named by the author the best known is Sir Mark Cubbon, who came to India in 1800, and died at Suez in 1861. During the interval he had never quitted India. He ruled over Mysore for nearly thirty years with almost despotic power, and reorganized the administration of that country with conspicuous success (Buckland, *Dict. of Indian Biography*, Sonnenschein, 1906).

The Hon. Frederick John Shore, of the Bengal Civil Service, officiated in 1836 as Civil Commissioner and Political Agent of the Sāgar and Nerbudda Territories. In 1837 he published his *Notes on Indian Affairs* (London, 2 vols. 8vo), a series of articles dealing in the most outspoken way with the abuses and weaknesses of Anglo-Indian administration at that time.

Mr. F. C. Smith was Agent to the Governor-General at Jubbulpore in 1830 and subsequent years. The author was then immediately subordinate to him. Messrs. Martin and Wellesley were Residents at Holkar's court at Indore. Mr. Stockwell tried some of the Thug prisoners at Cawnpore and Allahabad as Special Commissioner, in addition to his ordinary duties: correspondence between him and the author is printed in *Ramaseeana*. Mr. Charles Fraser preceded the author in charge of the Sāgar district, and in January, 1832, resumed charge of the revenue and civil duties of that district, leaving the criminal work to the author. The Hon. Mr. Cavendish was Resident at Sindhia's court at Gwālior. Mr. George Clerk became Sir George Clerk and Lieutenant-Governor of the North-Western Provinces, Governor of Bombay, and Permanent Under- Secretary of State for India; he died at a great age in 1889. Mr. Lancelot Wilkinson, Political Agent in Bhopal, was considered by the author to be 'one of the most able and estimable members of the India Civil Service' (*Journey*, ii. 403). Mr. Bax was Resident at Indore; Colonel (afterwards Sir John) Low, was Resident at Lucknow, and had served at Jubbulpore; Colonel Stewart and Major-General Fraser were Residents at Hyderabad; Major (Colonel) Alves was Political Agent in Bhopal and Agent in Rājputāna; Colonel Spiers was Agent at Nīmach, and officiated as Agent in Rājputāna; Colonel Caulfield had been Political Agent at Harautī; Colonel Sutherland was Resident at Gwālior, and afterwards Agent in Rājputāna; Colonel (Sir C. M.) Wade had been Political Agent at Lūdiāna; Major Borthwick was employed at Indore; Captain Paton was Assistant Resident at Lucknow (see *Journey through Kingdom of Oudh*, vol. ii, pp. 152-69).

Besides the officers above named, others are specified in *Ramaseeana* as having done good service.

Note.—Mr. Crooke suggests, and, I think, correctly, that the words *Megpunnia* and *Megpunnaism* (*ante*, note 20, and Bibliography No. 7) are corruptions of the Hindī *Mēkh-phandiyā*, from *mēkh*, 'a peg', and *phandā*, 'a noose', equivalent to the Persian *tasmabāz*, meaning 'playing tricks with a strap'. Creagh, a private in a British regiment at Cawnpore about 1803, is said to have initiated three men into the peg and strap trick, as practised by English rogues. These men became the leaders of three Tasmabāz Thug gangs, whose proceedings are described by Mr. R. Montgomery in *Selections of the Records of Government*, N.W.P., vol. i, p. 312. A strap is doubled and folded up in different shapes. The art consists in putting in a stick or peg in such a way that the strap when unfolded shall come out double. The Tasmabāz Thugs seem to be identical with the 'Megpunnia' (*N.I.N.& Qu.*, vol. i, p. 108, note 721, September 1891).

General Hervey records seven modern instances of strangulation by Megpunnia Thugs in Rājputāna (*Some Records of Crime* (1867), vol. i, pp. 126-31).

CHAPTER 14

Basaltic Cappings of the Sandstone Hills of Central India—Suspension Bridge—Prospects of the Nerbudda Valley—Deification of a Mortal.

On the 29th[1] we came on to Pathariā, a considerable little town thirty miles from Sāgar, supported almost entirely by a few farmers, small agricultural capitalists, and the establishment of a native collector,[2] On leaving Pathariā, we ascend gradually along the side of the basaltic hills on our left to the south for three miles to a point whence we see before us this plane of basaltic cappings extending as far as the eye can reach to the west, south, and north, with frequent breaks, but still preserving one uniform level. On the top of these tables are here and there little conical elevations of laterite, or indurated iron clay.[3] The cappings everywhere repose immediately upon the sandstone of the Vindhya range; but they have occasional beds of limestone, formed apparently by springs rising from their sides, and strongly impregnated with carbonic acid gas. For the most part this is mere travertine, but in some places they get good lime from the beds for building.

On the 1st of December we came to the pretty village of Sanodā, near the suspension bridge built over the river Biās by Colonel Presgrave, while he was assay master of the Sāgar mint.[4] I was present at laying the foundation-stone of this bridge in December 1827. Mr. Maddock was the Governor-General's representative in these territories, and the work was undertaken more with a view to show what could be done out of their own resources, under minds capable of developing them, than to supply any pressing or urgent want.

The work was completed in June, 1830; and I have several times seen upon the bridge as many as it could hold of a regiment of infantry while it moved over; and, at other times, as many of a corps of cavalry, and often several elephants at once. The bridge is between the points of suspension two hundred feet, and the clear portion of the platform measures one hundred and ninety feet by eleven and a half. The whole cost of the work amounted to about fifty thousand rupees; and, under a less able and careful person than Colonel Presgrave, would have cost, perhaps, double the amount. This work has been declared by a very competent judge to be equal to any structure of the same kind in Europe, and is eminently calculated to show what genius and perseverance can produce out of the resources of a country even in the rudest state of industry and the arts.

The river Nerbudda neither is nor ever can, I fear, be made navigable, and the produce of its valley would require to find its way to distant markets over the Vindhya range of hills to the north, or the Sātpura to the south. If the produce of the soil, mines, and industry of the valley cannot be transported to distant markets, the Government cannot possibly find in it any available net surplus revenue in money; for it has no mines of the precious metals, and the precious metals can flow in only in exchange for the produce of the land, and the industry of the valley that flows out. If the Government wishes to draw a net surplus revenue from the valley or from the districts that border upon it, that is, a revenue beyond its expenditure in support of the local public establishments, it must either draw it in produce, or for what can be got for that produce in distant markets.[5] Hitherto little beyond the rude produce of the soil has been able to find its way into distant markets from the valley of the Nerbudda; yet this valley abounds in iron mines,[6] and its soil, where unexhausted by cropping, is of the richest quality.[7] It is not then too much to hope that in time the iron of the mines will be worked with machinery for manufactures; and that multitudes, aided by this machinery, and subsisted on the rude agricultural produce, which now flows out, will invest the value of their labour in manufactured commodities adapted to the demand of foreign markets and better able from their superior value, compared with their bulk, to pay the cost of transport by land. Then, and not till then, can we expect to see these territories pay a considerable net surplus revenue to Government, and abound in a middle class of merchants, manufacturers, and agricultural capitalists.[8]

At Sanodā there is a very beautiful little fortress or castle now unoccupied, though still entire. It was built by an officer of the Rājā Chhatar Sāl of Bundēlkhand, about one hundred and twenty years ago.[9] He had a grant, on the tenure of military service, of twelve villages situated round this place; and a man who could build such a castle to defend the surrounding country from the inroads of freebooters, and to secure himself and his troops from any sudden impulse of the people's resentment, was as likely to acquire an increase of territorial possession in these parts as he would have been in Europe during the Middle Ages. The son of this chief, by name Rāi Singh, was, soon after the castle had been completed, killed in an attack upon a town near Chitrakōt;[10] and having, in the estimation of the people, *become a god*, he had a temple and a tomb raised to him close to our encampment. I asked the people how he had become a *god*; and was told that some one who had been long suffering from a quartan ague went to the tomb one night, and promised Rāi Singh, whose ashes lay under it, that if he could contrive to cure his ague for him, he would, during the rest of his life, make offerings to his shrine. After that he had never another attack, and was very punctual in his offerings. Others followed his example, and with like success, till Rāi Singh was recognized among them universally as a god, and a temple raised to his name. This is the way that gods were made all over the world at one time, and are still made all over India. Happy had it been for mankind if those only who were supposed to do good had been deified.[11]

On the 2nd we came on to the village of Khojanpur (leaving the town and cantonments of Sāgar to our left), a distance of some fourteen miles. The road for a great part of the way was over the bare back of the sandstone strata, the covering of basalt having been washed off. The hills, however, are, at this distance from the city and cantonments of Sāgar, nicely wooded; and, being constantly intersected by pretty little valleys, the country we came over was picturesque and beautiful. The soil of all these valleys is rich from the detritus of the basalt that forms or caps the hills; but it is now in a bad state of cultivation, partly from several successive seasons of great calamity, under which the people have been suffering, and partly from over-assessment; and this posture of affairs is continued by that loss of energy, industry, and character, among the farmers and cultivators, which must everywhere result from these two evils. In India, where the people have learnt so well to govern themselves, from the want of settled government, good or bad government really depends almost altogether upon *good or bad settlements of the land revenue.* Where the Government demand is imposed with moderation, and enforced with justice, there will the people be generally found happy and contented, and disposed to perform their duties to each other and to the state; except when they have the misfortune to suffer from drought, blight, and other calamities of season.[12]

I have mentioned that the basalt in the Sāgar district reposes for the most part immediately upon the sandstone of the Vindhya range; and it must have been deposited on the sand, while the latter was yet at the bottom of the ocean, though this range is now, I believe, nowhere less than from fifteen hundred to two thousand feet above the level of the sea. The marks of the ripple of the sea may be observed in some places where the basalt has been recently washed off, beautifully defined, as if formed only yesterday, and there is no other substance to be seen between the two rocks.

The texture of the sandstone at the surface, where it comes in contact with the basalt, has in some places been altered by it, but in others it seems to have been as little changed as the habitations of the people who were suffocated by the ashes of Vesuvius in the city of Pompeii. I am satisfied, from long and careful examination, that the greater part of this basalt, which covers the tableland of Central and Southern India, must have been held for some time in suspension in the ocean or lake into which it was first thrown in the shape of ashes, and then gradually deposited. This alone can account for its frequent appearance of stratification, for the gentle blending of its particles with those of the sand near the surface of the latter; and, above all, for those level steps, or tables, lying one above another horizontally in parallel bars on one range, corresponding exactly with the same parallel lines one above another on a range twenty or thirty miles across the valley. Mr. Scrope's theory is, I believe, that these are all mere flowing *coulées* of lava, which, in their liquid state, filled hollows, but afterwards became of a harder texture, as they dried and crystallized, than the higher rocks around them; the consequence of which is that the latter has been decomposed and washed away, while the basalt has been left to form the highest elevations. My opinion is that these steps, or stairs, at one time formed the beds of the ocean, or of great lakes, and that the substance of which they are composed was, for the most part, projected into the water, and there held in suspension till gradually deposited. There are, however, amidst these steps, and beneath them, masses of more compact and crystalline basalt, that bear evident signs of having been flows of lava.[13]

Reasoning from analogy at Jubbulpore, where some of the basaltic cappings of the hills had evidently been thrown out of craters long after this surface had been raised above the waters, and become the habitation both of vegetable and animal life, I made the first discovery of fossil remains in the Nerbudda valley. I went first to a hill within sight of my house in 1828,[14] and searched exactly between the plateau of basalt that covered it and the stratum immediately below, and there I found several small trees with roots, trunks, and branches, all entire, and beautifully petrified. They had been only recently uncovered by the washing away of a part of the basaltic plateau. I soon after found some fossil bones of animals.[15] Going over to Sāgar, in the end of 1830, and reasoning there upon the same analogy, I searched for fossil remains along the line of contact between the basalt and the surface upon which it had been deposited, and I found a grove of silicified palm- trees within a mile of the cantonments. These palm-trees had grown upon a calcareous deposit formed from springs rising out of the basaltic range of hills to the south. The commissariat officer had cut a road through this grove, and all the European officers of a large military station had been every day riding through it without observing the geological treasure; and it was some time before I could convince them that the stones which they had every day seen were really petrified palm-trees. The roots and trunks were beautifully perfect.[16]

Notes:

1. November, 1835.

2. In the Damoh District, twenty-four miles west of Damoh. The name appears to be derived from the 'great quantity of hewn stone (Hind. *patthar* or *pāthar*) lying about in all directions'. The C. P. *Gazetteer* (1870) calls the place 'a considerable village'.

3. A peculiar formation, of 'widespread occurrence in the tropical and subtropical regions of the world'. It is ordinarily of a reddish ferruginous or brick-dust colour, sometimes deepened into dark red. Apparently the special character which distinguishes laterite from other forms of red-coloured weathering is the presence of hydrous oxide of alumina in varying proportions. . . . 'Though there is still a great deal of uncertainty about the way in which laterite was formed, the facts which are known of its distribution seem to show that it is a distinct form of weathering, which is confined to low latitudes and humid climates; its formation seems to have been a slow process, only possible on flat or nearly flat surfaces, where surface rain-wash could not act' (Oldham, in *The Oxford Survey of the British Empire*, vol. ii, Asia, p. 10: Oxford, 1914). It hardens and darkens by exposure to air, and is occasionally used as a building stone.

4. The Sāgar mint was erected in 1820 by Captain Presgrave, the assay master, and used to employ four hundred men, but, after about ten or twelve years, the business was transferred to Calcutta, and the buildings converted to other uses (*C. P. Gazetteer*, 1870). Mints are now kept up at Calcutta and Bombay only. The Biās is a small stream flowing into the Sunār river, and belonging to the Jumna river system. The name is printed Beeose in the original edition.

5. Since the author's time the conditions have been completely changed by the introduction of railways. The East Indian, Great Indian Peninsular, and other railways now enter the Nerbudda Valley, so that the produce of most districts can be readily transported to distant markets. A large enhancement of the land revenue has been obtained by revisions of the settlement.

6. Details will be found in the *Central Provinces Gazetteer* (1870). The references are collected under the head 'Iron' in the index to that work. Chapter VIII of *Ball's Economic Geology of India* gives full information concerning the iron mines of the Central Provinces and all parts of India. That work forms Part III of the *Manual of the Geology of India*.

7. The soil of the valley of the Nerbudda, and that of the Nerbudda and Sāgar territories generally, is formed for the most part of the detritus of trap-rocks that everywhere covered the sandstone of the Vindhya and Sātpura

ranges which run through these territories. This basaltic detritus forms what is called the black cotton soil by the English, for what reason I know not. [W. H. S.] The reason is that cotton is very largely grown in the Nerbudda Valley, both on the black soil and other soils. In Bundēlkhand the black, friable soil, often with a high proportion of organic matter, is called 'mār', and is chiefly devoted to raising crops of wheat, gram, or chick-pea (*Cicer arietinum*), linseed, and joār (*Holcus sorghum*). Cotton is also sown in it, but not very generally. This black soil requires little rain, and is fertile without manure. It absorbs water too freely to be suitable for irrigation, and in most seasons does not need it. The 'black cotton soil' is often known as *regur*, a corruption of a Tamil word. 'The origin of *regur* is a doubtful question. . . . The dark coloration was attributed by earlier writers to vegetable matter, and taken to indicate a large amount of humus in the soil; more recent investigations make this doubtful, and in all probability the colour is due to mineral constitution rather than to the very scanty organic constituents of the soil,' It may possibly be formed of 'wind-borne dust', like the loess plains of China (Oldham, in *The Oxford Survey of the British Empire*, vol. ii, Asia, p. 9: Oxford, 1914).

8. The land revenue has been largely increased, and the resources and communications of the country have been greatly developed during the last half-century. The formation of the Central Provinces as a separate administration in 1861 secured for the Sāgar and Nerbudda territories the attention which they failed to obtain from the distant Government of the North-Western Provinces. Sir Richard Temple, the first Chief Commissioner, administered the Central Provinces with extraordinary energy and success.

9. Rājā Chhatarsāl Bundela was Rājā of Pannā. The history of Chhatarsāl is related in *I.G.* (1908), vol. xix, p. 400, s.v. Panna State. In 1729 he called in the Marāthās to help him against Muhammad Khan Bangash, and when he died in 1731 rewarded them by bequeathing one-third of his dominions to the Peshwa. The correct date of his death is Pūs Badi 3, Samvat 1788 (*Hamīrpur Settlement Report* (1880), note at end of chapter 2). The date is often given inaccurately.

10. Chitrakōt, in the Bānda district of Bundēlkhand, under the government of the United Provinces of Agra and Oudh, and seventy-one miles distant from Allahabad, is a famous place of pilgrimage, much frequented by the votaries of Rāma. Large fairs are held there.

11. The performance of miraculous cures at the tomb is not necessary for the deification of a person who has been specially feared in his lifetime, or has died a violent death. Either of these conditions is enough to render his ghost formidable, and worthy of propitiation. Shrines to such persons are very numerous both in Bundēlkhand and other parts of India, Miracles, of

course, occur at nearly every shrine, and are too common and well attested to attract much attention.

12. These observations are as true to-day as they were in the author's time. Disastrous cases of over-assessment were common in the early years of British rule, and the mischief so wrought has been sometimes traceable for generations afterwards. Since 1833 the error, though less common, has not been unknown.

13. Since writing the above, I have seen Colonel Sykes's notes on the formations of Southern India in the *Indian Review*. The facts there described seem all to support my conclusion, and his map would answer just as well for Central as for Southern India; for the banks of the Nerbudda and Chambal, Sōn, and Mahānadī, as well as for those of the Bām and the Bīmā. Colonel Sykes does not, I believe, attempt to account for the stratification of the basalt; he merely describes it. [W. H. S.]

The author's theory of the subaqueous origin of the greater part of the basalt of Central and Southern India, otherwise known as the 'Deccan Trap Series', had been supported by numerous excellent geologists, but W. T. Blanford proved the theory to be untenable, there being 'clear and unmistakable evidence that the traps were in great part of sub-aerial formation', The intercalation of sedimentary beds with fresh-water fossils is conclusive proof that the lava-flows associated with such beds cannot be submarine. The hypothesis that the lower beds of traps were poured out in a vast, but shallow, freshwater lake extending throughout the area over which the inter- trappean limestone formation extends appears to be extremely improbable. The lava seems to have been poured, during a long succession of ages, over a land surface, uneven and broken in parts, 'with intervals of rest sufficient for lakes, stocked with fresh- water mollusca, to form on the cold surfaces of several of the lava- flows' (Holland, in *I.G.* (1907), i. 88). A great tract of the volcanic region appears to have remained almost undisturbed to the present day, affected by sub-aerial erosion alone. The geological horizon of the Deccan trap cannot be precisely defined, but is now vaguely stated as 'the close of the cretaceous period'. The 'steps', or conspicuous terraces, traceable on the hill-sides for great distances, are explained as being 'due to the outcrop of the harder basaltic strata, or of those beds which resist best the disintegrating influences of exposure'.

The general horizontality of the Deccan trap over an area of not less than 200,000 square miles, and the absence of volcanic hills of the usual conical form, are difficulties which have caused much discussion. Some of the 'old volcanic vents' appear to have existed near Poona and Mahābleshwar. The entire area has been subjected to sub-aerial denudation on a gigantic scale, which explains the occurrence of the basalt as the caps of isolated hills. Much further investigation is required to clear up details (*Manual of the Geology of India*, ed. 1, Part I, chap. 13)

14. The author took charge of the Jubbulpore District in March 1828.

15. The fossiliferous beds near Jubbulpore, described in the text, seem to belong to the group now classed as the Lamētā beds. The bones of a large dinosaurian reptile (*Titanosaurus indicus*) have been identified (*I.G.*, 1907, vol. i, p. 88).

16. 'Many years ago Dr. Spry (*Note on the Fossil Palms and Shells lately discovered on the Table-Land of Sāgar in Central India*, in *J.A.S.B.* for 1833, vol. ii, p. 639) and, subsequently to him, Captain Nicholls (*Journal of Asiatic Soc. of Bombay*, vol. v, p. 614), studied and described certain trunks of palm-trees, whose silicified remains are found imbedded in the soft intertrappean mud-beds near Sāgar. . . . The trees are imbedded in a layer of calcareous black earth, which formed the surface soil in which they grew; this soil rests on, and was made up of the disintegration of, a layer of basalt. It is covered over by another and similar layer of the same rock near where the trees occur. . . . The palm-trees, now found fossilized, grew in the soil, which, in the condition of a black calcareous earthy bed, we now find lying round their prostrate stems. They fell (from whatever cause), and lay until their silicification was complete. A slight depression of the surface, or some local or accidental check of some drainage- course, or any other similar and trivial cause, may have laid them under water. The process of silicification proceeded gradually but steadily, and after they had there, in lapse of ages, become lapidified, the next outburst of volcanic matter overwhelmed them, broke them, partially enveloped, and bruised them, until long subsequent denudation once more brought them to light' (J. G. Medlicott, in *Memoirs of the Geological Survey of India*, vol. ii. Part II, pp. 200, 203, 204, 205, 216, as quoted in *C. P. Gazetteer* (1870), p. 435). The intertrappean fossils are all those of organisms which would occur in shallow fresh-water lakes or marshy ground.

Besides the author's friend and relative, Dr. H. H. Spry, Dr. Spilsbury contributed papers on the Nerbudda fossils to vols. iii, vi, viii, ix, x, and xiii of the *J.A.S.B.* Other writers also have treated of the subject, but it appears to be by no means fully worked out. James Prinsep, to whom no topic came amiss, discussed the Jubbulpore fossil bones in the volume in which Dr. Spry's paper appeared. Dr. Spry was the author of a work entitled *Modern India: with Illustrations of the Resources and Capabilities of Hindustan* (2 vols. 8vo, 1838). He became F.R.S.

CHAPTER 15

Legend of the Sāgar Lake — Paralysis from eating the Grain of the *Lathyrus sativus*.

The cantonments of Sāgar are about two miles from the city and occupied by three regiments of native infantry, one of local horse, and a company of European artillery.[1] The city occupies two sides of one of the most beautiful lakes of India, formed by a wall which unites two sandstone hills on the north side. The fort and part of the town stands upon this wall, which, according to tradition, was built by a wealthy merchant of the Banjāra caste.[2] After he had finished it, the bed of the lake still remained dry; and he was told in a dream, or by a priest, that it would continue so till he should consent to sacrifice his own daughter, then a girl, and the young lad to whom she was affianced, to the tutelary god of the place. He accordingly built a little shrine in the centre of the valley, which was to become the bed of the lake, put the two children in, and built up the doorway. He had no sooner done so than the whole of the valley became filled with water, and the old merchant, the priest, the masons, and spectators, made their escape with much difficulty. From that time the lake has been inexhaustible; but no living soul of the Banjāra caste has ever since been known to drink of its waters. Certainly all of that caste at present religiously avoid drinking the water of the lake; and the old people of the city say that they have always done so since they can remember, and that they used to hear from their parents that they had always done so. In nothing does the Founder of the Christian religion appear more amiable than in His injunction, 'Suffer little children to come unto me, and forbid them not'. In nothing do the Hindoo deities appear more horrible than in the delight they are supposed to take in their sacrifice — it is everywhere the helpless, the female, and the infant that they seek to devour — and so it was among the Phoenicians and their Carthaginian colonies. Human sacrifices were certainly offered in the cities of Sāgar during the whole of the Marātha government up to the year 1800, when they were put a stop to by the local governor, Āsā Sāhib, a very humane man; and I once heard a very learned Brahman priest say that he thought the decline of his family and government arose from this *innovation*. 'There is', said he, 'no sin in *not* offering human sacrifices to the gods where none have been offered; but, where the gods have been accustomed to them, they are naturally annoyed when the rite is abolished, and visit the place and people with all kinds of calamities.' He did not seem to think that there was anything singular in this mode of reasoning, and perhaps three Brahman priests out of four would have reasoned in the same manner.[3]

On descending into the valley of the Nerbudda over the Vindhya range of hills from Bhopal, one may see by the side of the road, upon a spur of the hill, a singular pillar of sandstone rising in two spires, one turning above and rising over the other, to the height of from twenty to thirty feet. On a spur of a hill half a mile distant is another sandstone pillar not quite so high. The tradition is that the smaller pillar was the affianced bride of the taller one, who was a youth of a family of great eminence in these parts. Coming with his uncle to pay his first visit to his bride in the procession they call the 'barāt', he grew more and more impatient as he approached nearer and nearer, and she shared the feeling. At last, unable to restrain himself, he jumped upon his uncle's shoulder, and looked with all his might towards the spot where his bride was said to be seated. Unhappily she felt no less impatient than he did, and raised 'the fringed curtains of her eye', as he raised his, [and] they saw each other at the same moment. In that moment the bride, bridegroom, and uncle were all converted into stone pillars; and there they stand to this day a monument, in the estimation of the people, to warn men and womankind against too strong an inclination to indulge curiosity. It is a singular fact that in one of the most extensive tribes of the Gond population of Central India, to which this couple is said to have belonged, the bride always goes to the bridegroom in the procession of the 'barāt', to prevent a recurrence of this calamity. It is the bridegroom who goes to the bride among every other class of the people of India, as well Muhammadans as Hindoos. Whether the usage grew out of the tradition, or the tradition out of the usage, is a question that will admit of much being said on both sides. I can only vouch for the existence of both. I have seen the pillars, heard the tradition from the people, and ascertained the usage; as in the case of that of the Sāgar lake.

The Mahādēo sandstone hills, which in the Sātpura range overlook the Nerbudda to the south, rise to between four and five thousand feet above the level of the sea;[4] and in one of the highest parts a fair was formerly, and is, perhaps, still held[5] for the enjoyment of those who assemble to witness the self devotion of a few young men, who offer themselves as a sacrifice to fulfil the vows of their mothers. When a woman is without children she makes votive offerings to all the gods, who can, she thinks, assist her, and promises of still greater in case they should grant what she wants. Smaller promises being found of no avail, she at last promises her first-born, if a male, to the god of destruction, Mahādēo. If she gets a son, she conceals from him her vows till he has attained the age of puberty; she then communicates it [sic] to him, and enjoins him to fulfil it. He believes it to be his paramount duty to obey his mother's call; and from that moment he considers himself as devoted to the god. Without breathing to any living soul a syllable of what she has told him, he puts on the habit of a pilgrim or religious mendicant, visits all the celebrated temples dedicated to this god in different parts of India;[6] and, at the annual fair on the Mahādēo hills, throws himself from a perpendicular height of four or five hundred feet, and is dashed to pieces upon the rocks below.[7] If the youth does not feel himself quite prepared for the sacrifice on the first visit, he spends another year in pilgrimages, and returns to fulfil his mother's vow at the next fair. Some have, I believe, been known to postpone the sacrifice to a third fair; but the interval is always spent in painful pilgrimages to the celebrated temples of the god. When Sir R. Jenkins was the Governor-General's representative at the court of Nāgpur,[8] great efforts were made by him and all the European officers under him to put a stop to these horrors by doing away with the fair; and their efforts were assisted by the *cholera morbus*, which broke out among the multitude one season while they were so employed, and carried off the greater part of them. This seasonable visitation was, I believe, considered as an intimation on the part of the god that the people ought to have been more attentive to the wishes of the white men, for it so happens that Mahādēo is the only one of the Hindoo gods who is represented with a white face. [9] He figures among the *dramatis personae* of the great pantomime of the Rāmlīlā[10] or fight for the recovery of Sitā from the demon king of Ceylon; and is the only one with a white face. I know not whether the fair has ever been revived, but [I] think not.

In 1829 the wheat and other spring crops in this and the surrounding villages were destroyed by a severe hail-storm; in 1830 they were deficient from the want of seasonable rains; and in 1831 they were destroyed by blight. During these three years the 'teorī', or what in other parts of India is called 'kesārī' (the *Lathyrus sativus* of botanists), a kind of wild vetch, which, though not sown itself, is left carelessly to grow among the wheat and other grain, and given in the green and dry state to cattle, remained uninjured, and thrived with great luxuriance.[11] In 1831 they reaped a rich crop of it from the blighted wheat-fields, and subsisted upon its grain during that and the following years, giving the stalks and leaves only to their cattle. In 1833 the sad effects of this food began to manifest themselves. The younger part of the population of this and the surrounding villages, from the age of thirty downwards, began to be deprived of the use of their limbs below the waist by paralytic strokes, in all cases sudden, but in some cases more severe than in others. About half the youth of this village of both sexes became affected during the years 1833 and 1834, and many of them have lost the use of their lower limbs entirely, and are unable to move. The youth of the surrounding villages, in which the 'teorī' from the same causes formed the chief article of food during the years 1831 and 1832, have suffered to an equal degree. Since the year 1834 no new case has occurred; but no person once attacked had been found to recover the use of the limbs affected; and my tent was surrounded by great numbers of the youth in different stages of the disease, imploring my advice and assistance under this dreadful visitation. Some of them were very fine-looking young men of good caste and respectable families; and all stated that their pains and infirmities were confined entirely to the parts below the waist. They described the attack as coming on suddenly, often while the person was asleep, and without any warning symptoms whatever; and stated that a greater portion of the young men were attacked than of the young women. It is the prevailing opinion of the natives throughout the country that both horses and bullocks, which have been much fed upon 'teorī', are liable to lose the use of their limbs; but, if the poisonous qualities abound more in the grain than in the stalk or leaves, man, who eats nothing but the grain, must be more liable to suffer from the use of this food than beasts, which eat it merely as they eat grass or hay.

I sent the son of the head man of the village and another, who were among the young people least affected, into Sāgar with a letter to my friend Dr. Foley, with a request that he would try what he could do for them; and if he had any fair prospect of being able to restore these people to the use of their limbs, that measures might be adopted through the civil authorities to provide them with accommodation and the means of subsistence, either by private subscription, or by application to Government. The civil authorities, however, could find neither accommodation nor funds to maintain these people while under Dr. Foley's care; and several seasons of calamity had deprived them of the means of maintaining themselves at a distance from their families. Nor is a medical man in India provided with the means found most effectual in removing such affections, such as baths, galvanic batteries, &c. It is lamentable to think how very little we have as yet done for the country in the healing art, that art which, above all others, a benevolent and enlightened Government should encourage among the people of India.

All we have as yet done has been to provide medical attendants for our European officers; regiments, and jails. It must not, however, be supposed that the people of India are without medical advice, for there is not a town or considerable village in India without its practitioners, the Hindoos following the Egyptian (Misrānī), and the Musalmāns the Grecian (Yunānī) practice. The first prescribe little physic and much fasting; and the second follow the good old rules of Hippocrates, Galen, and Avicenna, with which they are all tolerably well acquainted. As far as the office of physician goes, the natives of India of all classes, high and low, have much more confidence in their own practitioners than in ours, whom they consider too reckless and better adapted to treat diseases in a cold than a hot climate. They cannot afford to give the only fees which European physicians would accept; and they see them, in their hospital practice, trust much to their native assistants, who are very few of them able to read any book, much less to study the profound doctrines of the great masters of the science of medicine.[12] No native ventures to offer an opinion upon this abstruse subject in any circle where he is not known to be profoundly read in either Arabic or Sanskrit lore; nor would he venture to give a prescription without first consulting, 'spectacles on nose', a book as large as a church Bible. The educated class, as indeed all classes, say that they do not want our physicians, but stand much in need of our surgeons. Here they feel that they are helpless, and we are strong; and they seek our aid whenever they see any chance of obtaining it, as in the present case.[13] Considering that every European gentleman they meet is more or less a surgeon, or hoping to find him so, people who are afflicted, or have children afflicted, with any kind of malformation, or malorganization, flock round them [sic] wherever they go, and implore their aid; but implore in vain, for, when they do happen to fall in with a surgeon, he is a mere passer-by, without the means or the time to afford relief. In travelling over India there is nothing which distresses a benevolent man so much as the necessity he is daily under of telling poor parents, who, with aching hearts and tearful eyes, approach him with their suffering children in their arms, that to relieve them requires time and means which are not at a traveller's command, or a species of knowledge which he does not possess; it is bitter thus to dash to the ground the cup of hope which our approach has raised to the lip of mother, father, and child; but he consoles himself with the prospect, that at no distant period a benevolent and enlightened Government will distribute over the land those from whom the afflicted will not seek relief in vain.[14]

Notes:

1. The garrison is stated in the *Gazetteer* (1870) to consist of a European regiment of infantry, two batteries of European artillery, one native cavalry and one native infantry regiment. In 1893 it consisted of one battery of Royal Artillery, a detachment of British Infantry, a regiment of Bengal Cavalry, and a detachment of Bengal Infantry. According to the census of 1911, the population of Sāgar was 45,908.

2. The Banjāras, or Brinjāras, are a wandering tribe, principally employed as carriers of grain and salt on bullocks and cows. They used

to form the transport service of the Moghal armies, and of the Company's forces at least as late as 1819. Their organization and customs are in many ways peculiar. The development of roads and railways has much diminished the importance of the tribe. A good account of it will be found in Balfour, *Cyclopaedia of India*, 3rd ed., 1885, s. v. 'Banjāra'. Dubois (*Hindu Manners, &c.*, 3rd ed. (1906), p. 70) states that 'of all the castes of the Hindus, this particular one is acknowledged to be the most brutal'.

3. See note on human sacrifice, *ante*, Chapter 8, note 8.

4. In the Hoshangābād district of the Central Provinces. The sandstone formation here attains its highest development, and is known to geologists as the 'Mahādēo sandstones'. The new sanitarium of Pachmarhī is situated in these hills.

5. It has been long since suppressed.

6. Benares is the principal seat of the worship of Mahādēo (Siva), but his shrines are found everywhere throughout India. One hundred and eight of these are reckoned as important. In Southern India the most notable, perhaps, is the great temple at Tanjore (see chap. 17 of Monier Williams's *Religious Thought and Life in India*).

7. 'This mode of suicide is called Bhrigu-pātā, "throwing one's self from a precipice". It was once equally common at the rock of Girnār [in Kāthiāwār], and has only recently been prohibited' (ibid. p. 349).

8. Nagpore (Nāgpur) was governed by Marāthā rulers, with the title of Bhōnslā, also known as the Rājās of Berār. The last Rājā, Raghojī, died without heirs in 1853. His dominions were then annexed as lapsed territory by Lord Dalhousie. Sir Richard Jenkins was Resident at Nāgpur from 1810 to 1827. Nāgpur is now the head-quarters of the Chief Commissioner of the Central Provinces.

9. 'There is a legend that Siva appeared in the Kali age, for the good of the Brahmans, as "Sveta", "the white one", and that he had four disciples, to all of whom the epithet "Sveta" is applied' (Monier Williams, *Religious Thought and Life in India*, p. 80, note 2). Various explanations of the legend have been offered. Professor A. Weber is inclined to think that the various references to white teachers in Indian legends allude to Christian missionaries. The Mahābhārata mentions the travels of Nārada and others across the sea to 'Sveta-dwīpa', the 'Island of the White Men', in order to learn the doctrine of the unity of God. This tradition appears to be intelligible only if understood to commemorate the journeys of pious Indians to Alexandria, and their study of Christianity there (*Die Griechen in Indien*, 1890, p. 34).

10. The Rāmlīlā, a performance corresponding to the mediaeval European 'miracle-play', is celebrated in Northern India in the month of

Kuār (or Asvin, September-October), at the same time as the Durgā Pūjā is solemnized in Bengal. Rāma and his brother Lachhman are impersonated by boys, who are seated on thrones in state. The performance concludes by the burning of a wicker image of Rāvana, the demon king of Lankā (Ceylon), who had carried off Rāma's queen, Sitā. The story is the leading subject of the great epic called the Rāmāyana.

11. The *Lathyrus sativus* is cultivated in the Punjab and in Tibet. Its poisonous qualities are attributed to its excessive proportion of nitrogenous matter, which requires dilution. Another species of the genus, *L. cicer*, grown in Spain, has similar properties. The distressing effects described in the text have been witnessed by other observers (Balfour, *Cyclopaedia*, 3rd ed., 1885, s.v. 'Lathyrus').

12. One of the tent-pitchers one morning, after pitching our tent, asked the loan of a small extra one for the use of his wife, who was about to be confined. The basket-maker's wife of the village near which we were encamped was called; and the poor woman, before we had finished our breakfast, gave birth to a daughter. The charge is half a rupee, or one shilling for a boy, and a quarter, or sixpence, for a girl. The tent-pitcher gave her ninepence, which the poor midwife thought very handsome, The mother had come fourteen miles upon a loaded cart over rough roads the night before; and went the same distance with her child the night after, upon the same cart. The first midwife in Europe could not have done her duty better than this poor basket-maker's wife did hers. [W. H. S.]

13. The 'present case' was of a medical, not a surgical, nature.

14. The Hindoo practitioners are called 'baid' (Sanskrit 'vaidya', followers of the Veda, that is to say, the Ayur Veda). The Musalmān practitioners are generally called 'hakīm'. The Egyptian school (Misrānī, Misrī, or Suryānī, that is, Syrian) never practise bleeding, and are partial to the use of metallic oxides. The Yunānī physicians approve of bleeding, and prefer vegetable drugs. The older writers on India fancied that the Hindoo system of medicine was of enormous antiquity, and that the principles of Galenical medical science were ultimately derived from India. Modern investigation has proved that Hindoo medicine, like Hindoo astronomy, is largely of Greek origin. This conclusion has been expressed in an exaggerated form by some writers, but its general truth appears to be established. The Hindoo books treating of medicine are certainly older than Wilson supposed, for the Bower manuscript, written in the second half of the fourth century of our era, contains three Sanskrit medical treatises. The writers had, however, plenty of time to borrow from Galen, who lived in the second century. The Indian aversion to European medicine, as distinguished from surgery, still exists, though in a degree somewhat less than in the

author's time. Many municipal boards have insisted on employing 'baids' and 'hakīms' in addition to the practitioners trained in European methods. Well-to-do patients often delay resort to the English physician until they have exhausted all resources of the 'hakīm' and have been nearly killed by his drastic treatment. One medical innovation, the use of quinine as a febrifuge, has secured universal approbation. I never heard of an Indian who disbelieved in quinine. Chlorodyne also is fully appreciated, but most of the European medicines are regarded with little faith.

Since the author wrote, great progress has been made in providing hospital and dispensary accommodation. Each 'district', or unit of civil administration, has a fairly well equipped combined hospital and dispensary at head-quarters, and branch dispensaries exist in almost every district. An Inspector-General of Dispensaries supervises the medical administration of each province, and medical schools have been organized at Calcutta, Madras, Bombay, Lahore, and Agra. During Lord Dufferin's Viceroyalty and afterwards, energetic steps were taken to improve the system of medical relief for females. Pandit Madhusadan Gupta, on January 10, 1836, was the first Hindoo who ventured to dissect a human body and teach anatomy. India can now boast of a considerable number of Hindoo and Musalmān practitioners, trained in European methods, and skilful in their profession. Much has been done, infinitely more remains to be done. Details will be found in *I.G.* (1907), vol. iv, chap. 14, 'Medical Administration', The article 'Medicine' in Balfour, *Cyclopaedia*, 3rd ed., 1885, on which I have drawn for some of the facts above stated, gives a good summary of the earlier history of medicine in India, but greatly exaggerates the antiquity of the Hindoo books. On this question Weber's paper, 'Die Griechen in Indien' (Berlin, 1890, p. 28), and Dr. Hoernle's remarks on the Bower manuscript (in *J.A.S.B.*, vol. lx (1891), Part I, p. 145) may be consulted. Dr. Hoernle's annotated edition and translation of the Bower MS. were completed in 1912. Part of the work is reprinted with additions in the *Ind. Ant.* for 1913 and 1914.

CHAPTER 16

Suttee Tombs — Insalubrity of deserted Fortresses.

On the 3rd we came to Bahrol,[1] where I had encamped with Lord William Bentinck on the last day of December, 1832, when the quicksilver in the thermometer at sunrise, outside our tents, was down to twenty-six degrees of Fahrenheit's thermometer. The village stands upon a gentle swelling hill of decomposed basalt, and is surrounded by hills of the same formation. The Dasān river flows close under the village, and has two beautiful reaches, one above, the other below, separated by the dyke of basalt, over which lies the ford of the river.[2]

There are beautiful reaches of the kind in all the rivers in this part of India, and they are almost everywhere formed in the same manner. At Bahrol there is a very unusual number of tombs built over the ashes of women who have burnt themselves with the remains of their husbands. Upon each tomb stands erect a tablet of freestone, with the sun, the new moon, and a rose engraved upon it in bas-relief in one field;[3] and the man and woman, hand in hand, in the other. On one stone of this kind I saw a third field below these two, with the figure of a horse in bas-relief, and I asked one of the gentlemen farmers, who was riding with me, what it meant. He told me that he thought it indicated that the woman rode on horseback to bathe before she ascended the pile.[4] I asked him whether he thought the measure prohibiting the practice of burning good or bad.

'It is', said he, 'in some respects good, and in others bad. Widows cannot marry among us, and those who had no prospect of a comfortable provision among their husband's relations, or who dreaded the possibility of going astray, and thereby sinking into contempt and misery, were enabled in this way to relieve their minds, and follow their husbands, under the full assurance of being happily united to them in the next world.'

When I passed this place on horseback with Lord William Bentinck, he asked me what these tombs were, for he had never seen any of the kind before. When I told him what they were, he said not a word; but he must have felt a proud consciousness of the debt of gratitude which India owes to the statesman who had the courage to put a stop to this great evil, in spite of all the fearful obstacles which bigotry and prejudice opposed to the measure. The seven European functionaries in charge of the seven districts of the newly-acquired territories were requested, during the administration of Lord Amherst in 1826, to state whether the burning of widows could or should be prohibited; and I believe every one of them declared that it should not. And yet, when it was put a stop to only a few years after by Lord William, not a complaint or murmur was heard. The replies to the Governor-General's inquiries were, I believe, throughout India, for the most part, opposed to the measure.[5]

On the 4th we came to Dhamonī, ten miles. The only thing remarkable here is the magnificent fortress, which is built upon a small projection of the Vindhya range, looking down on each side into two enormously deep glens, through which the two branches of the Dasān river descend over the tableland into the plains of Bundēlkhand.[6] The rays of the sun seldom penetrate to the bottom of these glens, and things are, in consequence, grown there that could not be grown in parts more exposed.

Every inch of the level ground in the bed of the streams below seems to be cultivated with care. This fortress is said to have cost more than a million of money, and to have been only one of fifty-two great works, of which a former Rājā of Bundēlkhand, Bīrsingh Deo, laid the foundation in the same *happy hour* which had been pointed out to him by his astrologers. [7] The works form an acute triangle, with the base towards the tableland, and the two sides hanging perpendicularly over the glens, while the apex points to the course of the streams as they again unite, and pass out through a deep chasm into the plains of Bundēlkhand.

The fortress is now entirely deserted, and the town, which the garrison supported, is occupied by only a small police-guard, stationed here to see that robbers do not take up their abode among the ruins. There is no fear of this. All old deserted fortresses in India become filled by a dense stream of carbonic acid gas, which is found so inimical to animal life that those who attempt to occupy them become ill, and, sooner or later, almost all die of the consequences. This gas, being specifically much heavier than common air, descends into the bottom of such unoccupied fortresses, and remains stagnant like water in old reservoirs. The current of pure air continually passes over, without being able to carry off the mass of stagnant air below; and the only way to render such places habitable is to make large openings in the walls on all sides, from the top to the bottom, so that the foul air may be driven out by the current of pure atmospheric air, which will then be continually rushing in. When these fortresses are thickly peopled, the continual motion within tends, I think, to mix up this gas with the air above; while the numerous fires lighted within, by rarefying that below, tend to draw down a regular supply of the atmospheric air from above for the benefit of the inhabitants. When natives enter upon the occupation of an old fortress of this kind, that has remained long unoccupied, they always make a solemn religions ceremony of it; and, having fed the priests, the troops, and a crowd of followers, all rush in at once with beat of drums, and as much noise as they can make. By this rush, and the fires that follow, the bad air is, perhaps, driven off, and never suffered to collect again while the fortress remains fully occupied. Whatever may be the cause, the fact is certain that these fortresses become deadly places of abode for small detachments of troops, or small parties of any kind. They all get ill, and few recover from the diseases they contract in them.

From the year 1817, when we first took possession of the Sāgar and Nerbudda Territories, almost all the detachments of troops we required to keep at a distance from the headquarters of their regiments were posted in these old deserted fortifications. Our collections of revenue were deposited in them; and, in some cases, they were converted into jails for the accommodation of our prisoners. Of the soldiers so lodged, I do not believe that one in four ever came out well; and, of those who came out ill, I do not believe that one in four survived five years. They were all abandoned one after the other; but it is painful to think how many hundreds, I may say thousands, of our brave soldiers were sacrificed before this resolution was taken. I have known the whole of the survivors of strong detachments that went in, in robust health, three months before, brought away mere skeletons, and in a hopeless and dying state. All were sent to their homes on medical certificate, but they almost all died there, or in the course of their journey.

Notes:

1. December, 1835. The name of the village is spelled Behrole by the author.

2. The Dasān river rises in the Bhopāl State, flows through the Sāgar district of the Central Provinces, and along the southern boundary of the Lalitpur subdivision of the Jhānsī District, United Provinces of Agra and Oudh. It also forms the boundary between the Jhānsī and Hamīrpur Districts, and falls into the Betwa after a course of about 220 miles. The name is often, but erroneously, written Dhasān. It is the Sanskrit Dasārna.

3. This emblem is a lotus, not a rose flower. The latter is never used in Hindoo symbolism. The lotus is a solar emblem, and intimately associated with the worship of Vishnu.

4. It rather indicates that the husband was on horseback when killed. The sculptures on satī pillars often commemorate the mode of death of the

husband. Sometimes these pillars are inscribed. They usually face the east. An open hand is often carved in the upper compartment as well as the sun and moon. A drawing of such a pillar will be found in *J.A.S.B.*, vol. xlvi. Part I, 1877, pl. xiv. *A.S.R.*, vol. iii, p. 10; vol. vii, p. 137; vol. x, p. 75; and vol. xxi, p. 101, may be consulted.

5. The 'newly-acquired territories' referred to are the Sāgar and Nerbudda Territories, comprising the seven districts, Sāgar, Jubbulpore, Hoshangābād, Seonī, Damoh, Narsinghpur, and Baitūl, ceded in 1818, and now included in the Central Provinces. The tenor of the replies given to Lord Amherst's queries shows how far the process of Hindooizing had advanced among the European officials of the Company. Lord Amherst left India in March, 1828. See *ante*. Chapter 4 and Chapter 8, for cases of satī (suttees). For a good account of the suttee discussions and legislation, see D. Boulger, *Lord William Bentinck* (1897), chap. v, in 'Rulers of India' Series. No other biography of Lord William Bentinck exists.

6. Dhamonī is in the Sāgar district of the Central Provinces, about twenty-nine miles north of Sāgar. The fort was taken by General Marshall in 1818. It had been rebuilt by Rājā Bīrsingh Deo of Orchhā on an enormous scale about the end of the sixteenth century. In the original edition, the author's march is said to have taken place 'on the 24th'. This must be a mistake for 'on the 4th'; as the last date, that of the march to Bahrol, was the 3rd December. The author reached Agra on January 1, 1836,

7. The number fifty-two is one of the Hindoo favourite numbers, like seven, twelve, and eighty-four, held sacred for astronomical or astrological reasons. Bīrsingh Deo was the younger brother of Rāmchand, head of the Bundēla clan. To oblige Prince Salīm, afterwards the Emperor Jahāngīr, he murdered Abūl Fazl, the celebrated minister and historian of Akbar, on August 12, 1602, Jahāngīr, after his accession, rewarded the murderer by allowing him to supersede his brother in the headship of his clan, and by appointing him to the rank of 'commander of three thousand'. The capital of Bīrsingh was Orchhā. His successors are often spoken of as Rājās of Tehrī. The murder is fully described in *The Emperor Akbar* by Count von Noer, translated by A. S. Beveridge, Calcutta, 1890, vol. ii, pp. 384-404. Orchhā is described *post*, Chapters 22,23.

CHAPTER 17

Basaltic Cappings — Interview with a Native Chief — A Singular Character.

On the 5th[1] we came to the village of Seorī. Soon after leaving Dhamonī, we descended the northern face of the Vindhya range into the plains of Bundēlkhand. The face of this range overlooking the valley of the Nerbudda to the south is, as I have before stated, a series of mural precipices, like so many rounded bastions, the slight dip of the strata being to the north. The northern face towards Bundēlkhand, on the contrary, here descends gradually, as the strata dip slightly towards the north, and we pass down gently over their back. The strata have, however, been a good deal broken, and the road was so rugged that two of our carts broke down in descending. From the descent over the northern face of the tableland into Bundēlkhand to the descent over the southern face into the valley of the Nerbudda must be a distance of one hundred miles directly north and south.

The descent over the northern face is not everywhere so gradual; on the contrary, there are but few places where it is at all feasible; and some of the rivers of the tableland between Jubbulpore and Mirzapore have a perpendicular fall of more than four hundred feet over these mural precipices of the northern face of the Vindhya range.[2] A man, if he have good nerve, may hang over the summits, and suspend in his hand a plummet that shall reach the bottom.

I should mention that this tableland is not only intersected by ranges, but everywhere studded with isolated hills rising suddenly out of basins or valleys. These ranges and isolated hills are all of the same sandstone formation, and capped with basalt, more or less amygdaloidal. The valleys and cappings have often a substratum of very compact basalt, which must evidently have flowed into them after these islands were formed. The question is, how were these valleys and basins scooped out? 'Time, time, time!' says Mr. Scrope; 'grant me only time, and I can account for everything.' I think, however, that I am right in considering the basaltic cappings of these ranges and isolated hills to have once formed part of continued flat beds of great lakes. The flat parallel planes of these cappings, corresponding with each other, however distantly separated the hills they cover may be, would seem to indicate that they could not all have been subject to the convulsions of nature by which the whole substrata were upheaved above the ocean. I am disposed to think that such islands and ranges of the sandstone were formed before the deposit of the basalt, and that the form of the surface is now returning to what it then was, by the gradual decomposition and wearing away of the latter rock. Much, however, may be said on both sides of this, as of every other question. After descending from the sandstone of the Vindhya[3] range into Bundēlkhand, we pass over basalt and basaltic soil, reposing immediately on syenitic granite, with here and there beds and veins of pure feldspar, hornblende, and quartz.

Takht Singh, the younger brother of Arjun Singh, the Rājā of Shāhgarh,[4] came out several miles to meet me on his elephant. Finding me on horseback, he got off from his elephant, and mounted his horse, and we rode on till we met the Rājā himself, about a mile from our tents. He was on horseback, with a large and splendidly dressed train of followers, all mounted on fine sleek horses, bred in the Rājā's own stables. He was mounted on a snow-white steed of his own breeding (and I have rarely seen a finer animal), and dressed in a light suit of silver brocade made to represent the scales of steel armour, surmounted by a gold turban. Takht Singh was more plainly dressed, but is a much finer and more intelligent-looking man. Having escorted us to our tents, they took their leave, and returned to their own, which were pitched on a rising ground on the other side of a small stream, half a mile distant. Takht Singh resides here in a very pretty fortified castle on an eminence. It is a square building, with a round bastion at each corner, and one on each face, rising into towers above the walls.

A little after midday the Rājā and his brother came to pay us a visit; and about four o'clock I went to return it, accompanied by Lieutenant Thomas. As usual, he had a nautch (dance) upon carpets, spread upon the sward under awnings in front of the pavilion in which we were received. While the women were dancing and singing, a very fine panther was brought in to be shown to us. He had been caught, full-grown, two years before, and, in the hands of a skilful man, was fit for the chase in six months. It was a very beautiful animal, but, for the sake of the sport, kept wretchedly thin. [5] He seemed especially indifferent to the crowd and the music, but could not bear to see the woman whirling about in the dance with her red mantle floating in the breeze; and, whenever his head was turned towards her, he cropped his ears. She at last, in play, swept close by him, and with open mouth he attempted to spring upon her, but was pulled back by the keeper. She gave a shriek, and nearly fell upon her back in fright.

The Rājā is a man of no parts or character, and, his expenditure being beyond his income, he is killing his goose for the sake of her eggs—that is, he is ruining all the farmers and cultivators of his large estate by exactions, and thereby throwing immense tracts of fine land out of tillage. He was the heir to the fortress and territory of Garhā Kotā, near Sāgar, which was taken by Sindhia's army, under the command of Jean Baptiste Filose,[6] just before our conquest in 1817. I was then with my regiment, which was commanded by Colonel, afterwards Major- General, G— — —,[7] a very singular character. When our surgeon. Dr. E— — —, received the newspaper announcing the capture of Garhā Kotā in Central India by *Jean-Baptiste*, an officer of the corps was with him, who called on the colonel on his way home, and mentioned this as a bit of news. As soon as this officer had left him, the colonel wrote off a note to the doctor: 'My dear Doctor,—I understand that that fellow, *John the Baptist*, has got into Sindhia's service, and now commands an army—do send me the newspapers.' These were certainly the words of his note, and, at the only time I heard him speak on the subject of religion he discomfited his adversary in an argument at the mess by 'Why, sir, you do not suppose that I believe in those fellows, Luther, Calvin, and John the Baptist, do you?'

Nothing could stand this argument. All the party burst into a laugh, which the old gentleman took for an unequivocal recognition of his victory, and his adversary was silenced. He was an old man when I first became acquainted with him. I put into his hands, when in camp, Miss Edgeworth's novels, in the hope of being able to induce him to read by degrees; and I have frequently seen the tears stealing down over his furrowed cheeks, as he sat pondering over her pages in the corner of his tent. A braver soldier never lived than old G— — —; and he distinguished himself greatly in the command of his regiment, under Lord Lake, at the battle of Laswāri[8] and siege of Bharatpur.[9] It was impossible ever to persuade him that the characters and incidents of these novels were the mere creations of fancy— he felt them to be true—he wished them to be true, and he would have them to be true. We were not very anxious to undeceive him, as the illusion gave him pleasure and did him good. Bolingbroke says, after an ancient author, 'History is philosophy teaching by example.'[10] With equal truth may we say that fiction, like that of Maria Edgeworth, is philosophy teaching by emotion. It certainly taught old G— — — to be a better man, to leave much of the little evil he had been in the habit of doing, and to do much of the good he had been accustomed to leave undone.

Notes:

1. December 5, 1835, The date is misprinted '3rd' in the original edition. See note 2 to last preceding chapter, p. 110.

2. A good view of the precipices of the Kaimūr range, the eastern continuation of the Vindhyan chain, is given facing of vol. i of Hooker's *Himalayan Journals* (ed. 1855).

3. The author's theory is untenable. He failed, to realize the vast effects of sub-aerial denudation. All the evidence shows that the successive lava outflows which make up the Deccan trap series ultimately converted the surface of the land over which they welled out into an enormous, nearly uniform, plain of basalt, resting on the Vindhyan sandstone and other rocks. This great sheet of lava, extending, east and west, from Nāgpur to Bombay, a distance of about five hundred miles, was then, in succeeding millenniums, subjected to the denuding forces of air and water, until gradually huge tracts of it were worn away, forming beds of conglomerate, gravel, and clay. The flat-topped hills have been carved out of the basaltic surface by the agencies which wore away the massive sheet of lava. The basaltic cappings of the hills certainly cannot have 'formed part of continued flat beds of great lakes'. See the notes to Chapter 14, *ante*. Mr. Scrope was quite right. Vast periods of time must be allowed for geological history, and millions of years must have elapsed since the flow of the Deccan lava.

4. In the Sāgar district. The last Raja joined the rebels in 1857, and so forfeited his rank and territory.

5. The name panther is usually applied only to the large, fulvous variety of *Felis pardus (Linn.) (F. leopardus, Leopardus varius)*. The animal described in the text evidently was a specimen of the hunting leopard, *Felis jubata (F. guttata, F. venatica)*.

6. This officer was one of the many *'condottieri'* of various nationality who served the native powers during the eighteenth century, and the early years of the nineteenth. He commanded five infantry regiments at Gwālior. His 'kingdom- taking' raid in 1815 or 1816 is described *post* in Chapter 49. The history of the family is given by Compton in *European Military Adventures of Hindustan from 1784 to 1803* (Unwin, 1892), App. pp, 352-6. In 1911 Michael Filose of Gwālior was appointed K.C.I.E.

7.'G— — —' appears to have been Robert Gregory C.B.

8. The fiercely contested battle of Laswāri was fought on November 1, 1803, between the British force under Lord Lake and the flower of Sindhia's

army, known as the 'Deccan Invincibles'. Sindhia's troops lost about seven thousand killed and two thousand prisoners. The British loss in killed and wounded amounted to more than eight hundred. A medal to commemorate the victory was struck in London in 1851, and presented to the survivors. Laswāri is a village in the Alwar State, 128 miles south of Delhi.

9. Bharatpur (Bhurtpore), in the Jāt State of the same name, is thirty-four miles west of Agra. In January and February, 1805, Lord Lake four times attempted to take it by assault, and each time was repulsed with heavy loss. On January 18, 1826, Lord Combermere stormed the fortress. The fortifications were then dismantled. A large portion of the walls is now standing, and presents an imposing appearance. They seem to have been repaired. See *post*, Chapter 62.

10. 'I will answer you by quoting what I have read somewhere or other — in *Dionysius Halicarn.*, I think — that history is philosophy teaching by example' (Bolingbroke, *Letters on the Study and Use of History*, Letter II, p. 14 of vol. viii of edition printed by T. Cadell, London, 1770). The Greek words are ἱστορία φιλοσοφία ἐστὶν ἐκ παραδειγμάτ ων.

CHAPTER 18

Birds' Nests—Sports of Boyhood.

On the 6th[1] we came to Sayyidpur, ten miles, over an undulating country, with a fine soil of decomposed basalt, reposing upon syenite, with veins of feldspar and quartz. Cultivation partial, and very bad; and population extremely scanty. We passed close to a village, in which the children were all at play; while upon the bushes over their heads were suspended an immense number of the beautiful nests of the sagacious 'bayā' bird, or Indian yellow- hammer,[2] all within reach of a grown-up boy, and one so near the road that a grown-up man might actually look into it as he passed along, and could hardly help shaking it. It cannot fail to strike a European as singular to see so many birds' nests, situated close to a village, remain unmolested within reach of so many boisterous children, with their little proprietors and families fluttering and chirping among them with as great a feeling of security and gaiety of heart as the children themselves enjoy.

In any part of Europe not a nest of such a colony could have lived an hour within reach of such a population; for the bayā bird has no peculiar respect paid to it by the people here, like the wren and robin-redbreast in England. No boy in India has the slightest wish to molest birds in their nests; it enters not into their pastimes, and they have no feeling of pride or pleasure in it. With us it is different—to discover birds' nests is one of the first modes in which a boy exercises his powers, and displays his love of art. Upon his skill in finding them he is willing to rest his first claim to superior sagacity and enterprise. His trophies are his string of eggs; and the eggs most prized among them are those of the nests that are discovered with most difficulty, and attained with most danger. The same feeling of desire to display their skill and enterprise in search after birds' nests in early life renders the youth of England the enemy almost of the whole animal creation throughout their after career. The boy prides himself on his dexterity in throwing a stone or a stick; and he practises on almost every animal that comes in his way, till he never sees one without the desire to knock it down, or at least to hit it; and, if it is lawful to do so, he feels it to be a most serious misfortune not to have a stone within his reach at the time. As he grows up, he prides himself upon his dexterity in shooting, and he never sees a member of the feathered tribe within shot, without a desire to shoot it, or without regretting that he has not a gun in his hand to shoot it. That he is not entirely destitute of sympathy, however, with the animals he maims for his amusement is sufficiently manifest from his anxiety to put them out of pain the moment he gets them.

A friend of mine, now no more, Captain Medwin, was once looking with me at a beautiful landscape painting through a glass. At last he put aside the glass, saying: 'You may say what you like, S—, but the best landscape I know is a fine black partridge[3] falling before my Joe Manton.'

The following lines of Walter Scott, in his *Rokeby*, have always struck me as very beautiful:-

> As yet the conscious pride of art
> Had steel'd him in his treacherous part;
> A powerful spring of force unguessed
> That hath each gentler mood suppressed,
> And reigned in many a human breast;
> From his that plans the rude campaign,
> To his that wastes the woodland reign, &c.[4]

Among the people of India it is very different. Children do not learn to exercise their powers either in discovering and robbing the nests of birds, or in knocking them down with stones and staves; and, as they grow up, they hardly ever think of hunting or shooting for mere amusement. It is with them a matter of business; the animal they cannot eat they seldom think of molesting.

Some officers were one day pursuing a jackal, with a pack of dogs, through my grounds. The animal passed close to one of my guard, who cut him in two with his sword, and held up the reeking blade in triumph to the indignant cavalcade; who, when they came up, were ready to eat him alive. 'What have I done', said the poor man, 'to offend you?' 'Have you not killed the jackal?' shouted the whipper- in, in a fury.

'Of course I have; but were you not all trying to kill him?' replied the poor man. He thought their only object had been to kill the jackal, as they would have killed a serpent, merely because he was a mischievous and noisy beast.

The European traveller in India is often in doubt whether the peacocks, partridges, and ducks, which he finds round populous villages, are tame or wild, till he asks some of the villagers themselves, so assured of safety do these creatures become, and so willing to take advantage of it for the food they find in the suburbs. They very soon find the difference, however, between the white-faced visitor and the dark-faced inhabitants. There is a fine date-tree overhanging a kind of school at the end of one of the streets in the town of Jubbulpore, quite covered with the nests of the bayā birds; and they are seen, every day and all day, fluttering and chirping about there in scores, while the noisy children at their play fill the street below, almost within arm's length of them. I have often thought that such a tree so peopled at the door of a school in England might work a great revolution in the early habits and propensities of the youth educated in it. The European traveller is often amused to see the pariah dog[5] squatted close in front of the traveller during the whole time he is occupied in cooking and eating his dinner, under a tree by the roadside, assured that he shall have at least a part of the last cake thrown to him by the stranger, instead of a stick or a stone. The stranger regards him with complacency, as one that reposes a quiet confidence in his charitable disposition, and flings towards him the whole or part of his last cake, as if his meal had put him in the best possible humour with him and all the world.

Notes:

1. December, 1835. The name of the village is given in the author's text as Seindpore. It seems to be the place which is called Siedpore in the next chapter.

2. The common weaver bird, *Phoceus baya, Blyth*. '*Ploceinae*, the weaver birds. . . . They build nests like a crucible, with the opening downwards, and usually attach them to the tender branches of a tree hanging over a well or tank. *P. baya* is found throughout India; its nest is made of grasses and strips of the plantain or date-palm stripped while green. It is easily tamed and taught some tricks, such as to load and fire a toy cannon, to pick up a ring, &c,' (Balfour, *Cyclopaedia*, 3rd ed., 1885, s.v. 'Ploceinae').

3. *Francolinus vulgaris*; a capital game bird.

4. Canto V, stanza 22, line 3.

5. The author spells the word Pareear. The editor has used the form now customary. The word is the Tamil appellation of a large body of the population of Southern India, which stands outside the orthodox Hindoo castes, but has a caste organization of its own. Europeans apply the term to the low-caste mongrel dogs which infest villages and towns throughout India. See Yule and Burnell, *Glossary of Anglo-Indian Words (Hobson-Jobson)*, in either edition, s.v.; and Dubois, *Hindu Manners, &c.*, 3rd ed. (1906, index, s.v.).

CHAPTER 19

Feeding Pilgrims—Marriage of a Stone with a Shrub.

At Sayyidpur[1] we encamped in a pretty little mango grove, and here I had a visit from my old friend Jānkī Sewak, the high priest of the great temple that projects into the Sāgar lake, and is called Bindrāban.[2] He has two villages rent free, worth a thousand rupees a year; collects something more through his numerous disciples, who wander over the country; and spends the whole in feeding all the members of his fraternity (Bairāgīs), devotees of Vishnu, as they pass his temple in their pilgrimages. Every one who comes is considered entitled to a good meal and a night's lodging; and he has to feed and lodge about a hundred a day. He is a man of very pleasing manners and gentle disposition, and everybody likes him. He was on his return from the town of Ludhaura,[3] where he had been, at the invitation of the Rājā of Orchhā, to assist at the celebration of the marriage of Sālagrām with the Tulasī,[4] which there takes place every year under the auspices and at the expense of the Rājā, who must be present. 'Sālagrāms'[5] are rounded pebbles which contain the impressions of ammonites, and are washed down into the plains of India by the rivers from the limestone rocks in which these shells are imbedded in the mountains of the Himalaya.[6] The Spiti valley[7] contains an immense deposit of fossil ammonites and belemnites[8] in limestone rocks, now elevated above sixteen thousand feet above the level of the sea; and from such beds as these are brought down the fragments, which, when rounded in their course, the poor Hindoo takes for representatives of Vishnu, the preserving god of the Hindoo triad. The Sālagrām is the only stone idol among the Hindoos that is *essentially sacred*, and entitled to divine honours without the ceremonies of consecration.[9] It is everywhere held most sacred. During the war against Nepāl,[10] Captain B— — —, who commanded a reconnoitring party from the division in which I served, one day brought back to camp some four or five Sālagrāms, which he had found at the hut of some priest within the enemy's frontier. He called for a large stone and hammer, and proceeded to examine them. The Hindoos were all in a dreadful state of consternation, and expected to see the earth open and swallow up the whole camp, while he sat calmly cracking *their gods* with his hammer, as he would have cracked so many walnuts. The

Tulasī is a small sacred shrub (*Ocymum sanctum*), which is a metamorphosis of Sītā, the wife of Rāma, the seventh incarnation of Vishnu.

This little *pebble* is every year married to this little *shrub*; and the high priest told me that on the present occasion the procession consisted of eight elephants, twelve hundred camels, four thousand horses, all mounted and elegantly caparisoned. On the leading elephant of this *cortège*, and the most sumptuously decorated, was carried the *pebble god*, who was taken to pay his bridal visit (barāt) to the little *shrub goddess*. All the ceremonies of a regular marriage are gone through; and, when completed, the bride and bridegroom are left to repose together in the temple of Ludhaura[11] till the next season. 'Above a hundred thousand people', the priest said, 'were present at the ceremony this year at the Rājā's invitation, and feasted upon his bounty.'[12]

The old man and I got into a conversation upon the characters of different governments, and their effects upon the people; and he said that bad governments would sooner or later be always put down by the deity; and quoted this verse, which I took down with my pencil:

> Tulasī, gharīb na sātāe,
> Burī gharīb kī hai;
> Marī khāl ke phūnk se
> Lohā bhasm ho jāe.

'Oh, Rājā Tulasī! oppress not the poor; for the groans of the wretched bring retribution from heaven. The contemptible skin (in the smith's bellows) in time melts away the hardest iron.'[13]

On leaving our tents in the morning, we found the ground all round white with hoar frost, as we had found it for several mornings before;[14] and a little canary bird, one of the two which travelled in my wife's palankeen, having, by the carelessness of the servants been put upon the top without any covering to the cage, was killed by the cold, to her great affliction. All attempts to restore it to life by the warmth of her bosom were fruitless.

On the 7th[15] we came nine miles to Bamhaurī over a soil still basaltic, though less rich, reposing upon syenite, which frequently rises and protrudes its head above the surface, which is partially and badly cultivated, and scantily peopled. The silent signs of bad government could not be more manifest. All the extensive plains, covered with fine long grass, which is rotting in the ground from want of domestic cattle or distant markets. Here, as in every other part of Central India, the people have a great variety of good spontaneous, but few cultivated, grasses. They understand the character and qualities of these grasses extremely well. They find some thrive best in dry, and some in wet seasons; and that of inferior quality is often prized most because it thrives best when other kinds cannot thrive at all, from an excess or a deficiency of rain. When cut green they all make good hay, and have the common denomination of 'sahīa'. The finest of these grasses are two which are generally found growing spontaneously together, and are often cultivated together-'kēl' and 'musēl'; the third 'parwana'; fourth 'bhawār', or 'gūniār'; fifth 'sainā'.[16]

Notes:

1. Spelled Siedpore in the author's text.

2. More correctly Brindāban (Vrindāvana). The name originally belongs to one of the most sacred spots in India, situated near Mathurā (Muttra) on the Jumna, and the reputed scene of the dalliance between Krishna and the milkmaids (Gopīs); also associated with the legend Rāma.

3. Twenty-seven miles north-west of Tehrī in the Orchhā State.

4. The Tulasī plant, or basil, *Ocymum sanctum*, is 'not merely sacred to Vishnu or to his wife Lakshmi; it is pervaded by the essence of these deities, and itself worshipped as a deity and prayed to accordingly. . . . The Tulasī is the object of more adoration than any other plant at present worshipped in India. . . .It is to be found in almost every respectable household throughout India. It is a small shrub, not too big to be cultivated in a good-sized flower-pot, and often placed in rooms. Generally, however, it is planted in the courtyard of a well-to-do man's house, with a space round it for reverential circumambulation. In real fact the Tulasī is *par excellence* a domestic divinity, or rather, perhaps, a woman's divinity' (M. Williams, *Religious Thought and Life in India*, p. 333).

5. The fossil ammonites found in India include at least fifteen species. They occur between Trichinopoly and Pondicherry as well as in the Himalayan rocks. They are particularly abundant in the river Gandak, which rises near Dhaulagiri in Nepāl, and falls into the Ganges near Patna. The upper course of this river is consequently called Sālagrāmī. Various forms of the fossils are supposed to represent various *avatārs* of Vishnu (Balfour, *Cyclopaedia*, 3rd ed., s.v. 'Ammonite', 'Gandak', 'Salagrama'; M. Williams, *Religious Thought and Life in India*, pp. 69, 349). A good account of the reverence paid to both *sālagrāms* and the *tulasī* plant will be found in Dubois, *Hindu Manners*, &c., 3rd ed. (1906), pp. 648-51.

6. The author writes 'Himmalah'. The current spelling Himalaya is correct, but the word should be pronounced Himālaya. It means 'abode of snow'.

7. The north-eastern corner of the Punjāb, an elevated valley along the course of the Spiti or the Li river, a tributary of the Satlaj.

8. Fossils of the genus Belemnites and related genera are common, like the ammonites, near Trichinopoly, as well as in the Himalaya.

9. This statement is not quite correct. The pebbles representing the Linga of Siva, called Bāna-linga, or Vāna-linga, and apparently of white quartz, which are found in the Nerbudda river, enjoy the same distinction. 'Both are held to be of their own nature pervaded by the special presence of the deity, and need no consecration. Offerings made to these pebbles — such, for instance, as Bilwa leaves laid on the white stone of Vishnu — are believed to confer extraordinary merit' (M. Williams, *Religious Thought and Life in India*, p. 69).

10. In 1814-16.

11. 'Sadora' in author's text, which seems to be a misprint for Ludora or Ludhaura.

12. The Tulasī shrub is sometimes married to an image of Krishna, instead of to the sālagrāma, in Western India (M. Williams, *Religious Thought and Life in India*, p. 334). Compare the account of the marriage between the mango-tree and the jasmine, *ante*, Chapter 5, Note [3].

13. These Hindī verses are incorrectly printed, and loosely rendered by the author. The translation of the text, after necessary emendation, is: 'Tulasī, oppress not the poor; evil is the lot of the poor. From the blast of the dead hide iron becomes ashes.' Mr. W. Crooke informs me that the verses are found in the Kabīrkī Sakhī, and are attributable to Kabīr Dās, rather than to Tulasī Dās. But the authorship of such verses is very uncertain. Mr. Crooke further observes that the lines as given in the text do not scan, and that the better version is:

> Durbal ko na satāiye,
> Jāki māti hai;
> Mūē khāl ke sāns se
> Sār bhasm ho jāe.

Sār means iron. The author was, of course, mistaken in supposing the poet Tulasī Dās to be a Rājā. As usual in Hindī verse, the poet addresses himself by name.

14. Such slight frosts are common in Bundēlkhand, especially near the rivers, in January, but only last for a few mornings. They often cause great damage to the more delicate crops. The weather becomes hot in February.

15. December, 1835.

16. 'Musēl' is a very sweet-scented grass, highly esteemed as fodder. It belongs to the genus *Anthistiria*; the species is either *cimicina* or *prostrata*. 'Bhawār' is probably the 'bhaunr' of Edgeworth's list, *Anthistiria scandens*. I cannot identify the other grasses named in the text. The haycocks in Bundēlkhand are a pleasant sight to English eyes. Edgeworth's list of plants found in the Bāndā district, as revised by Messrs. Waterfield and Atkinson, is given in *N.W.P. Gazetteer*, 1st ed., vol. i, pp. 78-86.

CHAPTER 20

The Men-Tigers.

Rām Chand Rāo, commonly called the Sarīmant, chief of Deorī,[1] here overtook me. He came out from Sāgar to visit me at Dhamonī[2] and, not reaching that place in time, came on after me. He held Deorī under the Peshwā, as the Sāgar chief held Sāgar, for the payment of the public establishments kept up by the local administration. It yielded him about ten thousand a year, and, when we took possession of the country, he got an estate in the Sāgar district, in rent-free tenure, estimated at fifteen hundred a year. This is equal to about six thousand pounds a year in England. The tastes of native gentlemen lead them always to expend the greater part of their incomes in the wages of trains of followers of all descriptions, and in horses, elephants, &c.; and labour and the subsistence of labour are about four times cheaper in India than in England. By the breaking up of public establishments, and consequent diminution of the local demand for agricultural produce, the value of land throughout all Central India, after the termination of the Mahrātha War in 1817, fell by degrees thirty per cent.; and, among the rest, that of my poor friend the Sarīmant. While I had the civil charge of the Sāgar district in 1831 I represented this case of hardship; and Government, in the spirit of liberality which has generally characterized their measures in this part of India, made up to him the difference between what he actually received and what they had intended to give him; and he has ever since felt grateful to me.[3] He is a very small man, not more than five feet high, but he has the handsomest face I have almost ever seen, and his manners are those of the most perfect native gentleman. He came to call upon me after breakfast, and the conversation turned upon the number of people that had of late been killed by tigers between Sāgar and Deorī, his ancient capital, which lies about midway between Sāgar and the Nerbudda river.

One of his followers, who stood beside his chair, said[4] that 'when a tiger had killed one man he was safe, for the spirit of the man rode upon his head, and guided him from all danger. The spirit knew very well that the tiger would be watched for many days at the place where he had committed the homicide, and always guided him off to some other more secure place, when he killed other men without any risk to himself. He did not exactly know why the spirit of the man should thus befriend the beast that had killed him; but', added he, 'there is a mischief inherent in spirits; and the better the man the more mischievous is his ghost, if means are not taken to put him to rest.' This is the popular and general belief throughout India; and it is supposed that the only sure mode of destroying a tiger who has killed many people is to begin by making offerings to the spirits of his victims, and thereby depriving him of their valuable services.[5] The belief that men are turned into tigers by eating of a root is no less general throughout India.

The Sarīmant, on being asked by me what he thought of the matter, observed 'there was no doubt much truth in what the man said: but he was himself of opinion that the tigers which now infest the wood from Sāgar to Deorī were of a different kind—in fact, that they were neither more nor less than men turned into tigers—a thing which took place in the woods of Central India much more often than people were aware of. The only visible difference between the two', added the Sarīmant, 'is that the metamorphosed tiger has *no tail*, while the *bora*, or ordinary tiger, has a very long one. In the jungle about Deorī', continued he, 'there is a root, which, if a man eat of, he is converted into a tiger on the spot; and if, in this state, he can eat of another, he becomes a man again—a melancholy instance of the former of which', said he, 'occurred, I am told, in my own father's family when I was an infant. His washerman, Raghu, was, like all washermen, a great drunkard; and, being seized with a violent desire to ascertain what a man felt in the state of a tiger, he went one day to the jungle and brought home two of these roots, and desired his wife to stand by with one of them, and the instant she saw him assume the tiger shape, to thrust it into his mouth. She consented, the washerman ate his root, and became instantly a tiger; but his wife was so terrified at the sight of her husband in this shape that she ran off with the antidote in her hand. Poor old Raghu took to the woods, and there ate a good many of his old friends from neighbouring villages; but he was at last shot, and recognized from the circumstance of his *having no tail*. You may be quite sure,' concluded Sarīmant, 'when you hear of a tiger without a tail, that it is some unfortunate man who has eaten of that root, and of all the tigers he will be found the most mischievous.'

How my friend had satisfied himself of the truth of this story I know not, but he religiously believes it, and so do all his attendants and mine; and, out of a population of thirty thousand people in the town of Sāgar, not one would doubt the story of the washerman if he heard it.

I was one day talking with my friend the Rājā of Maihar.[6] on the road between Jubbulpore and Mirzapore, on the subject of the number of men who had been lately killed by tigers at the Katrā Pass on that road,[7] and the best means of removing the danger. 'Nothing', said the Rājā, 'could be more easy or more cheap than the destruction of these tigers, if they were of the ordinary sort; but the tigers that kill men by wholesale, as these do, are, you may be sure, men themselves converted into tigers by the force of their science, and such animals are of all the most unmanageable.'

'And how is it. Rājā Sāhib, that these men convert themselves into tigers?'

'Nothing', said he, 'is more easy than this to persons who have once acquired the science; but how they learn it, or what it is, we unlettered men know not.'

'There was once a high priest of a large temple, in this very valley of Maihar, who was in the habit of getting himself converted into a tiger by the force of this science, which he had thoroughly acquired. He had a necklace, which one of his disciples used to throw over his neck the moment the tiger's form became fully developed. He had, however, long given up the practice, and all his old disciples had gone off on their pilgrimages to distant shrines, when he was one day seized with a violent desire to take his old form of the tiger. He expressed the wish to one of his new disciples, and demanded whether he thought he might rely on his courage to stand by and put on the necklace. 'Assuredly you may', said the disciple; 'such is my faith in you, and in the God we serve, that I fear nothing.' The high priest upon this put the necklace into his hand with the requisite instructions, and forthwith began to change his form. The disciple stood trembling in every limb, till he heard him give a roar that shook the whole edifice, when he fell flat upon his face, and dropped the necklace on the floor. The tiger bounded over him, and out of the door, and infested all the roads leading to the temple for many years afterwards.'

'Do you think, Rājā Sahib, that the old high priest is one of the tigers at the Katrā Pass?'

'No, I do not; but I think they may be all men who have become imbued with a little too much of the high priest's *science*—when men once acquire this science they can't help exercising it, though it be to their own ruin, and that of others.'

'But, supposing them to be ordinary tigers, what is the simple plan you propose to put a stop to their depredations, Rājā Sahib?'

'I propose', said he, 'to have the spirits that guide them propitiated by proper prayers and offerings; for the spirit of every man or woman who has been killed by a tiger rides upon his head, or runs before him, and tells him where to go to get prey, and to avoid danger. Get some of the Gonds, or wild people from the jungles, who are well skilled in these matters—give them ten or twenty rupees, and bid them go and raise a small shrine, and there sacrifice to these spirits. The Gonds will tell them that they shall on this shrine have regular worship, and good sacrifices of fowls, goats, and pigs, every year at least, if they will but relinquish their offices with the tigers and be quiet. If this is done, I pledge myself', said the Raja, 'that the tigers will soon get killed themselves, or cease from killing men. If they do not, you may be quite sure that they are not ordinary tigers, but men turned into tigers, or that the Gonds have appropriated all you gave them to their own use, instead of applying it to conciliate the spirits of the unfortunate people.'[8]

Notes:

1. Deorī, in the Sāgar district, about forty miles south-east of Sāgar. In 1767, the town and attached tract called the Panj Mahāl were bestowed by the Peshwā, rent- free, on Dhōndo Dattātraya, a Marāthā pundit, ancestor of the author's friend. The Panj Mahal was finally made part of British territory by the treaty with Sindhia in 1860, and constitutes the District called Pānch Māhals in the Northern Division of the Bombay Presidency. The vernacular word pānch like the Persian panj, means 'five'. The title Sarīmant appears to be a popular pronunciation of the Sanskrit srīmant or srīmān, 'fortunate', and is still used by Marāthā nobles.

2. Ante, Chapter 16, note 6. The name is here erroneously printed 'Dhamoree' in the author's text.

3. He had good reason for his gratitude, inasmuch as the depression in rents was merely temporary.

4. An Indian chief is generally accompanied into the room by a confidential follower, who frequently relieves his master of the trouble of talking, and answers on his behalf all questions.

5. When Agrippina, in her rage with her son Nero, threatens to take her stepson, Britannicus, to the camp of the Legion, and there assert his right to the throne, she invokes the spirit of his father, whom she had poisoned, and the manes of the Silani, whom she had murdered. 'Simul attendere manus, aggerere probra; consecratum Claudium, infernos Silanorum manes invocare, et tot invita fari nova.'-(Tacitus, lib, xviii, sec. 14.) [W. H. S.] The quotation is from the Annals. Another reading of the concluding words is 'et tot irrita facinora', which gives much better sense. In the author's text 'aggerere' is printed 'aggere'.

6. A small principality, detached from the Pannā State. Its chief town is about one hundred miles north-east of Jubbulpore, on the route from Allahabad to Jubbulpore. The state is now traversed by the East

Indian Railway. It is under the superintendence of the Political Agent of Baghēlkhand, resident at Rīwā.

7. This pass is sixty-three miles south-east of Allahabad, on the road from that city to Rīwā.

8. These myths are based on the well-known facts that man-eating tigers are few, and exceptionally wary and cunning. The conditions which predispose a tiger to man-eating have been much discussed. It seems to be established that the animals which seek human prey are generally, though not invariably, those which, owing to old wounds or other physical defects, are unable to attack with confidence the stronger animals. The conversations given in the text are excellent illustrations of the mode of formation of modern myths, and of the kind of reasoning which satisfies the mind of the unconscious myth- maker.

The text may be compared with the following passage from the *Journey through the Kingdom of Oudh* (vol. i, p. 124): 'I asked him (the Rājā of Balrāmpur), whether the people in the Tarāi forest were still afraid to point out tigers to sportsmen. "I was lately out with a party after a tiger", he said, "which had killed a cowherd, but his companions refused to point out any trace of him, saying that their relative's spirit must be now riding upon his head, to guide him from all danger, and we should have no chance of shooting him. We did shoot him, however", said the Rājā exultingly, "and they were all afterwards very glad of it. The tigers in the Tarāi do not often kill men, sir, for they find plenty of deer and cattle to eat,"'

CHAPTER 21

Burning of Deorī by a Freebooter—A Suttee.

Sarīmant had been one of the few who escaped from the flames which consumed his capital of Deorī in the month of April 1813, and were supposed to have destroyed thirty thousand souls. I asked him to tell me how this happened, and he referred me to his attendant, a learned old pundit, Rām Chand, who stood by his side, as he was himself, he said, then only five years of age, and could recollect nothing of it.

'Mardān Singh,' said the pundit, 'the father of Rājā Arpan Singh, whom you saw at Seorī, was then our neighbour, reigning over Garhā Kotā;[1] and he had a worthless nephew, Zālim Singh, who had collected together an army of five thousand men, in the hope of getting a little principality for himself in the general scramble for dominion incident on the rise of the Pindhārīs and Amīr Khan,[2] and the destruction of all balance of power among the great sovereigns of Central India. He came to attack our capital, which was an emporium of considerable trade and the seat of many useful manufactures, in the expectation of being able to squeeze out of us a good sum to aid him in his enterprise. While his troops blocked up every gate, fire was, by accident, set to the fence of some man's garden within. There had been no rain for six months; and everything was so much dried up that the flames spread rapidly; and, though there was no wind when they began, it soon blew a gale. The Sarīmant was then a little boy with his mother in the fortress, where she lived with his father[3] and nine other relations. The flames soon extended to the fortress, and the powder- magazine blew up. The house in which they lived was burned down, and every soul, except the lieutenant [sic] himself, perished in it. His mother tried to bear him off in her arms, but fell down in her struggle to get out with him and died. His nurse, Tulsī Kurmin,[4] snatched him up, and ran with him outside of the fortress to the bank of the river, where she made him over unhurt to Harirām, the Mārwārī merchant.[5] He was mounted on a good horse, and, making off across the river, he carried him safely to his friends at Gaurjhāmar; but poor Tulsī the Kurmin fell down exhausted when she saw her charge safe, and died.

'The wind appeared to blow in upon the poor devoted city from every side; and the troops of Zālim Singh, who at first prevented the people from rushing out at the gates, made off in a panic at the horrors before them. All our establishments had been driven into the city at the approach of Zālim Singh's troops; and scores of elephants, hundreds of camels, and thousands of horses and ponies perished in the flames, besides twenty-five thousand souls. Only about five thousand persons escaped out of thirty thousand, and these were reduced to beggary and wretchedness by the loss of their dearest relations and their property. At the time the flames first began to spread, an immense crowd of people had assembled under the fortress on the bank of the Sonār river to see the widow of a soldier burn herself. Her husband had been shot by one of Zālim Singh's soldiers in the morning; and before midday she was by the side of his body on the funeral pile. People, as usual, begged her to tell them what would happen, and she replied, "The city will know in less than four hours"; in less than four hours the whole city had been reduced to ashes; and we all concluded that, since the event was so clearly foretold, it must have been decreed by God.'[6]

'No doubt it was,' said Sarīmant; 'how could it otherwise happen? Do not all events depend upon His will? Had it not been His will to save me, how could poor Tulsī the Kurmin have carried me upon her shoulders through such a scene as this, when every other member of our family perished?'

'No doubt', said Rām Chand, 'all these things are brought about by the will of God, and it is not for us to ask why.'[7]

I have heard this event described by many other people, and I believe the account of the old pundit to be a very fair one.

One day, in October 1833, the horse of the district surgeon, Doctor Spry, as he was mounting him, reared, fell back with his head upon a stone, and died upon the spot. The doctor was not much hurt, and the little Sarīmant called a few days after, and offered his congratulations upon his narrow escape. The cause of so quiet a horse rearing at this time, when he had never been known to do so before, was discussed; and he said that there could be no doubt that the horse, or the doctor himself, must have seen some unlucky face before he mounted that morning—that he had been in many places in his life, but in none where a man was liable to see so many ugly or unfortunate faces; and, for his part, he never left his house till an hour after sunrise, lest he should encounter them.[8]

Many natives were present, and every one seemed to consider the Sarīmant's explanation of the cause quite satisfactory and philosophical. Some days after, Spry was going down to sleep in the bungalow where the accident happened. His native assistant and all his servants came and prayed that he would not attempt to sleep in the bungalow, as they were sure the horse must have been frightened by a ghost, and quoted several instances of ghosts appearing to people there. He, however, slept in the bungalow, and, to their great astonishment, saw no ghost and suffered no evil.[9]

Notes:

1. A fortress, twenty-five miles cast of Sāgar, captured by a British force under General Watson in October 1818, For Seorī and Rājā Arjun Singh see *ante*, Chapter 17, text by notes 1 and 4.

2. Amīr Khān, a leader of predatory horse, has been justly described as 'one of the most atrocious villains that India ever produced'. He first came into notice in 1804, as an officer in Holkar's service, and in the following year opposed Lord Lake at Bharatpur. A treaty made with him in 1817 put an end to his activity. The Pindhārīs were organized bands of mounted robbers, who desolated Northern and Central India during the period of anarchy which followed the dissolution of the Moghal empire. They were associated with the Marāthās in the war which terminated with the capture of Asīrgarh in April 1819. In the same year the Pindhārī forces ceased to exist as a distinct and recognized, body.

> My father was an Afghān, and came from Kandahar:
> He rode with Nawāb Amir Khan in the old Marāthā war:
> From the Dekhan to the Himalay, five hundred of one clan,
> They asked no leave of prince or chief
> as they swept thro' Hindusthan.
>
> (Sir A. Lyall, 'The Old Pindaree'; in *Verses written in India*, London, 1889).

3. Named Govind Rāo. The proper name of the Sarīmant was Rāmchand Rāo (*C.P. Gazetteer*, 1870).

4. Kurmin is the feminine of Kurmī, the name of a widely spread and most industrious agricultural caste, closely connected, at least in Bundēlkhand, with the similar Lodhī caste.

5. Mārwār, or Jodhpur, is one of the leading states in Rājputāna. It supplies the rest of India with many of the keenest merchants and bankers.

6. See *ante*, Chapter 4, note 6, for remarks on the supposed prophetic gifts of satī women.

7. Such feelings of resignation to the Divine will, or fate, are common alike to Hindoos and Musalmāns.

8. 'One of a wife's duties should be to keep all bad omens out of her husband's way, or manage to make him look at something lucky in the early morning. . . . Different lists of inauspicious objects are given, which, if looked upon in the early morning, might cause disaster' (M. Williams, *Religious Thought and Life in India*, p. 397).

9. Dr. Spry died in 1842, and his estate was administered by the author. The doctor's works are described *ante*, Chapter 14, note 16.

CHAPTER 22

Interview with the Rājā who marries the Stone to the Shrub—
Order of the Moon and the Fish.

On the 8th,[1] after a march of twelve miles, we readied Tehrī, the present capital of the Rājā of Orchhā.[2] Our road lay over an undulating surface of soil composed of the detritus of the syenitic rock, and poor, both from its quality and want of depth. About three miles from our last territory we entered the boundary of the Orchhā Rājā's territory, at the village of Aslōn, which has a very pretty little fortified castle, built upon ground slightly elevated in the midst of an open grass plain.

This, and all the villages we have lately passed, are built upon the bare back of the syenitic rock, which seems to rise to the surface in large but gentle swells, like the broad waves of the ocean in a calm after a storm. A great difference appeared to me to be observable between the minds and manners of the people among whom we were now travelling, and those of the people of the Sāgar and Nerbudda territories. They seemed here to want the urbanity and intelligence we find among our subjects in the latter quarters.

The apparent stupidity of the people when questioned upon points the most interesting to them, regarding their history, their agriculture, their tanks, and temples, was most provoking; and their manners seemed to me more rude and clownish than those of people in any other part of India I had travelled over. I asked my little friend the Sarīmant, who rode with me, what he thought of this.

'I think', said he, 'that it arises from the harsh character of the government under which they live; it makes every man wish to appear a fool, in order that he may be thought a beggar and not worth the plundering.'

'It strikes me, my friend Sarīmant, that their government has made them in reality the beggars and the fools that they appear to be.'

'God only knows', said Sarīmant; 'certain it is that they are neither in mind nor in manners what the people of our districts are.'

The Rājā had no notice of our approach till intimation of it reached him at Ludhaura, the day before we came in. He was there resting, and dismissing the people after the ceremonies of the marriage between the Salagrām and the Tulasī. Ludhaura is twenty-seven miles north-west of Tehrī, on the opposite side from that on which I was approaching. He sent off two men on camels with a 'kharītā' (letter),[3] requesting that I would let him know my movements, and arrange a meeting in a manner that might prevent his appearing wanting in respect and hospitality; that is, in plain terms, which he was too polite to use, that I would consent to remain one stage from his capital, till he could return and meet me half-way, with all due pomp and ceremony. These men reached me at Bamhaurī,[4] a distance of thirty-nine miles, in the evening, and I sent back a kharītā, which reached him by relays of camels before midnight. He set out for his capital to receive me, and, as I would not wait to be met half-way in due form, he reached his palace, and we reached our tents at the same time, under a salute from his two brass field-pieces.

We halted at Tehrī on the 9th, and about eleven o'clock the Rājā came to pay his visit of congratulation, with a magnificent *cortège* of elephants, camels, and horses, all mounted and splendidly caparisoned, and the noise of his band was deafening. I had had both my tents pitched, and one of them handsomely fitted up, as it always is, for occasions of ceremony like the present. He came to within twenty paces of the door on his elephant, and from its back, as it sat down, he entered his splendid litter, without alighting on the ground.[5] In this vehicle he was brought to my tent door, where I received him, and, after the usual embraces, conducted him up through two rows of chairs, placed for his followers of distinction and my own, who are always anxious to assist in ceremonies like these.

At the head of this lane we sat upon chairs placed across, and facing down the middle of the two rows; and we conversed upon all the subjects usually introduced on such occasions, but more especially upon the august ceremonies of the marriage of the Salagrām with the Tulasī, in which his highness had been so *piously* engaged at Ludhaura.[6] After he had sat with me an hour and a half he took his leave, and I conducted him to the door, whence he was carried to his elephant in his litter, from which he mounted without touching the ground.

This litter is called a 'nālkī'. It is one of the three great insignia which the Mogul Emperors of Delhi conferred upon independent princes of the first class, and could never be used by any person upon whom, or upon whose ancestors, they had not been so conferred. These were the nālkī, the order of the Fish, and the fan of the peacock's feathers. These insignia could be used only by the prince who inherited the sovereignty of the one on whom they had been originally conferred. The order of the Fish, or Mahī Marātib, was first instituted by Khusrū Parvīz, King of Persia, and grandson of the celebrated Naushīrvān the Just. Having been deposed by his general, Bahrām, Khusrū fled for protection to the Greek emperor, Maurice, whose daughter, Shīrīn, he married, and he was sent back to Persia, with an army under the command of Narses, who placed him on the throne of his ancestors in the year A.D. 591.[7] He ascertained from his astrologer, Araz Khushasp, that when he ascended the throne the moon was in the constellation of the Fish, and he gave orders to have two balls made of polished steel, which were to be called Kaukabas (planets),[8] and mounted on long poles. These two planets, with large fish made of gold, upon a third pole in the centre, were ordered to be carried in all regal processions immediately after the king, and before the prime minister, whose *cortège* always followed immediately after that of the king. The two kaūkabas are now generally made of copper, and plated, and in the shape of a jar, instead of quite round as at first; but the fish is still made of gold. Two planets are always considered necessary to one fish, and they are still carried in all processions between the prince and his prime minister.

The court of this prince Khusrū Pārvīz was celebrated throughout the East for its splendour and magnificence; and the chaste love of the poet Farhad for his beautiful queen Shīrīn is the theme of almost as many poems in the East as that of Petrarch's for Laura is in the West. Nūh Samānī, who ascended the throne of Persia after the Sassanians,[9] ascertained that the moon was in the sign Leo at the time of his accession, and ordered that the gold head of a lion should thenceforward accompany the fishes, and the two balls, in all royal processions. The Persian order of knighthood is, therefore, that of the Fish, the Moon, and the Lion, and not the Lion and Sun, as generally supposed. The emperors of the house of Taimūr in Hindustan assumed the right of conferring the order upon all whom they pleased, and they conferred it upon the great territorial sovereigns of the country without distinction as to religion. He only who inherits the sovereignty can wear the order, and I believe no prince would venture to wear or carry the order who was not generally reputed to have received the investiture from one of the emperors of Delhi.[10]

As I could not wait another day, it was determined that I should return his visit in the afternoon; and about four o'clock we set out upon our elephant — Lieutenant Thomas, Sarīmant, and myself, attended by all my troopers and those of Sarīmant. We had our silver-stick men with us; but still all made a sorry figure compared with the splendid *cortège* of the Rājā. We dismounted at the foot of the stairs leading to the Rājā's hall of audience, and were there met by his two chief officers of state, who conducted us to the entrance of the hall, when we were received by the Rājā himself, who led us up through two rows of chairs laid out exactly as mine had been in the morning. In front were assembled a party of native comedians, who exhibited a few scenes of the insolence of office in the attendants of great men, and the obtrusive importunity of place- seekers, in a manner that pleased us much more than a dance would have done. Conversation was kept up very well, and the visit passed off without any feeling of ennui, or anything whatever to recollect with regret. The ladies looked at us from their apartments through gratings, and without our being able to see them very distinctly. We were anxious to see the tombs of the late Rājā, the elder brother of the present, who lately died, and that of his son, which are in progress in a very fine garden outside the city walls, and, in consequence, we did not sit above half an hour. The Rājā conducted us to the head of the stairs, and the same two officers attended us to the bottom, and mounted their horses, and attended us to the tombs.

After the dust of the town raised by the immense crowd that attended us, and the ceremonies of the day, a walk in this beautiful garden was very agreeable, and I prolonged it till dark. The Rājā had given orders to have all the cisterns filled during our stay, under the impression that we should wish to see the garden; and, as soon as we entered, the *jets d'eau* poured into the air their little floods from a hundred mouths. Our old cicerone told us that, if we would take the old capital of Orchhā in our way, we might there see the thing in perfection, and amidst the deluges of the rains of Sāwān and Bhādon (July and August) see the lightning and hear the thunder. The Rājās of this, the oldest principality in Bundēlkhand, were all formerly buried or burned at the old capital of Orchhā, even after they had changed their residence to Tehrī. These tombs over the ashes of the Rājā, his wife, and son, are the first that have been built at Tehrī, where their posterity are all to repose in future.

Notes:

1. December, 1835.

2. The State of Orchhā, also known as Tehrī or Tīkamgarh, situated to the south of the Jhānsī district, is the oldest and the highest in rank of the Bundela principalities. The town of Tehrī is seventy-two miles north- west of Sāgar. The town of Orchhā, founded in A.D. 1531, is 131 miles north of Sāgar, and about forty miles from Tehrī. Tīkamgarh is the fort of Tehrī.

3. A *kharītā* is a letter enclosed in a bag of rich brocade, contained in another of fine muslin. The mouth is tied with a string of silk, to which hangs suspended the great seal, which is a flat round mass of sealing-wax, with the seal impressed on each side of it. This is the kind of letter which

passes between natives of great rank in India, and between them and the public functionaries of Government. [W. H. S.]

4. *Ante*, Chapter 19, after note [15].

5. The Rājā's unwillingness to touch the ground is an example of a very widespread and primitive belief. 'Two of those rules or taboos by which . . . the life of divine kings or priests is regulated. The first is . . . that the divine personage may not touch the ground with his foot.' This prohibition applies to the Mikado of Japan and many other sacred personages. 'The second rule is that the sun may not shine upon the sacred person.' This second rule explains the use of the umbrella as a royal appendage in India and Burma. (Frazer, *The Golden Bough*, 1st ed., vol. ii, pp. 224, 225.)

6 *Ante*, Chapter 19, note 3.

7. During the time he remained the guest of the emperor he resided at Hierapolis, and did not visit Constantinople. The Greeks do not admit that Shīrīn was the daughter of Maurice, though a Roman by birth and a Christian by religion. The Persians and Turks speak of her as the emperor's daughter. [W. H. S.] Khusrū Pārvīz (Eberwiz), or Khusrū II, reigned as King of Persia from A.D. 591 to 628. In the course of his wars he took Jerusalem, and reduced Egypt, and a large part of northern Africa, extending for a time the bounds of the Persian empire to the Aegean and the Nile. Khusrū I, surnamed Naushīrvān, or (more correctly) Anushīrvān, reigned from A.D. 531 to 579. His successful wars with the Romans and his vigorous internal administration captivated the Oriental imagination, and he is generally spoken of as Ādil, or The Just. His name has become proverbial, and to describe a superior as rivalling Naushīrvān in justice is a commonplace of flattery. The prophet Muhammad was born during his reign, and was proud of the fact. The alleged expedition of Naushīrvān into India is discredited by the best modern writers. Gibbon tells the story of the wars between the two Khusrūs and the Romans in his forty- sixth chapter, and a critical history of the reigns of both Khusrū (Khosrau) I and Khusrū II will be found in Professor Rawlinson's *Seventh Great Oriental Monarchy* (London, 1876). European authors have, until recently, generally written the name Khusrū in its Greek form as Chosroes. The name of Shīrīn is also written Sira.

'With the name of Shirin and the rock of Bahistun the Persians have associated one of those poetic romances so dear to the national genius. Ferhad, the most famous sculptor of his time, who was very likely employed by Chosroes II to execute these bas-reliefs, is said in the legend to have fallen madly in love with Shīrīn, and to have received a promise of her from the king, if he would cut through the rock of Behistun, and divert a stream to the Kermanshah plain. The lover set to work, and had all but completed his gigantic enterprise (of which the remains, however interpreted, are still to be seen), when he was falsely informed by an emissary from the king of his lady's death. In despair he leaped from the rock, and was dashed to pieces. The legend of the unhappy lover is familiar throughout the East, and is used to explain many traces of rock- cutting or excavation as far east as Beluchistan' (*Persia and the Persian Question*, by the Hon. George N. Curzon, M.P. (London, 1892), vol. i, p. 562, note. See also Malcolm, *History of Persia*, vol. i, p. 129).

8. *Kaukab* in Arabic means 'a star'. Steingass (*Persian Dictionary*) defines *Kaukaba* as 'a polished steel ball suspended to a long pole, and carried as an ensign before the king; a star of gold, silver, or tinsel, worn as ornament or sign of rank; a concourse of people; a royal train, retinue, cavalcade; splendour'.

9. Yezdegird III (Isdigerd), the last of the Sassanians, was defeated in A.D. 641 at the battle of Nahavend by the Arab Nomān, general of the Khalīf Omar, and driven from his throne. The supremacy of the Khalīfs over Persia lasted till A.D. 1258. The subordinate Samāni dynasty ruled over Khurāsān, Seistān, Balkh, and the countries of Trans-Oxiana in the tenth century. Two of the princes of this line were named Nūh, or Noah. The author probably refers to the better known of the two, Amir Nūh II (Malcolm, *History of Persia*, ed. 1829, vol. i, pp. 158-66).

10. The poor old blind emperor. Shāh Alam, when delivered from the Marāthās in 1803 by Lord Lake, did all he could to show his gratitude by conferring on his deliverer honours and titles, and among them the 'Mahī Maratīb'. The editor has been unable to discover the source of the author's story of the origin of the Persian order of knighthood. Malcolm, an excellent authority, gives the following very different account: 'Their sovereigns have, for many centuries, preserved as the peculiar arms of the country,[e] the sign or figure of Sol in the constellation of Leo; and this device, a lion couchant and the sun rising at his back, has not only been sculptured upon their palaces[f] and embroidered upon their banners.[g] but has been converted into an Order,[h] which in the form of gold and silver medals, has been given to such as have distinguished themselves against the enemies of their country.[i]

Note e. The causes which led to the sign of Sol in Leo becoming the arms of Persia cannot be distinctly traced, but there is reason to believe that the use of this symbol is not of very great antiquity. We meet with it upon the coins of one of the Seljukian princes of Iconium; and, when this family had been destroyed by Hulākū [A.D. 1258], the grandson of Chengiz, that prince, or his successors, perhaps adopted this emblem as a trophy of their conquest, whence it has remained ever since among the most remarkable of the royal insignia. A learned friend, who has a valuable collection of Oriental coins, and whose information and opinion have enabled me to make this conjecture, believes that the emblematical representation of Sol in Leo was first adopted by Ghiās-ud-din Kai Khusrū bin Kaikobād, who began to reign A.H. 634, A.D. 1236, and died A.H. 642, A.D. 1244; and this emblem, he adds, is supposed to have reference either to his own horoscope or to that of his queen, who was a princess of Georgia.

Note f. Hanway states, vol. i, p. 199, that over the gate which forms the entrance of the palace built by Shah Abbās the Great [A.D. 1586 to 1628] at Ashrāf, in Mazenderan, are 'the arms of Persia, being a lion, and the sun rising behind it'.

Note g. The emblem of the Lion and Sun is upon all the banners given to the regular corps of infantry lately formed. They are presented to the regiments with great ceremony. A mūllā, or priest, attends, and implores the divine blessing on them.

Note h. This order, with additional decorations, has been lately conferred upon several ministers and representatives of European Governments in alliance with Persia.

Note i. The medals which have been struck with this symbol upon them have been chiefly given to the Persian officers and men of the regular corps who have distinguished themselves in the war with the Russians. An English officer, who served with these troops, informs me that those on whom these medals have been conferred are very proud of this distinction, and that all are extremely anxious to obtain them (*History of Persia*, ed. 1829, vol. ii, p. 406).

In Curzon's figure the lion is standing, not 'couchant', as stated by Malcolm, and grasps a scimitar in his off forepaw.

CHAPTER 23

The Rājā of Orchhā—Murder of his many Ministers.

The present Rājā, Mathurā Dās, succeeded his brother Bikramājīt, who died in 1834. He had made over the government to his only son, Rājā Bahādur, whom he almost adored; but, the young man dying some years before him, the father resumed the reins of government, and held them till his death. He was a man of considerable capacity, but of a harsh and unscrupulous character. His son resembled him; but the present Rājā is a man of mild temper and disposition, though of weak intellect. The fate of the last three prime ministers will show the character of the Rājā and his son, and the nature of their rule.

The minister at the time the old man made over the reins of government to his son was Khānjū Purōhit.[1] Wishing to get rid of him a few years after, this son, Rājā Bahādur, employed Muhram Singh, one of his feudal Rājpūt barons, to assassinate him. As a reward for this service he received the seals of office; and the Rājā confiscated all the property of the deceased, amounting to four lakhs of rupees[2] and resumed the whole of the estates held by the family.

The young Rājā died soon after; and his father, when he resumed the reins of government, wishing to remove the new minister, got him assassinated by Gambhīr Singh, another feudal Rājpūt baron, who, as his reward, received in his turn the seals of office. This man was a most atrocious villain, and employed the public establishments of his chief to plunder travellers on the high road. In 1833 his followers robbed four men, who were carrying treasure to the amount of ten thousand rupees from Sāgar to Jhānsī through Tehrī, and intended to murder them; but, by the sagacity of one of the party, and a lucky accident, they escaped, made their way back to Sāgar, and complained to the magistrate.[3] The[4] minister discovered the nature of their burdens as they lodged at Tehrī on their way, and sent after them a party of soldiers, with orders to put them in the bed of a rivulet that separated the territory of Orchhā from that of the Jhānsī Rājā. One of the treasure party discovered their object; and, on reaching the bank of the rivulet in a deep grass jungle, he threw down his bundle, dashed unperceived through the grass, and reached a party of travellers whom he saw ascending a hill about half a mile in advance. The myrmidons of the minister, when they found that one had escaped, were afraid to murder the others, but took their treasure. In spite of great obstacles, and with much danger to the families of three of those men, who resided in the capital of Tehrī, the magistrate of Sāgar brought the crime home to the minister, and the Rājā, anxious to avail himself of the occasion to fill his coffers, got him assassinated. The Rājā was then about eighty years of age, and his minister was a strong, athletic, and brave man. One morning while he was sitting with him in private conversation, the former pretended a wish to drink some of the water in which his household god had been washed (the 'chandan mirt'),[5] and begged the minister to go and fetch it from the place where it stood by the side of the idol in the court of the palace. As a man cannot take his sword before the idol, the minister put it down, as the Rājā knew he would, and going to the idol, prostrated himself before it preparatory to taking away the water. In that state he was cut down by Bihārī,[6] another feudal Rājpūt baron, who aspired to the seals, and some of his friends, who had been placed there on purpose by the Rājā. He obtained the seals by his service, and, as he was allowed to place one brother in command of the forces, and to make another chamberlain, he hoped to retain them longer than any of his predecessors had done. Gambhīr Singh's brother, Jhujhār Singh, and the husband of his sister, hearing of his murder, made off, but were soon pursued and put to death. The widows were all three put into prison, and all the property and estates were confiscated. The movable property amounted to three lakhs of rupees.[7] The Rājā boasted to the Governor-General's representative in Bundēlkhand of this act of retributive justice, and pretended that it was executed merely as a punishment for the robbery; but it was with infinite difficulty the merchants could recover from him any share of the plundered property out of that confiscated. The Rājā alleged that, according to our *rules*, the chief within whose boundary the robbery might have been committed, was obliged to make good the property. On inspection, it was found that the robbery was perpetrated upon the very boundary line, and 'in spite of pride, in erring reason's spite', the Jhānsī Rājā was made to pay one-half of the plundered treasure.

The old Rājā, Bikramājīt, died in June, 1834; and, though his death had been some time expected, he no sooner breathed his last than charges of 'dīnaī', slow poison, were got up, as usual, in the zenana (seraglio).

Here the widow of Rājā Bahādur, a violent and sanguinary woman, was supreme; and she persuaded the present Rājā, a weak old man, to take advantage of the funeral ceremonies to avenge the death of his brother. He did so; and Bihārī, and his three brothers, with above fifty of his relations, were murdered. The widows of the four brothers were the only members of all the families left alive. One of them had a son four months old; another one of two years; the four brothers had no other children. Immediately after the death of their husbands, the two children were snatched from their mothers' breasts, and threatened with instant death unless their mothers pointed out all their ornaments and other property. They did so; and the spoilers having got from them property to the amount of one hundred and fifty thousand rupees, and been assured that there was no more, threw the children over the high wall, by which they were dashed to pieces. The poor widows were tendered as wives to four sweepers, the lowest of all low castes; but the tribe of sweepers would not suffer any of its members to take the widows of men of such high caste and station as wives, notwithstanding the tempting offer of five hundred rupees as a present, and a village in rent-free tenure.[8] I secured a promise while at Tehrī that these poor widows should be provided for, as they had, up to that time, been preserved by the good feeling of a little community of the lowest of castes, on whom they had been bestowed as a punishment worse than death, inasmuch as it would disgrace the whole class to which they belonged, the Parihār Rājpūts.[9]

Tehrī is a wretched town, without one respectable dwelling- house tenanted beyond the palace, or one merchant, or even shopkeeper of capital and credit. There are some tolerable houses unoccupied and in ruins; and there are a few neat temples built as tombs, or cenotaphs, in or around the city, if city it can be called. The stables and accommodations for all public establishments seem to be all in the same ruinous state as the dwelling-houses. The revenues of the state are spent in feeding Brahmans and religious mendicants of all kinds; and in such idle ceremonies as those at which the Rājā and all his court have just been assisting—ceremonies which concentrate for a few days the most useless of the people of India, the devotee followers (Bairāgīs) of the god Vishnu, and tend to no purpose, either useful or ornamental, to the state or to the people.

This marriage of a stone to a shrub, which takes place every year, is supposed to cost the Rājā, at the most moderate estimate, three lakhs of rupees a year, or one-fourth of his annual revenue.[10] The highest officers of which his government is composed receive small beggarly salaries, hardly more than sufficient for their subsistence; and the money they make by indirect means they dare not spend like gentlemen, lest the Rājā might be tempted to take their lives in order to get hold of it. All his feudal barons are of the same tribe as himself, that is, Rājpūts; but they are divided into three clans—Bundēlas, Pawārs, and Chandēls. A Bundēla cannot marry a woman of his own clan, he must take a wife from the Pawārs or Chandēls; and so of the other two clans—no member of one can take a wife from his own clan, but must go to one of the other two for her. They are very much disposed to fight with each other, but not less are they disposed to unite against any third party, not of the same tribe. Braver men do not, I believe, exist than the Rājpūts of Bundēlkhand, who all carry their swords from their infancy.[11]

It may be said of the Rājpūts of Mālwa and Central India generally, that the Mogul Emperors of Delhi made the same use of them that the Emperors of Germany and the Popes made of the military chiefs and classes of Europe during the Middle Ages. Industry and the peaceful arts being reduced to agriculture alone under bad government or no government at all, the land remained the only thing worth appropriating; and it accordingly became appropriated by those alone who had the power to do so—by the Hindoo military classes collected around the heads of their clans, and powerful in their union. These held it under the paramount power on the feudal tenure of military service, as militia; or it was appropriated by the paramount power itself, who let it out on allodial tenure to peaceful peasantry. The one was the Zamīndārī, and the other the Mālguzārī tenure of India.[12]

The military chiefs, essentially either soldiers or robbers, were continually fighting, either against each other, or against the peasantry, or public officers of the paramount power, like the barons of Europe; and that paramount power, or its delegates, often found that the easiest way to crush one of these refractory vassals was to put him, as such men had been put in Germany, to *the ban of the empire*, and offer his lands, his castles, and his wealth to the victor. This victor brought his own clansmen to occupy the lands and castles of the vanquished; and, as these were the only things thought worth living for, the change commonly involved the utter destruction of the former occupants. The new possessors gave the name of their leader, their clan, or their former place of abode, to their new possession, and the tract of country over which they spread. Thus were founded the Bundēlas, Pawārs, and Chandēls [*sic*] upon the ruin of the Chandēls of Bundēlkhand, the Baghēlas in Baghēlkhand, or Rīwā, the Kachhwāhas, the Sakarwārs, and others along the Chambal river, and throughout all parts of India.[13]

These classes have never learnt anything, or considered anything worth learning, but the use of the sword; and a Rājpūt chief, next to leading a gang of his own on great enterprises, delights in nothing so much as having a gang or two under his patronage for little ones.

There is hardly a single chief of the Hindoo military class in the Bundēlkhand or Gwālior territories, who does not keep a gang of robbers of some kind or other, and consider it as a very valuable and legitimate source of revenue; or who would not embrace with cordiality the leader of a gang of assassins by profession who should bring him home from every expedition a good horse, a good sword, or a valuable pair of shawls, taken from their victims. It is much the same in the kingdom of Oudh, where the lands are for the most part held by the same Hindoo military classes, who are in a continual state of war with each other, or with the Government authorities. Three-fourths of the recruits for native infantry regiments are from this class of military agriculturists of Oudh, who have been trained up in this school of contest; and many of the lads, when they enter our ranks, are found to have marks of the cold steel upon their persons. A braver set of men is hardly anywhere to be found; or one trained up with finer feelings of devotion towards the power whose salt they eat.[14] A good many of the other fourth of the recruits for our native infantry are drawn from among the Ujainī Rājpūts, or Rājpūts from Ujain,[15] who were established many generations ago in the same manner at Bhōjpur on the bank of the Ganges. [16]

Notes:

1. A purōhit is a Brahman family priest.

2. Four hundred thousand rupees, worth at that time more than forty thousand pounds sterling.

3. The magistrate was the author.

4. 'That' in author's text.

5. The water of the Ganges, with which the image of the god Vishnu has been washed, is considered a very holy draught, fit for princes. That with which the image of the god Siva, alias Mahādēo, is washed must not be drunk. The popular belief is that in a dispute between him and his wife, Pārvatī, alias Kālī, she cursed the person that should thenceforward dare to drink of the water that flowed over his images on earth. The river Ganges is supposed to flow from the top-knot of Siva's head, and no one would drink of it after this curse, were it not that the sacred stream is supposed to come first from the *heel* of Vishnu, the Preserver. All the little images of Siva, that are made out of stones taken from the bed of the Nerbudda river, are supposed to be absolved from this curse, and water thrown upon *them* can be drunk with impunity. [W. H. S.] The natural emblems of Siva, the Bāna-linga quartz pebbles found in the Nerbudda, have already been referred to in the note to Chapter 19, *ante*, note 9. In the Marāthā country the 'household gods' generally comprise five sacred symbols, namely, the *sālagrāma* stone of Vishnu, the *bāna-linga* of Siva, a metallic stone representing the female principle in nature (Sakti), a crystal representing the sun, and a red stone representing Ganesh, the remover of obstacles. The details of the tiresome ritual observed in the worship of these objects occupy pp. 412 to 416 of Monier Williams's *Religious Thought and Life in India*.

6. 'Beearee' in author's text.

7. Then worth more than thirty thousand pounds sterling.

8. On the customs of the sweeper caste, see *ante*, Chapter 8, following note [11].

9. The Parihārs were the rulers of Bundēlkhand before the Chandēls. The chief of Uchhahara belongs to this clan.

10. Wealthy Hindoos, throughout India, spend money in the same ceremonies of marrying the stone to the shrub. [W. H. S.] Three lakhs of rupees were then worth thirty thousand pounds sterling or more.

11. The numerous clans, more or less devoted to war, grouped together under the name of Rājpūts (literally 'king's sons'), are in reality of multifarious origin, and include representatives of many races. They are the Kshatriyas of the law- books, and are still often called Chhattrī (*E.H.I.*, 3rd ed., pp. 407-15). In some parts of the country the word Thākur is more familiar as their general title. Thirty-six clans are considered as specially pure-blooded and are called, at any rate in books, the 'royal races'. All the clans follow the custom of exogamy. The Chandēls (Chandella) ruled Bundēlkhand from the ninth to the thirteenth centuries. Their capital was Mahoba, now a station on the Midland Railway. The Bundēlas became prominent at a later date, and attained their greatest power under Chhatarsāl (*circa* A.D. 1671-1731). Their territory is now known as Bundēlkhand. The country so designated is not an administrative division. It is partly in the United Provinces, partly in the Central Provinces, and partly in Native States. It is bounded on the north by the Jumna; on the north and west by the Chambal river; on the south by the Central Provinces, and on the south and east by Rīwā and the Kaimūr hills. The traditions of both the Bundēlas and Chandellas show that there is a strain of the blood of the earlier, so—called aboriginal, races in both clans. The Pawār (Pramara) clan ranks high, but is now of little political importance (See *N.W.P. Gazetteer*, 1st ed., vol. vii, p. 68).

12. The paramount power often assigned a portion of its reserved lands in 'Jāgīr' to public officers for the establishments they required for the performance of the duties, military or civil, which were expected from them. Other portions were assigned in rent-free tenure for services already performed, or to favourites; but, in both cases, the rights of the village or land owner, or allodial proprietors, were supposed to be unaffected, as the Government was presumed to assign only its own claim to a certain portion as revenue. [W. H. S.] The term 'ryotwar' (raiyatwār) is commonly used to designate the system under which the cultivators hold their lands direct from the State. The subject of tenures is further discussed by the author in Chapters 70, 71.

13. For elaborate comparisons between the Rājpūt policy and the feudal system of Europe, Tod's *Rajasthān* may be consulted. The parallel is not really so close as it appears to be at first sight. In some respects the organization of the Highland clans is more similar to that of the Rājpūts than the feudal system is. The Chambal river rises in Mālwā, and, after a course of some five hundred and seventy miles, falls into the Jumna forty miles below Etāwa. The statement in the text concerning the succession of clans is confused. The ruling family of Rīwā still belongs to the Baghēl clan. The Maharājā of Jaipur (Jeypore) is a Kachhwāha.

14. The barbarous habit of alliance and connivance with robber gangs is by no means confined to Rājpūt nobles and landholders. Men of all creeds and castes yield to the temptation and magistrates are sometimes startled to find that Honorary Magistrates, Members of District Boards, and others of apparently the highest respectability, are the abettors and secret organizers of robber bands. A modern example of this fact was discovered in the Meerut and Muzaffarnagar Districts of the United Provinces in 1890 and 1891. In this case the wealthy supporters of the banditti were Jāts and Muhammadans.

The unfortunate condition of Oudh previous to the annexation in 1856 is vividly described in the author's *Journey through the Kingdom of Oude*, published in 1858. The tour took place in 1849- 50. Some districts of the kingdom, especially Hardoī, are still tainted by the old lawlessness.

The remarks on the fine feelings of devotion shown by the sepoys must now be read in the light of the events of the Mutiny. Since that time the army has been reorganized, and depends on Oudh for its recruits much less than it did in the author's day.

15. Ujain (Ujjain, Oojeyn) is a very ancient city, on the river Sipra, in Mālwa, in the dominions of Sindhia, the chief of Gwālior.

16. Bhajpore in the author's text. The town referred to is Bhōjpur in the Shāhābād district of South Bihār.

CHAPTER 24

Corn Dealers — Scarcities — Famines in India.

Near Tehrī we saw the people irrigating a field of wheat from a tank by means of a canoe, in a mode quite new to me. The surface of the water was about three feet below that of the field to be watered. The inner end of the canoe was open, and placed to the mouth of a gutter leading into the wheat-field. The outer end was closed, and suspended by a rope to the outer end of a pole, which was again suspended to cross-bars. On the inner end of this pole was fixed a weight of stones sufficient to raise the canoe when filled with water; and at the outer end stood five men, who pulled down and sank the canoe into the water as often as it was raised by the stones, and emptied into the gutter. The canoe was more curved at the outer end than ordinary canoes are, and seemed to have been made for the purpose. The lands round the town generally were watered by the Persian wheel; but, where it [*scil.* the water] is near the surface, this [*scil.* the canoe arrangement] I should think a better method.[1]

On the 10th[2] we came on to the village of Bilgaī, twelve miles over a bad soil, badly cultivated; the hard syenitic rock rising either above or near to the surface all the way — in some places abruptly, in small hills, decomposing into large rounded boulders — in others slightly and gently, like the backs of whales in the ocean-in others, the whole surface of the country resembled very much the face of the sea, not after, but really in, a storm, full of waves of all sizes, contending with each other 'in most admired disorder'. After the dust of Tehrī, and the fatiguing ceremonies of its court, the quiet morning I spent in this secluded spot under the shade of some beautiful trees, with the surviving canary singing, my boy playing, and my wife sleeping off the fatigues of her journey, was to me most delightful. Henry was extremely ill when we left Jubbulpore; but the change of air, and all the other changes incident to a march, have restored him to health.

During the scarcity of 1833 two hundred people died of starvation in this village alone;[3] and were all thrown into one large well, which has, of course, ever since remained closed. Autumn crops chiefly are cultivated; and they depend entirely on the sky for water, while the poor people of the village depend upon the returns of a single season for subsistence during the whole year. They lingered on in the hope of aid from above till the greater part had become too weak from want of food to emigrate. The Rājā gave half a crown to every family;[4] but this served merely to kindle their hopes of more, and to prolong their misery. Till the people have a better government they can never be secure from frequent returns of similar calamities. Such security must depend upon a greater variety of crops, and better means of irrigation; better roads to bring supplies over from distant parts which have not suffered from the same calamities; and greater means in reserve of paying for such supplies when brought — things that can never be hoped for under a government like this, which allows no man the free enjoyment of property.

Close to the village a large wall has been made to unite two small hills, and form a small lake; but the wall is formed of the rounded boulders of the syenitic rock without cement, and does not retain the water. The land which was to have formed the bed of the lake is all in tillage; and I had some conversation with the man who cultivated it. He told me that the wall had been built with the money of *sin*, and not the money of *piety* (*pāp kē paisā sē, na pun kē paisā sē banā*), that the man who built it must have laid out his money with a *worldly*, and not a *religious* mind (*nīyat*); that on such occasions men generally assembled Brahmans and other deserving people, and fed and clothed them, and thereby *consecrated* a great work, and made it acceptable to God, and he had heard from his ancestors that the man who had built this wall had failed to do this; that the construction could never, of course, answer the purpose for which it was intended — and that the builder's name had actually been forgotten, and the work did him no good either in this world or the next. This village, which a year or two ago was large and populous, is now reduced to two wretched huts inhabited by two very miserable families.

Bundēlkhand suffers more often and more severely from the want of seasonable showers of rain than any other part of India; while the province of Mālwa, which adjoins it on the west and south, hardly ever suffers at all. [5] There is a couplet, which, like all other good couplets on rural subjects, is attributed to Sahdēo [Sahadeva], one of the five demigod brothers of the Mahābhārata, to this effect: 'If you hear not the thunder on such a night, you, father, go to Mālwa, I to Gujarāt;' — that is, there will be no rain, and we must seek subsistence where rains never fail, and the harvests are secure.

The province of Mālwa is well studded with hills and groves of fine trees, which intercept the clouds as they are wafted by the prevailing westerly winds, from the Gulf of Cambay to the valley of the Ganges, and make them drop their contents upon a soil of great natural powers, formed chiefly from the detritus of the decomposing basaltic rocks, which cap and intersect these hills.[6]

During the famine of 1833, as on all similar occasions, grain of every kind, attracted by high prices, flowed up in large streams from this favoured province towards Bundēlkhand; and the population of Bundēlkhand, as usual in such times of dearth and scarcity, flowed off towards Mālwa against the stream of supply, under the assurance that the nearer they got to the source, the greater would be their chance of employment and subsistence. Every village had its numbers of the dead and the dying; and the roads were all strewed with them; but they were mostly concentrated upon the great towns and civil and military stations, where subscriptions were open[ed] for their support, by both the European and native communities. The funds arising from these subscriptions lasted till the rains had set fairly in, when all able-bodied persons could easily find employment in tillage among the agricultural communities of villages around. After the rains have fairly set in, the *sick* and *helpless* only should be kept concentrated upon large towns and stations, where little or no employment is to be found; for the oldest and youngest of those who are able to work can then easily find employment in weeding the cotton, rice, sugar-cane, and other fields under autumn crops, and in preparing the lands for the reception of the wheat, gram,[7] and other spring seeds; and get advances from the farmers, agricultural capitalists[8] and other members of the village communities, who are all glad to share their superfluities with the distressed, and to pay liberally for the little service they are able to give in return.

It is very unwise to give from such funds what may be considered a full rate of subsistence to able-bodied persons, as it tends to keep concentrated upon such points vast numbers who would otherwise be scattered over the surface of the country among the village communities, who would be glad to advance them stock and the means of subsistence upon the pledge of their future services when the season of tillage commences. The rate of subsistence should always be something less than what the able-bodied person usually consumes, and can get for his labour in the field. For the sick and feeble this rate will be enough, and the healthy and able-bodied, with unimpaired appetites, will seek a greater rate by the offer of their services among the farmers and cultivators of the surrounding country. By this precaution, the mass of suffering will be gradually diffused over the country, so as best to receive what the country can afford to give for its relief. As soon as the rains set in, all the able-bodied men, women, and children should be sent off with each a good blanket, and a rupee or two, as the funds can afford, to last them till they can engage themselves with the farmers. Not a farthing after that day should be given out, except to the feeble and sick, who may be considered as hospital patients.[9]

At large places, where the greater numbers are concentrated, the scene becomes exceedingly distressing, for, in spite of the best dispositions and greatest efforts on the part of Government and its officers, and the European and native communities, thousands commonly die of starvation. At Sāgar, mothers, as they lay in the streets unable to walk, were seen holding up their infants, and imploring the passing stranger to take them in slavery, that they might at least live — hundreds were seen creeping into gardens, courtyards, and old ruins, concealing themselves under shrubs, grass, mats, or straw, where they might die quietly, without having their bodies torn by birds and beasts before the breath had left them. Respectable families, who left home in search of the favoured land of Mālwa, while yet a little property remained, finding all exhausted, took opium rather than beg, and husband, wife, and children died in each other's arms. Still more of such families lingered on in hope till all had been expended; then shut their doors, took poison and died all together, rather than expose their misery, and submit to the degradation of begging. All these things I have myself known and seen; and, in the midst of these and a hundred other harrowing scenes which present themselves on such occasions, the European cannot fail to remark the patient resignation with which the poor people submit to their fate; and the absence of almost all those revolting acts which have characterized the famines of which he has read in other countries — such as the living feeding on the dead, and mothers devouring their own children. No such things are witnessed in Indian famines;[10] here all who suffer attribute the disaster to its real cause, the want of rain in due season; and indulge in no feelings of hatred against their rulers, superiors, or more fortunate equals in society who happen to live beyond the range of such calamities. They gratefully receive the superfluities which the more favoured are always found ready to share with the afflicted in India; and, though their sufferings often subdue the strongest of all pride, the pride of caste, they rarely ever drive the people to acts of violence. The stream of emigration, guided as it always is by that of the agricultural produce flowing in from the more favoured countries, must necessarily concentrate upon the communities along the line it takes a greater number of people than they have the means of relieving, however benevolent their dispositions; and I must say that I have never either seen or read of a nobler spirit than seems to animate all classes of these communities in India on such distressing occasions.

In such seasons of distress, we often, in India, hear of very injudicious interference with grain dealers on the part of civil and military authorities, who contrive to persuade themselves that the interest of these corn-dealers, instead of being in accordance with the interests of the people, are entirely opposed to them; and conclude that, whenever grain becomes dear, they have a right to make them open their granaries, and sell their grain at such price as they, in their wisdom, may deem reasonable. If they cannot make them do this by persuasion, fine, or imprisonment, they cause their pits to be opened by their own soldiers or native officers, and the grain to be sold at an arbitrary price. If, in a hundred pits thus opened, they find one in which the corn happens to be damaged by damp, they come to the sage conclusion that the proprietors must be what they have all along supposed them to be, and treated as such — *the common enemies of mankind* — who, blind alike to their own interests and those of the people, purchase up the superabundance of seasons of plenty, not to sell it again in seasons of scarcity, but *to destroy it;* and that the whole of the grain in the other ninety-nine pits, but for their *timely interference,* must have inevitably shared the same fate.[11]

During the season here mentioned, grain had become very dear at Sāgar, from the unusual demand in Bundēlkhand and other districts to the north. As usual, supplies of land produce flowed up from the Nerbudda districts along the great roads to the east and west of the city; but the military authorities in the cantonments would not be persuaded out of their dread of a famine. There were three regiments of infantry, a corps of cavalry, and two companies of artillery cantoned at that time at Sāgar. They were a mile from the city, and the grain for their supply was exempted from town duties to which that for the city was liable. The people in cantonments got their supply, in consequence, a good deal cheaper than the people in the city got theirs; and none but persons belonging bona fide to the cantonments were ever allowed to purchase grain within them. When the dread of famine began, the commissariat officer, Major Gregory, apprehended that he might not be permitted to have recourse to the markets of the city in times of scarcity, since the people of the city had not been suffered to have recourse to those of the cantonments in times of plenty; but he was told by the magistrate to purchase as much as he liked, since he considered every man as free to sell his grain as his cloth, or pots and pans, to whom he chose. [12] He added that he did not share in the fears of the military authorities — that he had no apprehension whatever of a famine, or when prices rose high enough they would be sure to divert away into the city, from the streams then flowing up from the valley of the Nerbudda and the districts of Mālwa towards Bundēlkhand, a supply of grain sufficient for all.

This new demand upon the city increased rapidly the price of grain, and augmented the alarm of the people, who began to urge the magistrate to listen to their prayers, and coerce the sordid corn- dealers, who had, no doubt, numerous pits yet unopened. The alarm became still greater in the cantonments, where the commanding officer attributed all the evil to the inefficiency of the commissariat and the villany of the corn-dealers; and

Major Gregory was in dread of being torn to pieces by the soldiery. Only one day's supply was left in the cantonment bazaars—the troops had become clamorous almost to a state of mutiny—the people of the town began to rush in upon every supply that was offered for sale; and those who had grain to dispose of could no longer venture to expose it. The magistrate was hard pressed on all sides to have recourse to the old salutary method of searching for and forcibly opening the grain pits, and selling the contents at such price as might appear reasonable. The kotwāl[13] of the town declared that the lives of his police would be no longer safe unless this great and never-failing remedy, which had now unhappily been too long deferred, were immediately adopted.

The magistrate, who had already taken every other means of declaring his resolution never to suffer any man's granary to be forcibly opened, now issued a formal proclamation, pledging himself to see that such granaries should be as much respected as any other property in the city—that every man might keep his grain and expose it for sale, wherever and whenever he pleased; and expressing a hope that, as the people knew him too well not to feel assured that his word thus solemnly pledged would never be broken, he trusted they would sell what stores they had, and apply themselves without apprehension to the collecting of more.

This proclamation he showed to Major Gregory, assuring him that no degree of distress or clamour among the people of the city or the cantonments should ever make him violate the pledge therein given to the corn-dealers; and that he was prepared to risk his situation and reputation as a public officer upon the result. After issuing this proclamation about noon, he had his police establishments augmented, and so placed and employed as to give to the people entire confidence in the assurances conveyed in it. The grain-dealers, no longer apprehensive of danger, opened their pits of grain, and sent off all their available means to bring in more. In the morning the bazaars were all supplied, and every man who had money could buy as much as he pleased. The troops got as much as they required from the city. Major Gregory was astonished and delighted. The colonel, a fine old soldier from the banks of the Indus, who had commanded a corps of horse under the former government, came to the magistrate in amazement; every shop had become full of grain as if by supernatural agency.

'Kāle ādmī kī akl kahān talak chalēgī?' said he. 'How little could a black man's wisdom serve him in such an emergency?'

There was little wisdom in all this; but there was a firm reliance upon the truth of the general principle which should guide all public officers on such occasions. The magistrate judged that there were a great many pits of grain in the town known only to their own proprietors, who were afraid to open them, or get more grain, while there was a chance of the civil authorities yielding to the clamours of the people and the anxiety of the officers commanding the troops; and that he had only to remove these fears, by offering a solemn pledge, and manifesting the means and the will to abide by it, in order to induce the proprietors, not only to sell what they had, but to apply all their means to the collecting of more. But it is a singular fact that almost all the officers of the cantonments thought the conduct of the magistrate in refusing to have the grain pits opened under such pressing circumstances extremely reprehensible.

Had he done so, he might have given the people of the city and the cantonments the supply at hand; but the injury done to the corn- dealers by so very unwise a measure would have recoiled upon the public, since every one would have been discouraged from exerting himself to renew the supply, and from laying up stores to meet similar necessities in future. By acting as he did, he not only secured for the public the best exertions of all the existing corn- dealers of the place, but actually converted for the time a great many to that trade from other employments, or from idleness. A great many families, who had never traded before, employed their means in bringing a supply of grain, and converted their dwellings into corn shops, induced by the high profits and assurance of protection. During the time when he was most pressed the magistrate received a letter from Captain Robinson, who was in charge of the bazaars at Elichpur in the Hyderabad territory,[14] where the dearth had become even more felt than at Sāgar, requesting to know what measures had been adopted to regulate the price, and secure the supply of grain for the city and cantonments at Sāgar, since no good seemed to result from those hitherto pursued at Elichpur. He told him in reply that these things had hitherto been regulated at Sāgar as he thought 'they ought to be regulated everywhere else, by being left entirely to the discretion of the corn-dealers themselves, whose self-interest will always prompt them to have a sufficient supply, as long as they may feel secure of being permitted to do what they please with what they collect. The commanding officer, in his anxiety to secure food for the people, had hitherto been continually interfering to coerce sales and regulate prices, and continually aggravating the evils of the dearth by so doing'. On the receipt of the Sāgar magistrate's letter a different course was adopted; the same assurances were given to the corn-dealers, the same ability and inclination to enforce them manifested, and the same result followed. The people and the troops were steadily supplied; and all were astonished that so very simple a remedy had not before been thought of.

The ignorance of the first principles of political economy among European gentlemen of otherwise first-rate education and abilities in India is quite lamentable, for there are really few public officers, even in the army, who are not occasionally liable to be placed in the situations where they may, by false measures, arising out of such ignorance, aggravate the evils of dearth among great bodies of their fellow men. A soldier may, however, find some excuse for such ignorance, because a knowledge of these principles is not generally considered to form any indispensable part of a soldier's education; but no excuse can be admitted for a civil functionary who is so ignorant, since a thorough acquaintance with the principles of political economy must be, and, indeed, always is considered as an essential branch of that knowledge which is to fit him for public employment in India.[15]

In India unfavourable seasons produce much more disastrous consequences than in Europe. In England not more than one-fourth of the population derive their incomes from the cultivation of the lands around them. Three-fourths of the people have incomes independent of the annual returns from those lands; and with these incomes they can purchase agricultural produce from other lands when the crops upon them fail. The farmers, who form so large a portion of the fourth class, have stock equal in value to *four times the amount of the annual rent of their lands*. They have also a great variety of crops; and it is very rare that more than one or two of them fail, or are considerably affected, the same season. If they fail in one district or province, the deficiency is very easily supplied to a people who have equivalents to give for the produce of another. The sea, navigable rivers, fine roads, all are open and ready at all times for the transport of the superabundance of one quarter to supply the deficiencies of another. In India, the reverse of all this is unhappily to be found; more than three-fourths of the whole population are engaged in the cultivation of the land, and depend upon its annual returns for subsistence.[16] The farmers and cultivators have none of their stock equal in value to more than *half the amount of the annual rent of their lands*.[17] They have a great variety of crops; but all are exposed to the same accidents, and commonly fail at the same time. The autumn crops are sown in June and July, and ripen in October and November; and, if seasonable showers do not fall during July, August, and September, all fail. The spring crops are sown in October and November, and ripen in March; and, if seasonable showers do not happen to fall during December or January, all, save what are artificially irrigated, fail.[18] If they fail in one district or province, the people have few equivalents to offer for a supply of land produce from any other. Their roads are scarcely anywhere passable for wheeled carriages at *any season*, and nowhere *at all seasons* — they have nowhere a navigable canal, and only in one line a navigable river.

Their land produce is conveyed upon the backs of bullocks, that move at the rate of six or eight miles a day, and add one hundred per cent. to the cost of every hundred miles they carry it in the best seasons, and more than two hundred in the worst.[19] What in Europe is felt merely as a *dearth*, becomes in India, under all these disadvantages, a scarcity, and what is there a *scarcity* becomes here a *famine*. Tens of thousands die here of starvation, under calamities of season, which in Europe would involve little of suffering to any class. Here man does everything, and he must have his daily food or starve. In England machinery does more than three-fourths of the collective work of society in the production, preparation, and distribution of man's physical enjoyments, and it stands in no need of this daily food to sustain its powers; they are independent of the seasons; the water, fire, air, and other elemental powers which they require to render them subservient to our use are always available in abundance.

This machinery is the great assistant of the present generation, provided for us by the wisdom and industry of the past; wanting no food itself, it can always provide its proprietors with the means of purchasing what they require from other countries, when the harvests of their own fail. When calamities of season deprive men of employment for a time in tillage, they can, in England, commonly find it in other branches of industry, because agricultural industry forms so small a portion of the collective industry of the nation; and because every man can, without prejudice to his status in society, take to what branch of industry he pleases. But, when these calamities of season throw men out of employment in tillage for a time in India, they cannot find it in any other branch, because agricultural industry forms so very large a portion of the collective industry of every part of the country; and because men are often prevented by the prejudices of caste from taking to that which they can find.[20]

In societies constituted like that of India the trade of the corn-dealer is more essentially necessary for the welfare of the community than in any other, for it is among them that the superabundance of seasons of plenty requires most to be stored up for seasons of scarcity; and if public functionaries will take upon themselves to seize such stores, and sell them at their own arbitrary prices, whenever prices happen to rise beyond the rate which they in their short-sighted wisdom think just, no corn-dealer will ever collect such stores. Hitherto, whenever grain has become dear at any military or civil station, we have seen the civil functionaries urged to prohibit its egress—to search for the hidden stores, and to coerce the proprietors to the sale in all manner of ways; and, if they do not yield to the ignorant clamour, they are set down as indifferent to the sufferings of their fellow creatures around them, and as blindly supporting the worst enemies of mankind in the worst species of iniquity.

If those who urge them to such measures are asked whether silversmiths or linendrapers, who should be treated in the same manner as they wish the corn-dealers to be treated, would ever collect and keep stores of plate and cloth for their use, they readily answer — No; they see at once the evil effects of interfering with the free disposal of the property of the one, but are totally blind to that which must as surely follow any interference with that of the other, whose entire freedom is of so much more vital importance to the public. There was a time, and that not very remote, when grave historians, like Smollett, could, even in England, fan the flame of this vulgar prejudice against one of the most useful classes of society. That day is, thank God, past; and no man can now venture to write such trash in his history, or even utter it in any well-informed circle of English society; and, if any man were to broach such a subject in an English House of Commons, he would be considered as a fit subject for a madhouse.

But some, who retain their prejudices against corn-dealers, and are yet ashamed to acknowledge their ignorance of the first principles of political economy, try to persuade themselves and their friends that, however applicable these may be to the state of society in European or Christian countries, they are not so to countries occupied by Hindoos and Muhammadans. This is a sad delusion, and may be a very mischievous one, when indulged by public officers in India.[21]

Notes:

1. Irrigation by means of a 'dug-out' canoe used as a lever is commonly practised in many parts of the country. The author gives a rough sketch, not worth reproduction. The Persian wheel is suitable for use in wide-mouthed wells. It may be described as a mill-wheel with buckets on the circumference, which are filled and emptied as the wheel revolves. It is worked by bullock-power acting on a rude cog-wheel.

2. December, 1835.

3. A.D. 1833 corresponds to the year 1890 of the *Vikrama Samvat*, or era, current in Bundēlkhand. About 1880 the editor found this great famine still remembered as that of the year '90.

4. Half a crown seems to be used in this passage as a synonym for the rupee, now (1914) worth a shilling and four pence.

5. Bundēlkhand seems to be the meeting-place of the east and west monsoons, and the moist current is, in consequence, often feeble and variable. The country suffered again from famine in 1861 and 1877, although not so severely as in 1833. In northern Bundēlkhand a canal from the Betwa river has been constructed, but is of only very limited use. The peculiarities of the soil and climate forbid the wide extension of irrigation. For the

prevention of acute famine in this region the chief reliance must be on improved communications. The country has been opened up by the Indian Midland and other railways. In 1899-1900, notwithstanding improved communications, Mālwa suffered severely from famine. Aurangzēb considered Gujarāt to be 'the ornament and jewel of India' (Bilimoria, *Letters of Aurungzebie*, 1908, no. lxiv).

6. The influence of trees on climate is undoubted, but the author in this passage probably ascribes too much power to the groves of Mālwa. On the formation of the black soil see note 7 to Chapter 14, *ante*.

7. The word in the author's text is 'grain', a misprint for 'gram' (*Cicer arietinum*), a pulse, also known as chick-pea, and very largely grown in Bundēlkhand. 'Gram' is a corruption of the Portuguese word for grain, and, like many other Portuguese words, has passed into the speech of Anglo-Indians. See Yule and Burnell, *Glossary of Anglo-Indian Words*, s.v.

8. 'Agricultural capitalist' is a rather large phrase for the humble village money-lender, whose transactions are usually on a very small scale.

9. The author's advice on the subject of famine relief is weighty and perfectly sound. It is in accordance with the policy formulated by the Government of India in the Famine Relief Code, based on the Report of the Famine Commission which followed the terrible Madras famine of 1877.

10. This statement is too general. Examples of the horror alluded to are recorded in several Indian famines. Cases of cannibalism occurred during the Madras famine of 1877. But it is true that horrors of the kind are rare in India, and the author's praise of the patient resignation of the people is fully justified. An admirable summary of the history of Indian famines will be found in the articles 'Famines' and 'Food' in Balfour, *Cyclopaedia*, 3rd ed. (1885). For further and more recent information see *I.G.* (1907), vol. iii, chap. 10.

11. No European officer, military or civil, could now venture to adopt such arbitrary measures. In a Native State they might very probably be enforced.

12. 'The magistrate' was the author himself.

13. The chief police officer of a town. In the modern reorganized system he always holds the rank of either Inspector or Sub-Inspector. Under native governments he was a more important official.

14. Elichpur (Ilichpur) is in Berār, otherwise known as the Assigned Districts, a territory made over in Lord Dalhousie's time to British administration in order to defray the cost of the armed force called the Hyderabad Contingent. Since 1903 Berār has ceased to be a separate province. It is now merely a Division attached to the Central Provinces.

From the same date the Hyderabad Contingent lost its separate existence, being redistributed and merged in the Indian Army.

15. Political Economy was for many years a compulsory subject for the selected candidates for the Civil Service of India; but since 1892 its study has been optional.

16. The census of 1911 shows that about 71 per cent. of the 301,000,000 inhabiting India, excluding Burma, are supported by the cultivation of the soil and the care of cattle. The proportion varies widely in different provinces.

17. This proposition does not apply fully to Northern India at the present day. The amount of capital invested is small, although not quite so small as is stated in the text.

18. The times of harvest vary slightly with the latitude, being later towards the north. The cold-weather rains of December and January are variable and uncertain, and rarely last more than a few days. The spring crops depend largely on the heavy dews which occur daring the cold season.

19. Daring the years which have elapsed since the famine of 1833, great changes have taken place in India, and many of the author's remarks are only partially applicable to the present time. The great canals, above all, the wonderful Ganges Canal, have protected immense areas of Northern India from the possibility of absolute famine, and Southern India has also been to a considerable, though less, extent; protected by similar works. A few new staples, of which potatoes are the most important, have been introduced. The whole system of distribution has been revolutionized by the development of railways, metalled roads, wheeled vehicles, motors, telegraphs, and navigable canals. Carriage on the backs of animals, whether bullocks, camels, or donkeys, now plays a very subordinate part in the distribution of agricultural produce. Prices are, in great measure, dependent on the rates prevailing in Liverpool, Odessa, and Chicago. Food grains now stand ordinarily at prices which, in the author's time, would have been reckoned famine rates. The changes which have taken place in England are too familiar to need comment.

20. Since the author's time certain industries, the most important being cotton-pressing, cotton-spinning, and jute-spinning, have sprung up and assumed in Bombay, Calcutta, Cawnpore, and a few other places, proportions which, absolutely, are large. But India is so vast that these local developments of manufactures, large though they are, seem to be as nothing when regarded in comparison with the country as a whole. India is still, and, to all appearance, always must be, essentially an agricultural country.

21. The author's teaching concerning freedom of trade in times of famine and the function of dealers in corn is as sound as his doctrine of famine relief. The 'vulgar prejudice', which he denounces, still flourishes, and the 'sad delusion', which he deplores, still obscures the truth. As each period of scarcity or famine comes round, the old cries are again heard, and the executive authorities are implored and adjured to forbid export, to fix fair prices, and to clip the profits of the corn merchant. During the Bengal famine of 1873-4, the demand for the prohibition of the export of rice was urged by men who should have known better, and Lord Northbrook is entitled to no small credit for having firmly withstood the clamour. The more recent experiences of the Russian Government should be remembered when the clamour is again raised, as it will be. The principles on which the author acted in the crisis at Sāgar in 1833 should guide every magistrate who finds himself in a similar position, and should be applied with unhesitating firmness and decision.

CHAPTER 25

Epidemic Diseases — Scape-goat.

In the evening, after my conversation with the cultivator upon the wall that united the two hills,[1] I received a visit from my little friend the Sarīmant. His fine rose-coloured turban is always put on very gracefully; every hair of his jet-black eyebrows and mustachios seems to be kept always most religiously in the same place; and he has always the same charming smile upon his little face, which was never, I believe, distorted into an absolute laugh or frown. No man was ever more perfectly master of what the natives call 'the art of rising or sitting' (*nishisht wa barkhāst*), namely, good manners. I should as soon expect to see him set the Nerbudda on fire as commit any infringement of the *convenances* on this head established in good Indian society, or be guilty of anything vulgar in speech, sentiment, or manners. I asked him by what means it was that the old queen of Sāgar[2] drove out the influenza that afflicted the people so much in 1832, while he was there on a visit to me. He told me that he took no part in the ceremonies, nor was he aware of them till awoke one night by 'the noise, when his attendants informed him that the queen and the greater part of the city were making offerings to the new god, Hardaul Lāla. He found next morning that a goat had been offered up with as much noise as possible, and with good effect, for the disease was found to give way from that moment. About six years before, when great numbers were dying in his own little capital of Pithoria[3] from a similar epidemic, he had, he said, tried the same thing with still greater effect; but, on that occasion, he had the aid of a man very learned in such matters. This man caused a small carriage to be made up after a plan of his own, for *a pair of scape-goats*, which were harnessed to it, and driven during the ceremonies to a wood some distance from the town, where they were let loose. From that hour the disease entirely ceased in the town. The goats never returned. 'Had they come back,' said Sarīmant, 'the disease must have come back with them; so he took them a long way into the wood — indeed (he believed), the man, to make sure of them, had afterwards caused them to be offered up as a sacrifice to the shrine of Hardaul Lāla, in that very wood. He had himself never seen a *pūjā* (religious ceremony) so entirely and immediately efficacious as this, and much of its success was, no doubt, attributable to the *science* of the man who planned the carriage, and himself drove the pair of goats to the wood. No one had ever before heard of the plan of a pair of *scape- goats* being driven in a carriage; but it was likely (he thought) to be extensively adopted in future.'[4]

Sarīmant's man of affairs mentioned that when Lord Hastings took the field against the Pindhārīs, in 1817,[5] and the division of the grand army under his command was encamped near the grove in Bundēlkhand, where repose the ashes of Hardaul Lāla, under a small shrine, a cow was taken into this grove to be converted into beef for the use of the Europeans. The priest in attendance remonstrated, but in vain — the cow was killed and eaten. The priest complained, and from that day the cholera morbus broke out in the camp; and from this central point it was, he said, generally understood to have spread all over India.[6] The story of the cow travelled at the same time, and the spirit of Hardaul Lāla was everywhere supposed to be riding in the whirlwind, and *directing the storm*. Temples were everywhere erected, and offerings made to appease him; and in six years after, he had himself seen them as far as Lahore, and in almost every village throughout the whole course of his journey to that distant capital and back. He is one of the most sensible and freely spoken men that I have met with. 'Up to within the last few years', added he, 'the spirit of Hardaul Lāla had been propitiated only in cases of cholera morbus; but now he is supposed to preside over all kinds of epidemic diseases, and offerings have everywhere been made to his shrine during late influenzas.'[7]

'This of course arises', I observed, 'from the industry of his priests, who are now spread all over the country; and you know that there is hardly a village or hamlet in which there are not some of them to be found subsisting upon the fears of the people.'

'I have no doubt', replied he, 'that the cures which the people attribute to the spirit of Hardaul Lāla often arise merely from the firmness of their faith (*itikād*) in the efficacy of their offerings; and that any other ceremonies, that should give to their minds the same assurance of recovery, would be of great advantage in cases of epidemic diseases. I remember a singular instance of this,' said he. 'When Jeswant Rāo Holkar was flying before Lord Lake to the banks of the Hyphasis,[8] a poor trooper of one of his lordship's irregular corps, when he tied the grain-bag to his horse's mouth, said 'Take this in the name of Jeswant Rāo Holkar, for to him you and I owe all that we have.' The poor man had been suffering from an attack of ague and fever; but from that moment he felt himself relieved, and the fever never returned. At that time this fever prevailed more generally among the people of Hindustan than any I have ever known, though I am now an old man. The speech of the trooper and the supposed result soon spread; and others tried the experiment with similar success, and it acted everywhere like a charm. I had the fever myself, and, though by no means a superstitious man, and certainly no lover of Jeswant Rāo Holkar, I tried the experiment, and the fever left me from that day. From that time, till the epidemic disappeared, no man, from the Nerbudda to the Indus, fed his horse without invoking the spirit of Jeswant Rāo, though the chief was then alive and well. Some one had said he found great relief from plunging into the stream during the paroxysms of the fever; others followed the example, and some remained for half an hour at a time, and the sufferers generally found relief. The streams and tanks throughout the districts between the Ganges and Jumna became crowded, till the propitiatory offering to the spirit of the living Jeswant Rāo Holkar were [sic] found equally good, and far less troublesome to those who had horses that must have got their grain, whether in Holkar's name or not.'

There is no doubt that the great mass of those who had nothing but their horses and their *good blades* to depend upon for their subsistence did most fervently pray throughout India for the safety of this Marāthā chief, when he fled before Lord Lake's army; for they considered that, with his fall, the Company's dominion would become everywhere securely established, and that good soldiers would be at a discount. '*Company kē amal men kuchh rozgār nahin hai*,' — 'There is no employment in the Company's dominion,' is a common maxim, not only among the men of the sword and the spear, but among those merchants who lived by supporting native civil and military establishments with the luxuries and elegancies which, under the new order of things, they have no longer the means to enjoy.

The noisy *pūjā* (worship), about which our conversation began, took place at Sāgar in April, 1832, while I was at that station. More than four-fifths of the people of the city and cantonments had been affected by a violent influenza, which commenced with a distressing cough, was followed by fever, and, in some cases, terminated in death. I had an application from the old Queen Dowager of Sāgar, who received a pension of ten thousand pounds a year from the British Government,[9] and resided in the city, to allow of a *noisy* religious procession to implore deliverance from this great calamity. Men, women, and children in this procession were to do their utmost to add to the noise by 'raising their voices in *psalmody*', beating upon their brass pots and pans with all their might, and discharging fire-arms where they could get them; and before the noisy crowd was to be driven a buffalo, which had been purchased by a general subscription, in order that every family might participate in the merit. They were to follow it out for eight miles, where it was to be turned loose for any man who would take it. If the animal returned, the disease, it was said, must return with it, and the ceremony be performed over again. I was requested to intimate the circumstance to the officer commanding the troops in cantonments, in order that the hideous noise they intended to make might not excite any alarm, and bring down upon them the visit of the soldiery. It was, however, subsequently determined that the animal should be a goat, and he was driven before the crowd accordingly. I have on several occasions been requested to allow of such noisy *pūjās* in cases of epidemics; and the confidence they feel in their efficiency has, no doubt, a good effect.

While in civil charge of the district of Narsinghpur, in the valley of the Nerbudda, in April 1823, the cholera morbus raged in almost every house of Narsinghpur and Kandelī, situated near each other,[10] and one of them close to my dwelling-house and court. The European physicians lost all confidence in their prescriptions, and the people declared that the hand of God was upon them, and by appeasing Him could they alone hope to be saved.[11] A religious procession was determined upon; but the population of both towns was divided upon the point whether a silent or a noisy one would be most acceptable to God. Hundreds were dying around me when I was applied to to settle this knotty point between the parties. I found that both in point of numbers and respectability the majority was in favour of the silent procession, and I recommended that this should be adopted. The procession took place about nine the same night, with all due ceremony; but the advocates for noise would none of them assist in it. Strange as it may appear, the disease abated from that moment; and the great majority of the population of both towns believed that their prayers had been heard; and I went to bed with a mind somewhat relieved by the hope that this feeling of confidence might be useful. About one o'clock I was awoke from a sound sleep by the most hideous noise that I had ever heard; and, not at that moment recollecting the proposal for the noisy procession, ran out of my house, in expectation of seeing both towns in flames. I found that the advocates for noise, resolving to have their procession, had assembled together about midnight; and, apprehensive that they might be borne down by the advocates for silence and my police establishment, had determined to make the most of their time, and put in requisition all the pots, pans, shells, trumpets, pistols, and muskets that they could muster. All opened at once about one o'clock; and, had there been any virtue in discord, the cholera must soon have deserted the place, for such another hideous compound of noises I never heard. The disease, which seemed to have subsided with the silent procession before I went to bed, now returned with double violence, as I was assured by numbers who flocked to my house in terror; and the whole population became exasperated with the leaders of the noisy faction, who had, they believed, been the means of bringing back among them all the horrors of this dreadful scourge.

I asked the Hindoo Sadar Amīn, or head native judicial officer at Sāgar, a very profound Sanskrit scholar, what he thought of the efficacy of these processions in checking epidemic diseases. He said that 'there could be nothing more clear than the total inefficiency of medicine in such cases; and, when medicine failed, a man's only resource was in prayers; that the diseases of mankind were to be classed under three general heads: first, those suffered for sins committed in some former births; second, those suffered for sins committed in the present birth; third, those merely accidental. Now,' said the old gentleman, 'it must be clear to every unprejudiced mind that the third only can be cured or checked by the physician.' Epidemics, he thought, must all be classed under the second head, and as inflicted by the Deity for some very general sin; consequently, to be removed only by prayers; and, whether silent or noisy, was, he thought, matter of little importance, provided they were offered in the same spirit. I believe that, among the great mass of the people of India, three-fourths of the diseases of individuals are attributed to evil spirits and evil eyes; and for every physician among them there are certainly ten *exorcisers*. The faith in them is very great and very general; and, as the gift is supposed to be supernatural, it is commonly exercised without fee or reward. The gifted person subsists upon some other employment, and *exorcises* gratis.

A child of one of our servants was one day in convulsions from its sufferings in cutting its teeth. The Civil Surgeon happened to call that morning, and he offered to lance the child's gums. The poor mother thanked him, but stated that there could be no possible doubt as to the source of her child's sufferings — that the devil had got into it during the night, and would certainly not be frightened out by his little lancet; but she expected every moment my old tent- pitcher, whose exorcisms no devil of this description had ever yet been able to withstand.

The small-pox had been raging in the town of Jubbulpore for some time during one hot season that I was there, and a great many children had died from it. The severity of the disease was considered to have been a good deal augmented by a very untoward circumstance that had taken place in the family of the principal banker of the town, Khushhāl Chand. Sēwā Rām Sēth, the old man, had lately died, leaving two sons. Ram Kishan, the eldest, and Khushhāl Chand, the second. The eldest gave up all the management of the sublunary concerns of the family, and devoted his mind entirely to religious duties. They had a very fine family temple of their own, in which they placed an image of their god Vishnu, cut out of the choicest stone of the Nerbudda, and consecrated after the most approved form, and with very expensive ceremonies. This idol Rām Kishan used every day to wash with his own hands with rosewater, and anoint with precious ointments. One day, while he had the image in his arms, and was busily employed in anointing it, it fell to the ground upon the stone pavement, and one of the arms was broken. To live after such an untoward accident was quite out of the question, and poor Rām Kishan proceeded at once quietly to hang himself. He got a rope from the stable, and having tied it over the beam in the room where he had let the god fall upon the stone pavement, he was putting his head calmly into the noose, when his brother came in, laid hold of him, called for assistance, and put him under restraint. A conclave of the priests of that sect was immediately held in the town, and Rām Kishan was told that hanging himself was not absolutely necessary; that it might do if he would take the stone image, broken arm and all, upon his own back, and carry it two hundred and sixty miles to Benares, where resided the high priest of the sect, who would, no doubt, be able to suggest the proper measures for pacifying the god.

At this time, the only son of his brother, Khushhāl Chand, an interesting little boy of about four years of age, was extremely ill of the small-pox; and it is a rule with Hindoos never to undertake any journey, even one of pilgrimage to a holy shrine, while any member of the family is afflicted with this disease; they must all sit at home clothed in sackcloth and ashes. He was told that he had better defer his journey to Benares till the child should recover; but he could neither sleep nor eat, so great was his terror, lest some dreadful calamity should befall the whole family before he could expiate his crime, or take the advice of his high priest as to the best means of doing it: and he resolved to leave the decision of the question to God Himself. He took two pieces of paper, and having caused Benares to be written upon one, and Jubbulpore upon the other, he put them both into a brass vessel. After shaking the vessel well, he drew forth that on which Benares had been written. 'It is the will of God,' said Rām Kishan. All the family, who were interested in the preservation of the poor boy, implored him not to set out, lest Dēvī, who presides over small-pox, should become angry. It was all in vain. He would set out with his household god; and, unable to carry it himself, he put it into a small litter upon a pole, and hired a bearer to carry it at one end, while he supported it at the other. His brother, Khushhāl Chand, sent his second wife at the same time with offerings for Dēvī, to ward off the effects of his brother's rashness from his child. By the time the brother had got with his god to Adhartāl, three miles from Jubbulpore, on the road to Benares, he heard of the death of his nephew; but he seemed not to feel this slight blow in his terror of the dreadful but undefined calamity which he felt to be impending over him and the whole family, and he trotted on his road. Soon after, an infant son of their uncle died of the same disease; and the whole town became at once divided into two parties—those who held that the children had been killed by Dēvī as a punishment for Rām Kishan's presuming to leave Jubbulpore before they recovered; and those who held that they were killed by the god Vishnu himself, for having been so rudely deprived of one of his arms. Khushhāl Chand's wife sickened on the road, and died on reaching Mirzapore, of fever; and, as Dēvī was supposed to have nothing to do with fevers, this event greatly augmented the advocates of Vishnu. It is a rule with the Hindoos to bury, and not to burn, the bodies of those who die of the small-pox; 'for', say they, 'the small-pox is not only caused by the goddess Dēvī, but is, in fact, *Dēvī herself*, and to burn the body of the person affected with this disease is, in reality, neither more nor less than *to burn the goddess*'.

Khushhāl Chand was strongly urged to bury, and not burn, his child, particularly as it was usual with Hindoos to bury infants and children of that age, of whatever disease they might die; but he insisted upon having his boy burned with all due pomp and ceremony, and burned he was accordingly. From that moment, it is said, the disease began to rage with increased violence throughout the town of Jubbulpore. At least one-half of the children affected had before survived; but, from that hour, at least three out of four died; and, instead of the condolence which he expected from his fellow citizens, poor Khushhāl Chand, a very amiable and worthy man, received nothing but their execrations for bringing down so many calamities upon their heads; first, by maltreating his own god, and then by setting fire to theirs.

I had, a few days after, a visit from Gangādhar Rāo, the Sadar Amīn, or head native judicial officer of this district, whose father had been for a short time the ruler of the district, under the former government; and I asked him whether the small-pox had diminished in the town since the rains had now set in. He told me that he thought it had, but that a great many children had been taken off by the disease.[12]

'I understand, Rāo Sahib, that Khushhāl Chand, the banker, is supposed to have augmented the virulence of the disease by burning his boy; was it so?'

'Certainly,' said my friend, with a grave, long face; 'the disease was much increased by this man's folly.' I looked very grave in my turn, and he continued:- 'Not a child escaped after he had burned his boy. Such incredible folly! To set fire to the *goddess* in the midst of a population of twenty thousand souls; it might have brought destruction on us all!'

'What makes you think that the disease is itself the goddess?'

'Because we always say, when any member of a family becomes attacked by the small-pox, "*Dēvī nikalī*", that is, Dēvī has shown herself in that family, or in that individual. And the person affected can wear nothing but plain white clothing, not a silken or coloured garment, nor an ornament of any kind; nor can he or any of his family undertake a journey, or participate in any kind of rejoicings, lest he give offence to her. They broke the arm of their god, and he drove them all mad.[13] The elder brother set out on a journey with it, and his nephew, cousin, and sister-in-law fell victims to his temerity; and then Khushhāl Chand brings down the goddess upon the whole community by burning his boy![14] No doubt he was very fond of his child — so we all are — and wished to do him all honour; but some regard is surely due to the people around us, and I told him so when he was making preparations for the funeral; but he would not listen to reason.'

A complicated religious code, like that of the Hindoos, is to the priest what a complicated civil code, like that of the English, is to the lawyers. A Hindoo can do nothing without consulting his priest, and an Englishman can do nothing without consulting his lawyer.

Notes:

1. *Ante*, Chapter 24, following note [4].

2. Sāgar was ceded by the Peshwa in 1818, and a yearly sum of two and a half lakhs of rupees was allotted by Government for pensions to Rukmā Bāī, Vināyak Rāo, and the other officers of the Marāthā Government. A descendant of Rukmā Bāī continued for many years to enjoy a pension of R.10,000 per annum (*C.P. Gazetteer* (1870), p, 442). The lady referred to in the text seems to be Rukmā Bāī.

3. A village about twenty miles north-west of Sāgar. The estate consists of twenty-six revenue-free villages.

4. The Jewish ceremonial is described in Leviticus xvi. 20-26. After completing the atonement for the impurities of the holy place, the tabernacle, and the altar, Aaron was directed to lay 'his hands upon the head of the live goat', so putting all the sins of the people upon the animal, and then to 'send him away by the hand of a fit man into the wilderness; and the goat shall bear upon him all their iniquities unto a land not inhabited: and he shall let go the goat in the wilderness'. The subject of scape-goats is discussed at length and copiously illustrated by Mr. Frazer in *The Golden Bough*, 1st ed., vol. ii, section 15, pp. 182-217; 3rd ed. (1913) Part VI. The author's stories in the text are quoted by Mr. Frazer.

5. During the season of 1816-17 the ravages of the Pindhārīs were exceptionally daring and extensive. The Governor-General, the Marquis of Hastings, organized an army in several divisions to crush the marauders,

and himself joined the central division in October 1817. The operations were ended by the capture of Asīrgarh in March 1819.

6. The people in the Sāgar territories used to show several decayed mango-trees in groves where European troops had encamped during the campaigns of 1816 and 1817, and declared that they had been seen to wither from the day that beef for the use of these troops had been tied to their branches. The only coincidence was in the decay of the trees, and the encamping of the troops in the groves; that the withering trees were those to which the beef had been tied was of course taken for granted. [W. H. S.] The Hindoo veneration for the cow amounts to a passion, and its intensity is very inadequately explained by the current utilitarian explanations. The best analysis of the motives underlying the passionate Hindoo feeling on the subject is to be found in Mr. William Crooke's article 'The Veneration of the Cow in India' (*Folklore*, Sept. 1912, pp. 275-306). In modern times an active, though absolutely hopeless, agitation has been kept up, directed against the reasonable liberty of those communities in India who are not members of the Hindoo system. This agitation for the prohibition of cow-killing has caused some riots, and has evoked much ill-feeling. The editor had to deal with it in the Muzaffarnagar district in 1890, and had much trouble to keep the peace. The local leaders of the movement went so far as to send telegrams direct to the Government of India. Many other magistrates have had similar experiences. The authorities take every precaution to protect Hindoo susceptibilities from needless wounds, but they are equally bound to defend the lawful liberty of subjects who are not Hindoos. The Government of the United Provinces on one occasion yielded to the Hindoo demands so far as to prohibit cow- killing in at least one town where the practice was not fully established, but the legality and expediency of such an order are both open to criticism. The administrative difficulty is much enhanced by the fact that the Indian Muhammadans profess to be under a religious obligation to sacrifice cows at the Īdul Bakr festival. Cholera has been known to exist in India at least since the seventeenth century (Balfour, *Cyclopaedia of India*, 3rd ed. (1885), s.v.).

7. The cultus of Hardaul is further discussed *post* in Chapter 31. In 1875, the editor, who was then employed in the Hamīrpur district of Bundēlkhand, published some popular Hindi songs in praise of the hero, with the following abstract of the *Legend of Hardaul*: 'Hardaul, a son of the famous Bīr Singh Deo Bundēla of Orchhā, was born at Datiyā. His brother, Jhajhār Singh, suspected him of undue intimacy with his wife, and at a feast poisoned him with all his followers. After this tragedy, it happened that the daughter of Kunjāvatī, the sister of Jhajhār and Hardaul, was about to be married. Kunjāvatī accordingly sent an invitation to Jhajhār Singh,

requesting him to attend the wedding. He refused, and mockingly replied that she had better invite her favourite brother Hardaul. Thereupon she went in despair to his tomb and lamented aloud. Hardaul from below answered her cries, and said that he would come to the wedding and make all arrangements. The ghost kept his promise, and arranged the nuptials as befitted the honour of his house. Subsequently, he visited at night the bedside of Akbar, and besought the emperor to command *chabūtras* to be erected and honour paid to him in every village throughout the empire, promising that, if he were duly honoured, a wedding should never be marred by storm or rain, and that no one who first presented a share of his meal to Hardaul should ever want for food. Akbar complied with these requests, and since that time Hardaul's ghost has been worshipped in every village. He is chiefly honoured at weddings and in Baisākh (April-May), during which month the women, especially those of the lower castes, visit his *chabūtra* and eat there. His chabūtra is always built outside the village. On the day but one before the arrival of a wedding procession, the women of the family worship the gods and Hardaul, and invite them to the wedding. If any signs of a storm appears, Hardaul is propitiated with songs '(*J.A.S.B.*, vol. xliv (1875), Part I, p. 389). The belief that Hardaul worship and cholera had been introduced at the same time prevailed in Hamīrpur, as elsewhere. The *chabūtra* referred to in the above extract is a small platform built of mud or masonry.

8. The Hyphasis is the Greek name for the river Biās in the Panjāb. Holkar's flight into the Panjāb occurred in 1805, and in the same year the long war with him was terminated by a treaty, much too favourable to the marauding chief. He became insane a few years later, and died in 1811.

9. See note 2, *ante.*

10. Narsinghpur and Kandelī are practically one town. The Government offices and houses of the European residents are in Kandelī, which is a mile east of Narsinghpur. The original name of Narsinghpur was Gadariā Khērā. The modern name is due to the erection of a large temple to Narsingha, one of the forms of Vishnu. The district of Narsinghpur lies in the Nerbudda valley, west and south-west of Jubbulpore.

11. All classes of Indians still frequently refuse to employ any medicines in cases of either cholera or small-pox, supposing that the attempt to use ordinary human means is an insult to, and a defiance of, the Deity.

12. Vaccination was not practised in India in those days. The practice of it, although still unpopular in most places, has extended sufficiently to check greatly the ravages of small-pox. In many municipal towns vaccination is compulsory.

13. *Quem deus vult perdere, prius dementat.*

14. The judge cleverly combines the opinions of the adherents of both sects.

CHAPTER 26

Artificial Lakes in Bundēlkhand — Hindoo, Greek, and Roman Faith.

On the 11th[1] we came on twelve miles to the town of Bamhaurī, whence extends to the south-west a ridge of high and bare quartz hills, towering above all others, curling and foaming at the top, like a wave ready to burst, when suddenly arrested by the hand of Omnipotence, and turned into white stone. The soil all the way is wretchedly poor in quality, being formed of the detritus of syenitic and quartz rocks, and very thin. Bamhaurī is a nice little town,[2] beautifully situated on the bank of a fine lake, the waters of which preserved during the late famine the population of this and six other small towns, which are situated near its borders, and have their lands irrigated from it. Besides water for their fields, this lake yielded the people abundance of water-chestnuts[3] and fish. In the driest season the water has been found sufficient to supply the wants of all the people of those towns and villages, and those of all the country around, as far as the people can avail themselves of it.

This large lake is formed by an artificial bank or wall at the south-east end, which rests one arm upon the high range of quartz rocks, which run along its south-west side for several miles, looking down into the clear deep water, and forming a beautiful landscape.

From this pretty town, Ludhaura, where the great marriage had lately taken place, was in sight, and only four miles distant.[4] It was, I learnt, the residence of the present Rājā of Orchhā, before the death of his brother called him to the throne. Many people were returning from the ceremonies of the marriage of 'sālagrām' with 'Tulasī'; who told me that the concourse had been immense — at least one hundred and fifty thousand; and that the Rājā had feasted them all for four days during the progress of the ceremonies, but that they were obliged to defray their expenses going and coming, except when they came by special invitation to do honour to the occasion, as in the case of my little friend the Sāgar high priest, Jānkī Sewak. They told me that they called this festival the 'Dhanuk jag';[5] and that Janakrāj, the father of Sītā, had in his possession the 'dhanuk', or immortal bow of Parasrām, the sixth incarnation of Vishnu, with which he exterminated all the Kshatriyas, or original military class of India, and which required no less than four thousand men to raise it on one end.[6] The prince offered his daughter in marriage to any man who should bend this bow. Hundreds of heroes and demigods aspired to the hand of the fair Sītā, and essayed to bend the bow; but all in vain, till young Rām, the seventh incarnation of Vishnu,[7] then a lad of only ten years of age, came; and at the touch of his great toe the bow flew into a thousand pieces, which are supposed to have been all taken up into heaven. Sītā became the wife of Rām; and the popular poem of the Rāmāyana describes the abduction of the heroine by the monster king of Ceylon, Rāvana, and her recovery by means of the monkey general Hanumān. Every word of this poem, the people assured me, was written, if not by the hand of the Deity himself, at least by his inspiration, which was the same thing, and it must, consequently, be true. [8] Ninety-nine out of a hundred among the Hindoos implicitly believe, not only every word of this poem, but every word of every poem that has ever been written in Sanskrit. If you ask a man whether he really believes any very egregious absurdity quoted from these books, he replies with the greatest *naïveté* in the world, 'Is it not written in the book; and how should it be there written if not true?' The Hindoo religion reposes upon an entire prostration of mind, that continual and habitual surrender of the reasoning faculties, which we are accustomed to make occasionally. While engaged at the theatre, or in the perusal of works of fiction, we allow the scenes, characters, and incidents to pass before 'our mind's eye', and move our feelings, without asking, or stopping a moment to ask, whether they are real or true. There is only this difference that, with people of education among us, even in such short intervals of illusion or abandon, any extravagance in acting, or flagrant improbability in the fiction, destroys the charm, breaks the spell by which we have been so mysteriously bound, stops the smooth current of sympathetic emotion, and restores us to reason and to the realities of ordinary life. With the Hindoos, on the contrary, the greater the improbability, the more monstrous and preposterous the fiction, the greater is the charm it has over their minds;[9] and the greater their learning in the Sanskrit the more are they under the influence of this charm. Believing all to be written by the Deity, or by his inspiration, and the men and things of former days to have been very different from the men and things of the present day, and the heroes of these fables to have been demigods, or people endowed with powers far superior to those of the ordinary men of their own day, the analogies of nature are never for a moment considered; nor do questions of probability, or possibility, according to those analogies, ever obtrude to dispel the charm with which they are so pleasingly bound. They go on through life reading and talking of these monstrous fictions, which shock the taste and understanding of other nations, without once questioning the truth of one single incident, or hearing it questioned. There was a time, and that not very distant, when it was the same in England, and in every other European nation; and there are, I am afraid, some parts of Europe where it is so still. But the Hindoo faith, so far as religious questions are concerned, is not more capacious or absurd than that of the Greeks and Romans in the days of Socrates and Cicero—the only difference is, that among the Hindoos a greater number of the questions which interest mankind are brought under the head of religion.

There is nothing in the Hindoos more absurd than the *piety* of Tiberius in offering up sacrifices in the temple, and before the image of Augustus; while he was solicited by all the great cities of the empire to suffer temples to be built and sacrifices to be made to himself while still living; or than Alexander's attempt to make a goddess of his mother while yet alive, that he might feel the more secure of being made a god himself after his death.[10] In all religions there are points at which the professors declare that reason must stop, and cease to be a guide to faith. The pious man thinks that all which he cannot comprehend or reconcile to reason in his own religion must be above it. The superstitions of the people of India will diminish before the spread of science, art, and literature; and good works of history and fiction would, I think, make far greater havoc among these superstitions even than good works in any of the sciences, save the physical, such as astronomy, chemistry, &c.[11]

In the evening we went out with the intention of making an excursion of the lake, in boats that had been prepared for our reception by tying three or four fishing canoes together;[12] but, on reaching the ridge of quartz hills which runs along the south-east side, we preferred moving along its summit to entering the boats. The prospect on either side of this ridge was truly beautiful. A noble sheet of clear water, about four miles long by two broad, on our right; and on our left a no less noble sheet of rich wheat cultivation, irrigated from the lake by drains passing between small breaks in the ridges of the hills. The Persian wheel is used to raise the water.[13] This sheet of rich cultivation is beautifully studded with mango groves and fields of sugar-cane. The lake is almost double the size of that of Sāgar, and the idea of its great utility for purposes of irrigation made it appear to me far more beautiful; but my little friend the Sarīmant, who accompanied us in our walk, said that 'it could not be so handsome, since it had not a fine city and castle on two sides, and a fine Government house on the third'.

'But', said I, 'no man's field is watered from that lake.'

'No', replied he, 'but for every man that drinks of the waters of this, fifty drink of the waters of that; from that lake thirty thousand people get *ārām* (comfort) every day.'

This lake is called Kēwlas after Kēwal Varmma, the Chandēl prince by whom it was formed.[14] His palace, now in ruins, stood on the top of the ridge of rocks in a very beautiful situation. From the summit, about eight miles to the west, we could see a still larger lake, called the Nandanvārā Lake, extending under a similar range of quartz hills running parallel with that on which we stood.[15] That lake, we were told, answered upon a much larger scale the same admirable purpose of supplying water for the fields, and securing the people from the dreadful effects of droughts. The extensive level plains through which the rivers of Central India[16] generally cut their way have, for the most part, been the beds of immense natural lakes;[17] and there rivers sink so deep into their beds, and leave such ghastly chasms and ravines on either side, that their waters are hardly ever available in due season for irrigation. It is this characteristic of the rivers of Central India that makes such lakes so valuable to the people, particularly in seasons of drought.[18] The river Nerbudda has been known to rise seventy feet in the course of a couple of days in the rains; and, during the season when its waters are wanted for irrigation, they can nowhere be found within that [distance] of the surface; while a level piece of ground fit for irrigation is rarely to be met with within a mile of the stream.[19]

The people appeared to improve as we advanced farther into Bundēlkhand in appearance, manners, and intelligence. There is a bold bearing about the Bundēlas, which at first one is apt to take for rudeness or impudence, but which in time he finds not to be so.

The employés of the Rājā were everywhere attentive, frank, and polite; and the peasantry seemed no longer inferior to those of our Sāgar and Nerbudda territories. The females of almost all the villages through which we passed came out with their *Kalas* in procession to meet us — one of the most affecting marks of respect from the peasantry for their superiors that I know. One woman carries on her head a brass jug, brightly polished, full of water; while all the other families of the village crowd around her, and sing in chorus some rural song, that lasts from the time the respected visitor comes in sight till he disappears. He usually puts into the Kalas a rupee to purchase 'gur' (coarse sugar), of which all the females partake, as a sacred offering to the sex. No member of the other sex presumes to partake of it, and during the chorus all the men stand aloof in respectful silence. This custom prevails all over India, or over all parts of it that I have seen; and yet I have witnessed a Governor-General of India, with all his suite, passing by this interesting group, without knowing or asking what it was. I lingered behind, and quietly put my silver into the jug, as if from the Governor-General.[20]

The man who administers the government over these seven villages in all its branches, civil, criminal, and fiscal, receives a salary of only two hundred rupees a year. He collects the revenues on the part of Government; and, with the assistance of the heads and the elders of the villages, adjusts all petty matters of dispute among the people, both civil and criminal. Disputes of a more serious character are sent to be adjusted at the capital by the Rājā and his ministers. The person who reigns over the seven villages of the lake is about thirty years of age, of the Rājpūt caste, and, I think, one of the finest young men I have ever seen. His ancestors have served the Orchhā State in the same station for seven generations; and he tells me that he hopes his posterity will serve them [sic] for as many more, provided they do not forfeit their claims to do so by their infidelity or incapacity. This young man seemed to have the respect and affection of every member of the little communities of the villages through which we passed, and it was evident that he deserved their attachment. I have rarely seen any similar signs of attachment to one of our own native officers. This arises chiefly from the circumstance of their being less frequently placed in authority among those upon whose good feelings and opinions their welfare and comfort, as those of their children, are likely permanently to depend. In India, under native rule, office became hereditary, because officers expended the whole of their incomes in religious ceremonies, or works of ornament and utility, and left their families in hopeless dependence upon the chief in whose service they had laboured all their lives, while they had been educating their sons exclusively with the view of serving that chief in the same capacity that their fathers had served him before them. It is in this case, and this alone, that the law of primogeniture is in force in India.[21] Among Muhammadans, as well as Hindoos, all property, real and personal, is divided equally among the children;[22] but the duties of an office will not admit of the same subdivision; and this, therefore, when hereditary, as it often is, descends to the eldest son with the obligation of providing for the rest of the family. The family consists of all the members who remain united to the parent stock, including the widows and orphans of the sons or brothers who were so up to the time of their death.[23]

The old 'chobdār', or silver-stick bearer, who came with us from the Rājā, gets fifteen rupees a month, and his ancestors have served the Rājā for several generations. The Dīwān, who has charge of the treasury, receives only one thousand rupees a year, and the Bakshī, or paymaster of the army, who seems at present to rule the state as the prime favourite, the same. These latter are at present the only two great officers of state; and, though they are, no doubt, realizing handsome incomes by indirect means, they dare not make any display, lest signs of wealth might induce the Rājā or his successors to treat them as their predecessors in office were treated for some time past.[24] The Jāgīrdārs, or feudal chiefs, as I have before stated, are almost all of the same family or class as the Rājā, and they spend all the revenues of their estates in the maintenance of military retainers, upon whose courage and fidelity they can generally rely. These Jāgīrdārs are bound to attend the prince on all great occasions, and at certain intervals; and are made to contribute something to his exchequer in tribute. Almost all live beyond their legitimate means, and make up the deficiency by maintaining upon their estates gangs of thieves, robbers, and murderers, who extend their depredations into the country around, and share the prey with these chiefs, and their officers and under-tenants. They keep them as *poachers* keep their *dogs*; and the paramount power, whose subjects they plunder, might as well ask them for the best horse in the stable as for the best thief that lives under their protection.[25]

I should mention an incident that occurred during the Rājā's visit to me at Tehrī. Lieutenant Thomas was sitting next to the little Sarīmant, and during the interview he asked him to allow him to look at his beautiful little gold-hilted sword. The Sarīmant held it fast, and told him that he should do himself the honour of waiting upon him in his tent in the course of the day, when he would show him the sword and tell him its history. After the Rājā, left me, Thomas mentioned this, and said he felt very much hurt at the incivility of my little friend; but I told him that he was in everything he did and said so perfectly the gentleman, that I felt quite sure he would explain all to his satisfaction when he called upon him. During his visit to Thomas he apologized for not having given over his sword to him, and said, 'You European gentlemen have such perfect confidence in each other, that you can, at all times, and in all situations, venture to gratify your curiosity in these matters, and draw your swords in a crowd just as well as when alone; but, had you drawn mine from the scabbard in such a situation, with the tent full of the Rājā's personal attendants, and surrounded by a devoted and not very orderly soldiery, it might have been attended by very serious consequences. Any man outside might have seen the blade gloaming, and, not observing distinctly why it had been drawn, might have suspected treachery, and called out "To the rescue", when we should all have been cut down—the lady, child, and all.' Thomas was not only satisfied with the Sarīmant's apology, but was so much delighted with him, that he has ever since been longing to get his portrait; for he says it was really his intention to draw the sword had the Sarīmant given it to him. As I have said, his face is extremely beautiful, quite a model for a painter or a statuary, and his figure, though small, is handsome. He dresses with great elegance, mostly in azure-coloured satin, surmounted by a rose- coloured turban and a waistband of the same colour. All his motions are graceful, and his manners have an exquisite polish. A greater master of all the *convenances* I have never seen, though he is of slender capacity, and, as I have said, in stature less than five feet high.

A poor, half-naked man, reduced to beggary by the late famine, ran along by my horse to show me the road, and, to the great amusement of my attendants, exclaimed that he felt exactly as if he were always falling down a well, meaning as if he were immersed in cold water. He said that the cold season was suited only to gentlemen who could afford to be well clothed; but, to a poor man like himself, and the great mass of people, in Bundēlkhand at least, the hot season was much better. He told me that 'the late Rājā, though a harsh, was thought to be a just man;[26] and that his good sense, and, above all, his *good fortune* (ikbāl) had preserved the principality entire; but that God only, and the forbearance of the Honourable Company, could now serve it under such an imbecile as the present chief'. He seemed quite melancholy at the thought of living to see this principality, the oldest in Bundēlkhand, lose its independence. Even this poor, unclothed, and starving wretch had a feeling of patriotism, a pride of country, though that country had been so wretchedly governed, and was now desolated by a famine.

Just such a feeling had the impressed seamen who fought our battles in the great struggle. No nation has ever had a more disgraceful institution than that of the press-gang of England. This institution, if so it can be called, must be an eternal stain upon her glory—posterity will never be able to read the history of her naval victories without a blush—without reproaching her lawgivers who could allow them to be purchased with the blood of such men as those who fought for us the battles of the Nile and Trafalgar. *'England expected every man to do his duty'* on that day, but had England done her duty to every man who was on that day to fight for her? Was not every English gentleman of the Lords and Commons a David sending his Uriah to battle?[27]

The intellectual stock which we require in good seamen for our navy, and which is acquired in scenes of peril 'upon the high and giddy mast', is as much their property as that which other men acquire in schools and colleges; and we had no more right to seize and employ these seamen in our battles upon the wages of common, uninstructed labour, than we should have had to seize and employ as many clergymen, barristers, and physicians. When I have stood on the quarter-deck of a ship in a storm, and seen the seamen covering the yards in taking in sail, with the thunder rolling, and the lightning flashing fearfully around them—the sea covered with foam, and each succeeding billow, as it rushed by, seeming ready to sweep them all from their frail footing into the fathomless abyss below—I have asked myself, 'Are men like these to be seized like common felons, torn from their wives and children as soon as they reach their native land, subject every day to the lash, and put in front of those battles on which the wealth, the honour, and the independence of the nation depend, merely because British legislators know that when there, a regard for their own personal character among their companions in danger will make them fight like Englishmen?'

This feeling of nationality which exists in the little states of Bundēlkhand, arises from the circumstance that the mass of the landholders are of the same class as the chief Bundēlas; and that the public establishments of the state are recruited almost exclusively from that mass. The states of Jhānsī[28] and Jālaun[29] are the only exceptions. There the rulers are Brahmans and not Rājpūts, and they recruit their public establishments from all classes and all countries. The landed aristocracy, however, there, as elsewhere, are Rājpūts- either Pawārs, Chandēls, or Bundēlas.

The Rājpūt landholders of Bundēlkhand are linked to the soil in all their grades, from the prince to the peasant, as the Highlanders of Scotland were not long ago; and the holder of a hundred acres is as proud as the holder of a million.[30] He boasts the same descent, and the same exclusive possession of arms and agriculture, to which unhappily the industry of their little territories is almost exclusively confined, for no other branch can grow up among so turbulent a set, whose quarrels with their chiefs, or among each other, are constantly involving them in civil wars, which render life and property exceedingly insecure. Besides, as I have stated, their propensity to keep bands of thieves, robbers, and murderers in their baronial castles, as poachers keep their dogs, has scared away the wealthy and respectable capitalist and peaceful and industrious manufacturer.

All the landholders are uneducated, and unfit to serve in any of our civil establishments, or in those of any very civilized Governments; and they are just as unfitted to serve in our military establishments, where strict discipline is required. The lands they occupy are cultivated because they depend almost entirely upon the rents they get from them for subsistence; and because every petty chief and his family hold their lands rent-free, or at a trifling quit-rent, on the tenure of military service, and their residue forms all the market for land produce which the cultivators require. They dread the transfer of the rule to our Government, because they now form almost exclusively all the establishments of their domestic chief, civil as well as military; and know that, were our rule to be substituted, they would be almost entirely excluded from these, at least for a generation or two. In our regiments, horse or foot, there is hardly a man from Bundēlkhand, for the reasons above stated; nor are there any in the Gwālior regiments and contingents which are stationed in the neighbourhood; though the land among them is become minutely subdivided, and they are obliged to seek service or starve. They are all too proud for manual labour, even at the plough. No Bundēlkhand Rājpūt will, I believe, condescend to put his hand to one.

Among the Marāthā states, Sikhs, and Muhammadans, there is no bond of union of this kind. The establishments, military as well as civil, are everywhere among them composed for the most part of foreigners; and the landed interests under such Governments would dread nothing from the prospect of a transfer to our rule; on the contrary, they and the mass of the people would almost everywhere hail it as a blessing.

There are two reasons why we should leave these small native states under their own chiefs, even when the claim to the succession is feeble or defective; first, because it tends to relieve the minds of other native chiefs from the apprehension, already too prevalent among them, that we desire by degrees to absorb them all, because we think our government would do better for the people; and secondly, because, by leaving them as a contrast, we afford to the people of India the opportunity of observing the superior advantages of our rule.

'Tis distance lends enchantment to the view,' in governments as well as in landscapes; and if the people of India, instead of the living proofs of what perilous things native governments, whether Hindoo or Muhammadan, are in reality, were acquainted with nothing but such pictures of them as are to be found in their histories and in the imaginations of their priests and learned men (who lose much of their influence and importance under our rule), they would certainly, with proneness like theirs to delight in the marvellous, be far from satisfied, as they now are, that they never had a government so good as ours, and that they never could hope for another so good, were ours removed.[31]

For the advantages which we derive from leaving them independent, we are, no doubt, obliged to pay a heavy penalty in the plunder of our wealthy native subjects by the gangs of robbers of all descriptions whom they foster; but this evil may be greatly diminished by a judicious interposition of our authority to put down such bands.[32]

In Bundēlkhand, at present, the government and the lands of the native chiefs are in the hands of three of the Hindoo military classes, Bundēlas, Dhandēlas, and Pawārs. The principal chiefs are of the first, and their feudatories are chiefly of the other two. A Bundēla cannot marry the daughter of a Bundēla; he must take his wife from one or other of the other two tribes; nor can a member of either of the other two take his wife from his own tribe; he must take her from the Bundēlas, or the other tribe. The wives of the greatest chiefs are commonly from the poorest families of their vassals; nor does the proud family from which she has been taken feel itself exalted by the alliance; neither does the poorest vassal among the Pawārs and Dhandēls feel that the daughter of his prince has condescended in becoming his wife. All they expect is a service for a few more yeomen of the family among the retainers of the sovereign.

The people are in this manner, from the prince to the peasant, indissolubly linked to each other, and to the soil they occupy; for, where industry is confined almost exclusively to agriculture, the proprietors of the soil and the officers of Government, who are maintained out of its rents, constitute nearly the whole of the middle and higher classes. About one-half of the lands of every state are held on service tenure by vassals of the same family or clan as the chief; and there is hardly one of them who is not connected with that chief by marriage. The revenue derived from the other half is spent in the maintenance of establishments formed almost exclusively of the members of these families.

They are none of them educated for civil offices under any other rule, nor could they, for a generation or two, be induced to submit to wear military uniform, or learn the drill of regular soldiers. They are mere militia, brave as men can be, but unsusceptible of discipline. They have, therefore, a natural horror at the thought of their states coming under any other than a domestic rule, for they could have no chance of employment in the civil or military establishments of a foreign power; and their lands would, they fear, be resumed, since the service for which they had been given would be no longer available to the rulers. It is said that, in the long interval from the commencement of the reign of Alexander the third to the end of that of David the second,[33] not a single baron could be found in Scotland able to sign his own name. The Bundēlkhand barons have never, I believe, been quite so bad as this, though they have never yet learned enough to fit them for civil offices under us. Many of them can write and read their own language, which is that common to the other countries around them.[34]

Bundēlkhand was formerly possessed by another tribe of Rājpūts, the proud Chandēls, who have now disappeared altogether from this province. If one of that tribe can still be found, it is in the humblest rank of the peasant or the soldier; but its former strength is indicated by the magnificent artificial lakes and ruined castles which are traced to them; and by the reverence which is still felt by the present dominant classes of [sic] their old capital of Mahoba. Within a certain distance around that ruined city no one now dares to beat the 'nakkāra', or great drum used in festivals or processions, lest the spirits of the old Chandēl chiefs who there repose should be roused to vengeance;[35] and a kingdom could not tempt one of the Bundēlas, Pawārs, or Chandēls to accept the government of the parish ['mauza'] in which it is situated. They will take subordinate offices there under others with fear and trembling, but nothing could induce one of them to meet the governor. When the deadly struggle between these two tribes took place cannot now be discovered.[36]

In the time of Akbar, the Chandēls were powerful in Mahoba, as the celebrated Durgāvatī, the queen of Garhā Mandlā, whose reign extended over the Sāgar and Nerbudda territories and the greater part of Berār, was a daughter of the reigning Chandēl prince of Mahoba. He condescended to give his daughter only on condition that the Gond prince who demanded her should, to save his character, come with an army of fifty thousand men to take her. He did so, and 'nothing loth', Durgāvatī departed to reign over a country where her name is now more revered than that of any other sovereign it has ever had. She was killed above two hundred and fifty years ago, about twelve miles from Jubbulpore, while gallantly leading on her troops in their third and last attempt to stem the torrent of Muhammadan invasion. Her tomb is still to be seen where she fell, in a narrow defile between two hills; and a pair of large rounded stones which stand near are, according to popular belief, her royal drums turned into stone, which, in the dead of night, are still heard resounding through the woods, and calling the spirits of her warriors from their thousand graves around her. The travellers who pass this solitary spot respectfully place upon the tomb the prettiest specimen they can find of the crystals which abound in the neighbourhood; and, with so much of kindly feeling had the history of Durgāvatī inspired me, that I could not resist the temptation of adding one to the number when I visited her tomb some sixteen years ago.[37]

I should mention that the Rājā of Samthar in Bundēlkhand.[38] is by caste a Gūjar;[39] and he has not yet any landed aristocracy like that of the Bundēlas about him. One of his ancestors, not long ago, seized upon a fine open plain, and built a fort upon it, and the family has ever since, by means of this fort, kept possession of the country around, and drawn part of their revenues from depredations upon their neighbours and travellers. The Jhānsī and Jālaun chiefs are Brahmans of the same family as the Peshwā.

In the states governed by chiefs of the military classes, nearly the whole produce of the land goes to maintain soldiers, or military retainers, who are always ready to fight or rob for their chief. In those governed by the Brahmanical class, nearly the whole produce goes to maintain priests; and the other chiefs would soon devour them, as the black ants devour the white, were not the paramount power to interpose and save them. While the Peshwā lived, he interposed; but all his dominions were *running into priesthood*, like those in Sāgar and Bundēlkhand, and must soon have been swallowed up by the military chiefs around him, had we not taken his place. Jālaun and Jhānsī are preserved only by us, for, with all their religious, it is impossible for them to maintain efficient military establishments; and the Bundēla chiefs have always a strong desire to eat them up, since these states were all sliced out of their principalities when the Peshwā was all-powerful in Hindustan.

The Chhatarpur Rājā is a Pawār. His father had been in the service of the Bundēla Rājā; but, when we entered upon our duties as the paramount power in Bundēlkhand, the son had succeeded to the little principality seized upon by his father; and, on the principle of respecting actual possession, he was recognized by us as the sovereign.[40] The Bundela Rājās, east of the Dasān river, are descended from Rājā Chhatarsāl, and are looked down upon by the Bundēla Rājās of Orchhā, Chandērī, and Datiyā, west of the Dasān, as Chhatarsāl was in the service of one of their ancestors, from whom he wrested the estates which his descendants now enjoy. Chhatarsāl, in his will, gave one-third of the dominion he had thus acquired to the strongest power then in India, the Peshwā, in order to secure the other two-thirds to his two sons Hardī Sā and Jagatrāj, in the same manner as princes of the Roman empire used to bequeath a portion of theirs to the emperor. [41] Of the Peshwā's share we have now got all, except Jālaun. Jhānsī was subsequently acquired by the Peshwā, or rather by his subordinates, with his sanction and assistance.[42]

Notes:

1. December, 1835.

2. In the Orchhā State. This seems to be the same town which the author had already visited on his way to Tehrī on the 7th December. *Ante*, Chapter 19 note [15].

3. *Ante*, Chapter 12 following note [9].

4. Sodora in the author's text; see *ante*, Chapter 19, note 11.

5. 'Bow-sacrifice.'

6. The tradition is that a prince of this military class was sporting in a river with his thousand wives, when Renukā, the wife of Jamadagni, went to bring water. He offended her, and her husband cursed the prince, but was put to death by him. His son Parasrām was no less a person than the sixth incarnation of Vishnu, who had assumed the human shape merely to destroy these tyrants. He vowed, now that his mother had been insulted, and his father killed, not to leave one on the face of the earth. He destroyed them all twenty-one times, the women with child producing a new race each time. [W. H. S.] The legend is not narrated quite correctly.

7. Rāma Chandra, son of Dasaratha.

8. When Rām set out with his army for Ceylon, he is supposed to have worshipped the little tree called 'cheonkul', which stood near his capital

of Ajodhya. It is a wretched little thing, between a shrub and a tree; but I have seen a procession of more than seventy thousand persons attend their prince to the worship of it on the festival of the Dasahara, which is held in celebration of this expedition to Ceylon. [W. H. S.] 'As Arjuna and his brothers worshipped the shumee-tree, the *Acacia suma*, and hung up their arms upon it, so the Hindus go forth to worship that tree on the festival of the Dasahara. They address the tree under the name of Aparajita, the invincible Goddess, sprinkle it with five ambrosial liquids, the 'panchamrit', a mixture of milk, curds, sugar, clarified butter, and honey, wash it with water, and hang garments upon it. They light lamps and burn incense before the symbol of Aparajita, make 'chandlos' upon the tree, sprinkle it with rose-coloured water, and set offerings of food before it' (Balfour, *Cyclopaedia*, 3rd ed., s v. 'Dasahara'). The 'cheonkul' is the *chhonkar* or *chhaunkar* (*Prosopis spicigera*, Linn.), described by Growse as follows: —

'Very common throughout the district; occasionally grows to quite a large tree, as in the Dohani Kund at Chaksauli. It is used for religious worship at the festival of the Dasahara, and considered sacred to Siva. The pods (called *sangri*) are much used for fodder. Probably *chhonkar* and *sangri*, which latter is in some parts of India the name of the tree as well as of the pod, are both dialectical corruptions of the Sanskrit *sankara*, a name of Siva; for the palatal and sibilant are frequently interchangeable' ('List of Indigenous Trees' in *Mathurā, A. District Memoir*, 3rd ed., Allahabad, 1883, p. 422). Sundry leguminous trees are used in Dasahara ceremonies in the different parts of India, under varying local names.

9. *Credo quia impossibile.*

10. This comparison is not a happy one. The elements in some of the Hindoo myths specially repulsive to European taste are their monstrosity, their inartistic and hideous exaggeration, their accumulation of sanguinary horrors, and their childish triviality. Few of the classical myths exhibit these characteristics. The vanity or policy of Tiberius and Alexander in believing themselves to be, or wishing to be believed, divine, has nothing in common with the grotesque imagination of Puranic Hinduism.

11. The roots of Hinduism are so deeply fixed in a thick soil of custom and inherited sentiment, the growth of thousands of years, that English education has less effect than might be expected in loosening the bonds of beliefs which seem to every one but a Hindoo the merest superstition. Hindoos who can read English with fluency, and write it with accuracy, are often extremely devout, and Hindoo devoutness must ever appear to an outsider, even to a European as sympathetic as the author, to be no better than superstition. A Hindoo able to read English with ease has at his command all the rich stores of the knowledge of the West, but very

often does not care to taste them. Enmeshed in a web of ritual and belief inseparable from himself, he remains as much as ever a Hindoo, and uses his skill in English merely as an article of professional equipment. 'Good works of history and fiction' do not interest him, and he usually fails to digest and assimilate the physical or biological science administered to him at school or college. In fact, he does not believe it. The monstrous legends of the Purānas continue to be for his mind the realities; while the truths of science are to him phantoms, shadowy and unsubstantial, the outlandish notions of alien and casteless unbelievers. These observations, of course, are not universally true, and a few Hindoos, growing in number, are able to heartily accept and thoroughly assimilate the facts of history and the results of inductive science. But such Hindoos are few, and it may well be doubted if it is possible for a man really to believe the amount of history and science known to an ordinary English schoolboy, and still be a devout Hindoo. The old bottles cannot contain the new wine. The Hindoo scriptures do not treat of history and science in a merely incidental way; they teach, after their fashion, both history and science formally and systematically; grammar, logic, medicine, astronomy, the history of gods and men, are all taught in books which form part of the sacred canon. Inductive science and matter-of-fact history are absolutely destructive of, and irreconcilable with, veneration for the Hindoo scriptures as authoritative and infallible guides. It is impossible, within the narrow limits of a note, to discuss the problems suggested by the author's remarks. Enough, perhaps, has been said to show that the many-rooted banyan tree of Hinduism is in little danger of overthrow from the attacks either of history or of science, not to speak of 'good works of fiction'.

12. A 'dug-out' canoe is rather a shaky craft. When two or three are lashed together, and a native cot (chārpāi) is stretched across, the passenger can make himself very comfortable. The boats are poled by men standing in the stern.

13. *Ante*, Chapter 24, note 1.

14. This prince is not included in the authentic dynastic lists given in the Chandēl inscriptions. He was probably a younger son, who never reigned. The principal authorities for the history of the Chandēl dynasty are *A.S.R.*, vol. ii, pp. 439-51; vol. xxi, pp. 77-90, and V. A. Smith, 'Contributions to the History of Bundēlkhand', in *J.A.S.B.* vol. 1 (1881), Part I, p. 1; and 'The History and Coinage of the Chandēl (Chandella) Dynasty' in *Ind. Ant.*, 1908, pp. 114-48. A brief summary will be found in *Early History of India*, 3rd ed. (1914), pp. 390-4. Most of the great works of the dynasty date from the period A.D. 950- 1200.

15. The long ridges of quartz traversing the gneiss are marked features in the scenery of Bundēlkhand.

16. The author always uses the phrase Central India as a vague geographical expression. The phrase is now generally used to mean an administrative division, namely, the group of Native States under the Central India Agency at Indore, which deals with about 148 chiefs and rulers of various rank. Central India in this official sense must not be confounded with the Central Provinces, of which the capital is Nāgpur.

17. On this lake theory, see *ante*, Chapter 14, note 13.

18. During a residence of six years in Bundēlkhand the editor came to the conclusion that most of the ancient artificial lakes were not constructed for purposes of irrigation. The embankments seem generally to have been built as adjuncts to palaces or temples. Many of the lakes command no considerable area of irrigable ground, and there are no traces of ancient irrigation channels. In modern times small canals have been drawn from some of the lakes.

19. The desolation of the ravines of the rivers of Central India and Bundēlkhand offers a very striking spectacle, presenting to the geologist a signal example of the effects of sub-aerial denudation.

20. This pretty custom is also described, in Tod's *Rājasthān*; and is still common in Alwar, and perhaps in other parts of Rājputāna (*N.I. Notes and Queries*, vol. ii (Dec. 1892), p. 152), It does not seem to be now known in the Gangetic valley.

21. Principalities, and the estates of the talukdārs of Oudh also descend to the eldest son. The author states (*ante*, Chapter 10, see text before note [10].) that the same rule applied in his time to the small agricultural holdings in the Sāgar and Nerbudda territories.

22. This statement is inexact; Hindoo daughters, as a rule, inherit nothing from their fathers; a Muhammadan daughter takes half the share of a son.

23. But it is only the smaller local ministerial officers who are secure in their tenure of office under native Governments; those on whose efficiency the well-being of village communities depends. The greatest evil of Governments of the kind is the feeling of insecurity which pervades all the higher officers of Government, and the instability of all engagements made by the Government with them, and by them with the people. [W. H. S.]

24. *Ante*, Chapter 23, text at note [8].

25. In the Gwālior territory, the Marāthā 'āmils' or governors of districts, do the same, and keep gangs of robbers on purpose to plunder

their neighbours; and, if you ask them for their thieves, they will actually tell you that to part with them would be ruin, as they are their only defence against the thieves of their neighbours. [W. H. S.] These notions and habits are by no means extinct. In October, 1892, a force of about two hundred men, cavalry and infantry, was sent into Bundēlkhand to suppress robber gangs. Such gangs are constantly breaking out in that region, in most native states, and in many British districts. See *ante*, chapter 23, text following note [13].

26. My poor guide had as little sympathy with the prime ministers, whom the Tehrī Rājā put to death, as the peasantry of England had with the great men and women whom Harry the Eighth sacrificed. [W. H. S.] *Ante*, Chapter 23, beginning to note [9].

27. The cruel practice of impressment for the royal navy is authorized by a series of statutes extending from the reign of Philip and Mary to that of George III. Seamen of the merchant navy, and, with few exceptions, all seafaring men between the ages of eighteen and thirty-five, are liable, under the provisions of these harsh statutes, to be forcibly seized by the press-gang, and compelled to serve on board a man-of-war. The acts legalizing impressment were freely made use of during the Napoleonic wars, but since then have been little acted on, and no Government at the present day could venture to use them, though they have never been repealed. The fleet sent against the Russians in 1855 was the first English fleet ever manned without recourse to forcible impressment: see the article 'Impressment' by David Hannay, in *Encyclopaedia Britannica*, 11th ed., 1910. The work by J. B. Hutchinson entitled *The Press- gang Afloat and Ashore* (London: Nash, 1913) gives copious details of the infamous proceedings.

28. The Brahman chief of Jhānsī was originally a governor under the Peshwā. The treaty of November 18, 1817, recognized the then chief Rāmchand Rāo, his heirs and successors, as hereditary rulers of Jhānsī. Rāmchand Rāo was granted the title of Rājā by the British Government in 1832, and died without issue on August 20, 1835 (*N.W.P. Gazetteer*, 1st ed., vol. i, p. 296). See *post*, Chapter 29.

29. The chiefs of Jālaun also were officers under the Marātha Government of the Peshwā up to 1817. In consequence of gross misgovernment, an English superintendent was appointed in 1838, and the state lapsed to the British Government, owing to failure of heirs, in 1840 (ibid. p. 229).

30. *Ante* Chapter 23, note 13.

31. Lapse of years has increased the distance and the enchantment, so that modern agitators and sentimentalists discover marvellous excellences in the native Governments of the now remote past. The methods of

government in the existing native states have been so profoundly modified by the influence of the Imperial Government that these states are no longer as instructive in the way of contrast as they were in the author's day.

32. The author consistently held the views above enunciated, and defended the policy of maintaining the native states. He was of opinion that the system of annexation favoured by Lord Dalhousie and his Council 'had a downward tendency, and tended to crush all the higher and middle classes connected with the land'. He considered that the Government of India should have undertaken the management of Oudh, but that it had no right to annex the province, and appropriate its revenues (*Journey through the Kingdom of Oude*, p. 22, &c.). Since 1858 the policy of annexation has been repudiated. See Sir W. Lee-Warner, *The Protected Princes of India* (Macmillan, 1894), and *The Native States of India* (1910).

33. A.D. 1249 to A.D. 1371.

34. The Hindi spoken in different parts of Bundēlkhand comprises several distinct dialects: see Kellogg, *A Grammar of the Hindī Language*, 2nd ed., 1893; and Grierson, *Linguistic Survey*, vol. vi (1904), pp. 18-23, where the dialects of Eastern Bundēlkhand are discussed. Bundēlī, the speech of Bundēlkhand proper, will be treated as a dialect of Western Hindi in a volume of the *Survey* not yet published. Sir G. Grierson has favoured me with perusal of the proofs, and has used materials collected by me in the Hamīrpur District nearly forty years ago. Bundēlī has a considerable literature.

35. The editor was told of a case in which two chiefs suffered for beating their drums in Mahoba.

36. See *ante*, Chapter 23 note 11, and Chapter 26 note 14, and the authorities there cited. The Chandēl history occupies an important place in the mediaeval annals of India. Several important inscriptions of the dynasty have been correctly edited in the *Epigraphia Indica*. Mahoba is not now a 'ruined city'; it is a moderately prosperous country town, with a tolerable bazaar, and about eleven thousand inhabitants. It is the head-quarters of a 'tahsīldār', or sub-collector, and a station on the Midland Railway. The ruined temples and places in and near the town are of much interest. For many miles round the country is full of remarkable remains, some of which are in fairly good preservation. The published descriptions of these works are far from being exhaustive. The author was mistaken in supposing that the power of the Chandēls was broken by the Bundēlas. The last Chandēl king, who ruled over an extensive dominion, was Paramardi Deva, or Parmāl. This prince was defeated in a pitched battle, or rather a series of battles, near the Betwa river, by Prithīrāj Chauhān, king of Kanauj, in the

year 1182. A few years later, the victor was himself vanquished and slain by the advancing Muhammadans. Mahoba and the surrounding territories then passed through many vicissitudes, imperfectly recorded in the pages of history, and were ruled from time to time by Musalmāns, Bhars, Khangārs, and others. The Bundēlas, an offshoot of the Gaharwār clan, did not come into notice before the middle of the fourteenth century, and first became a power in India under the leadership of Champat Rāi, the contemporary of Jahāngīr and Shah Jāhan, in the first half of the seventeenth century. The line of Chandēl kings was continued in the persons of obscure local chiefs, whose very names are, for the most part, forgotten. The story of Durgāvatī, briefly told in the text, casts a momentary flash of light on their obscurity. The principal nobleman of the Chandēl race now occupying a dignified position is the Rājā of Gidhaur in the Mungir (Monghyr) district of Bengal, whose ancestor emigrated from Mahoba.

The war between the Chandēls and Chauhāns is the subject of a long section or canto of the Hindi epic, the *Chand-Rāisā*, written by Chand Bardāi, the court poet of Prithīrāj, of which the original MS. in 5,000 verses still exists. It was subsequently expanded to 125,000 verses (*E.H.I.*, 3rd ed., 1914, p. 387 note). The war is also the theme of the songs of many popular rhapsodists. The story is, of course, encrusted with a thick deposit of miraculous legend, and none of the details can be relied on. But the fact and the date of the war are fully proved by incontestable evidence.

37. The marriage of Durgāvatī is no proof that her father, the Chandēl Rājā, was powerful in Mahoba in the time of Akbar. It is rather an indication that he was poor and weak. If he had been rich and strong, he would probably have refused his daughter to a Gond, even though complaisant bards might invent a Rājpūt genealogy for the bridegroom. The story about the army of fifty thousand men cannot be readily accepted as sober fact. It looks like a courtly invention to explain a mésalliance. The inducement really offered to the proud but poor Chandēl was, in all likelihood, a large sum of money, according to the usual practice in such cases. Several indications exist of close relations between the Gonds and Chandēls in earlier times.

Early in Akbar's reign, in the year 1564, Āsaf Khān, the imperial viceroy of Karrā Mānikpur, obtained permission to invade the Gond territory. The young Rājā of Garhā Mandlā, Bīr Narāyan, was then a minor, and the defence of the kingdom devolved on Durgāvatī, the dowager queen. She first took up her position at the great fortress of Singaurgarh, north-west of Jabalpur, and, being there defeated, retired through Garhā, to the south-east, towards Mandlā. After an obstinately contested fight the invaders were again successful, and broke the queen's stout resistance. 'Mounted on an elephant, she refused to retire, though she was severely wounded, until her troops had time to recover the shock of the first discharge of artillery, and, notwithstanding that she had received an arrow-wound in her eye, bravely defended the pass in person. But, by an extraordinary coincidence, the river in the rear of her position, which had been nearly dry a few hours before the action commenced, began suddenly to rise, and soon became unfordable. Finding her plan of retreat thus frustrated, and seeing her troops give way, she snatched a dagger from her elephant-driver, and plunged it into her bosom. . . . Of all the sovereigns of this dynasty she lives most in the recollection of the people; she carried out many highly useful works in different parts of her kingdom, and one of the large reservoirs near Jabalpur is still called the Rānī Talāo in memory of her. During the fifteen years of her regency she did much for the country, and won the hearts of the people, while her end was as noble and devoted as her life had been useful' (C.P. Gazetteer (1870), p. 283; with references to Sleeman's article on the Rājās of Garhā Mandlā, and 'Briggs' Farishta', ed. 1829, vol. ii, pp. 217, 218). A memoir of Āsaf Khan Abdul Majīd, the general who overcame Durgāvatī, will be found in Blochmann's translation of the Aīn-i-Akbarī, vol. i, p. 366.

38. Samthar is a small state, lying between the Betwa and Pahūj rivers, to the south-west of the Jālaun district. It was separated from the Datiyā State only one generation previous to the British occupation of Bundēlkhand. A treaty was concluded with the Rājā in 1812 (N.W.P. Gazetteer (1st ed.), vol. i, p. 578).

39. Gūjars occupy more than a hundred villages in the Jālaun district, chiefly among the ravines of the Pahūj river. The Gūjar caste is most numerous in the Panjāb and the upper districts of the United Provinces. It is not very highly esteemed, being of about equal rank with the Āhīr caste and rather below the Jāt. Gūjar colonies are settled in the Hoshangābād and Nīmār districts of the Central Provinces. The Gūjars are inveterate cattle-lifters, and always ready to take advantage of any relaxation of the bonds of order to prey upon their neighbours. Many sections of the caste have adopted the Muhammadan faith.

40. The small state of Chhatarpur lies to the south of the Hamīrpur district, between the Dasān and Ken rivers. The town of Chhatarpur, on the military road from Bānda to Sāgar, is remarkable for the mausoleum and ruined palace of Rājā Chhatarsāl, after whom the town is named. Khajurāho, the ancient religious capital of the Chandēl monarchy, with its magnificent group of mediaeval Hindoo and Jain temples, is within the limits of the state, about eighteen miles south-east of Chhatarpur, and thirty-four miles south of Mahoba. The Pawār adventurer, who succeeded in separating Chhatarpur from the Panna state, was originally a common soldier.

41. Concerning Chhatarsāl (A.D. 1671 to 1731), see notes *ante*, Chapter 14 note 9, and chapter 23 note 11. He was one of the sons of Champat Rāi. The correct date of the death of Chhatarsāl is Pūs Badi 3, Sanwat, 1788 = A.D. 1731. Hardī (Hirdai) Sā succeeded to the Rāj, or kingdom, of Pannā, and Jagatrāj to that of Jaitpur. These kingdoms quickly broke up, and the fragments are now in part native states and in part British territory. The Orchhā State was formed about the beginning of the sixteenth century, and the Chandērī and Datiyā States are offshoots from it, which separated during the seventeenth century.

42. As already observed (*ante*, Chapter 26, note 29), the Jālaun State became British territory in 1840, four years after the tour described in the text, and four years before the, publication of the book. The Jhānsī State similarly lapsed on the death of Rājā Gangādhar Rāo in November, 1853. The Rānī Lachhmī Bāī joined the mutineers, and was killed in battle in June, 1858.

CHAPTER 27

Blights.

I had a visit from my little friend the Sarīmant, and the conversation turned upon the causes and effects of the dreadful blight to which the wheat crops in the Nerbudda districts had of late years been subject. He said that 'the people at first attributed this great calamity to an increase in the crime of adultery which had followed the introduction of our rule, and which', he said, 'was understood to follow it everywhere; that afterwards it was by most people attributed to our frequent measurement of the land, and inspection of fields, with a view to estimate their capabilities to pay; which the people considered a kind of *incest*, and which he himself, the Deity, can never tolerate. The land is', said he, 'considered as the *mother* of the prince or chief who holds it—the great parent from whom he derives all that maintains him—his family and his establishments. If well treated, she yields this in abundance to her son; but, if he presumes to look upon her with the eye of desire, she ceases to be fruitful; or the Deity sends down hail or blight to destroy all that she yields. The measuring the surface of the fields, and the frequent inspecting the crops by the chief himself, or by his immediate agents were considered by the people in this light; and, in consequence, he never ventured upon these things. They were', he thought, 'fully satisfied that we did it more with a view to distribute the burthen of taxation equally upon the people than to increase it collectively; still', he thought that, 'either we should not do it at all, or delegate the duty to inferior agents, whose close inspection of the great *parent* could not be so displeasing to the Deity.'[1]

Rām Chand Pundit said that 'there was no doubt much truth in what Sarīmant Sāhib had stated; that the crops of late had unquestionably suffered from the constant measuring going on upon the lands; but that the people (as he knew) had now become unanimous in attributing the calamities of season, under which these districts had been suffering so much, to the *eating of beef*- this was', he thought, 'the great source of all their sufferings.'

Sarīmant declared that he thought 'his Pundit was right, and that it would, no doubt, be of great advantage to them and to their rulers if Government could be prevailed upon to prohibit the eating of beef; that so great and general were the sufferings of the people from these calamities of seasons, and so firm, and now so general, the opinion that they arose chiefly from the practice of killing and eating cows that, in spite of all the other superior blessings of our rule, the people were almost beginning to wish their old Marāthā rulers in power again.'

I reminded him of the still greater calamities the people of Bundēlkhand had been suffering under.

'True,' said he, 'but among them there are crimes enough of everyday occurrence to account for these things; but, under your rule, the Deity has only one or other of these three things to be offended with; and, of these three, it must be admitted that the eating of beef so near the sacred stream of the Nerbudda is the worst.'

The blight of which we were speaking had, for several seasons from the year 1829, destroyed the greater part of the wheat crops over extensive districts along the line of the Nerbudda, and through Mālwā generally; and old people stated that they recollected two returns of this calamity at intervals from twenty to twenty-four years. The pores, with which the stalks are abundantly supplied to admit of their readily taking up the aqueous particles that float in the air, seem to be more open in an easterly wind than in any other; and, when this wind prevails at the same time that the air is filled with the farina of the small parasitic fungus, whose depredations on the corn constitute what they call the rust, mildew, or blight, the particles penetrate into these pores, speedily sprout and spread their small roots into the cellular texture, where they intercept, and feed on, the sap in its ascent; and the grain in the ear, deprived of its nourishment, becomes shrivelled, and the whole crop is often not worth the reaping.[2] It is at first of a light, beautiful orange-colour, and found chiefly upon the 'alsī' (linseed)[3] which it does not seem much to injure; but, about the end of February, the fungi ripen, and shed their seeds rapidly, and they are taken up by the wind, and carried over the corn-fields. I have sometimes seen the air tinted of an orange colour for many days by the quantity of these seeds which it has contained; and that without the wheat crops suffering at all, when any but an easterly wind has prevailed; but, when the air is so charged with this farina, let but an easterly wind blow for twenty-four hours, and all the wheat crops under its influence are destroyed — nothing can save them. The stalks and leaves become first of an orange colour from the light colour of the farina which adheres to them, but this changes to deep brown. All that part of the stalk that is exposed seems as if it had been pricked with needles, and had exuded blood from every puncture; and the grain in the ear withers in proportion to the number of fungi that intercept and feed upon its sap; but the parts of the stalks that are covered by the leaves remain entirely uninjured; and, when the leaves are drawn off from them, they form a beautiful contrast to the others, which have been exposed to the depredations of these parasitic plants.

Every pore, it is said, may contain from twenty to forty of these plants, and each plant may shed a hundred seeds,[4] so that a single shrub, infected with the disease, may disseminate it over the face of a whole district; for, in the warm month of March, when the wheat is attaining maturity, these plants ripen and shed their seeds in a week, and consequently increase with enormous rapidity, when they find plants with their pores open ready to receive and nourish them. I went over a rich sheet of wheat cultivation in the district of Jubbulpore in January, 1836, which appeared to me devoted to inevitable destruction. It was intersected by slips and fields of 'alsī', which the cultivators often sow along the borders of their wheat-fields, which are exposed to the road, to prevent trespass.[5] All this 'alsī' had become of a beautiful light orange colour from these fungi; and the cultivators, who had had every field destroyed the year before by the same plant, surrounded my tent in despair, imploring me to tell them of some remedy. I knew of none; but, as the 'alsī' is not a very valuable plant, I recommended them, as their only chance, to pull it all up by the roots, and fling it into large tanks that were everywhere to be found. They did so, and no 'alsī' was *intentionally* left in the district, for, like drowning men catching at a straw, they caught everywhere at the little gleam of hope that my suggestion seemed to offer. Not a field of wheat was that season injured in the district of Jubbulpore; but I was soon satisfied that my suggestion had had nothing whatever to do with their escape, for not a single stalk of the wheat was, I believe, affected; while *some* stalks of the affected 'alsī' must have been left by accident. Besides, in several of the adjoining districts, where the 'alsī' remained in the ground, the wheat escaped. I found that, about the time when the blight usually attacks the wheat, westerly winds prevailed, and that it never blew from the east for many hours together. The common belief among the natives was that the prevalence of an east wind was necessary to give full effect to the attack of this disease, though they none of them pretended to know anything of its *modus operandi* — indeed they considered the blight to be a demon, which was to be driven off only by prayers and sacrifices.

It is worthy of remark that hardly anything suffered from the attacks of these fungi but the wheat. The 'alsī', upon which it always first made its appearance, suffered something certainly, but not much, though the stems and leaves were covered with them. The gram (*Cicer arietinum*) suffered still less — indeed the grain in this plant often remained uninjured, while the stems and leaves were covered with the fungi, in the midst of fields of wheat that were entirely destroyed by ravages of the same kind. None of the other pulses were injured, though situated in the same manner in the midst of the fields of wheat that were destroyed. I have seen rich fields of uninterrupted wheat cultivation for twenty miles by ten, in the valley of the Nerbudda, so entirely destroyed by this disease that the people would not go to the trouble of gathering one field in four, for the stalks and the leaves were so much injured that they were considered as unfit or unsafe for fodder; and during the same season its ravages were equally felt in the districts along the tablelands of the Vindhya range, north of the valley and, I believe, those upon the Sātpura range, south. The last time I saw this blight was in March, 1832, in the Sāgar district, where its ravages were very great, but partial; and I kept bundles of the blighted wheat hanging up in my house, for the inspection of the curious, till the beginning of 1835.[6]

When I assumed charge of the district of Sāgar in 1831 the opinion among the farmers and landholders generally was that the calamities of season under which we had been suffering were attributable to the increase of *adultery*, arising, as they thought, from our indifference, as we seemed to treat it as a matter of little importance; whereas it had always been considered under former Governments as a case of *life and death*. The husband or his friends waited till they caught the offending parties together in criminal correspondence, and then put them both to death; and the death of one pair generally acted, they thought, as a sedative upon the evil passions of a whole district for a year or two. Nothing can be more unsatisfactory than our laws for the punishment of adultery in India, where the Muhammadan criminal code has been followed, though the people subjected to it are not one-tenth Muhammadans. This law was enacted by Muhammad on the occasion of his favourite wife Ayesha being found under very suspicious circumstances with another man. A special direction from heaven required that four witnesses should swear positively to the *fact*.

Ayesha and her paramour were, of course, acquitted, and the witnesses, being less than four, received the same punishment which would have been inflicted upon the criminals had the fact been proved by the direct testimony of the prescribed number—that is, eighty stripes of the 'korā', almost equal to a sentence of death. (See Korān, chap. 24, and chap. 4.)[7] This became the law among all Muhammadans. Ayesha's father succeeded Muhammad, and Omar succeeded Abū Bakr.[8] Soon after his accession to the throne, Omar had to sit in judgement upon Mughīra, a companion of the prophet, the governor of Basrah,[9] who had been accidentally seen in an awkward position with a lady of rank by four men while they sat in an adjoining apartment. The door or window which concealed the criminal parties was flung open by the wind, at the time when they wished it most to remain closed. Three of the four men swore directly to the point. Mughīra was Omar's favourite, and had been appointed to the government by him, Zāid, the brother of one of the three who had sworn to the fact, hesitated to swear to the entire fact.

'I think', said Omar, 'that I see before me a man whom God would not make the means of disgracing one of the companions of the holy prophet.'

Zāid then described circumstantially the most unequivocal position that was, perhaps, ever described in a public court of justice; but, still hesitating to swear to the entire completion of the crime, the criminals were acquitted, and his brother and the two others received the punishment described. This decision of the *Brutus of his age* and country settled the law of evidence in these matters; and no Muhammadan judge would now give a verdict against any person charged with adultery, without the four witnesses to the *entire fact*. No man hopes for a conviction for this crime in our courts; and, as he would have to drag his wife or paramour through no less than three—that of the police officer, the magistrate, and the judge—to seek it, he has recourse to poison, either secretly or with his wife's consent. She will commonly rather die than be turned out into the streets a degraded outcast. The seducer escapes with impunity, while his victim suffers all that human nature is capable of enduring. Where husbands are in the habit of poisoning their guilty wives from the want of *legal* means of redress, they will sometimes poison those who are suspected upon insufficient grounds. No magistrate ever hopes to get a conviction in the judge's court, if he commits a criminal for trial on this charge (under Regulation 17 of 1817), and, therefore, he never does commit. Regulation 7 of 1819 authorizes a magistrate to punish any person convicted of enticing away a wife or unmarried daughter for another's use; and an indignant functionary may sometimes feel disposed to stretch a point that the guilty man may not altogether escape.[10]

Redress for these wrongs is never sought in our courts, because they can never hope to get it. But it is a great mistake to suppose that the people of India want a heavier punishment for the crime than we are disposed to inflict—all they want is a fair chance of conviction upon such reasonable proof as cases of this nature admit of, and such a measure of punishment as shall make it appear that their rulers think the crime a serious one, and that they are disposed to protect them from it. Sometimes the poorest man would refuse pecuniary compensation; but generally husbands of the poorer classes would be glad to get what the heads of their caste or circle of society might consider the expenses of a second marriage. They do not dare to live in adultery, they would be outcasts if they did; they must be married according to the forms of their caste, and it is reasonable that the seducer of the wife should be obliged to defray the coats of the injured husband's second marriage. The rich will, of course, always refuse such a compensation, but a law declaring the man convicted of this crime liable to imprisonment in irons at hard labour for two years, but entitled to his discharge within that time on an application from the injured husband or father, would be extremely popular throughout India. The poor man would make the application when assured of the sum which the elders of his caste consider sufficient; and they would take into consideration the means of the offender to pay. The woman is sufficiently punished by her degraded condition. The *fatwa* of a Muhammadan law officer should be dispensed with in such cases.[11]

In 1832 the people began to search for other causes [*scilicet*, of bad seasons]. The frequent measurements of the land, with a view to equalize the assessments, were thought of; even the operations of the Trigonometrical Survey,[12] which were then making a great noise in Central India, where their fires were seen every night burning upon the peaks of the highest ranges, were supposed to have had some share in exasperating the Deity; and the services of the most holy Brahmans were put in requisition to exorcise the peaks from which the engineers had taken their angles, the moment their instruments were removed. In many places, to the great annoyance and consternation of the engineers, the landmarks which they had left to enable them to correct their work as they advanced, were found to have been removed during their short intervals of absence, and they were obliged to do their work over again. The priests encouraged the disposition on the part of the peasantry to believe that men who required to do their work by the aid of fires lighted in the dead of the night upon *high places*, and work which no one but themselves seemed able to comprehend, must hold communion with supernatural beings, a communion which they thought might be displeasing to the Deity.

At last, in the year 1833, a very holy Brahman, who lived in his cloister near the iron suspension bridge over the Biās river, ten miles from Sāgar, sat down with a determination to *wrestle with the Deity* till he should be compelled to reveal to him the real cause of all these calamities of season under which the people were groaning.[13] After three days and nights of fasting and prayer, he saw a vision which stood before him in a white mantle, and told him that all these calamities arose from the slaughter of cows; and that under former Governments this practice had been strictly prohibited, and the returns of the harvest had, in consequence, been always abundant, and subsistence cheap, in spite of invasion from without, insurrection within, and a good deal of misrule and oppression on the part of the local government. The holy man was enjoined by the vision to make this revelation known to the constituted authorities, and to persuade the people generally throughout the district to join in the petition for the prohibition of *beef-eating* throughout our Nerbudda territories. He got a good many of the most respectable of the landholders around him, and explained the wishes of the vision of the preceding night. A petition was soon drawn up and signed by many hundreds of the most respectable people in the district, and presented to the Governor-General's representative in these parts, Mr. F. C. Smith. Others were presented to the civil authorities of the district, and all stating in the most respectful terms how sensible the people were of the inestimable benefits of our rule, and how grateful they all felt for the protection to life and property, and to the free employment of all their advantages, which they had under it; and for the frequent and large reduction in the assessments, and remission in the demand, on account of calamities of seasons. These, they stated, were all that Government could do to relieve a suffering people, but they had all proved unavailing; and yet, under this truly paternal rule, the people were suffering more than under any former Government in its worst period of misrule—the hand of an *incensed God* was upon them; and, as they had now, at last after many fruitless attempts, discovered the real cause of this anger of the Deity, they trusted that we would listen to their prayers, and restore plenty and all its blessings to the country by prohibiting the *eating of beef*. All these dreadful evils had, they said, unquestionably originated in the (Sadr Bāzār) great market of the cantonments, where, for the first time, within one hundred miles of the sacred stream of the Nerbudda, men had purchased and eaten cows' flesh.

These people were all much attached to us and to our rule, and were many of them on the most intimate terms of social intercourse with us; and, at the time they signed this petition, were entirely satisfied that they had discovered the real cause of all their sufferings, and impressed with the idea that we should be convinced, and grant their prayers.[14] The day is past. Beef continued to be eaten with undiminished appetite, the blight, nevertheless, disappeared, and every other sign of vengeance from above; and the people are now, I believe, satisfied that they were mistaken. They still think that the lands do not yield so many returns of the seed under us as under former rulers; that they have lost some of the *barkat* (blessings) which they enjoyed under them—they know not why. The fact is that under us the lands do not enjoy the salutary fallows which frequent invasions and civil wars used to cause under former Governments. Those who survived such civil wars and invasions got better returns for their seed.

During the discussion of the question with the people, I had one day a conversation with the Sadr Amīn, or head native judicial officer, whom I have already mentioned. He told me that 'there could be no doubt of the truth of the conclusion to which the people had at length come. 'There are', he said, 'some countries in which punishments follow crimes after long intervals, and, indeed, do not take place till some future birth; in others, they follow crimes immediately; and such is the country bordering the stream of *Mother Nerbudda*. This', said he, 'is a stream more holy than that of the great Ganges herself, since no man is supposed to derive any benefit from that stream unless he either bathe in it or drink from it; but the sight of the Nerbudda from a distant hill could bless him, and purify him. In other countries, the slaughter of cows and bullocks might not be punished for ages; and the harvest, in such countries, might continue good through many successive generations under such enormities; indeed, he was not quite sure that there might not be countries in which no punishment at all would inevitably follow; but, so near the Nerbudda, this could not be the case.[15] Providence could never suffer beef to be eaten so near her sacred majesty without visiting the crops with blight, hail, or some other calamity, and the people with cholera morbus, small-pox, and other great pestilences. As for himself, he should never be persuaded that all these afflictions did not arise wholly and solely from this dreadful habit of eating beef. I declare', concluded he, 'that if the Government would but consent to prohibit the eating of beef, it might levy from the lands three times the revenue that they now pay.'

The great festival of the Holī, the Saturnalia of India, terminates on the last day of Phālgun, or 16th of March.[16] On that day the Holī is burned; and on that day the ravages of the monster (for monster they will have it to be) are supposed to cease. Any field that has remained untouched up to that time is considered to be quite secure from the moment the Holī has been committed to the flames. What gave rise to the notion I have never been able to discover, but such is the general belief. I suppose the siliceous epidermis must then have become too hard, and the pores in the stem too much closed up to admit of the further depredation of the fungi.

In the latter end of 1831, while I was at Sāgar, a cowherd in driving his cattle to water at a reach of the Biās river, called the Nardhardhār, near the little village of Jasrathī, was reported to have seen a vision that told him the waters of that reach, taken up and conveyed to the fields in pitchers, would effectually keep off the blight from the wheat, provided the pitchers were not suffered to touch the ground on the way. On reaching the field, a small hole was to be made in the bottom of the pitcher, so as to keep up a small but steady stream, as the bearer carried it round the borders of the field, that the water might fall in a complete ring, except at a small opening—which was to be kept dry, in order that the *monster* or *demon blight* might make his escape through it, not being able to cross over any part watered by the holy

stream. The waters Of the Bias river generally are not supposed to have any peculiar virtues. The report of this vision spread rapidly over the country; and the people who had been suffering under so many seasons of great calamity were anxious to try anything that promised the slightest chance of relief. Every cultivator of the district prepared pots for the conveyance of the water, with tripods to support them while they rested on the road, that they might not touch the ground. The spot pointed out for taking the water was immediately under a fine large pīpal- tree[17] which had fallen into the river, and on each bank was seated a Bairāgī, or priest of Vishṇu. The blight began to manifest itself in the alsī (linseed) in January, 1832, but the wheat is never considered to be in danger till late in February, when it is nearly ripe; and during that month and the following the banks of the river were crowded with people in search of the water. Some of the people came more than one hundred miles to fetch it, and all seemed quite sure that the holy water would save them. Each person gave the Bairāgī priest of his own side of the river two half-pence (copper pice), two pice weight of ghī (clarified butter), and two pounds of flour, before he filled his pitcher, to secure his blessings from it. These priests were strangers, and the offerings were entirely voluntary. The roads from this reach of the Bias river, up to the capital of the Orchhā Rājā, more than a hundred miles, were literally lined with these water-carriers; and I estimated the number of persons who passed with the water every day for six weeks at ten thousand a day.[18] After they had ceased to take the water, the banks were long crowded with people who flocked to see the place where priests and waters had worked such miracles, and to try and discover the source whence the water derived its virtues. It was remarked by some that the pīpal-tree, which had fallen from the bank above many years before, had still continued to throw out the richest foliage from the branches above the surface of the water. Others declared that they saw a *monkey* on the bank near the spot, which no sooner perceived it was observed than it plunged into the stream and disappeared. Others again saw some flights of steps under the water, indicating that it had in days of yore been the site of a temple, whose god, no doubt, gave to the waters the wonderful virtues it had been found to possess. The priests would say nothing but that 'it was the work of God, and, like all his works, beyond the reach of man's understanding.' They made their fortunes, and got up the vision and miracle, no doubt, for that especial purpose.[19] As to the effect, I was told by hundreds of farmers who had tried the waters that, though it had not anywhere kept the blight entirely off from the wheat, it was found that the fields which had not the advantages of water were entirely destroyed; and, where the pot had been taken all round the field without leaving any dry opening for the demon to escape through, it was almost as bad; but, when a small opening had been left, and the water carefully

dropped around the field elsewhere, the crops had been very little injured; which showed clearly the efficacy of the water, when all the ceremonies and observances prescribed by the vision had been attended to.

I could never find the cowherd who was said to have seen this vision, and, in speaking to my old friend, the Sadr Amīn, learned in the shāstras,[20] on the subject, I told him that we had a short saying that would explain all this: 'A drowning man catches at a straw.'

'Yes,' said he, without any hesitation, 'and we have another just as good for the occasion: "Sheep will follow each other, though it should be into a well".'

Notes:

1. We are told in 2 Samuel, chap. xxiv, that the Deity was displeased at a census of the people, taken by Joab by the order of David, and destroyed of the people of Israel seventy thousand, besides women and children. [W. H. S.] The editor, in the course of seven years' experience in the Settlement department, six of which were agent in Bundēlkhand, never heard of the doctrine as to the incestuous character of surveys. Probably it had died out. Even a census no longer gives rise to alarm in most parts of the country. The wild rumours and theories common in 1872 and 1881 did not prevail when the census of 1891 was taken, or during subsequent operations.

2. This theory is, of course, erroneous.

3. The flax plant (*Linum usitatissimum*) is grown in India solely for the sake of the linseed. Linen is never made, and the stalk of the plant, as ordinarily grown, is too short for the manufacture of fibre. The attempts to introduce flax manufacture into India, though not ultimately successful, have proved that good flax can be made in the country, from Riga seed. Indian linseed is very largely exported. (Article 'Flax' in Balfour, *Cyclopaedia*, 3rd ed.)

4. Spores is the more accurate word.

5. That is to say, cattle-trespass. Cattle do not care to eat the green flax plant. The fields are not fenced.

6. The rust, or blight, described in the text probably was a species of *Unedo*. The gram, or chick-pea, and various kinds of pea and vetch are grown intermixed with the wheat. They ripen earlier, and are plucked up by the roots before the wheat is cut.

7. Chap. 4 of the Korān is entitled 'Women', and chap. 24 is entitled 'Light'. The story of Ayesha's misadventure is given in Sale's notes to chap. 24.

8. Muhammad died A.D. 632. Abū Bakr succeeded him, and after a khalīfate of only two years, was succeeded by Omar, who was assassinated in the twelfth year of his reign.

9. Basrah (Bassorah, Bussorah) in the province of Baghdad, on the Shatt-ul-Arab, or combined stream of the Tigris and Euphrates, was founded by the Khalīf Omar.

10. In the author's time the Muhammadan criminal law was applied to the whole population by Anglo-Indian judges, assisted by Muhammadan legal assessors, who gave rulings called *fatwas* on legal points. The Penal Code enacted in 1859 swept away the whole jungle of Regulations and *fatwas*, and established a scientific System of criminal jurisprudence, which bas remained substantially unchanged to this day. Adultery is punishable under the Code by the Court of Session, but prosecutions for this offence are very rare. Enticing away a married woman is also defined as an offence, and is punishable by a magistrate. Complaints under this head are extremely numerous, and mostly false. Secret and unpunished murders of women undoubtedly are common, and often reported as deaths from snake-bite or cholera. An aggrieved husband frequently tries to save his honour, and at the same time satisfy his vengeance, by tromping up a false charge of burglary against the suspected paramour, who generally replies by an equally false *alibi*.

11. A prosecution under the Penal Code for adultery can be instituted only by the husband, or the guardian representing him, and the woman is not punishable. Although the Muhammadan law of evidence has been got rid of, the Anglo-Indian courts are still unsuitable for the prosecution of adultery cases, especially where Indians are concerned. The English courts, though they do not require any specified number of witnesses, demand strict proof given in open court, and no Indian, whose honour has really been touched, cares to expose his domestic troubles to be wrangled over by lawyers. Many officers, including the editor, would be glad to see the section which renders adultery penal struck out of the Code. The matrimonial delinquencies of Indians are better dealt with by the caste organizations, and those of Europeans by civil action.

12. The Trigonometrical Survey, originated by Colonel Lambton, was begun at Cape Comōrin in 1800. It is now almost, if not quite, complete, except in Burma. See Markham, *A Memoir of the Indian Surveys* (2nd ed., 1878). The stations are marked by masonry pillars, for the partial repair of which a small sum is annually allotted.

13. Hindoos believe that holy men, by means of great austerities, can attain power to compel the gods to do their bidding.

14. For some account of the modern agitation against cow-killing. See note *ante*, Chapter 26, note 6.

15. On the sacredness of the Nerbudda see note *ante*, Chapter 1, note 13.

16. The Holī festival marks approximately the time of the vernal equinox, ten days before the full moon of the Hindoo month Phālgun. The day of the bonfire does not always fall on the 16th of March. It is not considered lucky to begin harvest till the Holī has been burnt. Mr. Crooke holds that 'on the whole, there seems to be some reason to believe that the intention to promote the fertility of men, animals, and crops, supplies the basis of the rites' ('The Holī, a Vernal Festival of the Hindus', *Folklore*, vol. xxv (1914), p. 83). I agree.

17. The pīpal-tree (*Ficus religiosa*, Linn.; *Urostigma religiosum*, Gasp.) is sacred to Vishnu, and universally venerated throughout India.

18. About four hundred thousand persons.

19. Two pice x 400,000 = 800,000 pice, = 200,000 annas, = 12,500 rupees. Even if the author's estimate of the numbers be much too large, the pecuniary result must have been handsome, not to mention the butter and flour.

20. Hindoo sacred books.

CHAPTER 28

Pestle-and-Mortar Sugar-Mills — Washing away of the Soil.

On the 13th [December, 1885] we came to Barwā Sāgar,[1] over a road winding among small ridges and conical hills, none of them much elevated or very steep; the whole being a bed of brown syenite, generally exposed to the surface in a decomposing state, intersected by veins and beds of quartz rocks, and here and there a narrow and shallow bed of dark basalt. One of these beds of basalt was converted into grey syenite by a large granular mixture of white quartz and feldspar with the black hornblende. From this rock the people form their sugar-mills, which are made like a pestle and mortar, the mortar being cut out of the hornblende rock, and the pestle out of wood.[2]

We saw a great many of these mortars during the march that could not have been in use for the last half-dozen centuries, but they are precisely the same as those still used all over India. The driver sits upon the end of the horizontal beam to which the bullocks are yoked; and in cold mornings it is very common to see him with a pair of good hot embers at his buttocks, resting upon a little projection made behind him to the beam for the purpose of sustaining it [sic]. I am disposed to think that the most productive parts of the surface of Bundēlkhand, like that of some of the districts of the Nerbudda territories which repose upon the back of the sandstone of the Vindhya chain, is [sic] fast flowing off to the sea through the great rivers, which seem by degrees to extend the channels of their tributary streams into every man's field, to drain away its substance by degrees, for the benefit of those who may in some future age occupy the islands of their delta. I have often seen a valuable estate reduced in value to almost nothing in a few years by some new *antennae*, if I may so call them, thrown out from the tributary streams of great rivers into their richest and deepest soils. Declivities are formed, the soil gets nothing from the cultivator but the mechanical aid of the plough, and the more its surface is ploughed and cross-ploughed, the more of its substance is washed away towards the Bay of Bengal in the Ganges, or the Gulf of Cambay in the Nerbudda. In the districts of the Nerbudda, we often see these black hornblende mortars, in which sugar-canes were once pressed by a happy peasantry, now standing

upon a bare and barren surface of sandstone rock, twenty feet above the present surface of the culturable lands of the country. There are evident signs of the surface on which they now stand having been that on which they were last worked. The people get more juice from their small straw-coloured canes in these pestle-and-mortar mills than they can from those with cylindrical rollers in the present rude state of the mechanical arts all over India; and the straw-coloured cane is the only kind that yields good sugar. The large purple canes yield a watery and very inferior juice; and are generally and almost universally sold in the markets as a fruit. The straw-coloured canes, from being crowded under a very slovenly System, with little manure and less weeding, degenerate into a mere reed. The Otaheite cane, which was introduced into India by me in 1827, has spread over the Nerbudda, and many other territories; but that that will degenerate in the same manner under the same slovenly system of tillage, is too probable.[3]

Notes:

1. The lake known as Barwā Sāgar was formed by a Bundēla chief, who constructed an embankment nearly three- quarters of a mile long to retain the waters of the Barwā stream, a tributary of the Betwā. The work was begun in 1705 and completed in 1737. The town is situated at the north-west corner of the lake, on the road from Jhānsī to the cantonment of Nowgong (properly Naugāon, or Nayāgāon), at a distance of twelve miles from Jhānsī (N.W.P. Gazetteer, 1st ed., vol. i, pp. 243 and 387).

2. The rude sketch given here in the author's text is not worth reproduction.

3. The 'pestle-and-mortar' pattern of mill above described is the indigenous model formerly in universal use in India, but, in most parts of the country, where stone is not available, the 'mortar' portion was made of wood. The stone mills are expensive. In the Bānda and Hamīrpur districts of Bundēlkhand sugar-cane is now grown only in the small areas where good loam soil is found. The method of cultivation differs in several respects from that practised in the Gangetic plains, but the editor never observed the slovenliness of which the author complains. He always found the cultivation in sugar-cane villages to be extremely careful and laborious. Ancient stone mills are sometimes found in black soil country, and it is difficult to understand how sugarcane can ever have been grown there. The author was mistaken in supposing that the indigenous pattern of mill is superior to a good roller mill. The indigenous mill has been completely superseded in most parts of the Panjāb, United Provinces, and Bihār, by the roller mill patented by Messrs. Mylne and Thompson of Bihīa in 1869, and largely improved by subsequent modifications. The original patent having expired, thousands of roller mills are annually made by native artisans, with

little regard to the rights of the Bihīa firm. The iron rollers, cast in Delhi and other places, are completed on costly lathes in many country towns. The mills are generally hired out for the season, and kept in repair by the speculator. The Rājā of Nāhan or Sirmūr in the Panjāb, who has a foundry employing six hundred men, does a large business of this kind, and finds it profitable. Since the first patent was taken out, many improvements in the design have been effected, and the best mills squeeze the cane absolutely dry. Messrs. Mylne and Thompson have been successful in introducing other improved machinery for the manufacture of sugar in villages. The Rosa factory near Shahjahānpur in the United Provinces makes sugar on a large scale by European methods.

When the author says that the large canes are sold 'as a fruit' he means that the canes are used for eating, or rather sucking like a sugar-stick. The varieties of sugar-cane are numerous, and the names vary much in different districts. According to Balfour, the Otaheite (Tahiti) cane is 'probably *Saccharum violaceum*'. The ordinary Indian kinds belong to the species *Saccharum officinarum*. The Otaheite cane was introduced into the West Indies about 1794, and came to India from the Mauritius. It is more suitable for the roller mill than for the indigenous mill, the stems being hard (*Cyclopaedia of India*, 3rd ed., 1885, s.v. 'Saccharum'). In a letter dated December 15, 1844, the author refers to his introduction of the Otaheite cane, and mentions that the Indian Agricultural Society awarded him a gold medal for this service. The cane was first planted in the Government Botanical Garden at Calcutta.

CHAPTER 29

Interview with the Chiefs of Jhānsī—Disputed Succession.

On the 14th[1] we came on fourteen miles to Jhānsī.[2] About five miles from our last ground we crossed the Baitantī river over a bed of syenite. At this river we mounted our elephant to cross, as the water was waist-deep at the ford. My wife returned to her palankeen as soon as we had crossed, but our little boy came on with me on the elephant, to meet the grand procession which I knew was approaching to greet us from the city. The Rājā of Jhānsī, Rām Chandar Rāo, died a few months ago, leaving a young widow and a mother, but no child.[3]

He was a young man of about twenty-eight years of age, timid, but of good capacity, and most amiable disposition. My duties brought us much into communication; and, though we never met, we had conceived a mutual esteem for each other. He had been long suffering from an affection of the liver, and had latterly persuaded himself that his mother was practising upon his life, with a view to secure the government to the eldest son of her daughter, which would, she thought, ensure the real power to her for life. That she wished him dead with this view, I had no doubt; for she had ruled the state for several years up to 1831, during what she was pleased to consider his minority; and she surrendered the power into his hands with great reluctance, since it enabled her to employ her *paramour* as minister, and enjoy his society as much as she pleased, under the pretence of holding *privy councils* upon affairs of great public interest.[4] He used to communicate his fears to me; and I was not without apprehension that his mother might some day attempt to hasten his death by poison. About a month before his death he wrote to me to say that spears had been found stuck in the ground, under the water where he was accustomed to swim, with their sharp points upwards; and, had he not, contrary to his usual practice, walked into the water, and struck his foot against one of them, he must have been killed. This was, no doubt, a thing got up by some designing person who wanted to ingratiate himself with the young man; for the mother was too shrewd a woman ever to attempt her son's life by such awkward means. About four months before I reached the capital, this amiable young prince died, leaving two paternal uncles, a mother, a widow, and one sister, the wife of one of our Sāgar pensioners, Morīsar Rāo. The mother claimed the inheritance for her grandson by this daughter, a very handsome young lad, then at Jhānsī, on the pretence that her son had adopted him on his death-bed. She had his head shaved, and made him go through all the other ceremonies of mourning, as for the death of his real father. The eldest of his uncles, Raghunāth Rāo, claimed the inheritance as the next heir; and all his party turned the young lad out of caste as a Brahman, for daring to go into mourning for a father who was yet alive; one of the greatest of crimes, according to Hindoo law, for they would not admit that he had been adopted by the deceased prince.[5]

The question of inheritance had been referred for decision to the Supreme Government through the prescribed channel when I arrived, and the decision was every day expected. The mother, with her daughter and grandson, and the widow, occupied the castle, situated on a high hill overlooking the city; while the two uncles of the deceased occupied their private dwellings in the city below. Raghunāth Rāo, the eldest, headed the procession that came out to meet me about three miles, mounted upon a fine female elephant, with his younger brother by his side. The minister, Nārū Gopāl, followed, mounted upon another, on the part of the mother and widow. Some of the Rājā's relations were upon two of the finest male elephants I have ever seen; and some of their friends, with the 'Bakshī', or paymaster (always an important personage), upon two others. Raghunāth Rāo's elephant drew up on the right of mine, and that of the minister on the left; and, after the usual compliments had passed between us, all the others fell back, and formed a line in our rear. They had about fifty troopers mounted upon very fine horses in excellent condition, which curvetted before and on both sides of us; together with a good many men on camels, and some four or five hundred foot attendants, all well dressed, but in various costumes. The elephants were so close to each other that the conversation, which we managed to keep up tolerably well, was general almost all the way to our tents; every man taking a part as he found the opportunity of a pause to introduce his little compliment to the Honourable Company or to myself, which I did my best to answer or divert. I was glad to see the affectionate respect with which the old man was everywhere received, for I had in my own mind no doubt whatever that the decision of the Supreme Government would be in his favour. The whole *cortège* escorted me through the town to my tent, which was pitched on the other side; and then they took their leave, still seated on their elephants, while I sat on mine, with my boy on my knee, till all had made their bow and departed. The elephants, camels, and horses were all magnificently caparisoned, and the housings of the whole were extremely rich. A good many of the troopers were dressed in chain-armour, which, worn outside their light-coloured quilted vests, looked very like black gauze scarfs.

My little friend the Sarīmant's own elephant had lately died; and, being unable to go to the cost of another with all its appendages, he had come thus far on horseback. A native gentleman can never condescend to ride an elephant without a train of at least a dozen attendants on horseback—he would almost as soon ride a horse *without a tail*.[6] Having been considered at one time as the equal of all these Rājās, I knew that he would feel a little mortified at finding himself buried in the crowd and dust; and invited him, as we approached the city, to take a seat by my side. This gained him consideration, and evidently gave him great pleasure. It was late before we reached our tents, as we were obliged to move slowly through the streets of the city, as well for our own convenience as for the safety of the crowd on foot before and around us. My wife, who had gone on before to avoid the crowd and dust, reached the tents halt an hour before us.

In the afternoon, when my second large tent had been pitched, the minister came to pay me a visit with a large train of followers, but with little display; and I found him a very sensible, mild, and gentlemanly man, just as I expected from the high character he bears with both parties, and with the people of the country generally. Any unreserved conversation here in such a crowd was, of course, out of the question, and I told the minister that it was my intention early next morning to visit the tomb of his late master; where I should be very glad to meet him, if he could make it convenient to come without any ceremony. He seemed much pleased with the proposal, and next morning we met a little before sunrise within the railing that encloses the tomb or cenotaph; and there had a good deal of quiet and, I believe, unreserved talk about the affairs of the Jhānsī state, and the family of the late prince. He told me that, a few hours before the Rājā's death, his mother had placed in his arms for adoption the son of his sister, a very handsome lad of ten years of age—but whether the Rājā was or was not sensible at the time he could not say, for he never after heard him speak; that the mother of the deceased considered the adoption as complete, and made her grandson go through the funeral ceremonies as at the death of his father, which for nine days were performed unmolested; but, when it came to the tenth and last—which, had it passed quietly, would have been considered as completing the title of adoption—Raghunāth Rāo and his friends interposed, and prevented further proceedings, declaring that, while there were so many male heirs, no son could be adopted for the deceased prince according to the usages of the family.

The widow of the Rājā, a timid, amiable young woman, of twenty-five years of age, was by no means anxious for this adoption, having shared the suspicions of her husband regarding the practices of his mother; and found his sister, who now resided with them in the castle, a most violent and overbearing woman, who would be likely to exclude her from all share in the administration, and make her life very miserable, were her son to be declared the Rājā. Her wish was to be allowed to adopt, in the name of her deceased husband, a young cousin of his, Sadāsheo, the son of Nānā Bhāo. Gangādhar, the younger brother of Raghunāth Rāo, was exceedingly anxious to have his elder brother declared Rājā, because he had no sons, and from the debilitated state of his frame, must soon die, and leave the principality to him. Every one of the three parties had sent agents to the Governor-General's representative in Bundēlkhand to urge their claim; and, till the final decision, the widow of the late chief was to be considered the sovereign. The minister told me that there was one unanswerable argument against Raghunāth Rāo's succeeding, which, out of regard to his feelings, he had not yet urged, and about which he wished to consult me as a friend of the late prince and his widow; this was, that he was a leper, and that the signs of the disease were becoming every day more and more manifest.

I told him that I had observed them in his face, but was not aware that any one else had noticed them. I urged him, however, not to advance this as a ground of exclusion, since they all knew him to be a very worthy man, while his younger brother was said to be the reverse; and more especially I thought it would be very cruel and unwise to distress and exasperate him by so doing, as I had no doubt that, before this ground could be brought to their notice, Government would declare in his favour, right being so clearly on his side.

After an agreeable conversation with this sensible and excellent man, I returned to my tents to prepare for the reception of Raghunāth Rāo and his party. They came about nine o'clock with a much greater display of elephants and followers than the minister had brought with him. He and his friends kept me in close conversation till eleven o'clock, in spite of my wife's many considerate messages to say breakfast was waiting. He told me that the mother of the late Rājā, his nephew, was a very violent woman, who had involved the state in much trouble during the period of her regency, which she managed to prolong till her son was twenty-five years of age, and resigned with infinite reluctance only three years ago; that her minister during her regency, Gangadhar Mūlī, was at the same time her *paramour*, and would be surely restored to power and to her embraces, were her grandson's claim to the succession recognized; that it was with great difficulty he had been able to keep this atrocious character under surveillance pending the consideration of their claims by the Supreme Government; that, by having the head of her grandson shaved, and making him go through all the other funeral ceremonies with the other members of the family, she had involved him and his young *innocent wife* (who had unhappily continued to drink out of the same cup with her husband) *in the dreadful crime of mourning for a father whom they knew to be yet alive,* a crime that must be expiated by the 'prāyaschit,'[7] which-would be exacted from the young couple on their return to Sāgar before they could be restored to caste, from which they were now considered as excommunicated. As for the young widow, she was everything they could wish; but she was so timid that she would be governed by the old lady, if she should have any ostensible part assigned her in the administration.[8]

I told the old gentleman that I believed it would be my duty to pay the first visit to the widow and mother of the late prince, as one of pure condolence, and that I hoped my doing so would not be considered any mark of disrespect towards him, who must now be looked up to as the head of the family. He remonstrated against this most earnestly; and, at last, tears came into his eyes as he told me that, if I paid the first visit to the castle, he should never again be able to show his face outside his door, so great would be the indignity he would be considered to have suffered; but, rather than I should do this, he would come to my tents, and escort me himself to the castle. Much was to be said on both sides of the weighty question; but, at last, I thought that the arguments were in his favour—that, if I went to the castle first, he might possibly resent it upon the poor woman and the prime minister when he came into power, as I had no doubt he soon would—and that I might be consulting their interest as much as his feelings by going to his house first. In the evening I received a message from the old lady, urging the necessity of my paying the first visit of condolence for the death of my young friend to the widow and mother. 'The rights of mothers', said she, 'are respected in all countries; and, in India, the first visit of condolence for the death of a man is always due to the mother, if alive.' I told the messenger that my resolution was unaltered, and would, I trusted, be found the best for all parties under present circumstances. I told him that I dreaded the resentment towards them of Raghunāth Rāo, if he came into power.

'Never mind that,' said he: 'my mistress is of too proud a spirit to dread resentment from any one—pay her the compliment of the first visit, and let her enemies do their worst.' I told him that I could leave Jhānsī without visiting either of them, but could not go first to the castle; and he said that my departing thus would please the old lady better than the *second visit*. The minister would not have said this—the old lady would not have ventured to send such a message by him—the man was an understrapper; and I left him to mount my elephant and pay my two visits.[9]

With the best *cortège* I could muster, I went to Raghunāth Rāo's, where I was received with a salute from some large guns in his courtyard, and entertained with a party of dancing girls and musicians in the usual manner. Attar of roses and 'pān'[10] were given, and valuable shawls put before me, and refused in the politest terms I could think of; such as, 'Pray do me the favour to keep these things for me till I have the happiness of visiting Jhānsī again, as I am going through Gwālior, where nothing valuable is a moment safe from thieves'. After sitting an hour, I mounted my elephant, and proceeded up to the castle, where I was received with another salute from the bastions. I sat for half an hour in the hall of audience with the minister and all the principal men of the court, as Raghunāth Rāo was to be considered as a private gentleman till the decision of the Supreme Government should be made known; and the handsome lad, Krishan Rāo, whom the old woman wished to adopt, and whom I had often seen at Sāgar, was at my request brought in and seated by my side. By him I sent my message of condolence to the widow and mother of his deceased uncle, couched in the usual terms — that the happy effects of good government in the prosperity of this city, and the comfort and happiness of the people, had extended the fame of the family all over India; and that I trusted the reigning member of that family, whoever he might be, would be sensible that it was his duty to sustain that reputation by imitating the example of those who had gone before him. After attar of roses and pān had been handed round in the usual manner, I went to the summit of the highest tower in the castle, which commands an extensive view of the country around.

The castle stands upon the summit of a small hill of syenitic rock. The elevation of the outer wall is about one hundred feet above the level of the plain, and the top of the tower on which I stood about one hundred feet more, as the buildings rise gradually from the sides to the summit of the hill. The city extends out into the plain to the east from the foot of the hill on which the castle stands. Around the city there is a good deal of land, irrigated from four or five tanks in the neighbourhood, and now under rich wheat crops; and the gardens are very numerous, and abound in all the fruit and vegetables that the people most like. Oranges are very abundant and very fine, and our tents have been actually buried in them and all the other fruits and vegetables which the kind people of Jhānsī have poured in upon us. The city of Jhānsī contains about sixty thousand inhabitants, and is celebrated for its manufacture of carpets.[11] There are some very beautiful temples in the city, all built by Gosāins, one [*sic*] of the priests of Siva who here engage in trade, and accumulate much wealth.[12] The family of the chief do not build tombs; and that now raised over the place where the late prince was buried is dedicated as a temple to Siva, and was made merely with a view to secure the place from all danger of profanation.[13]

The face of the country beyond the influence of the tanks is neither rich nor interesting. The cultivation seemed scanty and the population thin, owing to the irremediable sterility of soil, from the poverty of the primitive rock from whose detritus it is chiefly formed. Raghunāth Rāo told me that the wish of the people in the castle to adopt a child as the successor to his nephew arose from the desire to escape the scrutiny into the past accounts of disbursements which he might be likely to order. I told him that I had myself no doubt that he would be declared the Rājā, and urged him to turn all his thoughts to the future, and to allow no inquiries to be made into the past, with a view to gratify either his own resentment, or that of others; that the Rajas of Jhānsī had hitherto been served by the most respectable, able, and honourable men in the country, while the other chiefs of Bundēlkhand could get no man of this class to do their work for them—that this was the only court in Bundēlkhand in which such men could be seen, simply because it was the only one in which they could feel themselves secure— while other chiefs confiscated the property of ministers who had served them with fidelity, on the pretence of embezzlement; the wealth thus acquired, however, soon disappearing, and its possessors being obliged either to conceal it or go out of the country to enjoy it. Such rulers thus found their courts and capitals deprived of all those men of wealth and respectability who adorned the courts of princes in other countries, and embellished, not merely their capitals, but the face of their dominions in general with their chateaus and other works of ornament and utility. Much more of this sort passed between us, and seemed to make an impression upon him; for he promised to do all that I had recommended to him. Poor man! he can have but a short and miserable existence, for that dreadful disease, the leprosy, is making sad inroads in his System already.[14] His uncle, Raghunāth Rāo, was afflicted with it; and, having understood from the priests that by *drowning* himself in the Ganges (taking the 'samādh'), he should remove all traces of it from his family, he went to Benares, and there drowned himself, some twenty years ago. He had no children, and is said to have been the first of his family in whom the disease showed itself.[15]

Notes:

1. December, 1835.

2. Now the head-quarters of the British district of the same name, and also of the Indian Midland Railway. Since the opening of this railway and the restoration of the Gwālior fort to Sindhia in 1886, the importance of Jhānsī, both civil and military, has much increased. The native town was given up by Sindhia in exchange for the Gwālior stronghold.

3. This chief is called Rājā Rāo Rāmchand in the *N.W.P. Gazetteer*, 1st ed. He died on August 20, 1835. His administration had been weak, and his finances were left in great disorder. Under his successor the disorder of the administration became still greater.

4. Dowagers in Indian princely families are frequently involved in such intrigues and plots. The editor could specify instances in his personal experience. Compare Chapter 34, *post*.

5. An adopted son passes completely out of the family of his natural, into that of his adoptive, father, all his rights and duties as a son being at the same time transferred. In this case, the adoption had not really taken place, and the lad's duty to his living natural father remained unaffected.

6. This statement will not apply to those districts in the United Provinces where elephants are numerous and often kept by gentry of no great rank or wealth, A Rājā, of course, always likes to have a few mounted men clattering behind him, if possible.

7. The 'prāyaschit' is an expiating atonement by which the person humbles himself in public. It is often imposed for crimes committed in a *former birth*, as indicated by inflictions suffered in this. [W. H. S.] The practical working of Hindoo caste rules is often frightfully cruel. The victims of these rules in the case described by the author were a boy ten years old, and his child- wife of still more tender years. Yet all the penalties, including rigorous fasts, would be mercilessly exacted from these innocent children. Leprosy and childlessness are among the afflictions supposed to prove the sinfulness of the sufferer in some former birth, perhaps thousands of years ago.

8. The poor young widow died of grief some months after my visit; her spirits never rallied after the death of her husband, and she never ceased to regret that she had not burned herself with his remains. The people of Jhānsī generally believe that the prince's mother brought about his death by (*dīnāī*) slow poison, and I am afraid that that was the impression on the mind of the poor widow. The minister, who was entirely on her side, and a most worthy and able man, was quite satisfied that this suspicion was without any foundation whatever in truth. [W. H. S.]

9. Considering the fact that, 'till the final decision, the widow of the late chief was to be considered the sovereign', it would be difficult to justify the anthor's decision. The reigning sovereign was clearly entitled to the first visit. Questions of precedence, salutes, and etiquette are as the very breath of their nostrils to the Indian nobility.

10. The leaf of *Piper betel*, handed to guests at ceremonial entertainments, along with the nut of *Areca catechu*, made up in a packet of gold or silver leaf.

11. This estimate of the population was probably excessive. The population in 1891, including the cantonments, was 53,779, and in 1911, 70,208. The fort of Gwālior and the cantonment of Morār were surrendered by the Government of India to Sindhia in exchange for the fort and town of Jhānsī on March 10, 1886. Sindhia also relinquished fifty-eight villages in exchange for thirty given up by the Government of India, the difference in value being adjusted by cash payments. The arrangements were finally sanctioned by Lord Dufferin on June 13, 1888.

12. These buildings are both tombs and temples. The Gosāins of Jhānsī do not burn, but bury their dead; and over the grave those who can afford to do so raise a handsome temple, and dedicate it to Siva. [W. H. S.] The custom of burial is not peculiar to the Saiva Gosāins of Jhānsī. It is the ordinary practice of Gosāins throughout India. Many of the Gosāins are devoted to the worship of Vishnu. Burial of the dead is practised by a considerable number of the Hindoo castes of the artisan grade, and by some divisions of the sweeper caste. See Crooke, 'Primitive Rites of Disposal of the Dead' (*J. Anthrop. Institute*, vol. xxix, N.S., vol. ii (1900), pp. 271-92).

13. This tact lends some support to W. Simpson's theory that the Hindoo temple is derived from a sepulchral structure.

14. This chief died of leprosy in May, 1838. [W. H. S.]

15. Raghunāth Rāo was the first of his family invested by the Peshwā with the government of the Jhānsī territory, which he had acquired from the Bundēlkhand chiefs. He went to Benares in 1795 to drown himself, leaving his government to his third brother, Sheorām Bhāo, as his next brother, Lachchhman Rāo, was dead, and his sons were considered incapable. Sheorām Bhāo died in 1815, and his eldest son, Krishan Rāo, had died four years before him, in 1811, leaving one son, the late Rājā, and two daughters. This was a noble sacrifice to what he had been taught by his spiritual teachers to consider as a duty towards his family; and we must admire the man while we condemn the religion and the priests. There is no country in the world where parents are more reverenced than in India, or where they more readily make sacrifices of all sorts for their children, or for those they consider as such. We succeeded in [June] 1817 to all the rights of the Peshwā in Bundēlkhand, and, with great generosity, converted the viceroys of Jhānsī and Jālaun into independent sovereigns of hereditary principalities, yielding each ten lakhs of rupees. [W. H. S.] The statement in the note that Raghunāth Rāo I 'went to Benares in 1795 to drown himself' is inconsistent with the statement in the text that this event happened 'some twenty years ago'. The word 'twenty' is evidently a mistake for 'forty'. The *N. W. P. Gazetteer*, 1st ed., names several persons who governed Jhānsī on behalf of the Peshwā between 1742 and 1770, in which latter year Raghunāth Rāo I

received charge. According to the same authority, Sheo (Shio) Rām Bhāo is called 'Sheo Bhāo Hari, better known as Sheo Rāo Bhāo', and is said to have succeeded Raghunāth Rāo I in 1794, and to have died in 1814, not 1816. A few words may here be added to complete the history. The leper Raghunāth Rāo II, whose claim the author strangely favoured, was declared Rājā, and died, as already noted, in May, 1838, 'his brief period of rule being rendered unquiet by the opposition made to him, professedly on the ground of his being a leper'. His revenues fell from twelve lākhs (£120,000) to three lākhs of rupees (£30,000) a year. On his death in 1838, the succession was again contested by four claimants. Pending inquiry into the merits of their claims, the Governor-General's Agent assumed the administration. Ultimately, Gangādhar Rāo, younger brother of the leper, was appointed Rājā. The disorder in the state rendered administration by British officers necessary as a temporary measure, and Gangādhar Rāo did not obtain power until 1842. His rule was, on the whole, good. He died childless in November, 1853, and Lord Dalhousie, applying the doctrine of lapse, annexed the estate in 1854, granting a pension of five thousand rupees, or about five hundred pounds, monthly to Lacchhmī Bāī, Gangādhar Rāo's widow, who also succeeded to personal property worth about one hundred thousand pounds. She resented the refusal of permission to adopt a son, and the consequent annexation of the state, and was further deeply offended by several acts of the English Administration, above all by the permission of cow-slaughter. Accordingly, when the Mutiny broke out, she quickly joined the rebels. On the 7th and 8th June, 1857, all the Europeans in Jhānsī, men, women, and children, to the number of about seventy persons, were cruelly murdered by her orders, or with her sanction. On the 9th June her authority was proclaimed. In the prolonged fighting which ensued, she placed herself at the head of her troops, whom she led with great gallantry. In June, 1858, after a year's bloodstained reign, she was killed in battle. By November, 1858, the country was pacified.

CHAPTER 30

Haunted Villages.

On the 16th[1] we came on nine miles to Amabāi, the frontier village of the Jhānsī territory, bordering upon Datiyā,[2] where I had to receive the farewell visits of many members of the Jhānsī parties, who came on to have a quiet opportunity to assure me that, whatever may be the final order of the Supreme Government, they will do their best for the good of the people and the state; for I have always considered Jhānsī among the native states of Bundēlkhand as a kind of oasis in the desert, the only one in which a man can accumulate property with the confidence of being permitted by its rulers freely to display and enjoy it. I had also to receive the visit of messengers from the Rājā of Datiyā, at whose capital we were to encamp the next day, and, finally, to take leave of my amiable little friend the Sarīmant, who here left me on his return to Sāgar, with a heavy heart I really believe.

We talked of the common belief among the agricultural classes of villages being haunted by the spirits of ancient proprietors whom it was thought necessary to propitiate. 'He knew', he said, 'many instances where these spirits were so very *froward* that the present heads of villages which they haunted, and the members of their little communities, found it almost impossible to keep them in good humour; and their cattle and children were, in consequence, always liable to serious accidents of one kind or another. Sometimes they were bitten by snakes, sometimes became possessed by devils, and, at others, were thrown down and beaten most unmercifully. Any person who falls down in an epileptic fit is supposed to be thrown down by a ghost, or possessed by a devil.[3] They feel little of our mysterious dread of ghosts; a sound *drubbing* is what they dread from them, and he who hurts himself in one of the fits is considered to have got it. 'As for himself, whenever he found any one of the villages upon his estate haunted by the spirit of an old "patēl" (village proprietor), he always made a point of giving him a *neat little shrine*, and having it well endowed and attended, to keep him in good humour; this he thought was a duty that every landlord owed to his tenants.' Rāmchand, the pundit, said that 'villages which had been held by old Gond (mountaineer) proprietors were more liable than any other to those kinds of visitations; that it was easy to say what village was and was not haunted, but often exceedingly difficult to discover to whom the ghost belonged. This once discovered, his nearest surviving relation was, of course, expected to take steps to put him to rest; but', said he, 'it is wrong to suppose that the ghost of an old proprietor must be always doing mischief—he is often the best friend of the cultivators, and of the present proprietor too, if he treats him with proper respect; for he will not allow the people of any other village to encroach upon their boundaries with impunity, and they will be saved all the expense and annoyance of a reference to the "adālat" (judicial tribunals) for the settlement of boundary disputes. It will not cost much to conciliate these spirits, and the money is generally well laid out.'

Several anecdotes were told me in illustration; and all that I could urge against the probability or possibility of such Visitation appeared to them very inconclusive and unsatisfactory. They mentioned the case of the family of village proprietors in the Sāgar district, who had for several generations, at every new settlement, insisted upon having the name of the spirit of the old proprietor inserted in the lease instead of their own, and thereby secured his good graces on all occasions. Mr. Fraser had before mentioned this case to me. In August, 1834, while engaged in the settlement of the land revenue of the Sāgar district for twenty years, he was about to deliver the lease of the estate made out in due form to the head of the family, a very honest and respectable old gentleman, when he asked him respectfully in whose name it had been made out. 'In yours, to be sure; have you not renewed your lease for twenty years?' The old man, in a state of great alarm, begged him to have it altered immediately, or he and his family would all be destroyed—that the spirit of the ancient proprietor presided over the village community and its interests, and that all affairs of importance were transacted is his name. 'He is', said the old man, 'a very jealous spirit, and will not admit of any living man being considered for a moment as a proprietor or joint proprietor of the estate. It has been held by me and my ancestors immediately under Government for many generations; but the lease deeds have always been made out in his name, and ours have been inserted merely as his managers or bailiffs—were this good old rule, under which we have so long prospered, to be now infringed, we should all perish under his anger.' Mr. Fraser found, upon inquiring, that this had really been the case; and, to relieve the old man and his family from their fears, he had the papers made out afresh, and the *ghost* inserted as the proprietor. The modes of flattering and propitiating these beings, natural and supernatural, who are supposed to have the power to do mischief, are endless.[4]

While I was in charge of the district of Narsinghpur, in the valley of the Nerbudda, in 1823, a cultivator of the village of Bēdū, about twelve miles distant from my court, was one day engaged in the cultivation of his field on the border of the village of Barkharā, which was supposed to be haunted by the spirit of an old proprietor, whose temper was so froward and violent that the lands could hardly be let for anything, for hardly any man would venture to cultivate them lest he might unintentionally incur his ghostship's displeasure. The poor cultivator, after begging his pardon in secret, ventured to drive his plough a few yards beyond the proper line of his boundary, and thus add half an acre of Barkharā to his own little tenement, which was situated in Bēdū. That very night his only son was bitten by a snake, and his two bullocks were seized with the murrain. In terror he went of to the village temple, confessed his sin, and vowed, not only to restore the half-acre of land to the village of Barkharā, but to build a very handsome shrine upon the spot as a perpetual sign of his repentance. The boy and the bullocks all three recovered, and the shrine was built; and is, I believe, still to be seen as the boundary mark.

The fact was that the village stood upon an elevated piece of ground rising out of a moist plain, and a colony of snakes had taken up their abode in it. The bites of these snakes had on many occasions proved fatal, and such accidents were all attributed to the anger of a spirit which was supposed to haunt the village. At one time, under the former government, no one would take a lease of the village on any terms, and it had become almost entirely deserted, though the soil was the finest in the whole district. With a view to remove the whole prejudices of the people, the governor, Goroba Pundit, took the lease himself at the rent of one thousand rupees a year; and, in the month of June, went from his residence, twelve miles, with ten of his own ploughs to superintend the commencement of so *perilous* an undertaking.

On reaching the middle of the village, situated on the top of the little hill, he alighted from his horse, sat down upon a carpet that had been spread for him under a large and beautiful banyan-tree, and began to refresh himself with a pipe before going to work in the fields. As he quaffed his hookah, and railed at the follies of the men, 'whose absurd superstitions had made them desert so beautiful a village with so noble a tree in its centre', his eyes fell upon an enormous black snake, which had coiled round one of its branches immediately over his head, and seemed as if resolved at once to pounce down and punish him for his blasphemy. He gave his pipe to his attendant, mounted his horse, from which the saddle had not yet been taken, and never pulled rein till he got home. Nothing could ever induce him to visit this village again, though he was afterwards employed under me as a native collector; and he has often told me that he verily believed this was the spirit of the old landlord that he had unhappily neglected to propitiate before taking possession.

My predecessor in the civil charge of that district, the late Mr. Lindsay of the Bengal Civil Service, again tried to remove the prejudices of the people against the occupation and cultivation of this fine village. It had never been measured, and all the revenue officers, backed by all the farmers and cultivators of the neighbourhood, declared that the spirit of the old proprietor would never allow it to be so. Mr. Lindsay was a good geometrician, and had long been in the habit of superintending his revenue surveys himself, and on this occasion be thought himself particularly called upon to do so. A new measuring cord was made for the occasion, and, with fear and trembling, all his officers attended him to the first field; but in measuring it the rope, by some accident, broke. Poor Lindsay was that morning taken ill and obliged to return to Narsinghpur, where he died soon after from fever. No man was ever more beloved by all classes of the people of his district than he was; and I believe there was not one person among them who did not believe him to have fallen a victim to the resentment of the spirit of the old proprietor. When I went to the village some years afterwards, the people in the neighbourhood all declared to me that they saw the cord with which he was measuring fly into a thousand pieces the moment the men attempted to straighten it over the first field.[5]

A very respectable old gentleman from the Concan, or Malabar coast,[6] told me one day that every man there protects his field of corn and his fruit-tree by dedicating it to one or other of the spirits which there abound, or confiding it to his guardianship. He sticks up something in the field, or ties on something to the tree, in the name of the said spirit, who from that moment feels himself responsible for its safe keeping. If any one, without permission from the proprietor, presumes to take either an ear of corn from the field, or fruit from the tree, he is sure to be killed outright, or made extremely ill. 'No other protection is required', said the old gentleman, 'for our fields and fruit-trees in that direction, though whole armies should have to march through them.' I once saw a man come to the proprietor of a jack-tree,[7] embrace his feet, and in the most piteous manner implore his protection. He asked what was the matter. 'I took', said the man, 'a jack from your tree yonder three days ago, as I passed at night; and I have been suffering dreadful agony in my stomach ever since. The spirit of the tree is upon me, and you only can pacify him.' The proprietor took up a bit of cow-dung, moistened it, and made a mark with it upon the man's forehead, *in the name of the spirit*, and put some of it into the knot of hair on the top of his head. He had no sooner done this than the man's pains all left him, and he went off, vowing never again to give similar cause of offence to one of these guardian spirits. 'Men', said my old friend, 'do not die there in the same regulated spirit, with their thoughts directed exclusively towards God, as in other parts; and whether a man's spirit is to haunt the world or not after his death all depends on that.'

Notes:

1. December, 1835.

2. Datiyā (Datia, Dutteeah) is a small state, with an area of about 911 square miles, and a cash revenue of about four lākhs of rupees. On the east it touches the Jhānsī district, but in all other directions it is enclosed by the territories of Sindhia, the Maharaja of Gwālior. The principality was separated from Orchhā by a family partition in the seventeenth century. The first treaty between the Rājā and the British Government was concluded on the 15th March, 1804.

3. The belief that epileptic patients are possessed by devils is, of course, in no wise peculiar to India. It is almost universal. Professor Lombroso discusses the belief in diabolical possession in chap. 4 of *The Man of Genius* (London ed., 1891).

4. 'The educated European of the nineteenth century cannot realize the dread in which the Hindoo stands of devils. They haunt his paths from the cradle to the grave. The Tamil proverb in fact says, "The devil who seizes yon in the cradle, goes with you to the funeral pile".' The fear and worship of ghosts, demons, and devils are universal throughout India, and the rites practised are often comical. The ghost of a bibulous European official with a hot temper, who died at Muzaffarnagar, in the United Provinces, many years ago, was propitiated by offerings of beer and whisky at 'his tomb. Much information on the subject is collected in the articles 'Demon', 'Devils', 'Dehwār', and 'Deified Warriors' in Balfour, *Cyclopaedia of India* (3rd ed.). Almost every number of Mr. Crooke's periodical *North Indian Notes and Queries* (Allahabad: Pioneer Press; London: A. Constable & Co., 5 vols., from 1891-2 to 1895-6) gave fresh instances of the oddities of demon-worship.

5. The officials of the native Governments were content to use either a rope or a bamboo for field measurements, and these primitive instruments continued to satisfy the early British officers. For many years past a proper chain has been always employed for revenue surveys.

6. 'The author uses the term 'Concan' (Konkan) in a wide sense, so as to cover all the territory between the Western Ghāts and the sea, including Malabar in the south. The term is often used in a more restricted sense to mean Bombay and certain other districts, to the north of Malabar.

7. *Artocarpus integrifolius.* The jack fruit attains an enormous size, and sometimes weighs fifty or sixty pounds. Indians delight in it, but to most Europeans it is extremely offensive.

CHAPTER 31

Interview with the Rājā of Datiyā — Fiscal Errors of Statesmen — Thieves and Robbers by Profession.

On the 17th[1] we came to Datiyā, nine miles over a dry and poor soil, thinly, and only partially, covering a bed of brown and grey syenite, with veins of quartz and feldspar, and here and there dykes of basalt, and a few boulders scattered over the surface. The old Rājā, Parīchhit,[2] on one elephant, and his cousin, Dalīp Singh, upon a second, and several of their relations upon others, all splendidly caparisoned, came out two miles to meet us, with a very large and splendid *cortège*. My wife, as usual, had gone on in her palankeen very early, to avoid the crowd and dust of this 'istikbāl', or meeting; and my little boy, Henry, went on at the same time in the palankeen, having got a slight fever from too much exposure to the sun in our slow and stately entrance into Jhānsī. There were more men in steel chain armour in this *cortège* than in that of Jhānsī; and, though the elephants were not quite so fine, they were just as numerous, while the crowd of foot attendants was still greater. They were in fancy dresses, individually handsome, and collectively picturesque; though, being all soldiers, not quite pleasing to the eye of a soldier. I remarked to the Rājā, as we rode side by side on our elephants, that we attached much importance to having our soldiers all in uniform dresses, according to their corps, while he seemed to care little about these matters. 'Yes,' said the old man, with a smile, 'with me every man pleases himself in his dress, and I care not what he wears, provided it is neat and clean.' They certainly formed a body more picturesque from being allowed individually to consult their own fancies in their dresses, for the native taste in dress is generally very good. Our three elephants came on abreast, and the Rājā and I conversed as freely as men in such situations can converse. He is a stout, cheerful old gentleman, as careless apparently about his own dress as about that of his soldiers, and a much more sensible and agreeable person than I expected; and I was sorry to learn from him that he had for twelve years been suffering from an attack of sciatica on one side, which had deprived him of the use of one of his legs. I was obliged to consent to halt the next day that I might hunt in his preserve (*ramnā*) in the morning, and return his visit in the evening. In the Rājā's cortege there were several men mounted on excellent horses, who carried guitars, and played upon them, and sang in a very agreeable style, I had never before seen or heard of such a band, and was both surprised and pleased.

The great part of the wheat, gram,[3] and other exportable land produce which the people consume, as far as we have yet come, is drawn from our Nerbudda districts, and those of Mālwa which border upon them; and, *par conséquent*, the price has been rapidly increasing as we recede from them in our advance northward. Were the soil of those Nerbudda districts, situated as they are at such a distance from any great market for their agricultural products, as bad as it is in the parts of Bundēlkhand that I came over, no net surplus revenue could possibly be drawn from them in the present state of arts and industry. The high prices paid here for land produce, arising from the necessity of drawing a great part of what is consumed from such distant lands, enables the Rājās of these Bundēlkhand states to draw the large revenue they do. These chiefs expend the whole of their revenue in the maintenance of public establishments of one kind or other; and, as the essential articles of subsistence, wheat and gram, &c., which are produced in their own districts, or those immediately around them, are not sufficient for the supply of these establishments, they must draw them from distant territories. All this produce is brought on the backs of bullocks, because there is no road from the districts whence they obtain it, over which a wheeled carriage can be drawn with safety; and, as this mode of transit is very expensive, the price of the produce, when it reaches the capitals, around which these local establishments are concentrated, becomes very high. They must pay a price equal to the collective cost of purchasing and bringing this substance from the most distant districts, to which they are at any time obliged to have recourse for a supply, or they will not be supplied; and, as there cannot be two prices for the same thing in the same market, the wheat and gram produced in the neighbourhood of one of these Bundēlkhand capitals fetch as high a price there as that brought from the most remote districts on the banks of the Nerbudda river; while it costs comparatively nothing to bring it from the former lands to the markets. Such lands, in consequence, yield a rate of rent much greater compared with their natural powers of fertility than those of the remotest districts whence produce is drawn for these markets or capitals; and, as all the lands are the property of the Rājās, they drew all those rents as revenue.[4]

Were we to take this revenue, which the Rajas now enjoy, in tribute for the maintenance of public establishments concentrated at distant seats, all these local establishments would, of course, be at once disbanded; and all the effectual demand which they afford for the raw agricultural produce of distant districts would cease. The price of this produce would diminish in proportion, and with it the value of the lands of the districts around such capitals. Hence the folly of conquerors and paramount powers, from the days of the Greeks and Romans down to those of Lord Hastings[5] and Sir John Malcolm,[6] who were all bad political economists, supposing that conquered and ceded territories could always be made to yield to a foreign state the same amount of gross revenue as they had paid to their domestic government, whatever their situation with reference to the markets for their produce — whatever the state of their arts and their industry — and whatever the character and extent of the local establishments maintained out of it. The settlements of the land revenue in all the territories acquired in Central India during the Marāthā war, which ended in 1817, were made upon the supposition that the lands would continue to pay the same rate of rent under the new as they had paid under the old government, uninfluenced by the diminution of all local establishments, civil and military, to one-tenth of what they had been; that, under the new order of things, all the waste lands must be brought into tillage, and be able to pay as high a rate of rent as before tillage, and, consequently, that the aggregate available net revenue must greatly and rapidly increase. Those who had the making of the settlements and the governing of these new territories did not consider that the diminution of every *establishment* was the removal of a *market*, of an effectual demand for land produce; and that, when all the waste lands should be brought into tillage, the whole would deteriorate in fertility, from the want of fallows, Under the prevailing system of agriculture, which afforded the lands no other means of renovation from over-cropping. The settlements of land which were made throughout our new land acquisitions upon these fallacious assumptions of course failed. During a series of quinquennial settlements the assessment has been everywhere gradually reduced to about two-thirds of what it was when our rule began, to less than one- half of what Sir John Malcolm, and all the other local authorities, and even the worthy Marquis of Hastings himself, under the influence of their opinions, expected it would be. The land revenues of the native princes of Central India, who reduced their public establishments, which the new order of things seemed to render useless, and thereby diminished the only markets for the raw produce of their lands, have been everywhere falling off in the same proportion; and scarcely one of them now draws two-thirds of the income he drew from the same lands in 1817.

There are in the valley of the Nerbudda districts that yield a great deal more produce every year than either Orchhā, Jhānsī, or Datiyā; and yet, from the want of the same domestic markets, they do not yield one-fourth of the amount of land revenue. The lands are, however, rated equally high to the assessment, in proportion to their value to the farmers and cultivators. To enable them to yield a larger revenue to Government, they require to have larger establishments as markets for land produce. These establishments may be either public, and paid by Government; or they may be private, as manufactories, by which the land produce of these districts would be consumed by people employed in investing the value of their labour in commodities suited to the demand of distant markets, and more valuable than land produce in proportion to their weight and bulk.[7] These are the establishments which Government should exert itself to introduce and foster; since the valley of the Nerbudda, in addition to a soil exceedingly fertile, has in its whole line, from its source to its embouchure, rich beds of coal reposing for the use of future generations, under the sandstone of the Sātpura and Vindhya ranges, and beds no less rich of very fine iron. These advantages have not yet been justly appreciated; but they will be so by and by.[8]

About half-past four in the afternoon of the day we reached Datiyā, I had a visit from the Rājā, who came in his palankeen, with a very respectable, but not very numerous or noisy, train, and he sat with me about an hour. My large tents were both pitched parallel to each other, about twenty paces distant, and united to each other at both ends by separate 'kanāts', or cloth curtains. My little boy was present, and behaved extremely well in steadily refusing, without even a look from me, a handful of gold mohurs, which the Rājā pressed several times upon his acceptance. I received him at the door of my tent, and supported him upon my arm to his chair, as he cannot walk without some slight assistance, from the affection already mentioned in his leg. A salute from the guns at his castle announced his departure and return to it. After the audience, Lieutenant Thomas and I ascended to the summit of a palace of the former Rājās of this state, which stands upon a high rock close inside the eastern gate of the city, whence we could see to the west of the city a still larger and handsomer palace standing, I asked our conductors, the Rājā's servants, why it was unoccupied. 'No prince these degenerate days', said they, 'could muster a family and court worthy of such a palace — the family and court of the largest of them would, within the walls of such a building, feel as if they were in a desert. Such palaces were made for princes of the older times, who were quite different beings from those of the present day.'

From the deserted palace we went to the new garden which is preparing for the young Rājā, an adopted son of about ten years of age. It is close to the southern wall of the city, and is very extensive and well managed. The orange-trees are all grafted, and sinking under the weight of as fine fruit as any in India. Attempting to ascend the steps of an empty bungalow upon a raised terrace at the southern extremity of the garden, the attendants told us respectfully that they hoped we would take off our shoes if we wished to enter, as the ancestor of the Rājā by whom it was built, Rām Chand, had lately *become a god*, and was there worshipped. The roof is of stone, supported on carved stone pillars. On the centre pillar, upon a ground of whitewash, is a hand or trident. This is the only sign of a sacred character the building has yet assumed; and I found that it owed this character of sanctity to the circumstance of some one having vowed an offering to the manes of the builder, if he obtained what his soul most desired; and, having obtained it, all the people believe that those who do the same at the same place in a pure spirit of faith will obtain what they pray for.

I made some inquiries about Hardaul Lāla, the son of Bīrsingh Deo, who built the fort of Dhamonī, one of the ancestors of the Datiyā Rājā, and found that he was as much worshipped here at his birthplace as upon the banks of the Nerbudda as the supposed great *originator* of the cholera morbus. There is at Datiyā a temple dedicated to him and much frequented; and one of the priests brought me a flower in his name, and chanted something indicating that Hardaul Lāla was now worshipped even so far as the British *capital of Calcutta*, I asked the old prince what he thought of the origin of the worship of this his ancestor; and he told me that when the cholera broke out first in the camp of Lord Hastings, then pitched about three stages from his capital, on the bank of the Sindh at Chāndpur Sunārī, several people recovered from the disease immediately after making votive offerings in his name; and that he really thought the spirit of his great-grandfather had worked some wonderful cures upon people afflicted with this dreadful malady.[9]

The town of Datiyā contains a population of between forty and fifty thousand souls. The streets are narrow, for, in buildings, as in dress, the Rājā allows every man to consult his own inclinations. There are, however, a great many excellent houses in Datiyā, and the appearance of the place is altogether very good. Many of his feudatory chiefs reside occasionally in the city, and have all their establishments with them, a practice which does not, I believe, prevail anywhere else among these Bundēlkhand chiefs, and this makes the capital much larger, handsomer, and more populous than that of Tehrī. This indicates more of mutual confidence between the chief and his vassals, and accords well with the character they bear in the surrounding countries. Some of the houses occupied by these barons are very pretty. They spend the revenue of their distant estates in adorning them, and embellishing the capital, which they certainly could not have ventured to do under the late Rājās of Tehrī, and may not possibly be able to do under the future Rajas of Datiyā. The present minister of Datiyā, Ganēsh, is a very great knave, and encourages the residence upon his master's estate of all kinds of thieves and robbers, who bring back from distant districts every season vast quantities of booty, which they share with him. The chief himself is a mild old gentleman, who would not suffer violence to be offered to any of his nobles, though he would not, perhaps, quarrel with his minister for getting him a little addition to his revenue from without, by affording a sanctuary to such kind of people. As in Tehrī, so here, the pickpockets constitute the entire population of several villages, and carry their depredations northward to the banks of the Indus, and southward to Bombay and Madras.[10] But colonies of thieves and robbers like these abound no less in our own territories than in those of native states. There are more than a thousand families of them in the districts of Muzaffarnagar, Sahāranpur, and Meerut in the Upper Doāb,[11] all well enough known to the local authorities, who can do nothing with them.

They extend their depredations into remote districts, and the booty they bring home with them they share liberally with the native police and landholders under whose protection they live. Many landholders and police officers make large fortunes from the share they get of this booty. Magistrates do not molest them, because they would despair of ever finding the proprietors of the property that might be found upon them; and, if they could trace them, they would never be able to persuade them to come and 'enter upon a worse sea of troubles' in prosecuting them. These thieves and robbers of the professional classes, who have the sagacity to avoid plundering near home, are always just as secure in our best regulated districts as they are in the worst native states, from the only three things which such depredators care about—the penal laws, the odium of the society in which they move, and the vengeance of the god they worship; and they are always well received in the society around them, as long as they can avoid having their neighbours annoyed by summons to give evidence for or against them in our courts. They feel quite sure of the goodwill of the god they worship, provided they give a fair share of their booty to his priests; and no less secure of immunity from penal laws, except on very rare occasions when they happen to be taken in the tact, in a country where such laws happen to be in force.[12]

Notes:

1. December, 1835.

2. Rājā Parīchhit died in 1839.

3. The word gram (*Cicer arietinum*) is misprinted 'grain' in the author's text, in this place and in many others.

4. Bundēlkhand exports to the Ganges a great quantity of cotton, which enables it to pay for the wheat, gram, and other land produce which

it draws from distant districts, [W. H. S.] Other considerable exports from Bundēlkhand used to be the root of the *Morinda citrifolia*, yielding a dark red dye, and the coarse *kharwā* cloth, a kind of canvas, dyed with this dye, which is known by the name of ' *āl'*. But modern chemistry has nearly killed the trade in vegetable dyes. The construction of railways and roads has revolutionized the System of trade, and equalized prices.

5. Governor-General from October 4, 1813, till January 1, 1823. He was Earl of Moira when he assumed office.

6. Sir John Malcolm was Agent to the Governor-General in Central India from 1817 to 1822, and was appointed Governor of Bombay in 1827.

7. The construction of railways and the development of trade with Europe have completely altered the conditions. The Nerbudda valley can now yield a considerable revenue.

8. The iron ore no doubt is good, but the difficulties in the way of working it profitably are so great that the author's sanguine expectations seem unlikely to be fully realized. V. Ball, in his day the best authority on the subject, observes, 'As will be abundantly shown in the course of the following pages, the manufacture of iron has, in many parts of India, been wholly crushed out of existence by competition with English iron, while in others it is steadily decreasing, and it seems destined to become extinct' (*Economic Geology* (1881), being part of the *Manual of the Geology of India*, p. 338). Ball thought that, if improved methods of reduction should be employed, the Chāndā ore might be worked profitably. As regards the rest of India, with the doubtful exception of Upper Assam, he had little hope of success. Full details of the working of the mines in the Jabalpur, Narsinghpur, and Chāndā districts of the Central Provinces are given in pp. 384 to 392 of the same work. See also *I. G.* (1908), vol. x, p. 51; and *The Oxford Survey of the British Empire* (Oxford, 1914), vol. ii, Asia, pp. 143, 160. A powerful company formed at Bombay in 1907, operating at a spot on the borders of the Central Provinces and Orissa, hopes to turn out 7,000 tons of 'steel shapes' per month.

Coal is not found below the very ancient sandstone rocks, classed by geologists under the name of the Vindhyan Series. The principal beds of coal are found in the great series of rocks, known collectively as the Gondwāna System, which is supposed to range in age from the Permian to the Upper Jurassic periods of European geologists (*Manual*, vol. i, p. 102). This Gondwāna System includes sandstones. A coalfield at Mohpāni, ninety-five miles west-south-west from Jabalpur by rail, was worked from 1862 to 1904 by the Nerbudda Coal and Iron Company; and is now worked by the G. I. P. Railway Company. The principal coal-field of the Central Provinces for some years was that near Warōrā in the Chāndā district, but the amount which can be extracted profitably is approaching exhaustion; in fact the colliery was closed in 1906. Thick seams are known to exist to the south of Chāndā near the Wardhā river. See *I. G.*, 1907, vol. iii, chap. iii, p. 135; vol. x. p. 51.

9. See note to Chapter 25, *ante*, note 7.

10. 'Pickpockets' is not a suitable term.

11. The Persian word 'doāb' means the tract of land between two rivers, which ultimately meet. The upper doāb referred to in the text lies between the Ganges and the Jumna.

12. These 'colonies of thieves and robbers' are still the despair of the Indian administrator. They are known to Anglo-Indian law as 'criminal tribes', and a special Act has been passed for their regulation. The principle of that Act is police supervision, exercised by means of visits of inspection, and the issue of passports. The Act has been applied from time to time to various tribes, but has in every case failed. In 1891, Sir Auckland Colvin, then Lieutenant-Governor of the North-Western Provinces, adopted the strong measure of suddenly capturing many hundreds of Sānsias, a troublesome criminal tribe, in the Muzaffarnagar, Meerut, and Alīgarh Districts. Some of the prisoners were sent to a special jail, or reformatory, called a 'settlement', at Sultānpur in Oudh, and the others were drafted off to various landlords' estates. These latter were supposed to devote themselves to agriculture. The editor, as Magistrate of Muzaffarnagar, effected the capture of more than seven hundred Sānsias in that district, and dispatched them in accordance with orders. As most people expected, the agricultural pupils promptly absconded. Multitudes of Sānsias in the Panjāb and elsewhere remained unaffected by the raid, which could not have any permanent effect. The milder expedient of settling and nursing a large colony, organized in villages, of another criminal tribe, the Bāwarias (Boureahs), was also tried many years ago in the same district of Muzaffarnagar. The people settled readily enough, and reclaimed a considerable area of waste land, but were not in the least degree reformed. At the beginning of the cold season, in October or November, most of the able-bodied men annually leave the villages, and remain absent on distant forays till March or April, when they return with their booty, enjoying almost complete immunity, for the reasons stated in the text. On one occasion some of these Bāwarias of Muzaffarnagar stole a lākh and a half of rupees (about £12,000 at that time), in currency notes at Tuticorin, in the south of the peninsula, 1,400 miles distant from their home. The number of such criminal tribes, or castes, is very great, and the larger of these communities, such as the Sānsias, each comprise many thousands of members, diffused over an enormous area in several provinces. It is, therefore, impossible to put them down, except by the use of

drastic measures such as no civilized European Government could propose or sanction. The criminal tribes, or castes, are, to a large extent, races; but, in many of these castes, fresh blood is constantly introduced by the admission of outsiders, who are willing to eat with the members of the tribe, and so become for ever incorporated in the brotherhood. The gipsies of Europe are closely related to certain of these Indian tribes. The official literature on the subject is of considerable bulk. Mr. W. Crooke's small book, *An Ethnographic Glossary*, published in 1891 (Government Press, Allahabad), is a convenient summary of most of the facts on record concerning the criminal and other castes of Northern India, and gives abundant references to other publications. See also his larger work, *Castes and Tribes of the N. W. P. and Oudh*, 4 vols. Calcutta, 1906. The author's folio book, *Report on the Budhuk alias Bagree Decoits and other Gang Robbers by Hereditary Profession, and on the Measures adopted by the Government of India for their Suppression* (Calcutta, 1849), *ante*, Bibliography No. 12, probably is the most valuable of the original authorities on the subject, but it is rare and seldom consulted.

CHAPTER 32

Sporting at Datiyā—Fidelity of Followers to their Chiefs in India—Law of Primogeniture wanting among Muhammadans.

The morning after we reached Datiyā, I went out with Lieutenant Thomas to shoot and hunt in the Rājā's large preserve, and with the *humane* and determined resolution of killing no more game than our camp would be likely to eat; for we were told that the deer and wild hogs were so very numerous that we might shoot just as many as we pleased.[1] We were posted upon two terraces, one near the gateway, and the other in the centre of the preserve; and, after waiting here an hour, we got each a shot at a hog. Hares we saw, and might have shot, but we had loaded all our barrels with ball for other game. We left the 'ramnā', which is a quadrangle of about one hundred acres of thick grass, shrubs, and brushwood, enclosed by a high stone wall. There is one gate on the west side, and this is kept open during the night, to let the game out and in. It is shut and guarded during the day, when the animals are left to repose in the shade, except on such occasions as the present, when the Rājā wants to give his guests a morning's sport. On the plains and woods outside we saw a good many large deer, but could not manage to get near them in our own way, and had not patience to try that of the natives, so that we came back without killing anything, or having had any occasion to exercise our *forbearance*. The Rājā's people, as soon as we left them, went about their sport after their own fashion, and brought us a fine buck antelope after breakfast. They have a bullock trained to go about the fields with them, led at a quick pace by a halter, with which the sportsman guides him, as he walks along with him by the side opposite to that facing the deer he is in pursuit of. He goes round the deer as he grazes in the field, shortening the distance at every circle till he comes within shot. At the signal given the bullock stands still, and the sportsman rests his gun upon his back and fires. They seldom miss. Others go with a fine buck and doe antelope, tame, and trained to browse upon the fresh bushes, which are woven for the occasion into a kind of hand-hurdle, behind which a man creeps along over the fields towards the herd of wild ones, or sits still with his matchlock ready, and pointed out through the leaves. The herd seeing the male and female strangers so very busily and agreeably employed upon their apparently inviting repast, advance to accost them, and are shot when they get within a secure distance.[2] The hurdle was filled with branches from the 'dhau' (*Lythrum fructuosum*) tree, of which the jungle is for the most part composed, plucked as we went along; and the tame antelopes, having been kept long fasting for the purpose, fed eagerly upon them. We had also two pairs of falcons; but a knowledge of the brutal manner in which these birds are fed and taught is enough to prevent any but a *brute* from taking much delight in the sport they afford.[3]

The officer who conducted us was evidently much disappointed, for he was really very anxious, as he knew his master the Rājā was, that we should have a good day's sport. On our way back I made him ride by my side, and talk to me about Datiyā, since he had been unable to show me any sport. I got his thoughts into a train that I knew would animate him, if he had any soul at all for poetry or poetical recollections, as I thought he had. 'The noble works in palaces and temples,' said he, 'which you see around you, Sir, mouldering in ruins, were built by princes who had beaten emperors in battle, and whose spirits still hover over and protect the place. Several times, under the late disorders which preceded your paramount rule in Hindustan, when hostile forces assembled around us, and threatened our capital with destruction, lights and elephants innumerable were seen from the tops of those battlements, passing and repassing under the walls, ready to defend them had the enemy attempted an assault. Whenever our soldiers endeavoured to approach near them, they disappeared; and everybody knew that they were spirits of men like Bīrsingh Deo and Hardaul Lāla that had come to our aid, and we never lost confidence.' It is easy to understand the devotion of men to their chiefs when they believe their progenitors to have been demigods, and to have been faithfully served by their ancestors for several generations. We neither have, nor ever can have, servants so personally devoted to us as these men are to their chiefs, though we have soldiers who will fight under our banners with as much courage and fidelity. They know that their grandfathers served the grandfathers of these chiefs, and they hope their grandchildren will serve their grandsons. The one feels as much pride and pleasure in so serving, as the other in being so served; and both hope that the link which binds them may never be severed. Our servants, on the contrary, private and public, are always in dread that some accident, some trivial fault, or some slight offence, not to be avoided, will sever for ever the link that binds them to their master.

The fidelity of the military classes of the people of India to their immediate chief, or leader, whose *salt they eat*, has been always very remarkable, and commonly bears little relation to his *moral virtues*, or conduct to *his* superiors. They feel that it is their duty to serve him who feeds and protects them and their families in all situations, and under all circumstances; and the chief feels that, while he has a right to their services, it is his imperative duty so to feed and protect them and their families. He may change sides as often as he pleases, but the relations between him and his followers remain unchanged. About the side he chooses to take in a contest for dominion, they ask no questions, and feel no responsibility. God has placed their destinies in dependence upon his; and to him they cling to the last. In Mālwa, Bhopāl, and other parts of Central India, the Muhammadan rule could be established over that of the Rājpūt chief only by the annihilation of the entire race of their followers.[4] In no part of the world has the devotion of soldiers to their immediate chief been more remarkable than in India among the Rājpūts; and in no part of the world bas the fidelity of these chiefs to the paramount power been more unsteady, or their devotion less to be relied upon. The laws of Muhammad, which prescribe that the property in land be divided equally among the sons,[5] leaves no rule for succession to territorial or political dominion. It has been justly observed by Hume: 'The right of primogeniture was introduced with the feudal law; an institution which is hurtful by producing and maintaining ari unequal division of property; but it is advantageous in another respect by accustoming the people to a preference for the eldest son, and thereby preventing a partition or disputed succession in the monarchy.'

Among the Muhammadan princes there was no law that bound the whole members of a family to obey the eldest son of a deceased prince. Every son of the Emperor of Hindustan considered that he had a right to set up his claim to the throne, vacated by the death of his father; and, in anticipation of that death, to strengthen his claim by negotiations and intrigues with all the territorial chiefs and influential nobles of the empire. However *prejudicial to the interests* of his elder brother such measures might be, they were never considered to be an *invasion of his rights*, because such rights had never been established by the laws of their prophet. As all the sons considered that they had an equal right to solicit the support of the chiefs and nobles, so all the chiefs and nobles considered that they could adopt the cause of whichever *son* they chose, without incurring the reproach of either *treason* or *dishonour*. The one who succeeded thought himself justified by the law of self-preservation to put, not only his brothers, but all their sons, to death; so that there was, after every new succession, an entire *clearance* of all the male members of the imperial family. Aurangzēb said to his pedantic tutor, who wished to be raised to high station on his accession to the imperial throne, 'Should not you, instead of your flattery, have taught me something of that point so important to a king, which is, what are the reciprocal duties of a sovereign to his subjects, and those of the subjects to their sovereign? And ought not you to have considered that one day I should be obliged, with the sword, to dispute my life and the crown with my brothers? Is not that the destiny, almost of all the sons of Hindustan?'[6] Now that they have become pensioners of the British Government, the members increase like white ants; and, as Malthus has it, 'press so hard against their means of subsistence' that a great many of them are absolutely starving, in spite of the enormous pension the head of the family receives for their maintenance.[7]

The city of Datiyā is surrounded by a stone wall about thirty feet high, with its foundation on a solid rock; but it has no ditch or glacis, and is capable of little or no defence against cannon. In the afternoon I went, accompanied by Lieutenant Thomas, and followed by the best *cortège* we could muster, to return the Rājā's visit. He resides within the walls of the city in a large square garden, enclosed with a high wall, and filled with fine orange-trees, at this time bending under the weight of the most delicious fruit. The old chief received us at the bottom of a fine flight of steps leading up to a handsome pavilion, built upon the wall of one of the faces of this garden. It was enclosed at the back, and in front looked into the garden through open arcades. The floors were spread with handsome carpets of the Jhānsī manufacture. In front of the pavilion was a wide terrace of polished stone, extending to the top of the flight of the steps; and, in the centre of this terrace, and directly opposite to us as we looked into the garden, was a fine *jet d'eau* in a large basin of water in full play, and, with its shower of diamonds, showing off the rich green and red of the orange-trees to the best advantage.

The large quadrangle thus occupied is called the 'kila', or fort, and the wall that surrounds it is thirty feet high, with a round embattled tower at each corner. On the east face is a fine large gateway for the entrance, with a curtain as high as the wall itself. Inside the gate is a piece of ordnance painted red, with the largest calibre I ever saw.[8] This is fired once a year, at the festival of the Dasahra.[9]

Our arrival at the wall was announced by a salute from some fine brass guns upon the bastions near the gateway. As we advanced from the gateway up through the garden to the pavilion, we were again serenaded by our friends with their guitars and excellent voices. They were now on foot, and arranged along both sides of the walk that we had to pass through. The open garden space within the walls appeared to me to be about ten acres. It is crossed and recrossed at right angles by numerous walks, having rows of plantain and other fruit trees on each side; and orange, pomegranate, and other small fruit trees to fill the space between; and anything more rich and luxuriant one can hardly conceive. In the centre of the north and west sides are pavilions with apartments for the family above, behind, and on each side of the great reception room, exactly similar to that in which we were received on the south face. The whole formed, I think, the most delightful residence that I have seen for a hot climate. There is, however, no doubt that the most healthy stations in this, and every other hot climate, are those situated upon dry, open, sandy plains, with neither shrubberies nor basins. [10]

We were introduced to the young Rājā, the old man's adopted son, a lad of about ten years of age, who is to be married in February next. He is plain in person, but has a pleasing expression of countenance; and, if he be moulded after the old man, and not after his minister, the country may perhaps have in him the 'lucky accident' of a good governor.[11] I have rarely seen a finer or more prepossessing man than the Rājā, and all his subjects speak well of him. We had an elephant, a horse, abundance of shawls, and other fine clothes placed before us as presents; but I prayed the old gentleman to keep them all for me till I returned, as I was a mere voyageur without the means of carrying such valuable things in safety; but he would not be satisfied till I had taken two plain hilts of swords and spears, the manufacture of Datiyā, and of little value, which Lieutenant Thomas and I promised to keep for his sake. The rest of the presents were all taken back to their places. After an hour's talk with the old man and his ministers, attar of roses and pān were distributed, and we took our leave to go and visit the old palace, which as yet we had seen only from a distance. There were only two men besides the Rājā, his son, and ourselves, seated upon chairs. All the other principal persons of the court sat around cross-legged on the carpet; but they joined freely in the conversation, I was told by these courtiers how often the young chief had, during the day, asked when he could have the happiness of seeing me; and the old chief was told, in my hearing, how many *good things* I had said since I came into his territories, all tending to his honour and my credit. This is a species of barefaced flattery to which we are all doomed to submit in our intercourse with these native chiefs; but still, to a man of sense, it never ceases to be distressing and offensive; for he can hardly ever help feeling that they must think him a mere child before they could venture to treat him with it. This is, however, to put too harsh a construction upon what in reality, the people mean only as civility; and they, who can so easily consider the grandfathers of their chiefs as gods, and worship them as such, may be suffered to treat *us* as heroes and sayers of good things without offence.[12]

We ascended to the summit of the old palace, and were well repaid for the trouble by the view of an extremely rich sheet of wheat, gram, and other spring crops, extending to the north and east, as far as the eye could reach, from the dark belt of forest, three miles deep, with which the Rājā has surrounded his capital on every side as hunting grounds. The lands comprised in this forest are, for the most part, exceedingly poor, and water for irrigation is unattainable within them, so that little is lost by this taste of the chief for the sports of the field, in which, however, he cannot himself now indulge.

On the 19th[13] we left Datiyā, and, after emerging from the surrounding forest, came over a fine plain covered with rich spring crops for ten miles, till we entered among the ravines of the river Sindh, whose banks are, like those of all rivers in this part of India, bordered to a great distance by these deep and ugly inequalities. Here they are almost without grass or shrubs to clothe their hideous nakedness, and have been formed by the torrents, which, in the season of the rains, rush from the extensive plain, as from a wide ocean, down to the deep channel of the river in narrow streams. These streams cut their way easily through the soft alluvial soil, which must once have formed the bed of a vast lake.[14] On coming through the forest, before sunrise we discovered our error of the day before, for we found excellent deer-shooting in the long grass and brushwood, which grow luxuriantly at some distance from the city. Had we come out a couple of miles the day before, we might have had noble sport, and really required the *forbearance and humanity* to which we had so magnanimously resolved to sacrifice our 'pride of art' as sportsmen; for we saw many herds of the nīlgāi, antelope, and spotted deer,[15] browsing within a few paces of us, within the long grass and brushwood on both sides of the road. We could not stay, however, to indulge in much sport, having a long march before us.

Notes:

1. Some readers may be shocked at the notion of the author shooting pig, but, in Bundēlkhand, where pig-sticking, or hog-hunting, as the older writers call it, is not practised, hog-shooting is quite legitimate.

2. The common antelope, or black buck (*Antilope bezoartica*, or *cervicapra*) feed in herds, sometimes numbering many hundreds, in the open plains, especially those of black soil. Men armed with matchlocks can scarcely get a shot except by adopting artifices similar to those described in the text.

3. Sixteen species of hawks, belonging to several genera, are trained in India. They are often fed by being allowed to suck the blood from the breasts of live pigeons, and their eyes are darkened by means of a silken thread passed through holes in the eyelids. 'Hawking is a very dull and

very cruel sport. A person must become insensible to the sufferings of the most beautiful and most inoffensive of the brute creation before he can feel any enjoyment in it. The cruelty lies chiefly in the mode of feeding the hawks' (*Journey through the Kingdom of Oude*, vol. i, p, 109). Asoka forbade the practice by the words: 'The living must not be fed with the living' (Pillar Edict V, c. 243 B.C., in V. A. Smith, *Asoka*, 2nd ed. (1909), p. 188).

4. The wording of this sentence is unfortunate, and it is not easy to understand why the author mentioned Bhopāl. The principality of Bhopāl was formed by Dost Mohammed Khān, an Afghān officer of Aurangzēb, who became independent a few years after that sovereign's death in 1707. Since that time the dynasty has always continued to be Muhammadan. The services of Sikandar Bēgam in the Mutiny are well known. Mālwa is the country lying between Bundēlkhand, on the east, and Rājputāna, on the west, and includes Bhopāl. Most of the states in this region are now ruled by Hindoos, but the local dynasty which ruled the kingdom of Mālwa and Māndū from A.D. 1401 to 1531 was Musalmān. (See Thomas, *Chronicles of the Pathan Kings of Dehli*, pp. 346-53.)

5. All near relatives succeed to a Muhammadan's estate, which is divided, under complicated rules, into the necessary number of shares. A son's share is double that of a daughter. As between themselves all sons share equally.

6. Bernier's *Revolutions of the Mogul Empire*. [W. H. S.] The author seems to have used either the London edition of 1671, entitled *The History of the Late Revolution of the Empire of the Great Mogul*, or one of the reprints of that edition. The anecdote referred to is called by Bernier 'an uncommonly good story'. Aurangzēb made a long speech, ending by dismissing the unlucky pedagogue with the words: 'Go! withdraw to thy native village. Henceforth let no man know either who thou art, or what is become of thee.' (Bernier, *Travels in the Mogul Empire*, pp. 154-161, ed. Constable and V. A, Smith, 1914.) Manucci repeats the story with slight variations (*Storie da Mogor*, vol. ii, pp. 29-33).

7. Compare the forcible description of the state of the Delhi royal family in Chapter 76, *post*. The old emperor's pension was one hundred thousand rupees a month. The events of the Mutiny effected a considerable clearance, though the number of persons claiming relationship with the royal house is still large. A few of these have taken service under the British Government, but have not distinguished themselves.

8. The author, unfortunately, does not give the dimensions of this piece. Rūmī Khān's gun at Bījāpur, which was cast in the sixteenth century at Ahmadnagar, is generally considered the largest ancient cannon in India. It is fifteen feet long, and weighs about forty-one tons, the calibre being two feet four inches. Like the gun at Datiyā, it is painted with red lead, and is worshipped by Hindoos, who are always ready to worship every manifestation of power. Another big gun at Bījāpur is thirty feet in length, built up of bars bound together. Other very large pieces exist at Gāwīlgarh in Berār, and Bīdar in the Nīzam's dominions. (Balfour, *Cyclopaedia*, 3rd ed., s.v. Gun, Bījāpur, Gawilgarh Hill Range, and Beder.)

9. The Dasahra festival, celebrated at the beginning of October, marks the close of the rains and the commencement of the cold season. It is observed by all classes of Hindus, but especially by Rājās and the military classes, for whom this festival has peculiar importance. In the old days no prince or commander, whether his command consisted of soldiers or robbers, ever undertook regular operations until the Dasahra had been duly observed. All Rājās still receive valuable offerings on this occasion, which form an important element in their revenue. In some places buffaloes are sacrificed by the Rājā in person. The soldiers worship the weapons which they hope to use during the coming season. Among the Marāthās the ordnance received especial attention and worship. The ceremony of worshipping certain leguminous trees at this festival has been noticed *ante*, Chapter 26 note 8.

10. Few Europeans nowadays could join in the author's enthusiastic admiration of the Datiyā garden. The arrangements seem to have been those usual in large formal native gardens in Northern India.

11. This lad has since succeeded his adoptive father as the chief of the Datiyā principality. The old chief found him one day lying in the grass, as he was shooting through one of his preserves. His elephant was very near treading upon the infant before he saw it. He brought home the boy, adopted him as his son, and declared him his successor, from having no son of his own. The British Government, finding that the people generally seemed to acquiesce in the old man's wishes, sanctioned the measure, as the paramount power. [W. H. S.] The old Rājā died in 1839, and the succession of the boy, Bijai Bahādur, thus strangely favoured by fortune, was unsuccessfully opposed by one of the nobles of the state. Bijai Bahādur governed the state with sufficient success until his death in 1857. The succession was then again disputed, and disturbances took place which were suppressed by an

armed British force. The state is still governed by its hereditary ruler, who has been granted the privilege of adoption (*N.W.P. Gazetteer*, 1st ed., vol. i, p. 410, s.v. Datiyā).

12. The fact is that all Oriental rulers thoroughly enjoy the most outrageous flattery, and would feel defrauded if they did not get it in abundance. Even Akbar, the greatest of them, could enjoy it, and allow the courtly poet to say 'See Akbar, and you see God'. Indians find it difficult to believe that European officials really dislike attentions which are exacted by rulers of their own races.

13. December, 1835.

14. This theory is probably incorrect. See *ante*, Chapter 14, note 7, on formation of black soil.

15. Nīlgāi, or 'blue-bull', a huge, heavy antelope of bovine form, common in India, scientifically named *Portax pictus*. By 'antelope' the author means the common antelope, or black buck, the *Antilope bezoartica*, or *cervicapra* of naturalists. The spotted deer, or 'chītal', a very handsome creature, is the *Axis maculata* of Gray, the *Cervus axis* of other zoologists.

CHAPTER 33

'Bhūmiāwat.'

Though no doubt very familiar to our ancestors during the Middle Ages, this is a thing happily but little understood in Europe at the present day. 'Bhūmiāwat', in Bundēlkhand, signifies a war or fight for landed inheritance, from 'bhūm', the land, earth, &c.; 'bhūmia', a landed proprietor. When a member of the landed aristocracy, no matter how small, has a dispute with his ruler, he collects his followers, and levies indiscriminate war upon his territories, plundering and burning his towns and villages, and murdering their inhabitants till he is invited back upon his own terms. During this war it is a point of honour not to allow a single acre of land to be tilled upon the estate which he has deserted, or from which he has been driven; and he will murder any man who attempts to drive a plough in it, together with all his family, if he can. The smallest member of this landed aristocracy of the Hindoo military class will often cause a terrible devastation during the interval that he is engaged in his bhūmiāwat; for there are always vast numbers of loose characters floating upon the surface of Indian society, ready to 'gird up their loins' and use their sharp swords in the service of marauders of this kind, when they cannot get employment in that of the constituted authorities of government.

Such a marauder has generally the sympathy of nearly all the members of his own class and clan, who are apt to think that his case may one day be their own. He is thus looked upon as contending for the interests of all; and, if his chief happens to be on bad terms with other chiefs in the neighbourhood, the latter will clandestinely support the outlaw and his cause, by giving him and his followers shelter in the hills and jungles, and concealing their families and stolen property in their castles. It is a maxim in India, and, in the less settled parts of it, a very true one, that 'one Pindhāra or robber makes a hundred'; that is, where one robber, by a series of atrocious murders and robberies, frightens the people into non- resistance, a hundred loose characters from among the peasantry of the country will take advantage of the occasion, and adopt his name, in order to plunder with the smallest possible degree of personal risk to themselves.

Some magistrates and local rulers, under such circumstances, have very unwisely adopted the measure of prohibiting the people from carrying or having arms in their houses, the very thing which, above all others, such robbers most wish; for they know, though such magistrates and rulers do not, that it is the innocent only, and the friends to order, who will obey the command. The robber will always be able to conceal his arms, or keep with them out of reach of the magistrate; and he is now relieved altogether from the salutary dread of a shot from a door or window. He may rob at his leisure, or sit down like a gentleman and have all that the people of the surrounding towns and villages possess brought to him, for no man can any longer attempt to defend himself or his family.[1] Weak governments are obliged soon to invite back the robber on his own terms, for the people can pay them no revenue, being prevented from cultivating their lands, and obliged to give all they have to the robbers, or submit to be plundered of it. Jhānsī and Jālaun are exceedingly weak governments, from having their territories studded with estates held rent-free, or at a quit-rent, by Pawār, Bundēla, and Dhandēl barons, who have always the sympathy of the numerous chiefs and their barons of the same class around.

In the year 1832, the Pawār barons of the estates of Noner, Jignī, Udgāon, and Bilharī in Jhānsī had some cause of dissatisfaction with their chief; and this they presented to Lord William Bentinck as he passed through the province in December. His lordship told them that these were questions of internal administration which they must settle among themselves, as the Supreme Government would not interfere. They had, therefore, only one way of settling such disputes, and that was to raise the standard of bhūmiāwat, and cry, 'To your tents, O Israel!' This they did; and, though the Jhānsī chief had a military force of twelve thousand men, they burnt down every town and village in the territory that did not come into their terms; and the chief had possession of only two, Jhānsī, the capital, and the large commercial town of Mau,[2] when the Bundēla Rājās of Orchhā and Datiyā, who had hitherto clandestinely supported the insurgents, consented to become the arbitrators. A suspension of arms followed, the barons got all they demanded, and the bhūmiāwat ceased. But the Jhānsī chief, who had hitherto lent large sums to the other chiefs in the province, was reduced to the necessity of borrowing from them all, and from Gwālior, and mortgaging to them a good portion of his lands.[3]

Gwālior is itself weak in the same way. A great portion of its lands are held by barons of the Hindoo military classes, equally addicted to bhūmiāwat, and one or more of them is always engaged in this kind of indiscriminate warfare; and it must be confessed that, unless they are always considered to be ready to engage in it, they have very little chance of retaining their possessions on moderate terms, for these weak governments are generally the most rapacious when they have it in their power.

A good deal of the lands of the Muhammadan sovereign of Oudh are, in the same manner, held by barons of the Rājpūt tribe; and some of them are almost always in the field engaged in the same kind of warfare against their sovereign. The baron who pursues it with vigour is almost sure to be invited back upon his own terms very soon. If his lands are worth a hundred thousand a year, he will get them for ten; and have this remitted for the next five years, until he is ready for another bhūmiāwat, on the ground of the injuries sustained during the last, from which his estate has to recover. The baron who is peaceable and obedient soon gets rack- rented out of his estate, and reduced to beggary.[4]

In 1818, some companies of my regiment were for several months employed in Oudh, after a young 'bhūmiāwatī' of this kind, Sheo Ratan Singh. He was the nephew and heir of the Rājā of Partābgarh,[5] who wished to exclude him from his inheritance by the adoption of a brother of his young bride. Sheo Ratan had a small village for his maintenance, and said nothing to his old uncle till the governor of the province, Ghulām Husani[6], accepted an invitation to be present at the ceremony of adoption. He knew that, if he acquiesced any longer, he would lose his inheritance, and cried, 'To your tents, 0 Israel!' He got a small band of three hundred Rājpūts, with nothing but their swords, shields, and spears, to follow him, all of the same clan and true men. They were bivouacked in a jungle not more than seven miles from our cantonments at Partābgarh, when Ghulām Husain marched to attack them with three regiments of infantry, one of cavalry, and two nine-pounders. He thought he should surprise them, and contrived so that he should come upon them about daybreak. Sheo Ratan knew all his plans. He placed one hundred and fifty of his men in ambuscade at the entrance to the jungle, and kept the other hundred and fifty by him in the centre. When they had got well in, the party in ambush rushed upon the rear, while he attacked them in front. After a short resistance, Ghulām Husain's force took to flight, leaving five hundred men dead on the field, and their guns behind them. Ghulām Husain was so ashamed of the drubbing he got that he bribed all the news-writers[7] within twenty miles of the place to say nothing about it in their reports to court, and he never made any report of it himself. A detachment of my regiment passed over the dead bodies in the course of the day, on their return to cantonments from detached command, or we should have known nothing about it. It is true, we heard the firing, but that we heard every day; and I have seen from my bungalow half a dozen villages in flames, at the same time, from this species of contest between the Rājpūt landholders and the government authorities. Our cantonments were generally full of the women and children who had been burnt out of house and home.

In Oudh such contests generally begin with the harvests. During the season of tillage all is quiet; but, when the crops begin to ripen, the governor begins to rise in his demands for revenue, and the Rājpūt landholders and cultivators to sharpen their swords and burnish their spears. One hundred of them always consider themselves a match for one thousand of the king's troops in a fair field, because they have all one heart and soul, while the king's troops have many.[8]

While the Pawārs were ravaging the Jhānsī state with their bhūmiāwat, a merchant of Sāgar had a large convoy of valuable cloths, to the amount, I think, of forty thousand rupees,[9] intercepted by them on its way from Mirzāpur[10] to Rājputāna. I was then at Sāgar, and wrote off to the insurgents to say that they had mistaken one of our subjects for one of the Jhānsī chiefs, and must release the convoy. They did so, and not a piece of the cloth was lost. This bhūmiāwat is supposed to have cost the Jhānsī chief above twenty lākhs of rupees,[11] and his subjects double that sum.

Gopāl Singh, a Bundēla, who had been in the service of the chief of Pannā,[12] took to bhūmiāwat in 1809, and kept a large British force employed in pursuit through Bundēlkhand and the Sāgar territories for three years, till he was invited back by our Government in the year 1812, by the gift of a fine estate on the banks of the Dasān river, yielding twenty thousand rupees[13] a year, which his son now enjoys, and which is to descend to his posterity, many of whom will, no doubt, animated by their fortunate ancestor's example, take to the same trade. He had been a man of no note till he took to this trade, but by his predatory exploits he soon became celebrated throughout India; and, when I came to the country, no other man's chivalry was so much talked of.

A Bundēla, or other landholder of the Hindoo military class, does not think himself, nor is he indeed thought by others, in the slightest degree less respectable for having waged this indiscriminate war upon the innocent and unoffending, provided he has any cause of dissatisfaction with his liege lord; that is, provided he cannot get his land or his appointment in his service upon his own terms, because all others of the same class and clan feel more or less interested in his success.

They feel that their tenure of land, or of office, is improved by the mischief he does; because every peasant he murders, and every field he throws out of tillage, affects their liege lord in his most tender point, his treasury; and indisposes him to interfere with their salaries, their privileges, or their rents. He who wages this war goes on marrying his sisters or his daughters to the other barons or landholders of the same clan, and receiving theirs in marriage during the whole of his bhūmiāwat,[14] as if nothing at all extraordinary had happened, and thereby strengthening his hand at the game he is playing.

Umrāo Singh of Jaklōn in Chandērī, a district of Gwālior bordering upon Sāgar,[15] has been at this game for more than fifteen years out of twenty, but his alliances among the baronial families around have not been in the slightest degree affected by it. His sons and his grandsons have, perhaps, made better matches than they might, had the old man been at peace with all the world, during the time that he has been desolating one district by his atrocities, and demoralizing all those around it by his example, and by inviting the youth to join him occasionally in his murderous enterprises. Neither age nor sex is respected in their attacks upon towns or villages; and no Muhammadan can take more pride and pleasure in defacing idols—the most monstrous idol—than a 'bhūmiāwatī' takes in maiming an innocent peasant, who presumes to drive his plough in lands that he chooses to put under the *ban*.

In the kingdom of Oudh, this bhūmiāwat is a kind of nursery for our native army; for the sons of Rājpūt yeomen who have been trained in it are all exceedingly anxious to enlist in our native infantry regiments, having no dislike to their drill or their uniform. The same class of men in Bundēlkhand and the Gwālior State have a great horror of the drill and uniform of our regular infantry, and nothing can induce them to enlist in our ranks. Both are equally brave, and equally faithful to their salt—that is, to the person who employs them; but the Oudh Rājpūt is a much more tameable animal than the Bundēla. In Oudh this class of people have all inherited from their fathers a respect for our rule and a love for our service. In Bundēlkhand they have not yet become reconciled to our service, and they still look upon our rule as interfering a good deal too much with their sporting propensities. [16]

Notes:

1. Since the author's time conditions have much changed. Then, and for long afterwards, up to the Mutiny, every village throughout the country was fall of arms, and almost every man was armed. Consequently, in those tracts where the Mutiny of the native army was accompanied by popular insurrection, the flame of rebellion burned fiercely, and was subdued with difficulty. The painful experience of 1857 and 1858 proved the necessity of general disarmament, and nearly the whole of British India has been disarmed under the provisions of a series of Acts. Licences to have and carry

ordinary arms and ammunition are granted by the magistrates of districts. Licences to possess artillery are granted only by the Governor-General in Council. The improved organization of the police and of the executive power generally renders possible the strict enforcement of the law. Some arms are concealed, but very few of these are serviceable. With rare exceptions, arms are now carried only for display, and knowledge of the use of weapons has died out in most classes of the population. The village forts have been everywhere dismantled. Robbery by armed gangs still occurs in certain districts (see ante, Chapter 23, note 14), but is much less frequent than it used to be in the author's days.

2. Many towns and villages bear the name of Mau (auglicè, Mhow), which may be, as Mr. Growse suggests, a form of the Sanskrit mahi, 'land' or 'ground'. The town referred to in the text is the principal town of the Jhānsī district, distinguished from its homonyms as Mau- Rānīpur, situated about east-south-east from Jhānsī, at a distance of forty miles from that city. Its special export used to be the 'kharwā' cloth, dyed with 'ai' (see ante., Chapter 31, note 4).

3. This insurrection continued into the year 1833. 'The inhabitants were reduced to the greatest distress, and have, even to the present day, scarcely recovered the losses they then sustained' (N.W.P. Gazetteer, vol. i (1870), p. 296).

4. See the author's Journey through the Kingdom of Oude, passim.

5. Partābgarh is now a separate district in the Fyzābād Division of Oudh. The chief town, also called Partābgarh, is thirty-two miles north of Allahabad, and still possesses a Rājā, who, at present (1914), is a most respectable gentleman, with no thoughts of violence. Further details about the Partābgarh family are given in the Journey, vol. i, p. 231.

6. Transcriber's note:- The author then uses the spelling 'Husain' consistently.

7. 'The news department is under a Superintendent-General, who has sometimes contracted for it, as for the revenues of a district, but more commonly holds it in amānī, as a manager. . . . He nominates his subordinates, and appoints them to their several offices, taking from each a present gratuity and a pledge for such monthly payments as he thinks the post will enable him to make. They receive from four to fifteen rupees a month each, and have each to pay to their President, for distribution among his patrons or patronesses at Court, from one hundred to five hundred rupees a month in ordinary times. Those to whom they are accredited have to pay them, under ordinary circumstances, certain sums monthly, to prevent their inventing or exaggerating cases of abuse of power or neglect of duty on their part; but, when they happen to be really guilty of great acts

of atrocity, or great neglect of duty, they are required to pay extraordinary sums, not only to the news-writers, who are especially accredited to them, but to all others who happen to be in the neighbourhood at the time. There are six hundred and sixty news-writers of this kind employed by the king, and paid monthly three thousand one hundred and ninety-four rupees, or, on an average, between four and five rupees each; and the sums paid by them to their President for distribution among influential officers and Court favourites averages [sic] above one hundred and fifty thousand rupees a year. . . . Such are the reporters of the circumstances in all the cases on which the sovereign and his ministers have to pass orders every day in Oudh. . . . the European magistrate of one of our neighbouring districts one day, before the Oudh Frontier Police was raised, entered the Oudh territory at the head of his police in pursuit of some robbers, who had found an asylum in one of the King's villages. In the attempt to secure them some lives were lost: and, apprehensive of the consequences, he sent for the official news-writer, and *gratified* him in the usual way. No report of the circumstances was made to the Oudh Darbār; and neither the King, the President, nor the British Government ever heard anything about it' (*Journey through the Kingdom of Oude*, vol. i, pp. 67- 69). Such a System of official news-writers was usually maintained by Asiatic despots from the most ancient times.

8. full details of the rotten state of the king's army are given in the *Journey through the Kingdom of Oude*.

9. Then worth £4,000, or more.

10. Mirzāpur (Mirzapore) on the Ganges, twenty-seven miles from Benares, was, in the author's time, the principal depot for the cotton and cloth trade of Northern India. Although the East Indian Railway passes through the city, the construction of the railway has diverted the bulk of the trade from Mirzāpur, which is now a declining place. The population, which wag 70,621 in 1881, fell to 32,332 in 1911. The carpets made there are well known.

11. Then equal to £200,000, or more.

12. The Pannā State lies between the British districts of Bāndā, in the United Provinces, on the north, and Damoh and Jabalpur, in the Central Provinces, on the south. The chief is a descendant of Chhatarsāl. For description and engraving of the diamond mines see *Economic Geology* (1881), p. 39.

13. Then equivalent to £2,000, or more.

14. The words 'of the same clan' are inexact. The author has shown (*ante*, Chapter 23 following [10], and Chapter 26 following [32]) that Rājpūts never marry into their own clan.

15. 'The Rājā of Chandērī belonged to the same family as the Orchhā chief. Sindhia annexed a great part of the Chandērī State in 1811. Chandērī was for a time British territory, but is now again in Sindhia's dominions. Its vicissitudes are related in *N.W.P. Gazetteer* (1870), vol. i, pp. 351-8.

16. In Oudh the misgovernment, anarchy, and cruel rapine, briefly alluded to in the text, and vividly described in detail by the author in his *Journey through the Kingdom of Oude*, lasted until the annexation of the kingdom by Lord Dalhousie in 1856, and, after a brief lull, were renewed during the insurrection of 1857 and 1858. The events of those years are a curious commentary on the author's belief that the people of Oudh entertained 'a respect for our rule and a love for our service'. The service of the British Government is sought because it pays, but a foreign Government must not expect love. Respect for the British rule depends upon the strength of that rule. Oudh still sends many recruits to the native army, though the young men no longer enjoy the advantage of a training in 'bhūmiāwat'. An occasional gang-robbery or bludgeon fight is the meagre modern substitute. The Rājpūts or Thākurs of Bundēlkhand and Gwālior still retain their old character for turbulence, but, of course, have less scope for what the author calls their 'sporting propensities' than they had in his time.

CHAPTER 34

The Suicide—Relations between Parents and Children in India.

The day before we left Datiyā our cook had a violent dispute with his mother, a thing of almost daily occurrence; for though a very fat and handsome old lady, she was a very violent one. He was a quiet man, but, unable to bear any longer the abuse she was heaping upon him, he first took up a pitcher of water and flung it at her head. It missed her, and he then snatched up a stick, and, for the first time in his life, struck her. He was her only son. She quietly took up all her things, and, walking off towards a temple, said she would leave him for ever; and he, having passed the Rubicon, declared that he was resolved no longer to submit to the parental tyranny which she had hitherto exercised over him. My water carrier, however, prevailed upon her with much difficulty to return, and take up her quarters with him and his wife and five children in a small tent we had given them. Maddened at the thought of a blow from her son, the old lady about sunset swallowed a large quantity of opium; and before the circumstance was discovered, it was too late to apply a remedy. We were told of it about eight o'clock at night, and found her lying in her son's arms— tried every remedy at hand, but without success, and about midnight she died. She loved her son, and he respected her; and yet not a day passed without their having some desperate quarrel, generally about the orphan daughter of her brother, who lived with them, and was to be married, as soon as the cook could save out of his pay enough money to defray the expenses of the ceremonies. The old woman was always reproaching him for not saving money fast enough. This little cousin had now stolen some of the cook's tobacco for his young assistant; and the old lady thought it right to admonish her. The cook likewise thought it right to add his admonitions to those of his mother; but the old lady would have her niece abused by nobody but herself, and she flew into a violent passion at his presuming to interfere. This led to the son's outrage, and the mother's suicide. The son is a mild, good-tempered young man, who bears an excellent character among his equals, and is a very good servant. Had he been less mild it had perhaps been better; for his mother would by degrees have given up that despotic sway over her child, which in infancy is necessary, in youth useful, but in manhood becomes intolerable. 'God defend us from the anger of the mild in spirit', said an excellent judge of human nature, Muhammad, the founder of this cook's religion;[1] and certainly the mildest tempers are those which become the most ungovernable when roused beyond a certain degree; and the proud spirit of the old woman could not brook the outrage which her son, so roused, had been guilty of. From the time that she was discovered to have taken poison till she breathed her last she lay in the arms of the poor man, who besought her to live, that her only son might atone for his crime, and not be a parricide.

There is no part of the world, I believe, where parents are so much reverenced by their sons as they are in India, in all classes of society. This is sufficiently evinced in the desire that parents feel to have sons. The duty of daughters is from the day of their marriage transferred entirely to their husbands and their husbands' parents, on whom alone devolves the duty of protecting and supporting them through the wedded and the widowed state. The links that united them to their parents are broken. All the reciprocity of rights and duties which have bound together the parent and child from infancy is considered to end with the consummation of her marriage; nor does the stain of any subsequent female backsliding ever affect the family of her parents; it can affect that only of her husband, who is held alone responsible for her conduct. If a widow inherits the property of her husband, on her death the property would go to her husband's brother, supposing neither had any children by their husbands, in preference to her own brother; but between the son and his parents this reciprocity of rights and duties follows them to the grave.[2] One is delighted to see in sons this habitual reverence for the mother; but, as in the present case, it is too apt to occasion a domineering spirit, which produces much mischief even in private families, but still more in sovereign ones. A prince, when he attains the age of manhood, and ought to take upon himself the duties of the government, is often obliged to witness a great deal of oppression and misrule, from his inability to persuade his widowed mother to resign the power willingly into his hands. He often tamely submits to see his country ruined, and his family dishonoured, as at Jhānsī, before he can bring himself, by some act of desperate resolution, to wrest it from her grasp.[3] In order to prevent his doing so, or to recover the reins he has thus obtained, the mother has often been known to poison her own son; and many a princess in India, like Isabella of England, has, I believe, destroyed her husband, to enjoy more freely the society of her paramour, and hold these reins during the minority of her son.[4]

In the exercise of dominion from behind the curtain (for it is those who live behind the curtain that seem most anxious to hold it), women select ministers who, to secure duration to their influence, become their paramours, or, at least, make the world believe that they are so, to serve their own selfish purposes. The sons are tyrannized over through youth by their mothers, who endeavour to subdue their spirit to the yoke, which they wish to bind heavy upon their necks for life; and they remain through manhood timid, ignorant, and altogether unfitted for the conduct of public affairs, and for the government of men under a despotic rule, whose essential principle is a *salutary fear* of the prince in all his public officers. Every unlettered native of India is as sensible of this principle [as] Montesquieu was; and will tell us that, in countries like India, a chief, to govern well, must have a *smack of the devil* ('shaitān') in him; for, if he has not, his public servants will prey upon his innocent and industrious subjects.[5] In India there are no universities or public schools, in which young men might escape, as they do in Europe, from the enervating and stultifying influence of the zanāna.[6] The state of mental imbecility to which a youth of naturally average powers of mind, born to territorial dominion, is in India often reduced by a haughty and ambitious mother, would be absolutely incredible to a man bred up in such schools. They are often utterly unable to act, think, or speak for themselves. If they happen, as they sometimes do, to get well informed in reading and conversation, they remain, Hamlet-like, nervous and diffident; and, however speculatively or *ruminatively* wise, quite unfit for action, or for performing their part in the great drama of life.

In my evening ramble on the bank of the river, which was flowing against the wind and rising into waves, my mind wandered back to the hours of infancy and boyhood when I sat with my brothers watching our little vessels as they scudded over the ponds and streams of my native land; and then of my poor brothers John and Louis, whose bones now he beneath the ocean. As we advance in age the dearest scenes of early days must necessarily become more and more associated in our recollection with painful feelings; for they who enjoyed such scenes with us must by degrees pass away, and be remembered with sorrow even by those who are conscious of having fulfilled all their duties in life towards them—but with how much more by those who can never remember them without thinking of occasions of kindness and assistance neglected or disregarded. Many of them have perhaps left behind them widows and children struggling with adversity, and soliciting from us aid which we strive in vain to give.

During my visit to the Rājā, a person in the disguise of one of my sipāhīs[7] went to a shop and purchased for me five-and-twenty rupees' worth of fine Europe chintz, for which he paid in good rupees, which were forthwith assayed by a neighbouring goldsmith. The sipāhī put these rupees into his own purse, and laid it down, saying that he should go and ascertain from me whether I wished to keep the whole of the chintz or not; and, if not, he should require back the same money—that I was to halt to-morrow, when he would return to the shop again. Just as he was going away, however, he recollected that he wanted a turban for himself, and requested the shopkeeper to bring him one. They were sitting in the verandah, and the shopkeeper had to go into his shop to bring out the turban. When he came out with it, the sipāhī said it would not suit his purpose, and went off, leaving the purse where it lay, cautioning the shopkeeper against changing any of the rupees, as he should require his own identical money back if his master rejected any of the chintz. The shopkeeper waited till four o'clock in the afternoon of the next day without looking into the purse.

Hearing then that I had left Datiyā, and seeing no signs of the sipāhī, he opened the purse, and found that the rupees were all copper, with a thin coating of silver. The man had changed them while he went into the shop for a turban, and substituted a purse exactly the same in appearance. After ascertaining that the story was true, and that the ingenious thief was not one of my followers, I insisted upon the man's taking the money from me, in spite of a great deal of remonstrance on the part of the Rājā's agent, who had come on with us.

Notes:

1. The editor has failed to trace this quotation, which may possibly be from the *Mishkat-ul-Masābih* (*ante*, Chapter 5, note 10). Compare '"There is nothing more horrible than the rebellion of a sheep", said de Marsay' (Balzac, *Lost by a Laugh*).

2. The English doggerel expresses the opposite sentiment,
'My son's my son till he gets him a wife;
My daughter's my daughter all her life.'

3. *Ante*, chap. 29, text at [4], and before [7].

4. Edward II, A.D. 1327.

5. The principle, so bluntly enunciated by the author, is true, though the truth may be unpalatable to people who think they know better, and it applies with as much force to European officials as it does to Indian princes. The 'shaitān' is more familiar in his English dress as Satan. The editor has failed to find any such phrase in the works of Montesquieu. In chapter 9 of Book III of *L'Esprit des Lois* that author lays down the principle that 'il faut de la crainte dans un gouvernement despotique; pour la vertu, elle n'y est point nécessaire,'

6. It can no longer be said that universities do not exist, at least in name, in India. Calcutta, Bombay, Madras, Lahore, and Allahabad are the seats of universities, and new foundations at Dacca and Patna are promised (1914).

The Indian universities, when first established, were mere examining bodies, on the model of the University of London. But changes, initiated by Lord Curzon, are in progress, and the University of London is being remodelled (1914). The Indian institutions are not frequented by young princes and nobles, and have little influence on their education. Attempts have been made, with partial success, to provide special boarding schools, or 'Chiefs' Colleges', for the sons of ruling princes and native nobles. The most notable of such institution are the colleges at Ajmēr, Rājkōt in Kāthiāwār, and Indore. The influence of the zanāna is invariably directed against every proposal to remove a young nobleman from home for the purpose of education, and obstacles of many kinds render the task of rightly educating such a youth extraordinarily difficult and unsatisfactory. In some cases a considerable degree of success has been attained.

7. Armed follower. The word is more familiar in the corrupt form 'sepoy'.

CHAPTER 35

Gwālior Plain once the Bed of a Lake — Tameness of Peacocks.

On the 19th, 20th, and 21st[1] we came on forty miles to the village of Antrī in the Gwālior territory, over a fine plain of rich alluvial soil under spring crops. This plain bears manifest signs of having been at no very remote period, like the kingdom of Bohemia, the bed of a vast lake bounded by the ranges of sandstone hills which now seem to skirt the horizon all round; and studded with innumerable islands of all shapes and sizes, which now rise abruptly in all directions out of the cultivated plain.[2] The plain is still like the unruffled surface of a vast lake; and the rich green of the spring crops, which cover the surface in one wide sheet unintersected by hedges, tends to keep up the illusion, which the rivers have little tendency to dispel; for, though they have cut their way down immense depths to their present beds through this soft alluvial deposit, the traveller no sooner emerges from the hideous ravines, which disfigure their banks, than he loses all trace of them. Their course is unmarked by trees, large shrubs, or any of the signs which mark the course of rivers in other quarters.

The soil over the vast plain is everywhere of good quality, and everywhere cultivated, or rather worked, for we can hardly consider a soil cultivated which is never either irrigated or manured, or voluntarily relieved by fallows or an alternation of crops, till it has descended to the last stage of exhaustion. The prince rack-rents the farmer, the farmer rack-rents the cultivator, and the cultivator rack-rents the soil. Soon after crossing the Sindh river we enter upon the territories of the Gwālior chief, Sindhia.

The villages are everywhere few, and their communities very small. The greater part of the produce goes for sale to the capital of Gwālior, when the money it brings is paid into the treasury in rent, or revenue, to the chief, who distributes it in salaries among his establishments, who again pay it for land produce to the cultivators, farmers, and agricultural capitalists, who again pay it back into the treasury in land revenue. No more people reside in the villages than are absolutely necessary to the cultivation of the land, because the chief takes all the produce beyond what is necessary for their bare subsistence; and, out of what he takes, maintains establishments that reside elsewhere. There is nowhere any jungle to be seen, and very few of the villages that are scattered over the plains have any fruit or ornamental trees left; and, when the spring crops, to which the tillage is chiefly confined, are taken off the ground, the face of the country must have a very naked and dreary appearance.[3] Near one village on the road I saw some men threshing corn in a field, and among them a peacock (which, of course, I took to be domesticated) breakfasting very comfortably upon the grain as it flew around him. A little farther on I saw another quietly working his way into a stack of corn, as if he understood it to have been made for his use alone. It was so close to me as I passed that I put out my stick to push it off in play, and, to my surprise, it flew off in a fright at my white face and strange dress, and was followed by the others. I found that they were all wild, if that term can be applied to birds that live on such excellent terms with mankind. On reaching our tents we found several feeding in the corn-fields close around them, undisturbed by our host of camp- followers; and were told by the villagers, who had assembled to greet us, that they were all wild. 'Why', said they, 'should we think of *keeping* birds that live among us on such easy terms without being *kept*?' I asked whether they ever shot them, and was told that they never killed or molested them, but that any one who wished to shoot them might do so, since they had here no religions regard for them.[4] Like the pariah dogs the peacocks seem to disarm the people by confiding in them—their tameness is at once the cause and the effect of their security. The members of the little communities among whom they live on such friendly terms would not have the heart to shoot them; and travellers either take them to be domesticated, or are at once disarmed by their tameness.

At Antrī a sufficient quantity of salt is manufactured for the consumption of the people of the town. The earth that contains most salt is dug up at some distance from the town, and brought to small reservoirs made close outside the walls. Water is here poured over it, as over tea and coffee. Passing through the earth, it flows out below into a small conduit, which takes it to small pits some yards' distance, whence it is removed in buckets to small enclosed platforms, where it is exposed to the Sun's rays, till the water evaporates, and leaves the salt dry.[5] The want of trees over this vast plain of fine soil from the Sindh river is quite lamentable. The people of Antrī pointed out the place close to my tents where a beautiful grove of mango-trees had been lately taken off to Gwālior for *gun-carriages* and firewood, in spite of all the proprietor could urge of the detriment to his own interest in this world, and to those of his ancestors in that to which they had gone. Wherever the army of this chief moved they invariably swept off the groves of fruit-trees in the same reckless manner. Parts of the country, which they merely passed through, have recovered their trees, because the desire to propitiate the Deity, and to perpetuate their name by such a work, will always operate among Hindoos as a sufficient incentive to secure groves, wherever man has be made to feel that their rights of property in the trees will be respected.[6] The lands around the village, which had a well for irrigation, paid four times as much as those of the same quality which had none, and were made to yield two crops in the year. As everywhere else, so here, those lands into which water flows from the town and can be made to stand for a time, are esteemed the best, as this water brings down with it manures of all kinds.[7] I had a good deal of talk with the cultivators as I walked through the fields in the evenings; and they seemed to dwell much upon the good faith which is observed by the farmers and cultivators in the Honourable Company's territories, and the total absence of it in those of Sindhia's, where no work, requiring an outlay of capital from the land, is, in consequence, ever thought of—both farmers and cultivators engaging from year to year, and no farmer ever feeling secure of his lease for more than one.

Notes:

1. December, 1835.

2. The anthor's favourite theory. See *ante*, Chapter 14 note 7, Chapter 24 note 6, on the formation of black cotton soil. The Gwālior plain is covered with this soil.

3. It has a very desolate appearance. The Indian Midland Railway now passes through Gwālior.

4. In many parts of India, especially in Mathurā (Mattra) on the Jumna, and the neighbouring districts, the peacock is held strictly sacred, and shooting one would be likely to cause a riot. Tavernier relates a story of a rich Persian merchant being beaten to death by the Hindoos of Gujarāt for shooting a peacock. (Tavernier, *Travels*, transl. Ball, vol. i, p. 70.) the bird is regarded as the vehicle of the Hindoo god of war, variously called Kumāra, Skanda, or Kārtikeya. the editor, like the author, has observed that in Bundēlkhand no objection is raised to the shooting of peacocks by any one who cares for such poor sport.

5. In British India the manufacture of salt can be practised only by persons duly licensed.

6. The Revenue Settlement Regulations now in force in British India provide liberally for the encouragement of groves, and hundred of miles of road are annually planted with trees.

7. Sanitation did not trouble native states in those days.

CHAPTER 36

Gwālior and its Government.

On the 22nd,[1] we came on fourteen miles to Gwālior, over some ranges of sandstone hills, which are seemingly continuations of the Vindhyan range. Hills of indurated brown and red iron clay repose upon and intervene between these ranges, with strata generally horizontal, but occasionally bearing signs of having been shaken by internal convulsions. These convulsions are also indicated by some dykes of compact basalt which cross the road.[2]

Nothing can be more unprepossessing than the approach to Gwālior; the hills being naked, black, and ugly, with rounded tops devoid of grass or shrubs, and the soil of the valleys a poor red dust without any appearance of verdure or vegetation, since the few autumn crops that lately stood upon them have been removed.[3] From Antrī to Gwālior there is no sign of any human habitation, save that of a miserable police guard of four or five, who occupy a wretched hut on the side of the road midway, and seem by their presence to render the scene around more dreary.[4] the road is a mere footpath unimproved and unadorned by any single work of art; and, except in this footpath, and the small police guard, there is absolutely no single sign in all this long march to indicate the dominion, or even the presence, of man; and yet it is between two contiguous [sic] capitals, one occupied by one of the most ancient, and the other by one of the greatest native sovereigns of Hindustan.[5] One cannot but feel that he approaches the capital of a dynasty of barbarian princes, who, like Attila, would choose their places of residence, as devils choose their pandemonia, for their ugliness, and rather reside in the dreary wastes of Tartary than on the shores of the Bosphorus. There are within the dominions of Sindhia seats for a capital that would not yield to any in India in convenience, beauty, and salubrity; but, in all these dominions, there is not, perhaps, another place so hideously ugly as Gwālior, or so hot and unhealthy. It has not one redeeming quality that should recommend it to the choice of a rational prince, particularly to one who still considers his capital as his camp, and makes every officer of his army feel that he has as little of permanent interest in his house as he would have in his tent.[6]

Phūl Bāgh, or the *flower-garden,* was suggested to me as the best place for my tents, where Sindhia had built a splendid summer-house. As I came over this most gloomy and uninteresting march, in which the heart of a rational man sickens, as he recollects that all the revenues of such an enormous extent of dominion over the richest soil and the most peaceable people in the world should have been so long concentrated upon this point, and squandered without leaving one sign of human art or industry, I looked forward with pleasure to a quiet residence in the *flower- garden,* with good foliage above, and a fine sward below, and an atmosphere free from dust, such as we find in and around all the residences of Muhammadan princes. On reaching my tents I found them pitched close outside the *flower-garden,* in a small dusty plain, without a blade of grass or a shrub to hide its deformity — just such a place as the pig-keepers occupy in the suburbs of other towns. On one side of this little plain, and looking into it, was the *summer-house* of the prince, without one inch of green sward or one small shrub before it.

Around the wretched little *flower-garden* was a low, naked, and shattered mud wall, such as we generally see in the suburbs thrown up to keep out and in the pigs that usually swarm in such places — 'and the swine they crawled out, and the swine they crawled in'.[7] When I cantered up to my tent-door, a sipāhī of my guard came up, and reported that as the day began to dawn a gang of thieves had stolen one of my best carpets, all the brass brackets of my tent-poles, and the brass bell with which the sentries on duty sounded the hour; all Lieutenant Thomas's cooking utensils, and many other things, several of which they had found lying between the tents and the prince's *pleasure- house,* particularly the contents of a large heavy box of geological specimens. They had, in consequence, concluded the gang to be lodged in the prince's pleasure-house. The guard on duty at this place would make no answer to their inquiries, and I really believe that they were themselves the thieves. The tents of the Rājā of Raghugarh, who had come to pay his respects to the Sindhia, his liege lord, were pitched near mine. He had the day before had five horses stolen from him, with all the plate, jewels, and valuable clothes he possessed; and I was told that I must move forthwith from the *flower-garden,* or cut off the tail of every horse in my camp. Without tails they might not be stolen, with them they certainly would. Having had sufficient proof of their dexterity, we moved our tents to a grove near the residency, four miles from the flower-garden and the court.[8]

As a citizen of the world I could not help thinking that it would be an immense blessing upon a large portion of our species if an earthquake were to swallow up this court of Gwālior, and the army that surrounds it. Nothing worse could possibly succeed, and something better might. It is lamentable to think how much of evil this court and camp inflict upon the people who are subject to them. In January, 1828, I was passing with a party of gentlemen through the town of Bhīlsā, which belongs to this chief, and lies between Sāgar and Bhopal,[9] when we found, lying and bleeding in one of the streets, twelve men belonging to a merchant at Mirzapore, who had the day before been wounded and plundered by a gang of robbers close outside the walls of the town. Those who were able ran in to the Āmil, or chief of the district, who resides in the town; and begged him to send some horsemen after the banditti, and intercept them as they passed over the great plains. 'Send your own people', said he, 'or hire men to send. Am I here to look after the private affairs of merchants and travellers, or to collect the revenues of the prince?' Neither he, nor the prince himself, nor any other officer of the public establishments ever dreamed that it was their duty to protect the life, property, or character of travellers, or indeed of any other human beings, save the members of their own families. In this pithy question the Āmil of Bhīlsā described the nature and character of the government. All the revenues of his immense dominions are spent entirely in the maintenance of the court and camps of the prince; and every officer employed beyond the boundary of the court and camp considers his duties to be limited to the collection of the revenue. Protected from all external enemies by our military forces, which surround him on every side, his whole army is left to him for purposes of parade and display; and having, according to his notions, no use for them elsewhere, he concentrates them around his capital, where he lives among them in the perpetual dread of mutiny and assassination. He has nowhere any police, nor any establishment whatever, for the protection of the life and property of his subjects; nor has he, any more than his predecessors, ever, I believe, for one moment thought that those from whose industry and frugality he draws his revenues have any right whatever to expect from him the use of such establishments in return. They have never formed any legitimate part of the Marāthā government, and, I fear, never will.[10]

The misrule of such states, situated in the midst of our dominions, is not without its use. There is, as Gibbon justly observes, 'a strong propensity in human nature to depreciate the advantages, and to magnify the evils, of the present times'; and, if the people had not before their eyes such specimens of native rule to contrast with ours, they would think more highly than they do of that of their past Muhammadan and Hindoo sovereigns; and be much less disposed than they are to estimate fairly the advantages of being under ours. The native governments of the present day are fair specimens of what they have always been—grinding military despotisms—their whole history is that of 'Saul has killed his thousands, and David his tens of thousands'; as if rulers were made merely to slay, and the ruled to be slain. In politics, as in landscape, "Tis distance lends enchantment to the view', and the past might be all *couleur de rose* in the imaginations of the people were it not represented in these ill-governed states, where the 'lucky accident' of a good governor is not to be expected in a century, and where the secret of the responsibility of ministers to the people is yet undiscovered.[11]

The fortress of Gwālior stands upon a tableland, a mile and a half long by a quarter of a mile wide, at the north-east end of a small insulated sandstone hill, running north-east and south-west, and rising at both ends about three hundred and forty feet above the level of the plain below. At the base is a kind of glacis, which runs up at an angle of forty-five from the plain to within fifty, and, in some places, within twenty feet of the foot of the wall.

The interval is the perpendicular face of the horizontal strata of the sandstone rock. The glacis is formed of a bed of basalt in all stages of decomposition, with which this, like the other sandstone hills of Central India, was once covered, and of the debris and chippings of the rocks above. The walls are raised a certain uniform height all round upon the verge of the precipice, and being thus made to correspond with the edge of the rock, the line is extremely irregular. They are rudely built of the fine sandstone of the rock on which they stand, and have some square and some semicircular bastions of different sizes, few of these raised above the level of the wall itself.[12] On the eastern face of the rock, between the glacis and foot of the wall, are cut out, in bold relief, the colossal figures of men sitting bareheaded under canopies, on each side of a throne or temple; and, in another place, the colossal figure of a man standing naked, and facing outward, which I took to be that of Buddha.[13]

The town of Gwālior extends along the foot of the hill on one side, and consists of a single street above a mile long. There is a very beautiful mosque, with one end built by a Muhammad Khan, A.D. 1665, of the white sandstone of the rock above it. It looks as fresh as if it had not been finished a month; and struck, as I passed it, with so noble a work, apparently new, and under such a government, I alighted from my horse, went in, and read the inscription, which told me the date of the building and the name of the founder. There is no stucco-work over any part of it, nor is any required on such beautiful materials; and the stones are all so nicely cut that cement seems to have been considered useless. It has the usual two minarets or towers, and over the arches and alcoves are carved, as customary, passages from the Korān, in the beautiful Kufic characters.[14] The court and camp of the chief extends out from the southern end of the hill for several miles.

The whole of the hill on which the fort of Gwālior stands had evidently, at no very distant period, been covered by a mass of basalt, surmounted by a crust of indurated brown and red iron clay, with lithomarge, which often assumes the appearance of common laterite. The boulders of basalt, which still cap some part of the hill, and form the greater part of the glacis at the bottom, are for the most part in a state of rapid decomposition; but some of them are still so hard and fresh that the hammer rings upon them as upon a bell, and their fracture is brilliantly crystalline. The basalt is the same as that which caps the sandstone hills of the Vindhya range throughout Mālwā. The sandstone hills around Gwālior all rise in the same abrupt manner from the plain as those through Mālwā generally; and they have almost all of them the same basaltic glacis at their base, with boulders of that rock scattered over the top, all indicating that they were at one time buried, in the same manner under one great mass of volcanic matter, thrown out from their submarine craters in streams of lava, or diffused through the ocean or lakes in ashes, and deposited in strata. The geological character of the country about Gwālior is very similar to that of the country about Sāgar; and I may say the same of the Vindhya range generally, as far as I have seen it, from Mirzapore on the Ganges to Bhopāl in Mālwā—hills of sandstone rising suddenly from alluvial plain, and capped, or bearing signs of having been capped, by basalt reposing immediately upon it, and partly covered in its turn by beds of indurated iron clay.[15]

The fortress of Gwālior was celebrated for its strength under the Hindoo sovereigns of India; but was taken by the Muhammadans after a long siege, A.D. 1197.[16] the Hindoos regained possession, but were again expelled by the Emperor Īltutmish, A. D. 1235.[17] the Hindoos again got possession, and after holding it one hundred years, again surrendered it to the forces of the Emperor Ibrāhīm, A.D. 1519.[18] In 1543 it was surrendered up by the troops of the Emperor Humāyūn[19] to Shēr Khān, his successful competitor for the empire.[20] It afterwards fell into the hands of a Jāt chief, the Rānā of Gohad,[21] from whom it was taken by the Marāthās. While in their possession, it was invested by our troops under the command of Major Popham; and, on the 3rd of August, 1780, taken by escalade.[22] The party that scaled the wall was gallantly led by a very distinguished and most promising officer, Captain Bruce, brother of the celebrated traveller.[23]

It was made over to us by the Rānā of Gohad, who had been our ally in the war. Failing in his engagement to us, he was afterwards abandoned to the resentment of Mādhojī Sindhia, chief of the Marāthās.[24] In 1783, Gwālior was invested by Mādhojī Sindhia's troops, under the command of one of the most extraordinary men that have ever figured in Indian history, the justly celebrated General De Boigne.[25] After many unsuccessful attempts to take it by escalade, he bought over part of the garrison, and made himself master of the place. Gohad itself was taken soon after in 1784;

but the Rānā, Chhatarpat, made his escape. He was closely pursued, made prisoner at Karaulī, and confined in the fortress of Gwālior, where he died in the year 1785.[26] He left no son, and his claims upon Gohad devolved upon his nephew, Kīrat Singh, who, at the close of our war with the Marāthās, got from Lord Lake, in lieu of these claims, the estate of Dholpur, situated on the left banks of the river Chambal, which is estimated at the annual value of three hundred thousand, or three lākhs, of rupees. He died this year, 1835, and has been succeeded by his son, Bhagwant Singh, a lad of seventeen years of age.[27]

Notes:

1. December, 1835.

2. Throughout the northern edge of the trap country in Rājputāna, Gwālior, and Bundēlkhand, dykes are rare or wanting.' (W. T. Blandford, in *Manual of the Geology of India*, 1st ed., Part 1, p. 328.) The dykes mentioned in the text may not have been visited by the officers of the Geological Surrey.

3. 'Basalt generally disintegrates into a reddish soil, quite different from *regar* in character. This reddish soil may be seen passing into *regar*, but, as a rule, the black soil is confined to the flatter ground at the bottom of the valleys, or on flat hill-tops, the brown or red soils occupying the slopes' (ibid. p. 433).

4. Johnson, in his *Journey to the Western Islands*, observes: 'Now and then we espied a little corn-field, which served to impress more strongly the general barrenness.' [W. H. S.] The remark referred to the shores of Loch Ness (p. 237 of volume viii of Johnson's Works, London, 1820).

5. By this awkward phrase the author seems to mean Lucknow, on the east, the capital of the kingdom of Oudh, and Udaipur, to the west, the capital of the long-descended chieftain of Mēwār. Alternatively, the author may possibly have referred to Agra and Gwālior, rather than Lucknow and Udaipur.

6. 'The new city at Gwālior below the fortress is, like the city of Jhānsī, known as the 'Lashkar', or camp. The old city of Gwālior encircles the north end of the fortress. The new city, or Lashkar, lies to the south, more than a mile distant. In January, 1859, the population of the two cities together amounted to 142,044 persons (*A.S.R.*, vol. ii, p. 331).

7. Only those readers who have lived in India can fully understand the reasons why the pigs should frequent such a place, and how great would be the horrors of encamping in it.

8. In the description of the author's encampment at Gwālior, he fell into a mistake, which he discovered too late for correction in his journal. His tents were not pitched within the Phūl Bāgh, as he supposed, but without; and

seeing nothing of this place, he imagined that the dirty and naked ground outside was actually the flower-garden. The Phūl Bāgh, however, is a very pleasing and well-ordered garden, although so completely secluded from observation by lofty walls that many other travellers must have encamped on the same spot without being aware of its existence. (*Publishers' note at end of volume ii of original edition.*)

9. Bhīlsā is the principal town of the Isāgarh subdivision in the Gwālior State. The famous Buddhist antiquities near it are described at length in Cunningham, *The Bhīlsā Topes, or Buddhist Monuments of Central India* (1854), and in Maisey, *Sānchi and its Remains. A full Description of the Ancient Buildings, Sculptures, and Inscriptions at Sānchi, near Bhīlsā, in Central India*. With an Introductory Note by Major-General Sir Alexander Cunningham, K.C.I.E. (1892). It is surprising that so keen an observer as the author appears not to have noticed any of the great Buddhist buildings of Central India.

10. The government of Gwālior has improved since the author wrote. Many reforms have been begun and more or less fully executed. In May, 1887, the vast hoard of rupees buried in pits in the fort, valued at five millions sterling, was exhumed, and lent to the Government of India to be usefully employed. The passive opposition of a court like that of Gwālior to the effectual execution of reforms is continuous and difficult to overcome.

11. The author's description of the ordinary Asiatic government at almost all times and in all places as 'a grinding military despotism' is correct. Sentimental persons in both India and England are apt to forget this weighty truth. The golden age of India, excepting, perhaps, the Gupta period between A.D. 330 and 455, is as mythical as that of Ireland. What Persia now is, that would India be, if she had been left to her own devices.

12. Sir A. Cunningham was stationed at Gwālior for five years, and had thus an exceptionally accurate knowledge of the fortress. His account, which corrects the text in some particulars, is as follows:-'the great fortress of Gwālior is situated on a precipitous, flat-topped, and isolated hill of sandstone, which rises 300 feet above the town at the north end, but only 274 feet at the upper gate of the principal entrance. The hill is long and narrow; its extreme length from north to south being one mile and three- quarters, while its breadth varies from 600 feet opposite the main entrance to 2,800 feet in the middle opposite the great temple. The walls are from 30 to 35 feet in height, and the rock immediately below them is steeply, but irregularly, scarped all round the hill. The long line of battlements which crowns the steep scarp on the east is broken only by the lofty towers and fretted domes of the noble palace of Rājā Mān Singh. On the opposite side, the line of battlements is relieved by the deep recess of the Urwāhi valley, and by the zigzag and serrated parapets and loopholed bastions which flank the

numerous gates of the two western entrances. At the northern end, where the rock has been quarried for ages, the jagged masses of the overhanging cliff seem ready to fall upon the city beneath them. To the south the hill is less lofty, but the rock has been steeply scarped, and is generally quite inaccessible. Midway over all towers the giant form of a massive Hindu temple, grey with the moss of ages. Altogether, the fort of Gwālior forms one of the most picturesque views in Northern India' (*A.S.R.*, vol. ii, p. 330).

13. The nakedness of the image in itself proves that Buddha could not be the person represented. His statues are never nude. The Gwālior figures are images of some of the twenty-four great saints (Tīrthankaras or Jinas) of the Digambara sect of the Jain religion. Jain statues are frequently of colossal size. The largest of those at Gwālior is fifty-seven feet high. The Gwālior sculptures are of late date—the middle of the fifteenth century. The antiquities of Gwālior, including these sculptures, are well described in *A.S.R.*, vol. ii, pp. 330-95, plates lxxxvi to xci.

14. This mosque is the Jāmi', or cathedral, mosque 'situated at the eastern foot of the fortress, near the Ālamgīrī Darwāza (gate). It is a neat and favourable specimen of the later Moghal architecture. Its beauty, however, is partly due to the fine light-coloured sandstone of which it is built. This at once attracted the notice of Sir Wm. Sleeman, who, &c.' (*A.S.R.*, vol. ii, p. 370). This mosque is in the old city, described as 'a crowded mass of small flat-roofed stone houses' (ibid. p. 330).

15. The Geological Survey recognizes a special group of 'transition' rocks between the metamorphic and the Vindhyan series under the name of the Gwālior area. 'The Gwālior area is . . . only fifty miles long from east to west, and about fifteen miles wide. It takes its name from the city of Gwālior, which stands upon it, surrounding the famous fort built upon a scarped outlier of Vindhyan sandstone, which rests upon a base of massive bedded trap belonging to the transition period' (*Manual of Geology of India*, 1st ed., Part l, p. 56). The writers of the manual do not notice the basaltic cap of the fort hill described by the author, and at p. 300 use language which implies that the hill is outside the limits of the Deccan trap. But the author's observations seem sufficiently precise to warrant the conclusion that he was right in believing the basaltic cap of the Gwālior hill to be an outlying fragment of the vast Deccan trap sheet. The relation between laterite and lithomarge is discussed in p. 353 of the *Manual*, and the occurrence of laterite caps on the highest ground of the country, at two places-near Gwālior, 'outside of the trap area', is noticed (ibid. p. 356). These two places are at Rāipur hill, and on the Kaimūr sandstone, about two miles to the north-west. No doubt these two hills are outliers of the Central India spread of laterite, which has been traced as far as Siprī, about sixty miles south of the

Rāipur hill (Hacket, *Geology of Gwālior and Vicinity*, in *Records of Geol. Survey of India*, vol. iii, p. 41). The geology of Gwālior is also discussed in Mallet's paper entitled 'Sketch of the Geology of Scindia's Territories' (*Records*, vol. viii, p. 55). Neither writer refers to the basaltic cap of Gwālior fort hill. For the refutation of the author's theory of the subaqueous origin of the Deccan trap see notes Chapters 14, note 13, and Chapter 17, note 3 *ante*.

16. In the reign of Muizz-ud-dīn, Muhammad bin Sām, also known by the names of Shibāb-ud-din, and Muhammad Ghorī. He struck billon coins at the Gwālior mint. the correct date is A.D. 1196. The Hījrī year 592 began on the 6th Dec., A.D. 1195.

17. Shams-ud-dīn Īltutmish, 'the greatest of the Slave Kings', reigned from A.D. 1210 to 1235 (A.H. 607-633). He besieged Gwālior in A.H. 629 and after eleven months' resistance captured the place in the month Safar, A.H. 630, equivalent to Nov.-Dec. A.D. 1232. The date given in the text is wrong. The correct name of this king is Īltutmish (*Z.D.M.G.*, vol. lxi (1907), pp. 192, 193). It is written Altumash by the author, and Altamsh by Thomas and Cunningham. A summary of the events of his reign, based on coins and other original documents, is given of Thomas, *Chronicles of the Pathān Kings of Delhi*. Īltutmish recorded an inscription dated A.H. 630 at Gwālior (ibid. p. 80). This inscription was seen by Bābur, but has since disappeared.

18. Ibrāhīm Lodī, A.D. 1517-26. He was defeated and killed by Bābur at the first battle of Pānīpat, A.D. 1526. the correct date of his capture of Gwālior, according to Cunningham (*A.S.R.*, vol. ii, p. 340), is 1518.

19. Humāyūn was son of Bābur, and father of Akbar the Great. His first reign lasted from A.D. 1530 to 1540; his second brief reign of less than six months was terminated by an accident in January A.D. 1556. The correct date of the surrender of Gwālior to Shēr Shāh was A.D. 1542, corresponding to A.H. 949 (*A. S.R.*, vol. ii, p. 393), which year began 17th April, 1542.

20. Shēr Khan is generally known as Shēr (or Shīr) Shāh. A good summary of his career from A.D. 1528 to his death in A.D. 1545 (A.H. 934 to 952) is given by Thomas (op. cit. p. 393). He struck coins at Gwālior in A.H. 950, 951, 952 (ibid. p. 403).

21. Gohad lies between Etawah (Itāwā) and Gwālior, twenty-eight miles north-east of the latter. The chief, originally an obscure Jāt landholder, rose to power during the confusion of the eighteenth century, and allied himself with the British in 1789 (Thornton, *Gazetteer*, s.v. 'Gohad').

22. This memorable exploit was performed during Warren Hastings's war with the Marāthās, Sir Eyre Coote being Commander- in-Chief. Captain Popham first stormed the fort of Lahar, a stronghold west of Kālpī (Calpee), and then, by a cleverly arranged escalade, captured 'with little trouble

and small loss' the Gwālior fortress, which was garrisoned by a thousand men, and commonly supposed to be impregnable. 'Captain Popham was rewarded for his gallant services by being promoted to the rank of Major' (Thornton, *The History of the British Empire in India*, 2nd ed., 1859, p. 149). 'It is said that the spot (for escalade) was pointed out to Popham by a cowherd, and that the whole of the attacking party were supplied with grass shoes to prevent them from slipping on the ledges of rock. There is a story also that the cost of these grass shoes was deducted from Popham's pay when he was about to leave India as a Major-General, nearly a quarter of a century afterwards' (*A.S.R.*, vol. ii, p. 340).

23. James Bruce, 'the celebrated traveller', was Consul at Algiers. He explored Tripoli, Tunis, Syria, and Egypt, and travelled in Abyssinia from November 1769 to December 1771. He returned to Egypt by the Nile, arriving at Cairo in January 1773. His travels were published in 1790. He died in 1794.

24. The Sindhia family of Gwālior was founded by Rānojī Sindhia, a man of humble origin, in the service of the Peshwā. Rānojī died about A.D. 1750, and was succeeded by one of his natural sons, Māhādajī (corruptly Mahdaju, &c.) Sindhia, whose turbulent and chequered career lasted till 1794, when he was succeeded by his grand-nephew, Daulat Rāo. The Marāthā power under Daulat Rāo was broken in 1803, by Sir Arthur Wellesley at Assaye and Argaum, and by Lord Lake at Laswārī. Māhādajī's career is treated fully by Grant Duff, *A History of the Mahrattas* (1826 and reprint). Mr. H. G. Keene in his little book (*Rulers of India*, Oxford, 1892) erroneously gives the chiefs name as 'Mādhava Rao'. The anthor's 'Mādhojī' also is wrong.

25. It is impossible within the limits of a note to give an account of the extraordinary career of General De Boigne. His Indian adventures began in 1778, and terminated in September 1796, when he retired from Sindhia's service, and sold his private regiment of Persian cavalry, six hundred strong, to Lord Cornwallis, on behalf of the East India Company, for three lakhs of rupees (about £30,000). He settled in his native town, Chambéri in Savoy, and lived, in the enjoyment of his great wealth, and of high honours conferred by the sovereigns of France and Italy, until 21st June, 1830. He was created a Count, and was succeeded in the title by his son. See G. M. Raymond, *Mémoire sur la Carrière Militaire et Politique de M. le Général Comte de Boigne*, 2ième ed., Chambéry, 1830. Nine chapters of Mr. Herbert Compton's book, *A Particular Account of European Military Adventurers of Hindustan* (London, 1892), are devoted to De Boigne.

26. The cession of Gohad to Sindhia, sanctioned in the year 1805, during the brief and inglorious second term of office of Lord Cornwallis,

was effected by Sir George Barlow. The transaction is severely censured by Thornton (*History*, p. 343) as a breach of faith. Gwālior was given up to Sindhia along with Gohad. In January 1844, shortly after the battle of Maharājpur, Gwālior was again occupied by the forces of the Company, and the fortress (save for the Mutiny period) continued in British occupation until the 2nd December 1885, when Lord Dufferin restored it to Sindhia in exchange for Jhānsī. In June 1857 the Gwālior soldiery mutinied and massacred the Europeans, but the Maharājā remained throughout loyal to the English Government.

Sir Hugh Rose recaptured the place by assault on the 28th June 1858. In the changed circumstances of the country, and with regard to the modern developments of the art of war, the Gwālior fortress is now of slight military value.

27. The territory of the Dholpur chief is about fifty-four miles long by twenty-three broad. The town of Dholpur is nearly midway between Agra and Gwālior. The revenue is estimated by Thornton (1858) as seven lākhs, not only three lākhs as stated by the author. It was about eight lākhs in 1904 (*I.G.*, 1908).

CHAPTER 37

Content for Empire between the Sons of Shāh Jahān.

Under the Emperors of Delhi the fortress of Gwālior was always considered as an imperial State prison, in which they confined those rivals and competitors for dominion whom they did not like to put to a violent death. They kept a large menagerie, and other things, for their amusement. Among the best of the princes who ended their days in this great prison was Sulaimān Shikoh, the eldest son of the unhappy Dārā.[1] A narrative of the contest for empire between the four sons of Shāh Jahān may, perhaps, prove both interesting and instructive; and, as I shall have occasion, in the course of my rambles, to refer to the characters who figured in it, I shall venture to give it a place. . . .[2]

Notes:

1. 'The prisons of Gwālior are situated in a small outwork on the western side of the fortress, immediately above the Dhondha gateway. They are called "nau chaukī", or "the nine cells", and are both well lighted and well ventilated. But in spite of their height, from fifteen to twenty-six feet, they must be insufferably close in the hot season. These were the State prisons in which Akbar confined his rebellious cousins, and Aurangzēb the troublesome sons of Dārā and Murād, as well as his own more dangerous son Muhammad. During these times the fort was strictly guarded, and no one was allowed to enter without a pass' (A.S.R., vol. ii, p. 369), Sulaimān Shikoh, whom Manucci credits with 'all the gifts of nature', was poisoned at Gwālior early in the reign of Aurangzēb, by order of that monarch, paternal uncle of the victim (Irvine, Storia do Mogor, i. 380). The author, following Bernier, always calls Shāhjahān's eldest son simply Dārā. His name really was Dārā Shikoh (or Shukoh), meaning 'in splendour like Darius'.

2. The following twelve chapters contain an historical piece, to the personages and events of which the author will have frequent occasion to refer; and it is introduced in this place from its connexion with Gwālior, the State prison in which some of its actors ended their days. [W. H. S.]

The 'historical piece' which occupies chapters 37 to 46, inclusive of the author's text is little more than a paraphrase of The History of the Late

Rebellion in the States of the Great Mogol by Bernier, as the disquisition is called in Brock's translation. Mr. A. Constable's revised and annotated translation of Bernier's work (Constable and Co., 1891; reprinted with corrections. Oxford University Press, 1914) renders superfluous the reprinting of Sleeman's paraphrase, which would require much correction and comment before it could be presented to readers of the present day. The main facts of the narrative are, moreover, now easily accessible in the histories of Elphinstone and innumerable other writers. Such explanations as may be required to elucidate allusions to the excised portion in the later chapters of the anthor's work will be found in the notes. The titles of the chapters which have not been reprinted follow here for facility of reference.

CHAPTER 38

Aurangzēb and Murād Defeat their Father's Army near Ujain.

CHAPTER 39

Dārā Marches in Person against his Brothers, and is Defeated.

CHAPTER 40

Dārā Retreats towards Lahore — Is robbed by the Jāts — Their Character.

CHAPTER 41

Shāh Jahān Imprisoned by his Two Sons, Aurangzēb and Murād.

CHAPTER 42

Aurangzēb Throws off the Mask, Imprisons his Brother Murād, and Assumes the Government of the Empire.

CHAPTER 43

Aurangzēb Meets Shujā in Bengal and Defeats him, after Pursuing Dārā to the Hyphasis.

CHAPTER 44

Aurangzēb Imprisons his Eldest Son—Shujā and all his Family are Destroyed.

CHAPTER 45

Second Defeat and Death of Dārā, and Imprisonment of his Two Sons.

CHAPTER 46

Death and Character of Amīr Jumla,

CHAPTER 47

Reflections on the Preceding History.

The contest for the empire of India here described is very like that which preceded it, between the sons of Jahāngīr, in which Shāh Jahān succeeded in destroying all his brothers and nephews; and that which succeeded it, forty years after,[1] in which Mu'azzam, the second of the four sons of Aurangzēb, did the same;[2] and it may, like the rest of Indian history, teach us a few useful lessons. First, we perceive the advantages of the law of primogeniture, which accustoms people to consider the right of the eldest son as sacred, and the conduct of any man who attempts to violate it as criminal. Among Muhammadans, property, as well real as personal, is divided equally among the sons;[3] and their Korān, which is their only civil and criminal, as well as religions, code, makes no provision for the successions to sovereignty. The death of every sovereign is, in consequence, followed by a contest between his sons, unless they are overawed by some paramount power; and he who succeeds in this contest finds it necessary, for his own security, to put all his brothers and nephews to death, lest they should be rescued by factions, and made the cause of future civil wars. But sons, who exercise the powers of viceroys and command armies, cannot, where the succession is unsettled, wait patiently for the natural death of their father—delay may be dangerous. Circumstances, which now seem more favourable to their views than to those of their brothers, may alter; the military aristocracy depend upon the success of the chief they choose in the enterprise, and the army more upon plunder than regular pay; both may desert the cause of the more wary for that of the more daring; each is flattered into an overweening confidence in his own ability and good fortune; and all rush on to seize upon the throne yet filled by their wretched parent, who, in the history of his own crimes, now reads those of his children. Gibbon has justly observed (chap. 7): 'the superior prerogative of birth, when it has obtained the sanction of time and popular opinion, is the plainest and least invidious of all distinctions among mankind. The acknowledged right extinguishes the hopes of faction; and the conscious security disarms the cruelty of the monarch. To the firm establishment of this idea we owe the peaceful succession and mild administration of European monarchies. To the defect of it we must attribute the frequent civil wars through which an Asiatic despot is obliged to cut his way to the throne of his fathers. Yet, even in the East, the sphere of contention is usually limited to the princes of the reigning house; and, as soon as the fortunate competitor has removed his brethren by the sword and the bowstring, he no longer entertains any jealousy of his meaner subjects.'

Among Hindoos, both real and personal property is divided in the same manner equally among the sons;[4] but a principality is, among them, considered as an exception to this rule; and every large estate, within which the proprietor holds criminal jurisdiction, and maintains a military establishment, is considered a principality. In such cases the law of primogeniture is rigorously enforced; and the death of the prince scarcely ever involves a contest for power and dominion between his sons. The feelings of the people, who are accustomed to consider the right of the eldest son to the succession as religiously sacred, would be greatly shocked at the attempt of any of his brothers to invade it. The younger brothers, never for a moment supposing they could be supported in such a sacrilegious attempt, feel for their eldest brother a reverence inferior only to that which they feel for their father; and the eldest brother, never supposing such attempts on their part as possible, feels towards them as towards his own children. All the members of such a family commonly live in the greatest harmony.[5] In the laws, usages, and feelings of the people upon this subject we had the means of preventing that eternal subdivision of landed property, which ever has been, and ever will be, the bane of everything that is great and good in India; but, unhappily, our rulers have never had the wisdom to avail themselves of them. In a great part of India the property, or the lease of a *village* held in farm under Government, was considered as a *principality*, and subject strictly to the same laws of primogeniture—it was a *fief*, held under Government on condition of either direct service, rendered to the State in war, in education, or charitable or religions duties, or of furnishing the means, in money or in kind, to provide for such service. In every part of the Sāgar and Nerbudda Territories the law of primogeniture in such leases was in force when we took possession, and has been ever since preserved.[6] The eldest of the sons that remain united with the father, at his death, succeeds to the estate, and to the obligation of maintaining all the widows and orphan children of those of his brothers who remained united to their parent stock up to their death, all his unmarried sisters, and, above all, his mother. All the younger brothers aid him in the management, and are maintained by him till they wish to separate, when a division of the stock takes place, and is adjusted by the elders of the village. The member, who thus separates from the parent stock, from that time forfeits for ever all claims to support from the possessor of the ancestral estate, either for himself, his widow, or his orphan children.[7]

Next, it is obvious that no existing Government in India could, in case of invasion or civil war, count upon the fidelity of their aristocracy either of land or of office. It is observed by Hume, in treating of the reign of King John in England, that 'men easily change sides in a civil war, especially where the power is founded upon an hereditary and independent authority, and is not derived from the opinion and favour of the people' — that is, upon the people collectively or the nation; for the hereditary and independent authority of the English baron in the time of King John was founded upon the opinion and fidelity of only that portion of the people over which he ruled, in the same manner as that of the Hindoo chiefs of India in the time of Shāh Jahān; but it was without reference either to the honesty of the cause he espoused, or to the opinion and feeling of the nation or empire generally regarding it. The Hindoo territorial chiefs, like the feudal barons of the Middle Ages in Europe, employed all the revenues of their estates in the maintenance of military followers, upon whose fidelity they could entirely rely, whatever side they might themselves take in a civil war; and the more of these resources that were left at their disposal, the more impatient they became of the restraints which settled governments imposed upon them. Under such settled governments they felt that they had an *arm* which they could not use; and the stronger that arm, the stronger was their desire to use it in the subjugation of their neighbours. The reigning emperors tried to secure their fidelity by assigning to them posts of honour about their court that required their personal attendance in all their pomp of pride; and by taking from each a daughter in marriage. If any one rebelled or neglected his duties, he was either crushed by the imperial forces, or put to the *ban of the empire*, and his territories were assigned to any one who would undertake to conquer them.[8] Their attendance at our viceroyal court would be a sad encumbrance;[9] and our Governor-General could not well conciliate them by matrimonial alliances, unless we were to alter a good deal in their favour our law against polygamy; nor would it be desirable to 'let slip the dogs of war' once more throughout the land by adopting the plan of putting the refractory chiefs to the ban of the empire. Their troops would be of no use to us in the way they are organized and disciplined, even if we could rely upon their fidelity in time of need; and this I do not think we ever can.[10]

If it be the duty of all such territorial chiefs to contribute to the support of the public establishments of the paramount power by which they are secured in the possession of their estates, and defended from all external danger, as it most assuredly is, it is the duty of that power to take such contribution in money, or the means of maintaining establishments more suited to its purpose than their rude militia can ever be; and thereby to impair the *powers* of that arm which they are so impatient to wield for their own aggrandizement, and to the prejudice of their neighbours; and to strengthen that of the paramount power by which the whole are kept in peace, harmony, and security. We give to India what India never had before our rule, and never could have without it, the assurance that there will always be at the head of the Government a sensible ruler trained up to office in the best school in the world; and that the security of the rights, and the enforcement of the duties, presented or defined by law, will not depend upon the will or caprice of individuals in power. These assurances the people in India now everywhere thoroughly understand and appreciate. They see in the native states around them that the lucky accident of an able governor is too rare ever to be calculated upon; while all that the people have of property, office, or character, depends not only upon their governor, but upon every change that he may make in his ministers.

The government of the Muhammadans was always essentially military, and the aristocracy was always one of military office. There was nothing else upon which an aristocracy could be formed. All high civil offices were combined with the military commands. The emperor was the great proprietor of all the lands, and collected and distributed their rents through his own servants. Every Musalmān with his Korān in his hand was his own priest and his own lawyer; and the people were nowhere represented in any municipal or legislative assembly—there was no bar, bench, senate, corporation, art, science, or literature by which men could rise to eminence and power. Capital had nowhere been concentrated upon great commercial or manufacturing establishments. There were, in short, no great men but the military servants of Government; and all the servants of Government held their posts at the will and pleasure of their sovereign.[11]

If a man was appointed by the emperor to the command of five thousand, the whole of this five thousand depended entirely on his favour for their employment, and upon their employment for their subsistence, whether paid from the imperial treasury, or by an assignment of land in some distant province.[12] In our armies there is a regular gradation of rank; and every officer feels that he holds his commission by a tenure as high in origin, as secure in possession, and as independent in its exercise, as that of the general who commands; and the soldiers all know and feel that the places of those officers, who are killed or disabled in action, will be immediately filled by those next in rank, who are equally trained to command, and whose authority none will dispute. In the Muhammadan armies there was no such gradation of rank. Every man held his office at the will of the chief whom he followed, and he was every moment made to feel that all his hopes of advancement must depend upon his pleasure. The relation between them was that of patron and client; the client felt bound to yield implicit obedience to the commands of his patron, whatever they might be; and the patron, in like manner, felt bound to protect and promote the interests of his client, as long as he continued to do so. As often as the patron changed sides in a civil war, his clients all blindly followed him; and when he was killed, they instantly dispersed to serve under any other leader whom they might find willing to take their services on the same terms.

The Hindoo chiefs of the military class had hereditary territorial possessions; and the greater part of these possessions were commonly distributed on conditions of military service among their followers, who were all of the same clan. But the highest Muhammadan officers of the empire had not an acre more of land than they required for their dwelling-houses, gardens, and cemeteries. They had nothing but their office to depend upon, and were always naturally anxious to hold it under the strongest side in any competition for dominion. When the star of the competitor under whom they served seemed to be on the wane, they soon found some plausible excuse to make their peace with his rival, and serve under his banners. Each competitor fought for his own life, and those of his children; the imperial throne could be filled by only one man; and that man dared not leave one single brother alive. His father had taken good care to dispose of all his own brothers and nephews in the last contest. The subsistence of the highest, as well as that of the lowest, officer in the army depended upon their employment in the public service, and all such employments would be given to those who served the victor in the struggle. Under such circumstances one is rather surprised that the history of civil wars in India exhibits so many instances of fidelity and devotion.

The mass of the people stood aloof in such contests without any feeling of interest, save the dread that their homes might become the seat of the war, or the tracks of armies which were alike destructive to the people in their course whatever side they might follow. The result could have no effect upon their laws and institutions, and little upon their industry and property. As ships are from necessity formed to weather the storms to which they are constantly liable at sea, so were the Indian village communities framed to weather those of invasion and civil war, to which they were so much accustomed by land; and, in the course of a year or two, no traces were found of ravages that one might have supposed it would have taken ages to recover from. The lands remained the same, and their fertility was improved by the fallow; every man carried away with him the implements of his trade, and brought them back with him when he returned; and the industry of every village supplied every necessary article that the community required for their food, clothing, furniture, and accommodation. Each of these little communities, when left unmolested, was in itself sufficient to secure the rights and enforce the duties of all the different members; and all they wanted from their government was moderation in the land taxes, and protection from external violence. Arrian says: 'If any intestine war happens to break forth among the Indians, it is deemed a heinous crime either to seize the husbandmen or spoil their harvest. All the rest wage war against each other, and kill and slay as they think convenient, while they live quietly and peaceably among them, and employ themselves at their rural affairs either in their fields or vineyards.'[13] I am afraid armies were not much more disposed to forbearance in the days of Alexander than at present, and that his followers must have supposed they remained untouched, merely because they heard of their sudden rise again from their ruins by that spirit of moral and political vitality with which necessity seems to have endowed them.[14]

During the early part of his life and reign, Aurangzēb was employed in conquering and destroying the two independent kingdoms of Golconda and Bījāpur in the Deccan, which he formed into two provinces governed by viceroys. Each had had an army of above a hundred thousand men while independent. The officers and soldiers of these armies had nothing but their courage and their swords to depend upon for their subsistence. Finding no longer any employment under settled and legitimate authority in defending the life, property, and independence of the people, they were obliged to seek it around the standards of lawless freebooters; and upon the ruins of these independent kingdoms and their disbanded armies rose the Marāthā power, the hydra-headed monster which Aurangzēb thus created by his ambition, and spent the last twenty years of his life in vain attempts to crush. [15] The monster has been since crushed by being deprived of its Peshwā, the head which alone could infuse into all the members of the confederacy a feeling of nationality, and direct all their efforts, when required, to one common object. Sindhia, the chief of Gwālior, is one of the surviving members of this great confederacy—the rest are the Holkars of Indore, the Bhōnslās of Nāgpur, and the Gaikwārs of Barodā,[16] the grandchildren of the commandants of predatory armies, who formed capital cities out of their standing camps in the countries they invaded and conquered in the name of their head, the Sātārā Rājā,[17] and afterwards in that of his mayor of the palace, the Peshwā. There is not now the slightest feeling of nationality left among the Marāthā States, either collectively or individually.[18] There is not the slightest feeling of sympathy between the mass of the people and the chief who rules over them, and his public establishments. To maintain these public establishments he everywhere plunders the people, who most heartily detest him and them. These public establishments are composed of men of all religions and sects, gathered from all quarters of India, and bound together by no common feeling, save the hope of plunder and promotion. Not one in ten is from, or has his family in, the country where he serves, nor is one in ten of the same clan with his chief. Not one of them has any hope of a provision either for himself, when disabled from wounds or old age from serving his chief any longer, or for his family, should he lose his life in his service.

In India[19] there are a great many native chiefs who were enabled, during the disorders which attended the decline and fall of the Muhammadan power and the rise and progress of the Marāthās and English, to raise and maintain armies by the plunder of their neighbours. The paramount power of the British being now securely established throughout the country, they are prevented from indulging any longer in such sporting propensities; and might employ their vast revenues in securing the blessing of good civil government for the territories in the possession of which they are secured by our military establishment. But these chiefs are not much disposed to convert their swords into ploughshares; they continue to spend their revenues on useless military establishments for purposes of parade and show. A native prince would, they say, be as insignificant without an army as a native gentleman upon an elephant without a cavalcade, or upon a horse without a tail. But the said army have learnt from their forefathers that they were to look to aggressions upon their neighbours—to pillage, plunder, and conquest, for wealth and promotion; and they continue to prevent their prince from indulging in any disposition to turn his attention to the duties of civil government. They all live in the hope of some disaster to the paramount power which secures the increasing wealth of the surrounding countries from their grasp; and threatened innovations from the north-west raise their spirits and hopes in proportion as they depress those of the classes engaged in all branches of peaceful industry.

There are, in all parts of India, thousands and tens of thousands who have lived by the sword, or who wish to live by the sword, but cannot find employment suited to their tastes. These would all flock to the standard of the first lawless chief who could offer them a fair prospect of plunder; and to them all wars and rumours of war are delightful. The moment they hear of a threatened invasion from the north-west, they whet their swords, and look fiercely around upon those from whose breasts they are 'to cut their pound of flesh'.[20]

Notes:

1. 'Fifty years after' would be more nearly correct. Aurangzēb wa crowned 23rd July, 1658, according to the author. See end of next note.

2. On the death of Aurangzēb, which took place in the Deccan, on the 3rd of March, 1707 (N.S.), his son 'Azam marched at the head of the troops which he commanded in the Deccan, to meet Mu'azzam, who was viceroy in Kabul. They met and fought near Agra. 'Azam was defeated and killed. The victor marched to meet his other brother, Kām Baksh, whom he killed near Hyderabad in the Deccan, and secured to himself the empire. On his death, which took place in 1713, his four sons contended in the same way for the throne at the head of the armies of their respective viceroyalties. Mu'izz- ud-dīn, the most crafty, persuaded his two brothers, Rafī-ash-Shān and Jahān Shāh, to unite their forces with his own against their ambitions brother, Azīm-ash-Shān, whom they defeated and killed, Mu'izz-ud- dīn then destroyed his two allies. [W. H. S.]

The above note is not altogether accurate. 'Azam, the third son of Aurangzēb, was killed in battle near Agra, in June 1707. During the interval between Aurangzēb's death and his own, he had struck coins. Mu'azzam, the second, and eldest then surviving son, after the defeat of his rival, ascended the throne under the title of Shāh Ālam Bahādur Shāh, and is generally known as Bahādur Shāh. He was then sixty-four years of age, his father having been eighty-seven years old when he died. The events following the death of Bahādur Shāh are narrated as follows by Mr. Lane-Poole; 'The Deccan was the weakest point in the empire from the beginning of the reign. Hardly had Bahādur appointed his youngest brother, Kām Baksh ('Wish-fulfiller'), viceroy of Bījāpur and Haidarābād, when that infatuated prince rebelled and committed such atrocities that the Emperor was compelled to attack him. Zū-l-Fikār engaged and defeated the rebel king (who was striking coins in full assumption of sovereignty) near Haidarābād, and Kām Baksh died of his wounds (1708, A.H. 1120).

'In the midst of this confusion, and surrounded by portents of coming disruption, Bahādur died, 1712 (1124). He left four sons, who immediately entered with the zest of their race upon the struggle for the crown. The eldest, 'Azīm-ash-Shān ("Strong of Heart"), first assumed the sceptre, but Zū-l- Fikār, the prime minister, opposed and routed him, and the prince was drowned in his flight. The successful general next defeated and slew two other brothers, Khujistah Akhtār Jahān-Shāh and Rafī-ash-Shān, and placed the surviving of the four sons of Bahādur [i.e. Mu'izz-ud- dīn] on the throne with the title of Jahāndār ("World-owner"). The new Emperor was an irredeemable poltroon and an abandoned debauchee.' (*The History of the Moghul Emperors of Hindustan illustrated by their Coins*, Constable, 1892, and in Introd. to *B. M. Catal. of Moghul Emperors*, same date.)

He was killed in 1713, and was succeeded by Farrukh-sīyar, the son of Azīm-ush-Shān. The chronology is as follows:-

No.	Soverign	A.H.	A.D.
VI.	Aurangzēb Ālamgīr, Muhayī-ud- dīn	1068	1658
	['Azam Shāh	1118	1707
	Kām Baksh	1119-20	1708]
VII	Bahādur Shāh-'Ālam, Kutb-ud-dīn	1119	1707
VIII	Jahāndār Shāh, Mu'izz-ud-dīn	1124	1713
IX	Farrukhsīyar	1124	1713

The question concerning the exact date from which the beginning of Aurangzēb's reign should be reckoned is obscured by the conflict of authorities and has given rise to much discussion. The results may be stated briefly as follow: —

Aurangzēb formally took possession of the throne in a garden outside Delhi on the 1st Zū'l Q'adah, A.H. 1068, July 31, A.D. 1658, but subsequently orders were passed to antedate the beginning of the reign to 1st Ramazān in the same year, equivalent to June 2, 1658. After the destruction of Shāh Shujā, Aurangzēb returned to Delhi in May, A.D. 1659, and was again enthroned with full ceremonial on June 15, 1659 (= A.H. 1069). Some authors consequently assume the accession to have taken place in 1659. But the reign certainly began in A.D. 1658, and should be reckoned as running from the official date, June 2 of that year. The dates given above are in New Style (N.S.). If recorded in Old Style (O.S.) they would be ten days earlier. (See Irvine and Hoernle in *J.A.S.B.*, Part I, vol. lxii (1893), pp. 256-67; and Irvine, in *Ind. Ant.*, vol. xl (1911), pp. 74, 75.)

3. The author invariably ignores the fact that daughters and other female relatives inherit under Muhammadan law.

4. Hindoo law does not ordinarily recognize any right of succession for daughters, and so differs essentially from the law of Islam. The exceptions to this general rule are unimportant.

5. The experience of most officials does not confirm this statement.

6. The statement now requires modification. After the Central Provinces were constituted in 1861, the principle of succession by primogeniture was maintained only in the Hoshangābād, Chhindwāra, Chāndā, and Chhattīsgarh Districts. But even there the legal effect of the restrictions on alienation and partition is 'not quite free from doubt' (*I.G.* 1908, x. 73). The tendency of the law courts is to apply everywhere uniform rules taken from the Hindoo law books.

7. 'See *ante*, Chapter 10, notes 10, 16. The gradual conversion of tenure by leases from Government into proprietary right in land has brought the

land under the operation of the ordinary Hindoo law, and each member of a joint family can now enforce partition of the land as well as of the stock upon it. The evils resulting from incessant partition are obvious, but no remedy can be devised. The people insist on partition, and will effect it privately, if the law imposes obstacles to a formal public division.

8. These remarks attribute too much System to the disorderly working of an Asiatic despotism. No institution resembling the formal 'ban of the empire' ever really existed in India.

9. The Rājās at Simla might now be considered by some people as an encumbrance.

10. The author could not foresee the gallant service to be rendered by the Chiefs of the Panjāb and other territories in the Mutiny, nor the institution of the Imperial Service Troops. Those troops, first organized in 1888, in response to the voluntary offers made by many princes as a reply to the Russian aggression on Panjdeh, are select bodies, picked from the soldiery of certain native states, and equipped and drilled in the European manner. Cashmere (Kāshmīr) and many States in the Panjāb and elsewhere furnish troops of this kind, officered by local gentlemen, under the guidance of English inspecting officers. The Kāshmīr Imperial Service Troops did excellent service during the campaign of 1892 in Hunza and Nagar. the System so happily introduced is likely to be much further developed. In 1907 the authorized strength was a little over 18,000 (*I.G.*, iv (1907), pp. 87, 373).

11. 'In Rome, as in Egypt and India, many of the great works which, in modern nations, form the basis of gradations of rank in society, were executed by Government out of public revenue, or by individuals gratuitously for the benefit of the public; for instance, roads, canals, aqueducts, bridges, &c., from which no one derived an income, though all derived benefit. There was no capital invested, with a view to profit, in machinery, railroads, canals, steam- engines, and other great works which, in the preparation and distribution of man's enjoyments, save the labour of so many millions to the nations of modern Europe and America, and supply the incomes of many of the most useful and most enlightened members of their middle and higher classes of society. During the republic, and under the first emperors, the laws were simple, and few derived any considerable income from explaining them. Still fewer derived their incomes from expounding the religion of the people till the establishment of Christianity.

Man was the principal machine in which property was invested with a view to profit, and the concentration of capital in hordes of slaves, and the farm of the public revenues of conquered provinces and tributary states, were, with the land, the great basis of the aristocracies of Rome, and the Roman world generally. The senatorial and equestrian orders were supported chiefly by lending out their slaves as gladiators and artificers, and by farming the revenues, and lending money to the oppressed subjects of the provinces, and to vanquished princes, at an exorbitant interest, to enable them to pay what the state or its public officers demanded. The slaves throughout the Roman empire were about equal in number to the free population, and they were for the most part concentrated in the hands of the members of the upper and middle classes, who derived their incomes from lending and employing them. They were to those classes in the old world what canals, railroads, steam-engines, &c., are to those of modern days. Some Roman citizens had as many as five thousand slaves educated to the one occupation of gladiators for the public shows of Rome. Julius Caesar had this number in Italy waiting his return from Gaul; and Gordianus used commonly to give five hundred pair for a public festival, and never less than one hundred and fifty.

In India slavery is happily but little known;[a] the church had no hierarchy either among the Hindoos or Muhammadans; nor had the law any high interpreters. In all its civil branches of marriage, inheritance, succession, and contract, it was to the people of the two religions as simple as the laws of the twelve tables; and contributed just as little to the support of the aristocracy as they did. In all these respects, China is much the same; the land belongs to the sovereign, and is minutely subdivided among those who farm and cultivate it—the great works in canals, aqueducts, bridges, roads, &c., are made by Government, and yield no private income. Capital is nowhere concentrated in expensive machinery; their church is without a hierarchy, their law without barristers-their higher classes are therefore composed almost exclusively of the public servants of the Government. The rule which prescribes that princes of the blood shall not be employed in the government of provinces and the command of armies, and that the reigning sovereign shall have the nomination of his successor, has saved China from a frequent return of the scenes which I have described. None of the princes are put to death, because it is known that all will acquiesce in the nomination when made known, supported as it always is by the popular sentiment throughout the empire. [W. H. S.]

a. the anthor's statement that in the year 1836 slavery was 'but little known in India' is a truly astonishing one. Slavery of various kinds—racial, predial, domestic—the slavery of captives, and of debtors, had existed in India from time immemorial, and still flourished in 1836. Slavery, so far as the law can abolish it, was abolished by the Indian Act v of 1843, but the final blow was not dealt until January l, 1862, when sections 370, &c., of the

Indian Penal Code came into force. In practice, domestic servitude exists to this day in great Muhammadan households, and multitudes of agricultural labourers have a very dim consciousness of personal freedom. The Criminal Law Commissioners, who reported previous to the passage of Act v of 1843, estimated that in British India, as then constituted, the proportion of the slave to the free population varied from one-sixth to two-fifths. Sir Bartle Frere estimated the slave population of the territories included in British India in the year 1841 as being between eight and nine millions. Slaves were heritable and transferable property, and could be mortgaged or let out on hire. The article 'Slave' in Balfour, *Cyclopaedia* (3rd ed.), from which most of the above particulars are taken, is copious, and gives references to various authorities. The following works may also be consulted: *The Law and Custom of Slavery in British India*, by William Adam, 8vo, 1840; *An Account of Slave Population in the Western Peninsula of India*, 1822, with an Appendix on Slavery in Malabar; *India's Cries to British Humanity*, by J. Peggs, 8vo, 1830; and *E.H.I.*, 3rd ed. (1914), pp. 100, 178, 180, 441.

12. In Akbar's time there were thirty-three grades of official rank, and the officers were known as 'commanders of ten thousand', 'commanders of five thousand', and so on. Only princes of the blood royal were granted the commands of seven thousand and of ten thousand. The number of troopers actually provided by each officer did not correspond with the number indicated by his title. The graded officials were called *mansabdārs*, no clear distinction between civil and military duties being drawn (*The Emperor Akbar*, by Count Von Noer; translated by Annette S. Beveridge, Calcutta, 1890, vol. i, p. 267).

13. Diodorus Siculus has the same observation. 'No enemy ever does any prejudice to the husbandmen; but, out of a due regard to the common good, forbear to injure them in the least degree; and, therefore, the land being never spoiled or wasted, yields its fruit in great abundance, and furnishes the inhabitants with plenty of victual and all other provisions.' Book II, chap. 3. [W. H. S.] These allegations certainly cannot be accepted as accurate statements of fact, however they may be explained. See *E.H.I.*, 3rd ed. (1914), p. 442.

14. The rapid recovery of Indian villages and villagers from the effects of war does not need for its explanation the evocation of 'a spirit of moral and political vitality'. The real explanation is to be found in the simplicity of the village life and needs, as expounded by the author in the preceding passage. Human societies with a low standard of comfort and a simple scheme of life are, like individual organisms of lowly structure and few functions, hard to kill. Human labour, and a few cattle, with a little grain and some sticks, are the only essential requisites for the foundation or reconstruction of a village.

15. Golconda was taken by Aurangzēb, after a protracted siege, in 1677. Bījāpur surrendered to him on the 15th October, 1686. The vast ruins of this splendid city, which was deserted after the conquest, occupy a space thirty miles in circumference. The town has partially recovered, and is now the head- quarters of a Bombay District, with about 24,000 inhabitants. Sivājī, the founder of the Marāthā power, died in 1680.

16. The Indore and Barodā States still survive, and the reigning chiefs of both have frequently visited England, and paid their respects to their Sovereign. Bhōnslā was the family name of the chiefs of Berār, also known as the Rājās of Nāgpur. The last Rājā, Raghojī III, died in December 1853, leaving no child begotten or adopted. Lord Dalhousie annexed the State as lapsed, and his action was confirmed in 1864 by the Court of Directors and the Crown.

17. The State of Sātārā, like that of Nāgpur, lapsed owing to failure of heirs, and was annexed in 1854. It is now a district in the Bombay Presidency.

18. During the early years of the twentieth century a spirit of Marāthā nationalism has been sedulously cultivated, with inconvenient results.

19. This paragraph, and that next following, are, in the original edition, printed as part of Chapter 48, 'The Great Diamond of Kohinūr', with which they have nothing to do. They seem to belong properly to Chapter 47, and are therefore inserted here. The observations in both paragraphs are merely repetitions of remarks already recorded.

20. It need hardly be said that these fire-eaters no longer exist.

CHAPTER 48

The Great Diamond of Kohinūr.

The foregoing historical episode occupies too large a space in what might otherwise be termed a personal narrative; but still I am tempted to append to it a sketch of the fortunes of that famous diamond, called with Oriental extravagance the Mountain of Light, which, by exciting the cupidity of Shāh Jahān, played so important a part in the drama.

After slumbering for the greater part of a century in the imperial treasury, it was afterwards taken by Nādir Shāh, the king of Persia, who invaded India under the reign of Muhammad Shāh, in the year 1738.[1] Nadir Shāh, in one of his mad fits, had put out the eyes of his son, Razā Kulī Mirzā, and, when he was assassinated, the conspirators gave the throne and the diamond to this son's son, Shāhrukh Mirza, who fixed his residence at Meshed.[2] Ahmad Shāh, the Abdālī, commanded the Afghān cavalry in the service of Nādir Shāh, and had the charge of the military chest at the time he was put to death. With this chest, he and his cavalry left the camp during the disorders that followed the murder of the king, and returned with all haste to Kandahār, where they met Tarīkī Khān, on his way to Nādir Shāh's camp with the tribute of the five provinces which he had retained of his Indian conquests, Kandahār, Kābul, Tatta, Bakkar, Multān, and Peshāwar. They gave him the first news of the death of the king, seized upon his treasure, and, with the aid of this and the military chest, Ahmad Shāh took possession of these five provinces, and formed them into the little independent kingdom of Afghānistan, over which he long reigned, and from which he occasionally invaded India and Khurāsān.[3]

Shāhrukh Mirzā had his eyes put out some time after by a faction. Ahmad Shāh marched to his relief, put the rebels to death, and united his eldest son, Taimūr Shāh, in marriage to the daughter of the unfortunate prince, from whom he took the diamond, since it could be of no use to a man who could no longer see its beauties. He established Taimūr as his viceroy at Herāt, and his youngest son at Kandahār; and fixed his own residence at Kābul, where he died.[4] He was succeeded by Taimūr Shāh, who was succeeded by his eldest son, Zamān Shāh, who, after a reign of a few years, was driven from his throne by his younger brother, Mahmūd. He sought an asylum with his friend Ashīk, who commanded a distant fortress, and who betrayed him to the usurper, and put him into confinement. He concealed the great diamond in a crevice in the wall of the room in which he was confined; and the rest of his jewels in a hole made in the ground with his dagger. As soon as Mahmūd received intimation of the arrest from Ashīk, he sent for his brother, had his eyes put out, and demanded the jewels, but Zamān Shāh pretended that he had thrown them into the river as he passed over. Two years after this, the third brother, the Sultān Shujā, deposed Mahmūd, ascended the throne by the consent of his elder brother, and, as a fair specimen of his notions of retributive justice, he blew away from the mouths of cannon, not only Ashīk himself, but his wife and all his innocent and unoffending children.

He intended to put out the eyes of his deposed brother, Mahmūd, but was dissuaded from it by his mother and Zamān Shāh, who now pointed out to him the place where he had concealed the great diamond. Mahmūd made his escape from prison, raised a party, drove out his brothers, and once more ascended the throne. The two brothers sought an asylum in the Honourable Company's territories; and have from that time resided at an out frontier station of Lūdiāna, upon the banks of the Hyphasis,[5] upon a liberal pension assigned for their maintenance by our Government. On their way through the territories of the Sikh chief, Ranjit Singh, Shujā was discovered to have this great diamond, the Mountain of Light, about his person; and he was, by a little torture skilfully applied to the mind and body, made to surrender it to his generous host.[6] Mahmūd was succeeded in the government of the fortress and province of Herāt by his son Kāmrān; but the throne of Kābul was seized by the mayor of the palace, who bequeathed it to his son Dost Muhammad, a man, in all the qualities requisite in a sovereign, immeasurably superior to any member of the house of Ahmad Shāh Abdālī. Ranjit Singh had wrested from him the province of Peshāwar in times of difficulty, and, as we would not assist him in recovering it from our old ally, he thought himself justified in seeking the aid of those who would, the Russians and Persians, who were eager to avail themselves of so fair an occasion to establish a footing in India. Such a footing would have been manifestly incompatible with the peace and security of our dominions in India, and we were obliged, in self-defence, to give to Shujā the aid which he had so often before in vain solicited, to enable him to recover the throne of his very limited number of legal ancestors.[7]

Notes:

1. Nādir Shāh was crowned king of Persia in 1736, entered the Panjāb, at the close of 1738, and occupied Delhi in March 1739. Having perpetrated

an awful massacre of the inhabitants, he retired after a stay of fifty-eight days, He was assassinated in May 1747.

2. Meshed, properly Mashhad ('the place of martyrdom'), is the chief city of Khurāsān. Nādir Shāh was killed while encamped there.

3. Ahmad Shāh defeated the Marāthās in the third great battle of Pānīpat, A.D. 1761. He had conquered the Panjāb in 1748. He invaded India five times.

4. In 1773.

5. Lūdiāna (misspelt 'Ludhiāna' in *I.G.*, 1908) is named from the Lodī Afghāns, who founded it in 1481. The town is now the headquarters of the district of the same name under the Panjāb Government. Part of the district lapsed to the British Government in 1836, other parts lapsed during the years 1846 and 1847, and the rest came from territory already British by rearrangement of jurisdiction. Hyphasis is the Greek name for the Biās river.

6. The above history of the Kohinūr may, I believe, be relied upon. I received a narrative of it from Shāh Zamān, the blind old king himself, through General Smith, who commanded the troops at Lūdiāna; forming a detail of the several revolutions too long and too full of new names for insertion here. [W. H. S.] The above note is, in the original edition, misplaced, and appended to two paragraphs of the text, which have no connexion with the story of the diamond, and really belong to Chapter 47, to which they have been removed in this edition.

The author assumes the identity of the Kohinūr with the great diamond found in one of the Golconda mines, and presented by Amīr Jumla to Shāh Jahān. The much-disputed history of the Kohinūr has been exhaustively discussed by Valentine Ball (Tavernier's *Travels in India*: Appendix I (1), 'The Great Mogul's Diamond and the true History of the Koh-i-nur; and (2) 'Summary History of the Koh-i-nur'). He has proved that the Kohinūr is almost certainly the diamond given by Amīr (Mīr) Jumla to Shāh Jahān, though now much reduced in weight by mutilation and repeated cutting. Assuming the identity of the Kohinūr with Amīr Jumla's gift, the leading incidents in the history of this famous jewel are as follows; —

Event.	Approximate Date.
Found at mine of Kollūr on the Kistna (Krishna) river	Not known
Presented to Shāh Jahān by Mīr Jumla, being uncut, and weighing about 756 English carats	1656 or 1657
Ground by Hortensio Borgio, and greatly reduced in weight	about 1657

Seen and weighed by Tavernier in Aurangzēb's treasury, its weight being 268 19/50 English carats	1665
Taken by Nadir Shāh of Persia from Muhammad Shāh of Delhi, and named Kohinūr	1739
Inherited by Shāh Rukh, grandson of Nadir Shāh	1747
Given up by Shāh Rukh to Ahmad Shāh Abdālī	1751
Inherited by Tīmūr, son of Ahmad Shāh	1772
Inherited by Shāh Zamān, son of Tīmūr	1793
Taken by Shāh Shujā, brother of Shāh Zamān	1795
Taken by Ranjit Singh, of Lahore, from Shāh Shujā	1813
Inherited by Dilīp (Dhuleep) Singh, reputed son of Ranjit Singh	1839
Annexed, with the Panjāb, and passed, through John Lawrence's waistcoat pocket (see his Life), into the possession of H.M. the Queen, its weight then being 186 1/16 English carats	1849
Exhibited at Great Exhibition in London	1851
Recut under supervision of Messrs. Garrards, and reduced in weight to 106 1/16 English carats	1852

The difference in weight between 268 19/50 carats in 1665 and 186 1/16 carats in 1849 seems to be due to mutilation of the stone during its stay in Persia and Afghanistan.

7. The policy of the first Afghan War has been, it is hardly necessary to observe, much disputed, and the author's confident defence of Lord Auckland's action cannot be accepted.

CHAPTER 49

Pindhārī System—Character of the Marāthā Administration—Cause of their Dislike to the Paramount Power.

The attempt of the Marquis of Hastings to rescue India from that dreadful scourge, the Pindhārī system, involved him in a war with all the great Marāthā states, except Gwālior; that is, with the Peshwā at Pūnā, Holkār at Indore, and the Bhonslā at Nāgpur; and Gwālior was prevented from joining the other states in their unholy league against us only by the presence of the grand division of the army, under the personal command of the Marquis, in the immediate vicinity of his capital. It was not that these chiefs liked the Pindhārīs, or felt any interest in their welfare, but because they were always anxious to crush that rising paramount authority which had the power, and had always manifested the will, to interpose and prevent the free indulgence of their predatory habits—the free exercise of that weapon, a standing army, which the disorders incident upon the decline and fall of the Muhammadan army had put into their hands, and which a continued series of successful aggressions upon their neighbours could alone enable them to pay or keep under control. They seized with avidity any occasion of quarrel with the paramount power which seemed likely to unite them all in one great effort to shake it off; and they are still prepared to do the same, because they feel that they could easily extend their depredations if that power were withdrawn; and they know no other road to wealth and glory but such successful depredations. Their ancestors rose by them, their states were formed by them, and their armies have been maintained by them. They look back upon them for all that seems to them honourable in the history of their families. Their bards sing of them in all their marriage and funeral processions; and, as their imaginations kindle at the recollection, they detest the arm that is extended to defend the wealth and the industry of the surrounding territories from their grasp. As the industrious classes acquire and display their wealth in the countries around during a long peace, under a strong and settled government, these native chiefs, with their little disorderly armies, feel precisely as an English country gentleman would feel with a pack of foxhounds, in a country swarming with foxes, and without the privilege of hunting them.[1]

Their armies always took the auspices and set out *kingdom taking* (mulk gīrī) after the Dasahra,[2] in November, as regularly as English gentlemen go partridge-shooting on the 1st of September; and I may here give, as a specimen, the excursion of Jean Baptiste Filose,[3] who sallied forth on such an expedition, at the head of a division of Sindhia's army, just before this Pindhārī war commenced. From Gwālior he proceeded to Karaulī,[4] and took from that chief the district of Sabalgarh, yielding four lākhs of rupees yearly.[5] He then took the territory of the Rājā of Chandērī,[6] Mor Pahlād, one of the oldest of the Bundēlkhand chiefs, which then yielded about seven lākhs of rupees,[7] but now yields only four. The Rājā got an allowance of forty thousand rupees a year. He then took the territories of the Rājās of Raghugarh and Bajranggarh,[8] yielding three lākhs a year; and Bahādurgarh, yielding two lākhs a year;[9] and the three princes got fifty thousand rupees a year for subsistence among them. He then took Lopar, yielding two lākhs and a half, and assigned the Rājā twenty-five thousand. He then took Garhā Kota,[10] whose chief gets subsistence from our Government. Baptiste had just completed his kingdom taking expedition, when our armies took the field against the Pindhārīs; and, on the termination of that war in 1817, all these acquisitions were confirmed and guaranteed to his master Sindhia by our Government. It cannot be supposed that either he or his army can ever feel any great attachment towards a paramount authority that has the power and the will to interpose, and prevent their indulging in such sporting excursions as these, or any great disinclination to take advantage of any occasion that may seem likely to unite all the native chiefs in a common effort to crush it. The Nepalese have the same feeling as the Marāthās in a still stronger degree, since their kingdom-taking excursions had been still greater and more successful; and, being all soldiers from the same soil, they were easily persuaded, by a long series of successful aggressions, that their courage was superior to that of all other men.[11]

In the year 1833, the Gwālior territory yielded a net revenue to the treasury of ninety-two lākhs of rupees, after discharging all the local costs of the civil and fiscal administration of the different districts, in officers, establishments, charitable institutions, religions endowments, military fiefs, &c.[12] In the remote districts, which are much infested by the predatory tribes of Bhīls,[13] and in consequence badly peopled and cultivated, the net revenue is estimated to be about one-third of the gross collections; but, in the districts near the capital, which are tolerably well cultivated, the net revenue brought to the treasury is about five-sixths of the gross collections; and these collections are equal to the whole annual rent of the land; for every man by whom the land is held or cultivated is a mere tenant at will, liable every season to be turned out, to give place to any other man that may offer more for the holding.

There is nowhere to be seen upon the land any useful or ornamental work, calculated to attach the people to the soil or to their villages; and, as hardly any of the recruits for the regiments are drawn from the peasantry of the country, the agricultural classes have nowhere any feeling of interest in the welfare or existence of the government. I am persuaded that there is not a single village in all the Gwālior dominions in which nine-tenths of the people would not be glad to see that government destroyed, under the persuasion that they could not possibly have a worse, and would be very likely to find a better.

The present force at Gwālior consists of three regiments of infantry, under Colonel Alexander; six under the command of Apājī, the adopted son of the late Bālā Bāī;[14] eleven under Colonel Jacobs and his son; five under Colonel Jean Baptiste Filose; two under the command of the Māmū Sāhib, the maternal uncle of the Mahārājā; three in what is called Bābū Bāolī's camp; in all thirty regiments, consisting, when complete, of six hundred men each, with four field-pieces. The 'Jinsī', or artillery, consists of two hundred guns of different calibre. There are but few corps of cavalry, and these are not considered very efficient, I believe.[15]

Robbers and murderers of all descriptions have always been in the habit of taking the field in India immediately after the festival of the Dasahrā,[16] at the end of October, from the sovereign of a state at the head of his armies, down to the leader of a little band of pickpockets from the corner of some obscure village. All invoke the Deity, and take the auspices to ascertain his will, nearly in the same way; and all expect that he will guide them successfully through their enterprises, as long as they find the omens favourable. No one among them ever dreams that his undertaking can be less acceptable to the Deity than that of another, provided he gives him the same due share of what he acquires in his thefts, his robberies, or his conquests, in sacrifices and offerings upon his shrines, and in donations to his priests.[17] Nor does the robber often dream that he shall be considered a less respectable citizen by the circle in which he moves than the soldier, provided he spends his income as liberally, and discharges all his duties in his relations with them as well; and this he generally does to secure their goodwill, whatever may be the character of his depredations upon distant circles of society and communities. The man who returned to Oudh, or Rohilkhand, after a campaign under a Pindhārī chief, was as well received as one who returned after serving one under Sindhia, Holkār, or Ranjīt Singh. A friend of mine one day asked a leader of a band of 'dacoits', or banditti, whether they did not often commit murder. 'God forbid', said he, 'that we should ever commit murder; but, if people choose to oppose us, we, of course, *strike and kill*; but you do the same. I hear that there is now a large assemblage of troops in the upper provinces going to take foreign countries; if they are opposed, they will kill people. We only do the same.'[18] The history of the rise of every nation in the world unhappily bears out the notion that princes are only robbers upon a large scale, till their ambition is curbed by a balance of power among nations.

On the 25th[19] we came on to Dhamēlā, fourteen miles, over a plain, with the range of sandstone hills on the left, receding from us to the west; and that on the right receding still more to the east. Here and there were some insulated hills of the same formation rising abruptly from the plain to our right. All the villages we saw were built upon masses of this sandstone rock, rising abruptly at intervals from the surface of the plain, in horizontal strata. These hillocks afford the people stone for building, and great facilities for defending themselves against the inroads of freebooters. There is not, I suppose, in the world a finer stone for building than these sandstone hills afford; and we passed a great many carts carrying them off to distant places in slabs or flags from ten to sixteen feet long, two to three feet wide, and six inches thick. They are white, with very minute pink spots, and of a texture so very fine that they would be taken for indurated clay on a slight inspection. The houses of the poorest peasants are here built of this beautiful freestone, which, after two hundred years, looks as if it had been quarried only yesterday.

About three miles from our tents we crossed over the little river Ghorapachhār,[20] flowing over a bed of this sandstone. The soil all the way very light, and the cultivation scanty and bad. Except within the enclosures of men's houses, scarcely a tree to be anywhere seen to give shelter and shade to the weary traveller; and we could find no ground for our camp with a shrub to shelter man or beast. All are swept away to form gun-carriages for the Gwālior artillery, with a philosophical disregard to the comforts of the living, the repose of the dead who planted them with a view to a comfortable berth in the next world, and to the will of the gods to whom they are dedicated. There is nothing left upon the land of animal or vegetable life to enrich it; nothing of stock but what is necessary to draw from the soil an annual crop, and which looks to one harvest for its entire return. The sovereign proprietor of the soil lets it out by the year, in farms or villages, to men who depend entirely upon the year's return for the means of payment. He, in his turn, lets the lands in detail to those who till them, and who depend for their subsistence, and for the means of paying their rents, upon the returns of the single harvest. There is no manufacture anywhere to be seen, save of brass pots and rude cooking utensils; no trade or commerce, save in the transport of the rude produce of the land to the great camp at Gwālior, upon the backs of bullocks, for want of roads fit for wheeled carriages. No one resides in the villages, save those whose labour is indispensably necessary to the rudest tillage, and those who collect the dues of government, and are paid upon the lowest possible scale. Such is the state of the Gwālior territories in every part of India where I have seen them.[21] The miseries and misrule of the Oudh, Hyderabad, and other Muhammadan governments, are heard of everywhere, because there are, under these governments, a middle and higher class upon the land to suffer and proclaim them; but those of the Gwālior state are never heard of, because no such classes are ever allowed to grow up upon the land. Had Russia governed Poland, and Turkey Greece, in the way that Gwālior has governed her conquered territories, we should never have heard of the wrongs of the one or the other.

In my morning's ride the day before I left Gwālior, I saw a fine leopard standing by the side of the most frequented road, and staring at every one who passed. It was held by two men, who sat by and talked to it as if it had been a human being. I thought it was an animal for show, and I was about to give them something, when they told me that they were servants of the Mahārājā, and were training the leopard to bear the sight and society of man. 'It had', they said, 'been caught about three months ago in the jungles, where it could never bear the sight and society of man, or of any animal that it could not prey upon; and must be kept upon the most frequented road till quite tamed. Leopards taken when very young would', they said, 'do very well as pets, but never answered for hunting; a good leopard for hunting must, before taken, be allowed to be a season or two providing for himself, and living upon the deer he takes in the jungles and plains.'

Notes:

1. For the characteristics of the Marāthās and Pindhārīs, see *ante*, Chapter 21, note 2.

2. *Ante*, Chapter 26, note 8, and Chapter 32, note 9.

3. *Ante*, Chapter 17, note 6.

4. A small principality, about seventy miles equidistant from Agra, Gwālior, Mathurā, Alwar, Jaipur, and Tonk. The attack on Karaulī occurred in 1813. Full details are given in the author's *Report on Budhuk alias Bagree Decoits*, pp. 99- 104.

5. Four hundred thousand rupees.

6. *Ante*, Chapter 33, note 15.

7. Seven hundred thousand rupees.

8. Raghugarh is now a mediatized chiefship in the Central India Agency, controlled by the Resident at Gwālior. Bajranggarh, a stronghold eleven miles south of Gūnā (Goonah), and about 140 miles distant from Gwālior, is in the Raghugarh territory.

9. Three hundred thousand and two hundred thousand rupees, respectively. Bahādurgarh is now included in the Isāgarh district of the Gwālior State.

10. I cannot find any mention of Lopar, if the name is correctly printed. Garhā Kota seems to be a slip of the pen for Garhā. Garhā Kota is in British territory, in the Sāgar District, C. P. But Garhā is a petty state, formerly included in the Raghugarh State. The town of Garhā is on the eastern slope of the Mālwā plateau in 25° 2′ N. and 78° 3′ E. (*I.G.*, 1908, s.v.).

11. On the coronation or installation of every new prince of the house of Sindhia, orders are given to plunder a few shops in the town as a part of the ceremony, and this they call or consider 'taking the auspices'. Compensation is *supposed* to be made to the proprietors, but rarely is made. I believe the same auspices are taken at the installation of a new prince of every other Marāthā house. The Moghal invaders of India were, in the same manner, obliged to allow their armies to *take the auspices* in the sack of a few towns, though they had surrendered without resistance. They were given up to pillage as a *religions duty*. Even the accomplished Bābar was obliged to concede this privilege to his army. [W. H. S.]

In reply to the editor's inquiries, Colonel Biddulph, officiating Resident at Gwālior, has kindly communicated the following information on the subject of the above note, in a letter dated 30th December, 1892. 'The custom of looting some "Banias'" shops on the installation of a new Maharaja in Gwālior is still observed. It was observed when the present Mādho Rāo Sindhia was installed on the *gadī* on 3rd July, 1886, and the looting was stopped by the police on the owners of the shops calling out "Dohai Mādho Mahārājkī!" five shops were looted on the occasion, and compensation to the amount of Rs. 427, 4, 3 was paid to the owners. My informant tells me that the custom has apparently no connexion with religion, but is believed to refer to the days when the period between the decease of one ruler and the accession of his successor was one of disorder and plunder. The maintenance of the custom is supposed to notify to the people that they must now look to the new ruler for protection.

'According to another informant, some "banias" are called by the palace officers and directed to open their shops in the palace precincts, and money is given them to stock their shops. The poor people are then allowed to loot them. No shops are allowed to be looted in the bazaar.

'I cannot learn that any particular name is given to the ceremony, and there appears to be some doubt as to its meaning; but the best information seems to show that the reason assigned above is the correct one.

'I cannot give any information as to the existence of the custom in other Mahratta states.'

The custom was observed late in the sixth century at the birth of King Harsha-vardhana (*Harsa-Caritā*, transl, Cowell and Thomas, p. 111). Anthropologists classify such practices as rites de passage, marking a transition from the old to the new.

'Bania', or 'baniyā', means shopkeeper, especially a grain dealer; 'gadī', or 'gaddī', is the cushioned seat, also known as 'masnad', which serves a Hindoo prince as a throne; and 'dohāi' is the ordinary form of a cry for redress.

12. Ninety-two lākhs of rupees were then worth more than £920,000. The *I.G.* (1908) states the normal revenue as 150 lākhs of rupees, equivalent (at the rate of exchange of 1s. 4d. to the rupee, or R 15 = £1) to one million pounds sterling. The fall in exchange has greatly lowered the sterling equivalent.

13. The Bhīl tribes are included in the large group of tribes which have been driven back by the more cultivated races into the hills and jungles. They are found among the woods along the banks of the Nerbudda, Taptī, and Mahī, and in many parts of Central India and Rājputāna. Of late years they have generally kept quiet; in the earlier part of the nineteenth century they gave much trouble in Khāndēsh. In Rājputāna two irregular corps of Bhīls have been organized.

14. Daughter of Māhādajī Sindhia. She died in 1834. See *post*, Chapter 70.

15. 'In 1886 the fort of Gwālior and the cantonment of Morār were surrendered by the Government of India to Sindhia in exchange for the fort and town of Jhānsī. Both forts were mutually surrendered and occupied on 10th March, 1886. As the occupation of the fort of Gwālior necessitated an increase of Sindhia's army, the Mahārāja was allowed to add 3,000 men to his infantry' (*Letter of Officiating Resident, dated 30th Dec.*, 1892). In 1908 the Gwālior army, comprising all arms, including three regiments of Imperial Service Cavalry, numbered more than 12,000 men, described as troops of 'very fair quality' (*I.G.*, 1908).

16. *Ante*, Chapter 26, note 8; Chapter 32, note 9; Chapter 49, note 2.

17. In *Ramaseeana* the author has fully described the practices of the Thugs in taking omens, and the feelings with which they regarded their profession. Similar information concerning other criminal classes is

copiously given in the *Report on Budhuk alias Bagree Decoits*. See also Meadows Taylor, *Confessions of a Thug*, in any edition.

18. These notions are still prevalent.

19. December, 1835, Christmas Day.

20. 'Overthrower of horses'; the same epithet is applied to the Utangan river, south of the Agra district, owing to the difficulty with which it is crossed when in flood (*N.W.P. Gazetteer*, 1st ed., vol. vii, p. 423).

21. Sindhia's territories, measuring 25,041 square miles, are in parts intermixed with those of other princes, and so extend over a wide space. Gwālior and its government have been discussed already in Chapter 36.

CHAPTER 50

Dhōlpur, Capital of the Jāt Chiefs of Gohad — Consequence of Obstacles to the Prosecution of Robbers.

On the morning of the 26th,[1] we sent on one tent, with the intention of following it in the afternoon; but about three o'clock a thunder-storm came on so heavily that I was afraid that which we occupied would come down upon us; and, putting my wife and child in a palankeen, I took them to the dwelling of an old Bairāgī, about two hundred yards from us. He received us very kindly, and paid us many compliments about the honour we had conferred upon him. He was a kind and, I think, a good old man, and had six disciples who seemed to reverence him very much. A large stone image of Hanumān, the monkey-god, painted red, and a good store of buffaloes, very comfortably sheltered from the pitiless storm, were in an inner court. The peacocks in dozens sought shelter under the walls and in the tree that stood in the courtyard; and I believe that they would have come into the old man's apartment had they not seen our white faces there. I had a great deal of talk with him, but did not take any notes of it. These old Bairāgīs, who spend the early and middle parts of life as disciples in pilgrimages to the celebrated temples of their god Vishnu in all parts of India, and the latter part of it as high priests or apostles in listening to the reports of the numerous disciples employed in similar wanderings are, perhaps, the most intelligent men in the country. They are from all the castes and classes of society. The lowest Hindoo may become a Bairāgī, and the very highest are often tempted to become so; the service of the god to which they devote themselves levelling all distinctions. Few of them can write or read, but they are shrewd observers of men and things, and often exceedingly agreeable and instructive companions to those who understand them, and can make them enter into unreserved conversation. Our tent stood out the storm pretty well, but we were obliged to defer our march till the next day. On the afternoon of the 27th we went on twelve miles, over a plain of deep alluvion, through which two rivers have cut their way to the Chambal; and, as usual, the ravines along their banks are deep, long, and dreary.

About half-way we were overtaken by one of the heaviest showers of rain I ever saw; it threatened us from neither side, but began to descend from an apparently small bed of clouds directly over our heads, which seemed to spread out on every side as the rain fell, and fill the whole vault of heaven with one dark and dense mass. The wind changed frequently; and in less than half an hour the whole surface of the country over which we were travelling was under water. This dense mass of clouds passed off in about two hours to the east; but twice, when the sun opened and beamed divinely upon us in a cloudless sky to the west, the wind changed suddenly round, and rushed back angrily from the east, to fill up the space which had been quickly rarefied by the genial heat of its rays, till we were again enveloped in darkness, and began to despair of reaching any human habitation before night. Some hail fell among the rain, but not large enough to hurt any one. The thunder was loud and often startling to the strongest nerves, and the lightning vivid, and almost incessant. We managed to keep the road because it was merely a beaten pathway below the common level of the country, and we could trace it by the greater depth of the water, and the absence of all shrubs and grass. All roads in India soon become watercourses—they are nowhere metalled; and, being left for four or five months every year without rain, their soil is reduced to powder by friction, and carried off by the winds over the surrounding country.[2] I was on horseback, but my wife and child were secure in a good palankeen that sheltered them from the rain. The bearers were obliged to move with great caution and slowly, and I sent on every person I could spare that they might keep moving, for the cold blast blowing over their thin and wet clothes seemed intolerable to those who were idle. My child's playmate, Gulāb, a lad of about ten years of age, resolutely kept by the side of the palankeen, trotting through the water with his teeth chattering as if he had been in an ague. The rain at last ceased, and the sky in the west cleared up beautifully about half an hour before sunset. Little Gulāb threw off his stuffed and quilted vest, and got a good dry English blanket to wrap round him from the palankeen. We soon after reached a small village, in which I treated all who had remained with us to as much coarse sugar (*gur*) as they could eat; and, as people of all castes can eat of sweetmeats from the hands of confectioners without prejudice to their caste, and this sugar is considered to be the best of all good things for guarding against colds in man or beast, they all ate very heartily, and went on in high spirits. As the sun sank below us on the left, a bright moon shone out upon us from the right, and about an hour after dark we reached our tents on the north bank of the Kuārī river, where we found excellent dinner for ourselves, and good fires, and good shelter for our servants. Little rain had fallen near the tents, and the river Kuārī, over which we had to cross, had not, fortunately, much swelled; nor did much fall on the ground we had left; and, as the tents there had been struck and laden before it came on, they came up the next morning early, and went on to our next ground.

On the 28th, we went on to Dhōlpur, the capital of the Jāt chiefs of Gohad,[3] on the left bank of the Chambal, over a plain with a variety of crops, but not one that requires two seasons to reach maturity. The soil excellent in quality and deep, but not a tree anywhere to be seen, nor any such thing as a work of ornament or general utility of any kind. We saw the fort of Dhōlpur at a distance of six miles, rising apparently from the surface of the level plain, but in reality situated on the summit of the opposite and high bank of a large river, its foundation at least one hundred feet above the level of the water. The immense pandemonia of ravines that separated us from this fort were not visible till we began to descend into them some two or three miles from the bed of the river. Like all the ravines that border the rivers in these parts, they are naked, gloomy, and ghastly, and the knowledge that no solitary traveller is ever safe in them does not tend to improve the impression they make upon us. The river is a beautiful clear stream, here flowing over a bed of fine sand with a motion so gentle, that one can hardly conceive it is she who has played such fantastic tricks along the borders, and made such 'frightful gashes' in them. As we passed over this noble reach of the river Chambal in a ferry- boat, the boatman told us of the magnificent bridge formed here by the Baiza Bāī for Lord William Bentinck in 1832, from boats brought down from Agra for the purpose. 'Little', said they, 'did it avail her with the Governor-General in her hour of need.[4]

The town of Dhōlpur lies some short way in from the north bank of the Chambal, at the extremity of a range of sandstone hills which runs diagonally across that of Gwālior. This range was once capped with basalt, and some boulders are still found upon it in a state of rapid decomposition. It was quite refreshing to see the beautiful mango groves on the Dhōlpur side of the river, after passing through a large tract of country in which no tree of any kind was to be seen. On returning from a long ride over the range of sandstone hills the morning after we reached Dhōlpur, I passed through an encampment of camels taking rude iron from some mines in the hills to the south towards Agra. They waited here within the frontier of a native state for a pass from the Agra custom house,[5] lest any one should, after they enter our frontier, pretend that they were going to smuggle it, and thus get them into trouble. 'Are you not', said I, 'afraid to remain here so near the ravines of the Chambal, when thieves are said to be so numerous?' 'Not at all,' replied they. 'I suppose thieves do not think it worth while to steal rude iron?' 'Thieves, sir, think it worth while to steal anything they can get, but we do not fear them much here.' 'Where, then, do you fear them much?' 'We fear them when we get into the Company's territories.' 'And how is this, when we have good police establishments, and the Dhōlpur people none?' 'When the Dhōlpur people get hold of a thief, they make him disgorge all that he has got of our property for us, and they confiscate all the rest that he has for themselves, and cut off his nose or his hands, and turn him adrift to deter others. You, on the contrary, when you get hold of a thief, worry us to death in the prosecution of your courts; and, when we have proved the robbery to your satisfaction, you leave all this ill-gotten wealth to his family,[6] and provide him with good food and clothing for himself, while he works for you a couple of years on the roads.[7] The consequence is, that here fellows are afraid to rob a traveller, if they find him at all on his guard, as we generally are, while in your districts they rob us where and when they like.'

'But, my friends, you are sure to recover what we do get of your property from the thieves.' 'Not quite sure of that neither,' said they, 'or the greater part is generally absorbed on its way back to us through the officers of your court; and we would always rather put up with the first loss than run the risk of a greater by prosecution, if we happen to get robbed within the Company's territories.'

The loss and annoyances to which prosecutors and witnesses are subject in our courts are a source of very great evil to the country. They enable police-officers everywhere to grow rich upon the concealment of crimes. The man who has been robbed will bribe them to conceal the robbery, that he may escape the further loss of the prosecution in our courts, generally very distant; and the witnesses will bribe them to avoid attending to give evidence; the whole village communities bribe them, because every man feels that they have the power of getting him summoned to the court in some capacity or other, if they like; and that they will certainly like to do so, if not bribed.

The obstacles which our system opposes to the successful prosecution of robbers of all denominations and descriptions deprive our Government of all popular support in the administration of criminal justice; and this is considered everywhere to be the worst, and, indeed, the only radically bad feature of our government. No magistrate hopes to get a conviction against one in four of the most atrocious gang of robbers and murderers of his district, and his only resource is in the security laws, which enable him to keep them in jail under a requisition of security for short periods. To this an idle or apathetic magistrate will not have recourse, and under him these robbers have a free licence.

In England, a judicial acquittal does not send back the culprit to follow the same trade in the same field, as in India; for the published proceedings of the court bring down upon him the indignation of society — the moral and religions feelings of his fellow men are arrayed against him, and from these salutary checks no flaw in the indictment can save him. Not so in India. There no moral or religions feelings interpose to assist or to supply the deficiencies of the penal law. Provided he eats, drinks, smokes, marries, and makes his offerings to his priest according to the rules of his caste, the robber and the murderer incurs no odium in the circle in which he moves, either religious or moral, and this is the only circle for whose feelings he has any regard.[8]

The man who passed off his bad coin at Datiyā, passed off more at Dhōlpur while my advanced people were coming in, pretending that he wanted things for me, and was in a great hurry to be ready with them at my tents by the time I came up. The bad rupees were brought to a native officer of my guard, who went with the shopkeepers in search of the knave, but he could nowhere be found. The gates of the town were shut up all night at my suggestion, and in the morning every lodging-house in the town was searched for him in vain—he had gone on. I had left some sharp men behind me, expecting that he would endeavour to pass off his bad money immediately after my departure; but in expectation of this he was now evidently keeping a little in advance of me. I sent on some men with the shopkeepers whom he had cheated to our next stage, in the hope of overtaking him; but he had left the place before they arrived without passing any of his bad coin, and gone on to Agra. The shopkeepers could not be persuaded to go any further after him, for, if they caught him, they should, they said, have infinite trouble in prosecuting him in our courts, without any chance of recovering from him what they had lost.

On the 29th, we remained at Dhōlpur to receive and return the visits of the young Rājā, or, as he is called, the young Rānā, a lad of about fifteen years of age, very plain, and very dull. He came about ten in the forenoon with a very respectable and well-dressed retinue, and a tolerable show of elephants and horses. The uniforms of his guards were made after those of our own soldiers, and did not please me half so much as those of the Datiyā guards, who were permitted to consult their own tastes; and the music of the drums and fifes seemed to me infinitely inferior to that of the mounted minstrels of my old friend Parīchhit.[9] The lad had with him about a dozen old public servants entitled to chairs, some of whom had served his father above thirty years; while the ancestors of others had served his grandfathers and great-grandfathers, and I could not help telling the lad in their presence that 'these were the greatest ornament of a prince's throne and the best signs and pledges of a good government'. They were all evidently much pleased at the compliment, and I thought they deserved to be pleased, from the good character they bore among the peasantry of the country. I mentioned that I had understood the boatmen of the Chambal at Dhōlpur never caught or ate fish. The lad seemed embarrassed, and the minister took upon himself to reply that 'there was no market for it, since the Hindoos of Dhōlpur never ate fish, and the Muhammadans had all disappeared'. I asked the lad whether he was fond of hunting. He seemed again confounded, and the minister said that 'his highness never either hunted or fished, as people of his caste were prohibited from destroying life'. 'And yet', said I, 'they have often showed themselves good soldiers in battle.' They were all pleased again, and said that they were not prohibited from killing tigers; but that there was no jungle of any kind near Dhōlpur, and, consequently, no tigers to be found. The Jāts are descendants of the Getae, and were people of very low caste, or rather of no caste at all, among the Hindoos, and they are now trying to raise themselves by abstaining from killing and eating animals.[10] Among Hindoos this is everything; a man of low caste is '*sab kuchh khātā*', sticks at nothing in the way of eating; and a man of high caste is a man who abstains from eating anything but vegetable or farinaceous food; if, at the same time, he abstains from using in his cook-room all woods but one, and has that one washed before he uses it, he is canonized.[11] Having attained to military renown and territorial dominion in the usual way by robbery, the Jāts naturally enough seek the distinction of high caste to enable them the better to enjoy their position in society.

It had been stipulated that I should walk to the bottom of the steps to receive the Rānā, as is the usage on such occasions, and carpets were accordingly spread thus far. Here he got out of his chair, and I led him into the large room of the bungalow, which we occupied during our stay, followed by all his and my attendants. The bungalow had been built by the former Resident at Gwālior, the Honourable R. Cavendish, for his residence during the latter part of the rains, when Gwālior is considered to be unhealthy. At his departure the Rānā purchased this bungalow for the use of European gentlemen and ladies passing through his capital.

In the afternoon, about four o'clock, I went to return his visit in a small palace not yet finished, a pretty piece of miniature fortification, surrounded by what they call their 'chhāonī', or cantonments. The streets are good, and the buildings neat and substantial; but there is nothing to strike or particularly interest the stranger. The interview passed off without anything remarkable; and I was more than ever pleased with the people by whom this young chief is surrounded. Indeed, I had much reason to be pleased with the manners of all the people on this side of the Chambal. They are those of a people well pleased to see English gentlemen among them, and anxious to make themselves useful and agreeable to us. They know that their chief is indebted to the British Government for all the country he has, and that he would be swallowed up by Sindhia's greedy army, were not the sevenfold shield of the Honourable Company spread over him. His establishments, civil and military, like those of the Bundēlkhand chiefs, are raised from the peasantry and yeomanry or the country; who all, in consequence, feel an interest in the prosperity and independent respectability of their chief. On the Gwālior side, the members of all the public establishments know and feel that it is we who interpose and prevent their master from swallowing up all his neighbours, and thereby having increased means of promoting their interest and that of their friends; and they detest us all most cordially in consequence. The peasantry of the Gwālior territory seem to consider their own government as a kind of minotaur, which they would be glad to see destroyed, no matter how or by whom; since it gives no lucrative or honourable employment to any of their members, so as to interest either their pride or their affections; nor throws back among them for purposes of local advantage any of the produce of their land and labour which it exacts. It is worthy of remark that, though the Dhōlpur chief is peculiarly the creature of the British Government, and indebted to it for all he has or ever will have, and though he has never had anything, and never can have, or can hope to have, anything from the poor pageant of the house of Tīmūr, who now sits upon the throne of Delhi;[12] yet, on his seal of office he declares himself to be the slave and creature of that imperial 'warrior for the faith of Islam'. As he abstains from eating the good fish of the river Chambal to enhance his claim to caste among Hindoos, so he abstains from acknowledging his deep debt of gratitude to the Honourable Company, or the British Government, with a view to give the rust of age to his rank and title. To acknowledge himself a creature of the British Government were to acknowledge that he was a man of yesterday; to acknowledge himself the slave of the Emperor is to claim for his poor veins 'the blood of a line of kings'. The petty chiefs of Bundēlkhand, who are in the same manner especially dependent on the British Government, do the same thing.

At Dhōlpur, there are some noble old mosques and mausoleums built three hundred years ago, in the reign of the Emperor Humāyūn, by some great officers of his government, whose remains still rest undisturbed among them, though the names of their families have been for many ages forgotten, and no men of their creed now live near to demand for them the respect of the living. These tombs are all elaborately built and worked out of the fine freestone of the country and the trellis-work upon some of their stone screens is still as beautiful as when first made. There are Persian and Arabic inscriptions upon all of them, and I found from them that one of the mosques had been built by the Emperor Shāh Jahān in A.D. 1634,[13] when he little dreamed that his three sons would here meet to fight the great fight for the throne while he yet sat upon it.[14]

Notes:

1. December, 1835.

2. The author's remark that in India the roads are 'nowhere metalled' must seem hardly credible to a modern traveller, who sees the country intersected by thousands of miles of metalled road. The Grand Trunk Road from Calcutta to Lahore, constructed in Lord Dalhousie's time, alone measures about 1,200 miles. The development of roads since 1850 ha been enormous, and yet the mileage of good roads would have to be increased tenfold to put India on an equality with the more advanced countries of Europe.

3. *Ante*, Chanter 36, notes 26 & 27.

4. The Baiza Bāī was the widow of Daulat Rāo Sindhia. He had died on March 21, 1827. With the consent of the Government of India, she adopted a boy as his successor, but, being an ambitions and intriguing woman, she tried to keep all power in her own hands. The young Mahārājā fled from her, and took refuge in the Residency in October, 1832. In December of the same year Lord William Bentinck visited Gwālior, and assumed an attitude of absolute neutrality. The result was that trouble continued, and seven months later the Mahārājā again fled to the Residency. The troops then revolted against the Baiza Bāī, and compelled her to retire to Dhōlpur. This event put an end to her political activity. Ultimately she was allowed to return to Gwālior, and died there in 1862 (Malleson, *The Native States of India*, pp. 160- 4). The author wrote an unpublished history of Baiza Bāī (*ante*, Bibliography).

5. Long since abolished.

6. The law now permits the person injured to be compensated out of any fine realized.

7. The system of employing gangs of prisoners on the roads was open to great abuses, and has been long given up. The prisoners are now, as a rule, employed only on the jail promises, and cannot be utilized for outside work, except under special circumstances by special sanction.

8. The notes to this edition have recorded many changes in India, but no change has taken place in the difficulties which beset the administration of criminal law. They are still those which the author describes, and Police Commissions cannot remove them. The power to exact security for good behaviour from known bad characters still exists, and, when discreetly used, is of great value. The conviction of atrocious robbers and murderers is, perhaps, less rare than it was in the author's time, though many still escape

even the minor penalty of arrest. The want of a sound moral public opinion is the fundamental difficulty in Indian police administration — a truth fully Understood by the author, but rarely realized by members of Parliament.

9. The title of the Dhōlpur chief is now Mahārājā Rānā. In 1905 his reduced army numbered 1,216 of all ranks (*I. G.*, 1908). The force is not of serious military value.

10. The identification of the Jāts, or Jats, with the Getae is not even probable. The anchor exaggerates the lowness of the social rank of the Jāts, who cannot properly be described as people of 'very low caste'. They are, and have long been, numerous and powerful in the Panjāb and the neighbouring countries. It is true that they hate Brahmans, care little for Brahman notions of propriety, either as regards food or marriage, and to a certain extent stand outside the orthodox Hindoo system; but they are heterodox rather than low-caste. The Rājās of Bharatpur, Dhōlpur, Nābha, Patiālā, and Jīnd are all Jāts. The Jāts are a fine and interesting people, who seem to suffer little deterioration from the notorious laxity of their matrimonial arrangements. They are skilled and industrious cultivators. A saying has been current in Upper India that, if the British power is ever broken, the succession will pass to the Jāts.

11. This is the Brahman and Baniyā theory. A high-spirited Rājpūt of Rājputāna, full of pride in his long ancestry, and yet fond of wild boar's flesh, would indeed be wroth if denounced as a low-caste man. It is, however, unfortunately, quite true that all races which become entangled in the meshes of Hinduism tend to gradually surrender their freedom, and to become proud of submission to the senseless formalities and restrictions which the Brahman loves.

12. Akbar II. He was titular emperor from A.D. 1806 to 1837, and was succeeded by Bahādur Shāh II, the last of his line. The portrait of Akbar II is the frontispiece to volume i of the original edition of this work, and a miniature portrait of him is given in the frontispiece of volume ii.

13. One of these tombs, namely, that of Bībī Zarīna, dated A.H. 942 = A.D. 1535-6, is described by Cunningham (*A.S.R.*, xx, p. 113, pl. xxxvii), who notes that according to an obviously false local popular story, the lady was a daughter of Shāh Jahān, who lived a century later. This story seems to have misled the author. No inscription of the reign of Shāh Jahān at Dhōlpur is recorded.

14. The three sons were Dārā Shikoh, Aurangzēb, and Murād Baksh.

CHAPTER 51

Influence of Electricity on Vegetation—Agra and its Buildings.

On the 30th and 31st,[1] we went twenty-four miles over a dry plain, with a sandy soil covered with excellent crops where irrigated, and a very poor one where not. We met several long strings of camels carrying grain from Agra to Gwālior. A single man takes charge of twenty or thirty, holding the bridle of the first, and walking on before its nose. The bridles of all the rest are tied one after the other to the saddles of those immediately preceding them, and all move along after the leader in single file. Water must tend to attract and to impart to vegetables a good deal of electricity and other vivifying powers that would otherwise he dormant in the earth at a distance. The mere circumstance of moistening the earth from within reach of the roots would not be sufficient to account for the vast difference between the crops of fields that are irrigated, and those that are not. One day, in the middle of the season of the rains, I asked my gardener, while walking with him over my grounds, how it was that some of the fine clusters of bamboos had not yet begun to throw out their shoots. 'We have not yet had a thunderstorm, sir,' replied the gardener. 'What in the name of God has the thunderstorm to do with the shooting of the bamboos?' asked I in amazement. 'I don't know, sir,' said he, 'but certain it is that no bamboos begin to throw out their shoots well till we get a good deal of thunder and lightning.' The thunder and lightning came, and the bamboo shoots soon followed in abundance. It might have been a mere coincidence; or the tall bamboo may bring down from the passing clouds, and convey to the roots, the electric fluid they require for nourishment, or for conductors of nourishment.[2]

In the Isle of France,[3] people have a notion that the mushrooms always come up best after a thunderstorm. Electricity has certainly much more to do in the business of the world than we are yet aware of, in the animal, mineral, and vegetable developments.[4]

At our ground this day, I met a very respectable and intelligent native revenue officer who had been employed to settle some boundary disputes between the yeomen of our territory and those of the adjoining territory of Dhōlpur.

'The Honourable Company's rights and those of its yeomen must', said he, 'be inevitably sacrificed in all such cases; for the Dhōlpur chief, or his minister, says to all their witnesses, "You are, of course, expected to speak the truth regarding the land in dispute; but, by the sacred stream of the Ganges, if you speak so as to lose this estate one inch of it, you lose both your ears" — and most assuredly would they lose them,' continued he, 'if they were not to swear most resolutely that all the land in question belonged to Dhōlpur. Had I the same power to cut off the ears of witnesses on our side, we should meet on equal terms. Were I to threaten to cut them off, they would laugh in my face.' There was much truth in what the poor man said, for the Dhōlpur witnesses always make it appear that the claims of their yeomen are just and moderate, and a salutary dread of losing their ears operates, no doubt, very strongly. The threatened punishment of the prince is quick, while that of the gods, however just, is certainly very slow —

Ut sit magna, tamen certe lenta ira deorum est.

On the 1st of January, 1836, we went on sixteen miles to Agra, and, when within about six miles of the city, the dome and minarets of the Tāj opened upon us from behind a small grove of fruit- trees, close by us on the side of the road. The morning was not clear, but it was a good one for a first sight of this building, which appeared larger through the dusty haze than it would have done through a clear sky. For five-and-twenty years of my life had I been looking forward to the sight now before me. Of no building on earth had I heard so much as of this, which contains the remains of the Emperor Shāh Jahān and his wife, the father and mother of the children whose struggles for dominion have been already described. We had ordered our tents to be pitched in the gardens of this splendid mausoleum, that we might have our fill of the enjoyment which everybody seemed to derive from it; and we reached them about eight o'clock. I went over the whole building before I entered my tent, and, from the first sight of the dome and minarets on the distant horizon to the last glance back from my tent-ropes to the magnificent gateway that forms the entrance from our camp to the quadrangle in which they stand, I can truly say that everything surpassed my expectations. I at first thought the dome formed too large a portion of the whole building; that its neck was too long and too much exposed; and that the minarets were too plain in their design; but, after going repeatedly over every part, and examining the *tout ensemble* from all possible positions, and in all possible lights, from that of the full moon at midnight in a cloudless sky to that of the noonday sun, the mind seemed to repose in the calm persuasion that there was an entire harmony of parts, a faultless congregation of architectural beauties, on which it could dwell for ever without fatigue.

After my quarter of a century of anticipated pleasure, I went on from part to part in the expectation that I must by and by come to something that would disappoint me; but no, the emotion which one feels at first is never impaired; on the contrary, it goes on improving from the first *coup d'œil* of the dome in the distance to the minute inspection of the last flower upon the screen round the tomb. One returns and returns to it with undiminished pleasure; and though at every return one's attention to the smaller parts becomes less and less, the pleasure which he derives from the contemplation of the greater, and of the whole collectively, seems to increase; and he leaves with a feeling of regret that he could not have it all his life within his reach, and of assurance that the image of what he has seen can never be obliterated from his mind 'while memory holds her seat'. I felt that it was to me in architecture what Kemble and his sister, Mrs. Siddons, had been to me a quarter of a century before in acting—something that must stand alone—something that I should never cease to see clearly in my mind's eye, and yet never be able clearly to describe to others.[5]

The Emperor and his Queen he buried side by side in a vault beneath the building, to which we descend by a flight of steps. Their remains are covered by two slabs of marble; and directly over these slabs, upon the floor above, in the great centre room under the dome, stand two other slabs, or cenotaphs, of the same marble exquisitely worked in mosaic. Upon that of the Queen, amid wreaths of flowers, are worked in black letters passages from the Korān, one of which, at the end facing the entrance, terminates with 'And defend us from the tribe of unbelievers'; that very tribe which is now gathered from all quarters of the civilized world to admire the splendour of the tomb which was raised to perpetuate her name.[6] On the slab over her husband there are no passages from the Korān—merely mosaic work of flowers with his name and the date of his death.[7] I asked some of the learned Muhammadan attendants the cause of this difference, and was told that Shāh Jahān had himself designed the slab over his wife, and saw no harm in inscribing the words of God upon it; but that the slab over himself was designed by his more pious son, Aurangzēb, who did not think it right to place these holy words upon a stone which the foot of man might some day touch, though that stone covered the remains of his own father. Such was this 'man of prayers', this 'Namāzī' (as Dara called him), to the last. He knew mankind well, and, above all, that part of them which he was called upon to govern, and which he governed for forty years with so much ability.[8]

The slab over the Queen occupies the centre of the apartments above and in the vault below, and that over her husband lies on the left as we enter. At one end of the slab in the vault her name is inwrought, 'Mumtāz-i-mahal Bānū Bēgam', the ornament of the palace, Bānū Bēgam, and the date of her death, 1631. That of her husband and the date of his death, 1666, are inwrought upon the other.[9]

She died in giving birth to a daughter, who is said to have been heard crying in the womb by herself and her other daughters. She sent for the Emperor, and told him that she believed no mother had ever been known to survive the birth of a child so heard, and that she felt her end was near. She had, she said, only two requests to make; first, that he would not marry again after her death, and get children to contend with hers for his favour and dominions; and, secondly, that he would build for her the tomb with which he had promised to perpetuate her name. She died in giving birth to the child, as might have been expected when the Emperor, in his anxiety, called all the midwives of the city, and all his secretaries of state and privy counsellors to prescribe for her. Both her dying requests were granted. Her tomb was commenced upon immediately. No woman ever pretended to supply her place in the palace; nor had Shāh Jahān, that we know of, children by any other.[10] Tavernier saw this building completed and finished; and tells us that it occupied twenty thousand men for twenty-two years.[11] The mausoleum itself and all the buildings that appertain to it cost 3,17,48,026 — three karōr, seventeen lākhs, forty-eight thousand and twenty-six rupees, or £3,174,802 sterling; — three million one hundred and seventy-four thousand eight hundred and two![12] I asked my wife, when she had gone over it, what she thought of the building. 'I cannot', said she, 'tell you what I think, for I know not how to criticize such a building, but I can tell you what I feel. I would die to-morrow to have such another over me.' This is what many a lady has felt, no doubt.

The building stands upon the north side of a large quadrangle, looking down into the clear blue stream of the river Jumna, while the other three sides are enclosed with a high wall of red sandstone.[13] The entrance to this quadrangle is through a magnificent gateway in the south side opposite the tomb; and on the other two sides are very beautiful mosques facing inwards, and corresponding exactly with each other in size, design, and execution. That on the left, or west, side is the only one that can be used as a mosque or church; because the faces of the audience, and those of all men at their prayers, must be turned towards the tomb of their prophet to the west. The pulpit is always against the dead wall at the back, and the audience face towards it, standing with their backs to the open front of the building. The church on the east side is used for the accommodation of visitors, or for any secular purpose, and was built merely as a 'jawāb' (answer) to the real one. [14] The whole area is laid out in square parterres, planted with flowers and shrubs in the centre, and with fine trees, chiefly the cypress, all round the borders, forming an avenue to every road. These roads are all paved with slabs of freestone, and have, running along the centre, a basin, with a row of *jets d'eau* in the middle from one extremity to the other. These are made to play almost every evening, when the gardens are much frequented by the European gentlemen and ladies of the station, and by natives of all religions and sects. The quadrangle is from east to west nine hundred and sixty-four feet, and from north to south three hundred and twenty-nine.[15]

The mausoleum itself, the terrace upon which it stands, and the minarets, are all formed of the finest white marble, inlaid with precious stones. The wall around the quadrangle, including the river face of the terrace, is made of red sandstone, with cupolas and pillars of the same white marble. The insides of the churches and apartments in and upon the walls are all lined with marble or with stucco work that looks like marble; but, on the outside, the red sandstone resembles uncovered bricks. The dazzling white marble of the mausoleum itself rising over the red wall is apt, at first sight, to make a disagreeable impression, from the idea of a whitewashed head to an unfinished building; but this impression is very soon removed, and tends, perhaps, to improve that which is afterwards received from a nearer inspection. The marble was all brought from the Jeypore territories upon wheeled carriages, a distance, I believe, of two or three hundred miles; and the sandstone from the neighbourhood of Dhōlpur and Fathpur Sīkrī. [16] Shāh Jāhan is said to have inherited his partiality for this colour from his grandfather, Akbar, who constructed almost all his buildings from the same stone, though he might have had the beautiful white freestone at the same cost. What was figuratively said of Augustus may be most literally said of Shāh Jahān; he found the cities (Agra and Delhi) all brick, and left them all marble; for all the marble buildings, and additions to buildings, were formed by him.[17]

This magnificent building and the palaces at Agra and Delhi were, I believe, designed by Austin de Bordeaux, a Frenchman of great talent and merit, in whose ability and integrity the Emperor placed much reliance. He was called by the natives 'Ustān [*sic*] Isā, Nādir-ul-asr', 'the wonderful of the age'; and, for his office of 'naksha navīs', or plan-drawer, he received a regular salary of one thousand rupees a month, with occasional presents, that made his income very large. He had finished the palace at Delhi, and the mausoleum and palace of Agra; and was engaged in designing a silver ceiling for one of the galleries in the latter, when he was sent by the Emperor to settle some affairs of great importance at Goa. He died at Cochin on his way back, and is supposed to have been poisoned by the Portuguese, who were extremely jealous of his influence at court. He left a son by a native, called Muhammad Sharīf, who was employed as an architect on a salary of five hundred rupees a month, and who became, as I conclude from his name, a Musalmān. Shāh Jahān had commenced his own tomb on the opposite side of the Jumna; and both were to have been united by a bridge. [18] The death of Austin de Bordeaux, and the wars between his [scil. Shāh Jahān's] sons that followed prevented the completion of these magnificent works.[19]

We were encamped upon a fine green sward outside the entrance to the south, in a kind of large court, enclosed by a high cloistered wall, in which all our attendants and followers found shelter. Colonel and Mrs. King, and some other gentlemen, were encamped in the same place, and for the same purpose; and we had a very agreeable party. The band of our friend Major Godby's regiment played sometimes in the evening upon the terrace of the Tāj; but, of all the complicated music ever heard upon earth, that of a flute blown gently in the vault below, where the remains of the Emperor and his consort repose, as the sound rises to the dome amidst a hundred arched alcoves around, and descends in heavenly reverberations upon those who sit or recline upon the cenotaphs above the vault, is, perhaps, the finest to an inartificial car. We feel as if it were from heaven, and breathed by angels; it is to the ear what the building itself is to the eye; but, unhappily, it cannot, like the building, live in our recollections. All that we can, in after life, remember is that it was heavenly, and produced heavenly emotions.

We went all over the palace in the fort, a very magnificent building constructed by Shāh Jahān within fortifications raised by his grandfather Akbar.[20]

The fretwork and mosaic upon the marble pillars and panels are equal to those of the Tāj; or, if possible, superior; nor is the design or execution in any respect inferior, and yet a European feels that he could get a house much more commodious, and more to his taste, for a much less sum than must have been expended upon it. The Marquis of Hastings, when Governor-General of India, broke up one of the most beautiful marble baths of this palace to send home to George IV of England, then Prince Regent, and the rest of the marble of the suite of apartments from which it had been taken, with all its exquisite fretwork and mosaic, was afterwards sold by auction, on account of our Government, by order of the then Governor-General, Lord W. Bentinck. Had these things fetched the price expected, it is probable that the whole of the palace, and even the Tāj itself, would have been pulled down, and sold in the same manner.[21]

We visited the Motī Masjid or Pearl Mosque. It was built by Shāh Jahān, entirely of white marble; and completed, as we learn from an inscription on the portico, in the year A.D. 1656.[22] There is no mosaic upon any of the pillars or panels of this mosque; but the design and execution of the flowers in bas- relief are exceedingly beautiful. It is a chaste, simple, and majestic building;[23] and is by some people admired even more than the Tāj, because they have heard less of it; and their pleasure is heightened by surprise. We feel that it is to all other mosques what the Tāj is to all other mausoleums, a *facile princeps*.

Few, however, go to see the 'mosque of pearls' more than once, stay as long as they will at Agra; and when they go, the building appears less and less to deserve their admiration; while they go to the Tāj as often as they can, and find new beauties in it, or new feelings of pleasure from it, every time[24]

I went out to visit this tomb of the Emperor Akbar at Sikandara, a magnificent building, raised over him by his son, the Emperor Jahāngīr. His remains he deposited in a deep vault under the centre, and are covered by a plain slab of marble, without fretwork or mosaic. On the top of the building, which is three or four stories high, is another marble slab, corresponding with the one in the vault below.[25] This is beautifully carved, with the 'nau nauwē nām'-the ninety-nine names, or attributes of the Deity, from the Korān.[26] It is covered by an awning, not to protect the tomb, but to defend the 'words of God' from the rain, as my cicerone assured me.[27] He told me that the attendants upon this tomb used to have the hay of the large quadrangle of forty acres in which it stands,[28] in addition to their small salaries, and that it yielded them some fifty rupees a year; but the chief native officer of the Tāj establishment demanded half of the sum, and when they refused to give him so much, he persuaded his master, the European engineer, *with much difficulty*, to take all this hay for the public cattle. 'And why could you not adjust such a matter between you, without pestering the engineer?' 'Is not this the way', said he, with emotion, 'that Hindustan has cut its own throat, and brought in the stranger at all times? Have they ever had, or can they ever have, confidence in each other, or let each other alone to enjoy the little they have in peace?' Considering all the circumstances of time and place, Akbar has always appeared to me among sovereigns what Shakespeare was among poets; and, feeling as a citizen of the world, I reverenced the marble slab that covers his bones more, perhaps, than I should that over any other sovereign with whose history I am acquainted. [29]

Notes:

1. December, 1835.

2. It is not, perhaps, generally known, though it deserves to be so, that the bamboo seeds only once, and dies immediately after seeding. All bamboos from the same seed die at the same time, whenever they may have been planted. The life of the common large bamboo is about fifty years. [W. H. S.] The period is said to vary between thirty and sixty years. Bamboo seed is eaten as rice when obtainable. The author's theories about electricity are more ingenious than satisfactory.

3. Better known as the Mauritius.

4. This proposition may be accepted with confidence. Electricity is a great mystery, which becomes more mysterious the more it is studied.

5. A letter of the author's, dated 13th March, 1809, is extant, in which he gives a full description of the performance of *Macbeth* at the Haymarket by Kemble and Mrs. Siddons on Saturday, 11th March. The author sailed in the *Devonshire* on the 24th March.

6. No European had ever before, I believe, noted this, [W. H. S.] Moīn-ud-dīn (p. 49) says that this phrase, 'Thou art our patron, help as therefore against the unbelieving nations,' is from the long chapter 2 ('The Cow') of the Korān, but I have not succeeded in finding the exact words in Sale's version of that chapter. I suspect that the words have been misread. Moīn-ud- dīn gives as the words at the north side of the tomb, 'the unbelieving nations', whereas Muh. Latīf (*Agra*, p. 111) says that the words 'on the head of the sarcophagus' are 'He is the everlasting. He is sufficient.' It will be observed that the characters in the two readings are almost identical.

7. The Empress had been a good deal exasperated against the Portuguese and Dutch by the treatment her husband received from them when a fugitive, after an unsuccessful rebellion against his father; and her hatred to them extended, in some degree, to all Christians, whom she considered to be included in the term 'Kāfir', or unbeliever. [W. H. S.] Prince Shāh Jahān (Khurram) rebelled against his father, Jahāngīr, in A.D. 1623, and submitted in A.D. 1625. The terrible punishment inflicted by Shāh Jahān when Emperor on the Portuguese of Hūgli (Hooghly) is related by Bernier (Constable's ed., pp. 177, 287). The Emperor had previously destroyed the Jesuits' church at Lahore completely, and the greater part of the church at Agra.

8. The cleverness, astuteness, energy, and business capacity of Aurangzēb are undoubted, and yet his long reign was a disastrous failure. The author reflects the praises of Muhammadans who cherish the memory

of the 'namāzī'. The Emperor himself knew better when, in his old ago, he wrote to his son Azam the pathetic words, 'I have not done well by the country or its people. My years have gone by profitless' (Lane-Poole's version in *Aurangzib* (Rulers of India), p. 203. Letter No. 72 in Bilimoria, *Letters of Aurungzbe*, Bombay, 1908. Another version in E. and D. vii, 562.) His reign lasted for almost forty-nine years, from June 1658 to February 1707, and not for only forty years.

9. The real tombs are in the vault below. Beautiful cenotaphs stand under the dome. The inscription on the tomb of the Empress is exactly repeated on her cenotaph, and runs thus:-
'The splendid sepulchre of Arjumand Bānō Bēgam, entitled Mumtāz Mahall, deceased in the year 1040 Hijrī.'

The epitaph on Shāh Jahān's tomb is as follows:- 'The sacred sepulchre of His Moat Exalted Majesty, nesting in Paradise, the Second Lord of the Conjunction, Shāh Jahān, the Emperor. May his mausoleum ever flourish. Year 1076 Hijrī.'

The inscription on Shāh Jahān's cenotaph adds more titles and gives the exact date of death as 'the night of Rajab 28, A.H. 1076'. 1040 Hījrī corresponds with the period from July 31, A.D. 1630 to July 19, 1631; and 1076 Hijrī with the period July 4, A. D. 1665 to June 23, 1666, Old Style. The dates in New Style would be ten days later.

The epithet 'nesting in Paradise' (*firdaus āshiyānī*) was the official posthumous title of Shāh Jahān, frequently used by historians instead of his name.

The title 'Second Lord of the Conjunction' means that Shāh Jahān was held to have been born under the fortunate conjunction of Venus and Jupiter, as his ancestor Tīmūr had been.

10. The details in the text are inaccurate. Arjumand Bānō Bēgam, daughter of Āsaf Khān, brother of Nūr Jahān, the queen of Jahāngīr, was born in A.D. 1592, married in 1612, and died July 7, 1631 (o.s.), at Burhānpur in the Deccan. After a delay of six months her remains were removed to Agra, and there rested six months longer at a spot in the Tāj gardens still remembered, until her tomb was sufficiently advanced for the final interment. Her titles were Mumtāz-i-Mahall, 'Exalted in the Palace'; Qudsia Bēgam, and Nawāb Aliyā Bēgam. She bore her husband eight sons and six daughters, fourteen children in all, of whom seven were alive at the time of her death. The child whose birth cost the mother's life was Gauharārā Bēgam, who survived for many years (Irvine, *Storia do Mogor*, iv. 425). Beale wrongly gives her name as Dahar Ārā.

Shāh Jahān, two years before his union with Arjumand Bāno Bēgam, had been married to a Persian princess, by whom he had a daughter who died young. Five and a half years after his marriage to Arjumand Bāno Bēgam, he espoused a third wife, daughter of Shāh Nawāz Khān, by whom he had a son, who died in infancy. This third marriage was dictated by motives of policy, and did not impair the Emperor's devotion to his favourite consort (Muh. Latīf, *Agra*, p. 101).

11. The testimony of Tavernier is doubtless correct if understood as referring to the whole complex of buildings connected with the mausoleum. He visited Agra several times. He left India in January, 1654, returning to the country in 1659. Work on the Tāj began in 1632, and so appears to have been completed about the close of, 1653 (Tavernier, *Travels*, transl. Ball, vol. i, pp. xxi, xxii, 25, 110, 142, 149). The latest dated inscription, that of the calligraphist Amānat Khan at the entrance to the domed mausoleum, was recorded in the twelfth year of the reign, A.H. 1048, equivalent to A.D. 1638-9. That year may be taken as the date of the completion of the mausoleum itself, as distinguished from the great mass of supplementary structures.

12. Various records of the cost differ enormously, apparently because they refer to different things. If all the buildings and the vast value of the materials be included, the highest estimate, namely, four and a half millions of pounds sterling, in round numbers, is not excessive (*H.F.A.*, 1911, p. 415) The figures are recorded with minute accuracy as 411 lākhs, 48,826 rupees, 7 annas, and 6 pies. A *karōr* (crore) is 100 lākhs, or 10 millions.

13. The enclosure occupies a space of more than forty-two acres.

14. This statement, though commonly made, is erroneous. The building is named the 'assembly house' (jamā'at khāna), or 'guest-house' (mihmān khāna) and was intended as the place for the congregation to assemble before prayers, or on the anniversaries of the deaths of the Emperor Shāh Jahān or his consort. Tāj Mahal (Muh. Latīf, *Agra*, p. 113). Of course, it also serves as an architectural balance for the mosque.

15. The gardens of the Tāj have been much improved since the author's time, and are now under the care of a skilled European superintendent, and full of beautiful shrubs and trees. The author's measurements of the quadrangle seem to be wrong. Different figures are given by Moīn-ud-dīn (*Hist. of the Tāj*, p. 29) and Fergusson (ed. 1910, vol. ii, p. 313). No official survey is available.

16. The white marble that forms the substance of the building came, Mr. Keene thinks, from Makrāna near Jaipur, but according to Mr. Hacket (*Records of the Geographical Survey of India*, x. 84), from Raiwāla in Jaipur, near the Alwar border [note]. The account of these marbles given in the *Rājputāna*

Gazetteer, 1st ed. (ii. 127) favours Mr. Keene's view' (*N.W.P. Gazetteer*, 1st ed., vol. vii, p. 707). The ornamental stones used for the inlay work in the Tāj are lapis lazuli, jasper, heliotrope, Chalcedon agate, chalcedony, cornelian, sarde, plasma (or quartz and chlorite), yellow and striped marble, clay slate, and nephrite, or jade (*Dr. Voysey, in Asiatic Researches*, vol. xv, p. 429, quoted by V. Bail in *Records of the Geological Survey of India*, vii. 109). Moīn-ud- dīn (pp. 27-9) gives a longer list, from the custodians' Persian account.

17. There is some exaggeration in this statement. Shāh Jahān's concern was with his wife's tomb, and his fortified palaces, more than with 'the cities'.

18. Sleeman's talk about Austin de Bordeaux is wholly based on his misreading of *Ustān* for *Ustād*, meaning 'Master', in the Persian account, which names Muhammed-i- Īsā Afandi (Effendi) as the chief designer. He had the title of Ustād, and some versions represent Muhammad Sharīf, the second draughtsman, as his son. Muhammad, the son of Īsā ('Jesus'), apparently was a Turk. He had the Turkish title of 'Effendi', and the Persian MS. used by Moīn- ud-dīn asserts that he came from Turkey. The same authority states that Muhammad Sharīf was a native of Samarkand.

Austin de Bordeaux was wholly distinct from Muhammad-i- Īsā, Ustād Afandi, and there is no reason to suppose that he had anything to do with the Tāj. Sleeman's story about his work at Agra and his death comes from Tavernier (i. 108, transl. Ball: see next note). Austin was in the service of Jahāngīr as early as 1621, and probably came out to India from Persia in 1614. He is described as an engineer (*ingénieur*), and is recorded to have made a golden throne for Jahāngīr (*J.R.A.S.*, 1910, pp. 494, 1343-5). Sleeman's misreading of *ustād* as *ustān*, and his consequent blunders, have misled innumerable writers. In cursive Persian the misreading is easy and natural. He took Ustān as intended for 'Austin'. Certain marks in the garden on the other side of the river indicate the spot where Shāh Jahān had begun work on his own tomb. Aurangzēb, as Tavernier observes, was 'not disposed to complete it' (see *A.S.R.*, iv. 180).

For a summary of the controversy concerning the alleged share of Geronimo Veroneo in the design of the Tāj, see *H.F.A.*, 1911, pp. 416-18. Personally, I am of opinion, as I was more than twenty years ago, that 'the incomparable Tāj is the product of a combination of European and Asiatic genius'. That opinion makes some people very angry.

19. I would not be thought very positive upon this point, I think I am right, but feel that I may be wrong. Tavernier says that Shāh Jahān was obliged to give up his intention of completing a silver ceiling to the great hall in the palace, because Austin de Bordeaux had been killed, and no other

person could venture to attempt it. Ustān [*sic*] Īsā, in all the Persian accounts, stands first among the salaried architects. [W. H. S.] Tavernier's words are, 'Shāh Jahān had intended to cover the arch of a great gallery which is on the right hand with silver, and a Frenchman, named Augustin de Bordeaux, was to have done the work. But the Great Mogul, seeing there was no one in his kingdom who was more capable to send to Goa to negotiate an affair with the Portuguese, the work was not done, for, as the ability of Augustin was feared, he was poisoned on his return from Cochin.' (*Tavernier*, transl. Ball, vol. i, p. 108.) The statement that Austin had 'finished the palace at Delhi, and the mausoleum and palace of Agra' is not warranted by any evidence known to the editor.

20. Akbar erected his works on the site of an older fort, named Bādalgarh, presumably of Hindu origin, 'which was of brick, and had become ruinous.' No existing building within the precincts can be referred with certainty to an earlier date than that of Akbar. The erection began in A.H. 972, corresponding to A.D. 1564-5, and the work continued for eight (or, according to another authority, four) years, costing 3,500,000 rupees, or about £350,000 sterling. The walls are of rubble, faced with red sandstone. The best account is the article by Nūr Baksh, entitled 'The Agra Fort and its Buildings', in *A.S. Ann. Rep.*, 1903-4, pp. 164-93.

21. It is difficult to understand how men like the Marquis of Hastings and Lord William Bentinck could have been guilty of such barbarous stupidity. But the fact is beyond doubt, and numberless officials of less exalted rank must share the disgrace of the ruin and spoliation, which, both at Agra and Delhi, have destroyed two noble palaces, and left but a few disconnected fragments. Fergusson's indignant protests (*History of Indian and Eastern Architecture*, ed. 1910, vol. ii, p. 312, &c.) are none too strong. Sir John Strachey, who was Lieutenant-Governor of the North- Western Provinces in 1876, is entitled to the credit of having done all that lay in his power to remedy the effects of the parsimony and neglect of his predecessors. The buildings which remain at both Agra and Delhi are now well cared for, and large sums are spent yearly on their reparation and conservation. The credit for the modern policy of reverence for the ancient monuments is due to Lord Curzon more than to any one else.

22. This date is erroneous. The inscription is dated A.H. 1063, in the 26th year of Shāh Jahān, equivalent practically to A.D. 1653. It is given in full, with both text and translation, in *A.S. Ann. Rep.* for 1903-4, p. 183. It states that the building was erected in the course of seven years at a cost of 300,000 rupees, which = £33,750, at the rate of 2*s*. 3*d*. to the rupee current at the time. Errors on the subject disfigure most of the guide-books and other works commonly read.

23. The beauty of the Motī Masjid, like that of most mosques, is all internal. The exterior is ugly. The interior deserves all praise. Fergusson describes this mosque as 'one of the purest and most elegant buildings of its class to be found anywhere', and truly observes that 'the moment you enter by the eastern gateway the effect of its courtyard is surpassingly beautiful'. 'I hardly know anywhere', he adds, 'of a building so perfectly pure and elegant.' (*Ind. and E. Arch.*, ed. 1910, vol. ii, p. 317. See also *H.F.A.*, p. 412, fig. 242.)

24. I would, however, here enter my humble protest against the quadrille and tiffin [*scil.* lunch] parties, which are sometimes given to the European ladies and gentlemen of the station at this imperial tomb; drinking and dancing are, no doubt, very good things in their season, even in a hot climate, but they are sadly out of place in a sepulchre, and never fail to shock the good feelings of sober-minded people when given there. Good church music gives us great pleasure, without exciting us to dancing or drinking; the Tāj does the same, at least to the sober-minded. [W. H. S.] The regulations now in force prevent any unseemly proceedings. The gardens at the Tāj, of Itimād-ud-daula's tomb, of Akbar's mausoleum at Sikandara, and the Rām Bāgh, are kept up by means of income derived from crown lands, aided by liberal grants from Government.

25. The anthor's curiously meagre description of the magnificent mausoleum of Akbar is, in the original edition, supplemented by coloured plates, prepared apparently from drawings by Indian artists. The structure is absolutely unique, being a square pyramid of five stories, the uppermost of which is built of pure white marble, while the four lower ones are of red sandstone. All earlier descriptions of the building have been superseded by the posthumous work of E. W. Smith, a splendidly illustrated quarto, entitled, *Akbar's Tomb, Sikandarah, Agra*, Allahabad Government Press, 1909, being vol. xxxv of A. S. India. Work had been begun in the lifetime of Akbar. The lower part of the enclosing wall of the park dates from his reign. The whole of the mausoleum itself probably is to be assigned to the reign of Jahāngīr, who in 1608 disapproved of the structure which had been three or four years in course of erection, and caused the design to be altered to please himself. The work was finished in 1613 at a cost of five millions of rupees (50 lākhs, more than half a million of pounds sterling). The exquisitely carved cenotaph on the top story is inadequately described by Sleeman as 'another marble slab'. It is a single block of marble 3¼ feet high. The tomb in the vault 'is perfectly plain with the exception of a few mouldings'.

26. The ninety-nine names of God do not occur in the Korān. They are enumerated in chapter 1 of Book X of the 'Mishkāt-ul-Masābih' (see note 10, Chapter 5 *ante*): 'Abū Hurairah said, "Verily there are ninety- nine names

for God; and whoever counts them shall enter into paradise. He is Allaho, than which there is no other; Al- Rahmān-ul-Rahīmo, the compassionate and merciful," &c., &c.' (Matthews, vol. i, p. 542.) The list is reproduced in the introduction to Palmer's translation of the Korān, and in Bosworth-Smith, *Muhammad and Muhammadanism*.

27. The court, 70 feet square, of the topmost story, is open to the sky, but the original intention was to provide a light dome, presumably similar to that built a little later to crown the mausoleum of Itimād-ud-daula. Finch, the traveller, who was at Agra about 1611, was informed that the cenotaph was 'to be inarched over with the most curious white and speckled marble, and to be seeled all within with pure sheet gold, richly inwrought.' The reason for omitting the dome is not recorded.

28. The area is much larger than 40 acres, being really about 150 acres. Each side is approximately 3½ furlongs.

29. This remarkable eulogium is quoted with approval by another enthusiastic admirer of Akbar, Count von Noer (Prince Frederick Augustus of Schleswig-Holstein), who observes that 'as Akbar was unique amongst his contemporaries, so was his place of burial among Indian tombs — indeed, one may say with confidence, among the sepulchres of Asia.' (*The Emperor Akbar, a Contribution towards the History of India in the 16th Century*, by Frederick Augustus, Count of Noer; edited from the Author's papers by Dr. Gustav von Buchwald; translated from the German by Annette S. Beveridge. Calcutta, 1890.) This work of Count von Noer, unsatisfactory though it is in many respects, is still the best exiting modern account of Akbar's reign. The competent scholar who will undertake the exhaustive treatment of the life and reign of Akbar will be in possession of perhaps the finest great historical subject as yet unappropriated. The editor long cherished the idea of writing such an exhaustive work, but if he should now attempt to deal with the fascinating theme, he must be content with a less ambitions performance. Colonel Malleson's little book in the 'Rulers of India' series, although serviceable as a sketch, adds nothing to the world's knowledge. Akbar's reign (1556-1605) was almost exactly coincident with that of Queen Elizabeth (1558-1603). The character and deeds of the Indian monarch will bear criticism as well as those of his great English contemporary. 'In dealing', observes Mr. Lane-Poole, 'with the difficulties arising in the Government of a peculiarly heterogeneous empire, he stands absently supreme among Oriental sovereigns, and may even challenge comparison with the greatest of European rulers.'

Unhappily, there is reason to believe that the marble slab no longer covers the bones of Akbar. Manucci states positively that 'During the time that Aurangzēb was actively at war with Shivā Jī [*scil.* the Marāthās], the villagers of whom I spoke before broke into the mausoleum in the year 1691 [in words], and after stealing all the stones and all the gold work to be found, extracted the king's bones and had the temerity to throw them on a fire and burn them' (*Storia do Mogor*, i. 142). The statement is repeated with some additional particulars in a later passage, which concludes with the words: 'Dragging out the bones of Akbar, they threw them angrily into the fire and burnt them' (ibid. ii. 320). Irvine notes that the plundering of the tomb by the Jāts is mentioned in detail by only one other writer, Ishar Dās Nāgar, author of the *Fatūhāt-I- Alamgīrī*, a manuscript in the British Museum. Manucci seems to be the sole authority for the alleged burning of Akbar's bones. I should be glad to disbelieve him, but cannot find any reason for doing so.

CHAPTER 52

Nūr Jahān, the Aunt of the Empress Nūr Mahal, over whose Remains the Tāj is built.[1]

I crossed over the river Jumna one morning to look at the tomb of Itimād-ud-daula, the most remarkable mausoleum in the neighbourhood after those of Akbar and the Tāj. On my way back, I asked one of the boatmen who was rowing me who had built what appeared to me a new dome within the fort. 'One of the Emperors, of course,' said he. 'What makes you think so?'

'Because such things are made only by Emperors,' replied the man quietly, without relaxing his pull at the oar.

'True, very true,' said an old Musalmān trooper, with large white whiskers and moustachios, who had dismounted to follow me across the river, with a melancholy shake of the head, 'very true; who but Emperors could do such things as these?'

Encouraged by the trooper, the boatman continued:—'The Jāts and the Marāthās did nothing but pull down and destroy while they held their *accursed dominion* here; and the European gentlemen who now govern seem to have no pleasure in building anything but *factories, courts of justice, and jails.*'

Feeling as an Englishman, as we all must sometimes do, be where we will, I could hardly help wishing that the beautiful panels and pillars of the bath-room had fetched a better price, and that palace, Tāj, and all at Agra, had gone to the hammer—so sadly do they exalt the past at the expense of the present in the imaginations of the people.

The tomb contains in the centre the remains of Khwāja Ghiās,[2] one of the most prominent characters of the reign of Jahāngīr, and those of his wife. The remains of the other members of his family repose in rooms all round them; and are covered with slabs of marble richly cut. It is an exceedingly beautiful building, but a great part of the most valuable stones of the mosaic work have been picked out and stolen, and the whole is about to be sold by auction, by a decree of the civil court, to pay the debt of the present proprietor, who is entirely unconnected with the family whose members repose under it, and especially indifferent as to what becomes of their bones. The building and garden in which it stands were, some sixty years ago, given away, I believe, by Nājīf Khān, the prime minister, to one of his nephews, to whose family it still belongs.[3] Khwaja Ghiās, a native of Western Tartary, left that country for India, where he had some relations at the imperial court, who seemed likely to be able to secure his advancement. He was a man of handsome person, and of good education and address. He set out with his wife, a bullock, and a small sum of money, which he realized by the sale of all his other property. The wife, who was pregnant, rode upon the bullock, while he walked by her side. Their stock of money had become exhausted, and they had been three days without food in the great desert, when she was taken in labour, and gave birth to a daughter. The mother could hardly keep her seat on the bullock, and the father had become too exhausted to afford her any support; and in their distress they agreed to abandon the infant. They covered it over with leaves, and towards evening pursued their journey. When they had gone on about a mile, and had lost sight of the solitary shrub under which they had left their child, the mother, in an agony of grief, threw herself from the bullock upon the ground, exclaiming, 'My child, my child!' Ghiās could not resist this appeal. He went back to the spot, took up his child, and brought it to its mother's breast. Some travellers soon after came up, and relieved their distress, and they reached Lahore, where the Emperor Akbar then held his court.[4]

Āsaf Khan, a distant relation of Ghiās, held a high place at court, and was much in the confidence of the Emperor. He made his kinsman his private secretary. Much pleased with his diligence and ability, Āsaf soon brought his merits to the special notice of Akbar, who raised him to the command of a thousand horse, and soon after appointed him master of the household. From this he was promoted afterwards to that of Itimād-ud-daula, or high treasurer, one of the first ministers.[5]

The daughter who had been born in the desert became celebrated for her great beauty, parts, and accomplishments, and won the affections of the eldest son of the Emperor, the Prince Salīm, who saw her unveiled, by accident, at a party given by her father. She had been betrothed before this to Shēr Afgan, a Turkoman gentleman of rank at court, and of great repute for his high spirit, strength, and courage.[6] Salīm in vain entreated his father to interpose his authority to make him resign his claim in his favour; and she became the wife of Shēr Afgan. Salīm dare not, during his father's life, make any open attempt to revenge himself; but he, and those courtiers who thought it their interest to worship the rising sun, soon made his [Afgan's] residence at the capital disagreeable, and he retired with his wife to Bengal, where he obtained from the governor the superintendency of the district of Bardwān.

Salīm succeeded his father on the throne;[7] and, no longer restrained by his (scil. Akbar's) rigid sense of justice, he recalled Shēr Afgan to court at Delhi. He was promoted to high offices, and concluded that time had removed from the Emperor's mind all feelings of love for his wife, and of resentment against his successful rival — but he was mistaken; Salīm had never forgiven him, nor had the desire to possess his wife at all diminished. A Muhammadan of such high feeling and station would, the Emperor knew, never survive the dishonour, or suspected dishonour, of his wife; and to possess her he must make away with the husband. He dared not do this openly, because he dreaded the universal odium in which he knew it would involve him; and he made several unsuccessful attempts to get him removed by means that might not appear to have been contrived or executed by his orders. At one time he designedly, in his own presence, placed him in a situation where the pride of the chief made him contend, single- handed, with a large tiger, which he killed; and, at another, with a mad elephant, whose proboscis he cut off with his sword; but the Emperor's motives in all these attempts to put him foremost in situations of danger became so manifest that Shēr Afgan solicited, and obtained, permission to retire with his wife to Bengal.

The governor of this province, Kutb,[8] having been made acquainted with the Emperor's desire to have the chief made away with, hired forty ruffians, who stole into his house one night. There happened to be nobody else in the house; but one of the party, touched by remorse on seeing so fine a man about to be murdered in his sleep, called out to him to defend himself. He seized his sword, placed himself in one corner of the room, and defended himself so well that nearly one-half of the party are said to have been killed or wounded. The rest all made off, persuaded that he was endowed with supernatural force. After this escape he retired from Tānda, the capital of Bengal,[9] to his old residence of Bardwān. Soon after, Kutb came to the city with a splendid retinue, on pretence of making a tour of inspection through the provinces under his charge, but in reality for the sole purpose of making away with Shēr Afgan, who as soon as he heard of his approach, came out some miles to meet him on horseback, attended by only two followers. He was received with marks of great consideration, and he and the governor rode on for some time side by side, talking of their mutual friends, and the happy days they had spent together at the capital. At last, as they were about to enter the city, the governor suddenly called for his elephant of state, and mounted, saying it would be necessary for him to pass through the city on the first visit in some state. Shēr sat on horseback while he mounted, but one of the governor's pikemen struck his horse, and began to drive him before them. Shēr drew his sword, and, seeing all the governor's followers with theirs ready drawn to attack him, he concluded at once that the affront had been put upon him by the orders of Kutb, and with the design to provoke him to an unequal fight. Determined to have his life first, he spurred his horse upon the elephant, and killed Kutb with his spear. He now attacked the principal of officers, and five noblemen of the first rank fell by his sword. All the crowd now rolled back, and formed a circle round Shēr and his two companions, and galled them with arrows and musket balls from a distance. His horse fell under him and expired; and, having received six balls and several arrows in his body, Shēr himself at last fell exhausted to the ground; and the crowd, seeing the sword drop from his grasp, rushed in and cut him to pieces.[10]

His widow was sent, 'nothing loth', to court, with her only child, a daughter. She was graciously received by the Emperor's mother, and had apartments assigned her in the palace; but the Emperor himself is said not to have seen her for four years, during which time the fame of her beauty, talents, and accomplishments filled the palace and city. After the expiration of this time the feelings, whatever they were, which prevented his seeing her, subsided; and when he at last surprised her with a visit, he found her to exceed all that his imagination had painted since their last separation. In a few days their marriage was celebrated with great magnificence;[11] and from that hour the Emperor resigned the reins of government almost entirely into her hands; and, till his death, under the name first of Nūr Mahall, 'Light of the Palace', and afterwards of Nūr Jahān, 'Light of the World ', she ruled the destinies of this great empire. Her father was now raised from the station of high treasurer to that of prime minister. Her two brothers obtained the titles of Āsaf Jāh and Itikād Khan; and the relations of the family poured in from Tartary in search of employment, as soon as they heard of their success.[12] Nūr Jahān had by Sher Afgan, as I have stated, one daughter; but she had never any child by the Emperor Jahāngīr.[13]

Āsaf Jāh became prime minister on the death of his father; and, in spite of his sister, he managed to secure the crown to Shāh Jahān, the third son of Jahāngīr, who had married his daughter, the lady over whose remains the Tāj was afterwards built. Jahāngīr's eldest son, Khusrū, had his eyes put out by his father's orders for repeated rebellions, to which he had been instigated by a desire to revenge his mother's murder, and by the ambition of her brother, the Hindoo prince, Mān Singh,[14] who wished to see his own nephew on the throne, and by his wife's father, the prime minister of Akbar, Khan Azam.[15] Nūr Jahān had invited the mother of Khusrū, the sister of Rājā Mān Singh, to look with her down a well in the courtyard of her apartments by moonlight, and as she did so she threw her in. As soon as she saw that she had ceased to struggle she gave the alarm, and pretended that she had fallen in by accident.[16]

By the murder of the mother of the heir-apparent she expected to secure the throne to a creature of her own. Khusrū was treated with great kindness by his father, after he had been barbarously deprived of sight;[17] but when his brother, Shāh Jahān, was appointed to the government of Southern India, he pretended great solicitude about the comforts of his *poor blind brother*, which he thought would not be attended to at court, and took him with him to his government in the Deccan, where he got him assassinated, as the only sure mode of securing the throne to himself.[18] Parwīz, the second son, died a natural death;[19] so also did his only son; and so also Dāniyāl, the fourth son of the Emperor.[20] Nūr Jahān's daughter by Shēr Afgan had married Shahryār, a young son of the Emperor by a concubine; and, just before his death he (the Emperor), at the instigation of Nūr Jahān, named this son as his successor in his will. He was placed upon the throne, and put in possession of the treasury, and at the head of a respectable army;[21] but the Empress's brother, Āsaf, designed the throne for his own son-in-law, Shāh Jahān; and, as soon as the Emperor died, he put up a puppet to amuse the people till he could come up with his army from the Deccan — Bulākī, the eldest son of the deceased Khusrū. Shahryār's troops were defeated; he was taken prisoner, and had his eyes put out forthwith, and the Empress was put into close confinement. As Shāh Jahān approached Lahore with his army, Āsaf put his puppet, Bulākī, and his younger brother, with the two young sons of Dāniyāl, into prison, where they were strangled by a messenger sent on for the purpose by Shāh Jahān, with the sanction of Āsaf. [22] This measure left no male heir alive of the house of Tīmūr (Tamerlane) in Hindustan, save Shāh Jahān himself and his four sons. Dārā was then thirteen years of age, Shujā twelve, Aurangzēb ten, and Murād four;[23] and all were present to learn from their father this sad lesson — that such of them who might be alive on his death, save one, must, with their sons, be hunted down and destroyed like mad dogs, lest they might get into the hands of the disaffected, and be made the tools of faction.

Monsieur de Thevenot, who visited Agra, as I have before stated, in 1666, says, 'Some affirm that there are twenty-five thousand Christian families in Agra; but all do not agree in that. The Dutch have a factory in the town, but the English have now none, because it did not turn to account.' The number must have been great, or so sober a man as Monsieur Thevenot would not have thought such an estimate worthy to be quoted without contradiction. [24] They were all, except those connected with the single Dutch factory, maintained from the salaries of office; and they gradually disappeared as their offices became filled with Muhammadans and Hindoos. The duties of the artillery, its arsenals, and foundries, were the chief foundation upon which the superstructure of Christianity then stood in India. These duties were everywhere entrusted exclusively to Europeans, and all Europeans were Christians, and, under Shāh Jahān, permitted freely to follow their own modes of worship. They were, too. Roman Catholic, and spent the greater part of their incomes in the maintenance of priests. But they could never forget that they were strangers in the land, and held their offices upon a precarious tenure; and, consequently, they never felt disposed to expend the little wealth they had in raising durable tombs, churches, and other public buildings, to tell posterity who or what they were. Present physical enjoyment, and the prayers of their priests for a good berth in the next world, were the only objects of their ambition. Muhammadans and Hindoos soon learned to perform duties which they saw bring to the Christians so much of honour and emolument; and, as they did so, they necessarily sapped the walls of the fabric. Christianity never became independent of office in India, and, I am afraid, never will; even under our rule, it still mainly rests upon that foundation.[25]

Notes:

1. The names and titles of the empress 'over whose remains the Tāj is built' were Nawāb Aliyā Begam, Arjumand Bānū, Mumtāz-i-Mahall. The title Nūr Mahall, as applied to her, is without authority: it properly belongs to her aunt. 'It is usual in this country', Bernier observes, 'to give similar names to the members of the reigning family. Thus the wife of *Chah-Jehan*— so renowned for her beauty, and whose splendid mausoleum is more worthy of a place among the wonders of the world than the unshapen masses and heaps of stones in Egypt—was named *Tāge Mehalle* [Mumtāz-i-Mahall], or the Crown of the Seraglio; and the wife of Jehan-Guyre, who so long wielded the sceptre, while her husband abandoned himself to drunkenness and dissipation, was known first by the name of *Nour Mehalle*, the Light of the Seraglio, and afterwards by that of *Nour-Jehan-Begum*, the Light of the World.' (Bernier, *Travels*, ed. Constable, and V. A. Smith, 1914, p. 5.)

2. Properly, Ghiās-ud-dīn, meaning 'succourer of religion'. The word Ghiās cannot stand as a name by itself.

3. The author's slight description of Itimād-ud-daula's exquisite sepulchre is, in the original edition, illustrated by two coloured plates, one of the exterior, and the other of the interior (restored). The lack of grandeur in this building is amply atoned for by its elegance and marvellous beauty of detail. An inscription, dated A.H. 1027 = A.D. 1618, alleged to exist in

connexion with the building, has not, apparently, been published. (*N.W.P. Gazetteer*, 1st ed., vol. vii, p. 687.)

Fergusson's description and just criticism deserve quotation. 'The tomb known as that of Itimād-ud-daula, at Agra, . . . cannot be passed over, not only from its own beauty of design, but also because it marks an epoch in the style to which it belongs. It was erected by Nūr-Jahān in memory of her father, who died in 1621, and [it] was completed in 1628. It is situated on the left bank of the river, in the midst of a garden surrounded by a wall measuring 540 feet on each side. In the centre of this, on a raised platform, stands the tomb itself, a square measuring 69 feet on each side. It is two stories in height, and at each angle is an octagonal tower, surmounted by an open pavilion. The towers, however, are rather squat in proportion, and the general design of the building very far from being so pleasing as that of many less pretentious tombs in the neighbourhood. Had it, indeed, been built in red sandstone, or even with an inlay of white marble like that of Humāyūn, it would not have attracted much attention, its real merit consists in being wholly in white marble, and being covered throughout with a mosaic in 'pietra dura' — the first, apparently, and certainly one of the most splendid, examples of that class of ornamentation in India....

'As one of the first, the tomb of Itimād-ud-daula was certainly one of the least successful specimens of its class. The patterns do not quite fit the places where they are put, and the spaces are not always those best suited for this style of decoration. [Altogether I cannot help fancying that the Italians had more to do with the design of this building than was at all desirable, and they are to blame for its want of grace.[a]] But, on the other hand, the beautiful tracery of the pierced marble slabs of its Windows, which resemble those of Salīm Chishtī's tomb at Fatehpur Sikrī, the beauty of its white marble walls, and the rich colour of its decorations, make up so beautiful a whole, that it is only on comparing it with the works of Shāh Jahān that we are justified in finding fault.' (*Indian and Eastern Architecture*, ed. 1910, pp. 305-7.) Further details will be found in Syad Muhammad Latīf, *Agra* (Calcutta, 1896); *A.S.R.* iv, pp. 137-41 (Calcutta, 1874); and more satisfactorily, in E. W. Smith, *Moghul Colour Decoration of Agra* (Allahabad, 1901), pp. 18-20, pl. lxv-lxxvii. Mr. E. W. Smith, if he had lived, would have produced a separate volume descriptive of this unique building.

The building is now carefully guarded and kept in repair. The restoration of the inlay of precious stones is so enormously expensive that much progress in that branch of the work is impracticable. The mausoleum contains seven tombs.

a. This sentence has been deleted by Dr. Burgess in his edition, 1910.

4. This tale is mythical. The alleged circumstances could not be known to any person besides the father and mother, neither of whom would be likely to make them public. Blochmann (transl. *Āīn*, i. 508) gives a full account of Itimād-ud-daula and his family. The historians state that Nūr Jahān was born at Kandahār, on the way to India. Her father was the son of a high Persian official, but for some reason or other was obliged to quit Persia with his family. He was a native of Teheran, not of 'Western Tartary'. The personal name of Nūr Jahān was Mihr-un-nisā.

5. This story is erroneous, and inconsistent with the correct statement in the heading of the chapter that Nūr Jahān, daughter of Ghias-ud-dīn, was aunt of the Lady of the Tāj. The author makes out Ghias-ud-dīn (whom he corruptly calls Aeeas) to be a distant relation of Āsaf Khan. In reality, Āsaf Khan (whose original name was Mirzā Abūl Hasan) was the second son of Ghiās-ud- dīn, and was elder brother of Nūr Jahān, The genealogy, so far as relevant, is best shown in a tabular form, thus:—

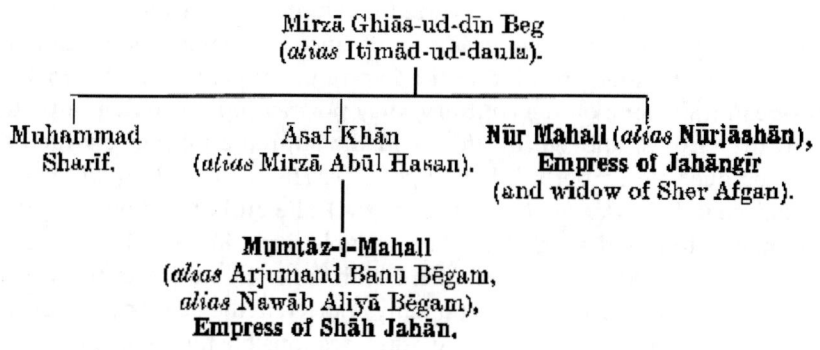

6. Alī Qulī Beg, from Persia entered Akbar's service, and in the war with the Rānā of Chitōr, served under Prince Salīm (Jahāngīr), who gave him the title of Shēr Afgan, 'tiger-thrower', with reverence to his deeds of prowess. The spelling *afgan* is correct. The word is the radical of the Persian verb *afgandan*, 'to throw down'.

7. In October, 1605.

8. Properly Kutb-ud-dīn Khan. He was foster-brother of Prince Salīm (Jahāngīr), and his appointment as viceroy alarmed Shēr Afgan, and caused the latter to throw up his appointment in Bengal. The word Kutb (Qutb) cannot stand alone as a name. Kutb (Qutb)-ud-dīn means 'pole-star of religion'.

9. **Tāndān, or Tānra.** Ancient town, now a petty village, in Mālda District, Bengal, the capital of Bengal after the decadence of Gaur. Its history is obscure, and the very site of the city has not been accurately determined. It is certain that it was in the immediate neighbourhood of Gaur, and south-west of that town beyond the Bhāgīrathī. Old Tāndān has been utterly swept away by the changes in the course of the Pāglā. It was occupied by the Afghan king of Bengal in A.D. 1564, and is not mentioned after 1660. (*I.G.*, 1908.)

10. This narrative, notwithstanding all the minute details with which it is garnished, cannot be accepted as sober history; and I do not know from what source the author obtained it. 'This lady, whose maiden name was Muhr-un-Nisā, or "Seal of Womankind", had attracted the admiration of Jahāngīr when he was crown prince, but Akbar married her to a young Turkomān and settled them in Bengal. After Jahāngīr's accession the husband was killed in a quarrel with the governor of the province, and the wife was placed under the care of one of Akbar's widows, with whom she remained four years, and then married Jahāngīr (1610). There is nothing to justify a suspicion of the Emperor's connivance in the husband's death; nor do Indian historians corroborate the invidious criticisms of "Normal" by European travellers; on the contrary, they portray Nūr-Mahall as a pattern of all the virtues, and worthy to wield the supreme influence which she obtained over the Emperor.' (Lane-Poole, *The History of the Moghul Emperors of Hindustan illustrated by their Coins*, p. xix.) The authorities on which this statement is founded are given in *E. & D.*, vol. vi, pp. 397 and 402-5. See also Blochmann, *Āīn*, vol. i, pp. 496, 524. Details of such stories in the various chronicles always differ. Jahāngīr openly rejoiced in the death of Shēr Afgan, and it is by no means clear that he was not responsible for the event. He was not troubled by nice scruples. The first element in the lady's personal name seems to be *Mihr*, 'sun', not *Muhr*, 'seal'. The words are identical in ordinary Persian writing.

11. The long interval which elapsed between Shēr Afgan's death and the marriage with the Emperor is a fact opposed to the assumptions which the author adopts that Nūr Mahall was 'nothing loth', and that the death of her first husband was contrived by Jahāngīr.

12. Quaint Sir Thomas Herbert thus expresses himself: 'Meher Metzia [Mihr-un-nisā] is forthwith espoused with all solemnity to the King, and her name changed to Nourshabegem [Nūr Shāh Bēgam], or Nor-mahal, i.e., Light or Glory of the Court; her Father upon this affinity advanced upon all the other Umbraes ['umarā', or nobles]; her brother, Assaph-Chan [Āsaf Khān], and most of her kindred, smiled upon, with the addition of Honours, Wealth, and Command. And in this Sun-shine of content Jangheer [Jahāngīr]

spends some years with his lovely Queen, without regarding ought save Cupid's Currantoes' (*Travels*, ed. 1677, p. 74). Authority exists for the title Āsaf Jāh, as well as for the variant Āsaf Khān.

Coins were struck in the joint names of Jahāngīr and his consort, bearing a rhyming Persian couplet to the effect that

'By command of Jahāngīr the King, from the name of Nūr Jahān his Queen, gold gained a hundred beauties.'

The Queen's administration is censured by some of the European travellers who visited India during Jahāngīr's reign as being venal and inefficient, and she is accused of cruelty and perfidy. She died on the 18th December (N.S.), 1645, and was buried by the aide of Jahāngīr in his mausoleum at Lahore. At her death she was in her 72nd year, according to the Muhammadan lunar reckoning, and would thus have been thirty-four solar years of age when the Emperor married her in 1610 (Beale: Blochmann).

13. According to Sir Thomas Herbert (*Travels*, ed. 1677, p. 99), 'Queen Normahal and her three daughters' were confined by order of Shāh Jahān in A.D. 1628.

14. Son of Bhagwān Dās, of Ambēr or Jaipur, in Rājputāna, and one of the greatest of Akbar's officers.

15. Also known as Azīz Kokah, a foster-brother of Akbar.

16. This story may or may not be true; but a charge of this kind is absolutely incapable of proof, and would be readily generated in the palace atmosphere.

17. According to a contemporary authority, the blinding was only partial, and the prince recovered the sight of one eye (*E. & D.* vi. 448). With regard to such details the discrepancies in the histories are innumerable.

18. A.H. 1031 = A.D. 1621-2. The charge seems to be true.

19. A.H. 1036 = A.D. 1626-7.

20. This is a blunder. Jahāngīr's fourth son was named Jahāndār, and died in or about A.H. 1035 = A.D. 1625-6. Dāniyāl was third son of Akbar, and younger brother of Jahāngīr. He died from *delirium tremens* in A.D. 1605, a few months before the death of Akbar,

21. Jahāngīr died, when returning from Kāshmīr, on the 8th November, A.D. 1627 (N.S.), and was buried near Lahore. The fight with Shahryār took place at Lahore.

22. Bulākī assumed the title of Dāwar Baksh during his short reign, and struck coins at Lahore. He 'vanished — probably to Persia — after his three months' pretence of royalty; and on 25th January, 1628 (18 Jumāda I, 1037), Shāh-Jahān ascended at Agra the throne which he was to occupy for

thirty years'. Shahryār was known by the nickname of *Nā-shudanī*, or 'Good-for-nothing' (Lane- Poole, *The History of the Moghul Emperors of Hindustan, illustrated by their Coins*, p. xxiii). The two nephews of Jahāngīr, the sons of Dāniyāl, slaughtered at this time, had been, according to Herbert, baptized as Christians (*Travels*, ed. 1677, pp. 74, 98). There are great discrepancies in the accounts given by various authorities concerning the fate of Bulākī and the other victims of Shāh Jahān. A dissuasion of the evidence would take too much apace, and must be inconclusive, the fact being that the proceedings were secret, and pains were taken to conceal the truth.

23. The dates of birth are, in Old Style:-Dārā Shikoh, March 20, 1615; Sultan Shujā, May 12, 1616; Aurangzēb, October 10, 1619; and Murād Baksh, not stated (Beale).

24. *Ante*, Chapter 2, text following [8]. The quotation is from Part III, chap. 19, p. 35 of *The Travels of Monsieur de Thevenot, now made English. London, Printed in the year MDCLXXXVII*. The author, in his quotation, omits between 'that' and 'The Dutch' the clause 'This indeed is certain that there are few Heathens and Parsis in respect of Mahometans there, and these surpass all the other sects in power as they do in number.'

25. During the reign of Akbar, many Christians, Portuguese, English, and others, visited Agra, and a considerable number settled there. A Roman Catholic church was built, the steeple of which was pulled down by Shāh Jahān. The oldest inscriptions in the cemetery adjoining the Roman Catholic cathedral are in the Armenian character. Three Catholic cemeteries exist at or near Agra, namely

(1) the old Catholic graveyard at the village of Lashkarpur, dating from the time of Akbar, who made a grant of the site about A.D. 1600. This cemetery includes the Martyrs' Chapel, also known as the Chapel of Father Santus (Santucci), which was erected in memory of Khoja Mortenepus, an Armenian merchant, whose epitaph is dated 1611. The next oldest tombstone, that of Father Emmanuel d' Anhaya, who died in prison, bears the date August, 1633. Father Joseph de Castro, who died at Lahore, on December 15, 1646, lies in the same building.

(2) A cemetery in Pādrītola, the native Christian ward of the city behind the old cathedral. Father Tieffenthaler is buried there.

(3) A cemetery in an unnamed village, granted by Jahāngīr, and situated a mile north of Lashkarpur. An unpublished letter in the British Museum shows that Jahāngīr closed the churches in his dominions in 1615. Notwithstanding, the College at Agra was founded about 1617 by

an Armenian who is known by his title Mirzā Zul-Qarnain. The acute persecution by Shāh Jahān occurred in 1631.

The artillery men in the Mogul service were not all European Christians. Turks from the Ottoman Empire were freely employed. (See *Ep. Ind.*, ii, 132 note.)

The facts concerning the early history of Christianity in Northern India have been imperfectly studied. In this note I have used chiefly a pamphlet by Father H. Hosten, S. J., entitled *Jesuit Missionaries in Northern India, &c.* (Catholic Orphan Press, Calcutta, 1907), and the confused little book by Fanthome, *Reminiscences of Agra* (2nd ed., Thacker, Spink & Co., Calcutta, 1895). The Jesuit and Capuchin Fathers are working at the subject and hope to elucidate it. From the *A.S. Progress Rep. N. Circle, Muhammadan Monuments*, for 1911-12, p. 21, it appears that arrangements for the proper maintenance of the Old Catholic cemetery are in hand.

The author's observations concerning the official relations of Christianity in India do not apply at all to the very ancient churches of the South (See *E.H.I.*, 3rd ed., 1914, App. M, pp. 245-7). Even in the north, the modern missionary operations may claim to be 'independent of office'.

CHAPTER 53

Father Gregory's Notion of the Impediments to Conversion in India —
Inability of Europeans to speak Eastern Languages.

Father Gregory, the Roman Catholic priest, dined with us one evening, and Major Godby took occasion to ask him at table, 'What progress our religion was making among the people?'

'Progress!' said he; 'why, what progress can we ever hope to make among a people who, the moment we begin to talk to them about the miracles performed by Christ, begin to tell us of those infinitely more wonderful performed by Krishna, who lifted a mountain upon his little finger, as an umbrella, to defend his shepherdesses at Govardhan from a shower of rain.[1] The Hindoos never doubt any part of the miracles and prophecies of our scripture — they believe every word of them; and the only thing that surprises them is that they should be so much less wonderful than those of their own scriptures, in which also they implicitly believe. Men who believe that the histories of the wars and amours of Rām and Krishna, two of the incarnations of Vishnu, were written some fifty thousand years before these wars and amours actually took place upon the earth, would of course easily believe in the fulfilment of any prophecy that might be related to them out of any other book;[2] and, as to miracles, there is absolutely nothing too extraordinary for their belief. If a Christian of respectability were to tell a Hindoo that, to satisfy some scruples of the Corinthians, St. Paul had brought the sun and moon down upon the earth, and made them rebound off again into their places, like tennis balls, without the slightest injury to any of the three planets [sic], I do not think he would feel the slightest doubt of the truth of it; but he would immediately be put in mind of something still more extraordinary that Krishna did to amuse the milkmaids, or to satisfy some sceptics of his day, and relate it with all the naïveté imaginable.'

I saw at Agra Mirzā Kām Baksh, the eldest son of Sulaimān Shikoh, the eldest son of the brother of the present Emperor. He had spent a season with us at Jubbulpore, while prosecuting his claim to an estate against the Rājā of Rīwā. The Emperor, Shāh Ālam, in his flight before our troops from Bengal (1762), struck off the high road to Delhi at Mirzapore, and came down to

Rīwā, where he found an asylum during the season of the rains with the Rīwā Rājā, who assigned for his residence the village of Makanpur.[3] His wife, the Empress, was here delivered of a son, the present Emperor, of Hindustān, Akbar Shāh;[4] and the Rājā assigned to him and his heirs for ever the fee simple of this village. As the members of this family increased in geometrical ratio, under the new system, which gave them plenty to eat with nothing to do, the Emperor had of late been obliged to hunt round for little additions to his income; and in his search he found that Makanpur gave name to a 'pargana', or little district, of which it was the capital, and that a good deal of merchandize passed through this district, and paid heavy dues to the Rājā. Nothing, he thought, would be lost by trying to get the whole district instead of the village; and for this purpose he sent down Kām Baksh, the ablest man of the whole family, to urge and prosecute his claim; but the Rājā was a close, shrewd man, and not to be done out of his revenue, and Kām Baksh was obliged to return minus some thousand rupees, which he had spent in attempting to keep up appearances.

The best of us Europeans feel our deficiencies in conversation with Muhammadans of high rank and education, when we are called upon to talk upon subjects beyond the everyday occurrences of life. A Muhammadan gentleman of education is tolerably acquainted with astronomy, as it was taught by Ptolemy; with the logic and ethics of Aristotle and Plato; with the works of Hippocrates and Galen, through those of Avicenna, or, as they call him, Abū- Alīsīna;[5] and he is very capable of talking upon all subjects of philosophy, literature, science, and the arts, and very much inclined to do so; and of understanding the nature of the improvements that have been made in them in modern times. But, however capable we may feel of discussing these subjects, or explaining these improvements in our own language, we all feel ourselves very much at a loss when we attempt to do it in theirs. Perhaps few Europeans have mixed and conversed more freely with all classes than I have; and yet I feel myself sadly deficient when I enter, as I often do, into discussions with Muhammadan gentlemen of education upon the subject of the character of the governments and institutions of different countries — their effects upon the character and condition of the people; the arts and the sciences; the faculties and operations of the human mind; and the thousand other things which are subjects of everyday conversation among educated and thinking; men in our country. I feel that they could understand me quite well if I could find words for my ideas; but these I cannot find, though their languages abound in them, nor have I ever met the European gentleman who could. East Indians can;[6] but they commonly want the ideas as much as we want the language. The chief cause of this deficiency is the want of sufficient intercourse with men in whose presence we should be ashamed to appear ignorant—this is the great secret, and all should know and acknowledge it.

We are not ashamed to convey our orders to our native servants in a barbarous language. Military officers seldom speak to their 'sipāhīs' (sepoys) and native officers, about anything but arms, accoutrements, and drill; or to other natives about anything but the sports of the field; and, as long as they are understood, they care not one straw in what language they express themselves. The conversation of the civil servants with their native officers takes sometimes a wider range; but they have the same philosophical indifference as to the language in which they attempt to convey their ideas; and I have heard some of our highest diplomatic characters talking,[7] without the slightest feeling of shame or embarrassment, to native princes on the most ordinary subjects of everyday interest in a language which no human being but themselves could understand. We shall remain the same till some change of system inspire us with stronger motives to please and conciliate the educated classes of the native community. They may be reconciled, but they can never be charmed out of their prejudices or the errors of their preconceived opinions by such language as the European gentlemen are now in the habit of speaking to them.[8] We must learn their language better, or we must teach them our own, before we can venture to introduce among them those free institutions which would oblige us to meet them on equal terms at the bar, on the bench, and in the senate.[9] Perhaps two of the best secular works that were ever written upon the facilities and operations of the human mind, and the duties of men in their relations with each other, are those of Imām-ud-dīn Ghazzālī, and Nasīr-ud-dīn of Tūs. [10] Their idol was Plato, but their works are of a more practical character than his, and less dry than those of Aristotle.

I may here mention the following, among many instances that occur to me, of the amusing mistakes into which Europeans are liable to fall in their conversation with natives.

Mr. J. W— — —n, of the Bengal Civil Service, commonly known by the name of Beau W— — —n,[11] was the Honourable Company's opium agent at Patna, when I arrived at Dinapore to join my regiment in 1810.[12] He had a splendid house, and lived in excellent style; and was never so happy as when he had a dozen young men from the Dinapore cantonments living with him. He complained that year, as I was told, that he had not been able to save more than one hundred thousand rupees that season out of his salary and commission upon the opium, purchased by the Government from the cultivators.[13] The members of the civil service, in the other branches of public service, were all anxious to have it believed by their countrymen that they were well acquainted with their duties, and able and willing to perform them; but the Honourable Company's commercial agents were, on the contrary, generally anxious to make their countrymen believe that they neither knew nor cared anything about their duties, because they were ashamed of them. They were sinecure posts for the drones of the service, or for those who had great interest and no capacity.[14] Had any young man made it appear that he really thought W— — —n knew or cared anything about his duties, he would certainly never have been invited to his house again; and if any one knew, certainly no one seemed to know that he had any other duty than that of entertaining his guests.

No one ever spoke the native language so badly, because no man had ever so little intercourse with the natives; and it was, I have been told, to his ignorance of the native languages that his bosom friend, Mr. P— — — —st, owed his life on one occasion. W. sat by the sick-bed of his friend with unwearied attention, for some days and nights, after the doctors had declared his case entirely hopeless. He proposed at last to try change of air, and take him on the river Ganges. The doctors, thinking that he might as well die in his boat on the river as in his house at Calcutta, consented to his taking him on board. They got up as far as Hooghly, when P. said that he felt better and thought he could eat something. What should it be? A little roasted kid perhaps. The very thing that he was longing for! W. went out upon the deck to give orders for the kid, that his friend might not be disturbed by the gruff voice of the old 'khānsāmā' (butler). P. heard the conversation, however.

'Khānsāmā', said the Beau W., 'you know that my friend Mr. P. is very ill?'

'Yes, sir.'

'And that he has not eaten anything for a month?'

'A long time for a man to fast, sir.'

'Yes, Khānsāmā, and his stomach is now become very delicate, and could not stand anything strong.'

'Certainly not, sir.'

'Well, Khānsāmā, then he has taken a fancy to a roasted *mare'* ('mādiyān'), meaning a 'halwān', or kid.'[15]

'A roasted mare, sir?'

'Yes, Khānsāmā, a roasted mare, which you must have nicely prepared.'

'What, the whole, sir?'

'Not the whole at one time; but have the whole ready as there is no knowing what part he may like best.'

The old butter had heard of the Tartars eating their horses when in robust health, but the idea of a sick man, not able to move in his bed without assistance, taking a fancy to a roasted mare, quite staggered him.

'But, sir, I may not be able to get such a thing as a mare at a moment's notice; and if I get her she will be very dear.'

'Never mind, Khānsāmā, get you the mare, cost what she will; if she costs a thousand rupees my friend shall have her. He has taken a fancy to the mare, and the mare he shall have, if she costs a thousand rupees.'

The butter made his salaam, said he would do his best, and took his leave, requesting that the boats might be kept at the bank of the river till he came back.

W. went into his sick friend, who, with great difficulty, managed to keep his countenance while he complained of the liberties old servants were in the habit of taking with their masters. 'They think themselves privileged', said W., 'to conjure up difficulties in the way of everything that one wants to have done.'

'Yes', said P — — —st, 'we like to have old and faithful servants about us, particularly when we are sick; but they are apt to take liberties, which new ones will not.'

In about two hours the butler's approach was announced from the deck, and W. walked out to scold him for his delay. The old gentleman was coming down over the bank, followed by about eight men bearing the four quarters of an old mare. The butler was very fat; and the proud consciousness of having done his duty, and met his master's wishes in a very difficult and important point, had made him a perfect Falstaff. He marshalled his men in front of the cooking-boat, and then came towards his master, who for some time stood amazed, and unable to speak. At last he roared out, 'And what the devil have you here?'

'Why, the *mare* that the sick gentleman took a fancy for; and dear enough she has cost me; not a farthing less than two hundred rupees would the fellow take for his mare.'

P — — —st could contain himself no longer; he burst into an immoderate fit of laughter, during which the abscess in his liver burst into the intestines, and he felt himself relieved, as if by enchantment. The mistake was rectified—he got his kid; and in ten days he was taken back to Calcutta a sound man, to the great astonishment of all the doctors.

During the first campaign against Nepāl, in 1815, Colonel, now Major-General, O.H., who commanded the — — — Regiment, N. I.,[16] had to march with his regiment through the town of Darbhanga, the capital of the Rājā, who came to pay his respects to him. He brought a number of presents, but the colonel, a high-minded, amiable man, never took anything himself, nor suffered any person in his camp to do so, in the districts they passed through without paying for it. He politely declined to take any of the presents; but said that he 'had heard that Darbhanga produced crows ("kauwā"), and should be glad to get some of them if the Rājā could spare them,' — meaning coffee, or 'kahwā'.

The Rājā stared, and said that certainly they had abundance of crows in Darbhanga; but he thought they were equally abundant in all parts of India.

'Quite the contrary, Rājā Sāhib, I assure you,' said the colonel; 'there is not such a thing as a crow to be found in any part of the Company's dominions that I have seen, and I have been all over them.'

'Very strange!' said the Rājā, turning round to his followers.

'Yes,' replied they,' it is very strange, Rājā Sāhib; but such is your 'ikbāl' (good fortune), that everything thrives under it; and, if the colonel should wish to have a few crows, we could easily collect them for him.'

'If', said the colonel, greatly delighted, 'you could provide us with a few of these crows, we should really feel very much obliged to you; for we have a long and cold campaign before us among the bleak hills of Nepal; and we are all fond of crows.'

'Indeed,' returned the Rājā, 'I shall be happy to send you as many as you wish.' ('Much' and 'many' are expressed by the same term.)

'Then we should be glad to have two or three bags full, if it would not be robbing you.'

'Not in the least,' said the Rājā; 'I will go home and order them to be collected immediately.'

In the evening, as the officers, with the colonel at their head, were sitting down to dinner, a man came up to announce the Rājā's present. Three fine large bags were brought in, and the colonel requested that one might be opened immediately. It was opened accordingly, and the mess butler ('khansāmān') drew out by the legs a fine old crow. The colonel immediately saw the mistake, and laughed as heartily as the rest at the result. A polite message was sent to the Rājā, requesting that he would excuse his having made it — for he had had half a dozen men out shooting crows all day with their matchlocks. Few Europeans spoke the language better than General — — —, and I do not believe that one European in a thousand, at this very moment, makes any difference, or knows any difference, in the sound of the two terms.

Kām Baksh had one sister married to the King of Oudh, and another to Mirzā Salīm, the younger son of the Emperor. Mirzā Salīm and his wife could not agree, and a separation took place, and she went to reside with her sister, the Queen of Oudh. The King saw her frequently; and, finding her more beautiful than his wife, he demanded her also in marriage from her father, who resided at Lucknow, the capital of Oudh, on a pension of five thousand rupees a month from the King. He would not consent, and demanded his daughter; the King, finding her willing to share his bed and board with her sister, would not give her up.[17] The father got his old friend, Colonel Gardiner, who had married a Muhammadan woman of rank, to come down and plead his cause. The King gave up the young woman, but at the same time stopped the father's pension, and ordered him and all his family out of his dominions. He set out with Colonel Gardiner and his daughter, on his road to Delhi, through Kāsganj, the residence of the colonel, who was one day recommending the prince to seek consolation for the loss of his pension in the proud recollection of having saved the honour of the *house of Tamerlane*, when news was brought to them that the daughter had run off from camp with his (Colonel Gardiner's) son James, who had accompanied him to Lucknow. The prince and the colonel mounted their horses, and rode after him; but they were so much heavier and older than the young ones, that they soon gave up the chase in despair. Sulaimān Shikoh insisted upon the colonel immediately fighting him, after the fashion of the English, with swords or pistols, but was soon persuaded that the honour of the house of Tīmūr would be much better preserved by allowing the offending parties to marry ![18] The King of Oudh was delighted to find that the old man had been so punished; and the Queen no less so to find herself so suddenly and unexpectedly relieved from all dread of her sister's return. All parties wrote to my friend Kām Baksh, who was then at Jubbulpore;[19] and he came off with their letters to me to ask whether I thought the incident might not be turned to account in getting the pension for his father restored.[20]

Notes:

1. Govardhan is a very sacred place of pilgrimage, full of temples, situated in the Mathurā (Muttra) district, sixteen miles west of Mathurā, Regulation V of 1826 annexed Govardhan to the Agra district. In 1832 Mathurā was made the head- quarters of a new district, Govardhan and other territory being transferred from Agra.

2. The Purānas, even when narrating history after a fashion, are cast in the form of prophecies. The Bhāgavat Purāna is especially devoted to the legends of Krishna. The Hindī version of the 10th Book (*skandha*) is known as the 'Prēm Sāgar', or 'Ocean of Love', and is, perhaps, the most wearisome book in the world.

3. This flight occurred during the struggles following the battle of Plassy in 1757, which were terminated by the battle of Buxar in 1764, and the grant to the East India Company of the civil administration of Bengal,

Bihār and Orissa in the following year. Shāh Ālam bore, in weakness and misery, the burden of the imperial title from 1759 to 1806. From 1765 to 1771 he was the dependent of the English at Allahabad. From 1771 to 1803 he was usually under the control of Marāthā chiefs, and from the time of Lord Lake's entry into Delhi, in 1803 he became simply a prisoner of the British Government. His successors occupied the same position. In 1788 he was barbarously blinded by the Rohilla chief, Ghulām Kādir.

4. Akbar II. His position as Emperor was purely titular.

5. The name is printed as Booalee Shina in the original edition. His full designation is Abū Alī al-Husain ibn Abdullah ibn Sīnā, which means 'that Sīnā was his grandfather. Avicenna is a corruption of either Abū Sīnā or Ibn Sīnā. He lived a strenuous, passionate life, but found time to compose about a hundred treatises on medicine and almost every subject known to Arabian science. He died in A.D. 1037. A good biography of him will be found in *Encyclo. Brit.*, 11th ed., 1910.

6. Otherwise called Eurasians, or, according to the latest official decree, Anglo-Indians.

7. 'Diplomatic characters' would now be described as officers of the Political Department.

8. These remarks of the author should help to dispel the common delusion that the English officials of the olden time spoke the Indian languages better than their more highly trained successors.

9. The author wrote these words at the moment of the inauguration by Lord William Bentinck and Macaulay of the new policy which established English as the official language of India, and the vehicle for the higher instruction of its people, as enunciated in the resolution dated 7th March, 1835, and described by Boulger in *Lord William Bentinck* (Rulers of India, 1897), chap. 8. The decision then formed and acted on alone rendered possible the employment of natives of India in the higher branches of the administration. Such employment has gradually year by year increased, and certainly will further increase, at least up to the extreme limit of safety. Indians now (1914) occupy seats in the Council of India in London, and in the Executive and Legislative Councils of the Governor- General, Provincial Governors, and Lieutenant-Governors. They hold most of the judicial appointments and fill many responsible executive offices.

10. Khojah Nasīr-ud-dīn of Tūs in Persia was a great astronomer, philosopher, and mathematician in the thirteenth century. The author's Imām-ud-dīn Ghazzālī is intended for Abū Hāmid Imām al Ghazzālī, one of the most famous of Musulmān doctors. He was born at Tūs, the modern Mashhad (Meshed) in Khurāsān, and died in A.D. 1111. His works are

numerous. One is entitled *The Ruin of Philosophies,* and another, the most celebrated, is *The Resuscitation of Religious Sciences* (F. J. Arbuthnot, *A Manual of Arabian History and Literature,* London, 1890). These authors are again referred to in a subsequent chapter. I am not able to judge the propriety of Sleeman's enthusiastic praise.

11. The gentleman referred to was Mr. John Wilton, who was appointed to the service in 1775.

12. The cantonments at Dinapore (properly Dānāpur) are ten miles distant from the great city of Patna.

13. The rupee was worth more than two shillings in 1810. The remuneration of high officials by commission has been long abolished.

14. There used to be two opium agents, one at Patna, and the other at Ghāzīpur, who administered the Opium Department under the control of the Board of Revenue in Calcutta. In deference to the demands of the Chinese Government and of public opinion in England, the Agency at Ghāzīpur has been closed, and the Government of India is withdrawing gradually from the opium trade. Such lucrative sinecures as those described in the text have long ceased to exist.

15. These Persian words would not now be used in orders to servants.

16. This officer was Sir Joseph O'Halloran, K.C.B., attached to the 18th Regiment, N.I. He became a Lieutenant-Colonel on June 4, 1814, and Major-General on January 10, 1837. He is mentioned in *Ramaseeana* (p 59) as Brigadier-General commanding the Sāgar Division.

17. The King's demand was improper and illegal. The Muhammadan law, like the Jewish (Leviticus xviii, 18), prohibits a man from being married to two sisters at once. 'Ye are also forbidden to take to wife two sisters; except what is already past: for God is gracious and merciful' (*Korān,* chap. iv). Compare the ruling in 'Mishkāt-ul-Masābih', Book XIII, chap. v, Part II (Matthews, vol. ii, p. 94).

18. The colonel's son has succeeded to his father's estates, and he and his wife are, I believe, very happy together. [W. H. S.] Such an incident would, of course, be now inconceivable. The family name is also spelled Gardner. The romantic history of the Gardners is summarized in the appendix to *A Particular Account of the European Military Adventures of Hindustan, from 1784 to 1803;* compiled by Herbert Compton: London, 1892.

19. *Ante,* Chapter 53 text between [2] and [3].

20. Kāsganj, the residence of Colonel Gardner, is in the Etah district of the United Provinces. In 1911 the population was 16,429.

CHAPTER 54

Fathpur-Sīkrī—The Emperor Akbar's Pilgrimage—Birth of Jahāngīr.

On the 6th January we left Agra, which soon after became the residence of the Governor of the North-Western Provinces, Sir Charles Metcalfe.[1] It was, when I was there, the residence of a civil commissioner, a judge, a magistrate, a collector of land revenue, a collector of customs, and all their assistants and establishments. A brigadier commands the station, which contained a park of artillery, one regiment of European and four regiments of native infantry.[2]

Near the artillery practice-ground, we passed the tomb of Jodh Bāī, the wife of the Emperor Akbar, and the mother of Jahāngīr. She was of Rājpūt caste, daughter of the Hindoo chief of Jodhpur, a very beautiful, and, it is said, a very amiable woman.[3] The Mogul Emperors, though Muhammadans, were then in the habit of taking their wives from among the Rājpūt princes of the country, with a view to secure their allegiance. The tomb itself is in ruins, having only part of the dome standing, and the walls and magnificent gateway that at one time surrounded it have been all taken away and sold by a thrifty Government, or appropriated to purposes of more practical utility.[4]

I have heard many Muhammadans say that they could trace the decline of their empire in Hindustan to the loss of the Rājpūt blood in the veins of their princes.[5] 'Better blood' than that of the Rājpūts of India certainly never flowed in the veins of any human beings; or, what is the same thing, no blood was ever believed to be finer by the people themselves and those they had to deal with. The difference is all in the imagination, and the imagination is all-powerful with nations as with individuals. The Britons thought their blood the finest in the world till they were conquered by the Romans, the Picts, the Scots, and the Saxons. The Saxons thought theirs the finest in the world till they were conquered by the Danes and the Normans. This is the history of the human race. The quality of the blood of a whole people has depended often upon the fate of a battle, which in the ancient world doomed the vanquished to the hammer; and the hammer changed the blood of those sold by it from generation to generation. How many

Norman robbers got their blood ennobled, and how many Saxon nobles got theirs plebeianized by the Battle of Hastings; and how difficult it would be for any of us to say from which we descended—the Britons or the Saxons, the Danes or the Normans; or in what particular action our ancestors were the victors or the vanquished, and became ennobled or plebeianized by the thousand accidents which influence the fate of battles. A series of successful aggressions upon their neighbours will commonly give a nation a notion that they are superior in courage; and pride will make them attribute this superiority to blood—that is, to an old date. This was, perhaps, never more exemplified than in the case of the Gūrkhas of Nepal, a small diminutive race of men not unlike the Huns, but certainly as brave as any men can possibly be. A Gūrkha thought himself equal to any four other men of the hills, though they were all much stronger; just as a Dane thought himself equal to four Saxons at one time in Britain. The other men of the hills began to think that he really was so, and could not stand before him.[6]

We passed many wells from which the people were watering their fields, and found those which yielded a brackish water were considered to be much more valuable for irrigation than those which yielded sweet water. It is the same in the valley of the Nerbudda, but brackish water does not suit some soils and some crops. On the 8th we reached Fathpur Sīkrī, which lies about twenty-four miles from Agra, and stands upon the back of a narrow range of sandstone hills, rising abruptly from the alluvial plains to the highest, about one hundred feet, and extends three miles north-north-east and south-south-west. This place owes its celebrity to a Muhammadan saint, the Shaikh Salīm of Chisht, a town in Persia, who owed his to the following circumstance:

The Emperor Akbar's sons had all died in infancy, and he made a pilgrimage to the shrine of the celebrated Muīn-ud-dīn of Chisht, at Ajmēr. He and his family went all the way on foot at the rate of three 'kōs', or four miles, a day, a distance of about three hundred and fifty miles. 'Kanāts', or cloth walls, were raised on each side of the road, carpets spread over it, and high towers of burnt bricks erected at every stage, to mark the places where he rested. On reaching the shrine he made a supplication to the saint, who at night appeared to him in his sleep, and recommended him to go and entreat the intercession of a very holy old man, who lived a secluded life upon the top of the little range of hills at Sīkrī. He went accordingly, and was assured by the old man, then ninety-six years of age, that the Empress Jodh Bāī, the daughter of a Hindoo prince, would be delivered of a son, who would live to a good old age. She was then pregnant, and remained in the vicinity of the old man's hermitage till her confinement, which took place 31st of August, 1569. The infant was called after the hermit, Mirzā Salīm, and became in

time Emperor of Hindostan, under the name of Jahāngīr.[7] It was to this Emperor Jahāngīr that Sir Thomas Roe, the ambassador, was sent from the English Court.[8] Akbar, in order to secure to himself, his family, and his people, the advantage of the continued intercessions of so holy a man, took up his residence at Sīkrī, and covered the hill with magnificent buildings for himself, his courtiers, and his public establishments.[9]

The quadrangle, which contains the mosque on the west side, and tomb of the old hermit in the centre, was completed in the year 1578, six years before his death; and is, perhaps, one of the finest in the world. It is five hundred and seventy-five feet square, and surrounded by a high wall, with a magnificent cloister all around within.[10] On the outside is a magnificent gateway, at the top of a noble flight of steps twenty-four feet high. The whole gateway is one hundred and twenty feet in height, and the same in breadth, and presents beyond the wall five sides of an octagon, of which the front face is eighty feet wide. The arch in the centre of this space is sixty feet high by forty wide.[11] This gateway is no doubt extremely grand and beautiful; but what strikes one most is the disproportion between the thing wanted and the thing provided—there seems to be something quite preposterous in forming so enormous an entrance for a poor diminutive man to walk through—and walk he must, unless carried through on men's shoulders; for neither elephant, horse, nor bullock could ascend over the flight of steps. In all these places the staircases, on the contrary, are as disproportionately small; they look as if they were made for rats to crawl through, while the gateways seem as if they were made for ships to sail under.[12] One of the most interesting sights was the immense swarms of swallows flying round the thick bed of nests that occupy the apex of this arch, and, to the spectators below, they look precisely like swarm of bees round a large honeycomb. I quoted a passage in the Korān in praise of the swallows, and asked the guardians of the place whether they did not think themselves happy in having such swarms of sacred birds over their heads all day long. 'Not at all,' said they; 'they oblige us to sweep the gateway ten times a day; but there is no getting at their nests, or we should soon get rid of them.' They then told me that the sacred bird of the Korān was the 'abābīl', or large black swallow, and not the 'partādīl', a little piebald thing of no religious merit whatever.[13] On the right side of the entrance is engraven on stone in large letters, standing out in bas-relief, the following passage in Arabic: 'Jesus, on whom be peace, has said, "The word is merely a bridge; you are to pass over it, and not to build your dwellings upon it".' Where this saying of Christ is to be found I know not, nor has any Mūhammadan yet been able to tell me; but the quoting of such a passage, in such a place, is a proof of the absence of all bigotry on the part of Akbar.[14]

The tomb of Shaikh Salīm, the hermit, is a very beautiful little building, in the centre of the quadrangle.[15] The man who guards it told me that the Jāts, while they reigned, robbed this tomb, as well as those at Agra, of some of the most beautiful and valuable portion of the mosaic work.[16] 'But,' said he, 'they were well plundered in their turn by your troops at Bharatpur; retribution always follows the wicked sooner or later.'[17] He showed us the little roof of stone tiles, close to the original little dingy mosque of the old hermit, where the Empress gave birth to Jahāngīr;[18] and told us that she was a very sensible woman, whose counsels had great weight with the Emperor.[19] 'His majesty's only fault was', he said, 'an inclination to learn the art of magic, which was taught him by an old Hindoo religious mendicant,' whose apartment near the palace he pointed out to us.

'Fortunately,' said our cicerone, 'the fellow died before the Emperor had learnt enough to practise the art without his aid.'

Shaikh Salīm had, he declared, gone more than twenty times on pilgrimage to the tomb of the holy prophet; and was not much pleased to have his repose so much disturbed by the noise and bustle of the imperial court. At last, Akbar wanted to surround the hill with regular fortifications, and the Shaikh could stand it no longer.[20] 'Either you or I must leave this hill,' said he to the Emperor; 'if the efficacy of my prayers is no longer to be relied upon, let me depart in peace.' 'If it be *your majesty's* will,' replied the Emperor, 'that one should go, let it be your slave, I pray.' The old story: 'There is nothing like relying upon the efficacy of our prayers,' say the priests, 'Nothing like relying upon that of our sharp swords,' say the soldiers; and, as nations advance from barbarism, they generally contrive to divide between them the surplus produce of the land and labour of society.

The old hermit consented to remain, and pointed out Agra as a place which he thought would answer the Emperor's purpose extremely well. Agra, then an unpeopled waste, soon became a city, and Fathpur- Sīkrī was deserted.[21] Cities which, like this, are maintained by the public establishments that attend and surround the courts of sovereign princes, must always, like this, become deserted when these sovereigns change their resting-places. To the history of the rise and progress, decline and fall, of how many cities is this the key?

Close to the tomb of the saint is another containing the remains of a great number of his descendants, who continue to enjoy, under the successors of Akbar, large grants of rent-free lands for their own support, and for that of the mosque and mausoleum. These grants have, by degrees, been nearly all resumed;[22] and, as the repair of the buildings is now entrusted to the public officers of our government, the surviving members of the saint's family, who still reside among the ruins, are extremely poor. What strikes a European most in going over these palaces of the Moghal Emperors is the want of what a gentleman of fortune in his own country would consider elegantly comfortable accommodations. Five hundred pounds a year would at the present day secure him more of this in any civilized country of Europe or America than the greatest of those Emperors could command. He would, perhaps, have the same impression in going over the domestic architecture of the most civilized nations of the ancient world, Persia and Egypt, Greece and Rome.[23]

Notes:

1. The Act of 1833 (3 & 4 William IV, c. 85), which reconstituted the government of India, provided that the upper Provinces should be formed into a separate Presidency under the name of Agra, and Sir Charles Metcalfe was nominated as the first Governor. On reconsideration, this arrangement was modified, and instead of the Presidency of Agra, the Lieutenant-Governorship of the North-Western Provinces was formed, with head-quarters at Agra. Sir C. Metcalfe became Lieutenant-Governor in 1836, but held the office for a short time only, until January, 1838, when Lord Auckland, the Governor-General, took over temporary charge. The seat of the Local Government was moved to Allahabad in 1868. From 1877 the Lieutenant-Governor of the North-Western Provinces was also Chief Commissioner of Oudh. The name North-Western Provinces, which had become unsuitable and misleading since the annexation of the Panjāb in 1849, could not be retained after the formation of the North-West Frontier Province in 1902. Accordingly, from that year the combined jurisdiction of the North-Western Provinces and Oudh received the new official name of the United Provinces of Agra and Oudh. The title of Chief Commissioner of Oudh was dropped at the same time, but the legal System and administration of the old kingdom of Oudh continued to be distinct in certain respects.

2. The civil establishment and garrison are still nearly the same as in the author's time. The inland customs department is now concerned only with the restrictions on the manufacture of salt. The offices of district magistrate and collector of land revenue have long been combined in a single officer.

3. Akbar married the daughter of Bihārī Mal, chief of Jaipur, in A.D. 1562. There is little doubt that she, *Mariam-uz- Zamānī*, was the mother of Jahāngīr. See Blochmann, transl. *Aīn*, vol. i, p. 619. Mr. Beveridge has given up the opinion which he formerly advocated in *J.A.S.B.*, vol. lvi (1887), Part I, pp. 164-7.

The Jodhpur princess was given the posthumous title of 'Mariam-uz-Zamānī', or 'Mary of the age', which circumstance probably originated the belief that Akbar had one Christian queen. Her tomb at Sikandara is locally known simply as Rauza Maryam, 'the mausoleum of Mary', a designation which has had much to do with the persistence of the erroneous belief in the existence of a Christian consort of Akbar. Mr. Beveridge holds, and I think rightly, that Jodh Bāī is not a proper name. It seems to mean merely 'princess of Jodhpur'. The only lady really known as Jodh Bāī was the daughter of Udai Singh (Mōth Rājā) of Jaipur, who became a consort of Jahāngīr. Sleeman's notion that Jahāngīr's mother also was called Jodh Bāī is mistaken (Blochmann, *ut supra*).

4. It was blown up about 1832 by order of the Government, and the materials of the gates, walls, and outer towns were used for the building of barracks. But the mausoleum itself resisted the spoiler and remained 'a huge shapeless heap of massive fragments of masonry'. The building consisted of a square room raised on a platform with a vault below. The marble tomb or cenotaph of the queen still exists in the vault. A fine gateway formerly stood at the entrance to the enclosure, and there was a small mosque to the west of the tomb (*A.S.R.* vol. iv. (1874), p. 121: Muh. Latif, *Agra*, p. 192). It is painful to be obliged to record so many instances of vandalism committed by English officials. This tomb is the memorial of Jodh Bāī, daughter of Udai Singh, *alias* Mōth Rājā, who was married to Jahāngīr in A.D. 1585, and was the mother of Shāh Jahān. Her personal names were Jagat Goshaini and Bālmatī. She died in A.D. 1619. Akbar's queen, Maryam- uz-Zamānī, daughter of Rājā Bihārī Mall of Jaipur (Ambēr), who died in A.D. 1623, is buried at Sīkandra. (See Beale, s.v. 'Jodh Bāī' and 'Mariam Zamānī'; Blochmann, transl. *Aīn*, pp. 429, 619.) The tomb of Maryam-uz- Zamānī has been purchased by Government from the missionaries, who had used it as a school, and has been restored. (*Ann. Rep. A.S., India*, 1910-11, pp. 92-6.)

5. Although it may be admitted that the Rājpūt strain of blood improved the constitution of the royal family of Delhi, the decline and fall of the Timuride dynasty cannot be truly ascribed to 'the loss of the Rājpūt blood in the veins' of the ruling princes. The empire was tottering to its fall long before the death of Aurangzēb, who 'had himself married two Hindoo wives; and he wedded his son Muazzam (afterwards the Emperor Bahādur) to a Hindoo princess, as his forefathers had done before him'. (Lane-Poole, *The History of the Moghul Emperors of Hindustan illustrated by their Coins*, p. xviii.) The wonder is, not that the empire of Delhi fell, but that it lasted so long.

6. When the author wrote the above remarks, Englishmen knew the gallant Gūrkhas as enemies only; they now know them as worthy and equal brethren in arms. The recruitment of Gūrkhas for the British service began in 1838. The spelling 'Gōrkhā' is more accurate.

7. The 'kōs' varies much in value, but in most parts of the United Provinces it is reckoned as equal to two miles. According to the *N.W.P. Gazetteer* (p. 568), the nearest approximate value for the Agra kōs is 1¾ mile. Three kōs would, therefore, be equal to about 5¼ miles. Muīn-ud- dīn died in A.D. 1236. Sleeman, on I know not what authority, represents Akbar as resorting to Salīm Chishtī, Shaikh of Fathpur- Sīkrī, on the advice given by a vision accorded at Ajmēr. The *Tabaqāt-i-Akbarī* simply records that Akbar had visited the Shaikh, the 'very holy old man' of Sleeman, several times, and had obtained the promise of a son. That promise was fulfilled by the birth of the princes Salīm and Murād, who both saw the light at Fathpur-Sīkrī. The pilgrimage of Akbar on foot to Ajmēr, which began on Friday, Shabān (8th month) 12, A.H. 977, took place *after* the birth of Prince Salīm, which occurred on the 18th of Rabī-ul-auwwal (3rd month) of the same Hijrī year. Akbar travelled at the rate of 7 or 8 *kōs* a day, and spent about 25 days on the journey (E. & D. v. 333, 334). If he had moved at the rate stated by Sleeman he would have been nearly three months on the road. He reached Ajmēr about the middle of February (N.S.). Shaikh Salīm Chishtī died in A.D. 1572 (A. H. 979) aged 96 lunar years.

8. Sir Thomas Roe was sent out by James I, and arrived at Jahāngīr's court in January, 1616. He remained there till 1618, and secured for his countrymen the privilege of trading at Surat. The best edition of his book is that by Mr. William Foster (Hakluyt Soc., 1899).

9. Fathpur-Sīkrī is fully described and illustrated in the late Mr. E. W. Smith's fine work in quarto entitled *The Moghul Architecture of Fathpur-Sīkrī* (4 Parts, Allahabad Govt. Press, 1894-8), which supersedes all other writings on the subject. The double name of the town means 'Fathpur at Sīkrī' according to a familiar Indian practice. The name Fathpur ('City of Victory') was bestowed in A.D. 1573 to commemorate the glorious campaign in Gujarāt, but building on the site had been begun in 1569. The historians usually call the town simply Fathpur, which name also is found on the coinage, from probably A.H. 977 (A.D. 1569-70). The mint was not in regular working order until eight years later (A.H. 985). Coins continued to be struck regularly at Fathpur until A.H. 989 (A.D. 1581-2). Akbar abandoned his costly foundation a little later. The only coin from the Fathpur mint of subsequent date is one of the first year of Shāhjahān (Wright, *Catalogue of Coins in Indian Museum, Mughal Emperors*, 1908, p. xlvii). But Rodgers believed in the genuineness of a zodiacal gold coin of Jahāngīr purporting to be struck at Fathpur (*J.A.S.B.*, vol. lvii (1888), Part I, p. 26).

10. Sleeman's dates and details require much correction. The mosque was completed at some time in the year A.H. 979 (May 26, 1571, to May 13, 1572, o.s.), excepting the Buland Darwāza, which was erected in A.H.

983 (1575-6). The 'old hermit', Shaikh Salīm, died on February 13, 1572 (Ramazān 27, A.H. 979). E. W. Smith (*op. cit.*, Part IV, p. 1) gives the correct measurements as follow: 'Exclusive of the bastions upon the angles it measures 542' from east to west to the outside of the *līwān* or sanctuary, or 515' 3" to the outside of the west main wall (which sets back from the outer wall of the līwān) and 438' from north to south. The general plan adopted by Muhammadans for their masjids has been followed. In the centre is a vast courtyard open to the heavens, measuring 359' 10" by 438' 9", surrounded on the north, south, and east sides by spacious cloisters 38' 3" in depth, and on the west by the līwān itself, 288' 2" in length by 65' deep. It is said to be copied from one at Makka [Mecca], and was erected according to a chronogram over the main arch in A.D. 1571, or at the same time as Rajah Bir Bal's house.' The 'six years before his death' of Sleeman's text should be 'six months' (Latif, *Agra*, p. 149).

11. The southern portal, known as the Buland Darwāza, or Lofty Gateway, does not match the other gateways. It was built in A.D. 1575-6 (A.H. 983), and was adorned in A.D. 1601-2 (A.H. 1010) with an inscription recording Akbar's triumphant return from his campaign in the Deccan. The date is fixed by a chronogram, preserved in Beale's work entitled *Miftāh-ul-tawārīkh* (*Ann. Progr. Rep. A. S. Northern Circle*, for 1905-6, p. 34, correcting E. W. Smith). Correct measurements are:

From roadway below to pavement	42 feet
From pavement to top of finial	134 "
Breadth across main front	130 "
Breadth across back facing the mosque	123 "
Depth	88½ "

Full details, with ample illustrations, are given by E. W. Smith, op. cit., Part IV, chap. ii. In the original edition of Sleeman a chromolithograph of the gateway is inserted. Photographs are reproduced in *H.F.A.*, Pl. xcvi, and Fergusson, *History of Indian and E. Archit.* (ed. 1910), fig. 425.

12. Fergusson (ed. 1910, vol. ii, p. 297) successfully justifies the vast size of the gateway. 'The semi-dome is the modulus of the design, and its scale that by which the imagination measures its magnificence.'

The cramped staircases criticized by Sleeman are those ascending from the pavement to the roof, one on the north-west, and the other on the north-east side of the gate. Each flight has 123 steep steps.

13. See the 105th chapter of the Korān. 'Hast thou not seen how thy Lord dealt with the masters of the elephant? Did he not make their treacherous

design an occasion of drawing them into error; and send against them flocks of *swallows* which cast down upon them stones of baked clay, and rendered them like the leaves of corn eaten by cattle?' [W. H. S.] The quotation is from Sale's translation, but Sale uses the word 'birds', and not '*swallows*'. In his note, where he tells the whole story, he speaks of 'a large flock of birds like swallows'. The Arabic, Persian, and Hindustānī dictionaries give no other word than 'abābīl' for swallow. The word 'partādīl' (purtadeel) occurs in none of them. According to Oates, *Fauna of British India* (London, 1890), the 'abābīl' is the common swallow, *Hirundo rustica*; and the 'mosque-swallow' ('masjid-abābīl'), otherwise called 'Sykes's striated swallow', is the *H. erythropygia, H. Daurica* of Balfour, *Cyclop. of India*, 3rd ed., s.v. Hirundinidae. This latter species is the 'little piebald thing' mentioned by the author.

14. Muh. Latif (Agra, pp. 146, 147) gives the text and English rendering of the inscription, which is in Persian, except the *logion* ascribed to Jesus, which is in Arabic. His translation of the Jesus saying is as follows:

'So said Jeans, on whom be peace! "The world is a bridge; pass over it, but build no house on it. He who reflected on the distresses of the Day of Judgement gained pleasure everlasting.

'"Worldly pleasures are but momentary; spend, then, thy life in devotion and remember that what remains of it is valueless".'

Like the author, I am unable to trace the source of the quotation. The inscription probably was recorded after Akbar's breach with Islam, which may be dated from 1579 or 1580. When he built the mosque, in 1571-5, he was still a devout Musalman, although entertaining liberal opinions. He died on October 25, 1605 (N.S.; October 15, O.S.)

15. For a full account of the exquisite sepulchre of Shaikh Salīm, see E. W. Smith, op. cit.. Part III, chap. ii. An inscription over the doorway is dated A.H. 979 = 1571-2, the year of the saint's death. The building, constructed regardless of expense, must be somewhat later. 'As originally built by Akbar, the tomb was of red sandstone, and the marble trellis-work, the chief ornament of the tomb, was erected subsequently by the Emperor Jahāngīr' (Latif, *Agra*, p. 144).

16. The first plundering of Akbar's tomb at Sikandra by the Jāts occurred in 1691 according to Manucci (*ante*, chapter 51, note 29.). The outrages at Fathpur-Sīkrī seem to have been later in date, and to have happened after the capture of Agra in 1761 by Sūraj Mall, the famous Rājā of Bhurtpore (Bharatpur). The Jāts retained possession of Agra until 1774 (*I.G.*, 1908, vol. viii, p. 76). That is the period while they reigned, to use the author's words. Tradition affirms that daring that time they shot away the tops of the minarets at the entrance to the Sikandra park; took the armour and books

of Akbar from his tomb, and sent them to Bharatpur, and also melted down two silver doors at the Tāj, which had cost Shāh Jahān more than 125,000 rupees (*N.W.P. Gazetteer*, 1st ed., vol. vii, p. 619)

17. We besieged and took Bharatpur in order to rescue the young prince, our ally, from his uncle, who had forcibly assumed the office of prime minister to his nephew. As soon as we got possession, all the property we found, belonging either to the nephew or the uncle, was declared to be prize-money, and taken for the troops. The young prince was obliged to borrow an elephant from the prize agents to ride upon. He has ever since enjoyed the whole of the revenue of his large territory. [W. H. S.] The final siege and capture of Bharatpur by Lord Combermere took place in January, 1826. The plundering, as Metcalfe observed, 'has been very disgraceful, and has tarnished our well-earned honours'. All the state treasures and jewels, amounting to forty-eight lākhs of rupees, or say half a million of pounds sterling, which should have been made over to the rightful Rājā, were treated as lawful prize, and at once distributed among the officers and men. Lord Combermere himself took six lākhs (Marshman, *History of India*, ed., 1869, vol. ii, p. 409).

18. The 'little dingy mosque' was built over the cave in which the saint dwelt, and was presented to him by the local quarry-men. It is therefore called The Stone-cutters' Mosque. It is fully described by E. W. Smith, op. cit., Part IV. chap. iii. It is earlier in date than any of Akbar's buildings, having been built in A. H. 945 (A.D. 1538-9), a year after the saint had settled in the 'dangerous jungle' (*Progr. Rep. A. S. N. Circle*, 1905-6, p. 35).

19. The people of India no doubt owed much of the good they enjoyed under the long reign of Akbar to this most excellent woman, who inspired not only her husband but the most able Muhammadan minister that India has ever had, with feelings of universal benevolence. It was from her that this great minister, Abūl Fazl, derived the spirit that dictated the following passages in his admirable work, the Aīn-i-Akbarī; 'Every sect becomes infatuated with its particular doctrines; animosity and dissension prevail, and each man deeming the tenets of his sect to be the dictates of truth itself, aims at the destruction of all others, vilifies reputation, stains the earth with blood, and has the vanity to imagine that he is performing meritorious actions. Were the voice of reason attended to, mankind would be sensible of their error, and lament the weaknesses which led them to interfere in the religious concerns of each other. Persecution, after all, defeats its own end; it obliges men to conceal their opinions, but produces no change in them.

'Summarily, the Hindoos are religious, affable, courteous to strangers, prone to inflict austerities on themselves, lovers of justice, given to retirement, able in business, grateful, admirers of truth, and of unbounded fidelity in all their dealings.

'This character shines brightest in adversity. Their soldiers know not what it is to fly from the field of battle; when the success of the combat becomes doubtful, they dismount from their horses, and throw away their lives in payment of the debt of valour. They have great respect for their tutors; and make no account of their lives when they can devote them to the service of their God.

'They consider the Supreme Being to be above all labour, and believe Brahmā to be the creator of the world, Vishnu its preserver, and Siva its destroyer. But one sect believes that God, who hath no equal, appeared on earth under the three above-mentioned forms, without having been thereby polluted in the smallest degree, in the same manner as the Christians speak of the Messiah; others hold that all these were only human beings, who, on account of their sanctity and righteousness, were raised to these high dignities.' [W. H. S.] The passage quoted is from Gladwin's translation, vol. ii, p. 318 (4th ed., London, 1800). The wording varies in different editions of Gladwin's work. A better version will be found in Jarrett, transl. Āīn (Calcutta, 1894), vol. iii, p. 8.

There is no substantial foundation for the author's statement that Abūl Fazl learned his charity and toleration from the Hindoo mother of Jahāngīr. The influences which really moulded the opinions of both Abūl Fazl and his royal master are well known. When Akbar and Abūl Fazl are compared with Elizabeth and Burleigh, Philip II and Alva, or the other sovereigns and ministers of the age in Europe, it seems to be little less than a miracle that the Indian statesmen should have held and practised the noble philosophy expounded in the above quotation from the 'Institutes of Akbar'. No man has deserved better than Akbar the stately eulogy pronounced by Wordsworth on a hero now obscure:

> A meteor wert thou in a darksome night;
>   Yet shall thy name, conspicuous and sublime,
>   Stand in the spacious firmament of time,
> Fixed as a star: such glory is thy right.
>   (*Sonnets dedicated to Liberty*, Part Second, No. XVII.)

20. The story is absurd, the saint having died early in 1572, when the Fathpur-Sīkrī buildings were in progress.

'The city . . . is enclosed on three sides by high embattlemented stone walls pierced by. . . gateways protected by heavy and grim semi- circular bastions of rubble masonry. The fourth side was protected by a large lake.' There were nine gateways (E. W. Smith, op. cit., pp. 1, 59; pl. xci, xciii). The Sangīn Burj, or Stone Tower, is a fine unfinished fortification (ibid.,

p. 34). The dam of the lake burst in the 27th year of the reign, A.D. 1582 (Latif, *Agra*, p. 159). The circumference of the town is variously stated as either six or seven miles.

21. Akbar began the works at the fort of Agra in A.H. 972, corresponding to A.D. 1564-65, several years before he began those at Fathpur in A.D. 1569-70 (E. & D., vol. v, pp. 295, 332); and the buildings at Agra and Fathpur were carried on concurrently. He continued building at Fathpur nearly to the close of his reign. Agra was never 'an unpeopled waste' during Akbar's reign. Sikandar Lodī had made it his capital in A.D. 1501.

22. That is to say, the grantees have now to pay land revenue, or rent, to the state.

23. No good general description of the buildings at Agra, Sikandra, and Fathpur-Sīkrī exists. The following list indicates the beat treatises available.

(1) Syad Muhammad Latif—*Agra, Historical and Descriptive., &c.*; 8vo, Calcutta, 1896, Useful, but crude and badly illustrated.

(2) E. W. Smith—*The Moghul Architecture of Fathpur- Sikri*; 4 Parts, 4to, Government Press, Allahabad, 1894-8.

(3) Same author—*Moghul Colour Decoration of Agra*; 4to, Government Press, Allahabad, 1901.

(4) Same author—*Akbar's Tomb, Sikandarah*; posthumous; 4to, Allahabad Government Press, 1909.

The three works by Mr. E. W. Smith are magnificently illustrated and worthy of the subject.

(5) Nūr Baksh—'The Agra Fort and its Buildings', in *A.S. Annual Report* for 1903-4, pp. 164-93.

(6) Moin-ud-din—*The History of the Taj, &c.*; thin 8vo, 116 pp.; Moon Press, Agra, 1905. Useful, as being the only book devoted to the Tāj and connected buildings, but crude and inadequate.

The Archaeological Survey of India, since its reorganization, has not had time to study the Tāj buildings, except for conservation purposes. The report by Mr. Carlleyle on the minor remains at and near Agra in *A.S.R.*, vol. iv, 1874, is almost worthless.

In 1873 Major Cole prepared a handsome volume entitled *Illustrations of Buildings near Muttra and Agra, &c.*

Some information, to be used with caution, is to be found in gazetteers of different dates.

The brief observations in Fergusson's *History of Indian and Eastern Architecture* (ed. 1910) are of permanent value. The plan of the editor's work, *A History of Fine Art in India and Ceylon* (H. F. A.), Oxford, 1911, does not permit of detailed descriptions. The well-known little Handbook by Mr. H. G. Keene contains many errors and is unworthy of the author's reputation as an historian.

A good guide-book, prepared with knowledge and accuracy, is badly wanted. It would be difficult to find an author possessed of the needful local knowledge and sufficiently well read to compile a satisfactory book. An adequate illustrated history of the Tāj buildings on the lines of Mr. E. W. Smith's work on Fathpur- Sīkrī is much to be desired, but would be a formidable undertaking, and is not likely to be written for a long time to come. Perhaps some wealthy admirer of Akbar and his achievements may appear and provide the considerable funds required for the preparation of the desired treatise. The Christian antiquities of Agra also deserve systematic treatment. At present the information on record is in a chaotic state.

CHAPTER 55

Bharatpur — Dīg — Want of employment for the Military and the Educated Classes under the Company's Rule.

Our old friends, Mr. Charles Fraser, the Commissioner of the Agra Division, then on his circuit, and Major Godby, had come on with us from Agra and made our party very agreeable. On the 9th, we went fourteen miles to Bharatpur, over a plain of alluvial, but seemingly poor, soil, intersected by one low range of sandstone hills running north-east and south-west. The thick belt of jungle, three miles wide, with which the chiefs of Bharatpur used to surround their fortress while they were freebooters, and always liable to be brought into collision with their neighbours, has been fast diminishing since the capture of the place by our troops in 1826; and will very soon disappear altogether, and give place to rich sheets of cultivation, and happy little village communities. Our tents had been pitched close outside the Mathurā gate, near a small grove of fruit- trees, which formed the left flank of the last attack on this fortress by Lord Combermere.[1] Major Godby had been present during the whole siege; and, as we went round the place in the evening on our elephants, he pointed out all the points of attack, and told all the anecdotes of the day that were interesting enough to be remembered for ten years. We went through the town, out at the opposite gate, and passed along the line of Lord Lake's attack in 1805.[2] All the points of his attack were also pointed out to us by our cicerone, an old officer in the service of the Rājā. It happened to be the anniversary of the first attempt to storm, which was made on the 9th of January, thirty-one years before. One old officer told us that he remembered Lord Lake sitting with three other gentlemen on chairs not more than half a mile from the ramparts of the fort.

The old man thought that the men of those days were quite a different sort of thing to the men of the present day, as well those who defended, as those who attacked the fort; and, if the truth must be told, he thought that the European lords and gentlemen had fallen off in the same scale as the rest.

'But', said the old man, 'all these things are matter of destiny and providence. Upon that very bastion (pointing to the right point of Lord

Lake's attack) stood a large twenty-four pounder, which was loaded and discharged three times by supernatural agency during one of your attacks—not a living soul was near it.' We all smiled, incredulous; and the old man offered to bring a score of witnesses to the fact, men of unquestionable veracity. The left point of Lord Lake's attack was the Baldēo bastion, so called alter Baldēo Singh, the second son of the then reigning chief, Ranjīt Singh. The feats which Hector performed in the defence of Troy sink into utter insignificance before those which Baldēo performed in the defence of Bharatpur, according to the best testimony of the survivors of that great day. 'But', said the old man, 'he was, of course, acting under supernatural influence; he condescended to measure swords only with Europeans'; and their bodies filled the whole bastion in which he stood, according to the belief of the people, though no European entered it, I believe, during the whole siege. They pointed out to us where the different corps were posted. There was one corps which had signalized itself a good deal, but of which I had never before heard, though all around me seemed extremely well acquainted with it—this was the *Antā Gurgurs*. At last Godby came to my side, and told me this was the name by which the Bombay troops were always known in Bengal, though no one seemed to know whence it came. I am disposed to think that they derive it from the peculiar form of the caps of their sepoys, which are in form like the common hookah, called a 'gurgurī', with a small ball at the top, like an 'antā', or tennis, or billiard ball; hence 'Antā Gurgurs'. The Bombay sepoys were, I am told, always very angry when they heard that they were known by this term—they have always behaved like good soldiers, and need not be ashamed of this or any other name.[3]

The water in the lake, about a mile to the west of Bharatpur, stands higher than the ground about the fortress; and a drain had been opened, through which the water rushed in and filled the ditch all round the fort and great part of the plain to the south and east, before Lord Lake undertook the siege in 1805.[4] This water might, I believe, have been taken off to the eastward into the Jumna, had the outlet been discovered by the engineers. An attempt was made to cut the same drain on the approach of Lord Combermere in 1826; but a party went on, and stopped the work before much water had passed, and the ditch was almost dry when the siege began.

The walls being all of mud, and now dismantled, had a wretched appearance;[5] and the town which is contained within them is, though very populous, a mere collection of wretched hovels; the only respectable habitation within is the palace, which consists of three detached buildings—one for the chief, another for the females of his family, and the third for his court of justice, I could not find a single trace of the European officers who had been killed there, either at the first or second siege, though I had been told that a small tomb had been built in a neighbouring grove over the remains of Brigadier-General Edwards, who fell in the last storm. It is, I believe, the only one that has ever been raised. The scenes of battles fought by the Muhammadan conquerors of India were commonly crowded with magnificent tombs, built over the slain, and provided for a time with the means of maintaining holy men who read the Korān over their graves. Not that this duty was necessary for the repose of their souls, for every Muhammadan killed in fighting against men who believed not in his prophet went, as a matter of course, to paradise; and every unbeliever, killed in the same action, went as surely to hell. There are only a few hundred men, exclusive of the prophets, who, according to Muhammad, have the first place in paradise—those who shared in one or other of his first three battles, and believed in his holy mission before they had the evidence of a single victory over the unbelievers to support it. At the head of these are the men who accompanied him in his flight from Mecca to Medina, when he had no evidence either from *victories* or *miracles*. In all such matters the less the evidence adduced in proof of a mission the greater the merit of those who believe in it, according to the person who pretends to it; and unhappily, the less the evidence a man has for his faith, the greater is his anger against other men for not joining in it with him. No man gets very angry with another for not joining with him in his faith in the demonstration of a problem in mathematics. Man likes to think that he is on the way to heaven upon such easy terms; but gets angry at the notion that others won't join him, because they may consider him an imbecile for thinking that he is so. The Muhammadan generals and historians are sometimes almost as concise as Caesar himself in describing very conscientiously a battle of this kind; instead of 'I came, I saw, I conquered', it is 'Ten thousand Musālmāns on that day tasted of the blessed fruit of paradise, after sending fifty thousand unbelievers to the flames of hell'.

On the 10th we came on twelve miles to Kumbhīr, over a plain of poor soil, much impregnated with salt, and with some works in which salt is made, with solar evaporation. The earth is dug up, water is filtered through it, and drawn off into small square beds, where it is evaporated by exposure to the solar heat. The gate of this fort leading out to the road we came is called, modestly enough, after Kumbhīr, a place only ten miles distant; that leading to Mathurā, three or four stages distant, is called the Mathurā gate. At Delhi, the gates of the city walls are called ostentatiously after distant places—the *Kashmīr*, the *Kābul*, the *Constantinople* gates. Outside the Kumbhīr gate, I saw, for the first time in my life, the well peculiar to Upper India. It is built up in the form of a round tower or cylindrical shell of burnt bricks, well cemented with good mortar, and covered inside and out with good stucco work, and let down by degrees, as the earth is removed by men at work in digging under the light earthy or sandy foundation inside and out. This well is about twenty feet below and twenty feet above the surface, and had to be built higher as it was let into the ground.[6]

On the 11th we came on twelve miles to Dīg (Deeg), over a plain of poor and badly cultivated soil, which must be almost all under water in the rains. This was, and still is, the country seat of the Jāts of Bharatpur, who rose, as I have already stated, to wealth and power by aggressions upon their immediate neighbours, and the plunder of tribute on its way to the imperial capital, and of the baggage of passing armies during the contests for dominion that followed the death of the Emperors, and during the decline and fall of the empire. The Jāts found the morasses with which they were surrounded here a source of strength. They emigrated from the banks of the Indus about Multān, and took up their abode by degrees on the banks of the Jumna, and those of the Chambal, from their confluence upwards, where they became cultivators and robbers upon a small scale, till they had the means to build garrisons, when they entered the lists with princes, who were only robbers upon a large scale. The Jāts, like the Marāthās, rose, by a feeling of nationality, among a people who had none. Single landholders were every day rising to principalities by means of their gangs of robbers; but they could seldom be cemented under one common head by a bond of national feeling.

They have a noble quadrangular garden at Dīg, surrounded by a high wall. In the centre of each of the four faces is one of the most beautiful Hindoo buildings for accommodation that I have ever seen, formed of a very fine sandstone brought from the quarries of Rūpbās, which he between thirty and forty miles to the south, and eight or ten miles west of Fathpur-Sīkrī. These stones are brought in in flags some sixteen feet long, from two to three feet wide, and one thick, with sides as flat as glass, the flags being of the natural thickness of the strata. The garden is four hundred and seventy-five feet long, by three hundred and fifty feet wide; and in the centre is an octagonal pond, with openings on the four sides leading up to the four buildings, each opening having, from the centre of the pond to the foot of the flight of steps leading into them, an avenue of *jets d'eau*.

Dīg as much surpassed, as Bharatpur fell short of, my expectations. I had seen nothing in India of architectural beauty to be compared with the buildings in this garden, except at Agra. The useful and the elegant are here everywhere happily blended; nothing seems disproportionate, or unsuitable to the purpose for which it was designed; and all that one regrets is that so beautiful a garden should be situated in so vile a swamp.[7] There was a general complaint among the people of the town of a want of 'rozgār' (employment), and its fruit, subsistence; the taking of Bharatpur had, they said, produced a sad change among them for the worse. Godby observed to some of the respectable men about us, who complained of this, that happily their chief had now no enemy to employ them against. 'But what', said they, 'is a prince without an army? and why do you keep up yours now that all your enemies have been subdued?' 'We want them', replied Godby, 'to prevent our friends from cutting each other's throats, and to defend them all against a foreign enemy.' 'True,' said they, 'but what are we to do who have nothing but our swords to depend upon, now that our chief no longer wants us, and you won't take us?' 'And what,' said some shopkeepers, 'are we to do who provided these troops with clothes, food, and furniture, which they can no longer afford to pay for?' *Company ke amal men kuchh rozgār nahīn* ('Under the Company's dominion there is no employment'). This is too true; we do the soldiers' work with one-tenth of the soldiers that had before been employed in it over the territories we acquire, and turn the other nine-tenths adrift. They all sink into the lowest class of religions mendicants, or retainers; or live among their friends as drones upon the land; while the manufacturing, trading, and commercial industry that provided them with the comforts, conveniences, and elegancies of life while they were in a higher grade of service is in its turn thrown out of employment; and the whole frame of society becomes, for a time, deranged by the local diminution in the demand *for the services of men and the produce of their industry.*

I say we do the soldiers' work with one-tenth of the numbers that were formerly required for it. I will mention an anecdote to illustrate this. In the year 1816 I was marching with my regiment from the Nepāl frontier, after the war, to Allahabad. We encamped about four miles from a mud fort in the kingdom of Oudh, and heard the guns of the Amil, or chief of the district, playing all day upon this fort, from which his batteries were removed at least two miles. He had three regiments of infantry, a corps or two of cavalry, and a good park of artillery; while the garrison consisted of only about two hundred stout Rājpūt landholders and cultivators, or yeomen. In the evening, just as we had sat down to dinner, a messenger came to the commanding officer, Colonel Gregory, who was a member of the mess, from the said Amil, and begged permission to deliver his message in private. I, as the senior staff officer, was requested to hear what he had to say.

'What do you require from the commanding officer?'

'I require the loan of the regiment.'

'I know the commanding officer will not let you have the regiment.'

'If the Amil cannot get more, he will be glad to get two companies; and I have brought with me this bag of gold, containing some two or three hundred gold mohurs.'

I delivered the message to Colonel Gregory, before all the officers, who desired me to say that he could not spare a single man, as he had no authority to assist the Amil, and was merely marching through the country to his destination, I did so. The man urged me to beg the commanding officer, if he could do no more, merely to halt the next day where he was, and lend the Amil the use of one of his drummers.

'And what will you do with him?'

'Why, just before daylight, we will take him down near one of the gates of the fort, and make him beat his drum as hard as he can; and the people within, thinking the whole regiment is upon them, will make out as fast as possible at the opposite gate.'

'And the bag of gold — what is to become of that?'

'You and the old gentleman can divide it between you, and I will double it for you, if you like.'

I delivered the message before all the officers to their great amusement; and the poor man was obliged to carry back his bag of gold to the Amil. The Amil is the collector of revenues in Oudh, and he is armed with all the powers of government, and has generally several regiments and a train of artillery with him.

The large landholders build these mud forts, which they defend by their Rājpūt cultivators, who are among the bravest men in the world. One hundred of them would never hesitate to attack a thousand of the king's regular troops, because they know the Amil would be ashamed to have any noise made about it at court; but they know also that, if they were to beat one hundred of the Company's troops, they would soon have a thousand upon them; and, if they were to beat one thousand, they would soon have ten. They provide for the maintenance of those who are wounded in their fight, and for the widows and orphans of those who are killed. Their prince provides for neither, and his soldiers are, consequently, somewhat chary of fighting. It is from this peasantry, the military cultivators of Oudh, that our Bengal native infantry draws three out of four of its recruits, and finer young men for soldiers can hardly anywhere be found.[8]

The advantage which arises to society from doing the soldiers' duty with a smaller number has never been sufficiently appreciated in India; but it will become every day more manifest, as our dominion becomes more and more stable — for men who have lived by the sword do not in India like to live by anything else, or to see their children anything but soldiers. Under the former government men brought their own arms and horses to the service, and took them away with them again when discharged. The supply always greatly exceeded the demand for soldiers, both in the cavalry and the infantry, and a very great portion of the men armed and accoutred as soldiers were always without service, roaming over the country in search of it. To such men the profession next in rank after that of the soldier robbing in the service of the sovereign was that of the robber plundering on his own account. '*Materia munificentiae per bella et raptus. Nec arare terram, aut expectare annum, tam facile persuaseris, quam vocare hostes et vulnera mereri; pigrum quinimmo et iners videtur sudore acquirere, quod possis sanguine parare.*' 'War and rapine supply the prince with the means of his munificence. You cannot persuade the German to cultivate the fields and wait patiently for the harvest so easily as you can to challenge the enemy, and expose himself to honourable wounds. They hold it to be base and dishonourable to earn by the sweat of their brow what they might acquire by their blood.'[9]

The equestrian robber had his horse, and was called 'ghurāsī', horse-robber, a term which he never thought disgraceful. The foot-robber under the native government stood in the same relation to the horse-robber as the foot-soldier to the horse- soldier, because the trooper furnished his own horses, arms, and accoutrements, and considered himself a man of rank and wealth compared with the foot-soldier; both, however, had the wherewithal to rob the traveller on the highway; and, in the intervals between wars, the high roads were covered with them. There was a time in England, it is said, when the supply of clergymen was so great compared with the demand for them, from the undue stimulus given to clerical education, that it was not thought disgraceful for them to take to robbing on the highway; and all the high roads were, in consequence, infested by them.[10] How much more likely is a soldier to consider himself justified in this pursuit, and to be held so by the feelings of society in general, when he seeks in vain for regular service under his sovereign and his viceroys.

The individual soldiers not only armed, accoutred, and mounted themselves, but they generally ranged themselves under leaders, and formed well-organized bands for any purpose of war or plunder. They followed the fortunes of such leaders whether in service or out of it; and, when dismissed from that of their sovereign, they assisted them in robbing on the highway, or in pillaging the country till the sovereign was compelled to take them back, or give them estates in rent-free tenure for their maintenance and that of their followers.

All this is reversed under our government. We do the soldiers' work much better than it was ever before done with one- tenth—nay, I may say, one-fiftieth—part of the numbers that were employed to do it by our predecessors; and the whole number of the soldiers employed by us is not equal to that of those who were under them actually in the transition state, or on their way from the place where they had lost service to the place where they hoped to find it; extorting the means of subsistence either by intimidation or by open violence. Those who are in this transition state under us are neither armed, accoutred, nor mounted; we do not disband en masse, we only dismiss individuals for offences, and they have no leaders to range themselves under. Those who come to seek our service are the sons of yeomen, bred up from their infancy with all those feelings of deference for superiors which we require in soldiers. They have neither arms, horses, nor accoutrements; and, when they leave us permanently or temporarily, they take none with them—they never rob or steal—they will often dispute with the shopkeepers on the road about the price of provisions, or get a man to carry their bundles gratis for a few miles, but this is the utmost of their transgressions, and for these things they are often severely handled by our police.

It is extremely gratifying to an Englishman to hear the general testimony borne by all classes of people to the merits of our rule in this respect; they all say that no former government ever devoted so much attention to the formation of good roads and to the protection of those who travel on them; and much of the security arises from the change I have here remarked in the character and number of our military establishments. It is equally gratifying to reflect that the advantages must go on increasing, as those who have been thrown out of employment in the army find other occupations for themselves and their children; for find them they must or turn mendicants, if India should be blessed with a long interval of peace. All soldiers under us who have served the government faithfully for a certain number of years, are, when no longer fit for the active duties of their profession, sent back with the means of subsistence in honourable retirement for the rest of their lives among their families and friends, where they form, as it were, fountains of good feeling towards the government they have served. Under former governments, a trooper was discharged as soon as his horse got disabled, and a foot- soldier as soon as he got disabled himself—no matter how—whether in the service of the prince, or otherwise; no matter how long they had served, whether they were still fit for any other service or not. Like the old soldier in *Gil Blas*, they tumed robbers on the highway, where they could still present a spear or a matchlock at a traveller, though no longer deemed worthy to serve in the ranks of the army. Nothing tended so much to the civilization of Europe as the substitution of standing armies for militia; and nothing has tended so much to the improvement of India under our rule.

The troops to which our standing armies in India succeeded were much the same in character as those licentious bodies to which the standing armies of the different nations of Europe succeeded; and the result has been, and will, I hope, continue to be the same, highly beneficial to the great mass of the people.

By a statute of Elizabeth it was made a capital offence, felony without benefit of clergy, for soldiers or sailors to beg on the high roads without a pass; and I suppose this statute arose from their frequently robbing on the highways in the character of beggars.[11] There must at that time have been an immense number of soldiers in the transition state in England; men who disdained the labours of peaceful life, or had by long habit become unfitted for them. Religions mendicity has hitherto been the great safety valve through which the unquiet transition spirit has found vent under our strong and settled government. A Hindoo of any caste may become a religious mendicant of the two great monastic orders – of Gosāins, who are disciples of Siva, and Bairāgīs, who are disciples of Vishnu; and any Muhammadan may become a Fakīr; and Gosāins, Bairāgīs, and Fakīrs, can always secure, or extort, food from the communities they visit.[12]

Still, however, there is enough of this unquiet transition spirit left to give anxiety to a settled government; for the moment insurrection breaks out at any point, from whatever cause, to that point thousands are found flocking from north, east, west, and south, with their arms and their horses, if they happen to have any, in the hope of finding service either under the local authorities or the insurgents themselves; as the troubled winds of heaven rush to the point where the pressure of the atmosphere has been diminished.[13]

Notes:

1. On the sieges of Bharatpur see *ante*, chapter 17, note 9.

2. In the original edition the year is misprinted 1804, though the correct date is indicated by the phrase 'thirty-one years before'. The operations on January 9, 1805, are described in considerable detail in Thornton's history, and Pearse, *The Life and Military Services of Viscount Lake* (Blackwood, 1908). Dīg was taken on December 24, 1804, and Lord Lake's army moved from Mathurā towards Bharatpur on January 1, 1805.

3. The Bombay column joined Lord Lake on February 11, and took part in the third and fourth assaults on the fortress.

4. As in the previous passage, this date is printed 1804 in the original edition.

5. They have been repaired to some extent, and the town has improved much since the author's time.

6. That is to say, the well-cylinder is gradually sunk by its own weight, aided, if necessary, by heavy additional weights piled upon it. The sinking often takes many months, and is continued till a suitable resting-place is found. The cylinder is built on a strong ring of timber. Indian bridge-piers commonly rest on wells of this kind. The ring is sometimes made of iron. Such a method of sinking is possible only in deep alluvium, free from rock, and consequently had not been seen in the Sāgar and Nerbudda territories.

7. In the original edition Dīg is illustrated by four coloured plates. The buildings are all the work of Sūraj Mal, the virtual founder of the Bharatpur dynasty, between A.D. 1725 and 1763. The palace wants, say Fergusson, 'the massive character of the fortified palaces of other Rājpūt states, but for grandeur of conception and beauty of detail it surpasses them all. . . . The greatest defect of the palace is that the style, when it was erected, was losing its true form of lithic propriety. The forms of its pillars and their ornaments are better suited for wood or metal than for stone architecture.' It is a 'fairy creation'. (*History of Indian and Eastern Architecture*, ed. 1910, vol. ii, pp. 178-81.)

8. On these topics see the 'Journey through the Kingdom of Oude', *passim*. The composition of the Bengal army has been much changed.

9. The quotation is from the end of chapter 14 of the *Germania* of Tacitus.

10. This picture of English roads infested by clergymen turned highwaymen is not to be found in the ordinary histories.

11. The Act alluded to probably is 14 Elizabeth, c. 5. Other Acts of the same reign dealing with vagrancy and the first poor-law are 39 Elizabeth, c. 3, and 43 Elizabeth, c. 2 (A.D. 1601). In 1595 vagrancy had assumed such alarming proportions in London that a provost- marshal was appointed to give the wanderers the short shrift of martial law. The course of legislation on the subject is summarized in the article 'Poor Laws' in Chambers's *Encyclopaedia* (1904), and the articles 'Poor-Law and Vagrancy' in the *Encyclopaedia Britannica*, 11th ed., 1910. See also the chapter entitled 'The England of Elizabeth' in Green's History of the English People.

12. As already observed, chapter 29, note 12, the term Gosāin is by no means restricted to the special devotees of Siva; many Gosāins—for example, those in Bengal and those at Gokul in the Mathurā district—are followers of Vishnu. The term 'fakīr' is vaguely used, and often applied to Hindoos.

13. Even still, something of this unquiet spirit hovers about India, and the incompatibility between the ideas of twentieth-century Englishmen and those of Indian peoples whose mental attitude approaches that of Europeans of the twelfth century is a perennial source of unrest.

CHAPTER 56

Govardhan, the Scene of Krishna's Dalliance with the Milkmaids.

On the 10th[1] we came on ten miles over a plain to Govardhan, a place celebrated in ancient history as the birthplace of Krishna, the seventh incarnation of the Hindoo god of preservation, Vishnu, and the scene of his dalliance with the milkmaids (*gōpīs*); and, in modern days, as the burial — or burning-place of the Jāt chiefs of Bharatpur and Dīg, by whose tombs, with their endowments, this once favourite abode of the god is prevented from being entirely deserted.[2] The town stands upon a narrow ridge of sandstone hills, about ten miles long, rising suddenly out of an alluvial plain and running north-east and south-west. The population is now very small, and composed chiefly of Brahmans, who are supported by the endowments of these tombs, and the contributions of a few pilgrims. All our Hindoo followers were much gratified as we happened to arrive on a day of peculiar sanctity; and they were enabled to bathe and perform their devotions to the different shrines with the prospect of great advantage. This range of hills is believed by Hindoos to be part of a fragment of the Himālaya mountains which Hanumān, the monkey general of Rāma, the sixth incarnation of Vishnu, was taking down to aid his master in the formation of his bridge from the continent to the island of Ceylon, when engaged in the war with the demon king of that island for the recovery of his wife Sītā. He made a false step by some accident in passing Govardhan, and this small bit of his load fell off. The rocks begged either to be taken on to the god Rāma, or back to their old place; but Hanumān was hard pressed for time, and told them not to be uneasy, as they would have a comfortable resting-place, and be worshipped by millions in future ages — thus, according to popular belief, foretelling that it would become the residence of a future incarnation, and the scene of Krishna's miracles. The range was then about twenty miles long, ten having since disappeared under the ground. It was of full length during Krishna's days; and, on one occasion, he took up the whole upon his little finger to defend his favourite town and its milkmaids from the wrath of Indra, who got angry with the people, and poured down upon them a shower of burning ashes.

As I rode along this range, which rises gently from the plains at both ends and abruptly from the sides, with my groom by my side, I asked him what made Hanumān drop all his burthen here.

'*All* his burthen!' exclaimed he with a smile; 'had it been all, would it not have been an immense mountain, with all its towns and villages? while this is but an insignificant belt of rock. A mountain upon the back of men of former days, sir, was no more than a bundle of grass upon the back of one of your grass-cutters in the present day.'

Nathū, whose mind had been full of the wonders of this place from his infancy, happened to be with us, and he now chimed in.

'It was night when Hanumān passed this place, and the lamps were seen burning in a hundred towns upon the mountain he had upon his back—the people were all at their usual occupations, quite undisturbed; this is a mere fragment of his great burthen.'

'And how was it that the men of those towns should have been so much smaller than the men who carried them?' 'God only knew; but the fact of the men of the plains having been so large was undisputed—their beards were as many miles long as those of the present day are inches. Did not Bhīm throw the forty-cubit stone pillar, that now stands at Eran,[3] a distance of thirty miles, after the man who was running away with his cattle?'

I thought of poor Father Gregory at Agra, and the heavy sigh he gave when asked by Godby what progress he was making among the people in the way of conversion.[4] The faith of these people is certainly larger than all the mustard-seeds in the world.

I told a very opulent and respectable Hindoo banker one day that it seemed to us very strange that Vishnu should come upon the earth merely to sport with milkmaids, and to hold up an umbrella, however large, to defend them from a shower. 'The earth, sir,' said he, 'was at that time infested with innumerable demons and giants, who swallowed up men and women as bears swallow white ants; and his highness, Krishna, came down to destroy them. His own mother's brother, Kans, who then reigned at Mathurā over Govardhan, was one of these horrible demons. Hearing that his sister would give birth to a son that was to destroy him, he put to death several of her progeny as soon as they were born.[5] When Krishna was seven days old, he sent a nurse, with poison on her nipple, to destroy him likewise; but his highness gave such a pull at it, that the nurse dropped down dead. In falling, she resumed her real shape of a she- demon, and her body covered no less than six square miles, and it took several thousand men to cut her up and burn her, to prevent the pestilence that must have followed. His uncle then sent a crane, which caught up his highness, who always looked very small for his age, and swallowed him as he would swallow a frog. But his highness kicked up such a rumpus in the bird's stomach that he was immediately thrown up again. When he was seven years old his uncle invited him to a feast, and got the largest and most ferocious elephant in India to tread him to death as he alighted at the door. His highness, though then not higher than my waist, took the enormous beast by one tusk, and, after whirling him round in the air with one hand half a dozen times, he dashed him on the ground and killed him.[6] Unable any longer to stand the wickedness of his uncle, he seized him by the beard, dragged him from his throne, and dashed him to the ground in the same manner.'

I thought of poor old Father Gregory and the mustard-seeds again, and told my rich old friend that it all appeared to us indeed passing strange.

The orthodox belief among the Muhammadans is that Moses was sixty yards high; that he carried a mace sixty yards long; and that he sprang sixty yards from the ground when he aimed the fatal blow at the giant Ūj, the son of Anak, who came from the land of Canaan, with a mountain on his back, to crush the army of Israelites. Still, the head of his mace could reach only to the ankle-bone of the giant. This was broken with the blow. The giant fell, and was crushed under the weight of his own mountain. Now a person whose ankle-bone was one hundred and eighty yards high must have been almost as prodigious as he who carried the fragment of the Himālaya upon his back; and he who believes in the one cannot fairly find fault with his neighbour for believing in the other.[7] I was one day talking with a very sensible and respectable Hindoo gentleman of Bundēlkhand about the accident which made Hanumān drop this fragment of his load at Govardhan. 'All doubts upon that point,' said the old gentleman, 'have been put at rest by holy writ. It is related in our scriptures.

'Bharat, the brother of Rāma, was left regent of the kingdom of Ajodhya,[8] during his absence at the conquest of Ceylon. He happened at night to see Hanumān passing with the mountain upon his back, and thinking he might be one of the king of Ceylon's demons about mischief, he let fly one of his blunt arrows at him. It hit him on the leg, and he fell, mountain and all, to the ground. As he fell, he called out in his agony, 'Rām, Rām', from which Bharat discovered his mistake. He went up, raised him in his arms, and with his kind attentions restored him to his senses. Learning from him the object of his journey, and fearing that his wounded brother Lachhman would die before he could get to Ceylon with the requisite remedy, he offered to send Hanumān on upon the barb of one of his arrows, mountain and all. To try him Hanumān took up his mountain and seated himself with it upon the barb of the arrow as desired. Bharat placed the arrow to the string of his bow, and drawing it till the barb touched the bow, asked Hanumān whether he was ready. 'Quite ready,' said Hanumān, 'but I am now satisfied that you really are the brother of our prince, and regent of his kingdom, which was all I desired. Pray let me descend; and be sure that I shall be at Ceylon in time to save your wounded brother.' He got off, knelt down, placed his forehead on Bharat's feet in submission, resumed his load, and was at Ceylon by the time the day broke next morning, leaving behind him the small and insignificant fragment, on which the town and temples of Govardhan now stand.

'While little Krishna was frisking about among the milkmaids of Govardhan,' continued my old friend, 'stealing their milk, cream, and butter, Brahmā, the creator of the universe, who had heard of his being an incarnation of Vishnu, the great preserver of the universe, visited the place, and had some misgivings, from his size and employment, as to his real character. To try him, he took off through the sky a herd of cattle, on which some of his favourite playmates were attending, old and young, boys and all. Krishna, knowing how much the parents of the boys and owners of the cattle would be distressed, created, in a moment, another herd and other attendants so exactly like those that Brahmā had taken, that the owners of the one, and the parents of the other, remained ignorant of the change. Even the new creations themselves remained equally ignorant; and the cattle walked into their stalls, and the boys into their houses, where they recognized and were recognized by their parents, as if nothing had happened.

'Brahmā was now satisfied that Krishna was a true incarnation of Vishnu, and restored to him the real herd and attendants. The others were removed out of the way by Krishna, as soon as he saw the real ones coming back.'

'But,' said I to the good old man, who told me this with a grave face, 'must they not have suffered in passing from the life given to death; and why create them merely to destroy them again?'

'Was he not God the Creator himself?' said the old man; 'does he not send one generation into the world after another to fulfil their destiny, and then to return to the earth from which they came, just as he spreads over the land the grass and corn? All is gathered in its season, or withers as that passes away and dies.' The old gentleman might have quoted Wordsworth:

> We die, my friend,
> Nor we alone, but that which each man loved
> And prized in his peculiar nook of earth
> Dies with him, or is changed; and very soon,
> Even of the good is no memorial left.[9]

I was one day out shooting with my friend, the Rājā of Maihar,[10] under the Vindhya range, which rises five or six hundred feet, almost perpendicularly. He was an excellent shot with an English double-barrel, and had with him six men just as good. I asked him whether we were likely to fall in with any hares, using the term 'khargosh', or 'ass-eared'.

'Certainly not,' said the Rājā, 'if you begin by abusing them with such a name; call them "lambkanās", sir, "long-eared", and we shall get plenty.'

He shot one, and attributed my bad luck to the opprobrious name I had used. While he was reloading, I took occasion to ask him how this range of hills had grown up where it was.

'No one can say,' replied the Rājā, 'but we believe that when Rāma went to recover his wife Sītā from the demon king of Ceylon, Rāvan, he wanted to throw a bridge across from the continent to the island, and sent some of his followers up to the Himālaya mountains for stones. He had completed his bridge before they all returned, and a messenger was sent to tell those who had not yet come to throw down their burdens, and rejoin him in all haste. Two long lines of these people had got thus far on their return when the messenger met them. They threw down their loads here, and here they have remained ever since, one forming the Vindhya range to the north of this valley, and the other the Kaimūr range to the south.'

The Vindhya range extends from Mirzapore, on the Ganges, nearly to the Gulf of Cambay, some six or seven hundred miles, so that my sporting friend's faith was as capacious as any priest could well wish it; and those who have it are likely never to die, or suffer much, from an over stretch of the reasoning faculties in a hot climate.

The town stands upon the belt of rocks, about two miles from its north-eastern extremity; and in the midst is the handsome tomb of Ranjit Singh, who defended Bharatpur so bravely against Lord Lake's army.[11] The tomb has on one side a tank filled with water, and, on the other, another much deeper than the first, but without any water at all. We were surprised at this, and asked what the cause could be. The people told us, with the air of men who had never known what it was to feel the uneasy sensation of doubt, that 'Krishna, one hot day, after skying with the milkmaids, had drunk it all dry; and that no water would ever stay in it, lest it might be quaffed by less noble lips'. No orthodox Hindoo would ever for a moment doubt that this was the real cause of the phenomenon. Happy people! How much do they escape of that pain which in hot climates wears us all down in our efforts to trace moral and physical phenomena to their real causes and sources! Mind! mind! mind! without any of it, those Europeans who eat and drink moderately might get on very well in this climate. Much of it weighs them down.

Oh, sir, the good die first, and those whose hearts (*brains*)
Are dry as summer dust burn to the socket.[12]

One is apt sometimes to think that Muhammad, Manu, and Confucius would have been great benefactors in saving so many millions of their species from the pain of thinking too much in hot climates, if they had only written their books in languages less difficult of acquirement. Their works are at once 'the bane and antidote' of despotism—the source whence it comes, and the shield which defends the people from its consuming fire.

The tomb of Sūraj Mall, the great founder of the Jāt power at Bharatpur, stands on the north-east extremity of this belt of rocks, about two miles from the town, and is an extremely handsome building, conceived in the very best taste, and executed in the very best style.[13] With its appendages of temples and smaller tombs, it occupies the whole of one side of a magnificent tank full of clear water; and on the other side it looks into a large and beautiful garden. All the buildings and pavements are formed of the fine white sandstone of Rūpbās, scarcely inferior either in quality or appearance to white marble. The stone is carved in relief with flowers in good taste. In the centre of the tomb is the small marble slab covering the grave, with the two feet of Krishna carved in the centre, and around them the emblems of the god, the discus, the skull, the sword, the rosary. These emblems of the god are put on that people may have something godly to fix their thoughts upon. It is by degrees, and with fear and trembling, that the Hindoos imitate the Muhammadans in the magnificence of their tombs. The object is ostensibly to keep the ground on which the bodies have been burned from being defiled; and generally Hindoos have been content to raise small open terraces of brick and stucco work over the spot, with some image or emblem of the god upon it. The Jāts here, like the princes and Gosāins in Bundēlkhand, have gone a stage beyond this, and raised tombs equal in costliness and beauty to those over Muhammadans of the highest rank; still they do not venture to leave it without a divine image or emblem, lest the gods might become jealous, and revenge themselves upon the souls of the deceased and the bodies of the living. On one side of Sūraj Mall's tomb is that of his wife, or some other female member of his family; and upon the slab over her grave, that is, over the precise spot where she was burned, are the same emblems, except the sword, for which a necklace is substituted. At each end of this range of tombs stands a temple dedicated to Baldēo, the brother of Krishna; and in one of them I found his image, with large eyes, a jet black complexion, and an *African countenance*. Why is this that Baldēo should be always represented of this countenance and colour, and his brother Krishna, either white, or of an azure colour, and the *Caucasian countenance*?[14] The inside of the tomb is covered with beautiful snow-white stucco work that resembles the finest marble; but this is disfigured by wretched paintings, representing, on one side of the dome, Sūraj Mall in 'darbār', smoking his hookah, and giving orders to his ministers; in another, he is at his devotions; on the third, at his sports, shooting hogs and deer; and on the fourth, at war, with some French officers of distinction figuring before him. He is distinguished by his portly person in all, and by his favourite light-brown dress in three places. At his devotions he is standing all in white before the tutelary god of his house, Hardēo.[15] In various parts, Krishna is represented at his sports with the milkmaids. The colours are gaudy, and apparently as fresh as when first put on eighty years ago; but the paintings are all in the worst possible taste and style.[16] Inside the dome of Ranjīt Singh's tomb the siege of Bharatpur is represented in the same rude taste and style. Lord Lake is dismounted, and standing before his white horse giving orders to his soldiers. On the opposite side of the dome, Ranjīt Singh, in a plain white dress, is standing erect before his idol at his devotions, with his ministers behind him. On the other two sides he is at his favourite field sports. What strikes one most in all this is the entire absence of priestcraft. He wanted all his revenue for his soldiers; and his tutelary god seems, in consequence, to have been well pleased to dispense with the mediatory services of priests.[17] There are few temples anywhere to be seen in the territories of these Jāt chiefs; and, as few of their subjects have yet ventured to follow them in this innovation upon the old Hindoo usages of building tombs,[18] the countries under their dominion are less richly ornamented than those of their neighbours. Those who build tombs or temples generally surround them with groves of mango and other fine fruit-trees, with good wells to supply water for them, and, if they have the means, they add tanks, so that every religions edifice, or work of ornament, leads to one or more of utility. So it was in Europe; often the Northern hordes swept away all that had grown up under the institution of the Romans and the Saracens; for almost all the great works of ornament and utility, by which these countries became first adorned and enriched, had their origin in church establishments. That portion of India, where the greater part of the revenue goes to the priesthood, will generally be much more studded with works of ornament and utility than that in which the greater part goes to the soldiery. I once asked a Hindoo gentleman, who had travelled all over India, what part of it he thought most happy and beautiful. He mentioned some part of Southern India, about Tanjore, I think, where you could hardly go a mile without meeting some happy procession, or coming to a temple full of priests, or find an acre of land uncultivated.

The countries under the Marāthā Government improved much in appearance, and in happiness, I believe, after the mayors of the palace, who were Brahmans, assumed the Government, and put aside the Sātārā Rajas, the descendants of the great Sivājī.[19] Wherever they could, they conferred the Government of their distant territories upon Brahmans, who filled all the high offices under them with men of the same caste, who spent the greater part of their incomes in tombs, temples, groves, and tanks, that embellished and enriched the face of the country, and thereby diffused a taste for such works generally among the people they governed. The appearance of those parts of the Marāthā dominion so governed is infinitely superior to that of the countries governed by the leaders of the military class, such as Sindhia, Holkār, and the Bhonslā, whose capitals are still mere standing camps—a collection of hovels, and whose countries are almost entirely devoid of all those works of ornament and utility that enrich and adorn those of their neighbours.[20] They destroyed all they found in those countries when they conquered them; and they have had neither the wisdom nor the taste to raise others to supply their places. The Sikh Government is of exactly the same character; and the countries they governed have, I believe, the same wretched appearance—they are swarms of human locusts, who prey upon all that is calculated to enrich and embellish the face of the land they infest, and all that can tend to improve men in their social relations, and to link their affection to their soil and their government.[21] A Hindoo prince is always running to the extreme; he can never take and keep a middle course. He is either ambitious, and therefore appropriates all his revenues to the maintenance of soldiers, to pour out in inroads upon his neighbours; or he is superstitious, and devotes all his revenue to his priesthood, who embellish his country at the same time that they weaken it, and invite invasion, as their prince becomes less and less able to repel it.

The more popular belief regarding this range of sandstone hills at Govardhan is that Lachhman, the brother of Rāma, having been wounded by Rāvan, the demon king of Ceylon, his surgeon declared that his wound could be cured only by a decoction of the leaves of a certain tree, to be found in a certain hill in the Himālaya mountains. Hanumān volunteered to go for it, but on reaching the place he found that he had entirely forgotten the description of the tree required; and, to prevent mistake, he took up the whole mountain upon his back, and walked off with it to the plains. As he passed Govardhan, where Bharat and Charat, the third and fourth brothers of Rāma, then reigned, he was seen by them.[22] It was night; and, thinking him a strange sort of fish, Bharat let fly one of his arrows at him. It hit him in the leg, and the sudden jerk caused this small fragment of his huge burden to fall off. He called out in his agony, 'Rām, Rām', from which they learned that he belonged to the army of their brother, and let him pass on; but he remained lame for life from the wound. This accounts very satisfactorily, according to popular belief, for the halting gait of all the monkeys of that species;[23] those who are descended lineally from the general inherit it, of course; and those who are not, adopt it out of respect for his memory, as all the soldiers of Alexander contrived to make one shoulder higher than the other, because one of his happened to be so. When he passed, thousands and tens of thousands of lamps were burning upon his mountain, as the people remained entirely unconscious of the change, and at their usual occupations. Hanumān reached Ceylon with his mountain, the tree was found upon it, and Lachhman's wound cured.[24]

Govardhan is now within the boundary of our territory, and a native collector resides here from Agra.[25]

Notes:

1. January, 1836.

2. See note on Govardhan, *ante*, chapter 53, note 1.

3. *Ante*, chapter 9, note 8.

4. *Ante*, beginning of chapter 53.

5. This Hindoo version of the Massacre of the Innocents necessarily recalls to mind the story in St. Matthew's Gospel. Numerous incidents of the Gospel narrative, including the birth among the cattle, the stable, the manger, and the imperial census, are repeated in the Indian legends of Krishna. The exact channel of communication is not known, but the intercourse between Alexandria and India is, in general terms, the explanation of the coincidences (Weber, *Die Griechen in Indien*, 1890, and *Abh. über Krishna's Geburtfest*, 1868).

6. This story may be an adaptation of the similar Buddhist tale.

7. Ūj is the Og, King of Bashan, of the Hebrew version of the legend. The extravagant stories quoted in the text are not in the Korān, but are the inventions of the commentators. Sale gives references in his notes to chap. 5 of the Korān.

8. The kingdom included the modern Oudh (Awadh). The capital was the ancient city, also named Ajodhya, adjoining Fyzabad, which is still a very sacred place of pilgrimage.

9. It is, I think, absolutely impossible for the most sympathetic European to understand, or enter into, the mental position of the learned and devout Hindoo who implicitly believes the wild myth related in the text, and sees no incongruity in the congeries of inconsistent ideas which are involved in the story. We may dimly apprehend that Brahmā is conceived as a δημιουργός, or Architect of the Universe, working in subordination to an impersonal higher power, and not as the infinite, omniscient, omnipotent Creator whom the Hebrews reverenced, but we shall still be a long way from attaining

the Hindoo point of view. The relations of Krishna, Vishnu, Brahma, Rāma, Siva, and all the other deities, with one another and with mankind, seem to be conceived by the Hindoo in a manner so confused and contradictory that every attempt at elucidation or explanation must necessarily fail. A Hindoo is born, not made, and the 'inwardness' of Hinduism is not to be penetrated, even by the most learned of 'barbarian' pundits.

10. *Ante,* chapter 20, note 6.

11. Rājā of Bharatpur, not to be confounded with the Lion of the Panjāb.

12. Wordsworth, *Excursion,* Book I.

13. The original edition gives a coloured plate of this tomb, which is not noticed by Fergusson. That author's remarks on the palace at Dīg would apply to this tomb also; the style is good, but not quite the best. Sūraj Mall was killed in a skirmish in 1763.

14. Baldēo, or in Sanskrit Bāladeva, Bālabhadra, or Bālarāma, was the elder brother of Krishna. His myth in some respects resembles that of Herakles, as that of Krishna is related to the myths of Apollo. The editor is not able to solve the queries propounded by the author.

15. i.e. Hari deva, a form of Vishnu. The temple of Hari deva at Govardhan was built about A.D. 1560. (*N.W.P. Gazetteer,* 1st ed., vol. viii, p. 94.)

16. Modern India shows little appreciation of good art, and the paintings ordinarily executed for decorative purposes are as crude as those described by the author. A school of clever artists in Bengal is doing something to raise the public taste. The high merit of the ancient Indian paintings at Ajantā and elsewhere is now fully recognized. A great revival of pictorial art took place about A.D. 1570 in the reign of Akbar. From that date the Indo-Persian and Indian schools of painting maintained a high standard of excellence, especially in portraiture, for a century approximately. During the eighteenth century marked deterioration may be observed. See *A History of Fine Art in India and Ceylon,* Oxford, 1911.

17. The Jāts detest Brahmans. The members of a Jāt deputation complained one day to the editor when in the Muzaffarnagar district that they suffered many evils by reason of the Brahmans.

18. The author's meaning seems to be that building tombs is not an old Hindoo usage.

19. Sivājī, the indomitable opponent of Aurangzēb in the Deccan, belonged to the agricultural Kunbī caste. He was born in May A.D. 1627, and died in April 1680. The Brahman ministers of the Rājās of Sātārā were known by the title of Peshwā. Bājī Rāo I, who died in 1740, the second

Peshwā, was the first who superseded in actual power his nominal master. The last of the Peshwās was Bājī Rāo II, who abdicated in 1818, after the termination of the great Marāthā war, and retired to Bithūr near Cawnpore. His adopted son was the notorious Nānā Sāhib. The Marquis of Hastings, in 1818, drew the Rājā of Sātārā from captivity, and re-established his dignity and power. In 1839 the Rājā's treachery compelled the Government of India to depose him. His territory is now a district of the Bombay Presidency. See Mānkar, *The Life and Exploits of Shivāji*, 2nd ed., Bombay, Nirnayasāgar Press, 1886.

20. The Rājā of Berār, also known as the Rājā of Nāgpur, was called the Bhonslā. The misrule of Gwālior has been described *ante*, in chapters 36 and 49. The condition of Gwālior and Indore, the capitals of Sindhia and Holkār respectively, is now very different. The Bhonslā has vanished.

21. Since the annexation of the Panjāb in 1849, the Sikhs have justly earned so much praise as loyal and gallant soldiers, the flower of the Indian army, that their earlier less honourable reputation has been effaced, Captain Francklin, writing in 1803, and apparently expressing the opinion of George Thomas, declares that 'the Seiks are false, sanguinary, and faithless; they are addicted to plunder and the acquirement of wealth by any means, however nefarious'. (*Military Memoirs of Mr. George Thomas, London reprint*, p. 112.) The Sikh states of the Panjāb are now sufficiently well governed.

22. I know of no authority for the name Charat (Churut), which seems to be a blunder for Satrughna. The sons of Dasaratha were Rāma, by the chief queen; Bharat, by a second; and Lachhman (Lakshmana), and Satrughna by a third consort.

23. The species referred to is the long-tailed monkey called 'Hanumān', and 'langūr' in Hindi, the *Presbytis entellus* of Jerdon (=*P. anchises*, Elliot; = *Semnopithecus*, Cuvier).

24. The author seems to have forgotten that he has already told this story, *ante*, this chapter following [8] in the text.

25. It is in the Mathurā district. The town of Mathurā (Muttra) became the head-quarters of a separate District in 1832. The official at Govardhan in 1836 must, therefore, have been subordinate to Mathurā, not to Agra.

CHAPTER 57

Veracity.

The people of Britain are described by Diodorus Siculus (Book V, chap. 2) as in a very simple and rude state, subsisting almost entirely on the produce of the land, but as being 'a people of much integrity and sincerity, far from the craft and knavery of men among us, contented with plain and homely fare, and strangers to the luxuries and excesses of the rich'. In India we find strict veracity most prevalent among the wildest and half-savage tribes of the hills and jungles in Central India, or the chain of the Himālaya mountains; and among those where we find it prevail most, we find cattle-stealing most common; the men of one tribe not deeming it to be any disgrace to *lift*, or steal, the cattle of another. I have known the man among the Gonds of the woods of Central India, whom nothing could induce to tell a lie, join a party of robbers to lift a herd of cattle from the neighbouring plains for nothing more than as much spirits as he could enjoy at one bout. I asked a native gentleman of the plains, in the valley of the Nerbudda, one day, what made the people of the woods to the north and south more disposed to speak the truth than those more civilized of the valley itself. 'They have not yet learned the value of a lie,' said he, with the greatest simplicity and sincerity, for he was a very honest and plain-spoken man.

Veracity is found to prevail most where there is least to tempt to falsehood, and most to be feared from it. In a very rude state of society, like that of which I have been speaking, the only shape in which property is accumulated is in cattle; things are bartered for each other without the use of a circulating medium, and one member of a community has no means of concealing from the other the articles of property he has. If they were to steal from each other, they would not be able to conceal what they stole—to steal, therefore, would be no advantage. In such societies every little community is left to govern itself; to secure the rights, and enforce the duties, of all its several members in their relations with each other; they are too poor to pay taxes to keep up expensive establishments, and their Governments seldom maintain among them any for the administration of justice, or the protection of life, property, or character. All the members of all such little communities will often unite in robbing the members of another community of their flocks and herds, the only kind of property they have, or in applauding those who most distinguish themselves in such enterprises; but the well- being of the community demands that each member should respect the property of the others, and be punished by the odium of all if he does not.[1]

It is equally necessary to the well-being of the community that every member should be able to rely upon the veracity of the other upon the very few points where their rights, duties, and interests clash. In the very rudest state of society, among the woods and hills of India, the people have some deity whose power they dread, and whose name they invoke when much is supposed to depend upon the truth of what one man is about to declare. The 'pīpal' tree (*Ficus religiosa*) is everywhere sacred to the gods, who are supposed to sit among its leaves and listen to the music of their rustling. The deponent takes one of these leaves in his hand, and invokes the god who sits above him to crush him, or those dear to him, as he crushes the leaf in his hand, if he speak anything but the truth; he then plucks and crushes the leaf, and states what he has to say.[2]

The large cotton-tree is, among the wild tribes of India, the favourite seat of gods still more terrible,[3] because their superintendence is confined exclusively to the neighbourhood; and having their attention less occupied, they can venture to make a more minute scrutiny into the conduct of the people immediately around them. The 'pīpal' is occupied by one or other of the Hindoo triad, the god of creation, preservation, or destruction, who have the affairs of the universe to look after;[4] but the cotton and other trees are occupied by some minor deities, who are vested with a local superintendence over the affairs of a district, or perhaps, of a single village. [5] These are always in the view of the people, and every man knows that he is every moment liable to be taken to their court, and to be made to invoke their vengeance upon himself, or those dear to him, if he has told a falsehood in what he has stated, or tells one in what he is about to state. Men so situated adhere habitually, and I may say religiously, to the truth; and I have had before me hundreds of cases in which a man's property, liberty, or life has depended upon his telling a lie, and he has refused to tell it to save either; as my friend told me, 'they had not learned the value of a lie', or rather, they had not learned with how much impunity a lie could be told in the tribunals of civilized society. In their own tribunals, under the pīpal-tree or cotton-tree, imagination commonly did what the deities, who were supposed to preside, had the credit of doing; if the deponent told a lie, he believed that the deity who sat on the sylvan throne above him, and searched the heart of man, must know it; and from that moment he knew no rest—he was always in dread of his vengeance; if any accident happened to him, or to those dear to him, it was attributed to this offended deity; and if no accident happened, some evil was brought about by his own disordered imagination.[6]

In the tribunals we introduce among them, such people soon find that the judges who preside can seldom search deeply into the hearts of men, or clearly distinguish truth from falsehood in the declarations of deponents; and when they can distinguish it, it is seldom that they can secure their conviction for perjury. They generally learn very soon that these judges, instead of being, like the judges of their own woods and wilds, the only beings who can search the hearts of men, and punish them for falsehood, are frequently the persons, of all others, most blind to the real state of the deponent's mind, and the degree of truth and falsehood in his narrative; that, however well-intentioned, they are often labouring in the 'darkness visible' created by the native officers around them. They not only learn this, but they learn what is still worse, that they may tell what lies they please in these tribunals; and that not one of them shall become known to the circle in which they move, and whose good opinion they value. If, by his lies told in such tribunals, a man has robbed another, or caused him to be robbed, of his property, his character, his liberty, or his life, he can easily persuade the circle in which he resides that it has arisen, not from any false statements of his, but from the blindness of the judge, or the wickedness of the native officers of his court, because all circles consider the blindness of the one, and the wickedness of the other, to be everywhere very great.

Arrian, in speaking of the class of supervisors in India, says: 'They may not be guilty of falsehood; and indeed none of the Indians were ever accused of that crime.'[7] I believe that as little falsehood is spoken by the people of India, in their village communities, as in any part of the world with an equal area and population. It is in our courts of justice where falsehoods prevail most, and the longer they have been anywhere established, the greater the degree of falsehood that prevails in them. Those entrusted with the administration of a newly-acquired territory are surprised to find the disposition among both principals and witnesses in cases to tell the plain and simple truth. As magistrates, they find it very often difficult to make thieves and robbers tell lies, according to the English fashion, to avoid running a risk of criminating themselves. In England, this habit of making criminals tell lies arose from the severity of the penal code, which made the punishment so monstrously disproportionate to the crime, that the accused, however clear and notorious his crimes, became an object of general sympathy.[8] In India, punishments have nowhere been, under our rule, disproportionate to the crimes; on the contrary, they have generally been more mild than the people would wish them to be, or think they ought to be, in order to deter from similar crimes; and, in newly- acquired territories, they have generally been more mild than in our old possessions. The accused are, therefore, nowhere considered as objects of public sympathy; and in newly-acquired territories they are willing to tell the truth, and are allowed to do so, in order to save the people whom they have injured, and their neighbours generally, the great loss and annoyance unavoidably attending upon a summons to our courts. In the native courts, to which ours succeed, the truth was seen through immediately, the judges who presided could commonly distinguish truth from falsehood in the evidence before them, almost as well as the sylvan gods who sat in the pīpal- or cotton-trees; though they were seldom supposed by the people to be quite so just in their decisions. When we take possession of such countries, they, for a time at least, give us credit for the same sagacity, with a little more integrity. The prisoner knows that his neighbours expect him to tell the truth to save them trouble, and will detest him if he does not; he supposes that we shall have the sense to find out the truth whether he tells it or not, and then humanity to visit his crime with the punishment it merits, and no more.

The magistrate asks the prisoner what made him steal; and the prisoner enters at once into an explanation of the circumstances which reduced him to the necessity of doing so, and offers to bring witnesses to prove them; but never dreams of offering to bring witnesses to prove that he did not steal, if he really had done so; because the general feeling would be in favour of his doing the one, and against his doing the other. Tavernier gives an amusing sketch of Amīr Jumla presiding in a court of justice, during a visit he paid him in the kingdom of Golconda, in the year 1648. (See Book I, Part II, chap. 11.)[9]

I asked a native law officer, who called on me one day, what he thought would be the effect of an Act to dispense with oaths on the Korān and Ganges water, and substitute a solemn declaration made in the name of God, and under the same penal liabilities, as if the Korān or Ganges water had been in the deponent's hand. 'I have practised In the courts thirty years, sir,' said he, 'and during that time I have found only three kinds of witnesses — two of whom would, by such an Act, be left precisely where they were, while the third would be released by it from a very salutary check.' 'And, pray, what are the three classes into which you divide the witnesses in our courts?'

'First, sir, are those who will always tell the truth, whether they are required to state what they know in the form of an oath or not.' 'Do you think this a large class?'

'Yes, I think it is; and I have found among them many whom nothing on earth could make to swerve from the truth; do what you please, you could never frighten or bribe them into a deliberate falsehood. The second are those who will not hesitate to tell a lie when they have a motive for it, and are not restrained by an oath. In taking an oath they are afraid of two things, the anger of God and the odium of men. Only three days ago, 'continued my friend,' I required a power of attorney from a lady of rank, to enable me to act for her in a case pending before the court in this town. It was given to me by her brother, and two witnesses came to declare that she had given it. "Now," said I, "this lady is known to live under the curtain; and you will be asked by the judge whether you saw her give this paper; what will you say?" They both replied: "If the judge asks us the question without an oath, we will say yes—it will save much trouble, and we know that she did give this paper, though we did not really see her give it; but if he puts the Korān into our hands we must say no, for we should otherwise be pointed at by all the town as perjured wretches—our enemies would soon tell everybody that we had taken a false oath." Now,' my friend went on, 'the form of an oath is a great check upon this sort of persons. The third class consists of men who will tell lies whenever they have sufficient motive, whether they have the Korān or Ganges water in their hands or not. Nothing will ever prevent their doing so; and the declaration which you propose would be just as well as any other for them.'

'Which class do you consider the most numerous of the three?'

'I consider the second the most numerous, and wish the oath to be retained for them.'

'That is of all the men you see examined in our courts, you think the most come under the class of those who will, under the influence of strong motives, tell lies if they have not the Korān or Ganges water in their hands?'

'Yes.'

'But do not a great many of those, whom you consider to be included among the second class, come from the village communities—the peasantry of the country?'

'Yes.'

'And do you not think that the greatest part of those men who tell lies in the court, under the influence of strong motives, unless they bear the Korān or Ganges water in their hands, would refuse to tell lies, if questioned before the people of their villages among the circle in which they live?'

'Of course I do; three-fourths of those who do not scruple to lie in our courts, would be ashamed to be before their neighbours, or the elders of their village.'

'You think that the people of the village communities are more ashamed to tell lies before their neighbours than the people of towns?'

'Much more[10] here is no comparison.'

'And the people of towns and cities bear in India but a small proportion to the people of the village communities?'

'I should think a very small proportion indeed.'

'Then you think that in the mass of the population of India out of our courts, and in their own circles, the first class, or those who speak truth, whether they have the Korān or Ganges water in their hands or not, would be found more numerous than the other two?'

'Certainly I do; if they were always to be questioned before their neighbours or elders, or so that they could feel that their neighbours and elders would know what they say.'

This man is a very worthy and learned Muhammadan, who has read all the works on medicine to be found in Persian and Arabia; gives up his time from sunrise in the morning till nine, to the indigent sick of the town, whom he supplies gratuitously with his advice and medicines, that cost him thirty rupees a month, out of about one hundred and twenty that he can make by his labours all the rest of the day.

There can be no doubt that, even in England, the fear of the odium of society, which is sure to follow the man who has perjured himself, acts more powerfully in making men tell the truth, when they have the Bible in their hands before a competent and public tribunal, and with a strong worldly motive to tell a lie, than the fear of punishment by the Deity in the next world for having 'taken his name in vain' in this. Christians, as well as other people, are too apt to think that there is yet abundance of time to appease the Deity by repentance and reformation; but they know that they cannot escape the odium of society, with a free press and high tone of moral and religions feeling, like those of England, if they deliberately perjure themselves in open court, whose proceedings are watched with so much jealousy. They learn to dread the name of 'perjured villain' or 'perjured wretch', which would embitter the rest of their lives, and perhaps the lives of their children.[11]

In a society much advanced in arts and the refinements of life, temptations to falsehood become very great, and require strong checks from law, religion, or moral feeling. Religion is seldom of itself found sufficient; for, though men cannot hope to conceal their transgressions from the Deity, they can, as I have stated, always hope in time to appease Him. Penal laws are not alone sufficient, for men can always hope to conceal their trespasses from those who are appointed to administer them, or at least to prevent their getting that measure of judicial proof required for their conviction; the dread of the indignation of their circle of society is everywhere the more efficient of the three checks; and this check will generally be found most to prevail where the community is left most to self- government—hence the proverb, 'There is honour among thieves'. A gang of robbers, who are outlaws, are, of course, left to govern themselves; and, unless these could rely on each other's veracity and honour in their relations with each other, they could do nothing. If Governments were to leave no degree of self-government to the communities of which the society is composed, this moral check would really cease—the law would undertake to secure every right, and enforce every duty; and men would cease to depend upon each other's good opinion and good feelings.[12]

There is perhaps no part of the world where the communities of which the society is composed have been left so much to self- government as in India. There has seldom been any idea of a reciprocity of duties and rights between the governing and the governed; the sovereign who has possession feels that he has a right to levy certain taxes from the land for the maintenance of the public establishments, which he requires to keep down rebellion against his rule, and to defend his dominions against all who may wish to intrude and seize upon them; and to assist him in acquiring the dominions of other princes when favourable opportunities offer; but he has no idea of a reciprocal duty towards those from whom he draws his revenues. The peasantry from whom the prince draws his revenues feel that they are bound to pay that revenue; that, if they do not pay it, he will, with his strong arm, turn them out and give to others their possessions—but they have no idea of any right on their part to any return from him. The village communities were everywhere left almost entirely to self-government; and the virtues of truth and honesty, in all their relations with each other, were indispensably necessary to enable them to govern themselves.[13] A common interest often united a good many village communities in a bond of union, and established a kind of brotherhood over extensive tracts of richly cultivated land. Self-interest required that they should unite to defend themselves against attacks with which they were threatened at every returning harvest in a country where every prince was a robber upon a scale more or less large according to his means, and took the field to rob while the lands were covered with the ripe crops upon which his troops might subsist; and where every man who practised robbery with open violence followed what he called an '*imperial* trade' (pādshāhī kām)—the only trade worthy the character of a gentleman. The same interest required that they should unite in deceiving their own prince, and all his officers, great and small, as to the real resources of their estates; because they all knew that the prince would admit of no other limits to his exactions than their abilities to pay at the harvest. Though, in their relations with each other, all these village communities spoke as much truth as those of any other communities in the world; still, in their relation with the Government, they told as many lies;—for falsehood, in the one set of relations, would have incurred the odium of the whole of their circles of society—truth, in the other, would often have involved the same penalty. If a man had told a lie to *cheat* his neighbour, he would have become an object of hatred and contempt—if he told a lie to *save* his neighbour's fields from an increase of rent or tax, he would have become an object of esteem and respect.[14] If the Government officers were asked whether there was any truth to be found among such communities, they would say, *No, that the truth was not in them*; because they would not cut each other's throats by telling them the real value of each other's fields.

If the peasantry were asked, they would say there was plenty of truth to be found everywhere except among a few scoundrels, who, to curry favour with the Government officers, betrayed their trust, and told the value of their neighbours'.fields. In their ideas, he might as well have gone off, and brought down the common enemy upon them in the shape of some princely robber of the neighbourhood.

Locke says: 'Outlaws themselves keep faith and rules of justice one with another—they practise them as rules of convenience within their own communities; but it is impossible to conceive that they embrace justice as a practical principle who act fairly with their fellow highwaymen, and at the same time plunder or kill the next honest man they meet.' (Vol. i, p. 37.) In India, the difference between the army of a prince and the gang of a robber was, in the general estimation of the people, only in *degree*—they were both driving an *imperial trade*, a 'pādshāhī kām'. Both took the auspices, and set out on their expedition after the Dasahrā, when the autumn crops were ripening; and both thought the Deity propitiated as soon as they found the omens favourable;[15] one attacked palaces and capitals, the other villages and merchants' storerooms. The members of the army of the prince thought as little of the justice or injustice of his cause as those of the gang of the robber; the people of his capital hailed the return of the victorious prince who had contributed so much to their wealth, to his booty, and to their self- love by his victory. The village community received back the robber and his gang with the same feelings: by their skill and daring they had come back loaded with wealth, which they were always disposed to spend liberally with their neighbours. There was no more of truth in the prince and his army in their relations with the princes and people of neighbouring principalities, than in the robber and his gang in their relations with the people robbed. The prince flatters the self-love of his army and his people; the robber flatters that of his gang and his village—the question is only in degree; the persons whose self-love is flattered are blind to the injustice and cruelty of the attack—the prince is the idol of a people, the robber the idol of a gang. Was ever robber more atrocious in his attacks upon a merchant or a village than Louis XIV of France in his attacks upon the Palatine and Palatinate of the Rhine? How many thousand similar instances might be quoted of princes idolized by their people for deeds equally atrocious in their relations with other people? What nation or sovereign ever found fault with their ambassadors for telling lies to the kings, courts, and people of other countries?[16]

Rome, during the whole period of her history, was a mere den of execrable thieves, whose feelings were systematically brutalized by the most revolting spectacles, that they might have none of those sympathies with suffering humanity, none of those 'compunctious visitings of conscience', which might be found prejudicial to the interests of the gang, and beneficial to the rest of mankind. Take, for example, the conduct of this atrocious gang under Aemilius Paulus, against Epirus and Greece generally after the defeat of Perseus, all under the deliberate decrees of the senate: take that of this gang under his son Scipio the younger, against Carthage and Numantia; under Cato, at Cyprus — all in the same manner under the *deliberate decrees of the senate*. Take indeed the whole of her history as a republic, and we find it that of the most atrocious band of robbers that was ever associated against the rest of their species. In her relations with the rest of mankind Rome was collectively devoid of truth; and her citizens, who were sent to govern conquered countries, were no less devoid of truth individually — they cared nothing whatever for the feelings or the opinions of the people governed; in their dealings with them, truth and honour were entirely disregarded. The only people whose favourable opinion they had any desire to cultivate were the members of the great gang; and the most effectual mode of conciliating them was to plunder the people of conquered countries, and distribute the fruits among them in presents of one kind or another. Can any man read without shuddering that it was the practice among this atrocious gang to have all the multitude of unhappy prisoners of both sexes, and of all ranks and ages, — who annually graced the triumphs of their generals, taken off and murdered just at the moment when these generals reached the Capitol, amid the shouts of the multitude, that their joys might be augmented by the sight or consciousness of the sufferings of others? (See Hooke's *Roman History*, vol. iii, p. 488; vol. iv, p. 541.) 'It was the custom that, when the triumphant conqueror turned his chariot towards the Capitol, he commanded the captives to be led to prison, and there put to death, that so the glory of the victor and the miseries of the vanquished might be in the same moment at the utmost.' How many millions of the most innocent and amiable of their species must have been offered up as human sacrifices to the triumphs of the leaders of this great gang! The women were almost as brutalized as the men; lovers met to talk 'soft nonsense', at exhibitions of gladiators. Valeria, the daughter and sister of two of the first men in Rome, was beautiful, gay, and lively, and of unblemished reputation. Having been divorced from her husband, she and the monster Sylla made love to each other at one of these exhibitions of gladiators, and were soon after married. Gibbon, in speaking of the lies which Severus told his two competitors in the contest for empire, says, 'Falsehood and insincerity, unsuitable as they seem to the dignity of public transactions, offend us with a less degrading idea of meanness than when they are found in the intercourse of private life. In the latter, they discover a want of courage; in the other, only a defect of power; and, as it is impossible for the most able statesmen to subdue millions of followers and enemies by their own personal strength, the world, under the name of *policy*, seems to have granted them a very liberal indulgence of craft and dissimulation.'[17]

But the weak in society are often obliged to defend themselves against the strong by the same weapons; and the world grants them the same liberal indulgence. Men advocate the use of the ballot in elections that the weak may defend themselves and the free institutions of the country, by dissimulation, against the strong who would oppress them.[18] The circumstances under which falsehood and insincerity are tolerated by the community in the best societies of modern days are very numerous; and the worst society of modern days in the civilized world, when slavery does not prevail, is immeasurably superior to the best in ancient days, or in the Middle Ages. Do we not every day hear men and women, in what are called the best societies, declaring to one individual or one set of acquaintances that the pity, the sympathy, the love, or the admiration they have been expressing for others is, in reality, all feigned to soothe or please? As long as the motive is not base, men do not spurn the falsehood as such. How much of untruth is tolerated in the best circles of the most civilized nations, in the relations between electors to corporate and legislative bodies and the candidates for election? between nominators to offices under Government and the candidates for nomination? between lawyers and clients, vendors and purchasers? (particularly of horses), between the recruiting sergeant and the young recruit, whom he has found a little angry with his widowed mother, whom he makes him kill by false pictures of what a soldier may hope for in the 'bellaque matribus detestata' to which he invites him?[19]

There is, I believe, no class of men in India from whom it is more difficult to get the true statement of a case pending before a court than the sepoys of our native regiments; and yet there are, I believe, no people in the world from whom it is more easy to get it in their own village communities, where they state it before their relations, elders, and neighbours, whose esteem is necessary to their happiness, and can be obtained only by adherence to truth. Every case that comes before a regimental court involves, or is supposed to involve, the interest or feelings of some one or other of their companions; and the question which the deponent asks himself is-not what religion, public justice, the interests of discipline and order, or the wishes of his officers require, or what would appear manly and honourable before the elders of his own little village, but what will secure the esteem, and what will excite the hatred, of his comrades. This will often be downright, deliberate falsehood, sworn upon the Korān or the Ganges water before his officers.

Many a brave sepoy have I seen faint away from the agitated state of his feelings, under the dread of the Deity if he told lies with the Ganges water in his hands, and of his companions if he told the truth, and caused them to be punished. Every question becomes a party question, and the 'point of honour' requires that every witness shall tell as many lies about it as possible.[20] When I go into a village, and talk with the people in any part of India, I know that I shall get the truth out of them on all subjects as long as I can satisfy them that I am not come on the part of the Government to inquire into the value of their fields with a view to new impositions, and this I can always do; but, when I go among the sepoys to ask about anything, I feel pretty sure that I have little chance of getting at the truth; they will take the alarm and try to deceive me, lest what I learn should be brought up at some future day against them or their comrades. The Duke of Wellington says, speaking of the English soldiers: 'It is most difficult to convict a prisoner before a regimental court-martial, for, I am sorry to say, that soldiers have little regard to the oath administered to them; and the officers who are sworn well and truly to try and determine *according to the evidence*, the matter before them, have too much regard to the strict *letter* of that administered to them.' Again: 'The witnesses being in almost every instance common soldiers, whose conduct this tribunal was instituted to control, the consequence is that perjury is almost as common an offence as drunkenness and plunder, &c.'[21]

In the ordinary civil tribunals of Europe and America a man commonly feels that, though he is removed far from the immediate presence of those whose esteem is necessary for him, their eyes are still upon him, because the statements he may give will find their way to them through the medium of the press. This he does not feel in the civil courts of India, nor in the military courts of Europe, or of any other part of the world, and the man who judges of the veracity of a whole people from the specimens he may witness in such courts, cannot judge soundly.

Shaikh Sādī, in his *Gulistān*, has the following tale: 'I have heard that a prince commanded the execution of a captive who was brought before him; when the captive, having no hope of life, told the prince that he disgraced his throne. The prince, not understanding him, turned to one of his ministers and asked him what he had said. "He says," replied the minister, quoting a passage from the Korān, "God loves those who subdue their passions, forgive injuries, and do good to his creatures." The prince pitied the poor captive, and countermanded the orders for the execution. Another minister, who owed a spite to the one who first spoke, said, "Nothing but truth should be spoken by such persons as we in the presence of the prince; the captive spoke abusively and insolently, and you have not interpreted his words truly". The prince frowned and said, "His false interpretation pleases me more than thy true one, because his was given for a good, and thine for a malignant, purpose; and wise men have said that 'a peace-making lie is better than a factious or anger exciting truth'."'[22]

He who would too fastidiously condemn this doctrine should think of the massacre of Thessalonica, and how much better it would have been for the great Theodosius to have had by his side the peace- making Ambrose, Archbishop of Milan, than the anger-exciting Rufinus, when he heard of the offence which that city had committed.[23]

In despotic governments, where lives, characters, and liberties are every moment at the mercy, not only of the prince but of all his public officers from the highest to the lowest, the occasions in which men feel authorized and actually called upon by the common feelings of humanity to tell 'peacemaking lies' occur every day—nay, every hour, every petty officer of government, 'armed with his little brief authority', is a little tyrant surrounded by men whose all depends upon his will, and who dare not tell him the truth—the 'point of honour' in this little circle demands that every one should be prepared to tell him 'peace-making lies'; and the man who does not do so when the occasion seems to call for it, incurs the odium of the whole circle, as one maliciously disposed to speak 'anger-exciting or factions truths'. Poor Cromwell and Anne Boleyn were obliged to talk of *love* and *duty* toward their brutal murderer, Henry VIII, and tell 'peace-making lies' on the scaffold to save their poor children from his resentment. European gentlemen in India often, by their violence surround themselves with circles of the same kind, in which the 'point of honour' demands that every member shall be prepared to tell 'peace-making lies', to save the others from the effects of their master's ungovernable passions—falsehood is their only safeguard; and, consequently, falsehood ceases to be odious. Countenanced in the circles of the violent, falsehood soon becomes countenanced in those of the mild and forbearing; their domestics pretend a dread of their anger which they really do not feel; and they gain credit for having the same good excuse among those who have no opportunity of becoming acquainted with the real character of the gentlemen in their domestic relations—all are thought to be more or less *tigerish* in these relations, particularly *before breakfast*, because some are *known* to be so.[24]

I have known the native officers of a judge who was really a very mild and worthy man, but who lived a very secluded life, plead as their excuse for all manner of bribery and corruption, that their persons and character were never safe from his violence; and urge that men whose tenure of office was very insecure, and who were every hour in the day exposed to so much indignity, could not possibly be blamed for making the most of their position. The society around believed all this, and blamed, not the native officers, but the judge, or the Government, who placed them in such a situation. Other judges and magistrates have been known to do what this person was merely reported to do, otherwise society would neither have given credit to his officers nor have held them excused for their malpractices. [25] Those European gentlemen who allow their passions to get the better of their reason among their domestics do much to lower the character of their countrymen in the estimation of the people; but the high officials who forget what they owe to themselves and the native officers of their courts, when presiding on the bench of justice, do ten thousand times more; and I grieve to say that I have known a few officials of this class.

We have in England known many occasions, particularly in the cases of prosecutions by the officers of Government for offences against the State, where little circles of society have made it a 'point of honour' for some individuals to speak untruths, and for others to give verdicts against their consciences; some occasions indeed where those who ventured to speak the truth, or give a verdict according to their conscience, were in danger from the violence of popular resentment. Have we not, unhappily, in England and among our countrymen in all parts of the world, experience of a wide difference between what is exacted from members of particular circles of society by the 'point of honour', and what is held to be strict religions truth by the rest of society? Do we not see gentlemen cheating their tradesmen, while they dare not leave a gambling debt unpaid? The 'point of honour' in the circle to which they belong demands that the one should be paid, because the non-payment would involve a breach of faith in their relations with each other, as in the case of the members of a gang of robbers; but the non-payment of a tradesman's bill involves only a breach of faith in a gentleman's relations with a lower order. At least, some gentlemen do not feel any apprehension of incurring the odium of the circle in which they move by cheating of this kind. In the same manner the roué, or libertine of rank, may often be guilty of all manner of falsehoods and crimes to the females of the class below him, without any fear of incurring the odium of either males or females of his own circle; on the contrary, the more crimes he commits of this sort, the more sometimes he may expect to be caressed by males and females of his own order. The man who would not hesitate a moment to destroy the happiness of a family by the seduction of the wife or the daughter, would not dare to leave one shilling of a gambling debt unpaid—the one would bring down upon him the odium of his circle, but the other would not; and the odium of that circle is the only kind of odium he dreads. Appius Claudius apprehended no odium from his own order—the patrician—from the violation of the daughter of Virginius, of the plebeian order; nor did Sextus Tarquinius of the royal order, apprehend any from the violation of Lucretia, of the patrician order—neither would have been punished by their own order, but they were both punished by the injured orders below them.

Our own penal code punished with death the poor man who stole a little food to save his children from starvation, while it left to exult in the caresses of his own order, the wealthy libertine who robbed a father and mother of their only daughter, and consigned her to a life of infamy and misery. The poor victim of man's brutal passions and base falsehood suffered inevitable and exquisite punishment, while the laws and usages of society left the man himself untouched. He had nothing to apprehend if the father of his victim happened to be of the lower order, or a minister of the Church of Christ; because his own order would justify his refusing to meet the one in single combat, and the other dared not invite him to it, and the law left no remedy.[26]

Take the two parties in England into which society is politically divided. There is hardly any species of falsehood uttered by the members of the party out of power against the members of the party in power that is not tolerated and even applauded by one party; men state deliberately what they know to be utterly devoid of truth regarding the conduct of their opponent; they basely ascribe to them motives by which they know they were never actuated, merely to deceive the public, and to promote the interests of their party, without the slightest fear of incurring odium by so doing in the minds of any but their political opponents. If a foreigner were to judge of the people of England from the tone of their newspapers, he would say that there was assuredly neither honour, honesty, nor truth to be found among the classes which furnished the nation with its ministers and legislators; for a set of miscreants more atrocious than the Whig and Tory ministers and legislators of England were represented to be in these papers never disgraced the society of any nation upon earth.

Happily, all foreigners who read these journals know that in what the members of one party say of those of the other, or are reported to say, there is often but little truth; and that there is still less of truth in what the editors and correspondents of the ultra journals of one party write about the characters, conduct, and sentiments of the members of the other.

There is one species of untruth to which we English people are particularly prone in India, and, I am assured, everywhere else. It is this. Young 'miss in her teens', as soon as she finds her female attendants in the wrong, no matter in what way, exclaims, 'It is so like the natives'; and the idea of the same error, vice, or crime, becomes so habitually associated in her mind with every native she afterwards sees, that she can no more separate them than she can the idea of ghosts and hobgoblins from darkness and solitude. The young cadet or civilian, as soon as he finds his valet, butler, or groom in the wrong, exclaims, 'It is so like blacky – so like the niggers; they are all alike!' And what could you expect from him? He has been constantly accustomed to the same vicious association of ideas in his native land – if he has been brought up in a family of Tories, he has constantly heard those he most reverenced exclaim, when they have found, or fancied they found, a Whig in the wrong, 'It is so like the Whigs – they are all alike – there is no trusting any of them.' If a Protestant, 'It is so like the Catholics; there is no trusting them in any condition of life.' The members of Whig and Catholic families may say the same, perhaps, of Tories and Protestants. An untravelled Englishman will sometimes say the same of a Frenchman; and the idea of everything that is bad in man will be associated in his mind with the image of a Frenchman. If he hears of an act of dishonour by a person of that nation, 'It is so like a Frenchman – they are all alike; there is no honour in them.' A Tory goes to America, predisposed to find in all who live under republican governments every species of vice and crime; and no sooner sees a man or woman misbehave than he exclaims, 'It is so like the Americans – they are all alike; but what could you expect from republicans?' At home, when he considers himself in relation to the members of the parties opposed to him in religion or politics, they are associated in his mind with everything that is vicious; abroad, when he considers the people of other countries in relation to his own, if they happen to be Christians, he will find them associated in his mind with everything that is good, or everything that is bad, in proportion as their institutions happen to conform to those which his party advocates. A Tory will abuse America and Americans, and praise the Austrians. A Whig will, *perhaps*, abuse the Austrians and others who live under paternal or despotic governments, and praise the Americans, who live under institutions still more free than his own. This has properly been considered by Locke as a species of madness to which all mankind are more or less subject, and from which hardly any individual can entirely free himself. 'There is', he says, 'scarce a man so free from it, but that if he should always, on all occasions, argue or do as in some cases he constantly does, would not be thought fitter for Bedlam than civil conversation. I do not here mean when he is under the power of an unruly passion, but in the steady, calm course of his life. That which thus captivates their reason, and leads men of sincerity blindfold from common sense will, when examined, be found to be what we are speaking of. Some independent ideas, of no alliance to one another, are, by education, custom, and the constant din of their party, so coupled in their minds, that they always appear there together, and they can no more separate them in their thoughts than if they were but one idea, and they operate as if they really were so.' (Book II, Chap. 33.)

Perjury had long since ceased to be considered disgraceful, or even discreditable, among the patrician order in Rome before the soldiers ventured to break their oaths of allegiance. Military service had, from the ignorance and selfishness of this order, been rendered extremely odious to free-born Romans; and they frequently mutinied and murdered their generals, though they would not desert, because they had sworn not to do so. To break his oath by deserting the standards of Rome was to incur the hatred and contempt of the great mass of the people — the soldier dared not hazard this. But patricians of senatorial and consular rank did not hesitate to violate their oaths whenever it promised any advantage to the patrician order collectively or individually, because it excited neither contempt nor indignation in that order. 'They have been false to their generals,' said Fabius, 'but they have never deceived the gods. I know they *can* conquer, and they shall swear to do so.' They swore, and conquered.

Instead of adopting measures to make the duties of a soldier less odious, the patricians turned their hatred of these duties to account, and at a high price sold an absolution from their oath. While the members of the patrician order bought and sold oaths among themselves merely to deceive the lower orders, they were still respected among the plebeians; but when they began to sell dispensations to the members of this lower order, the latter also, by degrees, ceased to feel any veneration for the oath, and it was no longer deemed disgraceful to desert duties which the higher order made no effort to render less odious.

'That they who draw the breath of life in a court, and pass all their days in an atmosphere of lies, should have any very sacred regard for truth, is hardly to be expected. They experience such falsehood in all who surround them, that deception, at least suppression of the truth, almost seems necessary for self-defence; and, accordingly, if their speech be not framed upon the theory of the French cardinal, that language was given to man for the better concealment of his thoughts, they at least seem to regard in what they say, not its resemblance to the tact in question, but rather its subserviency to the purpose in view.' (Brougham's *George IV*.) 'Yet, let it never be forgotten, that princes are nurtured in falsehood by the atmosphere of lies which envelops their palace; steeled against natural sympathies by the selfish natures of all that surround them; hardened in cruelty, partly indeed by the fears incident to their position, but partly too by the unfeeling creatures, the factions, the unnatural productions of a court whom alone they deal with; trained for tyrants by the prostration which they find in all the minds which they come in contact with; encouraged to domineer by the unresisting medium through which all their steps to power and its abuse are made.' (Brougham's *Carnot*.)

But Lord Brougham is too harsh. Johnson has observed truly enough, 'Honesty is not necessarily greater where elegance is less'; nor does a sense of supreme or despotic power necessarily imply the exercise or abuse of it. Princes have, happily, the same yearning as the peasant after the respect and affection of the circle around them, and the people under them; and they must generally seek it by the same means.

I have mentioned the village communities of India as that class of the population among whom truth prevails most; but I believe there is no class of men in the world more strictly honourable in their dealings than the mercantile classes of India. Under native governments a merchant's books were appealed to as 'holy writ', and the confidence in them has certainly not diminished under our rule. There have been instances of their being seized by the magistrate, and subjected to the inspection of the officers of his court. No officer of a native government ventured to seize them; the merchant was required to produce them as proof of particular entries, and, while the officers of government did no more, there was no danger of false accounts.

An instance of deliberate fraud or falsehood among native merchants of respectable station in society is extremely rare. Among the many hundreds of bills I have had to take from them for private remittances, I have never had one dishonoured, or the payment upon one delayed beyond the day specified; nor do I recollect ever hearing of one who had. They are so careful not to speculate beyond their means, that an instance of failure is extremely rare among them. No one ever in India hears of families reduced to ruin or distress by the failure of merchants or bankers; though here, as in all other countries advanced in the arts, a vast number of families subsist upon the interest of money employed by them.[27]

There is no class of men more interested in the stability of our rule in India than this of the respectable merchants; nor is there any upon whom the welfare of our Government and that of the people more depend. Frugal, first upon principle, that they may not in their expenditure encroach upon their capitals, they become so by habit; and when they advance in life they lay out their accumulated wealth in the formation of those works which shall secure for them, from generation to generation, the blessings of the people of the towns in which they have resided, and those of the country around. It would not be too much to say that one-half of the great works which embellish and enrich the face of India, in tanks, groves, wells, temples, &c., have been formed by this class of the people solely with the view of securing the blessings of mankind by contributing to their happiness in solid and permanent works.[28] 'The man who has left behind him great works in temples, bridges, reservoirs, and caravanserais for the public good, does not die,' says Shaikh Sādī,[29] the greatest of Eastern poets, whose works are more read and loved than those of any other uninspired man that has ever written, not excepting our own beloved Shakspeare.[30] He is as much loved and admired by Hindoos as by Muhammadans; and from boyhood to old age he continues the idol of the imaginations of both. The boy of ten, and the old man of seventy, alike delight to read and quote him for the music of his verses, and the beauty of his sentiments, precepts, and imagery.[31]

It was to the class last mentioned, whose incomes are derived from the profits of stock invested in manufactures and commerce, that Europe chiefly owed its rise and progress after the downfall of the Roman Empire, and the long night of darkness and desolation which followed it. It was through the means of mercantile industry, and the municipal institutions to which it gave rise, that the enlightened sovereigns of Europe were enabled to curb the licence of the feudal aristocracy, and to give to life, property, and character that security without which society could not possibly advance; and it was through the same means that the people were afterwards enabled to put those limits to the authority of the sovereign, and to secure to themselves that share in the government without which society could not possibly be free or well constituted. Upon the same foundation may we hope to raise a superstructure of municipal corporations and institutions in India, such as will give security and dignity to the society; and the sooner we begin upon the work the better.[32]

Notes:

1. Johnson says: 'Mountaineers are thievish because they are poor; and, having neither manufactures nor commerce, can grow rich only by robbery. They regularly plunder their neighbours, for their neighbours are commonly their enemies; and, having lost that reverence for property by which the order of civil life is preserved, soon consider all as enemies whom they do not reckon as friends, and think themselves licensed to invade whatever

they are not obliged to protect.' [W. H. S.] The quotation is from *A Journey to the Western Islands of Scotland.*

The observations in the text apply largely to the settled Hindoo villages, as well as to the forest tribes.

2. *Ficus religiosa* is the Linnaean name for the 'pīpal'. Other botanists call it *Urostigma religiosum*. In the original edition the botanical name is erroneously given as *Ficus indicus*. The *Ficus indica* (*F. Bengalensis,* or *Urostigma B.*) is the banyan. A story is current that the traders of a certain town begged the magistrate to remove a pīpal-tree which he had planted in the market-place, because, so long as it remained, business could not be conducted. They knew 'the value of a lie'.

3. The red cotton, or silk-cotton, tree, when in spring covered with its huge magnolia-shaped scarlet blossoms, is one of the most magnificent objects in nature. Its botanical name is *Salmalia malabarica* (*Bombax malabaricum; B. heptaphyllum*). This is the tree referred to in the text. The white silk-cotton tree (*Eriodendron anfractuosum; Bombax 'pentandrum; Ceiba pentandra; Gossampinus Rumphii*) has a more southern habitat. (Balfour, *Cyclopaedia,* 3rd ed., s.v. 'Salmalia' and 'Eriodendron'.)

4. The pīpal is usually regarded as sacred only to Vishnu, the Preserver. The *Ficus indica,* or banyan, is sacred to Siva, the Destroyer, and the *Butea frondosa* (Hind. 'dhāk', 'palās', or 'chhyūl ') to Brahmā, the Creator, or δημιουργός.

5. The sacred trees and plants of India are numerous. 'Balfour (Cyclop., 3rd ed., s.v. 'Sacred') enumerates eighty, and the list is by no mean complete. The same author's article, 'Tree', may also be consulted. The minor 'deities' alluded to by the author are the real gods of popular rural Hinduism. The observations of Mr. William Crooke, probably the best authority on the subject of Indian popular religion, though made with reference to a particular locality, are generally applicable. 'Hinduism certainly shows no signs of weakness, and is practically untouched by Christian and Muhammadan proselytism. The gods of the Vedas are as dead as Jupiter, and the Krishna worship only succeeds from its marvellous adaptability to the sensuous and romantic side of the native mind. But it would be too much to say that the creed exercises any real effect on life or morals. With the majority of its devotees it is probably more sympathetic than practical, and ranks with the periodical ablutions in the Ganges and Jumna, and the traditional worship of the local gods and ghosts, which really impress the rustic. He is enclosed on all sides by a ring of precepts, which attribute luck or ill-luck to certain things or actions. These and the bonds of caste, with its obligations for the performance of marriage, death, and other ceremonies, make up the

religions life of the peasant. Nearly every village and hamlet has its local ghost, usually the shrine of a childless man, or one whose funeral rites remained for some reason unperformed. In the expressive popular phrase, he is 'deprived of water' (aud). The pious make oblations to his cenotaph twice a year, and propitiate his ghost with offerings of water to allay his thirst in the lower world. The primaeval serpent-worship is perpetuated in the reverence paid to traditional village-snakes. Of the local ghosts some are beneficent. Sometimes they are only mischievous, like Robin Goodfellow, and will milk the cows, and sour the milk, or pull your hair, if you wander about at night in certain well-known uncanny places. A more dangerous demon is heard in the crackling of the dry leaves of the date-tree in the night wind; and some trees are haunted by a vampire, who will drag you up and devour you, if you venture near them in the darkness.' (*N.W.P. Gazetteer*, 1st ed., vol. vii. *Supplement*, p. 4.) See also the same author's work *Popular Religion and Folklore of Northern India*, 2nd ed., 2 vols. Constable, 1896.

6. Compare the story of Rāmkishan in Chapter 25. Books on anthropology cite many instances of deaths caused by superstitious fears.

7. Arrian, *Indica*, chap. 12: 'The sixth class consists of those called "superintendents". They spy out what goes on in country and town, and report everything to the king where the people have a king, and to the magistrates where the people are self-governed, and it is against use and wont for them to give a false report; — but indeed no Indian is accused of lying.' (McCrindle, *Ancient India, as described by Megasthenes and Arrian*, Trübner, 1877, p. 211). Arrian uses the word επίσκοποι; in the Fragments of Megasthenes quoted by Diodorus and Strabo, the word is έφοροι. The people referred to seem to be the well-known 'news-writers' employed by Oriental sovereigns (*ante*, chapter 33, note 7); a simple explanation missed by McCrindle (op. cit. p. 43, note). The remark about the truthfulness of the Indians appears to be Arrian's addition. It is not in the Fragment of Megasthenes from which Arrian copies, and the falsity of the remark is proved by the statement (ibid., p. 71) that 'a person convicted of bearing false witness suffers mutilation of his extremities'. But in Fragment XXVII from Strabo (op. cit., p. 70) Megasthenes says, 'Truth and virtue they hold alike in esteem'; and in Fragment XXXIII (ibid., p. 85) he asserts that 'the ablest and moat trustworthy men' are appointed έφοροι.

8. Up to the year 1827 'grand larceny', that is to say, stealing to a value exceeding twelve pence, was punishable with death. The Act 7 George IV, cap. 28, abolished the distinction of grand and petty larceny. In 1837, the first year of Queen Victoria's reign, the punishment of death was abolished in the case of between thirty and forty offences. Other statutes have further mitigated the ferocity of the old law.

9. The year was 1652, not 1648 (Tavernier, *Travels*, transl. Ball, vol. i, p. 260, note). The passages describing the criminal procedure of Amīr Jumla are not very long, and deserve quotation, as giving an accurate account of the administration of penal justice by an able native ruler. 'On the 14th [September] we went to the tent of the Nawāb to take leave of him, and to hear what he had to say regarding the goods which we had shown him. But we were told that he was engaged examining a number of criminals, who had been brought to him for immediate punishment. It is the custom in this country not to keep a man in prison; but immediately the accused is taken he is examined and sentence is pronounced on him, which is then executed without any delay. If the person whom they have seized is found innocent, he is released at once; and whatever the nature of the case may be, it is promptly concluded. . . . On the 15th, at seven o'clock in the morning, we went to the Nawāb, and immediately we were announced he asked us to enter his tent, where he was seated with two of his secretaries by him. . . . The Nawāb had the intervals between his toes full of letters, and he also had many between the fingers of his left hand. He drew them sometimes from his feet, sometimes from his hand, and sent his replies through his two secretaries, writing some also himself. . . . While we were with the Nawāb he was informed that four prisoners, who were then at the door of the tent, had arrived. He remained more than half an hour without replying, writing continually and making his secretaries write, but at length he suddenly ordered the criminals to be brought in; and after having questioned them, and made them confess with their own mouths the crime of which they were accused, he remained nearly an hour without saying anything, continuing to write and to make his secretaries write, . . . Among these four prisoners who were brought into his presence there was one who had entered a house and slain a mother and her three infants. He was condemned forthwith to have his feet and hands cut off, and to be thrown into a field near the high road to end his days. Another had stolen on the high road, and the Nawāb ordered him to have his stomach slit open and to be flung in a drain, I could not ascertain what the others had done, but both their heads were cut off. While all this passed the dinner was served, for the Nawāb generally eats at ten o'clock, and he made us dine with him.' (Ibid., pp. 290-3.) Such swift procedure and sharp punishments would still be highly approved of by the great mass of Indian opinion in the villages.

10. Misprinted 'much less' in original edition.

11. The new Act, V of 1840, prescribes the following declaration: 'I solemnly affirm, in the presence of Almighty God, that what I shall state shall be the truth, the whole truth, and nothing but the truth', — and declares that a false statement made on this shall be punished as perjury. [W. H.

S.] The law now in force is to the same effect. This form of declaration is absolutely worthless as a check on perjury, and never hinders any witness from lying to his heart's content. The use of the Korān and Ganges water in the courts has been given up.

12. The tendency of modern India is to rely too much on formal law and the exercise of the powers of the central government. The contemplation of the vast administrative machinery working with its irresistible force and unfailing regularity in obedience to the will of rulers, whose motives are not understood, undoubtedly has a paralysing influence on the life of the nations of India, which, if not counteracted, would work deep mischief. Something in the way of counteraction has been done, though not always with knowledge. The difficulties inherent in the problem of reconciling foreign rule with self-government in an Asiatic country are enormous.

13. But panegyrics on the self-government of Indian villages must always be read with the qualification that the standard of such government was low, and that hundreds of acts and omissions were tolerated, which are intolerable to a modern European Government. Hence comes the difficulty of enforcing numerous reforms loudly called for by European opinion. The vast Indian population hates reform and innovation for many reasons, and, above all, because they involve expense, which to the Indian mind appears wholly unwarrantable.

14. The same phenomenon is observable in rural Ireland, where, as in India, an unhappy history has generated profound distrust and dislike of official authority. The Irish peasant has always been ready to give his neighbour 'the loan of an oath', and a refusal to give it would be thought unneighbourly. An Irish Land Commission and an Indian Settlement Officer must alike expect to receive startling information about the value of land.

15. *Ante*, chapter 49, text at [16].

16. Hume, in speaking of Scotland in the fifteenth century, says, 'Arms more than laws prevailed; and courage, preferably to equity and justice, was the virtue most valued and respected. The nobility, in whom the whole power resided, were so connected by hereditary alliances, or so divided by inveterate enmities, that it was impossible, without employing an armed force, either to punish the most flagrant guilt, or to give security to the most entire innocence. Rapine and violence, when employed against a hostile tribe, instead of making a person odious among his own clan, rather recommended him to their esteem and approbation; and, by rendering him useful to the chieftain, entitled him to the preference above his fellows.' [W. H. S.]

17. Gibbon, chap. 5. The remark refers to Septimius Severus.

18. The Ballot Act became law in 1872.

19. All that the author says is true, and yet it does not alter the fact that Indian society is and always has been permeated and paralysed by almost universal distrust. Such universal distrust does not prevail in England. This difference between the two societies is fundamental, and its reality is fully recognized by natives of India.

20. Compare the author's account of the fraudulent practices of the Company's sepoys when on leave in Oudh. (*Journey through the Kingdom of Oude*, vol. i, pp. 286-304.)

21. The editor has failed to find these quotations in the Wellington Dispatches.

22. This is the first story in the first chapter of the *Gulistān*. The *Mishkāt-ul-Masābih* (Matthews, vol. ii, p. 427) teaches the same doctrine as Sādī: 'That person is not a liar who makes peace between two people, and speaks good words to do away their quarrel although they should be lies; and that person who carries good words from one to another is not a tale-bearer.'

23. Gibbon, chapter 27. In the year A.D. 390 Botheric, the general of Theodosius was murdered by a mob at Thessalonica. Acting on the advice of Rufinus, the emperor avenged his officer's death by an indiscriminate massacre of the inhabitants, in which numbers variously estimated at from 7,000 to 15,000 perished. The emperor quickly felt remorse for the atrocity of which he had been guilty, and submitted to do public penance under the direction of Ambrose.

24. The sum total of truth in India would not, I fear, be appreciably increased if every European had the temper of an angel.

25. The editor has never known a reputation for corruption in any way lower the social position of an official of Indian birth.

26. The argument in the anthor's mind seems to be that the unveracity practised and condoned by certain classes of the natives of India on certain occasions is, at least, not more reprehensible than the vices practised and condoned by certain classes of Europeans on certain occasions.

27. Since the author wrote the above remarks, the conditions of Indian trade have been revolutionized by the development of roads, railways, motors, telegraph, postal facilities, and exports. The Indian merchant has been drawn into the vortex of European and American commerce. He is, in consequence, not quite so cautions as he used to be, and is more liable to severe loss or failure, though he is still, as a rule, far more inclined to caution than are his Western rivals. The Indian private banker undoubtedly is honest in ordinary banking transactions and anxious to maintain his commercial credit, but he will often stoop to the most discreditable devices

in the purchase of a coveted estate, the foreclosure of a mortgage, and the like. His books, nowadays, are certainly not 'appealed to as holy writ', and many merchants keep a duplicate set for income-tax purposes. The happy people of 1836 had never heard of income tax. Private remittances are now made usually through the post office or the joint-stock banks, which did not exist in the author's days. In recent times failures of banks and merchants have been frequent.

28. These observations, which are perfectly true, form a corrective to the fashionable abuse of the Indian capitalist, whose virtues and merits are seldom noticed.

29. The editor has not succeeded in tracing this quotation, but several passages to a similar effect occur in the *Gulistān*.

30. I ought to except Confucius, the great Chinese moralist. [W. H. S.]

31. For a brief notice of Sādī (Sa'dī) see *ante*, chapter 12, note 6. The *Gulistān* is everywhere used as a text-book in schools where Persian is taught. The author's extant correspondence shows that he was fascinated by the charms of Persian poetry, even during the first year of his residence in India.

32. The work was 'begun upon' many years ago, and 'a superstructure of municipal corporations and institutions' now exists in every part of India. But 'the same foundation' does not exist. The stout burghers of the mediaeval English and German towns have no Indian equivalents. The superstructure of the municipal institutions is all that Acts of the Legislature can make it; the difficulty is to find or make a solid foundation. Still, it was right and necessary to establish municipal institutions in India, and, notwithstanding all weaknesses and defects, they are of considerable value, and are slowly developing.

CHAPTER 58

Declining Fertility of the Soil — Popular Notion of the Cause.

On the 18th[1] we came on ten miles to Sāhar, over a plain of poor soil, carelessly cultivated, and without either manure or irrigation. Major Godby left us at Govardhan to return to Agra. He would have gone on with us to Delhi; but having the command of his regiment, and being a zealous officer, he did not like to leave it so long during the exercising season. We felt much the loss of his society. He is a man of great observation and practical good sense; has an infinite fund of good humour, and a cheerfulness of temperament that never seems to flag — a more agreeable companion I have never met. The villages in these parts are literally crowded with peafowl. I counted no less than forty-six feeding close by among the houses of one hamlet on the road, all wild, or rather *unappropriated*, for they seemed on the best possible terms with the inhabitants. At Sāhar our water was drawn from wells eighty feet deep, and this is said to be the ordinary depth from which water is drawn; consequently irrigation is too expensive to be common. It is confined almost exclusively to small patches of garden cultivation in the vicinity of villages.

On the 14th we came on sixteen miles to Kosī, for the most part over a poor soil badly cultivated, and almost exclusively devoted to autumn crops, of which cotton is the principal. I lost the road in the morning before daylight,[2] and the trooper, who usually rode with me, had not come up. I got an old landholder from one of the villages to walk on with me a mile, and put me in the right road. I asked him what had been the state of the country under the former government of the Jāts and Marāthās, and was told that the greater part was a wild jungle. 'I remember,' said the old man, 'when you could not have got out of the road hereabouts without a good deal of risk. I could not have ventured a hundred yards from the village without the chance of having my clothes stripped off my back. Now the whole face of the country is under cultivation, and the roads are safe; formerly the governments kept no faith with their landholders and cultivators, exacting ten rupees where they had bargained for five, whenever they found the crops good; but, in spite of all this "zulm"' (oppression), said the old man, 'there was then more "barkat" (blessings from above) than now. The lands yielded more returns to the cultivator, and he could maintain his little family better upon five acres than he can now upon ten.'

'To what, my old friend, do you attribute this very unfavourable change in the productive powers of your soil?'

'A man cannot, sir, venture to tell the truth at all times, and in all places,' said he.

'You may tell it now with safety, my good old friend; I am a mere traveller ("musafir") going to the hills in search of health, from the valley of the Nerbudda, where the people have been suffering much from blight, and are much perplexed in their endeavour to find a cause.'

'Here, sir, we all attribute these evils to the dreadful System of *perjury*, which the practices of your judicial courts have brought among the people. You are perpetually putting the Ganges water into the hands of the Hindoos, and the Korān into those of Muhammadans; and all kinds of lies are every day told upon them. God Almighty can stand this no longer; and the lands have ceased to be blessed with that fertility which they had before this sad practice began. This, sir, is almost the only fault we have, any of us, to find with your government; men, by this System of perjury, are able to cheat each other out of their rights, and bring down sterility upon the land, by which the innocent are made to suffer for the guilty.'

On reaching our tents, I asked a respectable farmer, who came to pay his respects to the Commissioner of the division, Mr. Fraser, what he thought of the matter, telling him what I had heard from my old friend on the road. 'The diminished fertility is,' said he, 'owing no doubt to the want of those salutary fallows which the fields got under former governments, when invasions and civil wars were things of common occurrence, and kept at least two-thirds of the land waste; but there is, on the other hand, no doubt that you have encouraged perjury a good deal in your courts of justice; and this perjury must have some effect in depriving the land of the blessing of God.[3] Every man now, who has a cause in your civil courts, seems to think it necessary either to swear falsely himself, or to get others to do it for him. The European gentlemen, no doubt, do all they can to secure every man his right, but, surrounded as they are by perjured witnesses, and corrupt native officers, they commonly labour in the dark.'

Much of truth is to be found among the village communities of India, where they have been carefully maintained, if people will go among them to seek it. Here, as almost everywhere else, truth is the result of self-government, whether arising from choice, under municipal institutions, or necessity, under despotism and anarchy; self-government produces self-esteem and pride of character.

Close to our tents we found the people at work, irrigating their fields from several wells, whose waters were all brackish. The crops watered from these wells were admirable — likely to yield at least fifteen returns of the seed. Wherever we go, we find the signs of a great government passed away — signs that must tend to keep alive the recollections, and exalt the ideas of it in the minds of the people. Beyond the boundary of our military and civil stations we find as yet few indications of our reign or character, to link us with the affections of the people. There is hardly anything to indicate our existence as a people or a government in this country; and it is melancholy to think that in the wide extent of country over which I have travelled there should be so few signs of that superiority in science and arts which we boast of, and really do possess, and ought to make conducive to the welfare and happiness of the people in every part of our dominions. The people and the face of the country are just what they might have been had they been governed by police officers and tax-gatherers from the Sandwich Islands, capable of securing life, property, and character, and levying honestly the means of maintaining the establishments requisite for the purpose.[4] Some time after the journey here described, in the early part of November, after a heavy fall of rain, I was driving alone in my buggy from Garhmuktesar on the Ganges to Meerut. The roads were very bad, the stage a double one, and my horse became tired, and unable to go on.[5] I got out at a small village to give him a little rest and food; and sat down, under the shade of one old tree, upon the trunk of another that the storm had blown down, while my groom, the only servant I had with me, rubbed down and baited my horse. I called for some parched gram from the same shop which supplied my horse, and got a draught of good water, drawn from the well by an old woman in a brass jug lent to me for the purpose by the shopkeeper.[6]

While I sat contentedly and happily stripping my parched gram of its shell, and eating it grain by grain, the farmer, or head landholder of the village, a sturdy old Rājpūt, came up and sat himself, without any ceremony, down by my side, to have a little conversation. To one of the dignitaries of the land, in whose presence the aristocracy are alone entitled to chairs, this easy familiarity on the part of a poor farmer seems at first somewhat strange and unaccountable; he is afraid that the man intends to offer him some indignity, or, what is still worse, mistakes him for something less than the dignitary. The following dialogue took place.

'You are a Rājpūt, and a "zamīndār"?' (landholder).

'Yes; I am the head landholder of this village.'

'Can you tell me how that village in the distance is elevated above the ground? Is it from the debris of old villages, or from a rock underneath?'

'It is from the debris of old villages. That is the original seat of all the Rājpūts around; we all trace our descent from the founders of that village who built and peopled it many centuries ago.'

'And you have gone on subdividing your inheritances here, as elsewhere, no doubt, till you have hardly any of you anything to eat?'

'True, we have hardy any of us enough to eat; but that is the fault of the Government, that does not leave us enough, that takes from us as much when the season is bad as when it is good.'[7]

'But your assessment has not been increased, has it?' 'No, we have concluded a settlement for twenty years upon the same footing as formerly.'

'And if the sky were to shower down upon you pearls and diamonds, instead of water, the Government would never demand more from you than the rate fixed upon?'

'No.'

'Then why should you expect remissions in the bad seasons?'

'It cannot be disputed that the "barkat" (blessing from above) is less under you than it used to be formerly, and that the lands yield less to our labour.'

'True, my old friend, but do you know the reason why?'

'No.'

'Then I will tell you. Forty or fifty years ago, in what you call the times of the "barkat" (blessing from above), the cavalry of Sikh freebooters from the Panjāb used to sweep over this fine plain, in which stands the said village from which you are all descended; and to massacre the whole population of some villages, and a certain portion of that of every other village; and the lands of those killed used to be waste for want of cultivators. Is not this all true?'

'Yes, quite true.'

'And the fine groves which had been planted over the plain by your ancestors, as they separated from the great parent stock, and formed independent villages and hamlets for themselves, were all swept away and destroyed by the same hordes of freebooters, from whom your poor imbecile emperors, cooped up in yonder large city of Delhi, were utterly unable to defend you?'

'Quite true,' said the old man with a sigh. 'I remember when all this fine plain was as thickly studded with fine groves of mango- trees as Rohilkhand, or any other part of India.'

'You know that the land requires rest from labour, as well as men and bullocks, and that, if you go on sowing wheat and other exhausting crops, it will go on yielding less and less returns, and at last not be worth the tilling?'

'Quite well.'

'Then why do you not give the land rest by leaving it longer fallow, or by a more frequent alternation of crops relieve it?'

'Because we have now increased so much that we should not get enough to eat were we to leave it to fallow; and unless we tilled it with exhausting crops we should not get the means of paying our rents to the Government.'

'The Sikh hordes in former days prevented this; they killed off a certain portion of your families, and gave the land the rest which you now refuse it. When you had exhausted one part, you found another recovered by a long fallow, so that you had better returns; but now that we neither kill you, nor suffer you to be killed by others, you have brought all the cultivable lands into tillage; and under the old System of cropping to exhaustion, it is not surprising that they yield you less returns.'[8]

By this time we had a crowd of people seated around us upon the ground, as I went on munching my parched gram, and talking to the old patriarch.

They all laughed at the old man at the conclusion of my last speech, and he confessed I was right.

'This is all true, sir, but still your Government is not considerate; it goes on taking kingdom after kingdom, and adding to its dominions without diminishing the burden upon us, its old subjects. Here you have had armies away taking Afghanistan, but we shall not have one rupee the less to pay.'[9]

'True, my friend, nor would you demand a rupee less from those honest cultivators around us, if we were to leave you all your lands untaxed. You complain of the Government—they complain of you.' (Here the circle around us laughed at the old man again.) 'Nor would you subdivide the lands the less for having it rent-free; on the contrary, it would be every generation subdivided the more, inasmuch as there would be more of local ties, and a greater disinclination of families to separate and seek service abroad.'

'True, sir, very true—that is, no doubt, a very great evil.'

'And you know it is not an evil produced by us, but one arising out of your own laws of inheritance. You have heard, no doubt, that with us the eldest son gets the whole of the land, and the younger sons all go out in search of service, with such share as they can get of the other property of their father?'

'Yes, sir; but when shall we get service? — you have none to give us. I would serve to-morrow if you would take me as a soldier,' said he, stroking his white whiskers.

The crowd laughed heartily; and some wag observed that I should perhaps think him too old.

'Well,' said the old man, smiling, 'the gentleman himself is not very young, and yet I dare say he is a good servant of his Government.'

This was paying me off for making the people laugh at his expense.

'True, my old friend,' said I, 'but I began to serve when I was young, and have been long learning.'

'Very well,' said the old man, 'but I should be glad to serve the rest of my life upon a less salary than you got when you began to learn.'

'Well, my friend, you complain of our Government; but you must acknowledge that we do all we can to protect you, though it is true that we are often acting in the dark.'

'Often, sir? you are always acting in the dark; you, hardly any of you, know anything of what your revenue and police officers are doing; there is no justice or redress to be got without paying for it, and it is not often that those who pay can get it.'

'True, my old friend, that is bad all over the world. You cannot presume to ask anything even from the Deity Himself, without paying the priest who officiates in His temples; and if you should, you would none of you hope to get from your Deity what you asked for.'

Here the crowd laughed again, and one of them said that 'there was this certainly to be said for our Government, that the European gentlemen themselves never took bribes, whatever those under them might do'.

'You must not be too sure of that, neither. Did not the Lāl Bībī, the Red Lady, get a bribe for soliciting the judge, her husband, to let go Amīr Singh, who had been confined in jail?'

'How did this take place?'

'About three years ago Amīr Singh was sentenced to imprisonment, and his friends spent a great deal of money in bribes to the native officers of the court, but all in vain. At last they were recommended to give a handsome present to the Red Lady. They did so, and Amīr Singh was released.'

'But did they give the present into the lady's own hand?'

'No, they gave it to one of her women.'

'And how do you know that she ever gave it to her mistress, or that her mistress ever heard of the transaction?'

'She might certainly have been acting without her mistress' knowledge; but the popular belief is that the Lāl Bībī got the present.'

I then told the story of the affair at Jubbulpore, when Mrs. Smith's name had been used for a similar purpose, and the people around us were all highly amused; and the old man's opinion of the transaction with the Red Lady evidently underwent a change.[10]

We became good friends, and the old man begged me to have my tents, which he supposed were coming up, pitched among them, that he might have an opportunity of showing that he was not a bad subject, though he grumbled against the Government.

The next day at Meerut I got a visit from the chief native judge, whose son, a talented youth, is in my office. Among other things, I asked him whether it might not be possible to improve the character of the police by increasing the salaries of the officers, and mentioned my conversation with the landholder.

'Never, sir,' said the old gentleman; 'the man that now gets twenty-five rupees a month is contented with making perhaps fifty or seventy-five more; and the people subject to his authority pay him accordingly. Give him a hundred, sir, and he will put a shawl over his shoulders, and the poor people will be obliged to pay him at a rate that will make up his income to four hundred. You will only alter his style of living, and make him a greater burthen to the people. He will always take as long as he thinks he can with impunity.'

'But do you not think that when people see a man adequately paid by the Government they will the more readily complain of any attempt at unauthorized exactions?'

'Not a bit, sir, as long as they see the same difficulties in the way of prosecuting him to conviction. In the administration of civil justice' (the old gentleman is a civil judge), 'you may occasionally see your way, and understand what is doing; but in revenue and police you never have seen it in India, and never will, I think. The officers you employ will all add to their incomes by unauthorized means; and the lower these incomes, the less their pretensions, and the less the populace have to pay.'[11]

Notes:

1. January, 1836.

2. The old Anglo-Indian rose much earlier than his successor of the present day commonly does.

3. For other popular explanations of the alleged decrease in fertility of the soil, see *ante*, Chapter 27, where three explanations are offered, namely, the eating of beef, the prevalence of adultery, and the impiety of surveys.

4. The inapplicability of these observations of the author to the present time is a good measure of the material progress of India since his day. The Ganges Canal, the bridges over the Indus, Ganges, and other great rivers, and numberless engineering works throughout the empire, are permanent witnesses to the scientific superiority of the ruling race. Buildings which can claim any high degree of architectural excellence are, unfortunately, still rare, but the public edifices of Bombay will not suffer by comparison with those of most capital cities, and for some years past, considerable attention has been paid to architecture as an art. A great architectural experiment is in progress at the new official capital of Delhi (1914).

5. The road is now an excellent one.

6. Parched gram, or chick-pea, is commonly used by Indian travellers as a convenient and readily portable form of food. The 'brass jug' lent to the author could be purified by fire after his use of it.

7. Growls of this kind must not be interpreted too literally. Any village landholder, if encouraged, would grumble in the same strain.

8. This is the permanent difficulty of Indian revenue administration, which no Government measures can seriously diminish.

9. The mission to Kabul, under Captain Alexander Burnes, was not dispatched till September, 1837, and troops did not assemble before the conclusion of the treaty with the Sikhs in June, 1838. The army crossed the Indus in January, 1839. The conversation in the text is stated to have taken place 'some time after the journey herein described', and must, apparently, be dated in November, 1839. The author was in the North-Western Provinces in that year.

10. Some of Mrs. Smith's suitors entered into a combination to defraud a suitor in his court of a large sum of money, which he was to pay to

Mrs. Smith as she walked in the garden. A dancing girl from the town of Jubbulpore was made to represent Mrs. Smith, and a suit of Mrs. Smith's clothes was borrowed for her from the washerman. The butler took the suitor to the garden, and introduced him to the supposed Mrs. Smith, who received him very graciously, and condescended to accept his offer of five thousand rupees in gold mohurs. The plot was afterwards discovered, and the old butler, washerman, and all, were sentenced to work in a rope on the roads. [W. H. S.]

Penal labour on the roads has been discontinued long since. Similar plots probably have often escaped detection. The whole conversation is a valuable illustration of Indian habits and modes of thought.

11. The subject of the police administration is more fully discussed *post*, in Chapter 69.

CHAPTER 59

Concentration of Capital and its Effects.

Kosī[1] stands on the borders of Fīrōzpur, the estate of the late Shams-ud-dīn, who was hanged at Delhi on the 3rd of October, 1835, for the murder of William Fraser, the representative of the Governor-General in the Delhi city and territories.[2] The Mewātīs of Fīrōzpur are notorious thieves and robbers. During the Nawāb's time they dared not plunder within his territory, but had a free licence to plunder wherever they pleased beyond it.[3] They will now be able to plunder at home, since our tribunals have been introduced to worry prosecutors and their witnesses to death by the distance they have to go, and the tediousness of our process; and thereby to secure impunity to offenders, by making it the interest of those who have been robbed, not only to bear with the first loss without complaint, but largely to bribe police officers to conceal the crimes from their master, the magistrate, when they happen to come to their knowledge. Here it was that Jeswant Rāo Holkār gave a grand ball on the 14th of October, 1804, while he was with his cavalry covering the siege of Delhi by his regular brigade. In the midst of the festivity he had a European soldier of the King's 76th Regiment, who had been taken prisoner, strangled behind the curtain, and his head stuck upon a spear and placed in the midst of the assembly, where the 'nāch' (nautch) girls were made to dance round it. Lord Lake reached the place the next morning in pursuit of this monster; and the gallant regiment, who here heard the story, had soon an opportunity of revenging the foul murder of their comrade in the battle of Dīg, one of the most gallant passages of arms we have ever had in India.[4]

Near Kosī there is a factory in ruins belonging to the late firm of Mercer & Company. Here the cotton of the district used to be collected and screwed under the superintendence of European agents, preparatory to its embarkation for Calcutta on the river Jumna. On the failure of the firm, the establishment was broken up, and the work, which was then done by one great European merchant, is now done by a score or two of native merchants. There is, perhaps, nothing which India wants more than the concentration of capital; and the failure of a I [5] the great commercial houses in Calcutta, in the year 1833, was, unquestionably, a great calamity.

They none of them brought a particle of capital into the country, nor does India want a particle from any country; but they *concentrated* it; and had they employed the whole, as they certainly did a good deal of it, in judiciously improving and extending the industry of the natives, they might have been the source of incalculable good to India, its people, and government.[6]

To this concentration of capital in great commercial and manufacturing establishments, which forms the grand characteristic of European in contradistinction to Asiatic societies in the present day, must we look for those changes which we consider desirable in the social and religions institutions of the people. Where land is liable to eternal subdivision by the law and the religion of both the Muhammadan and Hindoo population; where every great work that improves its productive powers, and facilitates the distribution of its produce among the people, in canals, roads, bridges, &c., is made by Government; where capital is nowhere concentrated in great commercial or manufacturing establishments, there can be no upper classes in society but those of office; and of all societies, perhaps that is the worst in which the higher classes are so exclusively composed. In India, public office has been, and must continue to be, the only road to distinction, until we have a *law of primogeniture*, and a *concentration of capital*. In India no man has ever thought himself respectable, or been thought so by others, unless he is armed with his little 'hukūmat'; his 'little brief authority' under Government, that gives him the command of some public establishment paid out of the revenues of the State.[7] In Europe and America, where capital has been concentrated in great commercial and manufacturing establishments, and free institutions prevail almost as the natural consequence, industry is everything; and those who direct and command it are, happily, looked up to as the source of the wealth, the strength, the virtue, and the happiness of the nation. The concentration of capital in such establishments may, indeed, be considered, not only as the natural consequence, but as the prevailing cause of the free institutions by which the mass of the people in European countries are blessed.[8] The mass of the people were as much brutalized and oppressed by the landed aristocracy as they could have been by any official aristocracy before towns and higher classes were created by the concentration of capital.

The same observations are applicable to China. There the land all belongs to the sovereign, as in India; and, as in India, it is liable to the same eternal subdivision among the sons of those who hold it under him. Capital is nowhere more concentrated in China than in India; and all the great works that add to the fertility of the soil, and facilitate the distribution of the land labour of the country are formed by the sovereign out of the public revenue. The revenue is, in consequence, one of office;[9] and no man considers himself respectable,[10] unless invested with some office under Government, that is, under the Emperor. Subdivision of labour, concentration of capital, and machinery render an Englishman everywhere dependent upon the co-operation of multitudes; while the Chinaman, who as yet knows little of either, is everywhere independent, and able to work his way among strangers. But this very dependence of the Englishman upon the concentration of capital is the greatest source of his strength and pledge of his security, since it supports those members of the higher orders who can best understand and assert the rights and interests of the whole.[11]

If we had any great establishment of this sort in which Christians could find employment and the means of religious and secular instruction, thousands of converts would soon flock to them; and they would become vast sources of future improvement in industry, social comfort, municipal institutions, and religion. What chiefly prevents the spread of Christianity in India is the dread of exclusion from caste and all its privileges; and the utter hopelessness of their ever finding any respectable circle of society of the adopted religion, which converts, or would-be converts, to Christianity now everywhere feel. Form such circles for them, make the members of these circles happy in the exertion of honest and independent industry, let those who rise to eminence in them feel that they are considered as respectable and as important in the social system as the servants of Government, and converts will flock around you from all parts, and from all classes of the Hindoo community. I have, since I have been in India, had, I may say, at least a score of Hindoo grass-cutters turn Musalmāns, merely because the grooms and the other grass-cutters of my establishment happened to be of that religion, and they could neither eat, drink, nor smoke with them. Thousands of Hindoos all over India become every year Musalmāns from the same motive;[12] and we do not get the same number of converts to Christianity, merely because we cannot offer them the same advantages. I am persuaded that a dozen such establishments as that of Mr. Thomas Ashton of Hyde, as described by a physician at Manchester, and noticed in Mr. Baines's admirable work on the *Cotton Manufactures of Great Britain* , would do more in the way of conversion among the people of India than has ever yet been done by all the religious establishments, or ever will be done by them, without such aid.[13]

I have said that the great commercial houses of Calcutta, which in their ruin involved that of so many useful establishments scattered over India, like that of Kosī, brought no capital into the country.[14] They borrowed from one part of the civil and military servants of Government at a high interest that portion of their salary which they saved; and lent it at a higher interest to others of the same establishment, who for a time required or wished to spend more than they received; or they employed it at a higher rate of profit for great commercial and manufacturing establishments scattered over India, or spread over the ocean. Their great error was in mistaking nominal for real profits. Calculating their dividend on the nominal profits, and never supposing that there could be any such things as losses in commercial speculation, or bad debts from misfortunes and bad faith, they squandered them in lavish hospitality and ostentatious display, or allowed their retiring members to take them to England and to every other part of the world where their creditors might not find them, till they discovered that all the real capital left at their command was hardly sufficient to pay back with the stipulated interest one-tenth of what they had borrowed. The members of those houses who remained in India up to the time of the general wreck were of course reduced to ruin, and obliged to bear the burthen of the odium and indignation which the ruin of so many thousands of confiding constituents brought down upon them. Since that time the savings of civil and military servants have been invested either in Government securities at a small interest, or in banks, which make their profit in the ordinary way, by discounting bills of exchange, and circulating their own notes for the purpose, or by lending out their money at a high interest of 10 or 12 per cent. to other members of the same services.[15]

On the 16th of January we went on to Horal, ten miles over a plain, with villages numerous and large, and in every one some fine large building of olden times—sarāi, palace, temple, or tomb, but all going to decay.[16] The population much more dense than in any of the native states I have seen; villages larger and more numerous; trade in the transit of cotton, salt, sugar, and grain, much brisker. A great number of hares were here brought to us for sale at threepence apiece, a rate at which they sell at this season in almost all parts of Upper India, where they are very numerous, and very easily caught in nets.

Notes:

1. Kosī is twenty-five miles north-west of Mathurā.

2. The story of the murder of Mr. Fraser is fully detailed *post* in Chapter 64. After the execution of Shams-ud- dīn, the estate of the criminal was taken possession of by Government, and the town of Fīrōzpur is now the head- quarters of a sub-collectorship of the Gurgāon district in the Panjāb. The Delhi territories were placed under the government of the Lieutenant-Governor of the Panjāb in 1858.

3. The Mewātī depredations had gone on for centuries. The Sultān Balban (Ghiās-ud-dīn, alias Ulugh Khan), who reigned from A.D. 1265-87, temporarily suppressed them by punishments of awful cruelty, flaying the

criminals alive, and so forth. The Mewātīs now supply men to a few robber gangs, but are incapable of mischief on a large scale.

4. Delhi was most nobly defended against Holkār by a very small force under Lieutenant-Colonel Burn, who 'repelled an assault, and defended a city ten miles in circumference, and which had ever before been given up at the first appearance of an enemy at its gates'.

The battle of Dīg was fought on November 13, 1804, by the division under the command of General Fraser on the one side, and Holkār's infantry and artillery on the other. 'The 76th led the way, with its wonted alacrity and determination,' and forced its way into the village in advance of its supports. The fight resulted in the total defeat of the Marāthās, who lost nearly two thousand men, and eighty-seven pieces of cannon. The English loss also was heavy, amounting to upwards of six hundred and forty killed and wounded, including the brave commander, who was mortally wounded, and survived the victory only a few days.

On the night of November 17, General Lake in person routed Holkār and his cavalry, killing about three thousand men. The English loss on this occasion amounted to only two men killed, and about twenty wounded.

The fort of Dīg, with a hundred guns and a considerable quantity of ammunition and military stores, was captured on December 24 of the same year. (Thornton, *History of British India*, pp. 316-19, 2nd ed., 1859.)

5. Transcription note. This clause is not intelligible to the transcriber. The character '1' or 'I' appears in the text. Some words appear to be missing.

6. The author was grievously mistaken in supposing that India did not require 'a particle' of foreign capital. The railways, and the great tea, coffee, indigo, and other industries, built up and developed during the nineteenth century, and still growing, owe their existence to the hundreds of millions sterling of English capital poured into the country, and could not possibly have been financed from Indian resources. The author seems not to have expected the construction of railways in India, although when he wrote a beginning of the railway system in England had been made.

7. This sentiment is still potent, and explains the eagerness often shown by wealthy landholders of high social rank to obtain official appointments, which to the European mind seem unworthy of their acceptance.

8. Few readers are likely to accept this proposition.

9. This clause is not intelligible to the editor. The word 'revenue' probably is a misprint for 'aristocracy'.

10. The original edition prints, 'No man considers himself less respectable', which is nonsense.

11. This sentiment reads oddly in these days of social democracy and continual conflict between capital and labour.

12. The steady progress of Islam in Lower and Eastern Bengal, first made apparent by the census of 1872, has been confirmed by the enumerations of 1901 and 1911. The feeling that the religion of the Prophet gives its adherent a better position in both this world and the next than Hinduism can offer to a low-caste man is the most powerful motive for conversion. See Dr. James Wise's valuable treatise, 'The Muhammadans of Eastern Bengal' (*J.A.S.B.*, Part III (1894), pp. 28-63), and the Census Reports from 1872 to 1911.

13. The author's whimsical notion that a development of commercial and manufacturing organization in India would cause converts to flock from all parts, and from all classes of the Hindoo community, has not been verified by experience. Much capital is now concentrated in the great cities, and the number of cotton, jute, and other factories is considerable, but Christian converts are not among the goods produced.

14. The modern commercial houses bring a large proportion of their capital from Europe.

15. The three Presidency Banks, the Bank of Bengal, the Bank of Madras, and the Bank of Bombay, in which the Indian Government is interested, are the leading Indian banks. The Bank of Bengal was opened in 1806. No bank in India is allowed to issue notes. The paper money in use is issued by the Paper Currency Department of the Government of India, and the notes are known as 'currency notes'. The issue of these notes began in 1862-3. (Balfour, *Cyclopaedia*, 3rd ed., s.v. 'Bank and Paper Currency'). Much Indian capital is now invested in joint-stock companies of every kind.

16. More correctly, Hodal.

CHAPTER 60

Transit Duties in India — Mode of Collecting them.

At Horal[1] resides a Collector of Customs with two or three uncovenanted European assistants as patrol officers.[2] The rule now is to tax only the staple articles of produce from the west on their transit down into the valley of the Jumna and Ganges, and to have only one line on which these articles shall be liable to duties.[3] They are free to pass everywhere else without search or molestation. This has, no doubt, relieved the people of these provinces from an infinite deal of loss and annoyance inflicted upon them by the former System of levying the Customs duties, and that without much diminishing the net receipts of Government from this branch of its revenues. But the time may come when Government will be constrained to raise a greater proportion of its collective revenues than it has hitherto done from indirect taxation, and when this time comes, the rule which confines the impost to a single line must of course be abandoned.[4] Under the former system, one great man, with a very high salary, was put in to preside over a host of native agents with very small salaries, and without any responsible intermediate agent whatever to aid him, and to watch over them. The great man was selected without any reference to his knowledge of, or fitness for, the duties entrusted to him, merely because he happened to be of a certain standing in a certain exclusive service, which entitled him to a certain scale of salary, or because he had been found unfit for judicial or other duties requiring more intellect and energy of character. The consequence was that for every one rupee that went into the public treasury, ten were taken by these harpies from the merchants, or other people over whom they had, or could pretend to have, a right of search.[5]

Some irresponsible native officer who happened to have the confidence of the great man (no matter in what capacity he served him) sold for his own profit, and for that of those whose goodwill he might think it worth while to conciliate, the offices of all the subordinate agents immediately employed in the collection of the duties. A man who was to receive an avowed salary of seven rupees a month would give him three or four thousand for his post, because it would give him charge of a detached post, in which he could soon repay himself with a handsome profit. A poor 'peon', who was to serve under others, and could never hope for an independent charge, would give five hundred rupees for an office which yielded him avowedly only four rupees a month. All arrogated the right of search, and the state of Indian society and the climate were admirably suited to their purpose. A person of any respectability would feel himself dishonoured were the females of his family to be *seen*, much less *touched*, while passing along the road in their palanquin or covered carnage; and to save himself from such dishonour he was everywhere obliged to pay these custom-house officers. Many articles that pass in transit through India would suffer much damage from being opened along the road at any season, and be liable to be spoiled altogether during that of the rains; and these harpies could always make the merchants open them, unless they paid liberally for their forbearance. Articles were rated to the duty according to their value; and articles of the same weight were often, of course, of very different values. These officers could always pretend that packages liable to injury from exposure contained within them, among the articles set forth in the invoice, others of greater value in proportion to their weight. Men who carried pearls, jewels, and other articles very valuable compared with their bulk, always depended for their security from robbers and thieves on their concealment; and there was nothing which they dreaded so much as the insolence and rapacity of these custom-house officers, who made them pay large bribes, or exposed their goods. Gangs of thieves had members in disguise at such stations, who were soon able to discover through the insolence of the officers, and the fears and entreaties of the merchants, whether they had anything worth taking or not.

A party of thieves from Datiyā, in 1882, followed Lord William Bentinck's camp to the bank of the river Jumna near Mathurā, where they found a poor merchant humbly entreating an insolent custom-house officer not to insist upon his showing the contents of the little box he carried in his carriage, lest it might attract the attention of thieves, who were always to be found among the followers of such a camp, and offering to give him anything reasonable for his forbearance. Nothing he could be got to offer would satisfy the rapacity of the man; the box was taken out and opened. It contained jewels which the poor man hoped to sell to advantage among the European ladies and gentlemen of the Governor- General's suite. He replaced his box in his carriage; but in half an hour it was travelling post-haste to Datiyā, by relays of thieves who had been posted along the road for such occasions. They quarrelled about the division; swords were drawn, and wounds inflicted. One of the gang ran off to the magistrate at Sāgar, with whom he had before been acquainted;[6] and he sent him back with a small party, and a letter to the Datiyā Rājā requesting that he would get the box of jewels for the poor merchant. The party took the precaution of searching the house of the thieves before they delivered the letter to their friend the minister, and by this means recovered about half the jewels, which amounted in all to about seven thousand rupees. The merchant was agreeably surprised when he got back so much of his property through the magistrate of Mathurā, and confirmed the statement of the thief regarding the dispute with the custom-house officer which enabled them to discover the value of the box.

Should Government by and by extend the System that obtains in this single line to the Customs all over India they may greatly augment their revenue without any injury, and with but little necessary loss and inconvenience to merchants. The object of all just taxation is to make the subjects contribute to the public burthen in proportion to their means, and with as little loss and inconvenience to themselves as possible. The people who reside west of this line enjoy all their salt, cotton, and other articles which are taxed on crossing the line without the payment of any duties, while those to the east of it are obliged to pay. It is, therefore, not a just line. The advantages are, first, that it interposes a body of most efficient officers between the mass of harpies and the heads of the department, who now virtually superintend the whole System, whereas they used formerly to do so merely ostensibly. They are at once the *tapis* of Prince Husain and the telescope of Prince Alī; they enable the heads of departments to be everywhere and see everything, whereas before they were nowhere and saw nothing.[7] Secondly, it makes the great staple articles of general consumption alone liable to the payment of duties, and thereby does away in a great measure with the odious right of search.

At Kosī our friend, Charles Fraser, left us to proceed through Mathurā to Agra. He is a very worthy man and excellent public officer, one of those whom one always meets again with pleasure, and of whose society one never tires. Mr. Wilmot, the Collector of Customs, and Mr. Wright, one of the patrol officers, came to dine with us. The wind blew so hard all day that the cook and khānsāmān (butler) were long in despair of being able to give us any dinner at all. At last we managed to get a tent, closed at every crevice to keep out the dust, for a cook-room; and they were thus able to preserve their master's credit, which, no doubt, according to their notions, depended altogether on the quality of his dinner.

Notes:

1. The place is a small town in the Gurgāon District, Panjāb.

2. The term 'uncovenanted' may require explanation for readers not familiar with the details of Indian administration. The Civil Service of India,

commonly called Indian Civil Service, which supplies most of the higher administrative and judicial officers, used to be known as the Covenanted service, because its members sign a covenant with the Secretary of State. All the other departmental services—Public Works, Postal and the rest—were grouped together as uncovenanted. In accordance with the Report of the Public Service Commission (1886-7) the terms 'covenanted' and 'uncovenanted' have been disused.

3. The text refers to what was known as the 'customs hedge'. Before the establishment of the British supremacy each of the innumerable native jurisdictions levied transit duties on many kinds of goods at each of its frontiers, to the infinite vexation of traders. Such duties were gradually abolished in British territory, and few, if any, are now enforced by native states. Salt cannot be manufactured in British India without a licence, and the Salt (formerly called Inland Customs) Department is charged with the duty of preventing the manufacture or sale of illicit salt. In its later developments the Customs hedge was used for the collection of the salt duty only. Sir John Strachey took a leading part in its abolition. To secure the levy of the duty on salt, he writes, 'there grew up gradually a monstrous system, to which it would be almost impossible to find a parallel in any tolerably civilized country. A Customs line was established which stretched across the whole of India, which in 1869 extended from the Indus to the Mahānadī in Madras, a distance of 2,300 miles; and it was guarded by nearly 12,000 men and petty officers, at an annual cost of £162,000. It would have stretched from London to Constantinople. . . . It consisted principally of an immense impenetrable hedge of thorny trees and bushes . . . A similar line, 280 miles in length, was maintained in the north-eastern part of the Bombay Presidency from Dohud to the Runn of Cutch.' In 1878 the salt duties were revised, and the necessary arrangements with the native states were made. With effect from the 1st April, 1879, the whole Customs line was abolished, with the exception of a small portion on the Indus. (Sir J. Strachey, *The Finances and Public Works of India*, 1869-81, London, 1882, pp. 219, 220, 225.) Great mines of rock salt are worked near the Indus.

4. Most people who know India intimately are of opinion that indirect taxation is more suitable to the circumstances of the country than direct taxation. For municipal purposes, indirect taxation, under the name of octroi, is levied by most considerable towns, and notwithstanding its inconveniences, is far less unpopular and far more productive than any form of direct taxation. The people have been accustomed to indirect taxation of divers kinds from the most remote times, and hate income tax or any other direct impost, however reasonable it may be in theory. Since 1895 the general customs duty is 5 per cent. *ad valorem* on commodities imported into

British India by sea. (See *I.G.*, 1907, vol. iv, chapter 8). The above remarks on the suitability of indirect taxation for India are not intended as a defence of the barbarous device of the 'Customs hedge', which was indefensible.

5. That unsound System prevailed in all departments during the early years of the nineteenth century. 'In Bengal, the monopoly of salt in one form or other dates at least from the establishment of the Board of Trade there in 1765. The strict monopoly of salt commenced in 1780, under a System of agencies. The System introduced in 1780 continued in force with occasional modifications till 1862, when the several salt agencies were gradually abolished, leaving the Supply of salt, whether by importations or excise manufacture, to private enterprise. Since then, for Bengal Proper, the supply of the condiment has been obtained chiefly by importation, but in part by private manufacture under a System of excise.' (Balfour, *Cyclopaedia*, 3rd ed., s.v. Salt.) At present the Salt Department is controlled by a single Commissioner with the Government of India, The fee payable for a licence to manufacture salt is fifty rupees. It is inaccurate to describe the limitation imposed on the manufacture of salt as a monopoly. Any one can sell salt, but it can be made only under licence.

6. The author.

7. The same observations, *mutatis mutandis*, are applicable to the magistracy of the country; and the remedy for all the great existing evils must be sought in the same means, the interposition of a body of efficient officers between the magistrate and the 'thānadārs', or present head police officers of small divisions. [W. H. S.] Much has been done to carry out this advice. The 'most efficient officers' of the inland Customs department alluded to in the text were the European or Eurasian 'uncovenanted' Collectors of Customs and their assistants. The allusion to Prince Husain and Prince Alī refers to the well-known tale in the *Arabian Nights*, 'The story of Prince Ahmad and the Fairy Peri- Banu'. It is omitted, I believe, from Lane's version.

CHAPTER 61

Peasantry of India attached to no existing Government — Want of Trees in Upper India [1] — Cause and Consequence — Wells and Groves.

What strikes one most after crossing the Chambal is, I think, the improved size and bearing of the men; they are much stouter, and more bold and manly, without being at all less respectful. They are certainly a noble peasantry, full of courage, spirit, and intelligence; and heartily do I wish that we could adopt any system that would give our Government a deep root in their affections, or link their interests inseparably with its prosperity; for, with all its defects, life, property, and character are certainly more secure, and all their advantages more freely enjoyed under our Government than under any other they have ever heard of, or that exists at present in any other part of the country. The eternal subdivision of the landed property reduces them too much to one common level, and prevents the formation of that middle class which is the basis of all that is great and good in European societies — the great vivifying spirit which animates all that is good above it in the community.[2] It is a singular fact that the peasantry, and, I may say, the landed interest of the country generally, have never been the friends of any existing government, have never considered their interests and that of their government the same; and, consequently, have never felt any desire for its success or its duration.[3]

The towns and villages all stand upon high mounds formed of the debris of former towns and villages, that have been accumulating, most of them, for thousands of years. They are for the most part mere collections of wretched hovels built of frail materials, and destined only for a brief period.

> Man wants but little here below,
> Nor wants that little long.[4]

And certainly there is no climate in the world where man wants less than in this of India generally, and Upper India particularly. The peasant lives in the open air; and a house to him is merely a thing to eat and sleep in, and to give him shelter in the storm, which comes upon him but seldom, and never in a pitiless shape. The society of his friends he enjoys in the open air, and he never furnishes his house for their reception or for display. The peasantry of India, in consequence of living and talking so much in the open air, have all stentorian voices, which they find it exceedingly difficult to modulate to our taste when they come into our rooms.

Another thing in this part of India strikes a traveller from other parts — the want of groves of fruit-trees around the villages and along the roads. In every other part of India he can at every stage have his tents pitched in a grove of mango-trees, that defend his followers from the direct rays of the sun in the daytime, and from the cold dews at night; but in the district above Agra, he may go for ten marches without getting the shelter of a grove in one.[5] The Sikhs, the Marāthās, the Jāts, and the Pathāns destroyed them all during the disorders attending the decline of the Muhammadan empire; and they have never been renewed, because no man could feel secure that they would be suffered to stand ten years. A Hindoo believes that his soul in the next world is benefited by the blessings and grateful feelings of those of his fellow creatures who unmolested eat the fruit and enjoy the shade of the trees he has planted during his sojourn in this world; and, unless he can feel assured that the traveller and the public in general will be permitted to do so, he can have no hope of any permanent benefit from his good work. It might as well be cut down as pass into the hands of another person who had no feeling of interest in the eternal repose of the soul of the planter. That person would himself have no advantage in the next world from giving the fruit and the shade of the trees to the public, since the prayers of those who enjoyed them would be offered for the soul of the planter, and not for his — he, therefore, takes all their advantage to himself in this world, and the planter and the public are defrauded. Our Government thought they had done enough to encourage the renewal of these groves, when by a regulation they gave to the present lessees of villages the privilege of planting them themselves, or permitting others to plant them; but where they held their leases for a term of only five years, of course they would be unwilling to plant them. They might lose their lease when the term expired, or forfeit it before; and the successor would have the land on which the trees stood, and would be able to exclude the public, if not the proprietor, from the enjoyment of any of their advantages. Our Government has, in effect, during the thirty-five years that it has held the dominion of the North-Western Provinces,[6] prohibited the planting of mango groves, while the old ones are every year disappearing. On the resumption of rent-free lands, even the ground on which the finest of these groves stand has been recklessly resumed, and the proprietors told me that they may keep the trees they have, but cannot be allowed to renew them, as the lands are become the property of Government. The lands of groves that have been the pride of families for a century and a half have been thus resumed. Government is not aware of the irreparable mischief they do the country they govern by such measures.[7]

On my way back from Meerut, after the conversation already related with the farmer of a small village (*ante*, chapter 58, text at [7]), my tents were one day pitched, in the month of December, amidst some very fine garden cultivation in the district of Alīgarh;[8] and in the evening I walked out as usual to have some talk with the peasantry. I came to a neighbouring well at which four pair of bullocks were employed watering the surrounding fields of wheat for the market, and vegetables for the families of the cultivators. Four men were employed at the well, and two more in guiding the water into the little embanked squares into which they divide their fields.

I soon discovered that the most intelligent of the four was a Jāt; and I had a good deal of conversation with him as he stood landing the leather buckets, as the two pair of bullocks on his side of the well drew them to the top, a distance of forty cubits from the surface of the water beneath.

'Who built this well?' I began.

'It was built by one of my ancestors, six generations ago.'

'How much longer will it last?'

'Ten generations more, I hope; for it is now just as good as when first made. It is of 'pakkā' bricks without mortar cement.'[9]

'How many waterings do you give?'

'If there should be no rain, we shall require to give the land six waterings, as the water is sweet; had it been brackish four would do. Brackish water is better for wheat than sweet water; but it is not so good for vegetables or sugar-cane.'

'How many "bīghās" are watered from this well?'

'We water twenty "bīghās", or one hundred and five "jarības", from this well.'[10]

'And you pay the Government how much?'

'One hundred rupees, at the rate of five rupees the bīghā. But only the five immediately around the well are mine, the rest belong to others.'

'But the well belongs to you; and I suppose you get from the proprietors of the other fifteen something for your water?'

'Nothing. There is more water for my five bīghās, and I give them what they require gratis; they acknowledge that it is a gift from me, and that is all I want.'

'And what does the land beyond the range of your water of the same quality pay?'

'It pays at the rate of two rupees the bīghā, and it is with difficulty that they can be made to pay that. Water, sir, is a great thing, and with that and manure we get good crops from the land.'[11]

'How many returns of the seed?'

'From these twenty bīghās with six waterings, and cross ploughing, and good manure, we contrive to get twenty returns; that is, if God is pleased with us and blesses our efforts.'

'And you maintain your family comfortably out of the return from your five?'

'If they were mine I could; but we had two or three bad seasons seven years ago, and I was obliged to borrow eighty rupees from our banker at 24 per cent., for the subsistence of my family. I have hardly been able to pay him the interest with all I can earn by my labour, and I now serve him upon two rupees a month.'

'But that is not enough to maintain you and your family?'

'No; but he only requires my services for half the day, and during the other half I work with others to get enough for them.'

'And when do you expect to pay off your debt?'

'God only knows; if I exert myself, and keep a good "nīyat" (pure mind or intentions), he will enable me or my children to do so some day or other. In the meantime he has my five bīghās of land in mortgage, and I serve him in the cultivation.'

'But under those misfortunes, you could surely venture to demand something from the proprietors of the other fifteen bīghās for the water of your well?'

'Never, sir; it would be said all over the country that such an one sold God's water for his neighbours' fields, and I should be ashamed to show my face. Though poor, and obliged to work hard, and serve others, I have still too much pride for that.'

'How many bullocks are required for the tillage of these twenty bīghās watered from your well?'

'These eight bullocks do all the work; they are dear now. This was purchased the other day on the death of the old one, for twenty-six rupees. They cost about fifty rupees a pair — the late famine has made them dear.'[12]

'What did the well cost in making?'

'I have heard that it cost about one hundred and twenty rupees; it would cost about that sum to make one of this kind in the present day, not more.'

'How long have the families of your caste been settled in these parts?'

'About six or seven generations; the country had before been occupied by a peasantry of the Kalār caste. Our ancestors came, built up mud fortifications, dug wells, and brought the country under cultivation; it had been reduced to a waste; for a long time we were obliged to follow the plough with our swords by our sides, and our friends around us with their matchlocks in their hand, and their matches lighted.'

'Did the water in your well fail during the late seasons of drought?'

'No, sir, the water of this well never fails.'

'Then how did bad seasons affect you?'

'My bullocks all died one after the other from want of fodder, and I had not the means to till my lands; subsistence became dear, and to maintain my family, I was obliged to contract the debt for which my lands are now mortgaged. I work hard to get them back, and, if I do not succeed, my children will, I hope, with the blessing of God.'[13]

The next morning I went on to Kākā, fifteen miles; and finding tents, people, and cattle, without a tree to shelter them, I was much pleased to see in my neighbourhood a plantation of mango and other fruit-trees. It had, I was told, been planted only three years ago by Hīrāman and Mōtīrām, and I sent for them, knowing that they would be pleased to have their good work noticed by any European gentleman. The trees are now covered with cones of thatch to shelter them from the frost. The merchants came, evidently much pleased, and I had a good deal of talk with them.

'Who planted this new grove?'

'We planted it three years ago.'

'What did your well cost you, and how many trees have you?'

'We have about four hundred trees, and the well has cost us two hundred rupees, and will cost us two hundred more.'

'How long will you require to water them?'

'We shall require to water the mango and other large trees ten or twelve years; but the orange, pomegranate, and other small trees will always require watering.'

'What quantity of ground do the trees occupy?'

'They occupy twenty-two "bīghās" of one hundred and five "jarībs". We place them all twelve yards from each other, that is, the large trees; and the small ones we plant between them.'

'How did you get the land?'

'We were many years trying in vain to get a grant from the Government through the collector; at last we got him to certify on paper that, if the landholder would give us land to plant our grove upon, the Government would have no objection. We induced the landholder, who is a constituent of ours, to grant us the land; and we made our well, and planted our trees.'

'You have done a good thing; what reward do you expect?'

'We hope that those who enjoy the shade, the water, and the fruit, will think kindly of us when they are gone. The names of the great men who built the castles, palaces, and tombs at Delhi and Agra have been almost all forgotten, because no one enjoys any advantage from them; but the names of those who planted the few mango groves we see are still remembered and blessed by all who eat of their fruit, sit in their shade, and drink of their water, from whatever part of the world they come. Even the European gentlemen remember their names with kindness; indeed, it was at the suggestion of a European gentleman, who was passing this place many years ago, and talking with us as you are now, that we commenced this grove. "Look over this plain," said he, "it has been all denuded of the fine groves with which it was, no doubt, once studded; though it is tolerably well cultivated, the traveller finds no shelter in it from the noonday sun—even the birds seem to have deserted you, because you refuse them the habitations they find in other parts of India." We told him that we would have the grove planted, and we have done so; and we hope God will bless our undertaking.'

'The difficulty of getting land is, I suppose, the reason why more groves are not planted, now that property is secure?'

'How could men plant without feeling secure of the land they planted upon, and when Government would not guarantee it? The landholder could guarantee it only during the five years of lease;[14] and, if at the end of that time Government should transfer the lease of the estate to another, the land of the grove would be transferred with it. We plant not for worldly or immediate profits, but for the benefit of our souls in the next world—for the prayers of those who may derive benefit from our works when we are gone. Our landholders are good men, and will never resume the lands they have given us; and if the lands be sold at auction by Government, or transferred to others, we hope the certificate of the collector will protect us from his grasp.'[15]

'You like your present Government, do you not?'

'We like it much. There has never been a Government that gave so much security to life and property; all we want is a little more of public service, and a little more of trade; but we have no cause to complain; it is our own fault if we are not happy.'

'But I have been told that the people find the returns from the soil diminishing, and attribute it to the perjury that takes place in our courts occasionally.'

'That, sir, is no doubt true; there has been a manifest falling off in the returns; and people everywhere think that you make too much use of the Korān and the Ganges water in your courts. God does not like to hear lies told upon one or other, and we are apt to think that we are all punished for the sins of those who tell them. May we ask, sir, what office you hold?'

'It is my office to do the work which God assigns to me in this world.'

'The work of God, sir, is the greatest of all works, and those are fortunate who are chosen to do it.'

Their respect for me evidently increased when they took me for a clergyman. I was dressed in black.

'In the first place, it is my duty to tell you that God does not punish the innocent for the guilty, and that the perjury in courts has nothing to do with the diminution of returns from the soil. Where you apply water and manure, and alternate your crops, you always get good returns, do you not?'

'Very good returns; but we have had several bad seasons that have carried away the greater part of our population; but a small portion of our lands can be irrigated for want of wells, and we had no rain for two or three years, or hardly any in due season; and it was this deficiency of rain which the people thought a chastisement from heaven.'

'But the wells were not dried up, were they?'

'No.'

'And the people whose fields they watered had good returns, and high prices for produce?'

'Yes, they had; but their cattle died for want of food, for there was no grass any where to be found.'

'Still they were better off than those who had no wells to draw water from for their fields; and the only way to provide against such evils in future is to have a well for every field. God has given you the fields, and he has given you the water; and when it does not come from the clouds, you must draw it from your wells.'[16]

'True, sir, very true; but the people are very poor, and have not the means to form the wells they require.'

'And if they borrow the money from you, you charge them with interest?'

'From one to two per cent. a month according to their character and circumstances; but interest is very often merely nominal, and we are in most cases glad to get back the principal alone.'[17]

'And what security have you for the land of your grove in case the landholder should change his mind, or die and leave sons not so well disposed.'

'In the first place, we hold his bonds for a debt of nine thousand rupees which he owes us, and which we have no hopes of his ever paying. In the next, we have on stamped paper his deed of gift, in which he declares that he has given us the land, and that he and his heirs for ever shall be bound to make good the rents, should Government sell the estate for arrears of revenue. We wanted him to write this document in the regular form of a deed of sale; but he said that none of his ancestors had ever yet sold their lands, and that he would not be the first to disgrace his family, or record their disgrace on stamped paper — it should, he was resolved, be a deed of gift.'

'But, of course, you prevailed upon him to take the price?'

'Yes, we prevailed upon him to take two hundred rupees for the land, and got his receipt for the same; indeed, it is so mentioned in the deed of gift; but still the landlord, who is a near relation of the late chief of Hatrās, would persist in having the paper made out as a deed, not of sale, but of gift. God knows whether, after all, our grove will be secure — we must run the risk now we have begun upon it.'

Notes:

1. This phrase is misleading. There is no want of trees in Upper India generally; only certain limited areas are ill wooded. Most of the districts in the plains of the Ganges and Jumna are well wooded.

2. This is a favourite doctrine of the author, often reiterated. The absence of a powerful middle class is a characteristic, not of India only, but of all Oriental despotisms, and the subdivision of landed property is only one of the causes of the non-existence of such a class.

3. This is quite true. The rural population want two things, first a light assessment, secondly the minimum of official interference, They do not care a straw who the ruler is, and they like best that ruler, be his name or nationality what it may, who worries them least, and takes least money from them.

4. Goldsmith, 'The Hermit' (in chapter 8 of *The Vicar of Wakefield*).

5. Groves are still scarce in the Agra country, but much planting has been done on the roads.

6. Gorakhpur, Azamgarh, and some other districts, forming half of the old province of Oudh, ceded by the ruler of Oudh in 1801, were long known as the Ceded Provinces. The western districts of the North-Western Provinces, known as the Conquered Provinces, were taken from the Marāthās in 1803-5. The Province of Benares became British territory in 1775. The hill districts of the Kumaun Division were annexed in 1816, at the close of the war with Nepal. All the regions named are now included in the Agra Province of the United Provinces of Agra and Oudh, in which the editor served for twenty- nine years.

7. The author's remarks are not readily intelligible to readers unversed in the technicalities of Indian revenue administration. The author writes on the assumption that Government was the proprietor of the soil. While he was writing, the settlements under Regulation IX of 1833 were in progress. Those settlements, or revenue contracts, were ordinarily sanctioned for periods of thirty years, and the landholders, whom the author calls 'lessees', have gradually changed into 'proprietors', with full power over their land, subject only to the State lien for the 'land revenue' (Crown rent, or State share of the produce), and to the laws of inheritance and succession. The 'resumption of rent-free lands' simply means the subjection of those lands to the payment of 'land revenue'. It is inaccurate to say that the lands are become 'the property of Government' by reason of their being assessed. Even when land generally was regarded as the property of the State, and the landholders were considered to be only lessees, no objection would have been made to the planting of groves if payment of the 'land revenue' had been continued for the planted area as for cultivated land. Now that landholders have been recognized as proprietors, there is nothing to prevent them from planting as much land as they like with trees, although the State has not always been willing to exempt the whole planted area from assessment. No one ever objected to the renewal of trees except on the ground that the area under trees might be excluded from assessment. For many years past the Government of India has been most anxious to encourage tree- planting, and has sanctioned liberal rules respecting the exemption of grove land from assessment to 'land revenue', or 'rent', as the author calls it. The Government of the United Provinces certainly is not now liable to reproach for indifference to the value of groves. Enormous progress in the planting of road avenues has also been made. The deficiency of trees in the country about Agra is partly due to nature, much of the ground being cut up by ravines, and unfavourable for planting.

8. The Alīgarh district lies to the north and east of the Mathurā district. The fort of Alīgarh is fifty-five miles north of Agra, and eighty-four miles south-east of Delhi.

9. 'pakkā' here means 'burned in a kiln', as distinguished from 'sun-dried'.

10. The 'bīghā' is the unit of superficial land measure, varying, but often taken as five-eighths of an acre. The 'jarīb' is a smaller measure.

11. The rules now in force require assessing officers to make allowance for permanent improvements, such as the well described in the text, so as to give the fair benefit of the improvement to the maker. In the early settlements this important matter was commonly neglected.

12. Tolerable bullocks, fit for use at the well and in the plough, would now cost much more. This conversation appears to have taken place in the year 1839, The famine alluded to is that of 1837- 8.

13. This conversation gives a very vivid and truthful picture of rural life in Northern India. Most revenue officers have held similar conversations with rustics, but the author is almost the only writer on Indian affairs who has perceived that exact notes of casual chats in the fields would be found interesting and valuable.

14. The early settlements were made for short terms.

15. The certificate would not be of much avail in a civil court.

16. The Alīgarh district is now irrigated by canals.

17. This is the lender's view of his business; the borrowers might have a different story.

CHAPTER 62

Public Spirit of the Hindoos — Tree Cultivation and
Suggestions for extending it.

I may here be permitted to introduce as something germane to the matter of the foregoing chapter a recollection of Jubbulpore, although we are now far past that locality.

My tents are pitched where they have often been before, on the verge of a very large and beautiful tank in a fine grove of mango- trees, and close to a handsome temple. There are more handsome temples and buildings for accommodation on the other side of the tank, but they are gone sadly out of repair. The bank all round this noble tank is beautifully ornamented by fine banyan and pīpal trees, between which and the water's edge intervene numerous clusters of the graceful bamboo. These works were formed about eighty years ago by a respectable agricultural capitalist who resided at this place, and died about twenty years after they were completed. No relation of his can now be found in the district, and not one in a thousand of those who drink of the water or eat of the fruit knows to whom he is indebted. There are round the place some beautiful 'bāolīs', or large wells with flights of stone steps from the top to the water's edge, imbedded in clusters of beautiful trees. They were formed about the same time for the use of the public by men whose grandchildren have descended to the grade of cultivators of the soil, or belted attendants upon the present native collectors, without the means of repairing any of the injury which time is inflicting upon these magnificent works. Three or four young pīpal-trees have begun to spread their delicate branches and pale green leaves rustling in the breeze from the dome of this fine temple; which these infant Herculeses hold in their deadly grasp and doom to inevitable destruction. Pigeons deposit the seeds of the pīpal-tree, on which they chiefly feed, in the crevices of buildings.

No Hindoo dares, and no Christian or Muhammadan will condescend, to lop off the heads of these young trees, and if they did, it would only put off the evil and inevitable day; for such are the vital powers of their roots, when they have once penetrated deeply into a building, that they will send out their branches again, cut them off as often as you may, and carry on their internal attack with undiminished vigour.[1] No wonder that superstition should have consecrated this tree, delicate and beautiful as it is, to the gods. The palace, the castle, the temple, and the tomb, all those works which man is most proud to raise to spread and to perpetuate his name, crumble to dust beneath her withering grasp. She rises triumphant over them all in her lofty beauty, bearing high in air amidst her light green foliage fragments of the wreck she has made, to show the nothingness of man's greatest efforts.

While sitting at my tent-door looking out upon this beautiful sheet of water, and upon all the noble works around me, I thought of the charge, so often made against the people of this fine land, of the total want of *public spirit* among them, by those who have spent their Indian days in the busy courts of law, and still more busy commercial establishments of our great metropolis.

If by the term public spirit be meant a disposition on the part of individuals to sacrifice their own enjoyments, or their own means of enjoyment for the common good, there is perhaps no people in the world among whom it abounds so much as among the people of India. To live in the grateful recollections of their countrymen for benefits conferred upon them in great works of ornament and utility is the study of every Hindoo of rank and property.[2] Such works tend, in his opinion, not only to spread and perpetuate his name in this world, but, through the good wishes and prayers of those who are benefited by them, to secure the favour of the Deity in the next.

According to their notions, every drop of rain-water or dew that falls to the ground from the green leaf of a fruit-tree, planted by them for the common good, proves a refreshing draught for their souls in the next [world]. When no descendant remains to pour the funeral libations in their name, the water from the trees they have planted for the public good is destined to supply its place. Everything judiciously laid out to promote the happiness of their fellow creatures will in the next world be repaid to them tenfold by the Deity.

In marching over the country in the hot season, we every morning find our tents pitched on the green sward amid beautiful groves of fruit-trees, with wells of 'pakkā' (brick or stone) masonry, built at great expense, and containing the most delicious water; but how few of us ever dream of asking at whose cost the trees that afford us and our followers such agreeable shade were planted, or the wells that afford us such copious streams of fine water in the midst of dry, arid plains were formed! We go on enjoying all the advantages which arise from the *noble public spirit* that animates the people of India to benevolent exertions, without once calling in question the truth of the assertion of our metropolitan friends that 'the people of India have no public spirit'.

Mānmōr, a respectable merchant of Mirzapore, who traded chiefly in bringing cotton from the valley of the Nerbudda and Southern India through Jubbulpore to Mirzapore, and in carrying back sugar and spices in return, learning how much travellers on this great road suffered from the want of water near the Hiliyā pass, under the Vindhya range of hills, commenced a work to remedy the evil in 1822. Not a drop of wholesome water was to be found within ten miles of the bottom of the pass, where the laden bullocks were obliged to rest during the hot months, when the greatest thoroughfare always took place. Mānmōr commenced a large tank and garden, and had laid out about twenty thousand rupees in the work, when he died. His son, Lalū Mānmōr, completed the work soon after his father's death, at a cost of eighty thousand rupees more, that travellers might enjoy all the advantages that his good old father had benevolently intended for them. The tank is very large, always full of fine water even in the driest part of the dry season, with flights of steps of cut freestone from the water's edge to the top all round. A fine garden and shrubbery, with temples and buildings for accommodations, are attached, with an establishment of people to attend and keep them in order.[3]

All the country around this magnificent work was a dreary solitude — there was not a human habitation within many miles on any side. Tens of thousands who passed this road every year were blessing the name of the man who had created it where it was so much wanted, when the new road from the Nerbudda to Mirzapore was made by the British Government to descend some ten miles to the north of it. As many miles were saved in the distance by the new cut, and the passage down made comparatively easy at great cost, travellers forsook the Hiliyā road, and poor Mānmōr's work became comparatively useless. I brought the work to the notice of Lord William Bentinck, who, in passing Mirzapore some time after, sent for the son, and conferred upon him a rich dress of honour, of which he has ever since been extremely proud.[4]

Hundreds of works like this are undertaken every year for the benefit of the public by benevolent and unostentatious individuals, who look for their reward, not in the applause of newspapers and public meetings, but in the grateful prayers and good wishes of those who are benefited by them; and in the favour of the Deity in the next world, for benefits conferred upon his creatures in this.[5]

What the people of India want is not public spirit, for no men in the world have more of it than the Hindoos, but a disposition on the part of private individuals to combine their efforts and means in effecting great objects for the public good. With this disposition they will be, in time, inspired under our rule, when the enemies of all settled governments may permit us to divert a little of our intellect and our revenue from the duties of war to those of peace.[6]

In the year 1829, while I held the civil charge of the district of Jubbulpore, in this valley of the Nerbudda, I caused an estimate to be made of the public works of utility and ornament it contained. The population of the district at that time amounted to 500,000 souls, distributed among 4,053 occupied towns, villages, and hamlets. There were 1,000 villages more which had formerly been occupied, but were then deserted. There were 2,288 tanks, 209 'bāolīs', or large wells with flights of steps extending from the top down to the water when in its lowest stage; 1,560 wells lined with brick and stone, cemented with lime, but without stairs; 860 Hindoo temples, and 22 Muhammadan mosques. The estimated cost of these works in grain at the present price, had the labour been paid in kind at the ordinary rate, was R86,66,043 (£866,604 sterling).[7]

The labourer was estimated to be paid at the rate of about two- thirds the quantity of corn he would get in England if paid in kind, and corn sells here at about one-third the price it fetches in average seasons in England. In Europe, therefore, these works, supposing the labour equally efficient, would have cost at least four times the sum here estimated; and such works formed by private individuals for the public good, without any view whatever to return in profits, indicate a very high degree of *public spirit.*

The whole annual rent of the lands of this district amounts to R650,000 (£65,000 sterling), that is, 500,000 demandable by the Government, and 150,000 by those who hold the lands at lease immediately under Government, over and above what may be considered as the profits of their stock as farmers. These works must, therefore, have cost about thirteen times the amount of the annual rent of the whole of the lands of the district, or the whole annual rent for above thirteen years.[8]

But I have not included the groves of mango and tamarind, and other fine trees with which the district abounds. Two-thirds of the towns and villages are imbedded in fine groves of these trees, mixed with the banyan (*Ficus Indica*) and the pīpal (*Ficus religiosa*). I am sorry they were not numbered; but I should estimate them at three thousand, and the outlay upon a mango grove is, on an average, about four hundred rupees.

The groves of fruit-trees planted by individuals for the use of the public, without any view to a return in profit, would in this district, according to this estimate, have cost twelve lākhs [12,00,000] more, or about twice the amount of the annual rent of the whole of the lands. It should be remarked that the whole of these works had been formed under former governments. Ours was established in the year 1817.[9]

The Upper Doāb and the Delhi Territories were denuded of their trees in the wars that attended the decline and fall of the Muhammadan empire, and the rise and progress of the Sikhs, Jāts, and Marāthās in that quarter. These lawless freebooters soon swept all the groves from the face of every country they occupied with their troops, and they never attempted to renew them or encourage the renewal. We have not been much more sparing; and the finest groves of fruit-trees have everywhere been recklessly swept down by our barrack-masters to furnish fuel for their brick-kilns; and I am afraid little or no encouragement is given for planting others to supply their place in those parts of India where they are most wanted.

We have a regulation authorizing the lessee of a village to plant a grove in his grounds, but where the settlements of the land-revenue have been for short periods, as in all Upper and Central India, this authority is by no means sufficient to induce them to invest their property in such works. It gives no sufficient guarantee that the lessee for the next settlement shall respect a grant made by his predecessors; and every grove of mango-trees requires outlay and care for at least ten years. Though a man destines the fruit, the shade, and the water for the use of the public, he requires to feel that it will be held for the public in his name, and by his children and descendants, and never be exclusively appropriated by any man in power for his own use.

If the lands were still to belong to the lessee of the estate under Government, and the trees only to the planter and his heirs, he to whom the land belonged might very soon render the property in the trees of no value to the planter or his heirs.[10]

If Government wishes the Upper Doāb, the Delhi, Mathurā, and Agra districts again enriched and embellished with mango groves, they will not delay to convey this feeling to the hundreds, nay, thousands, who would be willing to plant them upon a single guarantee that the lands upon which the trees stand shall be considered to belong to them and their heirs as long as these trees stand upon them.[11] That the land, the shade, the fruit, and the water will be left to the free enjoyment of the public we may take for granted, since the good which the planter's soul is to derive from such a work in the next world must depend upon their being so; and all that is required to be stipulated in such grants is that mango tamarind, pīpal, or 'bar' (i.e. banyan) trees, at the rate of twenty-five the English acre, shall be planted and kept up in every piece of land granted for the purpose; and that a well of 'pakkā' masonry shall be made for the purpose of watering them, in the smallest, as well as in the largest, piece of ground granted, and kept always in repair.

If the grantee fulfil the conditions, he ought, in order to cover part of the expense, to be permitted to till the land under the trees till they grow to maturity and yield their fruit; if he fails, the lands, having been declared liable to resumption, should be resumed. The person soliciting such grants should be required to certify in his application that he had already obtained the sanction of the present lessee of the village in which he wishes to have his grove, and for this sanction he would, of course, have to pay the full value of the land for the period of his lease. When his lease expires, the land in which the grove is planted would be excluded from the assessment; and when it is considered that every good grove must cost the planter more than fifty times the annual rent of the land, Government may be satisfied that they secure the advantage to their people at a very cheap rate.[12]

Over and above the advantage of fruit, water, and shade for the public, these groves tend much to secure the districts that are well studded with them from the dreadful calamities that in India always attend upon deficient falls of rain in due season. They attract the clouds, and make them deposit their stores in districts that would not otherwise be blessed with them; and hot and dry countries denuded of their trees, and by that means deprived of a great portion of that moisture to which they had been accustomed, and which they require to support vegetation, soon become dreary and arid wastes. The lighter particles, which formed the richest portion of their soil, blow off, and leave only the heavy arenaceous portion; and hence, perhaps, those sandy deserts in which are often to be found the signs of a population once very dense.

In the Mauritius, the rivers were found to be diminishing under the rapid disappearance of the woods in the interior, when Government had recourse to the measure of preventing further depredations, and they soon recovered their size.

The clouds brought up from the southern ocean by the south-east trade wind are attracted, as they pass over the island, by the forests in the interior, and made to drop their stores in daily refreshing showers. In many other parts of the world governments have now become aware of this mysterious provision of nature; and have adopted measures to take advantage of it for the benefit of the people; and the dreadful sufferings to which the people of those of our districts, which have been the most denuded of their trees, have been of late years exposed from the want of rain in due season, may, perhaps, induce our Indian Government to turn its thoughts to the subject. [13]

The province of Mālwā, which is bordered by the Nerbudda on the south, Gujarāt on the west, Rājputāna on the north, and Allahabad on the east, is said never to have been visited by a famine; and this exemption from so great a calamity must arise chiefly from its being so well studded with hills and groves. The natives have a couplet, which, like all good couplets on rural subjects, is attributed to Sahadēo, one of the five demigod brothers of the Mahābhārata, to this effect: 'If it does not thunder on such a night, you, father, must go to Mālwā, and I to Gujarāt', meaning, 'The rains will fail us here, and we must go to those quarters where they never fail'[14]

Notes:

1. The Archaeological Survey is engaged in unceasing battle with the pīpal seedlings.

2. This proposition is too general.

3. The Hiliyā, or Haliyā, Pass is near the town of the same name in the Mirzāpur district, thirty-one miles south- west of Mirzāpur. A bilingual inscription, in English and Hindī, on a large slab on the bank of the river, records the capture of the fort of Bhōpārī in 1811 by the 21st Regiment Native Infantry. The tank described in the text is at Dibhōr, twelve miles south of Haliyā, and is 430 feet long by 352 broad. The full name of the builder is Srīmān Nāyak Mānmōr, who was the head of the Banjāra merchants of Mirzāpur. The inscription on his temple is dated 23 February, 1825, A.D. 'I suppose', remarks Cunningham, 'that the vagrant instinct of the old Banjāra preferred a jungle site. No doubt he got the ground cheap; and from this vantage point he was able to supply Mirzāpur with both wood and charcoal.' (A.S.R., vol. xxi, pp. 121-5, pl. xxxi.)

4. The new road passes through the Katrā Pass. The pass via Dibhōr and Haliyā, which the author calls the Hiliyā Pass, is properly called the Kerahi (Kerāi) Pass. Both old and new roads are now little used. The construction of railways has altogether changed the course of trade, and Cawnpore has risen on the ruins of Mirzāpur. Lalū, Nāyak's 'grandson, died in comparative obscurity some years ago, and only a few female relatives remain to represent the family—a striking example, if one were needed, of the instability of Oriental fortunes.' (A.S.R., vol. xxi, p. 124, quoting Gazetteer.)

5. Within a few miles of Gosalpur, at the village of Talwā, which stands upon the old high road leading to Mirzapore, is a still more magnificent tank with one of the most beautiful temples in India, all executed two or three generations ago at the expense of two or three lakhs of rupees for the benefit of the public, by a very worthy man, who became rich in the service of the former Government. His descendants, all save one, now follow the plough; and that one has a small rent-free village held on condition of appropriating the rents to the repair of the tank. [W. H. S.]

The name Talwā is only the rustic way of pronouncing 'tāl', meaning the tank. Gosalpur is nineteen miles north-east of Jabalpur. Two or three lakhs of rupees were then (in eighteenth century) worth about £22,000 to £33,000 sterling.

6. India, except on the frontiers, has been at peace since 1858, and much revenue has been spent on the duties of peace, but the power of combination for public objects has developed among the people to a less degree than the author seems to have expected, though some development undoubtedly has taken place.

7. In the original edition these statistics are given in words. Figures have been used in this edition as being more readily grasped. The *Central Provinces Gazetteer* (1870) gives the following figures: Area of district, 4,261 square miles; population, 620,201; villages, 2,707; wells in use, 5,515. The *Gazetteer* figures apparently include wells of all kinds, and do not reckon hamlets separately. Wells are, of course, an absolute necessity, and their construction could not be avoided in a country occupied by a fixed population. The number of temples and mosques was very small for so large a population. Many of the tanks, too, are indispensably necessary for watering the cattle employed in agriculture. The 'bāolīs' may fairly be reckoned as the fruit of the public spirit of individuals. This chapter is a reprint of a paper entitled 'On the Public Spirit of the Hindoos'. *See* Bibliography, *ante*, No. 10.

8. The *C.P. Gazetteer* (1870) states that in 1868-9 the land- revenue was R5,70,434, as compared with R500,000 in the author's time. It has since been largely enhanced. The lessees (zamīndārs) have now become proprietors, and the land- revenue, according to the rule in force for many years past, should not exceed half the estimated profit rental. The early settlements were made in accordance with the theory of native Governments that the land is the property of the State, and that the lessees are entitled only to subsistence, with a small percentage as payment for the trouble of collection from the actual cultivators. The author's estimate gives the zamīndārs only 15/80ths, or 3/16ths of the profit rental.

9. The people of the Jubbulpore district must have been very different from those of the rest of India if they planted their groves solely for the public benefit. The editor has never known the fruit, not to mention the timber and firewood, of a grove to be available for the use of the general public. Universal custom allows all comers to use the shade of any established grove, but the fruit is always jealousy guarded and gathered by the owners.

Even one tree is often the property of many sharing, and disputes about the division of mangoes and other fruits are extremely frequent. The framing of a correct record of rights in trees is one of the most embarrassing tasks of a revenue officer.

10. Under the modern System it often happens that the land belongs to one party, and the trees to another. Disputes, of course, occur, but, as a rule, the rights of the owner of the trees are not interfered with by the owner of the land. In thousands of such cases both parties exercise their rights without friction.

11. This sentence shows clearly how remote from the author's mind was the idea of private property in land in India. Government has long since parted with the power of giving grants such as the author recommends. The upper Doāb districts of Meerut, Muzaffarnagar, and Sahāranpur now have plenty of groves.

12. The cost of establishing a grove varies much according to circumstances, of which the distance of water from the surface is the most important. Where water is distant, the cost of constructing and working a well is very high. Where water is near, these items of expense are small, because the roots of the trees soon reach a moist stratum, and can dispense with irrigation.

13. The author, in his appreciation of the value of arboriculture and forest conservancy, was far in advance of his Anglo-Indian contemporaries. A modern meteorologist might object to some of his phraseology, but the substance of his remarks is quite sound. His statement of the ways in which trees benefit climate is incomplete. One important function performed by the roots of trees is the raising of water from the depths below the surface, to be dispersed by the leaves in the form of vapour. Trees act beneficially in many other ways also, which it would be tedious to specify.

The Indian Government long remained blind to the importance of the duty of saving the country from denudation. The first forest conservancy establishments were organized in 1852 for Madras and Burma, and, by Act vii of 1865, the Forest Department was established on a legal basis. Its operations have since been largely extended, and trained foresters are now sent out each year to India. The Department at the present time controls many thousand square miles of forest. The reader may consult the article 'Forests' in Balfour, *Cyclopaedia*, 3rd ed., and sundry official reports for further details.

A yearly grant for arboriculture is now made to every district. Thousands of miles of roads have been lined with trees, and multitudes of groves have been established by both Government and private individuals. The author was himself a great tree-planter. In a letter dated 15th December, 1844, he describes the avenue which he had planted along the road from Maihar to Jubbulpore in 1829 and 1830, and another, eighty-six miles long, from Jhānsī Ghāt on the Nerbudda to Chāka. The trees planted were banyan, pīpal, mango, tamarind, and jāman (*Eugenia jambolana*). He remarks that these trees will last for centuries.

14. 'In 1899-1900 Mālwā suffered from a severe famine, such as had not visited this favoured spot for more than thirty years. The people were unused to, and quite unprepared for, this calamity, the distress being aggravated by the great influx of immigrants from Rājputāna, who had hitherto always been sure of relief in this region, of which the fertility is proverbial. In 1903 a new calamity appeared in the shape of plague, which has seriously reduced the agricultural population in some districts' (*I.G.*, 1908, xvii. 105).

CHAPTER 63

Cities and Towns, formed by Public Establishments, disappear as
Sovereigns and Governors change their Abodes.

On the 17th and 18th,[1] we went on twenty miles to Palwal,[2] which
stands upon an immense mound, in some places a hundred feet high, formed
entirely of the debris of old buildings. There are an immense number of fine
brick buildings in ruins, but not one of brick or stone at present inhabited.
The place was once evidently under the former government the seat of some
great public establishments, which, with their followers and dependants,
constituted almost the entire population. The occasion which keeps such
establishments at a place no sooner passes away than the place is deserted
and goes to ruin as a matter of course. Such is the history of Nineveh,
Babylon,[3] and all cities which have owed their origin and support entirely
to the public establishments of the sovereign—any revolution that changed
the seat of government depopulated a city.

Sir Thomas Roe, the ambassador of James the First of England to the
court of Delhi during the reign of Jahāngīr, passing through some of the
old capital cities of Western India, then deserted and in ruins, writes to the
Archbishop of Canterbury: 'I know not by what policy the Emperors seek
the ruin of all the ancient cities which were nobly built, but now be desolate
and in rubbish. It must arise from a wish to destroy all the ancient cities in
order that there might appear nothing great to have existed before their
time.'[4] But these cities, like all which are supported in the same manner,
by the residence of a court and its establishments, become deserted as the
seat of dominion is changed. Nineveh, built by Ninus out of the spoils he
brought back from the wide range of his conquests, continued to be the
residence of the court and the principal seat of its military establishments
for thirteen centuries to the reign of Sardanapalus. During the whole of this
time it was the practice of the sovereigns to collect from all the provinces
of the empire their respective quotas of troops, and to canton them within
the city for one year, at the expiration of which they were relieved by fresh
troops.' In the last years of Sardanapalus, four provinces of the empire,
Media, Persia, Babylonia, and Arabia, are said to have furnished a quota of
four hundred thousand; and, in the rebellion which closed his reign, these

troops were often beaten by those from the other provinces of the empire, which could not have been much less in number. The successful rebel, Arbaces, transferred the court and his own appendages to its capital, and Nineveh became deserted, and for more than eighteen centuries lost to the civilized world.[5]

Babylon in the same manner; and Susa, Ecbatana, Persepolis, and Seleucia, all, one after the other, became deserted as sovereigns changed their residence, and with it the seats of their public establishments, which alone supported them. Thus Thebes became deserted for Memphis, Memphis for Alexandria, and Alexandria for Cairo, as the sovereigns of Egypt changed theirs; and thus it has always been in India, where cities have been almost all founded on the same bases—the residence of princes, and their public establishments, civil, military, or ecclesiastical.

The city of Kanauj, on the Ganges, when conquered by Mahmūd of Ghaznī,[6] is stated by the historians of the conqueror to have contained a standing army of five hundred thousand infantry, with a due proportion of cavalry and elephants, thirty thousand shops for the sale of 'pān' alone, and sixty thousand families of opera girls.[7] The 'pān' dealers and opera girls were part and parcel of the court and its public establishments, and as much dependent on the residence of the sovereign as the civil, military, and ecclesiastical officers who ate their 'pān', and enjoyed their dancing and music; and this great city no sooner ceased to be the residence of the sovereign, the great proprietor of all the lands in the country, than it became deserted.

After the establishment of the Muhammadan dominion in India almost all the Hindoo cities, within the wide range of their conquest, became deserted as the necessary consequence, as the military establishments were all destroyed or disbanded, and the religions establishments scattered, their lands confiscated, their idols broken, and their temples either reduced to ruins in the first ebullition of fanatical zeal, or left deserted and neglected to decay from want of those revenues by which alone they had been, or could be, supported.[8] The towns and cities of the Roman empire which owed their origin to the same cause, the residence of governors and their legions or other public establishments, resisted similar shocks with more endurance, because they had most of them ceased to depend upon the causes in which they originated, and began to rest upon other bases. When destroyed by wave after wave of barbarian conquest, they were restored for the most part by the residence of church dignitaries and their establishments; and the military establishments of the new order of things, instead of remaining as standing armies about the courts of princes, dispersed after every campaign like militia, to enjoy the fruits of the lands assigned for their maintenance, when alone they could be enjoyed in the rude state to which society had been reduced—upon the lands themselves.

For some time after the Muhammadan conquest of India, that part of it which was brought effectually under the new dominion can hardly be considered to have had more than one city with its dependent towns and villages;[9] because the emperor chose to concentrate the greater part of his military establishments around the seat of his residence, and this great city became deserted whenever he thought it necessary or convenient to change that seat.

But when the emperor began to govern his distant provinces by viceroys, he was obliged to confide to them a share of his military establishments, the only public establishments which a conqueror thought it worth while to maintain; and while they moved about in their respective provinces, the imperial camp became fixed. The great officers of state, enriched by the plunder of conquered provinces, began to spend their wealth in the construction of magnificent works for private pleasure or public convenience. In time, the viceroys began to govern their provinces by means of deputies, who moved about their respective districts, and enabled their masters, the viceroys of provinces, to convert their camps into cities, which in magnificence often rivalled that of the emperor their master. The deputies themselves in time found that they could govern their respective districts from a central point; and as their camps became fixed in the chosen spots, towns of considerable magnitude rose, and sometimes rivalled the capitals of the viceroys. The Muhammadans had always a greater taste for architectural magnificence, as well in their private as in their public edifices, than the Hindoos,[10] who sought the respect and good wishes of mankind through the medium of groves and reservoirs diffused over the country for their benefit. Whenever a Muhammadan camp was converted into a town or city almost all the means of individuals were spent in the gratification of this taste. Their wealth in money and movables would be, on their death, at the mercy of their prince—their offices would be conferred on strangers; tombs and temples, canals, bridges, and caravanserais, gratuitously for the public good, would tend to propitiate the Deity, and conciliate the goodwill of mankind, and might also tend to the advancement of their children in the service of their sovereign. The towns and cities which rose upon the sites of the standing camps of the governors of provinces and districts in India were many of them as much adorned by private and public edifices as those which rose upon the standing camps of the Muhammadan conquerors of Spain.[11] Standing camps converted into towns and cities, it became in time necessary to fortify with walls against any surprise under any sudden ebullition among the conquered people; and fortifications and strong garrisons often suggested to the bold and ambitions governors of distant provinces attempts to shake off the imperial yoke.[12] That portion of the annual revenue, which had hitherto flowed in copious streams of tribute to the imperial capital, was now arrested, and made to augment the local establishments, adorn the cities, and enrich the towns of the viceroys, now become the sovereigns of independent kingdoms. The lieutenant-governors of these new sovereigns, possessed of fortified towns, in their turn often shook off the yoke of their masters in the same manner, and became in their turn the independent sovereigns of their respective districts. The whole resources of the countries subject to their rule being employed to strengthen and improve their condition, they soon became rich and powerful kingdoms, adorned with splendid cities and populous towns, since the public establishments of the sovereigns, among whom all the revenues were expended, spent all they received in the purchase of the produce of the land and labour of the surrounding country, which required no other market.

Thus the successful rebellion of one viceroy converted Southern India into an independent kingdom; and the successful rebellion, of his lieutenant-governors in time divided it into four independent kingdoms, each with a standing army of a hundred thousand men, and adorned with towns and cities of great strength and magnificence.[13] But they continued to depend upon the causes in which they originated—the public establishments of the sovereign; and when the Emperor Akbar and his successors, aided by their own [sic] intestine wars, had conquered these sovereigns, and again reduced their kingdoms to tributary provinces, almost all these cities and towns became depopulated as the necessary consequence. The public establishments were again moving about with the courts and camps of the emperor and his viceroys; and drawing in their train all those who found employment and subsistence in contributing to their efficiency and enjoyment. It was not, as our ambassador in the simplicity of his heart supposed, the disinclination of the emperors to see any other towns magnificent, save those in which they resided, which destroyed them, but their ambition to reduce all independent kingdoms to tributary provinces.

Notes:

1. January, 1836.

2. A small town, thirty-six miles south of Delhi, situated in the Gurgāon district, now included in the Panjāb, but in the author's time attached to the North-Western Provinces. The town is the chief place in the 'pargana' of the same name.

3. Nineveh is not a well-chosen example, inasmuch as its decay was due to deliberate destruction, and not to mere desertion by a sovereign. It was

deliberately burned and ruined by Nabopolassar, viceroy of Babylon, and his allies, about 606 B.C. The decay of Babylon was gradual. See note *post*, note 5.

4. Extract from a letter to the Archbishop of Canterbury, dated from Ajmēr, January 29, 1616. The words immediately following 'rubbish' are 'His own [i.e. the King's] houses are of stone, handsome and uniform. His great men build not, for want of inheritance; but, as far as I have yet seen, live in tents, or in houses worse than our cottages. Yet, when the King likes, as at Agra, because it is a city erected by him, the buildings, as is reported, are fair and of carved stone.' (Pinkerton's *Collection*, vol. viii, p. 45.) The passage is not reprinted in the Hakluyt Society edition (vol. i, p. 122), where only extracts from the letter are given.

5. The site of Nineveh was forgotten for a period even longer than that stated by the author. Mr. Claudius Rich, the Resident at Baghdad, was the first European to make a tentative identification of Nineveh with the mounds opposite Mosal, in 1818. Real knowledge of the site and its history dates from the excavations of Botta begun in 1843, and those of Layard begun two years later. (Bonomi, *Nineveh and its Palaces*, 2nd ed., 1853; Layard, *Nineveh and its Remains*, 2 vols, 1849.) The author's account of the fall of Nineveh, based on that of Diodorus Siculus, is not in accordance with the conclusions of the best modern authorities. The destruction of the city in or about 606 B.C. was really effected some years after the death of Sardanapalus (Assurbanipal), in 625 B.C., by Nabopolassar (Nabupal-uzur), the rebel viceroy of Babylon, in alliance with Necho of Egypt, Cyaxares of Media, and the King of Armenia. The Assyrian monarch who perished in the assault was not Sardanapalus (Assur-banipal), but his son Assur-ebel-ili, or, according to Professor Sayce, a king called Saracus, After the destruction of Nineveh, Babylon became the capital of the Mesopotamian empire, and under Nebuchadrezzar (Nebuchadnezzar), son of Nabopolassar, who came to the throne in 604 B.C., attained the height of glory and renown. It was occupied by Cyrus in 539 B.C., and decayed gradually, but was still a place of importance in the time of Alexander the Great. The eponymous hero, Ninus, is of course purely mythical. The results of modern research will be found in the *Encycl. Brit.*, 11th ed., 1910, in the articles 'Babylon' (Sayce), 'Babylonia and Assyria' (Sayce and Jastrow), and 'Nineveh' (Johns). See also, ibid., 'Cyrus' (Meyer).

6. Kanauj, now in the Farrukhābād district of the United Provinces, was sacked by Mahmūd of Ghaznī in January, A.D. 1019. The name of Mahmūd's capital may be spelled Ghaznih, Ghaznī, or Ghaznīn. (Raverty, in *J.A.S.B.*, Part I, vol. lxi (1892), p. 156, note.)

7. 'Pān', the well-known Indian condiment (*ante*, chapter 29, note 10). 'Opera girls' is a rather whimsical rendering of the more usual phrase 'nāch (nautch) girls', or 'dancing girls'. The traditional numbers cited must not be accepted as historical facts. See V. A. Smith, 'The History of the City of Kanauj' (*J.R.A.S.*, 1908, pp. 767-93).

8. This statement is too general. Benares, Allahabad (Prayāg), and many other important Hindoo cities, were never deserted, and continued to be populous through all vicissitudes. It is true that in most places the principal temples were desecrated or destroyed, and were frequently converted into mosques.

9. The statement is much exaggerated. The Hindoo Rājās who paid tribute to the Sultans of Delhi often maintained considerable courts in populous towns.

10. This proposition, which is not true of Southern India at all, applies only to secular buildings in Northern India. The temples of Khajurāho, Mount Abū, and numberless other places, equal in magnificence the architecture of the Muhammadans, or, indeed, that of any people in the world.

11. The anthor's remarks seem likely to convey wrong notions. Very few of the capitals of the Muhammadan viceroys and governors were new foundations. Nearly all of them were ancient Hindoo towns adopted as convenient official residences, and enlarged and beautified by the new rulers, much of the old beauties being at the same time destroyed. Fyzabad certainly was a new foundation of the Nawāb Wazīrs of Oudh, but it lies so close to the extremely ancient city of Ajodhya that it should rather be regarded as a Muhammadan extension of that city. Lucknow occupies the site of a Hindoo city of great antiquity.

12. It would be difficult to point out an example of a *Muhammadan* standing camp which was first converted into an open, and then into a fortified town.

13. This abstract of the history of the Deccan, or Southern India, is not quite accurate. The Emperor, or Sultan, Muhammad bin Tughlak, after A.D. 1325, reduced the Deccan to a certain extent to submission, but the country revolted in A.D. 1347, when Hasan Gango founded the Bāhmani dynasty of Gulbarga, afterwards known as that of Bīdar. At the end of the fifteenth and the beginning of the sixteenth century, the kingdom so founded broke up into five, not four, separate states, namely, Bījāpur, Ahmadnagar, Golconda, Berār, and Bīdar. The Berār state had a separate existence for about eighty-five years, and then became merged in the kingdom of Ahmadnagar.

CHAPTER 64

Murder of Mr. Fraser, and Execution of the Nawāb Shams-ud-dīn.

At Palwal Mr. Wilmot and Mr. Wright, who had come on business, and Mr. Gubbins, breakfasted and dined with us. They complained sadly of the solitude to which they were condemned, but admitted that they should not be able to get through half so much business were they placed at a large station, and exposed to all the temptations and distractions of a gay and extensive circle, nor feel the same interest in their duties, or sympathy with the people, as they do when thrown among them in this manner. To give young men good feelings towards the natives, the only good way is to throw them among them at those out-stations in the early part of their career, when all their feelings are fresh about them. This holds good as well with the military as the civil officer, but more especially with the latter. A young officer at an outpost with his corps, or part of it, for the first season or two, commonly lays in a store of good feeling towards his men that lasts him for life; and a young gentleman of the Civil Service lays in, in the same manner, a good store of sympathy and fellow feeling with the natives in general.[1]

Mr. Gubbins is the Magistrate and Collector of one of the three districts into which the Delhi territories are divided, and he has charge of Fīrōzpur, the resumed estate of the late Nawāb Shams-ud-dīn, which yields a net revenue of about two hundred thousand rupees a year.[2] I have already stated that this Nawāb took good care that his Mewātī plunderers should not rob within his own estate; but he not only gave them free permission to rob over the surrounding districts of our territory, but encouraged them to do so, that he might share in their booty.[3] He was a handsome young man, and an extremely agreeable companion; but a most unprincipled and licentious character. No man who was reputed to have a handsome wife or daughter was for a moment safe within his territories. The following account of Mr. William Fraser's assassination by this Nawāb may, I think, be relied upon.[4]

The Fīrōzpur Jāgīr was one of the principalities created under the principle of Lord Cornwallis's second administration, which was to make the security of the British dominions dependent upon the divisions among the independent native chiefs upon their frontiers. The person receiving the grant or confirmation of such principality from the British Government 'pledged himself to relinquish all claims to aid, and to maintain the peace in his own possessions.'[5] Fīrōzpur was conferred by Lord Lake, in 1805, upon Ahmad Baksh, for his diplomatic services, out of the territories acquired by us west of the Jumna during the Marāthā wars. He had been the agent on the part of the Hindoo chiefs of Alwar in attendance upon Lord Lake during the whole of that war. He was a great favourite, and his lordship's personal regard for him was thought by those chiefs to have been so favourable to their cause that they conferred upon him the 'pargana' of Lohārū in hereditary rent-free tenure.

In 1822, Ahmad Baksh declared Shams-ud-dīn, his eldest son, his heir, with the sanction of the British Government and the Rājās of Alwar. In February, 1825, Shams-ud-dīn, at the request of his father, by a formal deed assigned over the pargana of Lohārū as a provision for his younger brothers by another mother, Amīn-ud-dīn and Ziā- ud-dīn;[6] and in October 1826 he was finally invested by his father with the management; and the circumstance was notified to the British Government, through the Resident at Delhi, Sir Charles Metcalfe. Ahmad Baksh died in October, 1827. Disputes soon after arose between the brothers, and they expressed a desire to submit their claims to the arbitration of Sir Edward Colebrooke,[7] who had succeeded Sir Charles Metcalfe in the Residency of Delhi.[8] He referred the matter to the Supreme Government; and by their instructions, under date 11th of April, 1828, he was authorized to adjust the matter. He decided that Shams-ud-dīn should make a complete and unencumbered cession to his younger brothers of the pargana of Lohārū, without the reservation of any right of interference in the management, or of any condition of obedience to himself whatever; and that Amīn-ud-dīn should, till his younger brother came of age, pay into the Delhi treasury for him the annual sum of five thousand two hundred and ten rupees, as his half share of the net proceeds, to be there held in deposit for him; and that the estate should, from the time he came of age, be divided between them in equal shares. This award was confirmed by Government; but Sir Edward was recommended to alter it for an annual money payment to the two younger brothers, if he could do so with the consent of the parties.

The pargana was transferred, as the money payment could not be agreed upon; and in September Mr. Martin, who had succeeded Sir E. Colebrooke, proposed to Government that the pargana of Lohārū should be restored to Shams-ud-dīn in lieu of a fixed sum of twenty-six thousand rupees a year to be paid by him annually to his two younger brothers. This proposal was made on the ground that Amīn-ud-dīn could not collect the revenues from the refractory landholders (instigated, no doubt, by the emissaries of Shams-ud-dīn), and consequently could not pay his younger brother's revenue into the treasury. In calculating the annual net revenue of 10,420 rupees, 15,000 of the *gross* revenue had been estimated as the annual expenses of the mutual [*sic*] establishments of the two brothers. To the arrangement proposed by Mr. Martin the younger brothers strongly objected; and proposed in preference to make over the pargana to the British Government, on condition of receiving the net revenue, whatever might be the amount. Mr. Martin was desired by the Governor-General to effect this arrangement, should Amīn-ud-dīn appear still to wish it; but he preferred retaining the management of it in his own hands, in the hope that circumstances would improve.

Shams-ud-dīn, however, pressed his claim to the restoration of the pargana so often that it was at last, in September, 1833, insisted upon by Government, on the ground that Amīn-ud-dīn had failed to fulfil that article of the agreement which bound him to pay annually into the Delhi treasury 5,210 rupees for his younger brother, though that brother had never complained; on the contrary, lived with him on the best possible terms, and was as averse as himself to the retransfer of the pargana, on condition that they gave up their claims to a large share of the movable property of their late father, which had been already decided in their favour in the court of first instance. Mr. W. Fraser, who had succeeded to the office of Governor-General's representative in the Delhi Territories, remonstrated strongly against this measure; and wished to bring it again under the consideration of Government; on the grounds that Ziā-ud-dīn had never made any complaint against his brother Amīn-ud-dīn for want of punctuality in the payment of his share of the net revenue after the payment of their mutual establishments; that the two brothers would be deprived by this measure of an hereditary estate to the value of sixty thousand rupees a year in perpetuity, burthened with the condition that they relinquished a suit already gained in the court of first instance, and likely to be gained in appeal, involving a sum that would of itself yield them that annual sum at the moderate interest of 6 per cent. The grounds alleged by him were not considered valid, and the pargana was made over to Shams-ud- dīn. The pargana now yields 40,000 rupees a year, and under good management may yield 70,000.

At Mr. Fraser's recommendation, Amīn-ud-dīn went himself to Calcutta, and is said to have prevailed upon the Government to take his case again into their consideration. Shams-ud- dīn had become a debauched and licentious character; and having criminal jurisdiction within his own estate, no one's wife or daughter was considered safe; for, when other means failed him, he did not scruple to employ assassins to effect his hated purposes, by removing the husband or father.[9] Mr. Fraser became so disgusted with his conduct that he would not admit him into his house when he came to Delhi, though he had, it may be said, brought him up as a child of his own; indeed he had been as fond of him as he could be of a child of his own; and the boy used to spend the greater part of his time with him. One day after Mr. Fraser had refused to admit the Nawāb to his house. Colonel Skinner, having some apprehensions that by such slights he might be driven to seek revenge by assassination, is said to have remonstrated with Mr. Fraser as his oldest and most valued friend.[10] Mr. Fraser told him that he considered the Nawāb to be still but a boy, and the only way to improve him was to treat him as such. It was, however, more by these slights than by any supposed injuries that Shams-ud-dīn was exasperated; and from that day he determined to have Mr. Fraser assassinated.[11]

Having prevailed upon a man, Karīm Khān, who was at once his servant and boon companion, he sent him to Delhi with one of his carriages, which he was to have sold through Mr. McPherson, a European merchant of the city. He was ordered to stay there ostensibly for the purpose of learning the process of extracting copper from the fossil containing the ore, and purchasing dogs for the Nawāb. He was to watch his opportunity and shoot Mr. Fraser whenever he might find him out at night, attended by only one or two orderlies; to be in no haste, but to wait till he found a favourable opportunity, though it should be for several months. He had with him a groom named Rūplā, and a Mewātī attendant named Aniā, and they lodged in apartments of the Nawāb's at Daryāoganj. He rode out morning and evening, attended by Aniā on foot, for three months, during which he often met Mr. Fraser, but never under circumstances favourable to his purpose; and at last, in despair, returned to Fīrōzpur. Aniā, had importuned him for leave to go home to see his children, who had been ill, and Karīm Khān did not like to remain without him. The Nawāb was displeased with him for returning without leave, and ordered him to return to his post, and effect the object of his mission. Aniā declined to return, and the Nawāb recommended Karīm to take somebody else, but he had, he said, explained all his designs to this man, and it would be dangerous to entrust the secret to another; and he could, moreover, rely entirely upon the courage of Aniā on any trying occasion.

Twenty rupees were due to the treasury by Aniā on account of the rent of the little tenement he held under the Nawāb; and the treasurer consented, at the request of Karīm Khān, to receive this by small instalments, to be deducted out of the monthly wages he was to receive from him. He was, moreover, assured that he should have nothing to do but to cook and eat; and should share liberally with Karīm in the one hundred rupees he was taking with him in money, and the letter of credit upon the Nawāb's bankers at Delhi for one thousand rupees more. The Nawāb himself came with them as far as the village of Nagīna, where he used to hunt; and there Karīm requested permission to change his groom, as he thought Rūplā too shrewd a man for such a purpose. He wanted, he said, a stupid, sleepy man, who would neither ask nor understand anything; but the Nawāb told him that Rūplā was an old and quiet servant, upon whose fidelity he could entirely rely; and Karīm consented to take him. Aniā's little tenement, upon which his wife and children resided, was only two miles distant, and he went to give instructions about gathering in the harvest, and to take leave of them. He told his wife that he was going to the capital on a difficult and dangerous duty, but that his companion Karīm would do it all, no doubt. Aniā asked Karīm before they left Nagīna what was to be his reward; and he told him that the Nawāb had promised them five villages in rent-free tenure. Aniā wished to learn from the Nawāb himself what he might expect; and being taken to him by Karīm, was assured that he and his family should be provided for handsomely for the rest of their lives, if he did his duty well on this occasion.

On reaching Delhi they took up their quarters near Colonel Skinner's house, in the Bulvemar's Ward,[12] where they resided for two months. The Nawāb had told Karīm to get a gun made for his purpose at Delhi, or purchase one, stating that his guns had all been purchased through Colonel Skinner, and would lead to suspicion if seen in his possession. On reaching Delhi, Karīm purchased an old gun, and desired Aniā to go to a certain man in the Chāndnī Chauk, and get it made in the form of a short blunderbuss, with a peculiar stock, that would admit of its being concealed under a cloak; and to say that he was going to Gwālior to seek service, if any one questioned him. The barrel was cut, and the instrument made exactly as Karīm wished it to be by the man whom he pointed out. They met Mr. Fraser every day, but never at night; and Karīm expressed regret that the Nawāb should have so strictly enjoined him not to shoot him in the daytime, which he thought he might do without much risk. Aniā got an attack of fever, and urged Karīm to give up the attempt and return home, or at least permit him to do so. Karīm himself became weary, and said he would do so very soon if he could not succeed; but that he should certainly shoot *some European gentleman* before he set out, and tell his master that he had taken him for Mr. Fraser — to save appearances. Aniā told him that this was a question between him and his master, and no concern of his.

At the expiration of two months, a peon came to learn what they were doing. Karīm wrote a letter by him to the Nawāb, saying that '*the dog* he wished was never to be seen without ten or twelve people about him; and that he saw no chance whatever of finding him, except in the midst of them; but that if he wished, he would purchase this *dog* in the midst of the crowd'. The Nawāb wrote a reply, which was sent by a trooper, with orders that it should be opened in presence of no one but Aniā. The contents were: 'I command you not to purchase *the dog* in presence of many persons, as its price will be greatly raised. You may purchase him before one person, or even two, but not before more; I am in no hurry, the longer the time you take the better; but do not return without purchasing *the dog*.'[13] That is, without killing Mr. Fraser.

They went on every day to watch Mr. Fraser's movements. Leaving the horse with the groom, sometimes in one old ruin of the city, and sometimes in another, ready saddled for flight, with orders that he should not be exposed to the view of passers-by, Karīm and Aniā used to pace the streets, and on several occasions fell in with him, but always found him attended by too many followers of one kind or another for their purpose. At last, on Sunday, the 13th of March, 1835, Karīm heard that Mr. Fraser was to attend a 'nāch' (dance), given by Hindoo Rāo, the brother of the Baiza Bāi,[14] who then resided at Delhi; and determining to try whether he could not shoot him from horseback, he sent away his groom as soon as he had ascertained that Mr. Fraser was actually at the dance. Aniā went in and mixed among the assembly; and as soon as he saw Mr. Fraser rise to depart, he gave intimation to Karīm, who ordered him to keep behind, and make off as fast as he could, as soon as he should hear the report of his gun.

A little way from Hindoo Rao's house the road branches off; that to the left is straight, while that to the right is circuitous. Mr. Fraser was known always to take the straight road, and upon that Karīm posted himself, as the road up to the place where it branched off was too public for his purpose. As it happened, Mr. Fraser, for the first time, took the circuitous road to the right, and reached his home without meeting Karīm. Aniā placed himself at the cross way, and waited there till Karīm came up to him. On hearing that he had taken the right road, Karīm said that 'a man in Mr. Fraser's situation must be a strange ('kāfir') unbeliever not to have such a thing as a torch with him in a dark night. Had he had what he ought', he said, 'I should not have lost him this time'.

They passed him on the road somewhere or other almost every afternoon after this for seven days, but could never fall in with him after dark. On the eighth day, Sunday, the 22nd of March, Karīm went, as usual, in the forenoon to the great mosque to say his prayers; and on his way back in the afternoon he purchased some plums which he was eating when he came up to Aniā, whom he found cooking his dinner. He ordered his horse to be saddled immediately, and told Aniā to make haste and eat his dinner, as he had seen Mr. Fraser at a party given by the Rājā of Kishangarh. 'When his time is come,' said Karīm, 'we shall no doubt find an opportunity to kill him, if we watch him carefully.' They left the groom at home that evening, and proceeded to the 'dargāh' (church) near the canal. Seeing Aniā with merely a Stick in his hand, Karīm bid him go back and change it for a sword, while he went in and said his evening prayers.

On being rejoined by Aniā, they took the road to cantonments, which passed by Mr. Fraser's house; and Aniā observed that the risk was hardly equal in this undertaking, he being on foot, while Karīm was on horseback; that he should be sure to be taken, while the other might have a fair chance of escape. It was now quite dark, and Karīm bid him stand by sword in hand; and if anybody attempted to seize his horse when he fired, cut him down, and be assured that while he had life he would never suffer him, Aniā, to be taken. Karīm continued to patrol up and down on the high-road, that nobody might notice him, while Aniā stood by the road-side. At last, about eleven o'clock, they heard Mr. Fraser approach, attended by one trooper, and two 'peons' on foot; and Karīm walked his horse slowly, as if he had been going from the city to the cantonments, till Mr. Fraser came up within a few paces of him, near the gate leading into his house. Karīm Khān, on leaving his house, had put one large ball into his short blunderbuss; and when confident that he should now have an opportunity of shooting Mr. Fraser, he put in two more small ones. As Mr. Fraser's horse was coming up on the left side, Karīm Khān turned round his, and, as he passed, presented his blunderbuss, fired, and all three balls passed into Mr. Fraser's breast. All three horses reared at the report and flash, and Mr. Fraser fell dead on the ground. Karīm galloped off, followed at a short distance by the trooper, and the two peons went off and gave information to Major Pew and Cornet Robinson, who resided near the place. They came in all haste to the spot, and had the body taken to the deceased's own house; but no signs of life remained. They reported the murder to the magistrate, and the city gates were closed, as the assassin had been seen to enter the city by the trooper.

Aniā ran home through the Kabul gate of the city, unperceived, while Karīm entered by the Ajmēr gate, and passed first through the encampment of Hindoo Rao, to efface the traces of his horse's feet. When he reached their lodgings, he found Aniā there before him; and Rūplā, the groom, seeing his horse in a sweat, told him that he had had a narrow escape—that Mr. Fraser had been killed, and orders given for the arrest of any horseman that might be found in or near the city. He told him to hold his tongue, and take care of the horse; and calling for a light, he and Aniā tore up every letter he had received from Fīrōzpur, and dipped the fragments in water, to efface the ink from them. Aniā asked him what he had done with the blunderbuss, and was told that it had been thrown into a well. Aniā now concealed three flints that he kept about him in some sand in the upper story they occupied, and threw an iron ramrod and two spare bullets into a well near the mosque.

The next morning, when he heard that the city gates had been all shut to prevent any one from going out till strict search should be made, Karīm became a good deal alarmed, and went to seek counsel from Moghal Beg, the friend of his master; but when in the evening he heard that they had been again opened, he recovered his spirits; and the next day he wrote a letter to the Nawāb, saying that he had purchased the dogs that he wanted, and would soon return with them. He then went to Mr. McPherson, and actually purchased from him for the Nawāb some dogs and pictures, and the following day sent Rūplā, the groom, with them to Fīrōzpur, accompanied by two bearers. A pilgrim lodged in the same place with these men, and was present when Karīm came home from the murder, and gave his horse to Rūplā. In the evening, after the departure of Rūplā with the dogs, four men of the Gūjar caste came to the place, and Karīm sat down and smoked a pipe with one of them,[15] who said that he had lost his bread by Mr. Fraser's death, and should be glad to see the murderer punished—that he was known to have worn a green vest, and he hoped he would soon be discovered. The pilgrim came up to Karīm shortly after these four men went away, and said that he had heard from some one that he, Karīm, was himself suspected of the murder. He went again to Moghal Beg, who told him not to be alarmed, that, happily, the Regulations were now in force in the Delhi Territory, and that he had only to stick steadily to one story to be safe.

He now desired Aniā to return to Fīrōzpur with a letter to the Nawāb, and to assure him that he would be stanch and stick to one story, though they should seize him and confine him in prison for twelve years. He had, he said, already sent off part of his clothes, and Aniā should now take away the rest, so that nothing suspicious should be left near him.

The next morning Aniā set out on foot, accompanied by Islāmullah, a servant of Moghal Beg's, who was also the bearer of a letter to the Nawāb. They hired two ponies when they became tired, but both flagged before they reached Nagīna, whence Aniā proceeded to Fīrōzpur, on a mare belonging to the native collector, leaving Islāmullah behind. He gave his letter to the Nawāb, who desired him to describe the affair of the murder. He did so. The Nawāb seemed very much pleased, and asked him whether Karīm appeared to be in any alarm. Aniā told him that he did not, and had resolved to stick to one story, though he should be imprisoned for twelve years. 'Karīm Khān,' said the Nawāb, turning to the brother-in-law of the former, Wāsil Khān, and Hasan Alī, who stood near him—'Karīm Khān is a very brave man, whose courage may be always relied on.' He gave Aniā eighteen rupees, and told him to change his name, and keep close to Wāsil Khān. They retired together; but, while Wāsil Khān went to his house, Aniā stood on the road unperceived, but near enough to hear Hasan Alī urge the Nawāb to have him put to death immediately, as the only chance of keeping the fatal secret. He went off immediately to Wāsil Khān, and prevailed upon him to give him leave to go home for that night to see his family, promising to be back the next morning early.

He set out forthwith, but had not been long at home when he learned that Hasan Alī, and another confidential servant of the Nawāb, were come in search of him with some troopers. He concealed himself in the roof of his house, and heard them ask his wife and children where he was, saying they wanted his aid in getting out some hyaenas they had traced into their dens in the neighbourhood. They were told that he had gone back to Fīrōzpur, and returned; but were sent back by the Nawāb to make a more careful search for him. Before they came, however, he had gone off to his friends Kamruddīn and Joharī, two brothers who resided in the Rāo Rājā's territory. To this place he was followed by some Mewātīs, whom the Nawāb had induced, under the promise of a large reward, to undertake to kill him. One night he went to two acquaintances, Makrām and Shahāmat, in a neighbouring village, and begged them to send to some English gentleman in Delhi, and solicit for him a pardon, on condition of his disclosing all the circumstances of Mr. Fraser's murder. They promised to get everything done for him through a friend in the police at Delhi, and set out for that purpose, while Aniā returned and concealed himself in the hills. In six days they came with a paper, purporting to be a promise of pardon from the court of Delhi, and desired Kamr-ud-dīn to introduce them to Aniā. He told them to return to him in three days, and he would do so; but he went off to Aniā in the hills, and told him that he did not think these men had really got the papers from the English gentlemen—that they appeared to him to be in the service of the Nawāb himself. Aniā was, however, introduced to them when they came back, and requested that the paper might be read to him. Seeing through their designs, he again made off to the hills, while they went out in search, they pretended, of a man to read it, but in reality to get some people who were waiting in the neighbourhood to assist in securing him, and taking him off to the Nawāb.

Finding on their return that Aniā had escaped, they offered high rewards to the two brothers if they would assist in tracing him out; and Joharī was taken to the Nawāb, who offered him a very high reward if he would bring Aniā to him, or, at least, take measures to prevent his going to the English gentlemen. This was communicated to Aniā, who went through Bharatpur to Bareilly, and from Bareilly to Secunderabad, where he heard, in the beginning of July, that both Karīm and the Nawāb were to be tried for the murder, and that the judge, Mr. Colvin, had already arrived at Delhi to conduct the trial. He now determined to go to Delhi and give himself up. On his way he was met by Mr. Simon Fraser's man, who took him to Delhi, when he confessed his share in the crime, became king's evidence at the trial, and gave an interesting narrative of the whole affair.

Two water-carriers, in attempting to draw up the brass jug of a carpenter, which had fallen into the well the morning after the murder, pulled up the blunderbuss which Karīm Khān had thrown into the same well. This was afterwards recognized by Aniā, and the man whom he pointed out as having made it for him. Two of the four Gūjars, who were mentioned as having visited Karīm immediately after the murder, went to Brigadier Fast, who commanded the troops at Delhi, fearing that the native officers of the European civil functionaries might be in the interest of the Nawāb, and get them made away with. They told him that Karīm Khān seemed to answer the description of the man named in the proclamation as the murderer of Mr. Fraser; and he sent them with a note to the Commissioner, Mr. Metcalfe, who sent them to the Magistrate, Mr. Fraser, who accompanied them to the place, and secured Karīm, with some fragments of important papers. The two Mewātīs, who had been sent to assassinate Aniā, were found, and they confessed the fact: the brother of Aniā, Rahmat, was found and he described the difficulty Aniā had to escape from the Nawāb's people sent to murder him. Rūplā, the groom, deposed to all that he had seen during the time he was employed as Karīm's groom at Delhi. Several men deposed to having met Karīm, and heard him asking after Mr. Fraser a few days before the murder. The two peons, who were with Mr. Fraser when he was shot, deposed to the horse which he rode at the time, and which was found with him.

Karīm Khān and the Nawāb were both convicted of the crime, sentenced to death, and executed at Delhi, I should mention that suspicion had immediately attached to Karīm Khān; he was known for some time to have been lurking about Delhi, on the pretence of purchasing dogs; and it was said that, had the Nawāb really wanted dogs, he would not have sent to purchase them by a man whom he admitted to his table, and treated on terms of equality. He was suspected of having been employed on such occasions before — known to be a good shot, and a good rider, who could fire and reload very quickly while his horse was in full gallop, and called in consequence the 'Bharmārū.'[16] His horse, which was found in the stable by the Gūjar spies, who had before been in Mr. Fraser's service, answered the description given of the murderer's horse by Mr. Fraser's attendants; and the Nawāb was known to cherish feelings of bitter hatred against Mr. Fraser.

The Nawāb was executed some time after Karīm, on Thursday morning, the 3rd of October, 1835, close outside the north, or Kashmir Gate, leading to the cantonments. He prepared himself for the execution in an extremely rich and beautiful dress of light green, the colour which martyrs wear; but he was made to exchange this, and he then chose one of simple white, and was too conscious of his guilt to urge strongly his claim to wear what dress he liked on such an occasion.

The following corps were drawn up around the gallows, forming three sides of a square: the 1st Regiment of Cavalry, the 20th, 39th, and 69th Regiments of Native Infantry, Major Pew's Light Field Battery, and a strong party of police. On ascending the scaffold, the Nawāb manifested symptoms of disgust at the approach to his person of the sweeper, who was to put the rope round his neck;[17] but he soon mastered his feelings, and submitted with a good grace to his fate. Just as he expired his body made a last turn, and left his face towards the *west*, or the *tomb of his Prophet*, which the Muhammadans of Delhi considered a miracle, indicating that he was a martyr—not as being innocent of the murder, but as being executed for the murder of an unbeliever. Pilgrimages were for some time made to the Nawāb's tomb,[18] but I believe they have long since ceased with the short gleam of sympathy that his fate excited. The only people that still recollect him with feelings of kindness are the prostitutes and dancing women of the city of Delhi, among whom most of his revenues were squandered[19] In the same manner was Wazīr Ali recollected for many years by the prostitutes and dancing women of Benares, after the massacre of Mr. Cherry and all the European gentlemen of that station, save one, Mr. Davis, who bravely defended himself, wife, and children against a host with a hog spear on the top of his house. No European could pass Benares for twenty years after Wazīr Alī's arrest and confinement in the garrison of Fort William, without hearing from the Windows songs in his praise, and in praise of the massacre.[20]

It is supposed that the Nawāb Faiz Muhammad Khan of Jhajjar was deeply implicated in this murder, though no proof of it could be found. He died soon after the execution of Shams-ud- dīn, and was succeeded in his fief by his eldest son, Faiz Alī Khān.[21] This fief was bestowed on the father of the deceased, whose name was Najābat Alī Khān, by Lord Lake, on the termination of the war in 1805, for the aid he had given to the retreating army under Colonel Monson.[22]

One circumstance attending the execution of the Nawāb Shams-ud-dīn seems worthy of remark. The magistrate, Mr. Frascott, desired his crier to go through the city the evening before the execution, and proclaim to the people that those who might wish to be present at the execution were not to encroach upon the line of sentries that would be formed to keep clear an allotted space round the gallows, nor to carry with them any kind of arms; but the crier, seemingly retaining in his recollection only the words *arms* and *sentries*, gave out after his 'Oyes, Oyes,'[23] that the sentries had orders to use their arms, and shoot any man, woman, or child that should presume to go outside the wall to look at the execution of the Nawāb. No person, in consequence, ventured out till the execution was over, when they went to see the Nawāb himself converted into smoke; as the general impression was that as life should leave it, the body was to be blown off into the air by a general discharge of musketry and artillery. Moghal Bēg was acquitted for want of judicial proof of his guilty participation in the crime.

Notes:

1. The author's remarks concerning military officers refer to officers serving with native regiments, now known as the Indian Army. Before the institution of the reformed police in 1861 the native troops used to be much scattered in detachments, guarding treasuries, and performing other duties since entrusted to the police. Detachments are now rarely sent out, except on frontier service.

2. Fīrōzpur, the Fīrozpur-Jhirka of the *I.G.*, is now the head-quarters of a sub-collectorate in the Gurgāon district. The three Districts of the Delhi Territories in Sleeman's time seem to have been Delhi, Pānīpat (= Karnāl), and Rohtak, which were under the jurisdiction of the Lieutenant-Governor of the North-Western Provinces. In 1858, after the Mutiny, they were transferred to the Panjāb. Since then, many administrative changes have occurred. The latest took place on October 1, 1912, on the occasion of Delhi becoming the official capital of India, instead of Calcutta. The city of Delhi with a small surrounding area, 557 square miles in all, now forms a tiny distinct province, ruled by a Chief Commissioner under the direct orders of the Government of India. The Delhi Division has ceased to exist, and six Districts, namely, Hissar, Rohtak, Karnāl, Ambāla (Umballa), Gurgāon, and Simla, now constitute the Commissioner's Division of Ambāla in the Panjāb.

3. *Ante*, chapter 31, text between [10] and [11]. Some great landholders of the present day pursue the same policy.

4. The story of the murder of Fraser is told very differently in Bosworth-Smith's *Life of Lord Lawrence*, where all the detective credit is given to Lord L., apparently on his own authority. See also an article in the *Quarterly*

Review for April 1883, by Sir H. Yule, and another in *Blackwoods Magazine* for January 1878.

Miniature medallion portraits of Nawāb Shams-ud-dīn and his servant Karīm Khān are given on the frontispiece of Volume II in the original edition.

5. The inglorious second administration of Lord Cornwallis lasted only from 30th of July, 1805, the date on which he relieved the Marquis Wellesley, to the 5th of October of the same year, the date of his death at Ghāzīpur. 'The Marquis Cornwallis arrived in India, prepared to abandon, as far as might be practicable, all the advantages gained for the British Government by the wisdom, energy, and perseverance of his predecessor; to relax the bands by which the Marquis Wellesley had connected the greater portion of the states of India with the British Government; and to reduce that Government from the position of arbiter of the destinies of India to the rank of one among many equals.' His policy was zealously carried out by Sir George Barlow, who succeeded him, and held office till July, 1807. That statesman was not ashamed to write that 'the British possessions in the Doāb will derive additional security from the contests of the neighbouring states'. (Thornton, *The History of the British Empire in India*, chap. 21.) This fatuous policy produced twelve years of anarchy, which were terminated by the Marquis of Hastings's great war with the Marāthās and Pindhārīs in 1817, so often referred to in this book. Lord Lake addressed the most earnest remonstrances to Sir George Barlow without avail.

6. Amīn-ud-dīn and Ziā-ud-dīn's mother was the Bhāo Bēgam, or wife; Shams-ud- dīn's the Bhāo Khānum, or mistress. [W. H. S.]

7. Sir James Edward, third baronet, who died November 5, 1838. He was paternal uncle of Henry Thomas Colebrooke, F.R.S., the greatest of Anglo-Indian Sanskritists. The fifth baronet, Edward Arthur, was created Baron Colebrooke in 1906.

8. Sir Charles Metcalfe was for a time Assistant Resident at Delhi, and was first appointed to the Residency at the extraordinarily early age of twenty-six. He was then transferred to other posts. In 1824 he returned to the Delhi Residency, superseding Sir David Ochterlony, whose measures had been disapproved by the Government of India. He left the Residency in 1827.

9. The editor once had occasion to deal with a similar case, which resulted in the loss by the offending Rājā of his rank and title. The orders were passed by the Government of Lord Dufferin.

10. Colonel Skinner, who raised the famous troops known as Skinner's Horse, died in 1841, and was buried in the church of St. James at Delhi

which he had built. The church still exists. The Colonel erected opposite the church, as a memorial of his friend Fraser, a fine inlaid marble cross, which was destroyed in the Mutiny (General Hervey, *Some Records of Crime*, vol. i, p. 403).

11. According to General Hervey, the provocation was that Mr. Fraser had inquired from the Nawāb about his sister by name (op. cit., p. 279).

12. I print this word 'Bulvemar's' as it stands in the original edition, not knowing what it means.

13. The habits of Europeans have now changed, and to most people escorts have become distasteful. High officials now constantly go about unattended, and could be assassinated with little difficulty. Happily crimes of the kind are rare, except on the Afghan frontier, where special precautions are taken.

14. For the 'Bāiza Bai' see *ante*, chapter 50 note 4. Hindoo Rāo's house became famous in 1857 as the head- quarters of the British force on the Ridge, during the siege of Delhi.

15. Many of the Gūjar caste are Muhammadans.

16. That is to say 'load and fire', or 'sharpshooter'.

17. No one but a member of one of the 'outcaste castes', if the 'bull' be allowable, will act as executioner.

18. This sinister incident shows clearly the real feeling of the Muhammadan populace towards the ruling power. That feeling is unchanged, and is not altogether confined to the Muslim populace. See the following remark about the populace of Benares.

19. This remark was evidently written some time after the author's first visit to Delhi, and probably was written in the year 1839.

20. On the death of Āsaf-ud-daula, Wazīr Alī was, in spite of doubts as to his legitimacy, recognized by Sir John Shore (Lord Teignmouth) as the Nawāb Wazīr of Oudh, in 1797. On reconsideration, the Governor-General cancelled the recognition of Wazīr Alī, and recognized his rival Saādat Alī. Wazīr Alī was removed from Lucknow, but injudiciously allowed to reside at Benares. The Marquis Wellesley, then Earl of Mornington, took charge of the office of Governor-General in 1798, and soon resolved that it was expedient to remove Wazīr Alī to a greater distance from Lucknow. Mr. Cherry, the Agent to the Governor-General, was accordingly instructed to remove him from Benares to Calcutta. The outbreak alluded to in the text occurred on January 14, 1799, and was the expression of Wazīr Ali's resentment at these orders. It is described as follows by Thornton (*History*,

chap. xvii): 'A visit which Wazīr Alī made, accompanied by his suite, to the British Agent, afforded the means of accomplishing the meditated revenge. He had engaged himself to breakfast with Mr. Cherry, and the parties met in apparent amity. The usual compliments were exchanged. Wazīr Alī then began to expatiate on his wrongs; and having pursued this subject for some time, he suddenly rose with his attendants, and put to death Mr. Cherry and Captain Conway, an English gentleman who happened to be present. The assassins then rushed out, and meeting another Englishman named Graham, they added him to the list of their victims. They thence proceeded to the house of Mr. Davis, judge and magistrate, who had just time to remove his family to an upper terrace, which could only be reached by a very narrow staircase. At the top of this staircase, Mr. Davis, armed with a spear, took his post, and so successfully did he defend it, that the assailants, after several attempts to dislodge him, were compelled to retire without effecting their object. The benefit derived from the resistance of this intrepid man extended beyond his own family: the delay thereby occasioned afforded to the rest of the English inhabitants opportunity of escaping to the place where the troops stationed for the protection of the city were encamped. General Erskine, on learning what had occurred, dispatched a party to the relief of Mr. Davis, and Wazīr Alī thereupon retired to his own residence.' Wazīr Alī escaped, but was ultimately given up by a chief with whom he had taken refuge, 'on condition that his life should be spared, and that his limbs should not be disgraced by chains'. Some of his accomplices were executed. 'He was confined at Port William, in a sort of iron cage, where he died in May, 1817, aged thirty-six, after an imprisonment of seventeen years and some odd months.' (*Men whom India has Known*, 2nd ed., 1874, art. 'Vizier Ali.') But Beale asserts that after many years' captivity in Calcutta, the prisoner was removed to Vellore, where he died (*Or. Biogr. Dict.*, ed. Keene, 1894, p. 416). It will be observed that the author was mistaken in supposing that 'all the European gentlemen, except Mr. Davis and his family, were included in the massacre.'

21. These names stand in the original edition as 'Tyz Mahomed Khan, of Ghujper,' and 'Tyz Alee Khan'. In 1857 the then Nawāb of Jhajjar joined the rebels. He was accordingly hanged, and his estate was confiscated. It is now included in the Rohtak District. See Fanshawe's *Settlement Report* of that District.

22. The disastrous retreat of Colonel Monson before Jeswant Rāo Holkār during the rainy season of 1804 is one of the few serious reverses which have interrupted the long series of British victories in India. A considerable

force under the command of Colonel Monson, sent out by General Lake at the beginning of May in pursuit of Holkār, was withdrawn too far from its base, and was compelled to retreat through Rājputāna, and fall back on Agra. During the retreat the rains broke, and, under pressure caused by the difficulties of the march and incessant attacks of the enemy, the Company's troops became disorganized, and lost their guns and baggage. The shattered remnants of the force straggled into Agra at the end of August. The disgrace of this retreat was speedily avenged by the great victory of Dīg.

23. This old Norman-French formula. Oyez, Oyez, meaning 'Hear!' is still, or recently was, used at the Assizes in the High Court, Calcutta. The formula would not now be heard at Delhi, or elsewhere beyond the precincts of the High Court.

CHAPTER 65

Marriage of a Jāt Chief.

ON the 19th[1] we came on to Balamgarh,[2] fifteen miles over a plain, better cultivated and more studded with trees than that which we had been coming over for many days before. The water was near the surface, more of the field were irrigated, and those which were not so looked better — [a] range of sandstone hills, ten miles off to the west, running north and south. Balamgarh is held in rent-free tenure by a young Jāt chief, now about ten years of age. He resides in a mud fort in a handsome palace built in the European fashion. In an extensive orange garden, close outside the fort, he is building a very handsome tomb over the spot where his father's elder brother was buried. The whole is formed of white and black marble, and the firm white sandstone of Rūpbās, and so well conceived and executed as to make it evident that demand is the only thing wanted to cover India with works of art equal to any that were formed in the palmy days of the Muhammadan empire.[3] The Rājā's young sister had just been married to the son of the Jāt chief of Nābhā, who was accompanied in his matrimonial visit (barāt) by the chief of Ludhaura, and the son of the Sikh chief of Patiālā,[4] with a *cortège* of one hundred elephants, and above fifteen thousand people.[5]

The young chief of Balamgarh mustered a *cortège* of sixty elephants and about ten thousand men to attend him out in the 'istikbāl', to meet and welcome his guests. The bridegroom's party had to expend about six hundred thousand rupees in this visit alone. They scattered copper money all along the road from their homes to within seven miles of Balamgarh. From this point to the gate of the fort they had to scatter silver, and from this gate to the door of the palace they scattered gold and jewels of all kinds. The son of the Patiālā chief, a lad of about ten years of age, sat upon his elephant with a bag containing six hundred gold mohurs of two guineas each, mixed up with an infinite variety of gold earrings, pearls, and precious stones, which he scattered in handfuls among the crowd. The scattering of the copper and silver had been left to inferior hands. The costs of the family of the bride are always much greater than that of the bridegroom; they are obliged to entertain at their own expense all the bridegroom's guests as well as their own, as long as they remain; and over and above this, on the present occasion, the Rājā gave a rupee to every person that came, invited or uninvited. An immense concourse of people had assembled to share in this donation, and to scramble for the money scattered along the road; and ready money enough was not found in the treasury. Before a further supply could be got, thirty thousand more had collected, and every one got his rupee. They have them all put into pens like sheep. When all are in, the doors are opened at a signal given, and every person is paid his rupee as he goes out. Some European gentlemen were standing upon the top of the Rājā's palace, looking at the procession as it entered the fort, and passed underneath; and the young chief threw up some handfuls of pearls, gold, and jewels among them. Not one of them would of course condescend to stoop to take up any; but their servants showed none of the same dignified forbearance.[6]

Notes:

1. January, 1836.

2. 'Balamgarh' is a mistake for Ballabgarh of I. G. (properly Ballabhgarh), which is about twenty-four miles from Delhi. In 1857 the chief was hanged for rebellion. The estate was confiscated and included in the Delhi District, under the Panjāb Government. From October 1, 1912, that District ceased to exist. Part of the Ballabhgarh sub-district has been included in the new Chief Commissioner's Province of Delhi, and part in the Gurgāon District.

3. Few observers will accept this proposition without considerable reservation.

4. Patiālā is the principal of the Cis-Satlaj Sikh Protected States. Nābhā belongs to the same group. Both states are very loyal, and supply Imperial Service troops. For a sketch of their history see chapters 2 and 9 of Sir Lepel Griffin's Ranjīt Singh.

5. The Sikh is a military nation formed out of the Jāts (who were without a place among the castes of the Hindoos),[a] by that strong bond of union, the love of conquest and plunder. Their religions and civil codes are the Granths, books written by their reputed prophets, the last of whom was Guru Govind,[b] in whose name Ranjīt Singh stamps his gold coins with this legend: 'The sword, the pot, victory, and conquest were quickly found in the grace of Guru Govind Singh,'[c] This prophet died insane in the end of the seventeenth century. He was the son of a priest Tēg Bahādur, who was made a martyr of by the bigoted Muhammadans of Patna in 1675. The son became a Peter the Hermit, in the same manner as Hargovind before him, when his father, Arjun Mal, was made a martyr by the fanaticism of the same people. A few more such martyrdoms would have set the Sikhs up for ever. They admit converts freely, and while they have a fair prospect of conquest and plunder they will find them; but, when they cease, they will be

swallowed up in the great ocean of Hinduism, since they have no chance of getting up an 'army of martyrs' while we have the supreme power.[d] They detest us for the same reason that the military followers of the other native chiefs detest us, because we say 'Thus far shall you go, and no farther' in your career of conquest and plunder.[e] As governors, they are even worse than the Marāthās—utterly detestable. They have not the slightest idea of a duty towards the people from whose industry they are provided. Such a thing was never dreamed of by a Sikh. They continue to receive in marriage the daughters of Jāts, as in this case; but they will not give their daughters to Jāts. [W. H. S.]

6. The Emperors of Delhi, from Jahāngīr onwards, used to strike special coins, generally of small size, bearing the word *nisār*, which means 'scattering', for the purpose of distribution among the crowd on the occasion of a wedding, or other great festivity.

a. It has already been observed that the author was completely mistaken in his estimate of the social position of Jāts. It is not correct to say that they 'were without a place among the castes of the Hindoos'. 'The Jāt is in every respect the most important of the Panjāb peoples. . . . The distinction between Jāt and Rājpūt is social rather than ethnic. . . . Socially the Jāt occupies a position which is shared by the Rōr, the Gūjar, and the Ahīr; all four eating and smoking together. Among the races of purely Hindoo origin I think that the Jāt stands next after the Brahman, the Rājpūt, and the Khatrī. . . . There are Jāts and Jāts. . . . His is the highest of the castes practising widow marriage.' (Ibbetson, *Outlines of Panjāb Ethnography*, Calcutta, 1883, pp. 220 sqq.) The Jāts in the United Provinces occupy much the same relative position.

b. The Sikhs are mostly, but not all, Jāts. The organization is essentially a religions one, and a few Brahmans and many members of various other castes join it. Even sweepers are admitted with certain limitations. The word Sikh means 'disciple'. Nānak Shāh, the founder, was born in A.D. 1469. The *Ādi Granth*, the Sikh Bible, containing compositions by Nānak, his next four successors, and other persons, was completed in 1604. A second *Granth* was compiled in 1734 by Govind Singh, the tenth Guru. The only authoritative version of the Sikh scriptures is the great work by Macauliffe, *The Sikh Religion* (Oxford, 1909, 6 vols.).

The political power of the sect rested on the institutions of Guru Govind, as framed between 1690 and 1708. In 1764 the Sikhs occupied Lahore. Full details of their history will be found in Cunningham, *A History of the Sikhs* (1st ed., 2 vols. 8vo, London, 1849, suppressed and scarce; 2nd ed. 1853); and more briefly in Sir Lepel Griffin's excellent little book, *Ranjīt Singh* (Oxford, 'Rulers of India' series, 1892).

c. See R. 0. Temple, 'The Coins of the Modern Chiefs of the Panjāb' (*Ind. Ant.*, vol. xviii (1889), pp. 321-41); and C. J. Rodgers, 'On the Coins of the Sikhs' (*J.A.S.B.*, vol. 1. Part I (1881), pp. 71-93). The couplet is in Persian, which may be transliterated thus:—

Dēg, tēgh, wa fath, wa nasrat bē darang
Yāft az Nānak Gūrū Govind Singh.

The word *dēg*, meaning pot or cauldron, is used as a symbol of plenty. The correct rendering is:—

Plenty, the sword, victory, and help without delay,
Gūrū Govind Singh obtained from Nānak.

d. This prophecy has not been fulfilled. The annexation of the Panjāb in 1849 put an end to Sikh hopes of 'conquest and plunder', and yet the sect has not been 'swallowed up in the great ocean of Hinduism'. At the census of 1881 its numbers were returned as 1,853,426, or nearly two millions, for all India. The corresponding figure for 1891 is 1,907,833. At the time of the first British census of 1855 the outside influences were depressing: the great Khālsa army had fallen, and Sikh fathers were slow to bring forward their sons for baptism (*pāhul*). The Mutiny, in the suppression of which the Sikhs took so great a part, worked a change. The Sikhs recovered their spirits and self-respect, and found honourable careers open in the British army and constabulary. 'Thus the creed received a new impulse, and many sons of Sikhs, whose baptism had been deferred, received the *pāhul*, while new candidates from among the Jāts and lower caste Hindoos joined the faith.' Some reaction then, perhaps, took place, but, on the whole, the numbers of the sect have been maintained or increased. (Sir Lepel Griffin, *Ranjīt Singh*, pp. 25-34.) For various reasons, which I have not space to explain, the statistics of Sikhism are untrustworthy. The returns for 1911 show an increase of 37 per cent. in the Panjāb. We may, at least, be assured that the numbers are not diminishing.

e. The Sikhs do not now detest us. They willingly furnish soldiers and military police of the best class, equal to the Gōrkhās, and fit to fight in line with English soldiers. The Panjāb chieftains have been among the foremost in offers of loyal assistance to the Government of India in times of danger, and in organizing the Imperial Service troops. The Sikh states are now sufficiently well governed.

CHAPTER 66

Collegiate Endowment of Muhammadan Tombs and Mosques.

On the 20th[1] we came to Badarpur, twelve miles over a plain, with the range of hills on our left approaching nearer and nearer the road, and separating us from the old city of Delhi. We passed through Farīdpur, once a large town, and called after its founder, Shaikh Farīd, whose mosque is still in good order, though there is no person to read or hear prayers in it.[2] We passed also two fine bridges, one of three, and one of four arches, both over what were once streams, but are now dry beds of sand.[3] The whole road shows signs of having been once thickly peopled, and highly adorned with useful and ornamental works when Delhi was in its glory.

Every handsome mausoleum among Muhammadans was provided with its mosque, and endowed by the founder with the means of maintaining men of learning to read their Korān over the grave of the deceased and in his chapel; and, as long as the endowment lasted, the tomb continued to be at the same time a college. They read the Korān morning and evening over the grave, and prayers in the chapel at the stated periods; and the rest of their time is commonly devoted to the instruction of the youths of their neighbourhood, either gratis or for a small consideration. Apartments in the tomb were usually set aside for the purpose, and these tombs did ten times more for education in Hindustan than all the colleges formed especially for the purpose.[4] We might suppose that rulers who formed and endowed such works all over the land must have had more of the respect and the affections of the great mass of the people than we, who, as my friend upon the Jumna has it, 'build nothing but private dwelling-houses, factories, courts of justice, and jails', can ever have; but this conclusion would not be altogether just.[5] Though every mosque and mausoleum was a seat of learning, that learning, instead of being a source of attraction and conciliation between the Muhammadans and Hindoos, was, on the contrary, a source of perpetual repulsion and enmity between them—it tended to keep alive in the breasts of the Musalmāns a strong feeling of religions indignation against the worshippers of idols; and of dread and hatred in those of the Hindoos.

The Korān was the Book of books, spoken by God to the angel Gabriel in parts as occasion required, and repeated by him to Muhammad; who, unable to write himself, dictated them to any one who happened to be present when he received the divine communications;[6] it contained all that it was worth man's while to study or know—it was from the Deity, but at the same time coeternal with Him—it was His divine eternal spirit, inseparable from Him from the beginning, and therefore, like Him, uncreated. This book, to read which was of itself declared to be the highest of all species of worship, taught war against the worshippers of idols to be of all merits the greatest in the eye of God; and no man could well rise from the perusal without the wish to serve God by some act of outrage against them. These buildings were, therefore, looked upon by the Hindoos, who composed the great mass of the people, as a kind of religions volcanoes, always ready to explode and pour out their lava of intolerance and outrage upon the innocent people of the surrounding country.

If a Hindoo fancied himself injured or insulted by a Muhammadan he was apt to revenge himself upon the Muhammadans generally, and insult their religion by throwing swine's flesh, or swine's blood, into one of their tombs or churches; and the latter either flew to arms at once to revenge their God, or retaliated by throwing the flesh or the blood of the cow into the first Hindoo temple at hand, which made the Hindoos fly to arms. The guilty and the wicked commonly escaped, while numbers of the weak, the innocent and the unoffending were slaughtered. The magnificent buildings, therefore, instead of being at the time bonds of union, were commonly sources of the greatest discord among the whole community, and of the most painful humiliation to the Hindoo population. During the bigoted reign of Aurangzēb and his successors a Hindoo's presence was hardly tolerated within sight of these tombs or churches; and had he been discovered entering one of them, he would probably have been hunted down like a mad dog. The recollection of such outrages, and the humiliation to which they gave rise, associated as they always are in the minds of the Hindoos with the sight of these buildings, are perhaps the greatest source of our strength in India; because they at the same time feel that it is to us alone they owe the protection which they now enjoy from similar injuries. Many of my countrymen, full of virtuous indignation at the outrages which often occur during the processions of the Muharram, particularly when these happen to take place at the same time with some religious procession of the Hindoos, are very anxious that our Government should interpose its authority to put down both. But these processions and occasional outrages are really sources of great strength to us; they show at once the necessity for the interposition of an impartial tribunal, and a disposition on the part of the rulers to interpose impartially. The Muhammadan festivals are regulated by the lunar, and those of the Hindoos by the solar year, and they cross each other every thirty or forty years, and furnish fair occasions for the local authorities to interpose effectually.[7] People who receive or imagine insults or injuries commonly postpone their revenge till these religious festivals come round, when they hope to be able to settle their accounts with impunity among the excited crowd. The mournful procession of the Muharram, when the Muhammadans are inflamed to madness by the recollection of the really affecting incidents of the massacre of the grandchildren of their prophet, and by the images of their tombs, and their sombre music,[8] crosses that of the Holī[9] (in which the Hindoos are excited to tumultuous and licentious joy by their bacchanalian songs and dances) every thirty- six years; and they reign together for some four or five days, during which the scene in every large town is really terrific. The processions are liable to meet in the street, and the lees of the wine of the Hindoos, or the red powder which is substituted for them, is liable to fall upon the tombs of the others. Hindoos pass on, forgetting in their saturnalian joy all distinctions of age, sex, or religion, their clothes and persons besmeared with the red powder, which is moistened and thrown from all kinds of machines over friend and foe; while meeting these come the Muhammadans, clothed in their green mourning, with gloomy downcast looks, beating their breasts, ready to kill themselves, and too anxious for an excuse to kill anybody else. Let but one drop of the lees of joy fall upon the image of the tomb as it passes, and a hundred swords fly from their scabbards; many an innocent person falls; and woe be to the town in which the magistrate is not at hand with his police and military force. Proudly conscious of their power, the magistrates refuse to prohibit one class from laughing because the other happens to be weeping; and the Hindoos on such occasions laugh the more heartily to let the world see that they are free to do so.

A very learned Hindoo once told me in Central India that the oracle of Mahādēo had been at the same time consulted at three of his greatest temples—one in the Deccan, one in Rājputāna, and one, I think, in Bengal—as to the result of the government of India by Europeans, who seemed determined to fill all the high offices of administration with their own countrymen, to the exclusion of the people of the country. A day was appointed for the answer; and when the priest came to receive it they found Mahādēo (Siva) himself with a European complexion, and dressed in European clothes. He told them that their European Government was in reality nothing more than a multiplied incarnation of himself; and that he had come among them in this shape to prevent their cutting each other's throats as they had been doing for some centuries past; that these, his incarnations, appeared to have no religion themselves in order that they might be the more impartial arbitrators between the people of so many different creeds and sects who now inhabited the country; that they must be aware that they never had before been so impartially governed, and that they must continue to obey these their governors, without attempting to pry further into futurity or the will of the gods. Mahādēo performs a part in the great drama of the Rāmāyana, or the Rape of Sīta, and he is the only figure there that is represented with a *white face*.[10]

I was one day praising the law of primogeniture among ourselves to a Muhammadan gentleman of high rank, and defending it on the ground that it prevented that rivalry and bitterness of feeling among brothers which were always found among the Muhammadans, whose law prescribes an equal division of property, real and personal, among the sons, and the *choice of the wisest* among them as successor to the government.[11] 'This', said he, 'is no doubt the source of our weakness, but why should you condemn a law which is to you a source of so much strength? I, one day', said he, 'asked Mr. Seaton, the Governor-General's representative at the court of Delhi, which of all things he had seen in India he liked best. "You have", replied he, smiling, "a small species of melon called 'phūt' (disunion); this is the thing we like best in your land." There was', continued my Muhammadan friend, 'an infinite deal of sound political wisdom in this one sentence. Mr. Seaton was a very good and a very wise man. Our European governors of the present day are not at all the same kind of thing. I asked Mr. B., a judge, the same question many years afterwards, and he told me that he thought the rupees were the best things he had found in India. I asked Mr. T., the Commissioner, and he told me that he thought the tobacco which he smoked in his hookah was the best thing. And pray, sir, what do you think the best thing?'

'Why, Nawāb Sāhib, I am always very well pleased when I am free from pain, and can get my nostrils full of cool air, and my mouth full of cold water in this hot land of yours; and I think most of my countrymen are the same. Next to these, the thing we all admire most in India, Nawāb Sāhib, is the entire exemption which you and I and every other gentleman, native or European, enjoy from the taxes which press so heavily upon them in other countries.[12] In Kāshmīr, no midwife is allowed to attend a woman in her confinement till a heavy tax has been paid to Ranjīt Singh for the infant; and in England, a man cannot let the light of heaven into his house till he has paid a tax for the window.'[13]

'Nor keep a dog, nor shoot a partridge in the jungle, I am told,' said the Nawāb.

'Quite true, Nawāb Sāhib.'

'Hindustan, sir,' said he, 'is, after all, the best country in the world; the only thing wanted is a little more (*rozgār*) employment for the educated classes under Government.'

'True, Nawāb Sāhib, we might, no doubt, greatly multiply this employment to the advantage of those who got the places, but we should have to multiply at the same time the taxes, to the great disadvantage of those who did not get them.'

'True, very true, sir,' said my old friend.

Notes:

1. January, 1836.

2. Farīdpur is a mistake for Farīdābād, a small town sixteen miles from Delhi, founded in 1607 by Shaikh Farīd, treasurer of Jahāngīr, to protect the high road between Agra and Delhi.

3. The beds are dry in the cold season, but the streams, which flow from the hills to the south of Delhi, are torrents in the rainy season.

4. But the education in such schools is of very little value, being commonly confined to the committing of the Korān to memory by boys ignorant of Arabic.

5. In modern India the British buildings are far more varied, and many aspire to some architectural merit.

6. Muhammad is said to have received these communications in all situations; sometimes when riding along the road on his camel, he became suddenly red in the face, and greatly agitated; he made his camel sit down immediately, and called for some one to write. His rhapsodies were all written at the time on leaves and thrown into a box. Gabriel is believed to have made him repeat over the whole once every year during the month of Ramazān. In the year he died Muhammad told his followers that the angel had made him repeat them over twice that year, and that he was sure he would not live to receive another visit. [W. H. S.]

7. The Muhammadan year consists of twelve lunar months of 30 and 29 days alternately. The common year, therefore, consists of only 354 days. But, when intercalary days in certain years are allowed for, the mean year consists of 354 11/30 days. Inasmuch as a solar year consists of about 365¼ days, the difference amounts to nearly 11 days, and any given month in the Muhammadan year consequently goes the round of the seasons in course of time.

8. The Muharram celebration takes its name from the first month of the Muhammadan year, during which it takes place. Alī, the cousin of

Muhammad, was married to the prophet's daughter Fatima, and, according to the Shīa sect, must be regarded as the lawful successor of Muhammad, who died in June, A.D. 632. But, as a matter of fact, Omar, Abū Bakr, and Othmān (Usmān) in turn succeeded to the Khalīfate, and Alī did not take possession of the office till A.D. 655. After five and a half years' reign he was assassinated in January, A.D. 661, and his son Hasan, who for a few months had held the vacant office, was poisoned in A.D. 670. Husain, the younger son of Alī, strove to assert his rights by force of arms, but was slain on the tenth day of the month Muharram (10th October, A.D. 680) in a great battle fought at Karbalā near the Euphrates. These events are commemorated yearly by noisy funeral processions. Properly, the proceedings ought to be altogether mournful, and confined to the Shīa sect, but in practice, Sunnī Muhammadans, and even Hindoos, take part in the ceremonies, which are regarded by many of the populace as no more solemn than a Lord Mayor's show.

9. The disgusting festival of the Holī, celebrated with drunkenness and obscenity, takes place in March, and is supposed to be the festival of the vernal equinox (see *ante*, chapter 27 note 16). The magistrates in India have no duty which requires more tact, discretion, and firmness than the regulation of conflicting religions processions. The general disarmament of the people has rendered collisions less dangerous and sanguinary than they used to be, but, in spite of all precautions, they still occur occasionally. The total prohibition of processions likely to cause collisions is, of course, impracticable.

10. Ante chapter 15 text at [9].

11. Muslim daughters also succeed, each taking half the share of a son.

12. *Tempora mutantur*. The land revenue, in the author's time, fully preserved its character of rent, and obviously was not a tax. Later legislation has obscured its real nature, and made it look like a tax. When the author wrote, the only taxes levied were indirect ones, as that on salt, which was paid unconsciously. The modern income-tax, local rates, municipal taxation, and gun licences were all unknown.

13. The window tax was levied at varying rates from 1697 to 1851.

CHAPTER 67

The Old City of Delhi.

On the 21st we went on eight miles to the Kutb Mīnār, across the range of sandstone hills, which rise to the height of about two hundred feet, and run north and south. The rocks are for the most part naked, but here and there the soil between them is covered with *famished* grass, and a few stunted shrubs; anything more unprepossessing can hardly be conceived than the aspect of these hills, which seem to serve no other purpose than to store up heat for the people of the great city of Delhi. We passed through a cut in this range of hills, made apparently by the stream of the river Jumna at some remote period, and about one hundred yards wide at the entrance. This cut is crossed by an enormous stone wall running north and south, and intended to shut in the waters, and form a lake in the opening beyond it. Along the brow of the precipice, overlooking the northern end of the wall, is the stupendous fort of Tughlakābād, built by the Emperor Tughlak the First[1] of the sandstones of the range of hills on which it stands, cut into enormous square blocks.[2]

On the brow of the opposite side of the precipice, overlooking the southern end of the wall, stands the fort of Muhammadābād, built by this Emperor's son and successor, Muhammad, and resembling in all things that built by his father.[3] These fortresses overlooked the lake, with the old city of Delhi spread out on the opposite side of it to the west. There is a third fortress upon an isolated hill, east of the great barrier wall, said to have been built in honour of his master by the Emperor Tughlak's *barber.* [4] The Emperor's tomb stands upon an isolated rock in the middle of the once lake, now plain, about a mile to the west of the barrier wall. The rock is connected with the western extremity of the northern fortress by a causeway of twenty- five arches, and about one hundred and fifty yards long. This is a fine tomb, and contains in a square centre room the remains of the Emperor Tughlak, his wife, and his son. The tomb is built of red sandstone, and surmounted by a dome of white marble. The three graves inside are built of brick covered with stucco work. The outer sides of the tomb slope slightly inwards from the base, in the form of a pyramid; but the inner walls are, of course, perpendicular.[5]

The impression left on the mind after going over these stupendous fortifications is that the arts which contribute to the comforts and elegancies of life must have been in a very rude state when they were raised. Domestic architecture must have been wretched in the extreme. The buildings are all of stone, and almost all without cement, and seem to have been raised by giants, and for giants, whose arms were against everybody, and everybody's arm against them. This was indeed the state of the Pathān sovereigns in India — they were the creatures of their armies; and their armies were also employed against the people, who feared and detested them all.[6]

The Emperor Tughlak, on his return at the head of the army, which he had led into Bengal to chastise some rebellious subjects, was met at Afghānpur by his eldest son, Jūnā, whom he had left in the government of the capital. The prince had in three days raised here a palace of wood for a grand entertainment to do honour to his father's return; and when the Emperor signified his wish to retire, all the courtiers rushed out before him to be in attendance, and among the rest, Jūnā himself. Five attendants only remained when the Emperor rose from his seat, and at that moment the building fell in and crushed them and their master. Jūnā had been sent at the head of an army into the Deccan, where he collected immense wealth from the plunder of the palaces of princes and the temples of their priests, the only places in which much wealth was to be found in those days. This wealth he tried to conceal from his father, whose death he probably thus contrived, that he might the sooner have the free enjoyment of it with unlimited power.[7]

Only thirty years before, Alā-ud-dīn, returning in the same manner at the head of an army from the Deccan loaded with wealth, murdered the Emperor Fīrōz the Second, the father of his wife, and ascended the throne. [8] Jūnā ascended the throne under the name of Muhammad the Third;[9] and, after the remains of his father had been deposited in the tomb I have described, he passed in great pomp and splendour from the fortress of Tughlakābād, which his father had just then completed, to the city in which the Mīnār stands, with elephants before and behind loaded with gold and silver coins, which were scattered among the crowd, who everywhere hailed him with shouts of joy. The roads were covered with flowers, the houses adorned with the richest stuffs, and the streets resounded with music.

He was a man of great learning, and a great patron of learned men; he was a great founder of churches, had prayers read in them at the prescribed times, and always went to prayers five times a day himself.[10] He was rigidly temperate himself in his habits, and discouraged all intemperance in others. These things secured him panegyrists throughout the empire during the twenty-seven years that he reigned over it, though perhaps he was the most detestable tyrant that ever filled a throne. He would take his armies out over the most populous and peaceful districts, and hunt down the innocent and unoffending people like wild beasts, and bring home their heads by thousands to hang them on the city gates for his mere amusement. He twice made the whole people of the city of Delhi emigrate with him to Daulatābād in Southern India, which he wished to make the capital, from some foolish fancy; and during the whole of his reign gave evident signs of being in an unsound state of mind.[11] There was at the time of his father's death a saint at Delhi named Nizāmuddīn Aulia, or the Saint, who was supposed by supernatural means to have driven from Delhi one night in a panic a large army of Moghals under Tarmasharīn, who invaded India from Transoxiana in 1303, and laid close siege to the city of Delhi, in which the Emperor Alā-ud-dīn was shut up without troops to defend himself, his armies being engaged in Southern India.[12] It is very likely that he did strike this army with a panic by getting some of their leaders assassinated in one night. He was supposed to have the 'dast ul ghaib', or supernatural purse' [literally, 'invisible hand'], as his private expenditure is said to have been more lavish even than that of the Emperor himself, while he had no ostensible source of income whatever. The Emperor was either jealous of his influence and display, or suspected him of dark crimes, and threatened to humble him when he returned to Delhi. As he approached the city, the friends of the saint, knowing the resolute spirit of the Emperor, urged him to quit the capital, as he had been often heard to say, 'Let me but reach Delhi, and this proud priest shall be humbled'.

The only reply that the saint would ever deign to give from the time the imperial army left Bengal, till it was within one stage of the capital, was 'Dihlī dūr ast'; 'Delhi is still far off'. This is now become a proverb over the East equivalent to our 'There is many a slip between the cup and the lip'. It is probable that the saint had some understanding with the son in his plans for the murder of his father; it is possible that his numerous wandering disciples may in reality have been murderers and robbers, and that he could at any time have procured through them the assassination of the Emperor. The Muhammadan Thugs, or assassins of India, certainly looked upon him as one of the great founders of their system, and used to make pilgrimages to his tomb as such; and, as he came originally from Persia, and is considered by his greatest admirers to have been in his youth a robber, it is not impossible that he may have been originally one of the 'assassins', or disciples of the 'old man of the mountains', and that he may have set up the system of Thuggee in India and derived a great portion of his income from it.[13] Emperors now prostrate themselves, and aspire to have their bones placed near it [scil. the tomb]. While wandering about the ruins, I remarked to one of the learned men of the place who attended us that it was singular Tughlak's buildings should be so rude compared with those of Iltutmish, who had reigned more than eighty years before him.[14] 'Not at all singular,' said he, 'was he not under the curse of the holy saint Nizām-ud-dīn?' 'And what had the Emperor done to merit the holy man's curse?' 'He had taken by force to employ upon his palaces several of the masons whom the holy man was employing upon a church,' said he.

The Kutb Mīnār was, I think, more beyond my expectations than the Tāj; first, because I had heard less of it; and secondly, because it stands as it were alone in India — there is absolutely no other tower in this Indian empire of ours.[15]

Large pillars have been cut out of single stones, and raised in different parts of India to commemorate the conquests of Hindoo princes, whose names no one was able to discover for several centuries, till an unpretending English gentleman of surprising talents and industry, Mr. James Prinsep, lately brought them to light by mastering the obsolete characters in which they and their deeds had been inscribed upon them.[16] These pillars would, however, be utterly insignificant were they composed of many stones. The knowledge that they are cut out of single stones, brought from a distant mountain, and raised by the united efforts of multitudes when the mechanical arts were in a rude state, makes us still view them with admiration.[17] But the single majesty of this Mīnār of Kutb-ud-dīn, so grandly conceived, so beautifully proportioned, so chastely embellished, and so exquisitely finished, fills the mind of the spectator with emotions of wonder and delight; without any such aid, he feels that it is among the towers of the earth what the Tāj is among the tombs — something unique of its kind that must ever stand alone in his recollections.[18]

It is said to have taken forty-four years in building, and formed the left of two 'mīnārs' of a mosque. The other 'mīnār' was never raised, but this has been preserved and repaired by the liberality of the British Government. [19] It is only 242 feet high, and 106 feet in circumference at the base. It is circular, and fluted vertically into twenty-seven semicircular and angular divisions. There are four balconies, supported upon large stone brackets, and surrounded with battlements of richly cut stone, to enable people to walk round the tower with safety. The first is ninety feet from the base, the second fifty feet further up, the third forty further; and the fourth twenty-four feet above the third. Up to the third balcony, the tower is built of fine, but somewhat ferruginous sandstone, whose surface has become red from exposure to the oxygen of the atmosphere. Up to the first balcony, the flutings are alternately semicircular and angular; in the second story they are all semicircular, and in the third all angular. From the third balcony to the top, the building is composed chiefly of white marble; and the surface is without the deep flutings. Around the first story there are five horizontal belts of passages from the Korān, engraved in bold relief, and in the Kufic character. In the second story there are four, and in the third three. The ascent is by a spiral staircase within, of three hundred and eighty steps; and there are passages from this staircase to the balconies, with others here and there for the admission of light and air.[20]

A foolish notion has prevailed among some people, over-fond of paradox, that this tower is in reality a Hindoo building, and not, as commonly supposed, a Muhammadan one. Never was paradox supported upon more frail, I might say absurd, foundations. They are these: 1st, that there is only one Mīnār, whereas there ought to have been two—had the unfinished one been intended as the second, it would not have been, as it really is, larger than the first; 2nd, that other Mīnārs seen in the present day either do not slope inward from the base up at all, or do not slope so much as this. I tried to trace the origin of this paradox, and I think I found it in a silly old 'munshī' (clerk) in the service of the Emperor. He told me that he believed it was built by a former Hindoo prince for his daughter, who wished to worship the rising sun, and view the waters of the Jumna from the top of it every morning.[21]

There is no other Hindoo building like, or of the same kind as this;[22] the ribbons or belts of passages from the Korān are all in relief; and had they not been originally inserted as they are, the whole surface of the building must have been cut down to throw them out in bold relief. The slope is the peculiar characteristic of all the architecture of the Pathāns, by whom the church to which this tower belongs was built.[23] Nearly all the arches of the church are still standing in a more or less perfect state, and all correspond in design, proportion, and execution to the tower. The ruins of the old Hindoo temples about the place, and about every other place in India, are totally different in all three; here they are all exceedingly paltry and insignificant, compared with the church and its tower, and it is evident that it was the intention of the founder to make them appear so to future generations of the faithful, for he has taken care to make his own great work support rather than destroy them, that they might for ever tend to enhance its grandeur. [24] It is sufficiently clear that the unfinished mīnār was commenced upon too large a scale, and with too small a diminution of the circumference from the base upwards. It is two-fifths larger than the finished tower in circumference, and much more perpendicular. Finding these errors when they had got some thirty feet from the foundation, the founder, Shams-ud-dīn (Īltutmish), began to work anew, and had he lived a little longer, there is no doubt that he would have raised the second tower in its proper place, upon the same scale as the one completed. His death was followed by several successive revolutions; five sovereigns succeeded each other on the throne of Delhi in ten years.[25] As usual on such occasions, works of peace were suspended, and succeeding sovereigns sought renown in military enterprise rather than in building churches. This church was entire, with the exception of the second mīnār, when Tamerlane invaded India.[26] He took back a model of it with him to Samarkand, together with all the masons he could find at Delhi, and is said to have built a church upon the same plan at that place, before he set out for the invasion of Syria.

The west face of the quadrangle, in which the tower stands, formed the church, which consisted of eleven large arched alcoves, the centre and largest of which contained the pulpit. In size and beauty they seem to have corresponded with the Mīnār, but they are now all in ruins.[27] In the front of the centre of these alcoves stands the metal pillar of the old Hindoo sovereign of Delhi, Prithī Rāj, across whose temple all the great mosque, of which this tower forms a part, was thrown in triumph. The ruins of these temples he scattered all round the place, and consist of colonnades of stone pillars and pedestals, richly enough carved with human figures, in attitudes rudely and obscenely conceived. The small pillar is of bronze, or a metal which resembles bronze, and is softer than brass, and of the same form precisely as that of the stone pillar at Eran, on the Bīnā river in Mālwā, upon which stands the figure of Krishna, with the glory around his head.[28]

It is said that this metal pillar was put down through the earth, so as to rest upon the very head of the snake that supports the world; and that the sovereign who made it, and fixed it upon so firm a basis, was told by his spiritual advisers that his dynasty should last as long as the pillar remained where it was. Anxious to see that the pillar was really where the priests supposed it to be, that his posterity might be quite sure of their position, Prithī Rāj had it taken up, and he found the blood and some of the flesh of the snake's head adhering to the bottom. By this means the charm was broken, and the priests told him that he had destroyed all the hopes of his house by his want of faith in their assurances. I have never met a Hindoo that doubted either that the pillar was really upon this snake's head, or that the king lost his crown by his want of faith in the assurance of his priests. They all believe that the pillar is still stuck into the head of the great snake, and that no human efforts of the present day could remove it. On my way back to my tents, I asked the old Hindoo officer of my guard, who had gone with me to see the metal pillar, what he thought of the story of the pillar?

'What the people relate about the "kīlī" (pillar) having been stuck into the head of the snake that supports the world, sir, is nothing more than a simple *historical* fact known to everybody. Is it not so, my brothers?' turning to the Hindoo sipāhīs and followers around us, who all declared that no fact could ever be better established.

'When the Rājā,' continued the old soldier, 'had got the pillar fast into the head of the snake, he was told by his chief priest that his dynasty must now reign over Hindustan for ever. "But," said the Rājā, "as all seems to depend upon the pillar being on the head of the snake, we had better see that it is so with our own eyes." He ordered it to be taken up; the clergy tried to dissuade him, but all in vain. Up it was taken—the flesh and blood of the snake were found upon it—the pillar was replaced; but a voice was heard saying: "Thy want of faith hath destroyed thee—thy reign must soon end, and with it that of thy race."'

I asked the old soldier from whence the voice came.

He said this was a point that had not, he believed, been quite settled. Some thought it was from the serpent himself below the earth, others that it came from the high priest or some of his clergy. 'Wherever it came from,' said the old man, 'there is no doubt that God decreed the Rājā's fall for his want of faith; and fall he did soon after.' All our followers concurred in this opinion, and the old man seemed quite delighted to think that he had had an opportunity of delivering his sentiments upon so great a question before so respectable an audience.

The Emperor Shams-ud-dīn Īltutmish is said to have designed this great Muhammadan church at the suggestion of Khwāja Kutb-ud-dīn, a Muhammadan saint from Ūsh in Persia, who was his religious guide and apostle, and died some sixteen years before him.[29] His tomb is among the ruins of this old city. Pilgrims visit it from all parts of India, and go away persuaded that they shall have all they have asked, provided they have given or promised liberally in a pure spirit of faith in his influence with the Deity. The tomb of the saint is covered with gold brocade, and protected by an awning—those of the Emperors around it he naked and exposed. Emperors and princes lie all around him; and their tombs are entirely disregarded by the hundreds that daily prostrate themselves before his, and have been doing so for the last six hundred years.[30] Among the rest I saw here the tomb of Mu'azzam, alias Bahādur Shāh, the son and successor of Aurangzēb, and that of the blind old Emperor Shāh Alam, from whom the Honourable Company got their Dīwanī grant.[31] The grass grows upon the slab that covers the remains of Mu'azzam, the most learned, most pious, and most amiable, l believe, of the crowned descendants of the great Akbar. These kings and princes all try to get a place as near as they can to the remains of such old saints, believing that the ground is more holy than any other, and that they may give them a lift on the day of resurrection. The heir apparent to the throne of Delhi visited the tomb the same day that I did. He was between sixty and seventy years of age.[32]

I asked some of the attendants of the tomb, on my way back, what he had come to pray for; and was told that no one knew, but every one supposed it was for the death of the Emperor, his father, who was only fifteen years older, and was busily engaged in promoting an intrigue at the instigation of one of his wives, to oust him, and get one of her sons, Mirza Salīm, acknowledged as his successor by the British Government. It was the Hindoo festival of the Basant,[33] and all the avenues to the tomb of this old saint were crowded when I visited it. Why the Muhammadans crowded to the tomb on a Hindoo holiday I could not ascertain.

The Emperor Īltutmish, who died A.D. 1235, is buried close behind one end of the arched alcove, in a beautiful tomb without its cupola. He built the tomb himself, and left orders that there should be no 'parda' (screen) between him and heaven; and no dome was thrown over the building in consequence. Other great men have done the same, and their tombs look as if their domes had fallen in; they think the way should be left clear for a start on the day of resurrection.[34] The church is stated to have been added to it by the Emperor Balban, and the Mīnār finished.[35] About the end of the seventeenth century, it was so shaken by an earthquake that the two upper stories fell down. Our Government, when the country came into our possession, undertook to repair these two stories, and entrusted the work to Captain Smith, who built up one of stone, and the other of wood, and completed the repairs in three years. The one was struck by lightning eight or nine years after, and came down. If it was anything like the one that is left, the lightning did well to remove it.[36]

About five years ago, while the Emperor was on a visit to the tomb of Kutb-ud-dīn, a madman got into his private apartments. The servants were ordered to turn him out. On passing the Mīnār he ran in, ascended to the top, stood a few minutes on the verge, laughing at those who were running after him, and made a spring that enabled him to reach the bottom, without touching the sides. An eye-witness told me that he kept his erect position till about half-way down, when he turned over, and continued to turn till he got to the bottom, when his fall made a report like a gun. He was of course dashed to pieces. About five months ago another fell over by accident, and was dashed to pieces against the sides. A new road has been here cut through the tomb of the Emperor Alā- ud-dīn, who murdered his father-in-law-the first Muhammadan conqueror of Southern India, and his remains have been scattered to the winds.[37]

A very pretty marble tomb, to the west of the alcoves, covers the remains of Imām Mashhadī, the religious guide of the Emperor Akbar; and a magnificent tomb of freestone covers those of his four foster-brothers. This was long occupied as a dwelling-house by the late Mr. Blake, of the Bengal Civil Service, who was lately barbarously murdered at Jaipur. To make room for his dining-tables he removed the marble slab, which covered the remains of the dead, from the centre of the building, against the urgent remonstrance of the people, and threw it carelessly on one side against the wall, where it now lies. The people appealed in vain, it is said, to Mr. Fraser, the Governor-General's representative, who was soon after assassinated; and a good many attribute the death of both to this outrage upon the remains of the dead foster-brother of Akbar. Those of Alā-ud-dīn were, no doubt, older and less sensitive. Tombs equally magnificent cover the remains of the other three foster- brothers of Akbar, but I did not enter them.[38]

Notes:

1. The Sultan, called by the author 'the Emperor Tughlak the First', as being the first of the Tughlak dynasty, was by birth a Karaunīah Turk, named Ghāzī Bēg Tughlak. He assumed the style of Ghiyās-ud-dīn Tughlak Shāh when he seized the throne in A.D. 1320, and he reigned till A.D. 1325.

2. This gigantic fortress is close to the village of Badarpur, about four miles due east of the Kutb Mīnār, and ten or twelve miles south of the modern city. The building of it occupied more than three years, but the whole undertaking 'proved eminently futile, as his son removed his Court to the old city within forty days after his accession.' (Thomas, *Chronicles of the Pathān Kings of Delhi*, 1871, p. 192.) The fort is described by Cunningham in *A.S.R.*, vol. i, p. 212, whose description is copied in the guide-books. See also Fanshawe, *Delhi Past and Present* (John Murray, 1902), p. 288 and plate. That work is cited as 'Fanshawe'.

3. Also called Adilābād. It is described in *A.S.R.*, vol. i, p. 21; Carr Stephen, *The Archaeology and Monumental Remains of Delhi*, Ludhiana, 1876, p. 98; and Fanshawe, p. 291.

4. '*The Barber's House*. This lies to the right of the road from Tughlākābad to Badarpur, and is close to the ruined city. It is said to have been built for Tughlak Shāh's barber about A.D. 1323. It is now a mere ruin.' (Harcourt, *The New Guide to Delhi*, Allahabad, 1866, p. 88.)

5. This fine tomb was built by Muhammad bin Tughlak (A.D. 1325- 51). It is described by Cunningham in *A.S.R.*, vol. i, p. 213. See also *Ann. Rep. A. S., India*, 1904-5, p. 19, fig. 11; *H.F.A.*, p. 397, fig. 234; and Fanshawe, p. 290, with plate. Thomas (*Chronicles*, p. 192) and Cunningham both say that the

causeway, or viaduct, has twenty-seven, not only twenty-five, arches, as stated in the text. The causeway is 600 feet in length. The sloping walls are characteristic of the period.

6. The blunder of calling the Sultāns of Delhi by the name Pathān, due to the translators of Firishta's History, has been perpetuated by Thomas's well-known work, *The Chronicles of the Pathān Kings of Delhi*, and in countless other books. The name is quite wrong. The only Pathān Sultāns were those of the Lodī dynasty, which immediately preceded Bābur, and those of the Sūr dynasty, the rivals of Bābur's son. 'He (*scil.* Ghiyās-ud-dīn Balban) was a *Turk* of the Ilbarī tribe, but compilers of Indian Histories and Gazetteers, and archaeological experts, turn him, like many Turks, Tājzīks, Jāts, and Sayyids, into *Pathāns*, which is synonymous with Afghan, it being the vitiated Hindī equivalent of Pushtūn, the name by which the people generally known as Afghans call themselves, in their own language. . . . It is quite time to give up Dow and Briggs' Ferishta.' (Raverty, in *J.A.S.B.*, vol. lxi (1892), Part I, p. 164, note.)

7. The murder of Ghiyās-ud-dīn Tughlak by his son Fakhr-ud-dīn Jūnā, also called Ulugh Khān, occurred in the year A.H. 725, which began on 18th December, 1324 (o.s.). The testimony of the contemporary traveller Ibn Batūtā establishes the fact that the fall of the pavilion was premeditated. (Thomas, *Chronicles*, pp. 187, 189.) The murderer, on his accession to the throne (1325), assumed the style of Muhammad bin Tughlak Shāh.

8. Jalāl-ud-dīn Fīrōz Shāh Khiljī was murdered by his son-in-law and nephew Alā-ud- dīn at Karrā on the Ganges in July, A.D. 1296. The murderer reigned until A.D. 1315 under the title of Alā-ud- dīn Muhammad Shāh, Sikandar Sānī.

9. As already noted, his proper style is Muhammad bin Tughlak Shāh. The word *bin* means 'son of'. The Sultan is never called 'Muhammad the Third'.

10. A Muhammadan must, if he can, say his prayers with the prescribed forms five times in the twenty-four hours; and on Friday, which is their sabbath, he must, if he can, say three prayers in the church *masjid*. On other days he may say them where he pleases. Every prayer must begin with the first chapter of the Korān—this is the grace to every prayer. This said, the person may put in what other prayers of the Korān he pleases, and ask for that which he most wants, as long as it does not injure other Musalmāns. This is the first chapter of the Korān: 'Praise be to God the Lord of all creatures— the most merciful—the King of the day of judgement. Thee do we worship, and of Thee do we beg assistance. Direct us in the right way—in the way of

those to whom Thou hast been gracious; not of those against whom Thou art incensed; nor of those who go astray.' [W. H. S.] The quotation is from Sale's version. The last clause may also be rendered, 'The way of those to whom Thou hast been gracious, against whom Thou art not incensed, and who have not erred,' as Sale points out in his note.

11. This mad tyrant, among other horrible deeds, flayed his nephew alive. He attempted to invade China through the Himālayas, and for three years issued a forced currency of brass and copper, which he vainly tried to make people take as equal in value to silver. Strange to say, he was allowed to reign for nearly twenty-seven years, and to die peacefully in his bed. The hunts of the 'innocent and unoffending people' were organized rather to gain the benefit of 'sending infidels to hell' than for 'mere amusement'. Daulatābād was the name given by Muhammad bin Tughlak to the ancient fortress of Deogīr (Deogiri, Deoghur), situated about ten miles from Aurangābād, in what is now the Hyderabad State.

12. In the original edition the Moghal leader's name is printed as 'Turmachurn', the Tarmasharīn (with variations in spelling) of Muhammadan authors (see E. and D., iii. 42, 450, 507; v. 485; vi. 222). The name Turghi is given by Thomas, who says he invested Delhi in A.H. 703, corresponding to A.D. 1303-4; and refers to an article in J.A.S.B., vol. xxxv (1866), Part I, pp. 199-218, entitled 'Notes on the History and Topography of the Ancient Cities of Delhi', by O. Campbell. (Chronicles, p. 175, note.) Campbell writes the leader's name as Turghai Khān. Apparently Tarmasharīn was identical with Turghi or Turghai Khān, but I am not sure that he was. The Moghals made several raids during the reign of Alā-ud-dīn Muhammad Shāh.

13. The tomb of Nizām-ud-dīn is further noticed in the next chapter of this work. It is situated in an enclosure which contains other notable tombs. The following extract from the author's Ramaseeana (p. 121) gives additional particulars concerning this saint of questionable sanctity: 'Nizām-ud-dīn Aulia. — A saint of the Sunnī sect of Muhammadans, said to have been a Thug of great note at some period of his life, and his tomb near Delhi is to this day visited as a place of pilgrimage by Thugs, who make votive offerings to it. He is said to have been of the Barsot class, born in the month of Safar [633], Hijrī, March A.D. 1236; died Rabī-ul-awwal, 725, October A.D. 1325. [The months as stated do not correspond.—Ed.] His tomb is visited by Muhammadan pilgrims from all parts as a place of great sanctity from containing the remains of so holy a man; but the Thugs, both Hindoo and Muhammadan, visit it as containing the remains of the most celebrated Thug of his day. He was of the Sunnī sect, and those of the Shīa sect find

no difficulty in believing that he was a Thug; but those of his own sect will never credit it. There are perhaps no sufficient grounds to pronounce him one of the fraternity; but there are some to suspect that he was so at some period of his life. The Thugs say he gave it up early in life, but kept others employed in it till late, and derived an income from it; and the 'dast-ul-ghaib', or supernatural purse, with which he was supposed to be endowed, gives a colour to this. His lavish expenditure, so much beyond his ostensible means, gave rise to the belief that he was supplied from above with money.'

The 'old man of the mountains' with whom the author compares Nizām-ud-dīn (or at least the original 'old man of the mountains', Shaikh-ul Jabal), was Hasan-ibn-Sabbāh (or, us- Sabbāh), who founded the sect of so-called Assassins in the mountains on the shores of the Caspian, and flourished from about A.D. 1089 to 1124. Hulākū the Mongol broke the power of the sect in A.D. 1256 (Thatcher, in Encycl. Brit., 11th ed., 1910, s. v. 'Assassin').

14. Shams-ud-dīn Īltutmish, who had been a slave, reigned from A.D. 1210 to 1235. His Turkish name is variously written as Yulteemush, Altamsh, Alitmish, &c. The form Īltutmish is correct (Z.D.M.G., 1907, p. 192). His tomb is discussed post.

15. This is not quite accurate. A similar mīnār, or mosque tower, built in the middle of the thirteenth century, formerly existed at Koil in the Alīgarh district (A.S.R., i. 191), and two mosques at Bayāna in the Bharatpur State, have each only one mīnār, placed outside the courtyard (ibid., vol. iv, p. ix). Chitor in Rajputānā possesses two noble Hindoo towers, one about 80 feet high, erected in connexion with Jain shrines, and the other, about 120 feet high, erected by Kumbha Rānā as a tower or pillar of victory. (Fergusson, Hist. of Indian and Eastern Architecture, ed. 1910, vol. ii, pp. 57-61.)

16. The short life of James Prinsep extended only from August 20, 1799, to April 22, 1840, and practically terminated in 1838, when his brain began to fail from the undue strain caused by incessant and varied activity. His memorable discoveries in archaeology and numismatics are recorded in the seven volumes of the J.A.S.B. for the years 1832-8. His contributions to those volumes were edited by B. Thomas, and republished in 1868 under the title of Essays on Indian Antiquities. Sir Alexander Cunningham, who was one of Prinsep's fellow workers, gives interesting details of the process by which the discoveries were made, in the Introduction to the first volume of the Reports of the Archaeological Survey. No adequate account of James Prinsep's remarkable career has been published. He was singularly modest and unassuming. A good summary of his life is given in Higginbotham's Men whom India has Known, 2nd ed., Madras, 1874. See also the editor's paper, 'James Prinsep', in East and West, Bombay, July, 1906.

17. The monolith pillars alluded to in the text are chiefly those of the great Emperor Piyadasi, Beloved of the Gods, also known by the name of Asoka. So far from being memorials of a time when 'the mechanical arts were in a rude state', the Asoka columns exhibit the arts of the stone-cutter and sculptor in perfection. They were erected about 242 to 230 B.C., and the inscriptions on them contain a code of moral and religions precepts. They do not commemorate conquests, although the Asoka pillar at Allahabad has been utilized by later sovereigns for the recording of magniloquent inscriptions in praise of their grandeur. The best-known of the Asoka pillars are the two at Delhi, and the one at Allahabad. Many scholars have devoted themselves to the study of the inscriptions of Asoka, which may be said to form the foundation of authentic Indian history. The reader interested in the subject should consult Senart, *Les Inscriptions de Piyadasi*, t. I and II, Paris, 1881, 1886; V. A. Smith, *Asoka, the Buddhist Emperor of India*, 2nd ed.. Oxford, 1909; and 'The Monolithic Pillars or Columns of Asoka' (*Z.D.M.G.*, 1911, pp. 221-10). See also *E.H.I.*, 3rd ed. (Oxford, 1914), chap. 6, 7, with Bibliography. Certain of the Gupta emperors in the fifth century A.C. also erected monolith pillars. Some of the pillars of the Gupta period commemorate victories; others are merely religious monuments.

18. Fergusson thought the Kutb Mīnār superior to Giotto's campanile at Florence in 'poetry of design and exquisite finish of detail'. He also held it to excel its taller Egyptian rival, the minaret of the mosque of Hasan at Cairo, in its nobler appearance, as well as in design and finish. To sum up, he held the Delhi monument to surpass any building of its class in the whole world. (*Hist. of Indian and Eastern Architecture*, ed. 1910, vol. ii, p. 206.)

19. Fergusson (ibid.) was mistaken in supposing that the Kutb Mīnār was intended for anything else than a *māzina*, or tower from which the call to prayers should be proclaimed. It is that and nothing else. Several examples of early mosques with only one *mīnār* each are known, at Koil and Bayāna, in India, as well as at Ghaznī and Cairo. The unfinished *mīnār* of Alāuddīn near the Kutb Mīnār was intended for a distinct building, namely, his addition to the original Kutb mosque. There was no 'other *mīnār*' connected with the Kutb Mīnār.(Cunningham, *A.S.R.* iv (1874), p. ix.)

The current name of the Kutb Mīnār refers to the saint Khwāja Kutb-ud-dīn of Ūsh, who lies near the tower, and not to Sultan Kutb-ud-dīn Aibāk or Ībak. The *mīnār* was erected, about A.D. 1232, by Sultan Shams-ud-dīn Īltutmish (V. A. Smith, 'Who Built the Kutb Mīnār?' *East and West*, Bombay, Dec. 1907, pp. 1200-5; B. N. Munshi, *The Kutb Mīnār, Delhi*, Bombay, 1911).

All the important monuments at or near Delhi are now carefully conserved, Lord Curzon having organized effective arrangements for the purpose.

20. The original edition gives a coloured plate of the Kutb Mīnār. The total height stated in the text, 242 feet, is said by Fergusson (p. 205, note) to be that ascertained in 1794; the present height of the *mīnār*, since the modern pavilion on the top has been removed, is 238 feet 1 inch, according to Cunningham. (*A.S.R.*, vol. i, p. 196.) Originally the building was ten, or perhaps twenty, feet higher. The deep flutings appear to have been suggested by the *mīnārs* of Mahmūd at Ghaznī, 'which are star polygons in plan, with deeply indented angles'. The Kutb Mīnār was built by Sultan Īltutmish alone about A.D. 1232. The statement in most books, including Fanshawe (pp. 265- 8, with plates), that it was *begun* by Sultan Kutb-ud- dīn, is erroneous.

21. The notion of the Hindoo origin of the Kutb Mīnār, which the author justly stigmatizes as 'foolish', was taken up by Sir Sayyid Ahmad Khān, the author of an Urdū work on the antiquities of Delhi, and by Sir A. Cunningham's assistant, Mr. Beglar, who wasted a great part of volume iv of the *Archaeological Survey Reports* in trying to prove the paradox. His speculations on the subject were conclusively refuted by his chief in the Preface (pp. v-x) of the same volume. The mīnār was built by Hindoo masons, and, in consequence, some of the details, notably its overlapping or corbelled arches, are Hindoo.

22. This is correct. The Hindoo 'towers of victory' are in a totally different style.

23. On the misnomer 'Pathāns', see *ante*, previous note 6.

24. The Kutb mosque was constructed from the materials of twenty-seven Hindoo temples. The colonnades retain much of their Hindoo character. (Fanshawe, p. 259 and plate.)

25. The author's description of the unfinished tower is far from accurate. The tower was begun, not by Shams-ud-dīn Īltutmish, but by Alā-ud-dīn Muhammad Shāh, in the year A.H. 711 (A.D. 1311). It is about 82 feet in diameter, and when cased with marble, as was intended, would have been at least 85 feet in diameter, or nearly double that of the Kutb Mīnār, which is 48 feet 4 inches. The total height of the column as it now stands is about 75 feet above the plinth, or 87 feet above the ground level. (*A.S.R.*, vol. i, p. 205; vol. iv, p. 62, pl. vii; Thomas, *Chronicles*, p. 173, citing original authorities.) Carr Stephen (p. 67) gives the circumference as 254 feet, and the height as about 80 feet.

26. Alā-ud-dīn's additions were never completed. The sack of Delhi by Tīmūr Lang (Tamerlane) took place in December 1398. The Delhi sacked by him was the city known as Fīrōzābād.

27. The glory of the mosque is . . . the great range of arches on the western side, extending north and south for about 385 feet, and consisting of three greater and eight smaller arches; the central one 22 feet wide, and 53 feet high; the larger side-arches, 24 feet 4 inches, and about the same height as the central arch; the smaller arches, which are unfortunately much ruined, are about half these dimensions.' The great arch 'has since been carefully restored by Government under efficient superintendence, and is now as sound and complete as when first erected. The two great side arches either were never completed, or have fallen down in consequence of the false mode of construction.' (Fergusson, *Hist. of I. and E. Archit.*, ed. 1910, vol. ii, pp. 203, 204). The centre arch bears an inscription dated in A.H. 594, or A.D. 1198 (Thomas, *Chronicles*, p. 24).

28. Most of the description of the Iron Pillar in the text is erroneous. The pillar has nothing to do with Prithī Rāj, who was slain by the Muhammadans in A.D. 1192 (A.H. 588). The earliest inscription on it records the victories of a Rājā Chandra, probably Chandra-varman, chief of Pokharan in Rājputāna in the fourth century A.C. (*E.H.I.*, 3rd ed., 1914, p. 290, note). The pillar is by no means 'small' when its material is considered; on the contrary, it is very large. That material is not 'bronze, or a metal which resembles bronze', but is pure malleable iron, as proved by analysis. It has been suggested that this pillar must have been formed by gradually welding pieces together; if so, it has been done very skilfully, since no marks of such welding are to be seen. . . . The famous iron pillar at the Kutb, near Delhi, indicates an amount of skill in the manipulation of a large mass of wrought iron which has been the marvel of all who have endeavoured to account for it. It is not many years since the production of such a pillar would have been an impossibility in the largest foundries of the world, and even now there are comparatively few where a similar mass of metal could be tumed out. . . . The total weight must exceed six tons.' (V. Ball, *Economic Geology of India*, pp. 338, 339.) The metal is uninjured by rust, and the inscription is perfect. An exact facsimile is set up in the Indian Section of the Victoria and Albert Museum at South Kensington, The pillar is shown, with the smaller arches of the mosque, in *H.F.A.* fig. 232. See also Fanshawe, pp. 260, 264, and plates. The inscription was edited by Fleet (*Gupta Inscriptions*, 1888, No. 32). The dimensions of the pillar are as follows: Height above ground (total), 22 ft,; height below ground, 1 ft. 8 in.; diameter at base, 16.4 in.; diameter at the capital, 12.05 in.; height of capital, 3½ ft. At a distance of a few inches below the surface it expands in a bulbous form to a diameter of 2 ft. 4 in., and rests on a gridiron of iron bars, which are fastened with lead into the stone pavement. (*A.S.R.*, vol. iv, p. 28, pl. v.)

This last prosaic fact, established by actual excavation, destroys the basis of all the current local legends and spurious traditions.

29. This name is printed Ouse in the author's text. The saint referred to is the celebrated Kutb-ud-dīn Bakhtyār Kākī, commonly called Kutb Shāh, who died on the 27th of November, A.D. 1235. Īltutmish died in April, A.D. 1236 (Beale).

30. The royal tombs are in the village of Mihraulī, close to the Kutb. See Carr Stephen, op. cit., pp. 180-4, and Fanshawe, pp. 280-4.

31. That is to say, the revenue administration of Bengal, Bihār, and Orissa in 1765.

32. He is now Emperor, having succeeded his father, Akbar Shāh, in 1837. [W. H. S.] He is known as Bahādur Shāh II. In consequence of his having joined the rebels in 1857, he was deposed and banished. He died at Rangoon in 1862, and with him ended the line of Emperors of Delhi. He was born on the 24th of October, 1775, and so was in his sixty-first year when the author met him. His father was about seventy-eight (eighty lunar) years of age at his death.

33. 'Basant' means the spring. The full name of this festival of the spring time is the Basant Panchamī.

34. According to Harcourt (The New Guide to Delhi, 1866), the tomb of Īltutmish was erected by his children, the Sultānas Rukn-ud-dīn and Razīa, who reigned in succession after him for short periods, that is to say, Rukn-ud- dīn Fīrōz Shāh for six months and twenty- eight days, and the Empress Razīa for about three years, from A.D. 1236 to 1239. (See Carr Stephen, p. 73.) Īltutmish died in April, A.D. 1236, not in 1235. Fergusson observes that this tomb is of special interest as being the oldest Muhammadan tomb known to exist in India. He also remarks (p. 509) that the effect at present is injured by the want of a roof, which, 'judging from appearance, was never completed, if ever commenced'. Harcourt (p. 120) states that 'Fīrōz Shāh, who reigned from A.D. 1351 to A.D. 1385 [sic, 1388], is said to have placed a roof to the building, but it is doubtful if there ever was one, as there are no traces of the same. Cunningham and Carr Stephen (p. 74) both find sufficient evidence remaining to satisfy them that a dome once existed. Fanshawe (p. 269) says 'that the chamber was intended to be roofed is clear from the remains of the lowest course of a dome on the top of the south wall; but, if it was built for her father by Sultan Raziya, as seems probable, it is quite possible that the dome was never completed'. The interior, a square of 29½ feet, is beautifully and elaborately decorated, and in wonderful preservation considering its

age and the exposure to which it has been subjected. The walls are over seven feet thick, the principal entrance being to the east. The tomb is built of red sandstone and marble; the sarcophagus is in the centre, and is of pale marble.

35. Sultan Ghiyās-ud-dīn Balban reigned from February, A.D. 1266 to 1286. I cannot discover any authority for the statement that he finished the Kutb Mīnār, and 'added the church'. It is not clear which 'church', or mosque, the author refers to. For a notice of Balban's tomb and buildings, see Carr Stephen, pp. 79-81, He certainly did not finish the Kutb Mīnār.

36. See *A.S.R.*, vol. i, p. 199. *'Top of the Kutb Mīnār.*—This octagonal stone pavilion was put up in A.D. 1826 over the Mīnār by Major Smith, of the Engineers, who had the superintendence of the repairs of the Kutb, but it was taken down by the order of Government' (Harcourt, *The New Guide to Delhi*, p. 123). This 'grotesque ornament' was removed in 1848 by order of Lord Hardinge, and bereft of its wooden pavilion, which had carried a flag-staff (Carr Stephen, p. 64; Fanshawe, p. 266). It has now been moved farther and more out of sight.

37. This alleged outrage does not appear to have really occurred. The author seems to have been misinformed about the position of Alā-ud-dīn's tomb, which still exits in the central room of a building, the eastern wall of which is in part identical with the western wall of the extension of the Kutb Mosque, built by Īltutmish (Carr Stephen, op. cit., p. 88). Fanshawe agrees (p. 272).

38. The tomb desecrated by Mr. Blake is on the right of the road leading from the Kutb Mīnār to the village of Mihraulī, and is either that of Adham Khān, whom Akbar put to death in A.D. 1562 for the murder of Shams-ud-dīn Muhammad Atgah Khān, one of the Emperor's foster fathers, or the neighbouring 'family grave enclosure' of his brothers, known as the *Chaunsath Khambhā*, or Hall of Sixty-four Pillars. Adham Khān's tomb is still, or was until recently, used as a rest-house (Fanshawe, pp. 14, 228, 242, 256, 278; Carr Stephen, pp. 31, 200, pl. ii). The best-known of the 'kokahs', or foster-brothers, of Akbar is Azīz, the son of Shams-ud-dīn above mentioned. Azīz received the title of Khān-i-Azam (Von Noer, *The Emperor Akbar*, transl. by Beveridge, vol. i, pp. 78, 95; and Blochmann, *Āīn-t-Akbarī*, vol. i, pp. 321, 323, &c.). The young chief of Jaipur died in 1834, and in the course of disturbances which followed, the Political Agent was wounded, and Mr. Blake, his assistant, was killed (D. Boulger, *Lord William Bentinck*, 'Rulers of India' series, p. 143). I cannot find mention in any authority of Imām Mashhadī. Mr. Fraser's murder has been fully described *ante* chapter 64.

CHAPTER 68

New Delhi, or Shāhjahānābād.

On the 22nd of January, 1836, we went on twelve miles to the new city of Delhi, built by the Emperor Shāhjahān, and called after him Shāhjahānābād; and took up our quarters in the palace of the Bēgam Samrū, a fine building, agreeably situated in a garden opening into the great street, with a branch of the great canal running through it, and as quiet as if it had been in a wilderness.[1] We had obtained from the Bēgam permission to occupy this palace during our stay. It was elegantly furnished, the servants were all exceedingly attentive, and we were very happy.

The Kutb Mīnār stands upon the back of the sandstone range of low hills, and the road descends over the north- eastern face of this range for half a mile, and then passes over a level plain all the way to the new city, which lies on the right bank of the river Jumna. The whole plain is literally covered with the remains of splendid Muhammadan mosques and mausoleums. These Muhammadans seem as if they had always in their thoughts the saying of Christ which Akbar has inscribed on the gateway at Fathpur Sīkrī: 'Life is a bridge which you are to pass over, and not to build your dwellings upon.'[2] The buildings which they have left behind them have almost all a reference to a future state—they laid out their means in a church, in which the Deity might be propitiated; in a tomb where leaned and pious men might chant their Korān over their remains, and youth be instructed in their duties; in a serai, a bridge, a canal built gratuitously for the public good, that those who enjoyed these advantages from generation to generation might pray for the repose of their souls. How could it be otherwise where the land was the property of Government, where capital was never concentrated or safe, when the only aristocracy was that of office, while the Emperor was the sole recognized heir of all his public officers?

The only thing that he could not inherit were his tombs, his temples, his bridges, his canals, his caravanserais. I was acquainted with the history of most of the great men whose tombs and temples I visited along the road; but I asked in vain for a sight of the palaces they occupied in their day of pride and power. They all had, no doubt, good houses agreeably situated, like that of the Bēgam Samrū, in the midst of well-watered gardens and shrubberies, delightful in their season; but they cared less about them — they knew that the Emperor was heir to every member of the great body to which they belonged, the *aristocracy of office*; and might transfer all their wealth to his treasury, and all their palaces to their successors, the moment the breath should be out of their bodies.[3] If their sons got office, it would neither be in the same grades nor in the same places as those of their fathers.

How different it is in Europe, where our aristocracy is formed upon a different basis; no one knows where to find the tombs in which the remains of great men who have passed away repose; or the churches and colleges they have founded; or the serāis, the bridges, the canals they formed gratuitously for the public good; but everybody knows where to find their 'proud palaces'; life is not to them 'a bridge over which they are to pass, and not build their dwellings upon'. The eldest sons enjoy all the patrimonial estates, and employ them as best they may to get their younger brothers into situations in the church, the army, the navy, and other public establishments, in which they may be honourably and liberally provided for out of the public purse.

About half-way between the great tower and the new city, on the left-hand side of the road, stands the tomb of Mansūr Alī Khān, the great-grandfather of the present King of Oudh. Of all the tombs to be seen in this immense extent of splendid ruins, this is perhaps the only one raised over a subject, the family of whose inmates are now in a condition even to keep it in repair. It is a very beautiful mausoleum, built after the model of the Tāj at Agra; with this difference, that the external wall around the quadrangle of the Tāj is here, as it were, thrown back, and closed in upon the tomb. The beautiful gateway at the entrance of the gardens of the Tāj forms each of the four sides of the tomb of Mansūr Alī Khān, with all its chaste beauty of design, proportion, and ornament.[4] The quadrangle in which this mausoleum stands is about three hundred and fifty yards square, surrounded by a stone wall, with handsome gateways, and filled in the same manner as that of the Tāj at Agra, with cisterns and fruit-trees. Three kinds of stones are used — white marble, red sandstone, and the fine white and flesh- coloured sandstone of Rupbās. The dome is of white marble, and exactly of the same form as that of the Tāj; but it stands on a neck or base of sandstone with twelve sides, and the marble is of a quality very inferior to that of the Tāj. It is of coarse dolomite, and has become a good deal discoloured by time, so as to give it the appearance, which Bishop Heber noticed, of *potted meat*. The neck is not quite so long as that of the Tāj, and is better covered by the marble cupolas that stand above each face of the building. The four noble minarets are, however, wanting. The apartments are all in number and form exactly like those of the Tāj, but they are somewhat less in size. In the centre of the first floor lies the beautiful marble slab that bears the date of this small pillar of a *tottering state*, A.H. 1167;[5] and in a vault underneath repose his remains by the side of those of one of his grand-daughters. The graves that cover these remains are of plain earth strewed with fresh flowers, and covered with plain cloth. About two miles from this tomb to the east stands that of the father of Akbar, Humāyūn, a large and magnificent building. As I rode towards this building to see the slab that covers the head of poor Dārā Shikoh, I frequently cast a lingering look behind to view, as often as I could, this very pretty imitation of the most beautiful of all the tombs of the earth.[6]

On my way I turned in to see the tomb of the celebrated saint, Nizām-ud-dīn Auliā, the defeater of the Transoxianian army under Tarmah Shīrīn in 1303, to which pilgrimages are still made from all parts of India.[7] It is a small building, surmounted by a white marble dome, and kept very clean and neat.[8] By its side is that of the poet Khusrū, his contemporary and friend, who moved about where he pleased through the palace of the Emperor Tughlak Shāh the First, five hundred years ago, and sang extempore to his lyre while the greatest and the fairest watched his lips to catch the expressions as they came warm from his soul. His popular songs are still the most popular; and he is one of the favoured few who live through ages in the every-day thoughts and feelings of many millions, while the crowned heads that patronized them in their brief day of pomp and power are forgotten, or remembered merely as they happened to be connected with them. His tomb has also a dome, and the grave is covered with rich brocade,[9] and attended with as much reverence and devotion as that of the great saint himself, while those of the emperors, kings, and princes that have been crowded around them are entirely disregarded. A number of people are employed to read the Korān over the grave of the old saint (*scil.* Nizām-ud-dīn), who died A.H. 725 [A.D. 1324-5], and are paid by contributions from the present Emperor, and the members of his family, who occasionally come in their hour of need to entreat his intercession with the Deity in their favour, and by the humble pilgrims who flock from all parts for the same purpose. A great many boys are here educated by those readers of their sacred volume. All my attendants bowed their heads to the dust before the shrine of the saint, but they seemed especially indifferent to those of the royal family, which are all open to the sky. Respect shown or neglect towards them could bring neither good nor evil, while any slight to the tomb of the *crusty old saint* might be of serious consequence.

In an enclosure formed by marble screens beautifully carved is the tomb of the favourite son of the present Emperor,[10] Mirzā Jahāngīr, whom

I knew intimately at Allahabad in 1816,[11] when he was killing himself as fast as he could with Hoffman's cherry brandy. 'This ', he would say to me, 'is really the only liquor that you Englishmen have worth drinking, and its only fault is that it makes one drunk too soon.' To prolong his pleasure, he used to limit himself to one large glass every hour, till he got dead drunk. Two or three sets of dancing women and musicians used to relieve each other in amusing him during this interval. He died, of course, soon, and the poor old Emperor was persuaded by his mother, the favourite sultana, that he had fallen a victim to sighing and grief at the treatment of the English, who would not permit him to remain at Delhi, where he was continually employed in attempts to assassinate his eldest brother, the heir apparent, and to stir up insurrections among the people. He was not in confinement at Allahabad, but merely prohibited from returning to Delhi. He had a splendid dwelling, a good income, and all the honours due to his rank.[12]

In another enclosure of the same kind are the Emperor Muhammad Shāh,[13]—who reigned when Nādir Shāh invaded Delhi—his mother, wife, and daughter; and in another close by is the tomb which interested me most, that of Jahānārā Bēgam, the favourite sister of poor Dārā Shikoh, and daughter of Shāh Jahān.[14] It stands in the same enclosure, with the brother of the present Emperor on one side, and his daughter on the other. Her remains are covered with a marble slab hollow at the top, and exposed to the sky—the hollow is filled with earth covered with green grass. Upon her tomb is the following inscription, the three first lines of which are said to have been written by herself:-

> Let no rich canopy cover my grave.
> This grass is the best covering for the tombs
>   of the poor in spirit.
> The humble, the transitory Jahānārā,
> The disciple of the holy men of Chisht,
> The daughter of the Emperor Shāh Jahān.'

I went over the magnificent tomb of Humāyūn, which was raised over his remains by the Emperor Akbar. It stands in the centre of a quadrangle of about four hundred yards square, with a cloistered wall all round; but I must not describe any more tombs.[15] Here, under a marble slab, lies the head of poor Dārā Shikoh, who, but for a little infirmity of temper, had perhaps changed the destinies of India, by changing the character of education among the aristocracy of the countries under his rule, and preventing the birth of the Marāthā powers by leaving untouched the independent kingdoms of the Deccan, upon whose ruins, under his bigoted brother, the former rose. Secular and religions education were always inseparably combined among the Muhammadans, and invited to India from Persia by the public offices, civil and military, which men of education and courtly manners could alone obtain. These offices had long been exclusively filled by such men, who flocked in crowds to India from Khorāsān and Persia. Every man qualified by secular instruction to make his way at court and fill such offices was disposed by his religions instruction to assert the supremacy of his creed, and to exclude the followers of every other from the employments over which he had any control. The aristocracy of office was the ocean to which this stream of Muhammadan education flowed from the west, and spread all over India; and had Dārā subdued his brothers and ascended the throne, he would probably have arrested the flood by closing the public offices against these Persian adventurers, and filling them with Christians and Hindoos. This would have changed the character of the aristocracy and the education of the people.[16]

While looking upon the slab under which his head reposes, I thought of the slight 'accidents by flood and field', the still slighter thought of the brain and feeling of the heart, on which the destinies of nations and of empires often depend — on the discovery of the great diamond in the mines of Golconda — on the accident which gave it into the hands of an ambitions Persian adventurer — on the thought which suggested the advantage of presenting it to Shāh Jahān — on the feeling which made Dārā get off, and Aurangzēb sit on his elephant at the battle of Samūgarh, on which depended the fate of India, and perhaps the advancement of the Christian religion and European literature and science over India.[17] But for the accident which gave Charles Martel the victory over the Saracens at Tours,[18] Arabic and Persian had perhaps been the classical languages, and Islamism the religion of Europe; and where we have cathedrals and colleges we might have had mosques and mausoleums; and America and the Cape, the compass and the press, the steam-engine, the telescope, and the Copernican System, might have remained still undiscovered; and but for the accident which turned Hannibal's face from Rome after the battle of Cannae, or that which intercepted his brother Asdrubal's letter, we might now all be speaking the languages of Tyre and Sidon, and roasting our own children in offerings to Siva or Saturn, instead of saving those of the Hindoos. Poor Dārā! but for thy little jealousy of thy father and thy son, thy desire to do all thy work without their aid, and those occasional ebullitions of passion which alienated from thee the most powerful of all the Hindoo princes, whom it was so much thy wish and thy interest to cherish, thy generous heart and enlightened mind had reigned over this vast empire, and made it, perchance, the garden it deserves to be made.

I visited the celebrated mosque known by the name of Jāmi (Jumma) Masjid, a fine building raised by Shāh Jahān, and finished in six years, A.H. 1060, at a cost of ten lākhs of rupees or one hundred thousand pounds. Money compared to man's labour and subsistence is still four times more valuable in India than in England; and a similar building in England would cost at least four hundred thousand pounds. It is, like all the buildings raised by this Emperor, in the best taste and style.[19] I was attended by three well-dressed and modest Hindoos, and a Muhammadan servant of the Emperor. My attention was so much taken up with the edifice that I did not perceive, till I was about to return, that the doorkeepers had stopped my three Hindoos. I found that they had offered to leave their shoes behind, and submit to anything to be permitted to follow me; but the porters had, they said, strict orders to admit no worshippers of idols; for their master was a man of the book, and had, therefore, got a little of the truth in him, though unhappily not much, since his heart had not been opened to that of the Korān. Nathū could have told him that he also had a book, which he and some fourscore millions more thought as good as his or better; but he was afraid to descant upon the merits of his 'shāstras', and the miracles of Kishan Jī [Krishna], among such fierce, cut-throat-looking people; he looked, however, as if he could have eaten the porter, Korān and all, when I came to their rescue. The only volumes which Muhammadans designate by the name of the book are the Old and New Testaments, and the Korān.

I visited also the palace, which was built by the same Emperor. It stands on the right bank of the Jumna, and occupies a quadrangle surrounded by a high wall built of red sandstone, about one mile in circumference; one side looks down into the clear stream of the Jumna, while the others are surrounded by the streets of the city.[20] The entrance is by a noble gateway to the west;[21] and facing this gateway on the inside, a hundred and twenty yards distant, is the Dīwān-ī-Amm, or the common hall of audience. This is a large hall, the roof of which is supported upon four colonnades of pillars of red sandstone, now white-washed, but once covered with stucco work and gilded. On one of these pillars is shown the mark of the dagger of a Hindoo prince of Chitōr, who, in the presence of the Emperor, stabbed to the heart one of the Muhammadan ministers who made use of some disrespectful language towards him. On being asked how he presumed to do this in the presence of his sovereign he answered in the very words almost of Roderic Dhu,

I right my wrongs where they are given,
Though it were in the court of Heaven.[22]

The throne projects into the hall from the back in front of the large central arch; it is raised ten feet above the floor, and is about ten feet wide, and covered by a marble canopy, all beautifully inlaid with mosaic work exquisitely finished, but now much dilapidated. The room or recess in which the throne stands is open to the front, and about fifteen feet wide and six deep. There is a door at the back by which the Emperor entered from his private apartments, and one on his left, from which his prime minister or chief officer of state approached the throne by a flight of steps leading into the hall. In front of the throne, and raised some three feet above the floor, is a fine large slab of white marble, on which one of the secretaries stood during the hours of audience to hand up to the throne any petitions that were presented, and to receive and convey commands. As the people approached over the intervening one hundred and twenty yards between the gateway and the hall of audience they were made to bow down lower and lower to the figure of the Emperor, as he sat upon his throne, without deigning to show by any motion of limb or muscle that he was really made of flesh and blood, and not cut out of the marble he sat upon.

The marble walls on three sides of this recess are inlaid with precious stones representing some of the most beautiful birds and flowers of India, according to the boundaries of the country when Shāh Jahān built this palace, which included Kābul and Kāshmīr, afterwards severed from it on the invasion of Nadir Shāh.[23]

On the upper part of the back wall is represented, in the same precious stones, and in a graceful attitude, a European in a kind of Spanish costume, playing upon his guitar, and in the character of Orpheus charming the birds and beasts which he first taught the people of India so well to represent in this manner. This I have no doubt was intended by Austin de Bordeaux for himself. The man from Shīrāz, Amānat Khān, who designed all the noble Tughra characters in which the passages from the Korān are inscribed upon different parts of the Tāj at Agra, was permitted to place his own name in the same bold characters on the right-hand side as we enter the tomb of the Emperor and his queen. It is inscribed after the date, thus, A.H. 1048 [A.D. 1638-9], 'The humble fakīr Amānat Khān of Shirāz.' Austin was a still greater favourite than Amānat Khān; and the Emperor Shāh Jahān, no doubt, readily acceded to his wishes to have himself represented in what appeared to him and his courtiers so beautiful a picture.[24]

The Dīwān-i-Khās, or hall of private audience, is a much more splendid building than the other from its richer materials, being all built of white marble beautifully ornamented. The roof is supported upon colonnades of marble pillars. The throne stands in the centre of this hall, and is ascended by steps, and covered by a canopy, with four artificial peacocks on the four corners.[25] Here, thought I, as I entered this apartment, sat Aurangzēb when he ordered the assassination of his brothers Dārā and Murād, and the imprisonment and destruction by slow poison of his son Muhammad, who had so often fought bravely by his side in battle. Here also, but a few months before, sat the great Shāh Jahān to receive the insolent commands of this same grandson Muhammad when flushed with victory, and to offer him the throne, merely to disappoint the hopes of the youth's father, Aurangzēb. Here stood in chains the graceful Sulaimān, to receive his sentence of death by slow poison with his poor young brother Sipihr Shikoh, who had shared all his father's toils and dangers, and witnessed his brutal murder.[26] Here sat Muhammad Shāh, bandying compliments with his ferocious conqueror, Nādir Shāh, who had destroyed his armies, plundered his treasury, stripped his throne, and ordered the murder of a hundred thousand of the helpless inhabitants of his capital, men, women, and children, in a general massacre. The bodies of these people lay in the streets tainting the air, while the two sovereigns sat here sipping their coffee, and swearing to the most deliberate lies in the name of their God, Prophet, and Korān;—all are now dust; that of the oppressor undistinguishable from that of the oppressed.[27]

Within this apartment and over the side arches at one end is inscribed in black letters the celebrated couplet, 'If there be a paradise on the face of the earth, it is this—it is this—it is this.[28] Anything more unlike paradise than this place now is can hardly be conceived. Here are crowded together twelve hundred *kings* and *queens* (for all the descendants of the Emperors assume the title of Salātīn, the plural of Sultan) literally eating each other up.[29]

Government, from motives of benevolence, has here attempted to apportion out the pension they assign to the Emperor, to the different members of his great family circle who are to be subsisted upon it, instead of leaving it to his own discretion. This has perhaps tended to prevent the family from throwing off its useless members to mix with the common herd, and to make the population press against the means of subsistence within these walls. Kings and queens of the house of Tīmūr are to be found lying about in scores, like broods of vermin, without food to eat or clothes to cover their nakedness. It has been proposed by some to establish colleges for them in the palace to fit them by education for high offices under our Government. Were this done, this pensioned family, which never can possibly feel well affected towards our Government or any Government but their own, would alone send out men enough to fill all the civil offices open to the natives of the country, to the exclusion of the members of the humbler but better affected families of Muhammadans and Hindoos. If they obtained the offices they would be educated for, the evil to Government and to society would be very great; and if they did not get them, the evil would be great to themselves, since they would be encouraged to entertain hopes that could not be realized. Better let them shift for themselves and quietly sink among the crowd. They would only become rallying points for the dissatisfaction and multiplied sources of disaffection; everywhere doing mischief, and nowhere doing good. Let loose upon society, they everywhere disgust people by their insolence and knavery, against which we are every day required to protect the people by our interference; the prestige of their name will by degrees diminish, and they will sink by and by into utter insignificance. During his stay at Jubbulpore, Kāmbaksh, the nephew of the Emperor, whom I have already mentioned as the most sensible member of the family,[30] did an infinite deal of good by cheating almost all the tradesmen of the town. Till he came down among them with all his ragamuffins from Delhi, men thought the Padshāhs and their progeny must be something superhuman, something not to be spoken of, much less approached, without reverence. During the latter part of his stay my court was crowded with complaints; and no one has ever since heard a scion of the house of Tīmūr spoken of but as a thing to be avoided—a person more prone than others to take in his neighbours. One of these *kings*, who has not more than ten shillings a month to subsist himself and family upon, will, in writing to the representative of the British Government, address him as 'Fidwī Khās', 'Your particular slave'; and be addressed in reply with 'Your majesty's commands have been received by your slave.'[31]

I visited the college which is in the mausoleum of Ghāzī-ud-dīn, a fine building, with its usual accompaniment of a mosque and a college. The slab that covers the grave, and the marble screens that surround the ground that contains it, are amongst the most richly cut things that I have seen. The learned and pious Muhammadans in the institution told me in my morning visit that there should always be a small hollow in the top of marble slabs, like that on Jahānārā's, whenever any of them were placed over graves, in order to admit water, earth, and grass; but that, strictly speaking, no slab should be allowed to cover the grave, as it could not fail to be in the way of the dead when summoned to get up by the trumpet of Azrāil on the day of the resurrection.'[32] 'Earthly pride,' said they, 'has violated this rule; and now everybody that can afford it gets a marble slab put over his grave. But it is not only in this that men have been falling off from the letter and spirit of the law; for we now hear drums beating and trumpets sounding even among the tombs of the saints, a thing that our forefathers would not have considered possible. In former days it was only a prophet like Moses, Jesus, or Muhammad, that was suffered to have a stone placed over his head.' I asked them how it was that the people crowded to the tombs of their saints, as I saw them at that of Kutb Shāh in old Delhi, on the Basant, a Hindoo festival. 'It only shows,' said they 'that the end of the world is approaching. Are we not divided into seventy-two sects among ourselves, all falling off into Hinduism, and every day committing greater and greater follies? These are the manifest signs long ago pointed out by wise and holy men as indicating the approach of the *last day*.'[33]

A man might make a curious book out of the indications of the end of the world according to the notions of different people or different individuals. The Hindoos have had many different worlds or ages; and the change from the good to the bad, or the golden to the iron age, is considered to have been indicated by a thousand curious incidents.[34] I one day asked an old Hindoo priest, a very worthy man, what made the five heroes of the Mahābhārata, the demigod brothers of Indian story, leave the plains and bury themselves no one knew where, in the eternal snows of the Himālaya mountains. 'Why, sir,' said he, 'there is no question about that. Yudhisthira, the eldest, who reigned quietly at Delhi after the long war, one day sat down to dinner with his four brothers and their single wife, Draupadī; for you know, sir, they had only one among them all. The king said grace and the covers were removed, when, to their utter consternation, a full-grown fly was seen seated upon the dish of rice that stood before his majesty. Yudhisthira rose in consternation. 'When flies begin to blow upon men's dinners,' said his majesty, 'you may be sure, my brothers, that the end of the world is near—the golden age is gone—the iron one has commenced, and we must all be off; the plains of India are no longer a fit abode for gentlemen.' Without taking one morsel of food,' added the priest, 'they set out, and were never after seen or heard of. They were, however, traced by manifest supernatural signs up through the valley of the Ganges to the snow tops of the Himālaya, in which they no doubt left their mortal coils.' They seem to feel a singular attachment for the birthplace of their great progenitrix, for no place in the world is, I suppose, more infested by them than Delhi, at present; and there a dish of rice without a fly would, in the iron, be as rare a thing as a dish with one in the golden, age.

Muhammadans in India sigh for the restoration of the old Muhammadan regime, not from any particular attachment to the descendants of Tīmūr, but with precisely the same feelings that Whigs and Tories sigh for the return to power of their respective parties in England; it would give them all the offices in a country where office is everything. Among them, as among ourselves, every man is disposed to rate his own abilities highly, and to have a good deal of confidence in his own good luck; and all think that if the field were once opened to them by such a change, they should very soon be able to find good places for themselves and their children in it. Perhaps there are few communities in the world among whom education is more generally diffused than among Muhammadans in India. He who holds an office worth twenty rupees a month commonly gives his sons an education equal to that of a prime minister. They learn, through the medium of the Arabic and Persian languages, what young men in our colleges learn through those of the Greek and Latin—that is, grammar, rhetoric, and logic. After his seven years of study, the young Muhammadan binds his turban upon a head almost as well filled with the things which appertain to these branches of knowledge as the young man raw from Oxford—he will talk as fluently about Socrates and Aristotle, Plato, and Hippocrates, Galen and Avicenna: (*alias* Sokrāt, Aristotalis, Aflātūn, Bokrāt, Jālīnus, and Bū Alī Sena); and, what is much to his advantage in India, the languages in which he has learnt what he knows are those which he most requires through life. [35] He therefore thinks himself as well fitted to fill the high offices which are now filled exclusively by Europeans, and naturally enough wishes the establishments of that power would open them to him. On the faculties and operations of the human mind, on man's passions and affections, and his duties in all relations of life, the works of Imām Muhammad Ghazālī[36] and Nāsir-ud- dīn Tūsī[37] hardly yield to those of Plato and Aristotle, or to those of any other authors who have written on the same subjects in any country. These works, the *Ihya-ul- ulūm*, epitomized into the *Kīmiā-i- Saādat*, and the *Akhlāk-i- Nāsirī*, with the didactic poems of Sādī,[38] are the great 'Pierian spring' of moral instruction from which the Muhammadan delights to 'drink deep' from infancy to old age; and a better spring it would be difficult to find in the works of any other three men.

It is not only the desire for office that makes the educated Muhammadans cherish the recollection of the old regime in Hīndustan: they say, 'We pray every night for the Emperor and his family, because our forefathers ate the salt of his forefathers'; that is, our ancestors were in the service of his ancestors; and, consequently, were the *aristocracy* of the country. Whether they really were so matters not; they persuade themselves or their children that they were. This is a very common and a very innocent sort of vanity. We often find Englishmen in India, and I suppose in all the rest of our foreign settlements, sporting high Tory opinions and feelings, merely with a view to have it supposed that their families are, or at some time were, among the aristocracy of the land. To express a wish for Conservative predominance is the same thing with them as to express a wish for the promotion in the Army, Navy, or Church of some of their near relations; and thus to indicate that they are among the privileged class whose wishes the Tories would be obliged to consult were they in power.[39]

Man is indeed 'fearfully and wonderfully made'; to be fitted himself for action in the world, or for directing ably the actions of others, it is indispensably necessary that he should mix freely from his youth up with his fellow men. I have elsewhere mentioned that the state of imbecility to which a man of naturally average powers of intellect may be reduced when brought up with his mother in the seraglio is inconceivable to those who have not had opportunities of observing it.[40] The poor old Emperor of Delhi, to whom so many millions look up, is an instance. A more venerable-looking man it is difficult to conceive, and had he been educated and brought up with his fellow men, he would no doubt have had a mind worthy of his person.[41] As it is, he has never been anything but a baby. Rājā Jīvan Rām, an excellent portrait painter, and a very honest and agreeable person, was lately employed to take the Emperor's portrait. After the first few sittings, the portrait was taken into the seraglio to the ladies. The next time he came, the Emperor requested him to remove the great *blotch from under the nose.* 'May it please your majesty, it is impossible to draw any person without *a shadow*; and I hope many millions will long continue to repose under that of your majesty.' 'True, Rājā,' said his majesty, 'men must have shadows; but there is surely no necessity for placing them immediately under their noses. The ladies will not allow mine to be put there; they say it looks as if I had been taking snuff all my life, and it certainly has a most filthy appearance; besides, it is all awry, as I told you when you began upon it.' The Rājā was obliged to remove from under the imperial, and certainly very noble, nose, the shadow which he had thought worth all the rest of the picture. Queen Elizabeth is said, by an edict, to have commanded all artists who should paint her likeness, 'to place her in a garden with a full light upon her, and the painter to put *any shadow* in her face at his peril'. The next time the Rājā came, the Emperor took the opportunity of consulting him upon a subject that had given him a good deal of anxiety for many months, the dismissal of one of his personal servants who had become negligent and disrespectful. He first took care that no one should be within hearing, and then whispered in the artist's ear that he wished to dismiss this man. The Rājā said carelessly, as he looked from the imperial head to the canvas, 'Why does your majesty not discharge the man if he displeases you?'

'Why do I not discharge him? I wish to do so, of course, and have wished to do so for many months, but *kuchh tadbīr chāhiye*, some plan of operations must be devised.' 'If your majesty dislikes the man, you have only to order him outside the gates of the palace, and you are relieved from his presence at once.' 'True, man, I am relieved from his presence, but his enchantments may still reach me; it is them that I most dread—he keeps me in a continual state of alarm; and I would give anything to get him away in a good humour.'

When the Rājā return to Meerut, he received a visit from one of the Emperor's sons or nephews, who wanted to see the place. His tents were pitched upon the plain not far from the theatre; he arrived in the evening, and there happened to be a play that night. Several times during the night he got a message from the prince to say that the ground near his tents was haunted by all manner of devils. The Rājā sent to assure him that this could not possibly be the case. At last a man came about midnight to say that the prince could stand it no longer, and had given orders to prepare for his immediate return to Delhi; for the devils were increasing so rapidly that they must all be inevitably devoured before daybreak if they remained. The Rājā now went to the prince's camp, here he found him and his followers in a state of utter consternation, looking towards the theatre. The last carriages were leaving the theatre, and going across the plain; and these silly people had taken them all for devils.[42]

The present pensioned imperial family f Delhi are commonly considered to be of the house of Tīmūr lang (the Lame), because Bābur, the real founder of the dynasty, was descended from him in the seventh stage.[43] Tīmūr merely made a predatory inroad into India, to kill a few million of unbelievers,[44] plunder the country of all the movable valuables he and his soldiers could collect, and take back into slavery all the best artificers of all kinds that they could lay their hands upon. He left no one to represent him in India, he claimed no sovereignty, and founded no dynasty there. There is no doubt much in the prestige of a name; and though six generations had passed away, the people of Northern India still trembled at that of the lame monster. Bābur wished to impress upon the minds of the people the notion that he had at his back the same army of demons that Tīmūr had commanded; and be boasted his descent from him for the same motive that Alexander boasted his from the horned and cloven-footed god of the Egyptian desert, as something to sanctify all enterprises, justify the use of all means, and carry before him the belief in his invincibility.

Bābur was an admirable chief — a fit founder of a great dynasty — a very proper object for the imagination of future generations to dwell upon, though not quite so good as his grandson, the great Akbar. Tīmūr was a ferocious monster, who knew how to organize and command the set of demons who composed his army, and how best to direct them for the destruction of the civilized portion of mankind and their works; but who knew nothing else. [45] In his invasion of India he caused the people of the towns and villages through which he passed to be all massacred without regard to religion, age, or sex. If the soldiers in the town resisted, the people were all murdered because they did so; if they did not, the people were considered to have forfeited their lives to the conquerors for being conquered; and told to purchase them by the surrender of all their property, the value of which was estimated by commissaries appointed for the purpose. The price was always more than they could pay; and after torturing a certain number to death in the attempt to screw the sum out of them, the troops were let in to murder the rest; so that no city, town, or village escaped; and the very grain collected for the army, over and above what they could consume at any stage, was burned, lest it might relieve some hungry infidel of the country who had escaped from the general carnage.

All the soldiers, high and low, were murdered when taken prisoners, as a matter of course; but the officers and soldiers of Tīmūr's army, after taking all the valuable movables, thought they might be able to find a market for the artificers by whom they were made, and for their families; and they collected together an immense number of men, women, and children. All who asked for mercy pretended to be able to make something that these Tartars had taken a liking to. On coming before Delhi, Tīmūr's army encamped on the opposite or left bank of the river Jumna; and here he learned that his soldiers had collected together above one hundred thousand of these artificers, besides their women and children. There were no soldiers among them; but Tīmūr thought it might be troublesome either to keep them or to turn them away without their women and children; and still more so to make his soldiers send away these women and children immediately. He asked whether the prisoners were not for the most part unbelievers in his prophet Muhammad; and being told that the majority were Hindoos, he gave orders that every man should be put to death; and that any officer or soldier who refused to kill or have killed all such men, should suffer death. 'As soon as this order was made known,' says Tīmūr's historian and great eulogist, 'the officers and soldiers began to put it in execution; and, in less than one hour, one hundred thousand prisoners, according to the smallest computation, were put to death and their bodies thrown into the river Jumna. Among the rest, Mulānā Nasīr-ud- dīn Amr, one of the most venerable doctors of the court, who would never consent so much as to kill a single sheep, was constrained to order fifteen slaves, whom he had in his tents, to be slain. Tīmūr then gave orders that one-tenth of his soldiers should keep watch over the Indian women, children, and camels taken in the pillage.'[46]

The city was soon after taken, and the people commanded, as usual, to purchase their lives by the surrender of their property — troops were sent in to take it — numbers were tortured to death — and then the usual pillage and massacre of the whole people followed without regard to religion, age, or sex; and about a hundred thousand more of innocent and unoffending people were murdered. The troops next massacred the inhabitants of the old city, which had become crowded with fugitives from the new;[47] the last remnant took refuge in a mosque, where two of Tīmūr's most distinguished generals rushed in upon them at the head of five hundred soldiers; and, as the amiable historian tells us, 'sent to the abyss of hell the souls of these infidels, of whose heads they erected towers, and gave their bodies for food to birds and beasts of prey'. Being at last tired of slaughter, the soldiers made slaves of the survivors, and drove them out in chains; and, as they passed, the officers were allowed to select any they liked except the masons, whom Tīmūr required to build for him at Samarkand a church similar to that of Īltutmish in old Delhi.

He now set out to take Meerut, which was at that time a fortified town of much note. The people determined to defend themselves, and happened to say that Tarmah Shirīn, who invaded India at the head of a similar body of Tartars a century before,[48] had been unable to take the place. This so incensed Tīmūr that he brought all his forces to bear on Meerut, took the place, and having had all the Hindoo men found in it *skinned alive*, he distributed their wives and children among his soldiers as slaves. He now sent out a division of his army to murder unbelievers, and collect plunder, over the cultivated plains between the Ganges and Jumna, while he led the main body on the same *pious duty* along the hills from Hardwār[49] on the Ganges to the west. Having massacred a few thousands of the hill people, Tīmūr read the noon prayer, and returned thanks to God for the victories he had gained, and the numbers he had murdered through his goodness; and told his admiring army that a religions war like this produced two great advantages: it secured eternal happiness in heaven, and a good store of valuable spoils on earth—that his design in all the fatigues and labours which he had undertaken was solely to render himself *pleasing to God*, treasure up *good works* for his eternal happiness, and get riches to bestow upon his soldiers and the poor. The historian makes a grave remark upon this invasion: The Korān declares that the highest glory man can attain in this world is unquestionably waging a successful war in person against the enemies of his religion (no matter whether those against whom it is waged happen ever to have heard of this religion or not). Muhammad inculcated the same doctrine in his discourses with his friends; and, in consequence, the great Tīmūr always strove to exterminate all the unbelievers, with a view to acquire that glory, and to spread the renown of his conquests. 'My name', said he, 'has spread terror through the universe, and the least motion I make is capable of shaking the whole earth.'

Tīmūr returned to his capital of Samarkand in Transoxiana in May, 1399. His army, besides other things which they brought from India, had an immense number of men, women, and children, whom they had reduced to slavery, and driven along like flocks of sheep to forage for their subsistence in the countries through which they passed, or perish. After the murder on the banks of the Jumna of part of the multitude they had collected before taking the capital, amounting to one hundred thousand men, Tīmūr was obliged to assign one-tenth of his army to guard what were left, the women and children. 'After the murder in the capital of Delhi,' says the historian, an eye-witness, 'there were some soldiers who had a hundred and fifty slaves, men, women, and children, whom they drove out of the city before them; and some soldiers' boys had twenty slaves to their own share.' On reaching Samarkand, they employed these slaves as best they could; and Tīmūr employed his, the masons, in raising his great church from the quarries of the neighbouring hills.[50]

In October following, Tīmūr led this army of demons over the rich and polished countries of Syria, Anatolia, and Georgia, levelling all the cities, towns, and villages, and massacring the inhabitants without any regard to age or sex, with the same *amiable view* of correcting the notions of people regarding his creed, propitiating the Deity, and rewarding his soldiers. He sent to the Christian inhabitants of Smyrna, then one of the first commercial cities in the world, to request that they would at once embrace Muhammadanism, in the *beauties* of which the general and his soldiers had orders generously and diligently to instruct them. They refused, and Tīmūr repaired immediately to the spot, that he might 'share in the merit of sending their souls to the abyss of hell'. Bajazet, the Turkish emperor of Anatolia, had recently terminated an unavailing siege of seven years. Tīmūr took the city in fourteen days, December, 1402;[51] had every man, woman, and child that he found in it murdered; and caused some of the heads of the Christians to be thrown by his balistas or catapultas into the ships that had come from different European nations to their succour. All other Christian communities found within the wide range of this dreadful tempest were swept off in the same manner, nor did Muhammadan communities fare better. After the taking of Baghdad, every Tartar soldier was ordered to cut off and bring away the head of one or more prisoners, because some of the Tartar soldiers had been killed in the attack; 'and they spared', says the historian, 'neither old men of fourscore, nor young children of eight years of age; no quarter was given either to rich or poor, and the number of dead was so great that they could not be counted; towers were made of their heads to serve as an example to posterity.' Ninety thousand were murdered in cold blood, and one hundred and twenty pyramids were made of the heads for trophies. Damascus, Nice, Aleppo, Sebastē,[52] and all the other rich and populous cities of Palestine, Syria, Asia Minor, and Georgia, then the most civilized region of the world, shared in the same fate; all were reduced to ruins, and their people, without regard to religion, age, or sex, barbarously and brutally murdered.

In the beginning of 1405, this man recollected that, among the many millions of unbelieving Christians and Hindoos 'whose souls he had sent to the abyss of hell', there were many Muhammadans, who had no doubt whatever in the divine origin or co-eternal existence of the Korān; and, as their death might, perhaps, not have been altogether pleasing to his God and his prophet, he determined to appease them both by undertaking the murder of some two hundred millions of industrious and unoffending Chinese; among whom there was little chance of finding one man who had ever even *heard of the Korān* — much less believed in its divinity and co- eternity — or of its interpreter, Muhammad. At the head of between two and three hundred thousand well-mounted Tartars and their followers, he departed from his capital of Samarkand on the 8th of January, 1405, and crossed the Jaxartes[53] on the ice. In the words of his *judicious* historian, 'he thus *generously* undertook the conquest of China, which was inhabited only by unbelievers that by so good a work he might atone for what had been done amiss in other wars, in which the blood of so many of the faithful had been shed'.

'As all my vast conquests', said Tīmūr himself,[54] 'have caused the destruction of a good many of the faithful, I am resolved to perform some good action, to atone for the crimes of my past life; and to make war upon the infidels, and exterminate the idolaters of China, which cannot be done without very great strength and power. It is therefore fitting, my dear companions in arms, that those very soldiers, who were the instruments whereby those my faults were committed, should be the means by which I work out my repentance, and that they should march into China, to acquire for themselves and their Emperor the merit of that holy war, in demolishing the temples of those unbelievers and erecting good Muhammadan mosques in their places. By this means we shall obtain pardon for all our sins, for the holy Korān assures us that good works efface the sins of this world.' At the close of the Emperor's speech, the princes of the blood and other officers of rank besought God to bless his generous undertaking, unanimously applauding his sentiments, and loading him with praises. 'Let the Emperor but display his standard, and we will follow him to the end of the world.' Tīmūr died soon after crossing the Jaxartes, on the 1st of April, 1406, and China was saved from this dreadful scourge. But, as the *philosophical* historian, Sharaf- ud-dīn,[55] *profoundly* observes, 'The Korān remarks that if any one in his pilgrimage to Mecca should be surprised by death, the merit of the good work is still written in heaven in his name, as surely as if he had had the good fortune to accomplish it. It is the same with regard to the "ghaza" (holy war), where an eternal merit is acquired by troubles, fatigues, and dangers; and he who dies during the enterprise, at whatever stage, is deemed to have completed his design.' Thus Tīmūr the Lame had the merit, beyond all question of doubt, of sending to the abyss of hell two hundred millions of men, women, and children, for not believing in a certain book of which they had never heard or read; for the Tartars had not become Muhammadans when they conquered China in the beginning of the thirteenth century. Indeed, the *amiable* and *profound* historian is of opinion, after the most mature deliberation, that 'God himself must have arranged all this in favour of so great and good a prince; and knowing that his end was nigh, inspired him with the idea of undertaking this enterprise, that he might have the merit of having completed it; otherwise, how should he have thought of leading out his army in the dead of winter to cross countries covered with ice and snow?'

The heir to the throne, the Prince Pīr Muhammad, was absent when Tīmūr died; but his wives, who had accompanied him, were all anxious to share in the merit of the holy undertaking; and in a council of the chiefs held after his death, the opinions of these amiable princesses prevailed that the two hundred millions of Chinese ought still to be sent to 'the abyss of hell', since it had been the earnest wish of their deceased husband, and must undoubtedly have been the will of God, to send them thither without delay. Fortunately quarrels soon arose among his sons and grandsons about the succession, and the army recrossed the Jaxartes, still over the ice, in the beginning of April, and China was saved from this scourge. Such was Timūr the Lame, the man whose greatness and goodness are to live in the hearts of the people of India, nine-tenths of whom are Hindoos, and to fill them with overflowing love and gratitude towards his descendants.

In this brief sketch will perhaps be found the true history of the origin of the gipsies, the tide of whose immigration began to flow over all parts of Europe immediately after the return of Tīmūr from India. The hundreds of thousands of slaves which his army brought from India in men, women, and children, were cast away when they got as many as they liked from the more beautiful and polished inhabitants of the cities of Palestine, Syria, Asia Minor, and Georgia, which were all, one after the other, treated in the same manner as Delhi had been. The Tartar soldiers had no time to settle down and employ them as they intended for their convenience; they were marched off to ravage Western Asia in October, 1399, about three months after their return from India. Tīmūr reached Samarkand in the middle of May, but he had gone on in advance of his army, which did not arrive for some time after. Being cast off, the slaves from India spread over those countries which were most likely to afford them the means of subsistence as beggars; for they knew nothing of the manners, the arts, or the language of those among whom they were thrown; and as Arabia, Palestine, Syria, Anatolia,

Georgia, Circassia, and Russia, had been, or were being, desolated by the army of this Tartar chief, they passed into Egypt and Bulgaria, whence they spread over all other countries. Scattered over the face of these countries, they found small parties of vagrants who were from the same regions as themselves, who spoke the same language, and who had in all probability been drawn away by the same means of armies returning from the invasion of India. Chingīz Khān invaded India two centuries before; his descendant, Tarmah Shirīn, invaded India in 1303, and must have taken back with him multitudes of captives. The unhappy prisoners of Tīmūr the Lame gathered round these nuclei as the only people who could understand or sympathize with them. From his sixth expedition into India Mahmūd is said to have carried back with him to Ghaznī two hundred thousand Hindoo captives in a state of slavery, A.D. 1011. From his seventh expedition in 1017, his army of one hundred and forty thousand fighting men returned 'laden with Hindoo captives, who became so cheap, that a Hindoo slave was valued at less than two rupees'. Mahmūd made several expeditions to the west immediately after his return from India, in the same manner as Tīmūr did after him, and he may in the same manner have scattered his Indian captives. They adopted the habits of their new friends, which are indeed those of all the vagrant tribes of India, and they have continued to preserve them to the present day. I have compared their vocabularies with those of India, and find so many of the words the same that I think a native of India would, even in the present day, be able without much difficulty to make himself understood by a gang of gipsies in any part of Europe.[56]

A good Christian may not be able exactly to understand the nature of the merit which Tamerlane expected to acquire from sending so many unoffending Chinese to the abyss of hell. According to the Muhammadan creed, God has vowed 'to fill hell chock full of men and genii'. Hence his reasons for hardening their hearts against that faith in the Korān which might send them to heaven, and which would, they think, necessarily follow an impartial examination of the evidence of its divinity and certainty. Tīmūr thought, no doubt, that it would be very meritorious on his part to assist God in this his labour of filling the great abyss by throwing into it all the existing population of China: while he spread over their land in pastoral tribes the goodly seed of Muhammadanism, which would give him a rich supply of recruits for paradise.

The following dialogue took place one day between me and the 'muftī', or head Muhammadan law officer, of one of our regulation courts.[57]

'Does it not seem to you strange, Muftī Sāhib, that your prophet, who, according to your notions, must have been so well acquainted with the universe and the laws that govern it, should not have revealed to his followers some great truths hitherto unknown regarding these laws, which might have commanded their belief, and that of all future generations, in his divine mission?'

'Not at all,' said the Muftī; 'they would probably not have understood him; and if they had, those who did not believe in what he did actually reveal to them, would not have believed in him had he revealed all the laws that govern the universe.'

'And why should they not have believed in him?'

'Because what he revealed was sufficient to convince all men whose hearts had not been hardened in unbelief. God said, "As for the unbelievers, it is the same with them whether you admonish them or do not admonish them; they will not believe. God hath sealed up their hearts, their ears, and their eyes; and a grievous punishment awaits them."'[58]

'And why were the hearts of any men thus hardened to unbelief, when by unbelief they were to incur such dreadful penalties?'

'Because they were otherwise wicked men.'

'But you think, of course, that there was really much of good in the revelations of your prophet?'

'Of course we do.'

'And that those who believed in it were likely to become better men for their faith?'

'Assuredly.'

'Then why harden the hearts of even bad men against a faith that might make them good?'

'Has not God said, "If we had pleased, we had certainly given unto every soul its direction; but the word which hath proceeded from me must necessarily be fulfilled when I said, *Verily, I will fill hell with men and genii altogether*".[59] And again, "Had it pleased the Lord, he would have made all men of one religion; but they shall not cease to differ among them, unless those on whom the Lord shall have mercy; and unto this hath he created them; for the word of thy Lord shall be fulfilled when he said, *Verily, I will fill hell altogether with genii and men*".'[60]

'You all believe that the devil, like all the angels, was made of fire?'

'Yes.'

'And that he was doomed to hell because he would not fall down and worship Adam, who was made of clay?'

'Yes, God commanded him to bow down to Adam; and when he did not do as he was bid, God said, "Why, Iblīs, what hindered thee from bowing down to Adam as the other angels did?" He replied, "It is not fit that I should worship man, whom thou hast formed of dried clay, or black mud". God said, "Get thee, therefore, hence, for thou shalt be pelted with stones; and a curse shall be upon thee till the day of judgement". The devil said, "O Lord, give me respite unto the day of resurrection". God said, "Verily, thou shalt be respited until the appointed time ".'[61]

'And does it not appear to you, Mufti Sāhib, that in respiting the devil Iblīs till the day of resurrection, some injustice was done to the children of Adam?'

'How?'

'Because he replies, "O Lord, because thou hast seduced me, I will surely tempt men to disobedience in the earth".'

'No, sir, because he could only tempt those who were *predestined* to go astray, for he adds, "I will seduce all, except such of them as shall be *thy chosen servants*". God said, "This is the right way with me. Verily, as to my servants, thou shalt have no power over them; but over those only who shall be seduced, and who shall follow thee; and hell is surely denounced to them all ".'[62]

'Then you think, Mufti Sāhib, that the devil could seduce only such as were predestined to go astray, and who would have gone astray whether he, the devil, had been respited or not?'

'Certainly I do.'

'Does it not then appear to you that it is as unjust to predestine men to do that for which they are to be sent to hell, as it would be to leave them all unguided to the temptations of the devil?'

'These are difficult questions,' replied the Muftī, 'which we cannot venture to ask even ourselves. All that we can do is to endeavour to understand what is written in the holy book, and act according to it. God made us all, and he has the right to do what he pleases with what he has made; the potter makes two vessels, he dashes the one on the ground, but the other he sells to stand in the palaces of princes.'

'But a pot has no soul, Muftī Sāhib, to be roasted to all eternity in hell!'

'True, sir; these are questions beyond the reach of human understanding.'

'How often do you read over the Korān?'

'I read the whole over about three times a month,' replied the Muftī.
[63]

I mentioned this conversation one day to the Nawāb Alī-ud-dīn,[64] a most estimable old gentleman of seventy years of age, who resides at Murādābād, and asked him whether he did not think it a singular omission on the part of Muhammad, after his journey to heaven, not to tell mankind some of the truths that have since been discovered regarding the nature of the bodies that fill these heavens, and the laws that govern their motions. Mankind could not, either from the Korān, or from the traditions, perceive that he was at all aware of the errors of the System of astronomy that prevailed in his day, and among his people.'

'Not at all', replied the Nawāb; 'the prophets had, no doubt, abundant opportunities of becoming acquainted with the heavenly bodies, and the laws which govern them, particularly those who, like Muhammad, had been up through the seven heavens; but their thoughts were so entirely taken up with the Deity that they probably never noticed the objects by which he was surrounded; and if they had noticed them, they would not, perhaps, have thought it necessary to say anything about them. Their object was to direct men's thoughts towards God and his commandments, and to instruct them in their duties towards him and towards each other.

'Suppose', continued the Nawāb, 'you were to be invited to see and converse with even your earthly sovereign, would not your thoughts be too much taken up with him to admit of your giving, on your return, an account of the things you saw about him? I have been several times to see you, and I declare that I have been so much taken up with the conversations which have passed, that I have never noticed the many articles I now see around me, nor could I have told any one on my return home what I had seen in your room—the wall- shades, the pictures, the sofas, the tables, the book-cases,' continued he, casting his eyes round the room,' all escaped my notice, and might have escaped it had my eyes been younger and stronger than they are. What then must have been the state of mind of those great prophets, who were admitted to see and converse with the great Creator of the universe, and were sent by him to instruct mankind?

'I told my old friend that I thought his answer the best that could be given; but still, that we could not help thinking that if Muhammad had really been acquainted with the nature of the heavenly bodies, and the laws which govern them, he would have taken advantage of his knowledge to secure more firmly their faith in his mission, and have explained to them the real state of the case, instead of talking about the stars as merely made to be thrown at devils, to give light to men upon this little globe of ours, and to guide them in their wanderings upon it by sea and land.

'But what', said the Nawāb, 'are the great truths that you would have had our holy prophet to teach mankind?'

'Why, Nawāb Sahib, I would have had him tell us, amongst other things, of that law which makes this our globe and the other planets revolve round the sun, and their moons around them. I would have had him teach us something of the nature of the things we call comets, or stars with large tails, and of that of the fixed stars, which we suppose to be suns, like our sun, with planets revolving round them like ours, since it is clear that they do not borrow their light from our sun, nor from anything that we can discover in the heavens. I would also have had him tell us the nature of that white belt which crosses the sky, which you call the ovarious belt, "Khatt- i-abyāz", and we the milky-way, and which we consider to be a collection of self-lighted stars, while many orthodox but unlettered Musalmāns think it the marks made in the sky by "Borak", the rough-shod donkey, on which your prophet rode from Jerusalem to heaven. And you think, Nawāb Sāhib, that there was quite evidence enough to satisfy any person whose heart had not been hardened to unbelief? and that no description of the heavenly bodies, or of the laws which govern their motion, could have had any influence on the minds of such people? '[65]

'Assuredly I do, sir! Has not God said, "If we should open a gate in the heavens above them, and they should ascend thereto all the day long, they would surely say, our eyes are only dazzled, or rather we are a people deluded by enchantments."[66] Do you think, sir, that anything which his majesty Moses could have said about the planets, and the comets, and the milky way, would have tended so much to persuade the children of Israel of his divine mission as did the single stroke of his rod, which brought a river of delicious water gushing from a dry rock when they were all dying from thirst? When our holy prophet', continued the Nawāb (placing the points of the four fingers of his right hand on the table), 'placed his blessed hand thus on the ground, and caused four streams to gush out from the dug plain, and supply with fresh water the whole army which was perishing from thirst; and when out of only *five small dates* he afterwards feasted this immense army till they could eat no more, he surely did more to convince his followers of his divine mission than he could have done by any discourse about the planets, and the milky way (Khatt-i-abyāz).'

'No doubt, Nawāb Sāhib, these were very powerful arguments for those who saw them, or believed them to have been seen; and those who doubt the divinity of your prophets mission are those who doubt their ever having been seen.'

'The whole army saw and attested them, sir, and that is evidence enough for us; and those who saw them, and were not satisfied, must have had their hearts hardened to unbelief.'

'And you think, Nawāb Sāhib, that a man is not master of his own belief or disbelief in religions matters; though he is rewarded by an eternity of bliss in paradise for the one, and punished by an eternity of scorching in hell for the other?

'I do, sir, faith is a matter of feeling; and over our feelings we have no control. All that we can do is to prevent their influencing our actions, when these actions would be mischievous. I have a desire to stretch out this arm, and crush that fly on the table, I can control the act, and do so; but the desire is not under my control.'

'True, Nawāb Sāhib; and in this life we punish men not for their feelings, which are beyond their control, but for their acts, over which they have no control; and we are apt to think that the Deity will do the same.'

'There are, sir,' continued the Nawāb, 'three kinds of certainty—the moral certainty, the mathematical, and the religious certainty, which we hold to be the greatest of all—the one in which the mind feels entire repose. This repose I feel in everything that is written in the Korān, in the Bible, and, with the few known exceptions, in the New Testament.[67] We do not believe that Christ was the son of God, though we believe him to have been a great prophet sent down to enlighten mankind; nor do we believe that he was crucified. We believe that the wicked Jews got hold of a thief, and crucified him in the belief that he was the Christ; but the real Christ was, we think, taken up into heaven, and not suffered to be crucified.'

'But, Nawāb Sāhib, the Sikhs have their book, in which they have the same faith.'

'True, sir, but the Sikhs are unlettered, ignorant brutes; and you do not, I hope, call their "Granth" a book—a thing written only the other day, and full of nonsense. No "book" has appeared since the Korān came down from heaven; nor will any other come till the day of judgement. And how', said the Nawāb, 'have people in modern days made all the discoveries you speak of in astronomy?'

'Chiefly, Nawāb Sāhib, by means of the telescope, which is an instrument of modern invention.'

'And do you suppose, sir, that I would put the evidence of your "dūrbīns" (telescopes) in opposition to that of the holy prophet? No, sir, depend upon it that there is much fallacy in a telescope—it is not to be relied upon. I have conversed with many excellent European gentlemen, and their great fault appears to me to be in the implicit faith they put in these *telescopes* — they hold their evidence above that of the prophets, Moses, Abraham, and Elijah. It is dreadful to think how much mischief these telescopes may do. No, sir, let us hold fast by the prophets; what they tell us is the truth, and the only truth that we can entirely rely upon in this life. I would not hold the evidence of all the telescopes in the world as anything against one word uttered by the humblest of the prophets named in the Old or New Testament, or the holy Korān. The prophets, sir, keep to the prophets, and throw aside your telescopes — there is no truth in them; some of them turn people upside down, and make them walk upon their heads; and yet you put their evidence against that of the prophets.'[68]

Nothing that I could say would, after this, convince the Nawāb that there was any virtue in telescopes; his religions feeling had been greatly excited against them; and had Galileo, Tycho Brahe, Kepler, Newton, Laplace, and the Herschels, all been present to defend them, they would not have altered his opinion of their demerits. The old man has, I believe, a shrewd suspicion that they are inventions of the devil to lead men from the right way; and were he told all that these great men have discovered through their means, he would be very much disposed to believe that they were incarnations of his satanic majesty playing over again with 'dūrbīns' (telescopes) the same game which the serpent played with the apple in the garden of Eden.

> Solicit not thy thoughts with matters hid;
> Leave them to God above: him serve and fear;
> Of other creatures, as him pleases best,
> Wherever placed, let him dispose: joy thou
> In what he gives to thee, this Paradise
> And thy fair Eve: heaven is for thee too high
> To know what passes there: be lowly wise:
> Think only what concerns thee, and thy being:
> Dream not of other worlds, what creatures there
> Live, in what state, condition, or degree:
> Contented that thus far hath been revealed,
> Not of earth only, but of highest heaven.'[69]

Notes:

1. Chapter 75 *post* is devoted to the history of the Bēgam Samrū (Sumroo). The 'great street' is the celebrated Chāndnī Chauk, a very wide thoroughfare. The branch of the canal which runs down the middle of it is now covered over. The Bēgam's house is now occupied by the Delhi Bank (Fanshawe, p, 49).

2. *Ante*, chapter 54, note 14.

3. The Emperors were not in the least ashamed of this practice, and robbed the families of rich merchants as well as those of officials. In fact they levied in a rough way the high 'death duties' so much admired by Radicals with small expectations. Some remarkable cases are related in detail by Bernier (Bernier, *Travels*, ed. Constable, and V. A. Smith (1914), pp. 163-7). When Aurangzēb heard of the death of the Governor of Kābul, he gave orders to seize the belongings of the deceased, so that 'not even a piece of straw be left' (Bilimoria, *Letters of Aurungzebe*, No. xcix).

4. The meaning of this sentence is obscure.

5. Corresponding to A.D. 1753-4. In the original edition the date is misprinted A.D. 1167.

6. The tomb of Mansūr Alī Khān is better known as that of Safdar Jang, which was the honorary title of the noble over whom the edifice was raised. He was the wazīr, or chief minister, of the Emperor Ahmad Shāh from 1748 to 1752, and was practically King of Oudh, where he had succeeded to the power of his father-in-law, the well-known Saādat Khān: Safdar Jang died in A.D. 1754 and was succeeded in Oudh by his son Shujā-ud-daula.

The author's praise of the beauty of Safdar Jang's tomb will seem extravagant to most critics. In the editor's judgement the building is a very poor attempt to imitate the inimitable Tāj. Fergusson (ed. 1910, vol. ii, p. 324, pl. xxxiv) gives it the qualified praise that 'it looks grand and imposing at a distance, but it will not bear close inspection'. See Fanshawe, p. 246 and plate. In the original edition a coloured plate of this mausoleum is given.

7. Nizām-ud-dīn was the disciple of Farīd-ud- dīn Ganj Shakar, so called from his look being sufficient to convert *cods of earth into lumps of sugar*. Farīd was the disciple of Kutb-ud-dīn of Old Delhi, who was the disciple of Mūin-ud-dīn of Ajmēr, the greatest of all their saints. [W. H. S.] Mūin-ud-dīn died A.D. 1236. For further particulars of the three saints see Beale, *Oriental Biographical Dictionary*, ed. Keene, 1894. Dr. Horn (*Ep. Ind.* ii, 145 n., 426 n.) gives information about the Persian biographies of Nizām-ud-dīn and other Chishtī saints.

8. For the personal history of Nizām-ud-dīn see the last preceding chapter, [13]. His tomb is situated in a kind of cemetery, which also contains the tombs of the poet Khusrū, the Princess Jahānārā, and the Emperor Muhammad Shāh, which will be noticed presently. Fanshawe (p. 236) gives a plan of the enclosure. Nizām-ud-dīn's tomb 'has a very graceful appearance, and is surrounded by a verandah of white marble, while a cut screen encloses the sarcophagus, which is always covered with a cloth. Round the gravestone runs a carved wooden guard, and from the four corners rise stone pillars draped with cloth, which support an angular

wooden frame-work, and which has something the appearance of a canopy to a bed. Below this wooden canopy there is stretched a cloth of green and red, much the worse for wear. The interior of the tomb is covered with painted figures in Arabic, and at the head of the grave is a stand with a Korān. The marble screen is very richly cut, and the roof of the arcade-like verandah is finely painted in a flower pattern. Altogether there is a quaint look about the building which cannot fail to strike any one. A good deal of money has at various times been spent on this tomb; the dome was added to the roof in Akbar's time by Muhammad Imām-ud- dīn Hasan, and in the reign of Shāh Jahān (A.D. 1628 [*sic., leg.* 1627]-58) the whole building was put into thorough repair. . . . The tomb is in the village of Ghyāspur, and is reached after passing through the 'Chaunsath Khambhā'. (Harcourt, *The New Guide to Delhi* (1866), p. 107.)

In the original edition a small coloured illustration of this tomb, from a miniature, is given on Plate 24. Carr Stephen (pp. 102- 7) gives a good and full account of Nizām-ud-dīn and his tomb.

9. According to Harcourt (p. 108), the tomb of Khusrū was erected about A.D. 1350, but this is a misprint for 1530. The poet, whose proper name was Abūl Hasan, is often called Amīr Khusrū, and was of Turkish origin. He was born A.D. 1253, and died in September, 1325. His works are numerous. (Beale.) The grave, and wooden railing round it, were built in A.H. 937 (A.D. 1530-1). . . . The present tomb was built in A.H. 1014 (A.D. 1605-6) by Imād-ud-dīn Hasan, in the reign of Jahāngīr, and this date occurs in an inscription under the dome and over the red sandstone screens. (Carr Stephen, p. 115.) In the original edition a small coloured illustration of this tomb, from a miniature, is given on Plate 24. See Fanshawe, p. 241.

10. Akbar II, who died in 1837.

11. When the author was with his regiment, after the close of the Nepalese war.

12. Harcourt (p. 109) truly observes that this tomb 'is a most exquisite piece of workmanship. The tomb itself, raised some few feet from the ground, is entered by steps, and is enclosed in a beautiful cut marble screen, the sarcophagus being covered with a very artistic representation of leaves and flowers carved in marble. Mirzā Jahāngīr was the son of Akbar II, and the tomb was built in A.D. 1832 '.

'He was, in consequence of having fired a pistol at Mr. Seton, the Resident at Delhi, sent as a State prisoner to Allahabad, where he resided in the garden of Sultān Khusro for several years, and died there in A.D. 1821 (A.H. 1236), aged thirty-one years; a salute of thirty-one guns was fired from the ramparts of the fort of Allahabad at the time of his burial. He was at first interred in the same garden, and subsequently his remains were transferred to Delhi, and buried in the courtyard of the mausoleum of Nizām-ud- dīn Auliā.' (Beale, *Dictionary*.) The young man's 'overt act of rebellion' occurred in 1808, and his body was removed to Delhi in 1832. The form of the monument is that ordinarily used for a woman, 'but it was put over the remains of the Prince on a dispensation being granted for the purpose by Muhammadan lawyers'. (Carr Stephen, p. 111.)

13. Muhammad Shāh reigned feebly from September, 1719, to April, 1748. 'He is the last of the Mughals who enjoyed even the semblance of power, and has been called "the seal of the house of Bābar", for "after his demise everything went to wreck".' (Lane-Poole, p. xxxviii.) Nadir Shāh occupied Delhi in 1738, and is said to have massacred 120,000 people. The tomb is described by Carr Stephen, p. 110.

14. Jahānārā Bēgam, or the Bēgam Sāhib, was the elder daughter of Shāhjahān, a very able intriguer, the partisan of Dārā Shikoh and the opponent of Aurangzēb during the struggle for the throne. She was closely confined in Agra till her father's death in 1666. After that event she was removed to Delhi, where she died in 1682. (Tavernier, *Travels*, transl. Ball, vol. i, p. 345.) She built the Bēgam Sarāi at Delhi. Her amours, real or supposed, furnished Bernier with some scandalous and sensational stories. (Bernier, *Travels*, transl. Constable, and V. A. Smith (1914), pp. 11-14.) Some writers credit her with all the virtues, e.g., Beale in his *Oriental Biographical Dictionary*. The author has omitted the last line of the inscription-'May God illuminate his intentions. In the year 1093 ', corresponding to A.D. 1682. The first line is, 'Let nothing but the green [grass] conceal my grave.' (Carr Stephen, p. 109.)

15. The tomb of Humāyūn was erected by the Emperor's widow, Hājī Bēgam, or Bēgā Bēgam, not by Akbar. She was the senior widow of Humāyūn, entitled Hājī or 'pilgrim ', because she performed the pilgrimage to Mecca. Carr Stephen and other writers confound her with Hamīda Bānū Bēgam, the mother of Akbar. For her true history see Beveridge, *The History of Humāyūn by Gulbadan Begam* (R.A.S., 1902). Carr Stephen (p. 203) says that the mausoleum was completed in A.D. 1565, or, according to some, in A.D. 1569, at a coat of fifteen lākhs of rupees. The true date is A.D. 1570, late in A.H. 977 (Badūouī, tr. Lowe, ii. 135). It is of special interest as being one of the earliest specimens of the architecture of the Moghal dynasty, The massive dome of white marble is a landmark for many miles round. The body of the building is of red sandstone with marble decorations. It stands on two noble terraces. Humāyūn rests in the central hall under an

elaborately carved marble sarcophagus. The head of Dārā Shikoh and the bodies of many members of the royal family are interred in the side rooms. After the fall of Delhi in September, 1857, the rebel princes took refuge in this mausoleum. The story of their execution by Hodson on the road to Delhi is well known, and has been the occasion of much controversy.

In the original edition a small coloured illustration of this tomb, from a miniature, is given on Plate 24. See Fergusson, ed. 1910, pl. xxxiii; *H.F.A.,* fig. 240; Fanshawe, p. 230 and plate.

16. The tragic history of Dārā Shikoh, the elder brother, and unsuccessful rival, of Aurangzēb, is fully given by Bernier. The notes in Constable's edition of that traveller's work and those to Irvine's *Storia do Mogor* (John Murray, 1907, 1908) give many additional particulars. Dārā Shikoh was executed by Aurangzēb in 1659, and it is alleged that with a horrid refinement of cruelty, the emperor, acting on the advice of his sister, Roshanārā Bēgam, caused the head to be embalmed and sent packed in a box as a present to the old ex- emperor, Shāh Jahān, the father of the three, in his prison at Agra. The prince died invoking the aid of Jesus, and was favourably disposed towards Christianity. He was also attracted by the doctrines of Sūfism, or heretical Muhammadan mysticism, and by those of the Hindoo Upanishads. In fact, his religions attitude seems to have much resembled that of his great-grandfather Akbar. The 'Broad Church' principles and practice of Akbar failed to leave any permanent mark on Muhammadan institutions or the education of the people, and if Dārā Shikoh had been victorious in the contest for the throne, it is not probable that he would have been able to effect lasting reforms which were beyond the power of his illustrious ancestor. The name of the unfortunate prince was Dārā Shikoh ('in splendour like Darius'), not merely Dārā (Darius), as Bernier has it.

17. The 'great diamond' alluded to is the Kohinūr, presented by the 'Persian adventurer', Amīr Jumla, to Shāh Jahān, who was advised to attack and conquer the country which produced such gems, (*Ante,* Chapter 48.) The decisive battle between Dārā Shikoh, on the one aide, and Aurangzēb, supported by his brother and dupe, Murād Baksh, on the other, was fought on the 28th May, 1658 [O. S.], at the small village of Samūgarh (Samogar), four miles from Agra. Dārā Shikoh was winning the battle, when a traitor persuaded him to come down from his conspicuous seat on an elephant and mount a horse. The report quickly spread that the prince had been killed. 'In a few minutes', says Bernier, 'the army seemed disbanded, and (strange and sudden reverse!) the conqueror became the vanquished. Aurangzēb remained during a quarter of an hour steadily on his elephant, and was rewarded with the crown of Hindustan; Dārā left his own elephant a

few minutes too soon, and was hurled from the pinnacle of glory, to be numbered among the most miserable of Princes; so short-sighted is man, and so mighty are the consequences which sometimes flow from the most trivial incident.'

According to another account the prince's change from the elephant to the horse was due to want of personal courage, and not to treacherous advice. (Bernier, *Travels*, ed. Constable, and V. A. Smith (1914), p. 54.)

18. Battle fought between Tours and Poitiers, A.D. 732.

19. The principal mosque of every town is known as the Jāmi Masjid, and is filled by large congregations on Fridays. The great mosque of Delhi stands on a natural rocky eminence, completely covered by the building, and approached on three sides by magnificent flights of steps, which give it peculiar dignity. It is, perhaps, the finest mosque in the world, and certainly has few rivals. It differs from most mosques in that its exterior is more magnificent than its interior. The two minarets are each about 130 feet high. The year A.H. 1060 corresponds to A.D. 1650. The mosque was begun in that year, and finished six years later. It is close to the palace, and seems to have been designed to serve as the mosque for the palace, as well as the city, for which reason no place of worship was included in his residence by Shāh Jahān. The pretty little Motī Masjid in the private apartments was added by Aurangzēb. Fergusson (ed. 1910, vol. ii, p. 319) gives a view of the mosque. Carr Stephen (pp. 260-6) gives approximate measurements, translations of the inscriptions, and many details. See Fanshawe, pp. 44-8 and plates.

20. Since the Mutiny multitudes of houses between the palace and the mosque have been cleared away.

21. 'Entering within its deeply recessed portal, you find yourself beneath the vaulted hall, the sides of which are in two stories, and with an octagonal break in the centre. This hall, which is 375 feet in length over all, has very much the effect of the nave of a gigantic Gothic cathedral, and forms the noblest entrance known to belong to any existing palace' (Fergusson, ed. 1910, vol. ii, p. 309). This is the Lahore Gate.

22. What recked the Chieftain if he stood
On Highland heath, or Holy- rood?
He rights such wrong where it is given,
If it were in the court of heaven.'
— (Scott, *Lady of the Lake*, Canto V, stanza 6).

23. The foundation-stone of the palace was laid on the 12th of May, 1639 (N.S. — 9 Muharrum, A.H. 1049). (E. & D., vii, p. 86), and the work continued for nine years, three months, and some days. Nadir Shāh's invasion took place in 1738. Kāshmīr was annexed by Akbar in 1587. Kābul had been more or less closely united with the empire since Bābur's time.

24. 'In front, at the entrance, was the Naubat Khāna, or music hall, beneath which the visitor entered the second or great court of the palace, measuring 550 feet north and south, by 385 feet east and west. In the centre of this stood the Dīwān-i- Amm, or great audience hall of the palace, very similar in design to that at Agra, but more magnificent. Its dimensions are about 200 feet by 100 feet over all. In its centre is a highly ornamental niche, in which on a platform of marble richly inlaid with previous stones, and directly facing the entrance, once stood the celebrated peacock throne, the most gorgeous example of its class that perhaps even the East could ever boast of. Behind this again was a garden-court; on its eastern side was the Rang Mahall, or painted hall, containing a bath and other apartments' (Fergusson, ed. 1910, vol. ii, p. 310).

The inlaid pictures were carried off, sold by the spoiler to Government, set as table-tops, and deposited in the Indian Section of the Victoria and Albert Museum at South Kensington (Hist. of Ind. and E. Archit., ed. 1910, vol. ii, p. 311, note); but in November, 1902, the Orpheus mosaic, along with several other inlaid panels, was returned to Delhi, where the panels were reset in due course. The representation of Orpheus is 'a bad copy from Raphael's picture of Orpheus charming the beasts'. Austin de Bordeaux has been already noticed. Many of the mosaics in the panels which had not been disturbed were renewed by Signor Menegatti of Florence during the years 1906-9.

The peacock throne and the six other thrones in the palace are fully described by Tavernier. (Transl. and ed. by V. Ball, vol. i, pp. 381-7.) Further details will be found in Carr Stephen, *Archaeology of Delhi*, pp. 220-7.

25. The throne here referred to was a makeshift arrangement used by the later emperors. Nādir Shāh in 1738 cleared the palace of the peacock throne and almost everything portable of value. The little that was left the Marāthās took. Their chief prize was the silver filagree ceiling of the Dīwān-i- Khās. This hall was, 'if not the most beautiful, certainly the most highly ornamented of all Shāh Jahān's buildings. It is larger certainly, and far richer in ornament than that of Agra, though hardly so elegant in design; but nothing can exceed the beauty of the inlay of precious stones with which it is adored, or the general poetry of the design, It is round the roof of this hall that the famous inscription runs: "If there is a heaven on earth, it is this, it is this ", which may safely be rendered into the sober English assertion that no palace now existing in the world possesses an apartment of such singular elegance as this' (Fergusson, ed. 1910, vol. ii, p. 311).

26. All the events alluded to are related in detail by Bernier and Manucci. Sulaimān and Sipihr Shikoh were the sons of Dārā Shikoh. The author makes a slip in saying that Shāh Jahān sat in the palace at Delhi

to negotiate with his grandson. During that negotiation Shāh Jahān was at Agra.

27. It is related that the coffee was delivered to the two sovereigns in this room upon a gold salver by the most polished gentleman of the court. His motions, as he entered the gorgeous apartment, amidst the splendid train of the two Emperors, were watched with great anxiety; if he presented the coffee first to his own master, the furious conqueror, before whom the sovereign of India and all his courtiers trembled, might order him to instant execution; if he presented it to Nādir first, he would insult his own sovereign out of fear of the stranger. To the astonishment of all, he walked up with a steady step direct to his own master. 'I cannot', said he, 'aspire to the honour of presenting the cup to the king of kings, your majesty's honoured guest, nor would your majesty wish that any hand but your own should do so.' The Emperor took the cup from the golden salver, and presented it to Nādir Shāh, who said with a smile as he took it, 'Had all your officers known and done their duty like this man, you had never, my good cousin, seen me and my Kizil Bāshis at Delhi; take care of him for your own sake, and get round you as many like him as you can.' [W. H. S.]

28. The famous inscription of Saād-Ullah Khān, supposed to be in the handwriting of Rashīd, the greatest caligraphist of his time; *Agar Firdaus bar rūe zamīn ast — hamīn ast, to hamīn ast, to hamīn ast'* (Carr Stephen, p. 229; Fanshawe, p. 35 and plate).

29. All these people were cleared out by the events of 1867, and the few beautiful fragments of the palace which have retained anything of their original magnificence are now clean and in good order. The elaborate decorations of the Dīwān-i- Khās have been partially restored, and the interior of this building is still extremely rich and elegant.

'Of the public parts of the palace all that now remains is the entrance hall, the Naubat Khāna, Dīwān-i-Amm and Khās, and the Rang Mahall — now used as a mess-room, and one or two small pavilions. They are the gems of the palace it is true, but without the courts and corridors connecting them they lose all their meaning and more than half their beauty. Being now situated in the middle of a British barrack-yard, they look like precious stones torn from their settings in some exquisite piece of Oriental jeweller's work and set at random in a bed of the commonest plaster' (Fergusson, ed. 1910, vol. ii, p. 312). Since Fergusson wrote an immense amount of work has been done in restoration and conservation, but it is difficult to obtain a general view of the result.

The books about Delhi are even more tantalising and unsatisfactory than those which deal with Agra. Mr. Beglar's contribution to Vol. IV of the *Archaeological Survey Reports* is a little, but very little, better than Mr.

Carlleyle's disquisition on Agra in that volume. Sir A. Cunningham's observations in the first and twentieth volumes of the same series are of greater value, but are fragmentary and imperfect, and scarcely notice at all the city of Shāhjahān. Fergusson's criticisms, so far as they go, are of permanent importance, though the scheme of his work did not allow him to treat in detail of any particular section. Guide-books by Beresford Cooper, Harcourt, and Keene, of which Keene's is the latest, and, consequently, in some respects the best, are all extremely unsatisfactory. Mr. H. C. Fanshawe's *Delhi Past and Present* (John Murray, 1902), a large, handsome work something between a guide-book and a learned treatise, is not quite satisfying. The late Mr. Carr Stephen, a resident of Delhi, wrote a valuable book on the Archaeology of the city, but it has no illustrations, except a few plans on a small scale. (8vo, Ludhiana, 1876.) A good critical, comprehensive, well illustrated description of the remains of the cities, said to number thirteen, all grouped together by European writers under the name of Delhi, does not exist, and it seems unlikely that the Panjāb Government will cause the blank to be filled. No Government in India has such opportunities, or has done so little, to elucidate the history of the country, as the Government of the Panjāb. But it has shown greater interest in the matter of late. The reorganized Archaeological Survey of India, under the capable guidance of Sir J. H. Marshall, C.I.E., has not yet had time to do much at Delhi beyond the work of conservation. A fourteenth Delhi is now being built (1914).

30. *Ante*, chapter 53, [19].

31. These epistolary formulas mean no more than the similar official phrases in English, 'Your most obedient humble servant', and the like. The 'fortunate occurrence' of the Mutiny—for such it was, in spite of all the blood and suffering—cut out many plague-spots from the body politic of India. Among these the reeking palace swarm of Delhi was not the least malignant.

32. Azraīl is the angel of death, whose duty it is to separate the souls from the bodies of men. Isrāfīl is entrusted with the task of blowing the last trump.

33. The resurrection, and the signs foretelling it, are described in the *Mishkat-ul-Masābih*, book xxiii, chapters 3 to 11. (Matthews, vol. ii, pp. 556-620.)

34. The Hindoo 'ages' are (1) Krita, or Satya, (2) Treta, (3) Dwāpara, (4) Kali, the present evil age. The long periods assigned to these are merely the result of the calculations of astronomers, who preferred integral to fractional numbers.

35. This kind of education does not now pay, and is, consequently, going out of fashion. The Muhammadans are slowly, and rather unwillingly, yielding to the pressure of necessity and beginning to accept English education.

36. Imam Muhammad Ghazzālī, who is also entitled Hujjat-ul-Islām, is the surname of Abu Hāmid Muhammad Zain-ud-dīn Tūsī, one of the greatest and most celebrated Musalmān doctors, who was born A.D. 1058, and died A.D. 1111. (Beale, s.v. 'Ghazzālī'.) The length of these Muhammadan names is terrible. They are much mangled in the original edition. See *ante*, chapter 53, note 10, and Blochmann (Aīn) pp. 103, 182.

37. Khwāja Nāsir-ud-dīn Tūsī, the famous philosopher and astronomer, the most universal scholar that Persia ever produced. Born A.D. 1201, died A.D. 1274. (Beale.) See *ante*, loc. cit.

38. Especially the *Būstān* and *Gulistān*. Beale gives a list of Sādī's works. See *ante*, chapter 12, note 6.

39. This is a very cynical and inadequate explanation of the prevalence of Conservative opinions among Englishmen in the East.

40. Ante, chapter 30, [6].

41. In the original edition the portrait of Akbar II is twice given, namely, in the frontispiece of Volume I as a full-page plate, and again as a miniature, dated 1836, in the frontispiece of Volume II.

42. The most secluded native prince of the present day could not be guilty of this absurdity.

43. Bābur was sixth in descent from Tīmūr, not seventh. Bābur's grandfather, Abu Sayyid, was great- grandson of Tīmūr. Bābur, not Bābar, is the correct spelling.

44. This may be an exaggeration. The undoubted facts are sufficiently horrible.

45. Tīmūr was a man of surpassing ability, and knew much 'else'. See Malcolm, *History of Persia*, ed. 1859, chapter 11.

46. Tīmūr's 'historian and great eulogist' was Sharaf-ud-dīn (died 1446), whose *Zafarnāma*, or 'Book of Victories', was translated into French by Petis de la Croix in 1722. That version was used by Gibbon and rendered into English in 1723, Copious extracts from an independent rendering are given in E. & D., iii, pp. 478-522. The details do not always agree exactly with Sleeman's account.

47. The 'old city' was that of Kutb-ud-dīn and Īltutmish; the 'new city' was that of Fīrōz Shāh, which partly coincided with the existing city, and partly lay to the south, outside the Delhi gate.

48. In A.D. 1303.

49. Now in the Sahāranpur district.

50. This is a repetition of the statement made above. According to *Encycl. Brit.*, ed. 1910, Tīmūr returned to his capital in April not May.

51. Bajazet, or more accurately Bayazīd I, was defeated by Tīmūr at the battle of Angora in 1402, and died the following year. The story of his confinement in an iron cage is discredited by modern critics, though Gibbon (chapter 65) shows that it is supported by much good evidence. Anatolia is a synonym for Asia Minor. It is a vague term, the Greek equivalent of 'the Levant'.

52. Sebastē, also called Elaeusa or Ayash, was in Cilicia.

53. Otherwise called Sihōn, or Syr Daryā.

54. Two autobiographical works, the *Malfūzāt* and the Tuzukāt, are attributed to Tīmūr and probably were composed under his direction. The latter was translated by Major Davey (Oxford, 1783), and the former, in part, by Major Stewart (Or. Transl. Fund, 1830). An independent version of the portion of the *Malfūzāt* relating to India will be found in E. & D., iii, pp. 389-477.

55. Alī Yazdī, commonly called Sharaf-ud- dīn, author of the *Zafarnāma* in Persian (see *ante*, chapter 68, note 46), Ibn Arabshāh, in an Arabic work, describes Tīmūr from a hostile point of view. (Encycl. Brit., 11th ed., s. v. 'Tīmūr').

56. It is impossible within the limits of a note to discuss the problem of the origin of the gipsies. Much has been written about it, though nothing quite satisfactory. The gipsy, or Romany, language (*Romani chiv*, or 'tongue') certainly is closely related to, though not derived from, the existing languages of Northern India. Some of the forms are very archaic. A valuable English-Gipsy vocabulary compiled by Mr. (Sir George) and Mrs. Grierson was published in *Ind. Ant.*, vols. xv, xvi (1886,1887). The author's theory does not tally with the facts. Gipsies existed in Persia and Europe long before Tīmūr's time. It is practically certain that they did not come through Egypt. The article 'Gypsies' by F. H. Groome in Chambers's *Encycl.* (1904) is good, and seems to the editor to be preferable to Dr. Gaster's article 'Gipsies' in *Encycl. Brit.*, 11th ed., 1910.

57. Before the Codes were passed (1859-1861) the criminal law administered in India was, in the main, that of the Muhammadans, and each judge's court had a Muhammadan law officer attached, who pronounced a 'fatwa', or decision, intimating the law applicable to the case, and the penalty which might be inflicted. Several examples of these 'fatwas' will be found among the papers bound up with the author's 'Ramaseeana'.

58. See Korān, chapter 2. [W. H. S.] The passage is the second sentence in chapter 2. The wording, as quoted, differs slightly from Sale's version.

59. See Korān, chapter 32. [W. H. S.]

60. Ibid., chapter 11. [W. H. S.] Sale's version, with trifling verbal differences. The 'mufti's' reasoning has been heard in Europe.

61. See Korān, chapter 15. [W. H. S.] Sale's version, with modifications.

62. 'This is a revelation of the most mighty, the merciful God; that thou mayest warn a people whose fathers were not warned, and who live in negligence. Our sentence hath justly been pronounced against the greater part of them, wherefore they shall not believe. It shall be equal unto them whether thou preach unto them, or do not preach unto them; they shall not believe.' Korān, chapter 36. [W. H. S.] From beginning of the chapter. Sale's version; a sentence being omitted between 'believe' and 'It shall'.

63. I have never met another man so thoroughly master of the Korān as the Muftī, and yet he had the reputation of being a very corrupt man in his office. [W. H. S.]

64. Aleeoodeen; an unusual name; probably a misprint for Alā-ud-dīn.

65. The 17th chapter of the Korān opens with the words, 'Praise be unto him who transported his servant by night from the sacred temple of Mecca to the farther temple of Jerusalem', 'from whence', as Sale observes, 'he was carried through the seven heavens to the presence of God, and brought back again to Mecca the same night'. The commentators dispute whether the journey to heaven was corporeally performed, or merely in a vision. 'But the received opinion is that it was no vision, but that he was actually transported in the body to his journey's end; and if any impossibility be objected, they think it a sufficient answer to say that it might easily be effected by an omnipotent agent.'

66. See Korān, chapter 15. [W. H. S.]

67. The Muhammadans believe that the Christians have tampered with the Scriptures.

68. It would be difficult to give more vivid expression to the eternal conflict between the theological and the scientific spirit. Compare the remarks *ante*, chapter 26, note 11, on the attitude of Hindoos towards modern science.

69. *Paradise Lost*, Book VIII. [W. H. S.] Line 167; from Raphael's address to Adam.

CHAPTER 69

Indian Police—Its Defects—and their Cause and Remedy.

On the 26th[1] we crossed the river Jumna, over a bridge of boats, kept up by the King of Oudh for the use of the public, though his majesty is now connected with Delhi only by the tomb of his ancestor;[2] and his territories are separated from the imperial city by the two great rivers, Ganges and Jumna.

We proceeded to Farrukhnagar, about twelve miles over an execrable road running over a flat but rugged surface of unproductive soil.[3] India is, perhaps, the only civilized country in the world where a great city could be approached by such a road from the largest military Station in the empire,[4] not more than three stages distant. After breakfast the head native police officer of the division came to pay his respects. He talked of the dreadful murders which used to be perpetrated in this neighbourhood by miscreants, who found shelter in the territories of the Bēgam Samrū,[5] whither his followers dared not hunt for them; and mentioned a case of nine persons who had been murdered just within the boundary of our territories about seven years before, and thrown into a dry well. He was present at the inquest held on their bodies, and described their appearance; and I found that they were the bodies of a news writer from Lahore, who, with his eight companions, had been murdered by Thugs on his way back to Rohilkhand. I had long before been made acquainted with the circumstances of this murder and the perpetrators had all been secured, but we wanted this link in the chain of evidence. It had been described to me as having taken place within the boundary of the Bēgam's territory, and I applied to her for a report on the inquest. She declared that no bodies had been discovered about the time mentioned; and I concluded that the ignorance of the people of the neighbourhood was pretended, as usual in such cases, with a view to avoid a summons to give evidence in our courts. I referred forthwith to the magistrate of the district, and found the report that I wanted, and thereby completed the chain of evidence upon a very important case. The Thānadār seemed much surprised to find that I was so well acquainted with the circumstances of this murder, but still more that the perpetrators were not the poor old Bēgam's subjects, but our own.

The police officers employed on our borders find it very convenient to trace the perpetrators of all murders and gang robberies into the territories of native chiefs, whose subjects they accuse often when they know that the crimes have been committed by our own. They are, on the one hand, afraid to seize or accuse the real offenders, lest they should avenge themselves by some personal violence, or by thefts or robberies, which they often commit with a view to get them turned out of office as inefficient; and, on the other, they are tempted to conceal the real offenders by a liberal share of the spoil, and a promise of not offending again within their beat. Their tenure of office is far too insecure, and their salaries are far too small. They are often dismissed summarily by the magistrate if they send him in no prisoners; and also if they send in to him prisoners who are not ultimately convicted, because a magistrate's merits are too often estimated by the proportion that his convictions bear to his acquittals among the prisoners committed for trial to the sessions. Men are often ultimately acquitted for want of judicial proof, when there is abundance of that moral proof on which a police officer or magistrate has to act in the discharge of his duties; and in a country where gangs of professional and hereditary robbers and murderers extend their depredations into very remote parts, and seldom commit them in the districts in which they reside, the most vigilant police officer must often fail to discover the perpetrators of heavy crimes that take place within his range.[6]

When they cannot find them, the native officers either seize innocent persons, and frighten them into confession, or else they try to conceal the crime, and in this they are seconded by the sufferers in the robbery, who will always avoid, if they can, a prosecution in our courts, and by their neighbours, who dread being summoned to give evidence as a serious calamity. The man who has been robbed, instead of being an object of compassion among his neighbours, often incurs their resentment for subjecting them to this calamity; and they not only pay largely themselves, but make him pay largely, to have his losses concealed from the magistrate. Formerly, when a district was visited by a judge of circuit to hold his sessions only once or twice a year, and men were constantly bound over to prosecute and appear as evidence from sessions to sessions, till they were wearied and worried to death, this evil was much greater than at present, when every district is provided with its judge of sessions, who is, or ought to be, always ready to take up the cases committed for trial by the magistrate.[7] This was one of the best measures of Lord W. Bentinck's admirable, though much abused, administration of the government of India.[8] Still, however, the inconvenience and delay of prosecution in our courts are so great, and the chance of the ultimate conviction of great offenders is so small, that strong temptations are held out to the police to conceal or misrepresent the character of crimes; and they must have a great feeling of security in their tenure of office, and more adequate salaries, better chances of rising, and better supervision over them, before they will resist such temptation. These Thānadārs, and all the public officers under them, are all so very inadequately paid that corruption among them excites no feeling of odium or indignation in the minds of those among whom they live and serve. Such feelings are rather directed against the government that places them in such situations of so much labour and responsibility with salaries so inadequate; and thereby confers upon them virtually a licence to pay themselves by preying upon those whom they are employed ostensibly to protect. They know that with such salaries they can never have the reputation of being honest, however faithfully they may discharge their duties; and it is too hard to expect that men will long submit to the necessity of being thought corrupt, without reaping some of the advantages of corruption. Let the Thānadārs have everywhere such salaries as will enable them to maintain their families in comfort, and keep up that appearance of respectability which their station in society demands; and over every three or four Thānadārs' jurisdiction let there be an officer appointed upon a higher scale of salary, to supervise and control their proceedings, and armed with powers to decide minor offences. To these higher stations the Thānadārs will be able to look forward as their reward for a faithful and zealous discharge of their duties.[9]

He who can suppose that men so inadequately paid, who have no promotion to look forward to, and feel no security in their tenure of office, and consequently no hope of a provision for old age,[10] will be zealous and honest in the discharge of their duties, must be very imperfectly acquainted with human nature, and with the motives by which men are influenced in all quarters of the world; but we are none of us so ignorant, for we all know that the same motives actuate public servants in India as elsewhere. We have acted successfully upon this knowledge in the scale of salaries and gradation of rank assigned to European civil functionaries, and to all native functionaries employed in the judicial and revenue branches of the public service; and why not act upon it in that of the salaries assigned to the native officers employed in the police? The magistrate of a district gets a salary of from two thousand to two thousand five hundred rupees a month.[11] The native officer next under him is the Thānadār, or head native police officer of a subdivision of his district, containing many towns and villages, with a population of a hundred thousand souls. This officer gets a salary of twenty-five rupees a month. He cannot possibly do his duty unless he keeps one or two horses; indeed, he is told by the magistrate that he cannot; and that he must have one or two horses, or resign his post. The people, seeing how much we expect from the Thānadār, and how little we give him, submit to his demands for contributions without murmuring, and consider almost any demand trivial from a man so employed and so paid. They are confounded at our inconsistency, and say, 'We see you giving high salaries and high prospects of advancement to men who have nothing to do but collect your rents, and decide our disputes about pounds, shillings, and pence, which we used to decide much better ourselves, when we had no other court but that of our elders—while those who are to protect life and property, to keep peace over the land, and enable the industrious to work in security, maintain their families, and pay the government revenue, are left with hardly any pay at all.'

There is really nothing in our rule in India which strikes the people so much as this inconsistency, the evil effects of which are so great and manifest; the only way to remedy the evil is to give a greater feeling of security in the tenure of office, a higher rate of salary, the hope of a provision for old age, and, above all, the gradation of rank, by interposing the officers I speak of between the Thānadārs and the magistrate.[12] This has all been done in the establishments for the collection of the revenue, and administration of civil justice.

Hobbes, in his *Leviathan*, says, 'And seeing that the end of punishment is not revenge and discharge of choler, but correction, either of the offender, or of others by his example, the severest punishments are to be inflicted for those crimes that are of most danger to the public; such as are those which proceed from malice to the government established; those that spring from contempt of justice; those that provoke indignation in the multitude; and those which, unpunished, seem authorized, as when they are committed by sons, servants, or favourites of men in authority.[13] For indignation carrieth men, not only against the actors and authors of injustice, but against all power that is likely to protect them; as in the case of Tarquin, when, for the insolent act of one of his sons, he was driven out of Rome, and the monarchy itself dissolved.' (Para. 2, chapter 30.) Almost every one of our Thānadārs is, in his way, a little Tarquin, exciting the indignation of the people against his rulers; and no time should be lost in converting him into something better.

By the obstacles which are still everywhere opposed to the conviction of offenders, in the distance of our courts, the forms of procedure, and other causes of 'the law's delay', we render the duties of our police establishment everywhere 'more honoured in the breach than the observance', by the mass of the people among whom they are placed. We must, as I have before said, remove some of these obstacles to the successful prosecution of offenders in our criminal courts, which tend so much to deprive the government of all popular aid and support in the administration of justice; and to convert all our police establishments into instruments of oppression, instead of what they should be, the efficient means of protection to the persons, property, and character of the innocent. Crimes multiply from the assurance the guilty are everywhere apt to feel of impunity to crime; and the more crimes multiply, the greater is the aversion the people everywhere feel to aid the government in the arrest and conviction of criminals, because they see more and more the innocent punished by attendance upon distant courts at great cost and inconvenience, to give evidence upon points which seem to them unimportant, while the guilty escape owing to technical difficulties which they can never understand.[14]

The best way to remove these obstacles is to interpose officers between the Thānadār and the magistrate, and arm them with judicial powers to try minor cases, leaving an appeal open to the magistrate, and to extend the final jurisdiction of the magistrate to a greater range of crimes, though it should involve the necessity of reducing the measure of punishment annexed to them.[15] Beccaria has justly observed that 'Crimes are more effectually prevented by the certainty than by the severity of punishment. The certainty of a small punishment will make a stronger impression than the fear of one more severe, if attended with the hope of escaping; for it is the nature of mankind to be terrified at the approach of the smallest inevitable evil; whilst hope, the best gift of Heaven, has the power of dispelling the apprehensions of a greater, especially if supported by examples of impunity, which weakness or avarice too frequently affords.'

I ought to have mentioned that the police of a district, in our Bengal territories, consists of a magistrate and his assistant, who are European gentlemen of the Civil Service; and a certain number of Thānadārs, from twelve to sixteen, who preside over the different sub-divisions of the district in which they reside with their establishments. These Thānadārs get twenty-five rupees a month, have under them four or five Jemadārs upon eight rupees, and thirty or forty Barkandāzes upon four rupees a month. The Jemadārs are, most of them, placed in charge of 'nākas', or sub-divisions of the Thānadār's jurisdiction, the rest are kept at their headquarters, ready to move to any point where their services may be required. These are all paid by government; but there is in each village one watchman, and in larger villages more than one, who are appointed by the heads of villages, and paid by the communities, and required daily or periodically to report all the police matters of their villages to the Thānadārs.[16]

The distance between the magistrates and Thānadārs is at present immeasurable; and an infinite deal of mischief is done by the latter and those under them, of which the magistrates know nothing whatever. In the first place, they levy a fee of one rupee from every village at the festival of the Holī in February, and another at that of the Dasehra in October, and in each Thānadār's jurisdiction there are from one to two hundred villages. These and numerous other unauthorized exactions they share with those under them, and with the native officers about the person of the magistrate, who, if not conciliated, can always manage to make them appear unfit for their places.[17]

A robbery affords a rich harvest. Some article of stolen property is found in one man's house, and by a little legerdemain it is conveyed to that of another, both of whom are made to pay liberally; the man robbed also pays, and all the members of the village community are made to do the same. They are all called to the court of the Thānadār to give evidence as to what they have seen or heard regarding either the fact or the persons in the remotest degree connected with it—as to the arrests of the supposed offenders—the search of their house—the character of their grandmothers and grandfathers—and they are told that they are to be sent to the magistrate a hundred miles distant, and then made to stand at the door among a hundred and fifty pairs of shoes, till *his excellency* the Nāzir, the under-sheriff of the court, may be pleased to announce them to his highness the magistrate, which, of course, he will not do without a *consideration*. To escape all these threatened evils, they pay handsomely and depart in peace. The Thānadār reports that an attempt to rob a house by persons unknown had been defeated by his exertions, and the *good fortune* of the magistrate; and sends a liberal share of spoil to those who are to read his report to that functionary.[18] This goes on more or less in every district, but more especially in those where the magistrate happens to be a man of violent temper, who is always surrounded by knaves, because men who have any regard for their character will not approach him—or a weak, good-natured man, easily made to believe anything, and managed by favourites—or one too fond of field- sports, or of music, painting, European languages, literature, and sciences, or lastly, of his own ease.[19] Some magistrates think they can put down crime by dismissing the Thānadār; but this tends only to prevent crimes being reported to him; for in such cases the feelings of the people are in exact accordance with the interests of the Thānadārs; and crimes augment by the assurance of impunity thereby given to criminals. The only remedy for all this evil is to fill up the great gulf between the magistrate and Thānadār by officers who shall be to him what I have described the patrol officers to be to the collectors of customs, at once the *tapis* of Prince Husain, and the *telescope* of Prince Ali—a medium that will enable him to be everywhere, and see everything.[20] And why is this remedy not applied? Simply and solely because such appointments would be given to the uncovenanted, and might tend indirectly to diminish the appointments open to the covenanted servants of the company. Young gentlemen of the Civil Service are supposed to be doing the duties which would be assigned to such officers, while they are at school as assistants to magistrates and collectors; and were this great gulf filled up by efficient covenanted officers, they would have no school to go to. There is no doubt some truth in this; but the welfare of a whole people should not be sacrificed to keep this school or play-ground open exclusively for them; let them act for a time as they would unwillingly do with the uncovenanted, and they will learn much more than if they occupied the ground exclusively and acted alone — they will be always with people ready and willing to tell them the real state of things; whereas, at present, they are always with those who studiously conceal it from them.[21]

It is a common practice with Thānadārs all over the country to connive at the residence within their jurisdiction of gangs of robbers, on the condition that they shall not rob within those limits, and shall give them a share of what they bring back from their distant expeditions.

They [*scil.* the gangs] go out ostensibly in search of service, on the termination of the rains of one season in October, and return before the commencement of the next in June; but their vocation is always well known to the police, and to all the people of their neighbourhood, and very often to the magistrates themselves, who could, if they would, secure them on their return with their booty; but this would not secure their conviction unless the proprietors could be discovered, which they scarcely ever could. Were the police officers to seize them, they would be all finally acquitted and released by the judges — the magistrate would get into disrepute with his superiors, by the number of acquittals compared with convictions exhibited in his monthly tables; and he would vent his spleen upon the poor Thānadār, who would at the same time have incurred the resentment of the robbers; and between both, he would have no possible chance of escape. He therefore consults his own interest and his own case by leaving them to carry on their trade of robbery or murder unmolested; and his master, the magistrate, is well pleased not to be pestered with charges against men whom he has no chance of getting ultimately convicted. It was in this way that so many hundred families of assassins by profession were able for so many generations to reside in the most cultivated and populous parts of our territories, and extend their depredations into the remotest parts of India, before our System of operations was brought to bear upon them in 1830. Their profession was perfectly well known to the people of the districts in which they resided, and to the greater part of the police; they murdered not within their own district, and the police of that district cared nothing about what they might do beyond it.[22]

The most respectable native gentleman in the city and district told me one day an amusing instance of the proceedings of a native officer of that district, which occurred about five years ago. 'In a village which he had purchased and let in farms, a shopkeeper was one day superintending the cutting of some sugar-cane which he had purchased from a cultivator as it stood. His name was Girdhārī, I think, and the boy who was cutting it for him was the son of a poor man called Madārī. Girdhārī wanted to have the cane cut down as near as he could to the ground, while the boy, to save himself the trouble of stooping, would persist in cutting it a good deal too high up. After admonishing him several times, the shopkeeper gave him a smart clout on the head. The boy, to prevent a repetition, called out, "Murder! Girdhārī has killed me—Girdhārī has killed me!" His old father, who was at work carrying away the cane at a little distance out of sight, ran off to the village watchman, and, in his anger, told him that Girdhārī had murdered his son. The watchman went as fast as he could to the Thānadār, or head police officer of the division, who resided some miles distant. The Thānadār ordered off his subordinate officer, the Jemadār, with half a dozen policemen, to arrange everything for an inquest on the body, by the time he should reach the place, with all due pomp. The Jemadār went to the house of the murderer, and dismounting, ordered all the shopkeepers of the village, who were many and respectable, to be forthwith seized, and bound hand and feet. "So", said the Jemadār, "you have all been aiding and abetting your friend in the murder of poor Madārī's only son." "May it please your excellency, we have never heard of any murder." "Impudent scoundrels," roared the Jemadār, "does not the poor boy lie dead in the sugar-cane field, and is not his highness the Thānadar coming to hold an inquest upon it? and do you take us for fools enough to believe that any scoundrel among you would venture to commit a deliberate murder without being aided and abetted by all the rest?" The village watchman began to feel some apprehension that he had been too precipitate; and entreated the Jemadār to go first and see the body of the boy. "What do you take us for," said the Jemadār, "a thing without a stomach? Do you suppose that government servants can live and labour on air? Are we to go and examine bodies upon empty stomachs? Let his father take care of the body, and let these murdering shopkeepers provide us something to eat." Nine rupees' worth of sweetmeats, and materials for a feast were forthwith collected at the expense of the shopkeepers, who stood bound, and waiting the arrival of his highness the Thānadār, who was soon after seen approaching majestically upon a richly caparisoned horse. "What," said the Jemadār, "is there nobody to go and receive his highness in due form?" One of the shopkeepers was untied, and presented with fifteen rupees by his family, and those of the other shopkeepers. These he took up and presented to his highness, who deigned to receive them through one of his train, and then dismounted and partook of the feast that had been provided. "Now", said his highness, "we will go and hold an inquest on the body of the poor boy"; and off moved all the great functionaries of government to the sugar-cane field, with the village watchman leading the way. The father of the boy met them as they entered, and was pointed out by the village watchman. "Where", said the Thānadār, "is your poor boy?" "There," said Madārī, "cutting the canes." "How, cutting the canes? Was he not murdered by the shopkeepers?" "No," said Madārī, "he was beaten by Girdhārī, and richly deserved it! I find." Girdhārī and the boy were called up, and the little urchin said that he called out murder merely to prevent Girdhārī from giving him another clout on the side of the head. His father was then fined nine rupees for giving a false alarm, and Girdhārī fifteen for so unmercifully beating the boy; and they were made to pay on the instant, under the penalty of all being sent off forty miles to the magistrate. Having thus settled this very important affair, his highness the Thānadār walked back to the shop, ordered all the shopkeepers to be set at liberty, smoked his pipe, mounted his horse, and rode home, followed by all his police officers, and well pleased with his day's work.'

The farmer of the village soon after made his way to the city, and communicated the circumstances to my old friend, who happened to be on intimate terms with the magistrate.[23] He wrote a polite note to the Thānadār to say that he should never get any rents from his estate if the occupants were liable to such fines as these, and that he should take the earliest opportunity of mentioning them to his friend the magistrate. The Thānadār ascertained that he was really in the habit of visiting the magistrate, and communicating with him freely; and hushed up the matter by causing all, save the expenses of the feast, to be paid back. These are things of daily occurrence in all parts of our dominions, and the Thānadārs are not afraid to play such 'fantastic tricks' because all those under and all those above them share more or less in the spoil, and are bound in honour to conceal them from the European magistrate, whom it is the interest of all to keep in the dark. They know that the people will hardly ever complain, from the great dislike they all have to appear in our courts, particularly when it is against any of the officers of those courts, or their friends and creatures in the district police.[24]

When our operations commenced, in 1830, these assassins [*scil.* the Thugs] revelled over every road in India in gangs of hundreds, without the fear of punishment from divine or human laws; but there is not now, I believe, a road in India infested by them. That our government has still defects, and great ones, must be obvious to every one who has travelled much over India with the requisite qualifications and disposition to observe; but I believe that in spite of all the defects I have noticed above in our police System, the life, property, and character of the innocent are now more secure, and all their advantages more freely enjoyed, than they ever were under any former government with whose history we are acquainted, or than they now are under any native government in India.[25]

Those who think they are not so almost always refer to the reign of Shāh Jahān, when men like Tavernier travelled so securely all over India with their bags of diamonds; but I would ask them whether they think that the life, property, and character of the innocent could be anywhere very secure, or their advantages very freely enjoyed, in a country where a man could do openly with impunity what the traveller describes to have been done by the Persian physician of the Governor of Allahabad? This governor, being sickly, had in attendance upon him *eleven physicians*, one of whom was a European gentleman of education, Claudius Maille, of Bourges.[26] The chief favourite of the eleven was, however, a Persian, 'who one day threw his wife from the top of a battlement to the ground in a fit of jealousy. He thought the fall would kill her, but she had only a few ribs broken; whereupon the kindred of the woman came and demanded justice at the feet of the governor. The governor, sending for the physician, commanded him to be gone, resolving to retain him no longer in his service. The physician obeyed; and putting his poor maimed wife in a palankeen, he set forward upon the road with all his family. But he had not gone above three or four days' journey from the city, when the governor, finding himself worse than he was wont to be, sent to recall him; which the physician perceiving, stabbed his wife, his four children, and thirteen female slaves, and returned again to the Governor, who said not a word to him, but entertained him again in his service.' This occurred within Tavernier's own knowledge and about the time he visited Allahabad; and is related as by no means a very extraordinary circumstance.[27]

Notes:

1. January, 1836.

2. The tomb of Safdar Jang, or Mansūr Alī Khān, described *ante*, chapter 68 [4]. The bridges over the Jumna are now, of course, maintained by Government and the railway companies.

3. The main highways approaching Delhi are now excellent metalled roads.

4. By the term 'the largest military station in the empire', the author means Meerut. At present the largest military station in Northern India is, I believe, Rāwal Pindi, and the combined cantonments of Secunderābād and Bolarum in the Nizam's dominions constitute the largest military station in the empire.

5. Comprising parts of the Meerut and Muzaffarnagar districts of the North-Western Provinces, now the Agra Province in the United Provinces of Agra and Oudh. The Bēgam's history will be discussed in chapter 75, *post*.

6. The members of the reformed police force, constituted under Act V of 1861, generally on the model of the Royal Irish Constabulary, have no reason to complain of insecurity of tenure. It is now very difficult to obtain sanction to the dismissal of a corrupt or inefficient officer, unless he has been judicially convicted of a statutory offence.

7. Ordinarily there is for each district, or administrative unit, a separate Sessions and District Judge, who tries both civil and criminal cases of the more serious kind. Occasionally two or three districts have only one judge between them, who is then usually in arrear with his work. Sessions for the trial of grave criminal cases are held monthly, bimonthly, or quarterly, according to circumstances. In some districts, and for some classes of cases, the jury system has been introduced, but, as a rule, in Northern India the responsibility rests with the judge alone, who receives some slight aid from assessors. Capital sentences passed by a Sessions Judge must be confirmed by two Judges of a High Court, or equivalent tribunal.

8. The historian Thornton (chapter 27) went so far as to declare that Lord William Bentinck has 'done less for the interest of India, and for his own reputation, than any who had occupied his place since the commencement of the nineteenth century, with the single exception of Sir George Barlow'. The abolition of widow-burning is the only act of the Bentinck administration which this writer could praise. Such a criticism is

manifestly unjust, the outcome of contemporary anger and prejudice. The inscription written by Macaulay, the friend and coadjutor of Lord William, and placed on the statue of the reforming Governor-General in Calcutta, does not give undeserved praise to the much abused statesman. Sir William Sleeman so much admired Lord William Bentinck, and formed such a favourable estimate of the merits of his government, that it may be well to support his opinion by that of Macaulay. The text of the inscription is:

TO

WILLIAM CAVENDISH BENTINCK,

who during seven years ruled India with eminent prudence,
    integrity, and benevolence;
who, placed at the head of a great Empire, never laid aside
the simplicity and moderation of a private citizen;
who infused into Oriental despotism the spirit
    of British freedom;
who never forgot that the end of Government is the happiness
    of the governed;
who abolished cruel rites;
    who effaced humiliating distinctions;
who gave liberty to the expression of public opinion;
whose constant study it was to elevate the intellectual and
moral character of the nation committed to his charge,

THIS MONUMENT

was erected by men
who, differing in race, in manners, in language and in religion,
    cherish with equal veneration and gratitude
the memory of his wise, reforming,
and paternal administration.

(*Lord William Bentinck*, by D. Boulger, p. 203; 'Rulers of India' series.)

9. A European District Superintendent of Police, under the general supervision of the Magistrate of the District, now commands the police of each district, and sometimes has one or two European Assistants. He is also aided by well-paid Inspectors, who are for the most part natives of India. Measures have recently been taken, especially in the United Provinces, to

improve the pay, training, and position of the police force, European and Indian.

10. Police officers and men now obtain pensions, like public servants in other departments.

11. In some provinces the highest salaries of magistrates are much lower than the rates stated by the author, which are the highest paid to the most senior officers in certain provinces; and, in all provinces, officiating incumbents, who form a large proportion of the officers employed, draw only a part of the full salary. The fall in exchange has enormously reduced the real value of all Indian salaries.

12. Another popular view of this subject, and, I think, the one more commonly taken, is expressed in the anecdote told *ante*, chapter 58 following [10]. Well-paid Inspectors of Police, drawing salaries of 150 to 200 rupees a month, are often extremely corrupt, and retire with large fortunes, I knew many cases, but could never obtain judicial proof of one.

13. When 'sons, servants, or favourites of men in authority', in India, no longer oppress their fellows, the millennium will have arrived.

14. It is some slight satisfaction to a zealous magistrate of the present day, when he sees a great and influential criminal escape his just doom, to think that even the best magistrates many years ago had to submit to similar painful experiences. India cannot truly be described as an uncivilized or barbarous country, but, side by side with elements of the highest civilization, it contains many elements of primitive and savage barbarism. The savagery of India cannot be dealt with by barristers or moral text-books.

15. The number of subordinate magistrates, paid and unpaid, has of late years been enormously increased, and courts are, consequently, much more numerous than they used to be. The vast increase in facility of communication has also diminished the inconveniences which the author deplores. In Oudh, and certain other provinces, which used to be called Non-Regulation, the chief Magistrate of the District has power to try and adequately punish all offences, except capital ones. The power is useful, when the district officer has time to exercise it, which is not always the case.

16. There is a Superintendent of Police for the Province of Bengal; but in the North-Western Provinces his duties are divided among the Commissioners of Revenue. [W. H. S.] By 'Superintendent of Police' the author means the high officer now called the Inspector- General of Police, under the present System each Local Government or Administration has one of these officers, who is aided by one or more staff officers as Assistant-Inspectors-General. The Commissioners in the United Provinces have been relieved of police duties. The organization of police stations has been much

modified since the author's time. 'Our Bengal territories', as understood by the author, included, in addition to Bengal, the 'North-Western Provinces', now the Province, of Agra, the Saugor and Nerbudda Territories, now in the Central Provinces, and the Delhi Territories. Oudh, of course, was then independent; and the Panjāb was under the rule of Ranjit Singh.

17. All these practices are still carried on; and experienced magistrates are well aware of their existence, though powerless to stop them. People will often give private information of malpractices, but will hardly ever come into court, and speak out openly. A magistrate cannot take action on statements which the makers will not submit to cross-examination.

18. This is still a favourite trick. Every year Inspectors- General of Police and Secretaries to Government make the same sarcastic remarks about the wonderful number of 'attempts at burglary', and the apparent contentment of the criminal classes with the small results of their labours. But the Thānadār is too much for even Inspectors-General and Secretaries to Government. No amount of reorganization changes him.

19. Mr. R., when appointed magistrate of the district of Fathpur on the Ganges, had a wish to translate the 'Henriade', and, in order to secure leisure, he issued a proclamation to all the Thānadārs of his district to put down crime, declaring that he would hold them responsible for what might be committed, and dismiss from his situation every one who should suffer any to be committed within his charge. This district, lying on the borders of Oudh, had been noted for the number and atrocious character of its crimes. From that day all the periodical returns went up to the superior court blank — not a crime was reported. Astonished at this sudden result of the change of magistrates, the superior court of Calcutta (the Sadr Nizāmat Adālat) requested one of the judges, who was about to pass through the district on his way down, to inquire into the nature of the System which seemed to work so well, with a view to its adoption in other districts. He found crimes were more abundant than ever; and the Thānadārs showed him the proclamation, which had been understood, as all such proclamations are, not as enjoining vigilance in the prosecution of crime, but as prohibiting all report of them, so as to *save the magistrate trouble*, and get him a good name with his superiors. [W. H. S.]

Great caution should always be used by local officers in making comments on statistics. The subordinate cares nothing for the facts. When a superior objects that the birth-rate is too low and the death- rate too high in any police circle, the practical conclusion drawn by the police is that the figures of the next return must be made more palatable, and they are cooked accordingly. So, if burglaries are too numerous, they cease to be reported, and so forth.

The old Superior Court was known as the Sadr Nizāmat Adālat, on the criminal, and as the Sadr Dīwānī Adālat, on the civil side. These courts have now been replaced by the High Courts, and equivalent tribunals. In the author's time the High Court for the Agra Province had not yet been established. Its seat is now at Allahabad, but was formerly at Agra.

20. The gap has been filled up by numbers of Deputy Magistrates, Tahsīldār, &c., invested with magisterial powers, Honorary Magistrates, District Superintendents, and Inspectors, and yet all the old games still go on merrily. The reason is that the character of the people has not changed. The police must have the power to arrest, and that power, when wielded by unscrupulous hands, must always be formidable.

21. A magistrate who can find in his district even one man, official or unofficial, who will tell him 'the real state of things', and not merely repeat scandal and malignant gossip, is unusually fortunate.

22. The Thugs were suppressed because a special organization was devised and directed for the purpose, the English rules as to the admissibility of evidence being judiciously relaxed. The ordinary law and methods of procedure are of little effect against the secret societies known as 'criminal tribes'. These criminal tribes number hundreds of thousands of persona, and present a problem almost unknown to European experience. The gipsies, who are largely of Indian origin, are, perhaps, the only European example of an hereditary criminal tribe. But they are not sheltered and abetted by the landowners as their brethren in India are.

23. The magistrate, of course, was the author.

24. These motives all retain their full force, and are unaffected by Police Commissions and reorganization schemes. Some people think that the character of the police will be raised by the employment as officers of young Indians of good family. I am sorry to say that I found these young men to be the worst offenders. They are more daring in their misdeeds than the ordinary policeman, and no better in their morals.

25. This is quite true; and it is also true that our police administration is the weakest part of our System. But the fault is not entirely that of the police. In some provinces, especially in Bengal, the action of the High Courts has almost paralysed the arm of the Executive.

26. 'M. Claude Maille, of Bourges. As we shall see in Book I, chapter 18, a man of this name, who had escaped from the Dutch service, was, in the year 1652, a not very successful amateur gun- founder for Mīr Jumla; he had, after his escape, set up as a surgeon to the Nawāb, with an equipment consisting of a case of instruments and a box of ointments which he had stolen from M. Cheteur, the Dutch Ambassador to Golconda. Tavernier

throws no light upon his identity with this physician.' (Tavernier, *Travels*, ed. Ball, vol. i, p. 116, note). M. Maille befriended Manucci, who mentions him several times (Irvine, *Storia do Mogor*, i, 92, &c.)

27. Ball's version of this horrible story (vol. i, p. 117) does not differ materially from that quoted in the text. Tavernier does not mention the name of the governor, though he observes that he was 'one of the greatest nobles in India'. Tavernier visited Allahabad in December, 1665, and then heard the story, the governor concerned being at the time in the fort. I have no doubt that in the reign of Shāh Jahān ordinary offences committed by ordinary criminals were ruthlessly punished, and to some extent suppressed. But, under the best Asiatic Governments, great men and their dependants have usually been able to do pretty much what they pleased. The English Government has the merit of refusing to give formal recognition to difference of rank in criminals, and of often trying to punish influential offenders, though seldom succeeding in the attempt. From time to time a conspicuous example, like that of the Nawāb Shams-ud-dīn, is made, and a few such examples, combined with the greater vigilance and more complete organization of the English executive, prevent the occurrence of atrocities so great as that described, without a word of comment, by the French traveller. I have not the slightest doubt, nor has any magistrate of long experience any doubt, that women are frequently made away with quietly in the recesses of the 'zanāna'. I have known several such cases, which were notorious, though incapable of judicial proof. The amount of serious secret crime which occurs in India, and never comes to light, is very considerable.

CHAPTER 70

Rent-free Tenures — Right of Government to Resume such Grants.

ON the 27th[1] we went on fifteen miles to Bēgamābād, over a sandy and level country. All the peasantry along the roads were busy watering their fields; and the singing of the man who stood at the well to tell the other who guides the bullocks when to pull, after the leather bucket had been filled at the bottom, and when to stop as it reached the top, was extremely pleasing.[2] It is said that Tānsēn of Delhi, the most celebrated singer they have ever had in India, used to spend a great part of his time in these fields, listening to the simple melodies of these water-drawers, which he learned to imitate and apply to his more finished vocal music. Popular belief ascribes to Tānsēn the power of stopping the river Jumna in its course. His contemporary and rival, Birjū Baulā, who, according to popular belief, could split a rock with a single note, is said to have learned his bass from the noise of the stone mills which the women use in grinding the corn for their families.[3] Tānsēn was a Brahman from Patna, who entered the service of the Emperor Akbar, became a Musalmān, and after the service of twenty-seven years, during which he was much beloved by the Emperor and all his court, he died at Gwālior in the thirty-fourth year of the Emperor's reign. His tomb is still to be seen at Gwālior. All his descendants are said to have a talent for music, and they have all Sēn added to their names.[4]

While Mādhojī Sindhia, the Gwālior chief, was prime minister, he made the emperor assign to his daughter the Bālā Bāī in jāgīr, or rent- free tenure, ninety-five villages, rated in the imperial 'sanads' [deeds of grant] at three lākhs of rupees a year. When the Emperor had been released from the 'durance vile' in which he was kept by Daulat Rāo Sindhia, the adopted son of this chief,[5] by Lord Lake in 1803, and the countries, in which these villages were situated, taken possession of, she was permitted to retain them on condition that they were to escheat to us on her death. She died in 1834, and we took possession of the villages, which now yield, it is said, four lākhs of rupees a year. Bēgamābād was one of them. It paid to the Bālā Bāī only six hundred rupees a year, but it pays now to us six hundred and twenty rupees; but the farmers and cultivators do not pay a farthing more — the difference was taken by the favourite to whom she assigned the duties of collection, and who always took as much as he could get from them, and paid as little as he could to her.[6] The tomb of the old collector stood near my tents, and his son, who came to visit it, told me that he had heard from Gwālior that a new Governor-General was about to arrive,[7] who would probably order the villages to be given back, when he should be made collector of the village, as his father had been.

Had our Government acted by all the rent-free lands in our territories on the same principle, they would have saved themselves a vast deal of expense, trouble, and odium. The justice of declaring all lands liable to resumption on the death of the present incumbents when not given by competent authority for, and actually applied to, the maintenance of religious, charitable, educational, or other establishments of manifest public utility, would never have been for a moment questioned by the people of India, because they would have all known that it was in accordance with the customs of the country. If, at the same time that we declared all land liable to resumption, when not assigned by such authority for such purposes and actually applied to them, we had declared that all grants by competent authority registered in due form before the death of the present incumbents should be liable on their death to the payment to Government of only a quarter or half the rent arising from them, it would have been universally hailed as an act of great liberality, highly calculated to make our reign popular. As it is, we have admitted the right of former rulers of all descriptions to alienate in perpetuity the land, the principal source of the revenue of the state, in favour of their relatives, friends, and favourites, leaving upon the holders the burthen of proving, at a ruinous cost in fees and bribes, through court after court, that these alienations had been made by the authorities we declare competent, before the time prescribed; and we have thus given rise to an infinite deal of fraud, perjury, and forgery, and to the opinion, I fear, very generally prevalent, that we are anxious to take advantage of unavoidable flaws in the proof required, to trick them out of their lands by tedious judicial proceedings, while we profess to be desirous that they should retain them. In this we have done ourselves great injustice. [8]

Though these lands were often held for many generations under former Governments, and for the exclusive benefit of the holders, it was almost always, when they were of any value, in collusion with the local authorities, who concealed the circumstances from their sovereign for a certain stipulated sum or share of the rents while they held office. This of course the holders were always willing to pay, knowing that no sovereign would hesitate much to resume their lands, should the circumstance of their holding them for their private use alone be ever brought to his notice.

The local authorities were, no doubt, always willing to take a moderate share of the rent, knowing that they would get nothing should the lands be resumed by the sovereign. Sometimes the lands granted were either at the time the grant was made, or became soon after, waste and depopulated, in consequence of invasion or internal disorders; and remaining in this state for many generations, the intervening sovereigns either knew nothing or cared nothing about the grants. Under our rule they became by degrees again cultivated and peopled, and in consequence valuable, not by the exertions of the rent-free holders, for they were seldom known to do anything but collect the rents, but by those of the farmers and cultivators who pay them.

When Saādat Alī Khan, the sovereign of Oudh, ceded Rohilkhand and other districts to the Honourable Company in lieu of tribute in 1801, he resumed every inch of land held in rent-free tenure within the territories that remained with him, without condescending to assign any other reason than state necessity. The measure created a good deal of distress, particularly among the educated classes; but not so much as a similar measure would have created within our territories, because all his revenues are expended in the maintenance of establishments formed exclusively out of the members of Oudh families, and retained within the country, while ours are sent to pay establishments formed and maintained at a distance; and those whose lands are resumed always find it exceedingly difficult to get employment suitable to their condition.

The face of the country between Delhi and Meerut is sadly denuded of its groves; not a grove or an avenue is to be seen anywhere, and but few fine solitary trees.[9] I asked the people of the cause, and was told by the old men of the village that they remembered well when the Sikh chiefs who now bask under the sunshine of our protection used to come over at the head of 'dalas' (bodies) of ten or twelve horse each, and plunder and lay waste with fire and sword, at every returning harvest, the fine country which I now saw covered with rich sheets of cultivation, and which they had rendered a desolate waste, 'without a man to make, or a man to grant, a petition', when Lord Lake came among them.[10] They were, they say, looking on at a distance when he fought the battle of Delhi, and drove the Marāthās, who were almost as bad as the Sikhs, into the Jumna river, where ten thousand of them were drowned. The people of all classes in Upper India feel the same reverence as our native soldiery for the name of this admirable soldier and most worthy man, who did so much to promote our interests and sustain our reputation in this country.[11]

The most beautiful trees in India are the 'bar' (banyan), the 'pīpal', and the tamarind.[12] The two first are of the fig tribe, and their greatest enemies are the elephants and camels of our public establishments and public servants, who prey upon them wherever they can find them when under the protection of their masters or keepers, who, when appealed to, generally evince a very philosophical disregard to the feeling of either property or piety involved in the trespass. It is consequently in the driest and hottest parts of the country, where the shade of these trees is most wanted, that it is least to be found; because it is there that camels thrive best, and are most kept, and it is most difficult to save such trees from their depredations.

In the evening a trooper passed our tents on his way in great haste from Meerut to Delhi, to announce the death of the poor old Bēgam Samrū, which had taken place the day before at her little capital of Sardhana. For five-and-twenty years had I been looking forward to the opportunity of seeing this very extraordinary woman, whose history had interested me more than that of any other character in India during my time; and I was sadly disappointed to hear of her death when within two or three stages of her capital.[13]

Notes:

1. January, 1836.

2. Mr. Fox Strangways gives specimens of songs sung at wells in his learned and original book, *The Music of Hindostan* (Oxford, 1914, pp. 20, 21).

3. Brij Bowla in the original edition. The name is correctly written Birjū Baulā or Baurā. A legend of the rivalry between him and Tānsēn is given in *Linguistic Survey of India*, vi, 47. His name is not included in Abūl Fazl's list of eminent musicians, or in Blochmann's notes to it (Āīn trans. i, 612), and I have not succeeded in obtaining any trustworthy information about him. Marvellous legends of the rival singers will be found in *N.I.N. & Qu.* vol. v, para. 207.

4. Abūl Fazl describes Tānsēn as being of Gwālior, adding that 'a singer like him has not been in India for the last thousand years'. Nos. 2-5 and several others in Abūl Fazl's list of eminent musicians in Akbar's reign are all noted as belonging to Gwālior, which evidently was the most musical of cities (Blochmann, transl. Āīn, i, 612). Sleeman appears to have been mistaken in connecting Tānsēn with Patna. But the musician must really have become a Musalmān, because his tomb stands close to the south- western corner of the sepulchre at Gwālior of Muhammad Ghaus, an eminent Muslim saint. No Hindu could have been buried in such a spot (*A.S.R.*, vol. ii, p. 370). According to one account Tānsēn died in Lahore, his body being removed to Gwālior by order of Akbar (Forbes, *Oriental Memoirs*, London, 1813, vol. iii, p. 32). The leaves of the tamarind-tree overshadowing the tomb are believed to improve the voice marvellously when chewed.

Mr. Fox Strangways notes that Hindu critics hold Tānsēn 'principally responsible for the deterioration of Hindu music. He is said to have falsified the rāgs, and two, Hindol and Megh, of the original six have disappeared since his time' (op. cit., p. 84).

Akbar, in the seventh year of his reign (1562-3), compelled the Rājā of Rīwā (Bhath) to give up Tānsēn, who was in the Rājā's service. The emperor gave the musician Rs. 200,000. 'Most of his compositions are written in Akbar's name, and his melodies are even nowadays everywhere repeated by the people of Hindustān' (Blochmann, op. cit., p. 406). Tānsēn died in A.D. 1588 (Beale).

5. Shāh Alam is the sovereign alluded to. Māhādajī (Mādhojī or Mādhava Rāo) Sindhia died in February, 1794. His successor, Daulat Rāo, was then a boy of fourteen or fifteen (Grant Duff, *History of the Mahrattas*, ed. 1826, vol. iii, p. 86). The formal adoption of Daulat Rāo had not been completed (ibid., p. 91).

6. This observation is a good illustration of the tendency of administrators in a country so poor as India to take note of the infinitely little. In Europe no one would take the trouble to notice the difference between £60 and £62 rental.

7. Lord Auckland, in March, 1836, relieved Sir Charles Metcalfe, who, as temporary Governor-General, had succeeded Lord William Bentinck.

8. The resumption, that is to say, assessment, of revenue-free lands was a burning question in the anthor's day. It has long since got settled. The author was quite right in his opinion. All native Governments freely exercised the right of resumption, and did not care in the least what phrases were used in the deed of grant. The old Hindoo deeds commonly directed that the grant should last 'as long as the sun and moon shall endure', and invoked awful curses on the head of the resumer. But this was only formal legal phraseology, meaning nothing. No ruler was bound by his predecessor's acts.

9. This is not now the case.

10. 'It is difficult to realize that the dignified, sober, and orderly men who now fill our regiments are of the same stock as the savage freebooters whose name, a hundred years ago, was the terror of Northern India. But the change has been wrought by strong and kindly government and by strict military discipline under sympathetic officers whom the troops love and respect.' (Sir Lepel Griffin, *Ranjīt Singh*, p. 37.)

11. Gerard Lake was born on the 27th July, 1744, and entered the army before he was fourteen. He served in the Seven Years' War in Germany, in the American War, in the French campaign of 1793, and against the Irish rebels in 1798. In the year 1801 he became Commander-in-Chief in India, and proceeded to Cawnpore, then our frontier station. Two years later the second Marāthā War began, and gave General Lake the opportunity of winning a series of brilliant victories. In rapid succession he defeated the enemy at Kōil, Alīgarh, Delhi (the battle alluded to in the text), Agra, and Laswārī. Next year, 1804, the glorious record was marred by the disaster to Colonel Monson's force, but this was quickly avenged by the decisive victories of Dīg and Farrukhābād, which shattered Holkār's power. The year 1805 saw General Lake's one personal failure, the unsuccessful siege of Bharatpur. The Commander-in-Chief then resumed the pursuit of Holkār, and forced him to surrender. He sailed for England in February, 1807, and on his arrival at home was created a Viscount. On the 21st February, 1808, he died. (Pearse, *Memoir of the Life and Military Services of Viscount Lake.* London, Blackwood, 1908.) The village of Patparganj, nearly due east from Humāyūn's Tomb, marks the site of the battle. Fanshawe (p. 70) gives a plan.

12. The banyan is the *Ficus indica,* or *Urostigma bengalense;* the 'pīpal' is *Ficus religiosa,* or *Urostigma religiosum;* and the tamarind is the *Tamarindus indica,* or *occidentalis,* or *officinalis.*

13. The history of the Bēgam is given in Chapter 76, *post.*

CHAPTER 71

The Station of Meerut—'Atālīs' who Dance and Sing gratuitously for the Benefit of the Poor.

On the 30th,[1] we went on twelve miles to Meerut, and encamped close to the Sūraj Kund, so called after Sūraj-mal, the Jāt chief of Dīg, whose tomb I have described at Govardhan.[2] He built here a very large tank, at the recommendation of the spirit of a Hindoo saint, Manohar Nāth, whose remains had been burned here more than two hundred years before, and whose spirit appeared to the Jāt chief in a dream, as he was encamped here with his army during one of his *kingdom-taking* expeditions. This is a noble work, with a fine sheet of water, and flights of steps of 'pakkā' masonry from the top to its edge all round. The whole is kept in repair by our Government. [3] About half a mile to the north-west of the tank stands the tomb of Shāh Pīr, a Muhammadan saint, who is said to have descended from the mountains with the Hindoo, and to have been his bosom friend up to the day of his death. Both are said to have worked many wonderful miracles among the people of the surrounding country, who used to see them, according to popular belief, quietly taking their morning ride together upon the backs of two enormous tigers who came every morning at the appointed hour from the distant jungle. The Hindoo is said to have been very fond of music; and though he has been now dead some three centuries, a crowd of amateurs (atālīs) assemble every Sunday afternoon at his shrine, on the bank of the tank, and sing gratis, and in a very pleasing style, to an immense concourse of people, who assemble to hear them, and to solicit the spirit of the old saint, softened by their melodies. At the tomb of the Muhammadan saint a number of professional dancers and singers assemble every Thursday afternoon, and dance, sing, and play gratis to a large concourse of people, who make offerings of food to the poor, and implore the intercession of the old man with the Deity in return.

The Muhammadan's tomb is large and handsome, and built of red sandstone, inlaid with marble, but without any cupola, that there may be no *curtain* between him and heaven when he gets out of his 'last long sleep' at the resurrection.[4] Not far from his tomb is another, over the bones of a pilgrim they call Ganj-i-fann, or the granary of science. Professional singers and dancers attend it every Friday afternoon, and display their talents gratis to a large concourse, who bestow what they can in charity to the poor, who assemble on all these occasions to take what they can get. Another much frequented tomb lies over a Muhammadan saint, who has not been dead more than three years, named Gohar Sāh. He owes his canonization to a few circumstances of recent occurrence, which are, however, universally believed. Mr. Smith, an enterprising merchant of Meerut, who had raised a large windmill for grinding corn in the Sadr Bāzār, is said to have abused the old man as he was one day passing by, and looked with some contempt on his method of grinding, which was to take the bread from the mouths of so many old widows. 'My child,' said the old saint, 'amuse thyself with this toy of thine, for it has but a few days to run.' In four days from that time the machine stopped. Poor Mr. Smith could not afford to set it going again, and it went to ruin. The whole native population of Meerut considered this a miracle of Gohar Sāh. Just before his death the country round Meerut was under water, and a great many houses fell from incessant rain. The old man took up his residence during this time in a large sarāi in the town, but finding his end approach, he desired those who had taken shelter with him to have him taken to the jungle where he now reposes. They did so, and the instant they left the building it fell to the ground. Many who saw it told me they had no doubt that the virtues of the old man had sustained it while he was there, and prevented its crushing all who were in it. The tomb was built over his remains by a Hindoo officer of the court, who had been long out of employment and in great affliction. He had no sooner completed the tomb, and implored the aid of the old man, than he got into excellent service, and has been ever since a happy man. He makes regular offerings to his shrine, as a grateful return for the saint's kindness to him in his hour of need. Professional singers and dancers display their talents here gratis, as at the other tombs, every Wednesday afternoon.

The ground all round these tombs is becoming crowded with the graves of people, who in their last moments request to be buried (zēr-sāya) under the shadow of these saints, who in their lifetime are all said to have despised the pomps and vanities of this life, and to have taken nothing from their disciples and worshippers but what was indispensably necessary to support existence — food being the only thing offered and accepted, and that taken only when they happened to be very hungry. Happy indeed was the man whose dish was put forward when the saint's appetite happened to be sharp. The death of the poor old Bēgam has, it is said, just canonized another saint, Shākir Shāh, who lies buried at Sardhana, but is claimed by the people of Meerut, among whom he lived till about five years ago, when he desired to be taken to Sardhana, where he found the old lady very dangerously ill and not expected to live. He was himself very old and ill when he set out from Meerut; and the journey is said to have shaken him so much that he found his end approaching, and sent a messenger to the princess in these words: 'Ayā torē, chale ham'; that is, 'Death came for thee, but I go in thy place'; and he told those around him that she had precisely five years more to live. She is said to have caused a tomb to be built over him, and is believed by the people to have died that day five years.

All these things I learned as I wandered among the tombs of the old saints the first few evenings after my arrival at Meerut. I was interested in their history from the circumstance that amateur singers and professional dancers and musicians should display their talents at their shrines gratis, for the sake of getting alms for the poor of the place, given in their name—a thing I had never before heard of—though the custom prevails no doubt in other places; and that Musalmāns and Hindoos should join promiscuously in their devotions and charities at all these shrines. Manohar Nāth's shrine, though he was a Hindoo, is attended by as many Musalmān as Hindoo pilgrims. He is said to have 'taken the *samādh*', that is, to have buried himself alive in this place as an offering to the Deity. Men who are afflicted with leprosy or any other incurable disease in India often take the samādh, that is, bury or drown themselves with due ceremonies, by which they are considered as acceptable sacrifices to the Deity. I once knew a Hindoo gentleman of great wealth and respectability, and of high rank under the Government of Nāgpur, who came to the river Nerbudda, two hundred miles, attended by a large retinue, to *take the samādh* in due form, from a painful disease which the doctors pronounced incurable. After taking an affectionate leave of all his family and friends, he embarked on board the boat, which took him into the deepest part of the river. He then loaded himself with sand, as a sportsman who is required to carry weights in a race loads himself with shot, and stepping into the water disappeared. The funeral ceremonies were then performed, and his family, friends, and followers returned to Nāgpur, conscious that they had all done what they had been taught to consider their duty. Many poor men do the same every year when afflicted by any painful disease that they consider incurable.[5] The only way to prevent this is to carry out the plan now in progress of giving to India in an accessible shape the medical science of Europe—a plan first adopted under Lord W. Bentinck, prosecuted by Lord Auckland, and superintended by two able and excellent men, Doctors Goodeve and O'Shaughnessy. It will be one of the greatest blessings that India has ever received from England.[6]

Notes:

1. January, 1836. The date is misprinted 20th in the original edition.

2. *Ante*, chapter 56 [13].

3. 'Amongst the remains of former times in and around Meerut may be noticed the Sūraj kund, commonly called by Europeans 'the monkey tank'. It was constructed by Jawāhir Mal, a wealthy merchant of Lāwār, in 1714. It was intended to keep it full of water from the Abū Nāla but at present the tank is nearly dry in May and June. There are numerous small temples, 'dharmsālās' [i.e. rest-houses], and 'satī' pillars on its banks, but none of any note. The largest of the temples is dedicated to Manohar Nāth, and is said to have been built in the reign of Shāh Jahān. Lāwār, a large village . . . is distant twelve miles north of the civil station. . . . There is a fine house here called Mahal Sarāi, built about A.D. 1700 by Jawāhir Singh, Mahājan, who constructed the Sūraj kund near Meerut' (*N.W.P. Gazetteer*, 1st ed., vol. iii, pp. 406,400). This information, supplied by the local officials, is more to be depended on than the author's statement.

4. 'The "dargāh" [i.e. shrine] of Shāh Pīr is a fine structure of red sandstone, erected about A.D. 1620 by Nūr Jahān, the wife of the Emperor Jahāngīr, in memory of a pious fakīr named Shāh Pīr. An "urs", or religions assembly, is held here every year in the month of Ramazān. The "dargāh" is supported from the proceeds of the revenue-free village of Bhagwānpur' (ibid., vol. iii, p. 406). The text of the original edition gives the pilgrim's name as 'Gungishun', which has no meaning.

5. An interesting collection of modern cases of a similar kind is given in Balfour, *Cyclopaedia*, 3rd ed., s.v. 'Samadhi'.

6. See *ante*, chapter 15, note 14. Dr. W. B. O'Shaughnessy contributed many scientific papers to the *J.A.S.B.* (vols. viii, ix, x, xii, and xvi).

CHAPTER 72

Subdivisions of Lands — Want of Gradations of Rank — Taxes.

The country between Delhi and Meerut is well cultivated and rich in the latent power of its soil; but there is here, as everywhere else in the Upper Provinces, a lamentable want of gradations in society, from the eternal subdivision of property in land, and the want of that concentration of capital in commerce and manufactures which characterizes European — or I may take a wider range, and say Christian societies.[1] Where, as in India, the landlords' share of the annual returns from the soil has been always taken by the Government as the most legitimate fund for the payment of its public establishments; and the estates of the farmers, and the holdings of the immediate cultivators of the soil, are liable to be subdivided in equal shares among the sons in every succeeding generation, the land can never aid much in giving to society that without which no society can possibly be well organized — a gradation of rank. Were the Government to alter the System, to give up all the rent of the lands, and thereby convert all the farmers into proprietors of their estates, the case would not be much altered, while the Hindoo and Muhammadan law of inheritance remained the same; for the eternal subdivision would still go on, and reduce all connected with the soil to one common level; and the people would be harassed with a multiplicity of taxes, from which they are now free, that would have to be imposed to supply the place of the rent given up. The agricultural capitalists who derived their incomes from the interest of money advanced to the farmers and cultivators for subsistence and the purchase of stock were commonly men of rank and influence in society; but they were never a numerous class. [2] The mass of the people in India are really not at present sensible that they pay any taxes at all. The only necessary of life, whose price is at all increased by taxes, is salt, and the consumer is hardly aware of this increase. The natives never eat salted meat; and though they require a great deal of salt, living, as they do, so much on vegetable food, still they purchase it in such small quantities from day to day as they require it, that they really never think of the tax that may have been paid upon it in its progress.[3]

To understand the nature of taxation in India, an Englishman should suppose that all the non-farming landholders of his native country had, a century or two ago, consented to resign their property into the hands of their sovereign, for the maintenance of his civil functionaries, army, navy, church, and public creditors, and then suddenly disappeared from the community, leaving to till the lands merely the farmers and cultivators; and that their forty millions of rent were just the sum that the Government now required to pay all these four great establishments.[4]

To understand the nature of the public debt of England a man has only to suppose one great national establishment, twice as large as those of the civil functionaries, the Army, Navy, and the Church together, and composed of members with fixed salaries, who purchased their commissions from *the wisdom of our ancestors*, with liberty to sell them to whom they please—who have no duty to perform for the public,[5] and have, like Adam and Eve, the privilege of going to 'seek their place of rest' in what part of the world they please—a privilege of which they will, of course, be found more and more anxious to avail themselves as taxation presses on the one side, and prohibition to the import of the necessaries of life diminishes the means of paying them on the other.

The repeal of the Corn Laws may give a new lift to England; it may greatly increase the foreign demand for the produce of its manufacturing industry; it may invite back a large portion of those who now spend their incomes in foreign countries, and prevent from going abroad to reside a vast number who would otherwise go. These laws must soon be repealed, or England must reduce one or other of its great establishments—the National Debt, the Church, the Army, or the Navy. The Corn Laws press upon England just in the same manner as the discovery of the passage to India by the Cape of Good Hope pressed upon Venice and the other states whose welfare depended upon the transit of the produce of India by land. But the navigation of the Cape benefited all other European nations at the same time that it pressed upon these particular states, by giving them all the produce of India at cheaper rates than they would otherwise have got it, and by opening the markets of India to the produce of all other European nations. The Corn Laws benefit only one small section of the people of England, while they weigh, like an incubus, upon the vital energies of all the rest; and at the same time injure all other nations by preventing their getting the produce of manufacturing industry so cheap as they would otherwise get it. They have not, therefore, the merit of benefiting other nations, at the same time that they crush their own.[6]

For some twenty or thirty years of our rule, too many of the collectors of our land revenue in what we call the Western Provinces,[7] sought the 'bubble reputation' in an increase of assessment upon the lands of their district every five years when the settlement was renewed. The more the assessment was increased, the greater was the praise bestowed upon the collector by the revenue boards, or the revenue secretary to Government, in the name of the Governor-General of India.[8] These collectors found an easy mode of acquiring this reputation—they left the settlements to their native officers, and shut their ears to all complaints of grievances, till they had reduced all the landholders of their districts to one common level of beggary, without stock, character, or credit; and transferred a great portion of their estates to the native officers of their own courts through the medium of the auction sales that took place for the arrears, or pretended arrears, of revenue. A better feeling has for some years past prevailed, and collectors have sought their reputation in a real knowledge of their duties, and real good feeling towards the farmers and cultivators of their districts. For this better tone of feeling the Western Provinces are, I believe, chiefly indebted to Mr. R. M. Bird, of the Revenue Board, one of the most able public officers now in India. A settlement for twenty years is now in progress that will leave the farmers at least 35 per cent. upon the gross collections from the immediate cultivators of the soil; that is, the amount of the revenue demandable by Government from the estate will be that less than what the farmer will, and would, under any circumstances, levy from the cultivators in his detailed settlement.[9]

The farmer lets all the land of his estate out to cultivators, and takes in money this rate of profit for his expense, trouble, and risk; or he lets out to the cultivators enough to pay the Government demand, and tills the rest with his own stock, rent-free. When a division takes place between his sons, they either divide the estate, and become each responsible for his particular share, or they divide the profits, and remain collectively responsible to Government for the whole, leaving one member of the family registered as the lessee and responsible head.[10]

In the Ryotwār System of Southern India, Government officers, removable at the pleasure of the Government collector, are substituted for these farmers, or more properly proprietors, of estates; and a System more prejudicial to the best interests of society could not well be devised by the ingenuity of man.[11] It has been supposed by some theorists, who are practically unacquainted with agriculture in this or any other country, that all who have any interest in land above the rank of cultivator or ploughman are mere *drones*, or useless consumers of that rent which, under judicious management, might be added to the revenues of Government—that all which they get might, and ought to be, either left with the cultivators or taken by the Government. At the head of these is the justly celebrated historian, Mr. Mill. But men who understand the subject practically know that the intermediate agency of a farmer, who has a permanent interest in the estate, or an interest for a long period, is a thousand times better both for the Government and the people than that of a Government officer of any description, much less that of one removable at the pleasure of the collector. Government can always get more revenue from a village under the management of the farmer; the character of the cultivators and village community generally is much better; the tillage is much better; and the produce, from more careful weeding and attention of all kinds, sells much better in the market. The better character of the cultivators enables them to get the loans they require to purchase stock, and to pay the Government demand on more moderate terms from the capitalists, who rely upon the farmer to aid in the recovery of their outlays, without reference to civil courts, which are ruinous media, as well in India as in other places. The farmer or landlord finds in the same manner that he can get much more from lands let out on lease to the cultivators or yeomen, who depend upon their own character, credit, and stock, than he can from similar lands cultivated with his own stock; and hired labourers can never be got to labour either so long or so well. The labour of the Indian cultivating lessee is always applied in the proper quantity, and at the proper time and place—that of the hired field-labourer hardly ever is. The skilful coachmaker always puts on the precise quantity of iron required to make his coach strong, because he knows where it is required; his coach is, at the same time, as light as it can be with safety. The unskilful workman either puts on too much, and makes his coach heavy; or he puts it in the wrong place, and leaves it weak.

If government extends the twenty years' settlement now in progress to fifty years or more, they will confer a great blessing upon the people[12] and they might, perhaps, do it on the condition that the incumbent consented to allow the lease to descend undivided to his heirs by the laws of primogeniture. To this condition all classes would readily agree, for I have heard Hindoo and Muhammadan landholders all equally lament the evil effects of the laws by which families are so quickly and inevitably broken up; and say that 'it is the duty of government to take advantage of their power as the great proprietor and leaser of all the lands to prevent the evil by declaring leases indivisible. 'There would then', they say, 'be always one head to assist in maintaining the widows and orphans of deceased members, in educating his brothers and nephews; and by his influence and respectability procuring employment for them.' In such men, with feelings of permanent interest in their estates, and in the stability of the government that secured them possession on such favourable terms, and with the means of educating their children, we should by and by find our best support, and society its best element. The law of primogeniture at present prevails only where it is most mischievous under our rule, among the feudal chiefs, whose ancestors rose to distinction and acquired their possessions by rapine in times of invasion and civil wars. This law among them tends to perpetuate the desire to maintain those military establishments by which the founders of their families arose, in the hope that the times of invasion and civil wars may return and open for them a similar field for exertion. It fosters a class of powerful men, essentially and irredeemably opposed in feeling, not only to our rule, but to settled government under any rule; and the sooner the Hindoo law of inheritance is allowed by the paramount power to take its course among these feudal chiefs, the better for society. There is always a strong tendency to it in the desire of the younger brothers to share in the loaves and fishes; and this tendency is checked only by the injudicious interposition of our authority.[13]

To give India the advantage of free institutions, or all the blessings of which she is capable under an enlightened paternal government, nothing is more essential than the supersession of this feudal aristocracy by one founded upon other bases, and, above all, upon that of the concentration of capital in commerce and manufactures. Nothing tends so much to prevent the accumulation and concentration of capital over India as this feudal aristocracy which tends everywhere to destroy that feeling of security without which men will nowhere accumulate and concentrate it. They do so, not only by the intrigues and combinations against the paramount power, which keep alive the dread of internal wars and foreign invasion, but by those gangs of robbers and murderers which they foster and locate upon their estates to prey upon the more favoured or better governed territories around them. From those gangs of freebooters who are to be found upon the estate of almost every native chief, no accumulation of movable property of any value is ever for a moment considered safe, and those who happen to have any such are always in dread of losing, not only their property, but their lives along with it, for these gangs, secure in the protection of such chief, are reckless in their attack, and kill all who happen to come in their way.[14]

Notes:

1. This phrase is meant to include America.

2. Money-lenders naturally have flourished daring the long period of internal peace since the Mutiny. They vary in wealth and position from the humblest 'gombeen man' to the millionaire banker. Many of these money-lenders are now among the largest owners of land in the country. Under native rule interests in land were generally too precarious to be saleable. The author did not foresee that the growth of private property in land would carry with it the right and desire of one party to sell and of another to buy, and would thus favour the growth of large estates, and, to a considerable

extent, counteract the evils of subdivision. Of course, like everything else, the large estates have their evils too. Much nonsense is written about sales of land in India, as well as in Ireland. The two countries have more than the initial letter in common.

3. Theorists declare that it is right that the tax-payers should know what is taken from them, and that, therefore, direct taxes are best; but practical men who have to govern ignorant and suspicious races, resentful of direct taxation, know that indirect taxation is, for such people, the best.

4. This illustration would give a very false idea of modern Indian finance.

5. They have no duty to perform as creditors; but as citizens of an enlightened nation they no doubt perform many of them, very important ones. [W. H. S.] The author's whimsical comparison between stockholders and Adam and Eve, and his notion that the creditors of the nation may be regarded as officials without duties, only obscure a simple matter. The emigration of owners of Consols never assumed very alarming dimensions.

6. The Corn Laws were repealed in 1846, and the shilling duty which was then left was abolished in 1869. Considering that the author belonged to a land-owning family, his clear perception of the evils caused by the Corn Laws is remarkable.

7. By the 'Western Provinces' the author means the region called later the North-Western Provinces, and now known as the Agra Province in the United Provinces of Agra and Oudh, with the Delhi Territories, which latter are now partly under the Government of the Panjāb, and partly in the new small Province, or Chief Commissionership of Delhi.

8. At the time referred to, the provincial Government had not been constituted.

9. Fifty per cent. may be considered as the average rate left to the lessees or proprietors of estates under this new settlement; and, if they take on an average one-third of the gross produce, Government takes two-ninths. But we may rate the Government share of the produce actually taken at one-fifth as the maximum, and one-tenth as the minimum. [W. H. S.]

It is unfortunately true that in the short-term settlements made previous to 1833 many abuses of the kinds referred to in the text occurred. The traditions of the people and the old records attest numerous instances. The first serious attempt to reform the system of revenue settlements was made by Regulation VII of 1822, but, owing to an excessive elaboration of procedure, the attempt produced no appreciable results. Regulation IX of 1833 established a workable system, and provided for the appointment of Indian Deputy Collectors with adequate powers. The settlements of the

North-Western Provinces made under this Regulation were, for the most part, reasonably fair, and were generally confirmed for a period of thirty years. Mr. Robert Mertins Bird, who entered the service in 1805, and died in 1853, took a leading part in this great reform. When the next settlements were made, between 1860 and 1880, the share of the profit rental claimed by the State was reduced from two-thirds to one-half. Full details will be found in the editor's *Settlement Officer's Manual for the N. W. P.* (Allahabad, 1882), or in Baden Powell's big book, *Land Systems of British India* (Clarendon Press, 1892).

10. Since 1833 the people whom the author calls 'farmers' have gradually become fall proprietors, subject to the Government lien on the land and its produce for the land revenue. For many years past the ancient custom of joint ownership and collective responsibility has been losing ground. Partitions are now continually demanded, and every year collective responsibility is becoming more unpopular and more difficult to enforce.

11. This judgement, I need hardly say, would not be accepted in Madras or Bombay. The issue raised is too large for discussion in footnotes.

12. The advantages of very long terms of settlements are obvious; the disadvantages, though equally real, are less obvious. Fluctuations in prices, and above all, in the price of silver, are among the many conditions which complicate the question. Except the Bengal landowners, most people now admit that the Permanent Settlement of Bengal in 1793 was a grievous mistake. It is also admitted that the mistake is irrevocable.

13. These two suggestions of the author that the law of primogeniture should be established to regulate the succession to ordinary estates, and that it should be abolished in the case of chieftainships, where it already prevails, are obviously open to criticism. It seems sufficient to say that both recommendations are, for many reasons, altogether impracticable. In passing, I may note that the term 'feudal' does not express with any approach to correctness the relation of the Native States to the Government of India.

14. The evils described in this paragraph, though diminished, have not disappeared. Nevertheless, no one would now seriously propose the deliberate supersession of the existing aristocracy by rich merchants and manufacturers. The proposal is too fanciful for discussion. During the long period of peace merchants and manufacturers have naturally risen to a position much more prominent than they occupied in the author's time.

CHAPTER 73

Meerut — Anglo-Indian Society.

Meerut is a large station for military and civil establishments; it is the residence of a civil commissioner, a judge, a magistrate, a collector of land revenue, and all their assistants and establishments. There are the Major-General commanding the division; the Brigadier commanding the station; four troops of horse and a company of foot artillery; one regiment of European cavalry, one of European infantry, one of native cavalry, and three of native infantry.[1] It is justly considered the healthiest station in India, for both Europeans and natives,[2] and I visited it in the latter end of the cold, which is the healthiest, season of the year; yet the European ladies were looking as if they had all come out of their graves, and talking of the necessity of going off to the mountains to renovate, as soon as the hot weather should set in. They had literally been fagging themselves to death with gaiety, at this the gayest and most delightful of all Indian stations, during the cold months when they ought to have been laying in a store of strength to carry them through the trying seasons of the hot winds and rains. Up every night and all night at balls and suppers, they could never go out to breathe the fresh air of the morning; and were looking wretchedly ill, while the European soldiers from the barracks seemed as fresh as if they had never left their native land. There is no doubt that sitting up late at night is extremely prejudicial to the health of Europeans in India.[3] I have never seen the European, male or female, that could stand it long, however temperate in habits; and an old friend of mine once told me that if he went to bed a little exhilarated every night at ten o'clock, and took his ride in the morning, he found himself much better than if he sat up till twelve or one o'clock without drinking, and lay abed in the mornings. Almost all the gay pleasures of India are enjoyed at night, and as ladies here, as everywhere else in Christian societies, are the life and soul of all good parties, as of all good novels, they often to oblige others sit up late, much against their own inclinations, and even their judgements, aware as they are that they are gradually sinking under the undue exertions.

When I first came to India there were a few ladies of the old school still much looked up to in Calcutta, and among the rest the grandmother of the Earl of Liverpool, the old Bēgam Johnstone, then between seventy and eighty years of age.[4] All these old ladies prided themselves upon keeping up old usages. They use to dine in the afternoon at four or five o'clock—take their airing after dinner in their carriages; and from the time they returned till ten at night their houses were lit up in their best style and thrown open for the reception of visitors. All who were on visiting terms came at this time, with any strangers whom they wished to introduce, and enjoyed each other's society; there were music and dancing for the young, and cards for the old, when the party assembled happened to be large enough; and a few who had been previously invited stayed supper. I often visited the old Bēgam Johnstone at this hour, and met at her house the first people in the country, for all people, including the Governor-General himself, delighted to honour this old lady, the widow of a Governor-General of India, and the mother-in-law of a Prime Minister of England.[5] She was at Murshīdābād when Sirāj-ud-daula marched from that place at the head of the army that took and plundered Calcutta, and caused so many Europeans to perish in the Black Hole; and she was herself saved from becoming a member of his seraglio, or perishing with the lest, by the circumstance of her being far gone in her pregnancy, which caused her to be made over to a Dutch factory.[6]

She had been a very beautiful woman, and had been several times married; the pictures of all her husbands being hung round her noble drawing-room in Calcutta, covered during the day with crimson cloth to save them from the dust, and uncovered at night only on particular occasions. One evening Mrs. Crommelin, a friend of mine, pointing to one of them, asked the old lady his name. 'Really, I cannot at this moment tell you, my dear; my memory is very bad,' (striking her forehead with her right hand, as she leaned with her left arm in Mrs. Crommelin's,) 'but I shall recollect in a few minutes.' The old lady's last husband was a clergyman, Mr. Johnstone, whom she found too gay, and persuaded to go home upon an annuity of eight hundred a year, which she settled upon him for life. The bulk of her fortune went to Lord Liverpool; the rest to her grandchildren, the Ricketts, Watts, and others.

Since those days the modes of intercourse in India have much altered. Society at all the stations beyond the three capitals of Calcutta, Madras, and Bombay, is confined almost exclusively to the members of the civil and military services, who seldom remain long at the same station—the military officers hardly ever more than three years, and the civil hardly ever so long. At disagreeable stations the civil servants seldom remain so many months. Every newcomer calls in the forenoon upon all that are at the station when he arrives, and they return his call at the same hour soon after. If he is a married man, the married men upon whom he has called take their wives to call upon his; and he takes his to return the call of theirs. These calls are all indispensable; and being made in the forenoon, become very disagreeable in the hot season; all complain of them, yet no one forgoes his claim upon them; and till the claim is fulfilled, people will not recognize each other as acquaintances.[7] Unmarried officers generally dine in the evening, because it is a more convenient hour for the mess; and married civil functionaries do the same, because it is more convenient for their office work. If you invite those who dine at that hour to spend the evening with you, you must invite them to dinner, even in the hot weather; and if they invite you, it is to dinner. This makes intercourse somewhat heavy at all times, but more especially so in the hot season, when a table covered with animal food is sickening to any person without a keen appetite, and stupefying to those who have it. No one thinks of inviting people to a dinner and ball—it would be vandalism; and when you invite them, as is always the case, to come after dinner, the ball never begins till late at night, and seldom ends till late in the morning. With all its disadvantages, however, I think dining in the evening much better for those who are in health, than dining in the afternoon, provided people can avoid the intermediate meal of tiffin. No person in India should eat animal food more than once a day; and people who dine in the evening generally eat less than they would if they dined in the afternoon. A light breakfast at nine; biscuit, or a slice of toast with a glass of water, or soda-water, at two o'clock, and dinner after the evening exercise, is the plan which I should recommend every European to adopt as the most agreeable.[8] When their digestive powers get out of order, people must do as the doctors tell them.

There is, I believe, no society in which there is more real urbanity of manners than in that of India—a more general disposition on the part of its different members to sacrifice their own comforts and conveniences to those of others, and to make those around them happy, without letting them see that it costs them an effort to do so.[9] There is assuredly no society where the members are more generally free from those corroding cares and anxieties which 'weigh upon the hearts' of men whose incomes are precarious, and position in the world uncertain. They receive their salaries on a certain day every month, whatever may be the state of the seasons or of trade; they pay no taxes; they rise in the several services by rotation;[10] religious feelings and opinions are by common consent left as a question between man and his Maker; no one ever thinks of questioning another about them, nor would he be tolerated if he did so. Most people take it for granted that those which they got from their parents were the right ones; and as such they cherish them. They remember with feelings of filial piety the prayers which they in their infancy offered to their Maker, while kneeling by the side of their mothers; and they continue to offer them up through life, with the same feelings and the same hopes.[11]

Differences of political opinion, which agitate society so much in England and other countries where every man believes that his own personal interests must always be more or less affected by the predominance of one party over another, are no doubt a source of much interest to people in India, but they scarcely ever excite any angry passions among them. The tempests by which the political atmosphere of the world is cleared and purged of all its morbid influences burst not upon us—we see them at a distance—we know that they are working for all mankind; and we feel for those who boldly expose themselves to their 'pitiless peltings' as men feel for the sailors whom they suppose to be exposed on the ocean to the storm, while they listen to it from their beds or winter firesides.[12] We discuss all political opinions, and all the great questions which they affect, with the calmness of philosophers; not without emotion certainly, but without passion; we have no share in returning members to parliament—we feel no dread of those injuries, indignities, and calumnies to which those who have are too often exposed; and we are free from the bitterness of feelings which always attend them.[13]

How exalted, how glorious, has been the destiny of England, to spread over so vast a portion of the globe her literature, her language, and her free institutions! How ought the sense of this high destiny to animate her sons in their efforts to perfect their institutions which they have formed by slow degrees from feudal barbarism; to make them in reality as perfect as they would have them appear to the world to be in theory, that rising nations may love and honour the source whence they derive theirs, and continue to look to it for improvement.

We return to the society of our wives and children after the labours of the day are over, with tempers unruffled by collision with political and religious antagonists, by unfavourable changes in the season and the markets, and the other circumstances which affect so much the incomes and prospects of our friends at home. We must look to them for the chief pleasures of our lives, and know that they must look to us for theirs; and if anything has crossed us we try to conceal it from them. There is in India a strong feeling of mutual dependence which prevents little domestic misunderstandings between man and wife from growing into quarrels so often as in other countries, where this is less prevalent. Men have not here their clubs, nor their wives their little coteries to fly to when disposed to make serious matters out of trifles, and both are in consequence much inclined to bear and forbear. There are, of course, on the other hand, evils in India that people have not to contend with at home; but, on the whole, those who are disposed to look on the fair, as well as on the dark side of all around them, can enjoy life in India very much, as long as they and those dear to them are free from physical pain.[14] We everywhere find too many disposed to look upon the dark side of all that is present, and the bright side of all that is distant in time and place—always miserable themselves, be they where they will, and making all around them miserable; this commonly arises from indigestion, and the habit of eating and drinking in a hot, as in a cold, climate; and giving their stomachs too much to do, as if they were the only parts of the human frame whose energies were unrelaxed by the temperature of tropical climates.

There is, however, one great defect in Anglo-Indian society; it is composed too exclusively of the servants of government, civil, military, and ecclesiastic, and wants much of the freshness, variety, and intelligence of cultivated societies otherwise constituted. In societies where capital is concentrated for employment in large agricultural, commercial, and manufacturing establishments, those who possess and employ it form a large portion of the middle and higher classes. They require the application of the higher branches of science to the efficient employment of their capital in almost every purpose to which it can be applied; and they require, at the same time, to show that they are not deficient in that conventional learning of the schools and drawing-rooms to which the circles they live and move in attach importance. In such societies we are, therefore, always coming in contact with men whose scientific knowledge is necessarily very precise, and at the same time very extensive, while their manners and conversation are of the highest polish. There is, perhaps, nothing which strikes a gentleman from India so much on his entering a society differently constituted, as the superior precision of men's information upon scientific subjects; and more especially upon that of the sciences more immediately applicable to the arts by which the physical enjoyments of men are produced, prepared, and distributed all over the world. Almost all men in India feel that too much of their time before they left England was devoted to the acquisition of the dead languages; and too little to the study of the elements of science. The time lost can never be regained—at least they think so, which is much the same thing. Had they been well grounded in the elements of physics, physiology, and chemistry before they left their native land, they would have gladly devoted their leisure to the improvement of their knowledge; but to go back to elements, where elements can be learnt only from books, is, unhappily, what so few can bring themselves to, that no man feels ashamed of acknowledging that he has never studied them at all till he returns to England, or enters a society differently constituted, and finds that he has lost the support of the great majority that always surrounded him in India.

[15] It will, perhaps, be said that the members of the official aristocracy of all countries have more or less of the same defects, for certain it is that they everywhere attach paramount or undue importance to the conventional learning of the grammar-school and the drawing-room, and the ignorant and the indolent have everywhere the support of a great majority. Johnson has, however, observed:

'But the truth is that the knowledge of external nature and the sciences, which that knowledge requires or includes, are not the great or the frequent business of the human mind. Whether we provide for action or conversation, whether we wish to be useful or pleasing, the first requisite is the religious and moral knowledge of right and wrong; the next is an acquaintance with the history of mankind, and with those examples which may be said to embody truth, and prove by events the reasonableness of opinions.[16] Prudence and justice are virtues and excellences of all times, and of all places — we are perpetually moralists; but we are geometricians only by chance. Our intercourse with intellectual nature is necessary; our speculations upon matter are voluntary and at leisure. Physiological learning is of such rare emergence, that one may know another half his life, without being able to estimate his skill in hydrostatics or astromony; but his moral and prudential character immediately appears. Those authors, therefore, are to be read at schools that supply most axioms of prudence, most principles of moral truth, and most materials for conversation; and these purposes are best served by poets, orators, and historians' (*Life of Milton*).

Notes:

1. In India officers have much better opportunities in time of peace to learn how to handle troops than in England, from having them more concentrated in large stations, with fine open plains to exercise upon. During the whole of the cold season, from the beginning of November to the end of February, the troops are at large stations exercised in brigades, and the artillery, cavalry, and infantry together. [W. H. S.] The normal garrison of Meerut in recent years has consisted of one British cavalry regiment, one battalion of British infantry, one native cavalry regiment, and one battalion of native infantry, with two batteries of horse and two of field artillery. The cantonment was established in 1806, from which date the town grew rapidly in size and population. The civil staff has been largely increased since Sleeman's time by the addition of numerous officers belonging to irrigation and other departmental services which did not exist in his day. The offices of District Magistrate and Collector have been united as a single person for many years.

2. The cantonments suffered severely from typhoid fever for several years in the latter part of the nineteenth century.

3. Few Anglo-Indians will dispute the truth of this dictum.

4. The late Earl of Liverpool, then Mr. Jenkinson, married this old lady's daughter. He was always very attentive to her, and she used with feelings of great pride and pleasure to display the contents of the boxes of millinery which he used every year to send out to her. [W. H. 8.] The author came out to India in 1809. Mr. Charles Jenkinson was created Baron Hawkesbury in 1786, and Earl of Liverpool in 1796. His first wife, who died in 1770, was Amelia, daughter of Mr. William Watts, Governor of Fort William, and of the lady described by the author. Their only son succeeded to the earldom in 1808, and died in 1828. The peerage became extinct on the death of the third earl in 1851. (Burke's *Peerage*.) It was revived in 1905.

5. Lord Liverpool, the second earl, became Prime Minister in 1812, after the murder of Perceval. Mrs. Johnson (not Johnstone) was not 'the widow of a Governor-General of India'. Her history is told in detail on her tombstone in St. John's churchyard, Calcutta, and is summarized in Buckland, *Dictionary of Indian Biography* (1906). She was born in 1725, and died in 1812. She had four husbands, namely (l) Parry Purple Temple, whom she married when she was only thirteen years of age; (2) James Altham, who died of smallpox a few days after his marriage; (3) William Watts, Senior Member of Council, and for a short time Governor or President of Fort William in 1758; (4) in 1774 Rev. William Johnson, who became principal chaplain of Fort William in 1784, and left India in 1788. She was known as 'the old Begum ', and her epitaph asserts that she was when she died 'the oldest British resident in Bengal, universally beloved, respected, and revered'. Mr. A. L. Paul kindly communicated the full text of the inscription on her tomb, with some additional notes. The author met her in 1810, when she was about eighty-five years of age.

6. The tragedy of the Black Hole occurred in June, 1756.

7. Of late years the rigour of the custom exacting midday calls has been relaxed in some places.

8. Moat people would require some training before they could find this very abstemious regimen 'the most agreeable'.

9. It will, I hope, be admitted that this observation still holds good.

10. When the author wrote the rupee was worth more than two shillings, the members of the Indian services were few in number, and mostly well paid, while living was cheap. Now all is changed. The rupee has an artificial value of 1s. 4d., the members of the services are numerous and often ill paid, while living is dear. The sharp fall in the value of silver, and consequently

in the gold equivalent of the rupee, began in 1874. 'Corroding cares and anxieties' are now the lot of most people who serve in India. They now have the privilege of paying taxes.

11. This perfect religious freedom, still generally characteristic of Anglo-Indian society, is one of its greatest charms; and the charms of the country do not increase.

12. The author probably had in his mind the famous lines of Lucretius:-

Suave, mari magno turbantibus aequora ventis,
E terra magnum alterius spectare laborem;
Non quia vexari quemquam 'st jucunda voluptas,
Sed, quibus ipse malis careas, quia cernere suave 'st.

(Book II, line 1.)

13. This delightful philosophic calm is no longer an Anglo-Indian possession; nor can the modern Indian official congratulate himself on his immunity from 'injuries, indignities, and calumnies'.

14. There are now clubs everywhere, and coteries are said to be not unknown. Few Anglo-Indians of the present day are able to share the author's cheery optimism.

15. In this matter also time has wrought great changes. The scientific branches of the Indian services, the medical, engineering, forestry, geological survey, and others, have greatly developed, and many officials, in India, whether of European or Indian race, now occupy high places in the world of science.

16. Compare Bolingbroke's observation, already quoted, that 'history is philosophy teaching by example'.

CHAPTER 74

Pilgrims of India.

There is nothing which strikes a European more in travelling over the great roads in India than the vast number of pilgrims of all kinds which he falls in with, particularly between the end of November [*sic*], when all the autumn harvest has been gathered, and the seed of the spring crops has been in the ground. They consist for the most part of persons, male and female, carrying Ganges water from the point at Hardwār, where the sacred stream emerges from the hills, to the different temples in all parts of India, dedicated to the gods Vishnu and Siva. There the water is thrown upon the stones which represent the gods, and when it falls upon these stones it is called 'Chandamirt', or holy water, and is frequently collected and reserved to be drunk as a remedy 'for a mind diseased'[1]

This water is carried in small bottles, bearing the seals of the presiding priest at the holy place whence it was brought. The bottles are contained in covered baskets, fixed to the ends of a pole, which is carried across the shoulder. The people who carry it are of three kinds — those who carry it for themselves as a votive offering to some shrine; those who are hired for the purpose by others as salaried servants; and, thirdly, those who carry it for sale. In the interval between the sowing and reaping of the spring crops, that is, between November and March, a very large portion of the Hindoo landholders and cultivators of India devote their leisure to this pious duty. They take their baskets and poles with them from home, or purchase them on the road; and having poured their libations on the head of the god, and made him acquainted with their wants and wishes, return home. From November to March three-fourths of the number of these people one meets consist of this class. At other seasons more than three-fourths consist of the other two classes — of persons hired for the purpose as servants, and those who carry the water for sale.

One morning the old Jemadār, the marriage of whose mango- grove with the jasmine I have already described,[2] brought his two sons and a nephew to pay their respects to me on their return to Jubbulpore from a pilgrimage to Jagannāth.[3] The sickness of the youngest, a nice boy of about six years of age, had caused this pilgrimage. The eldest son was about twenty years of age, and the nephew about eighteen.

After the usual compliments, I addressed the eldest son: 'And so your brother was really very ill when you set out?'

'Very ill, sir; hardly able to stand without assistance.'

'What was the matter with him?'

'It was what we call a drying-up, or withering of the System.'

'What were the symptoms?'

'Dysentery.'

'Good; and what cured him, as he now seems quite well?'

'Our mother and father vowed five pair of baskets of Ganges water to Gajādhar, an incarnation of the god Siva, at the temple of Baijnāth, and a visit to the temple of Jagannāth.'

'And having fulfilled these vows, your brother recovered?'

'He had quite recovered, sir, before we had set out on our return from Jagannāth.'

'And who carried the baskets?'

'My mother, wife, cousin, myself, and little brother, all carried one pair each.'

'This little boy could not surely carry a pair of baskets all the way?'

'No, sir, we had a pair of small baskets made especially for him; and when within about three miles of the temple he got down from his little pony, took up his baskets, and carried them to the god. Up to within three miles of the temple the baskets were carried by a Brahman servant, whom we had taken with us to cook our food. We had with us another Brahman, to whom we had to pay only a trifle, as his principal wages were made up of fees from families in the town of Jubbulpore, who had made similar vows, and gave him so much a bottle for the water he carried in their several names to the god.'

'Did you give all your water to the Baijnāth temple, or carry some with you to Jagannāth?'

'No water is ever offered to Jagannāth, sir; he is an incarnation of Vishnu.'[4]

'And does Vishnu never drink?'

'He drinks, sir, no doubt; but he gets nothing but offerings of food and money.'

'From this to Bindāchal on the Ganges, two hundred and thirty miles; thence to Baijnāth, a hundred and fifty miles; and thence to Jagannāth, some four or five hundred miles more.'[5]

'And your mother and wife walked all the way with their baskets?'

'All the way, sir, except when either of them got sick, when she mounted the pony with my little brother till she felt well again.'

Here were four members of a respectable family walking a pilgrimage of between twelve and fourteen hundred miles, going and coming, and carrying burthens on their shoulders for the recovery of the poor sick boy; and millions of families are every year doing the same from all parts of India. The change of air, and exercise, cured the boy, and no doubt did them all a great deal of good; but no physician in the world but a religions one could have persuaded them to undertake such a journey for the same purpose.

The rest of the pilgrims we meet are for the most part of the two monastic orders of Gosāins, or the followers of Siva, and Bairāgīs, or followers of Vishnu, and Muhammadan Fakīrs. A Hindoo of any caste may become a member of these monastic orders. They are all disciples of the high priests of the temples of their respective gods; and in their name they wander all over India, visiting the celebrated temples which are dedicated to them. A part of the revenues of these temples is devoted to subsisting these disciples as they pass; and every one of them claims the right of a day's food and lodging, or more, according to the rules of the temple. They make collections along the roads; and when they return, commonly bring back some surplus as an offering to their apostle, the high priest who has adopted them. Almost every high priest has a good many such disciples, as they are not costly; and from their returning occasionally, and from the disciples of others passing, these high priests learn everything of importance that is going on over India, and are well acquainted with the state of feeling and opinion.

What these disciples get from secular people is given not only from feelings of charity and compassion, but as a religions or propitiatory offering: for they are all considered to be armed by their apostle with a vicarious power of blessing or cursing; and as being in themselves men of God whom it might be dangerous to displease. They never condescend to feign disease or misery in order to excite feelings of compassion, but demand what they want with a bold front, as holy men who have a right to share liberally in the superfluities which God has given to the rest of the Hindoo community. They are in general exceedingly intelligent men of the world, and very communicative. Among them will be found members of all classes of Hindoo society, and of the most wealthy and respectable families.[6] While I had charge of the Narsinghpur district in 1822 a Bairāgī, or follower of Vishnu, came and settled himself down on the border of a village near my residence. His mild and paternal deportment pleased all the little community so much that they carried him every day more food than he required. At last, the proprietor of the village, a very respectable old gentleman, to whom I was much attached, went out with all his family to ask a blessing of the holy man. As they sat down before him, the tears were seen stealing down his cheeks as he looked upon the old man's younger sons and daughters. At last, the old man's wife burst into tears, ran up, and fell upon the holy man's neck, exclaiming, 'My lost son, my lost son!' He was indeed her eldest son. He had disappeared suddenly twelve years before, became a disciple of the high priest of a distant temple, and visited almost every celebrated temple in India, from Kedārnāth in the eternal snows to Sītā Baldī Rāmesar, opposite the island of Ceylon.[7] He remained with the family for nearly a year, delighting them and all the country around with his narratives. At last, he seemed to lose his spirits, his usual rest and appetite; and one night he again disappeared. He had been absent for some years when I last saw the family, and I know not whether he ever returned.

The real members of these monastic orders are not generally bad men; but there are a great many men of all kinds who put on their disguises, and under their cloak commit all kinds of atrocities.[8] The security and convenience which the real pilgrims enjoy upon our roads, and the entire freedom from all taxation, both upon these roads and at the different temples they visit, tend greatly to attach them to our rule, and through that attachment, a tone of good feeling towards it is generally disseminated over all India. They come from the native states, and become acquainted with the superior advantages the people under us enjoy, in the greater security of property, the greater freedom with which it is enjoyed and displayed; the greater exemption from taxation, and the odious right of search which it involves, the greater facilities for travelling in good roads and bridges; the greater respectability and integrity of public servants, arising from the greater security in their tenure of office and more adequate rate of avowed salaries; the entire freedom of the navigation of our great rivers, on which thousands and tens of thousands of laden vessels now pass from one end to the other without any one to question whence they come or whither they go. These are tangible proofs of good government, which all can appreciate; and as the European gentleman, in his rambles along the great roads, passes the lines of pilgrims with which the roads are crowded during the cold season, he is sure to hear himself hailed with grateful shouts, as one of those who secured for them and the people generally all the blessings they now enjoy.[9]

One day my sporting friend, the Rājā of Maihar, told me that he had been purchasing some water from the Ganges at its source, to wash the image of Vishnu which stood in one of his temples.[10] I asked him whether he ever drank the water after the image had been washed in it. 'Yes,' said he, 'we all occasionally drink the "chandamirt".' 'And do you in the same manner drink the water in which the god Siva has been washed?' 'Never,' said the Rājā. 'And why not?' 'Because his wife, Devī, one day in a domestic quarrel cursed him and said, "The water which falls from thy head shall no man henceforward drink." From that day', said the Rājā, 'no man has ever drunk of the water that washes his image, lest Devī should punish him.' 'And how is it, then, Rājā Sahib, that mankind continue to drink the water of the Ganges, which is supposed to flow from her husband Siva's top-knot?' 'Because', replied the Rājā, 'this sacred river first flows from the right foot of the god Vishnu, and thence passes over the head of Siva. The three gods', continued the Rājā, 'govern the world turn and turn about, twenty years at a time. While Vishnu reigns, all goes on well; rain descends in good season, the harvests are abundant, and the cattle thrive. When Brahma reigns, there is little falling off in these matters; but during the twenty years that Siva reigns, nothing goes on well—we are all at cross purposes, our crops fail, our cattle get the murrain, and mankind suffer from epidemic diseases.' The Rājā was a follower of Vishnu, as may be guessed.

Notes:

1. Tavernier notes that Ganges water is often given at weddings, 'each guest receiving a cup or two, according to the liberality of the host'. 'There is sometimes', he says, '2,000 or 3,000 rupees' worth of it consumed at a wedding.' (Tavernier, *Travels*, ed. Ball, vol. ii, pp. 231, 254.)

2. *Ante*, Chapter 5, [3].

3. Jagannāth (corruptly Juggernaut, &c.), or Purī, on the coast of Orissa, probably is the most venerated shrine in India. The principal deity there worshipped is a form of Vishnu.

4. Water may not be offered to Jagannāth, but the facts stated in this chapter show that it is offered in other temples of Vishnu.

5. Bindāchal is in the Mirzāpur district of the United Provinces. Baijnāth is in the Santāl Parganas District of the Bhāgalpur Division in the province of Bihār and Orissa. The group of temples at Deogarh dedicated to Siva is visited by pilgrims from all parts of India. The principal temple is called Baijnāth or Baidyanāth. Deogarh is a small town in the Santāl Parganas (*I.G.*, 1908, s.v. Deogarh; *A.S.R.*, vol. viii (1878), pp. 137-45, Pl. ix, x; vol. xix (1885), pp. 29-35 (crude notes), Pl. x, xi).

6. Pandit Sāligrām, who was Postmaster-General of the North-Western Provinces some years ago, became one of these wandering friars, and other similar cases are recorded.

7. Seet Buldee Ramesur in original edition. The temple alluded to is that called Rāmesvaram (Ramisseram) in the small island of Pāmban at the entrance of Palk's Passage in the Straits of Manaar, which is distinguished by its magnificent colonnade and corridors. (Fergusson, *Hist. Ind. and Eastern Arch.*, vol. i, pp. 380-3, ed. 1910.) The island forms part of the so-called Adam's Bridge, a reef of comparatively recent formation, which almost joins Ceylon with the mainland. A railway now runs along the 'bridge', and the pilgrims have an easy task.

The Kedārnāth temple is in the Himalayan District of Garhwāl (United Provinces), at an elevation of nearly 12,000 feet.

8. The author's other works show that the Thugs frequently assumed the guise of ascetics, and much of the secret crime of India is known to be committed by men who adopt the garb of holiness. A man disguised as a fakīr is often sent on by dacoits (gang- robbers) as a spy and decoy. 'Three-fourths of these religions mendicants, whether Hindoos or Muhammadans, rob and steal, and a very great portion of them murder their victims before they rob them; but they have not any of them as a class been found to follow the trade of murder so exclusively as to be brought properly within the scope of our operations. . . . There is hardly any species of crime that is not throughout India perpetrated by men in the disguise of these religious mendicants; and almost all such mendicants are really men in disguise; for Hindoos of any caste can become Bairāgīs and Gosāins; and Muhammadans of any grade can become Fakīrs.' (*A Report on the System of Megpunnaism*, 1839, p. 11.) In the same little work the author advises the compulsory registration of 'every disciple belonging to every high priest, whether Hindoo or Muhammadan', and a stringent Vagrant Act. His suggestions have not been acted on.

9. This incident still happens occasionally.

10. For the Rājā, see *ante*, chapter 20, [6].

CHAPTER 75

The Bēgam Sumroo.

On the 7th of February [1836] I went out to Sardhana and visited the church built and endowed by the late Bēgam Sombre, whose remains are now deposited in it.[1] It was designed by an Italian gentleman, M. Reglioni, and is a fine but not a striking building.[2] I met the bishop, Julius Caesar, an Italian from Milan, whom I had known a quarter of a century before, a happy and handsome young man — he is still handsome, though old; but very miserable because the Bēgam did not leave him so large a legacy as he expected. In the revenues of her church he had, she thought, quite enough to live upon; and she said that priests without wives or children to care about ought to be satisfied with this; and left him only a few thousand rupees. She made him the medium of conveying a donation to the See of Rome of one hundred and fifty thousand rupees,[3] and thereby procured for him the bishopric of Amartanta in the island of Cyprus; and got her grandson, Dyce Sombre, made a chevalier of the Order of Christ, and presented with a splint from the real cross, as a relic.

The Bēgam Sombre was by birth a Saiyadanī, or lineal descendant from Muhammad, the founder of the Musalmān faith; and she was united to Walter Reinhard, when very young, by all the forms considered necessary by persons of her persuasion when married to men of another.[4] Reinhard had been married to another woman of the Musalmān faith, who still lives at Sardhana,[5] but she had become insane, and has ever since remained so. By this first wife he had a son, who got from the Emperor the title of Zafar Yāb Khān, at the request of the Bēgam, his stepmother; but he was a man of weak intellect, and so little thought of that he was not recognized even as the nominal chief on the death of his father.

Walter Reinhard was a native of Salzburg. He enlisted as a private soldier in the French service, and came to India, where he entered the service of the East India Company, and rose to the rank of sergeant.[6] Reinhard got the sobriquet of Sombre from his comrades while in the French service from the sombre cast of his countenance and temper.[7] An Armenian, by name Gregory, of a Calcutta family, the virtual minister of Kāsim Alī Khān,[8] under the title of Gorgīn Khān,[9] took him into his service when the war was about to commence between his master and the English. Kāsim Alī was a native of Kāshmīr, and not naturally a bad man; but he was goaded to madness by the injuries and insults heaped upon him by the servants of the East India Company, who were not then paid, as at present, in adequate salaries, but in profits upon all kinds of monopolies; and they would not suffer the recognized sovereign of the country in which they traded to grant to his subjects the same exemption that they claimed for themselves exclusively; and a war was the consequence.[10]

Mr. Ellis, one of these civil servants and chief of the factory at Patna, whose opinions had more weight with the council in Calcutta than all the wisdom of such men as Vansittart and Warren Hastings, because they happened to be more consonant with the personal interests of the majority, precipitately brought on the war, and assumed the direction of all military operations, of which he knew nothing, and for which he seems to have been totally unfitted by the violence of his temper. All his enterprises failed — the city and factory were captured by the enemy, and the European inhabitants taken prisoners. The Nawāb, smarting under the reiterated wrongs he had received, and which he attributed mainly to the counsels of Mr. Ellis, no sooner found the chief within his grasp, than he determined to have him and all who were taken with him, save a Doctor Fullarton, to whom he owed some personal obligations, put to death. His own native officers were shocked at the proposal, and tried to dissuade him from the purpose, but he was resolved, and not finding among them any willing to carry it into execution he applied to Sumroo, who readily undertook and, with some of his myrmidons, performed the horrible duty in 1763.[11] At the suggestion of Gregory and Sombre, Kāsim Alī now attempted to take the small principality of Nepāl, as a kind of basis for his operations against the English. He had four hundred excellent rifles with flint locks and screwed barrels made at Monghyr (Mungēr) on the Ganges, so as to fit into small boxes. These boxes were sent up on the backs of four hundred brave volunteers for this forlorn hope. Gregory had got a passport for the boxes as rare merchandise for the palace of the prince at Kathmandū, in whose presence alone they were to be opened. On reaching the palace at night, these volunteers were to open their boxes, screw up the barrels, destroy all the inmates, and possess themselves of the palace, where it is supposed Kāsim Ali had already secured many friends. Twelve thousand soldiers had advanced to the foot of the hills near Betiyā, to support the attack, and the volunteers were in the fort of Makwānpur, the only strong fort between the plain and the capital. They had been treated with great consideration by the garrison, and were to set out at daylight the next morning; but one of the attendants, who had been let into the secret, got drunk, and in a quarrel with one of the garrison, told him that he should see in a few days who would be master of that garrison. This led to suspicion; the boxes were broken open, the arms discovered, and the whole of the party, except three or four, were instantly put to death; the three or four who escaped gave intelligence to the army at Betiyā, and the whole retreated upon Monghyr. But for this drunken man, Nepāl had perhaps been Kāsim Alī's.[12]

Kāsim Alī Khān was beaten in several actions by our gallant little band of troops under their able leader, Colonel Adams; and at last driven to seek shelter with the Nawāb Wazīr of Oudh, into whose service Sumroo afterwards entered. This chief being in his turn beaten, Sumroo went off and entered the service of the celebrated chief of Rohilkhand, Hāfiz Rahmat Khān. This he soon quitted from fear of the English. He raised two battalions in 1772, which he soon afterwards increased to four; and let out always to the highest bidder — first, to the Jāt chiefs of Dīg, then to the chief of Jaipur, then to Najaf Khān, the prime minister, and then to the Marāthās. His battalions were officered by Europeans, but Europeans of respectability were unwilling to take service under a man so precariously situated, however great their necessities; and he was obliged to content himself for the most part with the very dross of society — men who could neither read nor write, nor keep themselves sober. The consequence was that the battalions were often in a state of mutiny, committing every kind of outrage upon the persons of their officers, and at all times in a state of insubordination bordering on mutiny. These battalions seldom obtained their pay till they put their commandant into confinement, and made him dig up his hidden stores, if he had any, or borrow from bankers, if he had none. If the troops felt pressed for time, and their commander was of the necessary character, they put him astride upon a hot gun without his trousers. When our battalion had got its pay out of him in this manner, he was often handed over to another for the same purpose. The poor old Bēgam had been often subjected to the starving stage of this proceeding before she came under our protection; but had never, I believe, been grilled upon a gun. It was a rule, it was said, with Sombre, to enter the field of battle at the safest point, form line facing the enemy, fire a few rounds in the direction where they stood, without regard to the distance or effect, form square, and await the course of events. If victory declared for the enemy, he sold his unbroken force to him to great advantage; if for his friends, he assisted them in collecting the plunder, and securing all the advantages of the victory. To this prudent plan of action his corps afterwards steadily adhered; and they never took or lost a gun till they came in contact with our forces at Ajantā and Assaye.[13]

Sombre died at Agra on the 4th of May, 1778, and his remains were at first buried in his garden. They were afterwards removed to the consecrated ground in the Agra churchyard by his widow the Bēgam,[14] who was baptized, at the age of forty,[15] by a Roman Catholic priest, under the name of Joanna,[16] on the 7th of May, 1781.

On the death of her husband she was requested to take command of the force by all the Europeans and natives that composed it, as the only possible mode of keeping them together, since the son was known to be altogether unfit. She consented, and was regularly installed in the charge by the Emperor Shāh Alam. Her chief officer was a Mr. Paoli, a German, who soon after took an active part in providing the poor imbecile old Emperor with a prime minister, and got himself assassinated on the restoration, a few weeks after, of his rival.[17] The troops continued in the same state of insubordination, and the Bēgam was anxious for an opportunity to show that she was determined to be obeyed.

While she was encamped with the army of the prime minister of the time at Mathurā,[18] news was one day brought to her that two slave girls had set fire to her houses at Agra, in order that they might make off with their paramours, two soldiers of the guard she had left in charge. These houses had thatched roofs, and contained all her valuables, and the widows, wives, and children of her principal officers. The fire had been put out with much difficulty and great loss of property; and the two slave girls were soon after discovered in the bazaar at Agra, and brought out to the Bēgam's camp. She had the affair investigated in the usual summary form; and their guilt being proved to the satisfaction of all present, she had them flogged till they were senseless, and then thrown into a pit dug in front of her tent for the purpose, and buried alive. I had heard the story related in different ways, and I now took pains to ascertain the truth; and this short narrative may, I believe, be relied upon.[19]

An old Persian merchant, called the Agā, still resided at Sardhana, to whom I knew that one of the slave girls belonged. I visited him, and he told me that his father had been on intimate terms with Sombre, and when he died his mother went to live with his widow, the Bēgam—that his slave girl was one of the two- that his mother at first protested against her being taken off to the camp, but became on inquiry satisfied of her guilt—and that the Bēgam's object was to make a strong impression upon the turbulent spirit of her troops by a severe example. 'In this object', said the old Agā, 'she entirely succeeded; and for some years after her orders were implicitly obeyed; had she faltered on that occasion she must have lost the command—she would have lost that respect, without which it would have been impossible for her to retain it a month. I was then a boy; but I remember well that there were, besides my mother and sisters, many respectable females that would have rather perished in the flames than come out to expose themselves to the crowd that assembled to see the fires; and had the fires not been put out, a great many lives must have been lost; besides, there were many old people and young children who could not have escaped.' The old Agā was going off to take up his quarters at Delhi when this conversation took place; and I am sure that he told me what he thought to be true. This narrative corresponded exactly with that of several other old men from whom I had heard the story. It should be recollected that among natives there is no particular mode of execution prescribed for those who are condemned to die; nor, in a camp like this, any court of justice save that of the commander in which they could be tried, and, supposing the guilt to have been established, as it is said to have been to the satisfaction of the Bēgam and the principal officers, who were all Europeans and Christians, perhaps the punishment was not much greater than the crime deserved and the occasion demanded. But it is possible that the slave girls may not have set fire to the buildings, but merely availed themselves of the occasion of the fire to run off; indeed, slave girls are under so little restraint in India, that it would be hardly worth while for them to burn down a house to get out. I am satisfied that the Bēgam believed them guilty, and that the punishment, horrible as it was, was merited. It certainly had the desired effect. My object has been to ascertain the truth in this case, and to state it, and not to eulogize or defend the old Bēgam.

After Paoli's death, the command of the troops under the Bēgam devolved successively upon Baours, Evans, Dudrenec, who, after a short time, all gave it up in disgust at the beastly habits of the European subalterns, and the overbearing insolence to which they and the want of regular pay gave rise among the soldiers. At last the command devolved upon Monsieur Le Vaisseau, a French gentleman of birth, education, gentlemanly deportment, and honourable feelings.[20] The battalions had been increased to six, with their due proportion of guns and cavalry; part resided at Sardhana, her capital, and part at Delhi, in attendance upon the Emperor. A very extraordinary man entered her service about the same time with Le Vaisseau, George Thomas, who, from a quartermaster on board a ship, raised himself to a principality in Northern India.[21] Thomas on one occasion raised his mistress in the esteem of the Emperor and the people by breaking through the old rule of central squares: gallantly leading on his troops, and rescuing his majesty from a perilous situation in one of his battles with a rebellious subject, Najaf Kulī Khān, where the Bēgam was present in her palankeen, and reaped all the laurels, being from that day called 'the most beloved daughter of the Emperor'.[22] As his best chance of securing his ascendancy against such a rival, Le Vaisseau proposed marriage to the Bēgam, and was accepted. She was married to Le Vaisseau by Father Gregoris, a Carmelite monk, in 1793, before Saleur and Bernier, two French officers of great merit. George Thomas left her service, in consequence, in 1793, and set up for himself; and was afterwards crushed by the united armies of the Sikhs and Marāthās, commanded by European officers, after he had been recognized as a general officer by the Governor-General of India. George Thomas had latterly twelve small disciplined battalions officered by Europeans. He had good artillery, cast his own guns, and was the first person that applied iron calibres to brass cannon. He was unquestionably a man of very extraordinary military genius, and his ferocity and recklessness as to the means he used were quite in keeping with the times. His revenues were derived from the Sikh states which he had rendered tributary; and he would probably have been sovereign of them all in the room of Ranjit Singh, had not the jealousy of Perron and other French officers in the Marāthā army interposed.[23]

The Bēgam tried in vain to persuade her husband to receive all the European officers of the corps at his table as gentlemen, urging that not only their domestic peace, but their safety among such a turbulent set, required that the character of these officers should be raised if possible, and their feelings conciliated. Nothing, he declared, should ever induce him to sit at table with men of such habits; and they at last determined that no man should command them who would not condescend to do so. Their insolence and that of the soldiers generally became at last unbearable, and the Bēgam determined to go off with her husband, and seek an asylum in the Honourable Company's territory with the little property she could command, of one hundred thousand rupees in money, and her jewels, amounting perhaps in value to one hundred thousand more. Le Vaisseau did not understand English; but with the aid of a grammar and a dictionary he was able to communicate her wishes to Colonel McGowan, who commanded at that time (1795) an advanced post of our army at Anūpshahr on the Ganges. [24] He proposed that the Colonel should receive them in his cantonments, and assist them in their journey thence to Farrukhābād, where they wished in future to reside, free from the cáres and anxieties of such a charge. The Colonel had some scruples, under the impression that he might be censured for aiding in the flight of a public officer of the Emperor. He now addressed the Governor-General of India, Sir John Shore himself, April 1795,[25] who requested Major Palmer, our accredited agent with Sindhia, who was then encamped near Delhi, and holding the seals of prime minister of the empire, to interpose his good offices in favour of the Bēgam and her husband. Sindhia demanded twelve lākhs of rupees as the price of the privilege she solicited to retire; and the Bēgam, in her turn, demanded over and above the privilege of resigning the command into his hands, the sum of four lākhs of rupees as the price of the arms and accoutrements which had been provided at her own cost and that of her late husband. It was at last settled that she should resign the command, and set out secretly with her husband; and that Sindhia should confer the command of her troops upon one of his own officers, who would pay the son of Sombre two thousand rupees a month for life. Le Vaisseau was to be received into our territories, treated as a prisoner of war upon parole, and permitted to reside with his wife at the French settlement of Chandernagore. His last letter to Sir John Shore is dated the 30th April, 1795. His last letters describing this final arrangement are addressed to Mr. Even, a French merchant at Mirzapore, and a Mr. Bernier, both personal friends of his, and are dated 18th of May, 1795.[26]

The battalions on duty at Delhi got intimation of this correspondence, made the son of Sombre declare himself their legitimate chief, and march at their head to seize the Bēgam and her husband. Le Vaisseau heard of their approach, and urged the Bēgam to set out with him at midnight for Anūpshahr, declaring that he would rather destroy himself than submit to the personal indignities which he knew would be heaped upon him by the infuriated ruffians who were coming to seize them. The Bēgam consented, declaring that she would put an end to her life with her own hand should she be taken. She got into her palankeen with a dagger in her hand, and as he had seen her determined resolution and proud spirit before exerted on many trying occasions, he doubted not that she would do what she declared she would. He mounted his horse and rode by the side of her palankeen, with a pair of pistols in his holsters, and a good sword by his side. They had got as far as Kabrī, about three miles from Sardhana,[27] on the road to Meerut, when they found the battalions from Sardhana, who had got intimation of the flight, gaining fast upon the palankeen. Le Vaisseau asked the Bēgam whether she remained firm in her resolve to die rather than submit to the indignities that threatened them. 'Yes,' replied she, showing him the dagger firmly grasped in her right hand. He drew a pistol from his holster without saying anything, but urged on the bearers. He could have easily galloped off, and saved himself, but he would not quit his wife's side. At last the soldiers came up close behind them. The female attendants of the Bēgam began to scream; and looking in, Le Vaisseau saw the white cloth that covered the Bēgam's breast stained with blood. She had stabbed herself, but the dagger had struck against one of the bones of her chest, and she had not courage to repeat the blow. Her husband put his pistol to his temple and fired. The bail passed through his head, and he fell dead on the ground. One of the soldiers who saw him told me that he sprang at least a foot off the saddle into the air as the shot struck him. His body was treated with every kind of insult by the European officers and their men;[28] and the Bēgam was taken back into Sardhana, kept under a gun for seven days, deprived of all kinds of food, save what she got by stealth from her female servants, and subjected to all manner of insolent language.

At last the officers were advised by George Thomas, who had instigated them to this violence out of pique against the Bēgam for her preference of the Frenchman,[29] to set aside their puppet and reseat the Bēgam in the command, as the only chance of keeping the territory of Sardhana.[30] 'If', said he, 'the Bēgam should die under the torture of mind and body to which you are subjecting her, the minister will very soon resume the lands assigned for your payment, and disband a force so disorderly, and so little likely to be of any use to him or the Emperor.' A council of war was held—the Bēgam was taken out from under the gun, and reseated on the 'masnad'. A paper was drawn up by about thirty European officers, of whom only one, Monsieur Saleur, could sign his own name, swearing in the name of God and Jesus Christ,[31] that they would henceforward obey her with all their hearts and souls, and recognize no other person whomsoever as commander. They all affixed their seals to this covenant; but some of them, to show their superior learning, put their initials, or what they used as such, for some of these learned Thebans knew only two or three letters of the alphabet, which they put down, though they happened not to be their real initials. An officer on the part of Sindhia, who was to have commanded these troops, was present at this reinstallation of the Bēgam, and glad to take, as a compensation for his disappointment, the sum of one hundred and fifty thousand rupees, which the Bēgam contrived to borrow for him.

The body of poor Le Vaisseau was brought back to camp, and there lay several days unburied, and exposed to all kinds of indignities. The supposition that this was the result of a plan formed by the Bēgam to get rid of Le Vaisseau is, I believe, unfounded.[32] The Bēgam herself gave some colour of truth to the report by retaining the name of her first husband, Sombre, to the last, and never publicly or formally declaring her marriage with Le Vaisseau after his death. The troops in this mutiny pretended nothing more than a desire to vindicate the honour of their old commander Sombre, which had, they said, been compromised by the illicit intercourse between Le Vaisseau and his widow. She had not dared to declare the marriage to them lest they should mutiny on that ground, and deprive her of the command; and for the same reason she retained the name of Sombre after her restoration, and remained silent on the subject of her second marriage. The marriage was known only to a few European officers. Sir John Shore, Major Palmer, and the other gentlemen with whom Le Vaisseau corresponded. Some grave old native gentlemen who were long in her service have told me that they believed 'there really was too much of truth in the story which excited the troops to mutiny on that occasion—her too great intimacy with the gallant young Frenchman. God forgive them for saying so of a lady whose salt they had eaten for so many years'. Le Vaisseau made no mention of the marriage to Colonel McGowan; and from the manner in which he mentions it to Sir John Shore it is clear that he, or she, or both, were anxious to conceal it from the troops and from Sindhia before their departure. She stipulated in her will that her heir, Mr. Dyce, should take the name of Sombre, as if she wished to have the little episode of her second marriage forgotten.

After the death of Le Vaisseau, the command devolved on Monsieur Saleur, a Frenchman, the only respectable officer who signed the covenant; he had taken no active part in the mutiny; on the contrary, he had done all he could to prevent it; and he was at last, with George Thomas, the chief means of bringing his brother officers back to a sense of their duty. Another battalion was added to the four in 1787, and another raised in 1798 and 1802; five of the six marched under Colonel Saleur to the Deccan with Sindhia. They were in a state of mutiny the whole way, and utterly useless as auxiliaries, as Saleur himself declared in many of his letters written in French to his mistress the Bēgam. At the battle of Assaye, four of these battalions were left in charge of the Marāthā camps. One was present in the action and lost its four guns. Soon after the return of these battalions, the Bēgam entered into an alliance with the British Government; the force then consisted of these six battalions, a party of artillery served chiefly by Europeans, and two hundred horse. She had a good arsenal well stored, a foundry for cannon, both within the walls of a small fortress, built near her dwelling at Sardhana. The whole cost her about four lākhs of rupees a year; her civil establishments eighty thousand, and her household establishments and expenses about the same; total six lākhs of rupees a year. The revenues of Sardhana, and the other lands assigned at different times for the payment of the force had been at no time more than sufficient to cover these expenses; but under the protection of our Government they improved with the extension of tillage, and the improvements of the surrounding markets for produce, and she was enabled to give largely to the support of charitable institutions, and to provide handsomely for the support of her family and pensioners after her death.'[33]

Sombre's son, Zafaryāb Khān, had a daughter who was married to Colonel Dyce, who had for some time the management of the Bēgam's affairs; but he lost her favour long before her death by his violent temper and overbearing manners, and was obliged to resign the management to his son, who, on the Bēgam's death, came in for the bulk of her fortune, or about sixty lākhs of rupees. He has two sisters who were brought up by the Bēgam, one married to Captain Troup, an Englishman, and the other to Mr. Salaroli, an Italian, both very worthy men. Their wives have been handsomely provided for by the Bēgam, and by their brother, who trebled the fortunes left to them by the Bēgam.[34] She built an excellent church at Sardhana, and assigned the sum of 100,000 rupees as a fund to provide for its service and repairs; 50,000 rupees as another [fund] for the poor of the place; and 100,000 as a third, for a college in which Roman Catholic priests might be educated for the benefit of India generally. She sent to Rome 150,000 rupees to be employed as a charity fund at the discretion of the Pope; and to the Archbishop of Canterbury she sent 50,000 for the same purpose. She gave to the Bishop of Calcutta 100,000 rupees to provide teachers for the poor of the Protestant church in Calcutta. She sent to Calcutta for distribution to the poor, and for the liberation of deserving debtors, 50,000. To the Catholic missions at Calcutta, Bombay, and Madras she gave 100,000; and to that of Agra 50,000. She built a handsome chapel for the Roman Catholics at Meerut; and presented the fund for its support with a donation of 12,000; and she built a chapel for the Church Missionary at Meerut, the Reverend Mr. Richards, at a cost of 10,000, to meet the wants of the native Protestants. [35]

Among all who had opportunities of knowing her she bore the character of a kind-hearted, benevolent, and good woman; and I have conversed with men capable of judging, who had known her for more than fifty years. She had uncommon sagacity and a masculine resolution; and the Europeans and natives who were most intimate with her have told me that though a woman and of small stature, her 'ru'b' (dignity, or power of commanding personal respect) was greater than that of almost any person they had ever seen.[36] From the time she put herself under the protection of the British Government, in 1808, she by degrees adopted the European modes of social intercourse, appearing in public on an elephant, in a carriage, and occasionally on horseback with her hat and veil, and dining at table with gentlemen. She often entertained Governors-General and Commanders-in-Chief, with all their retinues, and sat with them and their staff at table, and for some years past kept an open house for the society of Meerut; but in no situation did she lose sight of her dignity. She retained to the last the grateful affections of the thousands who were supported by her bounty, while she never ceased to inspire the most profound respect in the minds of those who every day approached her, and were on the most unreserved terms of intimacy.[37]

Lord William Bentinck was an excellent judge of character; and the following letter will show how deeply his visit to that part of the country had impressed him with a sense of her extensive usefulness:

'To Her Highness the Begum Sumroo.

'My esteemed Friend,—I cannot leave India without expressing the sincere esteem I entertain for your highness's character. The benevolence of disposition and extensive charity which have endeared you to thousands, have excited in my mind sentiments of the warmest admiration; and I trust that you may yet be preserved for many years, the solace of the orphan and widow, and the sure resource of your numerous dependants. To-morrow morning I embark for England; and my prayers and best wishes attend you, and all others who, like you, exert themselves for the benefit of the people of India.

> 'I remain,
> 'With much consideration,
> 'Your sincere friend,
> (Signed) 'M. W. BENTINCK.[38]

'Calcutta, March 17th, 1835.'

Notes:

1. The reader will observe that the lady's name is spelt Sumroo in the heading and Sombre in the text. The form Samrū, or Shamrū, transliterates the Hindustāni spelling.

2. The author means General Regholini who was in the Bēgam's service at the time of her death. (*N.W.P. Gazetteer*, 1st ed., vol. iii, p. 295.) The church, or cathedral, was consecrated in 1822, and coat 400,000 rupees. A portrait of the General, from Sardhana, is now in the Indian Institute, Oxford, which also possesses a portrait of the Bishop.

The best account of Begum Sumroo is to be found in *A Tour through the Upper Provinces of Hindustan*, 1804-14, by A. D. = Ann Deane (1823). Walter Scott introduces more than one of the stories about the Begum into *The Surgeon's Daughter* (1827), e.g.: "But not to be interred alive under your seat, like the Circassian of whom you were jealous," said Middlemas, shuddering (vol. 48, Black's ed. of the novels, p. 382).

3. The Bēgam's benefactions are detailed *post*.

4. 'This remarkable woman was the daughter, by a concubine, of Asad Khān, a Musalmān of Arab decent settled in the town of Kutāna in the Meerut district. She was born about the year A.D. 1753 [see *post*.] On the death of her father, she and her mother became subject to ill-treatment from her half-brother, the legitimate heir, and they consequently removed to Delhi about 1760. There she entered the service of Sumru, and accompanied him

through all his campaigns. Sumru, on retiring to Sardhana, found himself relieved of all the cares and troubles of war, and gave himself entirely up to a life of ease and pleasure, and so completely fell into the hands of the Bēgam that she had no difficulty in inducing him to exchange the title of mistress for that of wife.' (E. T. Atkinson in *N.W.P. Gazetteer*, 1st ed., vol. ii, p. 95. The authorities for the history of Bēgum Samrū are very conflicting. Atkinson has examined them critically, and his account probably is the best in existence.) An anonymous pamphlet published apparently at Sardhana and sent to the editor anonymously long ago, gives the name of the Bēgam's father as 'Lutf Ali Khan, a decayed nobleman of Arabian descent' living at Kotana. Some writers state that the Bēgam was a dancing girl, and was bought by Sumroo. Her name was Zēb-un-nissa.

5. This first wife died at Sardhana during the rainy season of 1838. She must have been above one hundred years of age; and a good many of the Europeans that he buried in the Sardhana cemetery had lived above a hundred years. [W. H. S.] She was a concubine, named Bahā Bēgam. (*N.W.P. Gazetteer*, vol. iii, p. 96.)

6. His name is spelt Reinhard on his tombstone, as in the text. It is also spelt Renard. According to some authorities, his birthplace was Trèves, not Salzburg. He is said to have been a butcher by trade, and certainly deserted from both the French and the English services.

7. A more probable explanation is that the name is a corruption of an alias, Summers, assumed by the deserter.

8. Kāsim Alī Khān is generally referred to in the histories under the name of Mīr Kāsim (Meer Cossim). Mīr Jāfir was deposed in 1760, and his son-in- law Mīr Kāsim was placed on the throne of Bengal in his stead by the English. The history of Mīr Kāsim is told in detail by Thornton in his sixth chapter, and also by Mill.

9. Probably 'Gorgīn' is a corruption of 'Gregory'. This name may be a corruption of 'Georgian'.

10. Mill observes upon these transactions: 'The conduct of the Company's servants upon this occasion furnishes one of the most remarkable instances upon record of the power of self-interest to extinguish all sense of justice and even of shame. They had hitherto insisted, contrary to all right and all precedent, that the government of the country should exempt all their goods from duty; they now insisted that it should impose duties upon all other traders, and accused it as guilty of a breach of the peace towards the English nation, because it proposed to remit them.' [W. H. S.] The quotation is from Book iv, chapter 5 (5th ed., 1858, vol. iii, p. 237).

11. The 3rd of October was the day of slaughter at Patna. The Europeans at other places in Mīr Kāsim's power were also massacred; and the total number slain, men, women, and children, amounted to about two hundred. Sumroo personally butchered about one hundred and fifty at Patna.

12. Our troops, under Sir David Ochterlony, took the fort of Makwānpur in 1815, and might in five days have been before the defenceless capital; but they were here arrested by the romantic chivalry of the Marquis of Hastings. The country had been virtually conquered; the prince, by his base treachery towards us and outrages upon others, had justly forfeited his throne; but the Governor- General, by perhaps a misplaced lenity, left it to him without any other guarantee for his future good behaviour than the recollection that he had been soundly beaten. Unfortunately he left him at the same time a sufficient quantity of fertile land below the hills to maintain the same army with which he had fought us, with better knowledge how to employ them, to keep us out on a future occasion. Between the attempt of Kāsim Alī and our attack upon Nepāl, the Gōrkhā masters of the country had, by a long series of successful aggressions upon their neighbours, rendered themselves in their own opinion and in that of their neighbours the beat soldiers of India. They have, of course, a very natural feeling of hatred against our government, which put a stop to the wild career of conquest, and wrested from their grasp all the property and all the pretty women from Kathmandū to Kashmīr. To these beautify regions they were what the invading Huns were in former days to Europe, absolute fiends. Had we even exacted a good road into their country with fortifications at the proper places, it might have checked the hopes of one day resuming the career of conquest that now keeps up the army and military spirit, to threaten us with a renewal of war whenever we are embarrassed on the plains. [W. H. S.]

The author's uneasiness concerning the attitude of Nepal was justified. During the Afghan troubles of 1838-43 the Nepalese Government was in constant communication with the enemies of the Indian Government. The late Maharāja Sir Jang Bahādur obtained power in 1846, and, after his visit to England in 1850, decided to abide by the English alliance. He did valuable service in 1857 and 1858, and the two governments have ever since maintained an unbroken, though reserved, friendship. The Gōrkhā regiments in the English service are recruited in Nepāl.

13. Aasaye (Assye, Asāi) is in the Nizām's dominions. Here, on the 23rd of September, 1803, Sir Arthur Wellesley, afterwards Duke of Wellington, with less than 5,000 men, defeated the Marāthā host of at least 32,000 men, including more than 10,000 under European leaders. Ajantā, or Ajantā Ghāt, is in the same region. (Owen, *Sel. from Wellington Despatches* (1880), pp. 301-9.)

14. His tombstone bears a Portuguese inscription: 'Aqui iaz Walter Reinhard, morreo aos 4 de Mayo no anno de 1778.' (*N.W.P. Gazetteer*, vol. ii, p. 96.)

15. According to this statement she must have been born in or about 1741, not in 1753, as stated by Atkinson. If the earlier date were correct, she would have been ninety-five when she died in 1836. Higginbotham, referring to Bacon's work, says she died at the age of eighty-nine, which places her birth in 1747. According to Beale, she was aged eighty-eight lunar years when she died, on the 27th January, 1836, equivalent to about eighty-five solar years. This computation places her birth in A.D. 1751, which may be taken as the correct date. The date of her baptism is correctly stated in the text.

16. She added the name Nobilis, when she married Le Vaisseau. (*N.W.P. Gazetteer*, vol. ii, p. 106, note.)

17. The author spells the German's name Pauly; I have followed Atkinson's spelling. The man was assassinated in 1783.

18. This circumstance indicates that the execution of the slave girls took place in 1782. (See *N.W.P. Gazetteer*, vol. ii, p. 91.)

19. The darker aide of the Bēgam's character is shown by the story of the slave girl's murder. By some it is said that the girl's crime consisted in her having attracted the favourable notice of one of the Bēgam's husbands. Whatever may have been the offence, her barbarous mistress visited it by causing the girl to be buried alive. The time chosen for the execution was the evening, the place the tent of the Bēgam; who caused her bed to be arranged immediately over the grave, and occupied it until the morning, to prevent any attempt to rescue the miserable girl beneath. By acts like this the Bēgam inspired such terror that she was never afterwards troubled with domestic dissensions.' (*N.W.P. Gazetteer*, 1st ed., vol. ii, p. 110.) It will be observed that this version mentions only one girl. According to Higginbotham (*Men whom India has Known*, 2nd ed., s.v. 'Sumroo'), this execution took place on the evening of the day on which Le Vaisseau perished in 1795. (See *post.*) He adds that 'it is said that this act preyed upon her conscience in after life'. This account professes to be based on Bacon's *First Impressions and Studies from Nature in Hindustan*, which is said to be 'the most reliable, as the author saw the Bēgam, attended and conversed with her at one of her levées, and gained all his information at her Court'. But Bacon's account of the Bēgam's history, as quoted by Higginbotham, is full of gross errors; and Sir William Sleeman may be relied on as giving the most accurate obtainable version of the horrid story. He had the beat possible opportunities, as well as a desire, to ascertain the truth.

20. Atkinson (*N.W.P. Gazetteer*, vol. ii, p. 106) uses the spelling Le Vaisseau, which probably is correct, and observes that the name is also written Le Vassont. The author writes Le Vassoult; and Francklin (*Military Memoirs of Mr. George Thomas*, London, 8vo reprint (Stockdale), p. 55) spells the name phonetically as Levasso. 'On every occasion he was the declared and inveterate enemy of Mr. Thomas.'

21. Thomas was an Irishman, born in the county of Tipperary. 'From the best information we could procure, it appears that Mr. George Thomas first came to India in a British ship of war, in 1781- 2. His situation in the fleet was humble, having served as a quarter- master, or, as is affirmed by some, in the capacity of a common sailor. . . . His first service was among the Polygars to the southward, where he resided a few years. But at length setting out overland, he spiritedly traversed the central part of the peninsula, and about the year 1787 arrived at Delhi. Here he received a commission in the service of the Bēgam Sumroo. . . . Soon after his arrival at Delhi, the Bēgam, with her usual judgement and discrimination of character, advanced him to a command in her army. From this period his military career in the north-west of India may be said to have commenced.' Owing to the rivalry of Le Vaisseau, Thomas 'quitted the Bēgam Sumroo, and about 1792 betook himself to the frontier station of the British army at the post of Anopshire (Anūpshāhr). . . . Here he waited several months. . . . In the beginning of the year 1793, Mr. Thomas, being at Anopshire, received letters from Appakandarow (Apakanda Rāo), a Mahratta chief, conveying offers of service, and promises of a comfortable provision.' (Francklin, op. cit., p. 20.) The author states that Thomas left the Bēgam's service in 1793, after her marriage with Le Vaisseau in that year. Francklin (see also p. 55) was clearly under the impression that the marriage did not take place till after Thomas had thrown up his command under the Bēgam. He made peace with her in 1795. The capital of the principality which he carved out for himself in 1798 was at Hānsī, eighty-nine miles north-west of Delhi. He was driven out at the close of 1801, entered British territory in January 1802, and died on the 22nd of August in that year at Barhāmpur, being about forty-six years of age. A son of his was an officer in the Bēgam's service at the time of her death in 1836. A great-granddaughter of George Thomas was, in 1867, the wife of a writer on a humble salary in one of the Government offices at Agra. (Beale.)

22. This incident happened in 1788. (See *N.W.P. Gazetteer*, vol. ii, p. 99; *I.G.*, 1908, vol. xii, p. 106.)

23. 'A more competent estimate may perhaps be formed of his abilities if we reflect on the nature and extent of one of his plans, which he detailed to the compiler of these memoirs during his residence at Benares. When fixed

in his residence at Hānsī, he first conceived, and would, if unforeseen and untoward circumstances had not occurred, have executed the bold design of extending his conquests to the mouths of the Indus. This was to have been effected by a fleet of boats, constructed from timber procured in the forests near the city of Fīrōzpur, on the banks of the Satlaj river, proceeding down that river with his army, and settling the countries he might subdue on his route; a daring enterprise, and conceived in the true spirit of an ancient Roman. On the conclusion of this design it was his intention to turn his arms against the Panjāb, which he expected to reduce in a couple of years; and which, considering the wealth he would then have acquired, and the amazing resources he would have possessed, these successes combined would doubtless have contributed to establish his authority on a firm and solid basis.' He offered to conquer the Panjāb on behalf of the Government of India, for the welfare of his king and country. (Francklin, pp. 334- 6.)

24. A small town in the Bulandshahr district of the North-Western Provinces, seventy-three miles south-east of Delhi. Its fort used to be considered strong and of strategical importance.

25. Afterwards Lord Teignmouth.

26. Major Bernier was killed at the storm of Hānsī in 1801. His tombstone at Barsi village was found ninety years later (*Pioneer*, Dec. 14, 1894). For epitaph of Joseph Even Bahādur see *N.I.N. & Qu.*, vol. i, note 265.

27. Francklin says that the troops overtook the fugitives 'at the village of Kerwah, in the begum's jaghire, four miles distant from her capital', (p. 58.)

28. 'For three days it lay exposed to the insults of the rabble, and was at length thrown into a ditch.' (Francklin, p. 60.)

29. According to George Thomas (whose version of the story is given by his biographer), the Bēgam, when the mutiny broke out, was actually preparing to attack Thomas. A German officer, known only as the Liègeois, strenuously dissuaded the Bēgam from the proposed hostilities, and was, in consequence, degraded by Le Vaisseau. The troop then mutinied, and swore allegiance to Zafar Yāb Khān. (Francklin, p. 37.)

30. Thomas says that the overtures came from the Bēgam. 'In a manner the most abject and desponding, she addressed Mr. Thomas . . . implored him to come to her assistance, and, finally, offered to pay any sum of money the Marāthās should require, on condition they would reinstate her in the Jāgīr. On receipt of these letters, Mr. Thomas, by an offer of 120,000 rupees, prevailed on Bāpū Sindhia to make a movement towards Sardhana.' After negotiation, Thomas marched to Khataulī, and 'publicly gave out that unless the Bēgam was reinstated in her authority, those who resisted must expect

no mercy; and to give additional weight to this declaration, he apprised them that he was acting under the orders of the Marāthā chiefs.' After some difficulty, 'she was finally reinstated in the full authority of her Jāgīr'. This version of the affair, it will be noticed, does not quite agree with that given more briefly by the author.

31. The paper was written by a Muhammadan, and he would not write Christ *the Son of God*. It is written 'In the name of God, and his Majesty Christ'. The Muhammadans look upon Christ as the greatest of prophets before Muhammad; but the most binding article of their faith is this from the Korān, which they repeat every day: 'I believe in God, who was never begot, nor has ever begotten, nor will ever have an equal,' — alluding to the Christians' belief in the Trinity. [W. H. S.] For Mohammed's opinion of Jesus Christ see especially chapters 4 and 5 of the Korān.

32. To my mind the circumstances all tend to throw suspicion on the Bēgam. The author evidently was disposed to form the beat possible opinion of her character and acts.

33. After the Bēgam's death the revenue settlement of the estate was made by Mr. Plowden, who writes in his report, as quoted in *N.W.P. Gazetteer*, 1st ed., vol. iii, p. 432, 'The rule seems to have been fully recognized and acted up to by the Bēgam which declared that, according to Muhammadan law, "there shall be left for every man who cultivates his lands as much as he requires for his own support, till the next crop be reaped, and that of his family, and for seed. This much shall be left to him; what remains is land-tax, and shall go to the public treasury." For, considering her territory as a private estate and her subjects as serfs, she appropriated the whole produce of their labour, with the exception of what sufficed to keep body and soul together. It was by these means . . . that a factitious state of prosperity was induced and maintained, which, though it might, and I believe did, deceive the Bēgam's neighbours into an impression that her country was highly prosperous, could not delude the population into content and happiness. Above the surface and to the eye all was smiling and prosperous, but within was rottenness and misery. Under these circumstances the smallness of the above arrear is no proof of the fairness of the revenue. It rather shows that the collections were as much as the Bēgam's ingenuity could extract, and this balance being unrealizable, the demand was, by so much at least, too high.' The statistics alluded to are:

Average demand of the portions of the Bēgam's Rs.
Territory in the Meerut district 5.86.650
Average collections 5.67.211
Balances 19.439

'Ruin was impending, when the Bēgam's death in January, 1836, and the consequent lapse of the estate to the British, induced the cultivators to return to their homes.'

Details of the Bēgam's military forces are given in *N.W.P. Gazetteer*, vol. iii, p. 295. For the last thirty years of her life the Bēgam had no need for the large force (3,371 officers and men, with 44 guns) which she maintained. In her excessive expenditure on a superfluous army, in her niggardly provision for civil administration, and in her merciless rack- renting, she followed the evil example of the ordinary native prince, and was superior only in the unusual ability with which she worked an unsound and oppressive System. She left £700,000. The population of Sardhana town has risen from 3,313 in 1881 to 9,242 in 1911.

34 Zafaryāb Khān died in 1802 or 1803. His son-in- law, Colonel Dyce, was employed in the Bēgam's service. 'The issue of this marriage was: (l) David Ochterlony Dyce Sombre, who married Mary Anne, daughter of Viscount St. Vincent, by whom he had no issue. He died in Paris in July, 1851. In August, 1867, his body was conveyed to Sardhana and buried in the cathedral. (2) A daughter, who married Captain Rose Troup. (3) A daughter, who married Paul Salaroli, now Marquis of Briona. The present owner of Sardhana is the Honourable Mary Anne Forester, the widow of David Ochterlony Dyce Sombre, and the successful claimant in the suit against Government which has recently been decided in her favour.' (*N.W.P. Gazetteer*, vol. iii (1875), p. 296.) This lady, in 1862, married George Cecil-Weld, third Baron Forester, who died without issue in 1886. (*Burke's Peerage*.) Lady Forester died on March 7, 1893.

35. In the original edition these statistics are given in words. Figures have been used in this edition as being more readily grasped. The amounts stated by the author are approximate round sums. More accurate details are given in *N.W.P. Gazetteer*, vol. iii (1875), p. 295. The Bēgam also subscribed liberally to Hindoo and Muhammadan institutions. Her contemporary, Colonel Skinner, was equally impartial, and is said to have built a mosque and a temple, as well as the church at Delhi.

The Cathedral at Sardhana was built in 1822. St. John's College is intended to train Indians as priests, There are, or were recently, about 250 native Christians at Sardhana, partly the descendants of the converts who followed their mistress in change of faith. 'The Roman Catholic priests work hard for their little colony, and are greatly revered and respected. At St. John's College some of the boys are instructed for the priesthood, and others taught to read and write the Nāgarī and Urdū characters. The instruction for the priesthood is peculiar. There are some twelve little native boys who can quote whole chapters of the Latin Bible, and nearly all the prayers of the Missal. Those who cannot sympathize with the system mast admire the patience and devotion of the Italian priests who have put themselves to the trouble of imparting such instruction. The majority of the Christian population here are cultivators and weavers, while many are the pensioned descendants of the European servants of Bēgam Sumru, and still bear the appellation of Sāhib and Mem Sāhib.' (*N.W.P. Gazetteer*, vol. iii (1875), pp. 273, 430.)

The Bēgam's palace, built in 1834, was chiefly remarkable for a collection of about twenty-five portraits of considerable interest. They comprised likenesses of Sir David Ochterlony, Dyce Sombre, Lord Combermere, and other notable personages. (*Calcutta Review*, vol. lxx, p. 460; quoted in *North Indian N. & Q.*, vol. ii, p. 179.) The mansion and park were sold by auction in 1895. Some of the portraits are now in the Indian Institute, Oxford, some in the Indian Museum, Calcutta, and some in Government House, Allahabad. A long article by H. N. on Sardhana and its owners appeared in the *Pioneer* (Allahabad) on December 12,1894.

36. A miniature portrait of the Bēgam is given on the frontispiece to volume ii of the original edition. Francklin, describing the events of 1796, in his memoirs of George Thomas, first published in 1803, describes her personal appearance as follows: 'Begum Sumroo is about forty-five years of age, small in stature, but inclined to be plump. Her complexion is very fair, her eyes black, large and animated; her dress perfectly Hindustany, and of the most costly materials. She speaks the Persian and Hindustany languages with fluency, and in her conversation is engaging, sensible, and spirited.' (London ed., p. 92, note.) The liberal benefaction of her later years have secured her ecclesiastical approval, and I should not be surprised to hear of her beatification or canonization. Her earlier life certainly was not that of a saint.

37. In her younger days she strictly maintained Hindustani etiquette. 'It has been the constant and invariable usage of this lady to exact from her subjects and servants the most rigid attention to the customs of Hindoostan. She is never seen out of doors or in her public durbar unveiled.

'Her officers and others, who have business with her, present themselves opposite the place where she sits. The front of her apartment is furnished with *chicques* or Indian screens, these being let down from the roof.

In this manner she gives audience and transacts business of all kinds. She frequently admits to her table the higher ranks of her European officers, but never admits the natives to come within the enclosure,' (Francklin, p, 92.)

38. The Governor-General's name was William Henry Cavendish-Bentinck, I do not understand the signature M. W. Bentinck, which may be a misprint. The eulogium seems odd to a reader who remembers that the recipient had been for fifteen years the mistress and wife of the Butcher of Patna. But when it was written, the memory of the massacre had been dimmed by the lapse of seventy-two years, and His Excellency may not have been well versed in the lady's history.

Perhaps the author was mistaken, and the letter was sent by Lady Bentinck, whose name was Mary.

CHAPTER 76

ON THE SPIRIT OF MILITARY DISCIPLINE
IN THE NATIVE ARMY OF INDIA

Abolition of Corporal Punishment—Increase of Pay with Length of Service—Promotion by Seniority.

The following observations on a very important and interesting subject were not intended to form a portion of the present work.[1] They serve to illustrate, however, many passages in the foregoing chapters touching the character of the natives of India; and the Afghan war having occurred since they were written, I cannot deny myself the gratification of presenting them to the public, since the courage and fidelity, which it was my object to show the British Government had a right to expect from its native troops and might always rely upon in the hour of need, have been so nobly displayed.

I had one morning (November 14th, 1838) a visit from the senior native officer of my regiment, Shaikh Mahūb Alī, a very fine old gentleman, who had recently attained the rank of 'Sardār Bahādur', and been invested with the new Order of British India.[2] He entered the service at the age of fifteen, and had served fifty-three years with great credit to himself, and fought in many an honourable field. He had come over to Jubbulpore as president of a native general court-martial, and paid me several visits in company with another old officer of my regiment who was a member of the same court. The following is one of the many conversations I had with him, taken down as soon as he left me.

'What do you think, Sardār Bahādur, of the order prohibiting corporal punishment in the army; has it had a bad or a good effect?'

'It has had a very good effect.'

'What good has it produced?'

'It has reduced the number of courts martial to one-quarter of what they were before, and thereby lightened the duties of the officers; it has made the good men more careful, and the bad men more orderly than they used to be.'

'How has it produced this effect?'

'A bad man formerly went on recklessly from small offences to great ones in the hope of impunity; he knew that no regimental, cantonment, or brigade court martial could sentence him to be dismissed the service; and that they would not sentence him to be flogged, except for great crimes, because it involved at the same time dismissal from the service. If they sentenced him to be flogged, he still hoped that the punishment would be remitted. The general or officer confirming the sentence was generally unwilling to order it to be carried into effect, because the man must, after being flogged, be turned out of the service, and the marks of the lash upon his back would prevent his getting service anywhere else. Now he knows that these courts can sentence him to be dismissed from the service—that he is liable to lose his bread for ordinary transgressions, and be sentenced to work on the roads for graver ones.[3] He is in consequence much more under restraint than he used to be.'

'And how has it tended to make the well-disposed more careful?'

'They were formerly liable to be led into errors by the example of the bad men, under the same hope of impunity; but they are now more on their guard. They have all relations among the native officers, who are continually impressing upon them the necessity of being on their guard, lest they be sent back upon their families—their mothers and fathers, wives and children, as beggars. To be dismissed from a service like that of the Company is a very great punishment; it subjects a man to the odium and indignation of all his family. When in the Company's service, his friends know that a soldier gets his pay regularly, and can afford to send home a very large portion of it. They expect that he will do so; he feels that they will listen to no excuse, and he contracts habits of sobriety and prudence. If a man gets into the service of a native chief, his friends know that his pay is precarious, and they continue to maintain his family for many years without receiving a remittance from him, in the hope that his circumstances may one day improve. He contracts bad habits, and is not ashamed to make his appearance among them, knowing that his excuses will be received as valid. If one of the Company's sepoys[4] were not to send home remittances for six months, some members of the family would be sent to know the reason why. If he could not explain, they would appeal to the native officers of the regiment, who would expostulate with him; and, if all failed, his wife and children would be turned out of his father's house, unless they knew that he was gone to the wars; and he would be ashamed ever to show his face among them again.'

'And the gradual increase of pay with length of service has tended to increase the value of the service, has it not?'

'It has very much; there are in our regiment, out of eight hundred men, more than one hundred and fifty sepoys who get the increase of two rupees a month, and the same number that get the increase of one. This they feel as an immense addition to the former seven rupees a month.[5] A prudent sepoy lives upon two, or at the utmost three, rupees a month in seasons of moderate plenty, and sends all the rest to his family. A great number of the sepoys of our regiment live upon the increase of two rupees, and send all their former seven to their families. The dismissal of a man from such a service as this distresses, not only him, but all his relations in the higher grades, who know how much of the comfort and happiness of his family depend upon his remaining and advancing in it; and they all try to make their young friends behave as they ought to do.'

'Do you think that a great portion of the native officers of the army have the same feelings and opinions on the subject as you have?'

'They have all the same; there is not, I believe, one in a hundred that does not think as I do upon the subject. Flogging was an odious thing. A man was disgraced, not only before his regiment, but before the crowd that assembled to witness the punishment. Had he been suffered to remain in the regiment he could never have hoped to rise after having been flogged, or sentenced to be flogged; his hopes were all destroyed, and his spirit broken, and the order directing him to be dismissed was good; but, as I have said, he lost all hope of getting into any other service, and dared not show his face among his family at home.'

'You know who ordered the abolition of flogging?'

'Lord Bentinck.'[6]

'And you know that it was at his recommendation the Honourable Company gave the increase of pay with length of service?'

'We have heard so; and we feel towards him as we felt towards Lord Wellesley, Lord Hastings, and Lord Lake.'

'Do you think the army would serve again now with the same spirit as they served under Lord Lake?'

'The army would go to any part of the world to serve such masters — no army had ever masters that cared for them like ours. We never asked to have flogging abolished; nor did we ever ask to have an increase of pay with length of service; and yet both have been done for us by the Company Bahādur.'

The old Sardār Bahādur came again to visit me on the 1st of December, with all the native officers who had come over from Sāgar to attend the court, seven in number. There were three very smart, sensible men among them; one of whom had been a volunteer at the capture of Java,[7] and the other[s] at that of the Isle of France.[8] They all told me that they considered the abolition of corporal punishment a great blessing to the native army. 'Some bad men who had already lost their character, and consequently all hope of promotion, might be in less dread than before; but they were very few, and their regiments would soon get rid of them under the new law that gave the power of dismissal to regimental courts martial.'

'But I find the European officers are almost all of opinion that the abolition of flogging has been, or will be, attended with bad consequences.'

'They, sir, apprehend that there will not be sufficient restraint upon the loose characters of the regiment; but now that the sepoys have got an increase of pay in proportion to length of service there will be no danger of that. Where can they ever hope to get such another service if they forfeit that of the Company? If the dread of losing such a service is not sufficient to keep the bad in order, that of being put to work upon the roads in irons will. The good can always be kept in order by lighter punishments, when they have so much at stake as the loss of such a service by frequent offences. Some gentlemen think that a soldier does not feel disgraced by being flogged, unless the offence for which he has been flogged is in itself disgraceful. There is no soldier, sir, that does not feel disgraced by being tied up to the halberts and flogged in the face of all his comrades and the crowd that may choose to come and look at him; the sepoys are all of the same respectable families as ourselves, and they all enter the service in the hope of rising in time to the same stations as ourselves, if they conduct themselves well; their families look forward with the same hope. A man who has been tied up and flogged knows the disgrace that it will bring upon his family, and will sometimes rather die than return to it; indeed, as head of a family he could not be received at home.[9] But men do not feel disgraced in being flogged with a rattan at drill. While at the drill they consider themselves, and are considered by us all, as in the relation of scholars to their schoolmasters. Doing away with the rattan at drill had a very bad effect. Young men were formerly, with the judicious use of the rattan, made fit to join the regiment at furthest in six months; but since the abolition of the rattan it takes twelve months to make them fit to be seen in the ranks. There was much virtue in the rattan, and it should never have been given up. We have all been flogged with the rattan at the drill, and never felt ourselves disgraced by it-we were *shāgirds* (scholars), and the drill-sergeant, who had the rattan, was our *ustād* (schoolmaster); but when we left the drill, and took our station in the ranks as sepoys, the case was altered, and we should have felt disgraced by a flogging, whatever might have been the nature of the offence we committed. The drill will never get on so well as it used to do, unless the rattan be called into use again; but we apprehend no evil from the abolition of corporal punishment afterwards. People are apt to attribute to this abolition offences that have nothing to do with it; and for which ample punishments are still provided. If a man fires at his officer, people are apt to say it is because flogging has been done away with; but a man who deliberately fires at his officer is prepared to undergo worse punishment than flogging.[10]

'Do you not think that the increase of pay with length of service to the sepoys will have a good effect in tending to give to regiments more active and intelligent native officers? Old sepoys who are not so will now have less cause to complain if passed over, will they not?'

'If the sepoys thought that the increase of pay was given with this view, they would rather not have it at all. To pass over men merely because they happen to have grown old, we consider very cruel and unjust. They all enter the service young, and go on doing their duty till they become old, in the hope that they shall get promotion when it comes to their turn. If they are disappointed, and young men, or greater favourites with their European officers, are put over their heads, they become heart-broken. We all feel for them, and are always sorry to see an old soldier passed over, unless he has been guilty of any manifest crime, or neglect of duty. He has always some relations among the native officers who know his family, for we all try to get our relations into the same regiment with ourselves when they are eligible. They know what that family will suffer when they learn that he has no longer any hopes of rising in the service, and has become miserable. Supersessions create distress and bad feelings throughout a regiment, even when the best men are promoted, which cannot always be the case; for the greatest favourites are not always the best men. Many of our old European officers, like yourself, are absent on staff or civil employments; and the command of companies often devolves upon very young subalterns, who know little or nothing of the character of their men. They recommend those whom they have found most active and intelligent, and believe to be the best; but their opportunities of learning the characters of the men have been few. They have seen and observed the young, active, and forward; but they often know nothing of the steady, unobtrusive old soldier, who has done his duty ably in all situations, without placing himself prominently forward in any. The commanding officers seldom remain long with the same regiment, and, consequently, seldom know enough of the men to be able to judge of the justice of the selections for promotion. Where a man has been guilty of a crime, or neglected his duty, we feel no sympathy for him, and are not ashamed to tell him so, and put him down[11] when he complains.'

Here the old Sūbadār, who had been at the taking of the Isle of France, mentioned that when he was senior Jemadār of his regiment, and a vacancy had occurred to bring him in as Sūbadār, he was sent for by his commanding officer, and told that, by orders from headquarters, he was to be passed over, on account of his advanced age, and supposed infirmity. 'I felt,' said the old man, 'as if I had been struck by lightning, and *fell down dead*. The colonel was a good man, and had seen much service. He had me taken into the open air; and when I recovered, he told me that he would write to the Commander-in-Chief, and represent my case. He did so, and I was promoted; and I have since done my duty as Sūbadār for ten years.'[12]

The Sardār Bahādur told me that only two men in our regiment had been that year superseded, one for insolence, and the other for neglect of duty; and that officers and sepoys were all happy in consequence—the young, because they felt more secure of being promoted if they did their duty; and the old, because, they felt an interest in their young relations. 'In those regiments,' said he, 'where supersessions have been more numerous, old and young are dispirited and unhappy. They all feel that the *good old rule of right* (*hakk*), as long as a man does his duty well, can no longer be relied upon.'

When two companies of my regiment passed through Jubbulpore a few days after this conversation on their way from Sāgar to Seoni, I rode out a mile or two to meet them. They had not seen me for sixteen years, but almost all the native commissioned and non- commissioned officers were personally known to me. They were all very glad to see me, and I rode along with them to their place of encampment, where I had ready a feast of sweetmeats. They liked me as a young man, and are, I believe, proud of me as an old one. Old and young spoke with evident delight of the rigid adherence on the part of the present commanding officer, Colonel Presgrave, to the good old rule of 'hakk' (right) in the recent promotions to the vacancies occasioned by the annual transfer to the invalid establishment. We might, no doubt, have in every regiment a few smarter native officers by disregarding this rule than by adhering to it; but we should, in the diminution of the good feeling towards the European officers and the Government, lose a thousand times more than we gained. They now go on from youth to old age, from the drill to the retired pension, happy and satisfied that there is no service on earth so good for them.[13] With admirable *moral*, but little or no *literary* education, the native officers of our regiments never dream of aspiring to anything more than is now held out to them, and the mass of the soldiers are inspired with devotion to the service, and every feeling with which we could wish to have them inspired, by the hope of becoming officers in time, if they discharge their duties faithfully and zealously. Deprive the mass of this hope, give the commissions to an *exclusive class* of natives, or to a favoured few, chosen often, if not commonly, without reference to the feelings or qualifications we most want in our native officers, and our native army will soon cease to have the same feelings of devotion towards the Government, and of attachment and respect towards their European officers that they now have. The young, ambitions, and aspiring native officers will soon try to teach the great mass that their interest and that of the European officers and European Government are by no means one and the same, as they have been hitherto led to suppose; and it is upon the good feeling of this great mass that we have to depend for support. To secure this good feeling, we can well afford to sacrifice a little efficiency at the drill. It was unwise in one of the commanders-in-chief to direct that no soldier in our Bengal native regiments should be promoted unless he could read and write-it was to prohibit the promotion of the best, and direct the promotion of the worst, soldiers in the ranks. In India a military officer is rated as a gentleman by his birth, that is *caste*, and by his deportment in all his relations of life, not by his *knowledge of books*.

The Rājpūt, the Brahman, and the proud Pathān who attains a commission, and deports himself like an officer, never thinks himself, or is thought by others, deficient in anything that constitutes the gentleman, because he happens not to be at the same time a clerk. He has from his childhood been taught to consider the quill and the sword as two distinct professions, both useful and honourable when honourably pursued; and having chosen the sword, he thinks he does quite enough in learning how to use and support it through all grades, and ought not to be expected to encroach on the profession of the penman. This is a tone of feeling which it is clearly the interest of Government rather to foster than discourage, and the order which militated so much against it has happily been either rescinded or disregarded.

Three-fourths of the recruits of our Bengal native infantry are drawn from the Rājpūt peasantry of the kingdom of Oudh, on the left bank of the Ganges, where their affections have been linked to the soil for a long series of generations.[14] The good feelings of the families from which they are drawn continue through the whole period of their service to exercise a salutary influence over their conduct as men and as soldiers. Though they never take their families with them, they visit them on furlough every two or three years, and always return to them when the surgeon considers a change of air necessary to their recovery from sickness. Their family circles are always present to their imaginations; and the recollections of their last visit, the hopes of the next, and the assurance that their conduct as men and as soldiers in the interval will be reported to those circles by their many comrades, who are annually returning on furlough to the same parts of the country, tend to produce a general and uniform propriety of conduct, that is hardly to be found among the soldiers of any other army in the world, and which seems incomprehensible to those unacquainted with its source — veneration for parents cherished through life, and a never-impaired love of home, and of all the dear objects by which it is constituted.

Our Indian native army is perhaps the only entirely voluntary standing army that has been ever known, and it is, to all intents and purposes, entirely voluntary, and as such must be treated.[15] We can have no other native army in India, and without such an army we could not maintain our dominion a day. Our best officers have always understood this quite well; and they have never tried to flog and harass men out of all that we find good in them for our purposes. Any regiment in our service might lay down their arms and disperse to- morrow, without our having a chance of apprehending one deserter among them all.[16]

When Frederick the Great of Prussia reviewed his army of sixty thousand men in Pomerania, previous to his invasion of Silesia, he asked the Prince d'Anhalt, who accompanied him, what he most admired in the scene before him.

'Sire,' replied the prince, 'I admire at once the fine appearance of the men, and the regularity and perfection of their movements and evolutions.'

'For my part,' said Frederick, 'this is not what excites my astonishment, since with the advantage of money, time, and care, these are easily attained. It is that you and I, my dear cousin, should be in the midst of such an army as this in perfect safety. Here are sixty thousand men who are all *irreconcilable enemies to both you and myself*, not one among them that is not a man of more strength and better armed than either, yet they all tremble at our presence, while it would be folly on our part to tremble at theirs — such is the wonderful effect of order, vigilance, and subordination.'

But a reasonable man might ask, what were the circumstances which enabled Frederick to keep in a state of order and subordination an army composed of soldiers who were 'irreconcilable enemies' of their Prince and of their officers? He could have told the Prince d'Anhalt, had he chose to do so; for Frederick was a man who thought deeply. The chief circumstance favourable to his ambition was the imbecility of the old French Government, then in its dotage, and unable to see that an army of involuntary soldiers was no longer compatible with the state of the nation. This Government had reduced its soldiers to a condition worse than that of the common labourers upon the roads, while it deprived them of all hope of rising, and all feeling of pride in the profession.[17] Desertion became easy from the extension of the French dominion and from the circumstance of so many belligerent powers around requiring good soldiers; and no odium attended desertion, where everything was done to degrade, and nothing to exalt the soldier in his own esteem and that of society.

Instead of following the course of events and rendering the condition of the soldier less odious by increasing his pay and hope of promotion, and diminishing the labour and disgrace to which he was liable, and thereby filling her regiments with voluntary soldiers when involuntary ones could no longer be obtained, the Government of France reduced the soldier's pay to one-half the rate of wages which a common labourer got on the roads, and put them under restraints and restrictions that made them feel every day, and every hour, that they were slaves. To prevent desertions by severe examples under this high- pressure System, they had recourse first to slitting the noses and cutting off the ears of deserters, and, lastly, to shooting them as fast as they could catch them.[18] But all was in vain; and Frederick of Prussia alone got fifty thousand of the finest soldiers in the world from the French regiments, who composed one-third of his army, and enabled him to keep all the rest in that state of discipline that improved so much its efficiency, in the same manner as the deserters from the Roman legions, which took place under similar circumstances, became the flower of the army of Mithridates.[19]

Frederick was in position and disposition a despot. His territories were small, while his ambition was boundless. He was unable to pay a large army the rate of wages necessary to secure the services of voluntary soldiers; and he availed himself of the happy imbecility of the French Government to form an army of involuntary ones. He got French soldiers at a cheap rate, because they dared not return to their native country, whence they were hunted down and shot like dogs, and these soldiers enabled him to retain his own subjects in his ranks upon the same terms. Had the French Government retraced its steps, improved the condition of its soldiers, and mitigated the punishment for desertion during the long war, Frederick's army would have fallen to pieces 'like the baseless fabric of a vision'.

'Parmi nous,' says Montesquieu, 'les désertions sont fréquentes parce que les soldats sont la plus vile partie de chaque nation, et qu'il n'y en a aucun qui aie, ou qui croie avoir un certain avantage sur les autres. Chez les Romains elles étaient plus rares — des soldats tirés du sein d'un peuple si fier, si orgueilleux, si sûr de commander aux autres, ne pouvaient guère penser à s' aviler jusqu'à cesser d'être Romains.'[20] But was it the poor soldiers who were to blame if they were 'vile', and had 'no advantage over others', or the Government that took them from the vilest classes, or made their condition when they got them worse than that of the lowest class in society? The Romans deserted under the same circumstances, and, as I have stated, formed the elite of the army of Mithridates and the other enemies of Rome; but they respected their military oath of allegiance long after perjury among senators had ceased to excite any odium, since as a fashionable or political vice it had become common.

Did not our day of retribution come, though in a milder shape, to teach us a great political and moral lesson, when so many of our brave sailors deserted our ships for those of America, in which they fought against us?[21] They deserted from our ships of war because they were there treated like dogs, or from our merchant ships because they were every hour liable to be seized like felons and put on board the former. When 'England expected every man to do his duty' at Trafalgar, had England done its duty to every man who was that day to fight for her? Is not the intellectual stock which the sailor acquires in scenes of peril 'upon the high and giddy mast' as much his property as that which others acquire in scenes of peace at schools and colleges? And have not our senators, morally and religiously, as much right to authorize their sovereign to seize clergymen, lawyers, and professors, for employment in his service, upon the wages of ordinary uninstructed labour, as they have to authorize him to seize able sailors to be so employed in her navy? A feeling more base than that which authorized the able seaman to be hunted down upon such conditions, torn from his wife and children, and put like Uriah in front of those battles upon which our welfare and honour depended, never disgraced any civilized nation with whose history we are acquainted.[22]

Sir Matthew Decker, in a passage quoted by Mr. McCulloch, says, 'The custom of impressment put a freeborn British sailor on the same footing as a Turkish slave. The Grand Seignior cannot do a more absolute act than to order a man to be dragged away from his family, and against his will run his head against the mouth of a cannon; and if such acts should be frequent in Turkey upon any one set of useful men, would it not drive them away to other countries, and thin their numbers yearly? And would not the remaining few double or triple their wages, which is the case with our sailors in time of war, to the great detriment of our commerce?' The Americans wisely relinquished the barbarous and unwise practice of their parent land, and, as McCulloch observes, 'While the wages of all labourers and artisans are uniformly higher in the United States than in England, those of sailors are generally lower,' as the natural consequence of manning their navy by means of voluntary enlistment alone. At the close of the last war, sixteen thousand British sailors were serving on board of American ships; and the wages of our seamen rose from forty or[23] fifty to a hundred or one hundred and twenty shillings a month, as the natural consequence of our continuing to resort to impressment after the Americans had given it up.[24]

Frederick's army consisted of about one hundred and fifty thousand men. Fifty thousand of these were French deserters, and a considerable portion of the remaining hundred thousand were deserters from the Austrian army, in which desertion was punished in the same manner with death. The dread of this punishment if they quitted his ranks, enabled him to keep up that state of discipline that improved so much the efficacy of his regiments, at the same time that it made every individual soldier his 'irreconcilable enemy'. Not relying entirely upon this dread on the part of deserters to quit his ranks under his high-pressure system of discipline, and afraid that the soldiers of his own soil might make off in spite of all their vigilance, he kept his regiments in garrison towns till called on actual service; and that they might not desert on their way from one garrison to another during relief, he never had them relieved at all. A trooper was flogged for falling from his horse, though he had broken a limb in his fall; it was difficult, he said, to distinguish an involuntary fault from one that originated in negligence, and to prevent a man hoping that his negligence would be forgiven, all blunders were punished, from whatever cause arising. No soldier was suffered to quit his garrison till led out to fight; and when a desertion took place, cannons were fired to announce it to the surrounding country. Great rewards were given for apprehending, and severe punishments inflicted for harbouring, the criminal; and he was soon hunted down, and brought back. A soldier was, therefore, always a prisoner and a slave.

Still, all this rigour of Prussian discipline, like that of our navy, was insufficient to extinguish that ambition which is inherent in our nature to obtain the esteem and applause of the circle in which we move; and the soldier discharged his duty in the hour of danger, in the hope of rendering his life more happy in the esteem of his officers and comrades. 'Every tolerably good soldier feels ', says Adam Smith, 'that he would become the scorn of his companions if he should be supposed capable of shrinking from danger, or of hesitating either to expose or to throw away his life, when the good of the service required it.' So thought the philosopher-King of Prussia, when he let his regiments out of garrison to go and face the enemy. The officers were always treated with as much lenity in the Prussian as any other service, because the king knew that the hope of promotion would always be sufficient to bind them to their duties; but the poor soldiers had no hope of this kind to animate them in their toils and their dangers.

We took our System of drill from Frederick of Prussia; and there is still many a martinet who would carry his high-pressure system of discipline into every other service over which he had any control, unable to appreciate the difference of circumstances under which they may happen to be raised and maintained.[25]

The sepoys of the Bengal army, the only part of our native army with which I am much acquainted, are educated as soldiers from their infancy — they are brought up in that feeling of entire deference for constituted authority which we require in soldiers, and which they never lose through life. They are taken from the agricultural classes of Indian society — almost all the sons of yeomen — cultivating proprietors of the soil, whose families have increased beyond their means of subsistence. One son is sent one after another to seek service in our regiments as necessity presses at home, from whatever cause — the increase of taxation, or the too great increase of numbers in families.[26] No men can have a higher sense of the duty they owe to the state that employs them, or whose 'salt they eat'; nor can any men set less value on life when the service of that state requires that it shall be risked or sacrificed. No persons are brought up with more deference for parents. In no family from which we drew our recruits is a son through infancy, boyhood, or youth, heard to utter a disrespectful word to his parents — such a word from a son to his parents would shock the feelings of the whole community in which the family resides, and the offending member would be visited with their highest indignation. When the father dies the eldest son takes his place, and receives the same marks of respect, the same entire confidence and deference as the father. If he be a soldier in a distant land, and can afford to do so, he resigns the service, and returns home to take his post as the head of the family. If he cannot afford to resign, if the family still want the aid of his regular monthly pay, he remains with his regiment, and denies himself many of the personal comforts he has hitherto enjoyed, that he may increase his contribution to the general stock.

The wives and children of his brothers, who are absent on service, are confided to his care with the same confidence as to that of the father. It is a rule to which I have through life found but few exceptions that those who are most disposed to resist constituted authority are those most disposed to abuse such authority when they get it. The members of these families, disposed, as they always are, to pay deference to such authority, are scarcely ever found to abuse it when it devolves upon them; and the elder son, when he succeeds to the place of his father, loses none of the affectionate attachment of his younger brothers.

They never take their wives or children with them to their regiments, or to the places where their regiments are stationed.[27] They leave them with their fathers or elder brothers, and enjoy their society only when they return on furlough. Three-fourths of their incomes are sent home to provide for their comfort and subsistence, and to embellish that home in which they hope to spend the winter of their days. The knowledge that any neglect of the duty they owe their distant families will be immediately visited by the odium of their native officers and brother soldiers, and ultimately communicated to the heads of their families, acts as a salutary check on their conduct; and I believe that there is hardly a native regiment in the Bengal army in which the twenty drummers who are Christians, and have their families with the regiment, do not cause more trouble to the officers than the whole eight hundred sepoys.

To secure the fidelity of such men all that is necessary is to make them feel secure of three things – their regular pay, at the handsome rate at which it has now been fixed; their retiring pensions upon the scale hitherto enjoyed; and promotion by seniority, like their European officers, unless they shall forfeit all claims to it by misconduct or neglect of duty.[28] People talk about a demoralized army, and discontented army! No army in the world was certainly ever more moral or more contented than our native army; or more satisfied that their masters merit all their devotion and attachment; and I believe none was ever more devoted or attached to them.[29] I do not speak of the European officers of the native army. They very generally believe that they have had just cause of complaint, and sufficient care has not always been taken to remove that impression. In all the junior grades the Honourable Company's officers have advantages over the Queen's in India. In the higher grades the Queen's officers have advantages over those of the Honourable Company. The reasons it does not behove me here to consider.[30]

In all armies composed of involuntary soldiers, that is, of soldiers who are anxious to quit the ranks and return to peaceful occupations, but cannot do so, much of the drill to which they are subjected is adopted merely with a view to keep them from pondering too much upon the miseries of their present condition, and from indulging in those licentious habits to which a strong sense of these miseries, and the recollection of the enjoyments of peaceful life which they have sacrificed, are too apt to drive them. No portion of this is necessary for the soldiers of our native army, who have no miseries to ponder over, or superior enjoyments in peaceful life to look back upon; and a very small quantity of drill is sufficient to make a regiment go through its evolutions well, because they have all a pride and pleasure in their duties, as long as they have a commanding officer who understands them. Clarke, in his *Travels*, speaking of the three thousand native infantry from India whom he saw paraded in Egypt under their gallant leader, Sir David Baird, says, 'Troops in such a state of military perfection, or better suited for active service, were never seen – not even on the famous parade of the chosen ten thousand belonging to Bonaparte's legions, which he was so vain of displaying before the present war in the front of the Tuileries at Paris. Not an unhealthy soldier was to be seen. The English, inured to the climate of India, considered that of Egypt as temperate in its effects, and the sipāhees seemed as fond of the Nile as the Ganges.'[31]

It would be much better to devise more innocent amusements to lighten the miseries of European soldiers in India than to be worrying them every hour, night and day, with duties which are in themselves considered to be of no importance whatever, and imposed merely with a view to prevent their having time to ponder on these miseries.[32] But all extra and useless duties to a soldier become odious, because they are always associated in his mind with the ideas of the odious and degrading punishment inflicted for the neglect of them. It is lamentable to think how much of misery is often wantonly inflicted upon the brave soldiers of our European regiments of India on the pretence of a desire to preserve order and discipline.[33]

Sportsmen know that if they train their horses beyond a certain point they 'train off'; that is, they lose the spirit and with it the condition they require to support them in their hour of trial. It is the same with soldiers; if drilled beyond a certain point, they 'drill off', and lose the spirit which they require to sustain them in active service, and before the enemy. An over-drilled regiment will seldom go through its evolutions well, even in ordinary review before its own general. If it has all the mechanism, it wants all the real spirit of military discipline—it becomes dogged, and is, in fact, a body with but a soul. The martinet, who is seldom a man of much intellect, is satisfied as long as the bodies of his men are drilled to his liking; his narrow mind comprehends only one of the principles which influence mankind—fear; and upon this he acts with all the pertinacity of a slave-driver. If he does not disgrace himself when he comes before the enemy, as he commonly does, by his own incapacity, his men will perhaps try to disgrace him, even at the sacrifice of what they hold dearer than their lives—their reputation. The real soldier, who is generally a man of more intellect, cares more about the feelings than the bodies of his men; he wants to command their affections as well as their limbs, and he inspires them with a feeling of enthusiasm that renders them insensible to all danger—such men were Lord Lake, and Generals Ochterlony, Malcolm, and Adams, and such are many others well known in India.

Under the martinet the soldiers will never do more than what a due regard for their own reputation demands from them before the enemy, and will sometimes do less. Under the real soldier, they will always do more than this; his reputation is dearer to them even than their own, and they will do more to sustain it. The army of the consul, Appius Claudius, exposed themselves to almost inevitable destruction before the enemy to disgrace him in the eyes of his country, and the few survivors were decimated on their return; he cared nothing for the spirit of his men. The army of his colleague,

Quintius, on the contrary, though from the same people, and levied and led out at the same time, covered him with glory because they loved him. [34] We had an instance of this in the war with Nepāl in-1813, in which a king's regiment played the part of the army of Appius.[35] There were other martinets, king's and Company's, commanding divisions in that war, and they all signally failed; not, however, except in the above one instance, from backwardness on the part of their troops, but from utter incapacity when the hour of trial came. Those who succeeded were men always noted for caring something more about the hearts than the whiskers and buttons of their men. That the officer who delights in harassing his regiment in times of peace will fail with it in times of war and scenes of peril seems to me to be a rule almost as well established as that he, who in the junior ranks of the army delights most to kick against authority, is always found the most disposed to abuse it when he gets to the higher. In long intervals of peace, the only prominent military characters are commonly such martinets; and hence the failures so generally experienced in the beginning of a war after such an interval. Whitelocks are chosen for command, till Wolfes and Wellingtons find Chathams and Wellesleys to climb up by.

To govern those whose mental and physical energies we require for our subsistence and support by the lash alone is so easy, so simple a mode of bending them to our will, and making them act strictly and instantly in conformity to it, that it is not at all surprising to find so many of those who have been accustomed to it, and are not themselves liable to have the lash inflicted upon them, advocating its free use. In China the Emperor has his generals flogged, and finds the lash so efficacious in bending them to his will that nothing would persuade him that it could ever be safely dispensed with. In some parts of Germany they had the officers flogged, and princes and generals found this so very efficacious in making those act in conformity to their will that they found it difficult to believe that any army could be well managed without it. In other Christian armies the officers are exempted from the lash, but they use it freely upon all under them; and it would be exceedingly difficult to convince the greater part of these officers that the free use of the lash is not indispensably necessary, nay, that the men do not themselves like to be flogged, as eels like to be skinned, when they once get used to it. Ask the slave-holders of the southern states of America whether any society can be well constituted unless the greater part of those upon the sweat of whose brow the community depends for their subsistence are made by law liable to be bought, sold, and driven to their daily labour with the lash; they will one and all say No; and yet there are doubtless many very excellent and amiable persons among these slave-holders. If our army, as at present constituted, cannot do without the free use of the lash, let its constitution be altered; for no nation with free institutions should suffer its soldiers to be flogged. *'Laudabiliores tamen duces sunt, quorum exercitum ad modestiam labor et usus instituit, quam illi, quorum milites ad obedientiam suppliciorum formido compellit.'*[36]

Though I reprobate that wanton severity of discipline in which the substance is sacrificed to the form, in which unavoidable and trivial offences are punished as deliberate and serious crimes, and the spirit of the soldier is entirely disregarded, while the motion of his limbs, cut of his whiskers, and the buttons of his coat are scanned with microscopic eye, I must not be thought to advocate idleness. If we find the sepoys of a native regiment, as we sometimes do at a healthy and cheap station, become a little unruly like schoolboys, and ask an old native officer the reason, he will probably answer others as he has me by another question, *'Ghora ārā kyūn? Pānī sarā kyūn?'* 'Why does the horse become vicious? Why does the water become putrid?'-For want of exercise. Without proper attention to this exercise no regiment is ever kept in order; nor has any commanding officer ever the respect or the affection of his men unless they see that he understands well all the duties which his Government entrusts to him, and is resolved to have them performed in all situations and under all circumstances. There are always some bad characters in a regiment, to take advantage of any laxity of discipline, and lead astray the younger soldiers, whose spirits have been rendered exuberant by good health and good feeding; and there is hardly any crime to which they will not try to excite these young men, under an officer careless about the discipline of his regiment, or disinclined, from a mistaken *esprit de corps*, or any other cause, to have those crimes traced home to them and punished.[37]

There can be no question that a good tone of feeling between the European officers and their men is essential to the well-being of our native army; and I think I have found this tone somewhat impaired whenever our native regiments are concentrated at large stations. In such places the European society is commonly large and gay; and the officers of our native regiments become too much occupied in its pleasures and ceremonies to attend to their native officers or sepoys. In Europe there are separate classes of people who subsist by catering for the amusements of the higher classes of society, in theatres, operas, concerts, balls, &c., &c.; but in India this duty devolves entirely upon the young civil and military officers of the Government, and at large stations it really is a very laborious one, which often takes up the whole of a young man's time. The ladies must have amusement; and the officers must find it for them, because there are no other persons to undertake the arduous duty. The consequence is that they often become entirely alienated from their men, and betray signs of the greatest impatience while they listen to the necessary reports of their native officers, as they come on or go off duty.[38]

It is different when regiments are concentrated for active service. Nothing tends so much to improve the tone of feeling between the European officers and their men, and between European soldiers and sepoys, as the concentration of forces on actual service, where the same hopes animate, and the same dangers unite them in common bonds of sympathy and confidence. '*Utrique alteris freti, finitimos armis aut metu sub imperium cogere, nomen gloriamque sibi addidere.*' After the campaigns under Lord Lake, a native regiment passing Dinapore, where the gallant King's 76th, with whom they had fought side by side, was cantoned, invited the soldiers to a grand entertainment provided for them by the sepoys. They consented to go on one condition—that the sepoys should see them all back safe before morning. Confiding in their sable friends, they all got gloriously drunk, but found themselves lying every man upon his proper cot in his own barracks in the morning. The sepoys had carried them all home upon their shoulders. Another native regiment, passing within a few miles of a hill on which they had buried one of their European officers after that war, solicited permission to go and make their 'salām' to the tomb, and all went who were off duty.[39] The system which now keeps the greater part of our native infantry at small stations of single regiments in times of peace tends to preserve this good tone of feeling between officers and men, at the same time that it promotes the general welfare of the country by giving confidence everywhere to the peaceful and industrious classes.

I will not close this chapter without mentioning one thing which I have no doubt every Company's officer in India will concur with me in thinking desirable to improve the good feeling of the native soldiery—that is, an increase in the pay of the Jemadārs. They are commissioned officers, and seldom attain the rank in less than from twenty-five to thirty years;[40] and they have to provide themselves with clothes of the same costly description as those of the Sūbadār; to be as well mounted, and in all respects to keep the same respectability of appearance, while their pay is only twenty-four rupees and a half a month; that is, ten rupees a month only more than they had been receiving in the grade of Havildārs, which is not sufficient to meet the additional expenses to which they become liable as commissioned officers. Their means of remittance to their families are rather diminished than increased by promotion, and but few of them can hope ever to reach the next grade of Sūbadār. Our Government, which has of late been so liberal to its native civil officers, will, I hope, soon take into consideration the claims of this class, who are universally admitted to be the worst paid class of native public officers in India. Ten rupees a month addition to their pay would be of great importance; it would enable them to impart some of the advantages of promotion to their families, and improve the good feeling of the circles around them towards the Government they serve.[41]

Notes:

1. This chapter and the following one were printed as a separate tract at Calcutta in 1841 (see Bibliography). That small volume included an Introduction and two statistical tables which the author did not reprint. He has utilized extracts from the Introduction in various parts of the *Rambles and Recollections*. I am not sure that the tract was ever published, though it was printed; for the author says in his Introduction: 'They (*scil.* these two essays) may never be published; but I cannot deny myself the gratification of printing them.'

2. This order is confined to the Indian Army.

3. The punishment of working on the roads is long obsolete.

4. The author spells this word 'sipahee'. I have thought it better to use throughout the now familiar corruption.

5. The ordinary infantry pay was raised from seven to nine rupees in 1895.

6. General Orders by the Commander-in-Chief of the 5th of January, 1797, declare that no sepoy or trooper of our native army shall be dismissed from the service by the sentence of any but a general court martial. General Orders by the Commander-in-Chief, Lord Combermere, of the 19th of March, 1827, declare that his Excellency is of opinion that the quiet and orderly habits of the native soldiers are such that it can very seldom be necessary to have recourse to the punishment of flogging, which might be almost entirely abolished with great advantage to their character and feelings; and directs that no native soldier shall in future be sentenced to corporal punishment unless for the crime of *stealing, marauding, or gross insubordination,* where the individuals are deemed unworthy to continue in the ranks of the army. No such sentence by a regimental, detachment, or brigade court martial was to be carried into effect till confirmed by the general officer commanding the division. When flogged the soldier was invariably to be discharged from the service.

A circular letter from the Commander-in-Chief, Lord Combermere, on the 16th of June, 1827, directs that sentence to corporal punishment is not to be restricted to the three crimes of *theft, marauding, or gross insubordination;* but that it is not to be awarded except for very serious offences against discipline, or actions of a disgraceful or infamous nature, which show those who committed them to be unfit for the service; that the officer who assembles the court may remit the sentence of corporal punishment, and the dismissal involved in it; but cannot carry it into effect till confirmed by the officer commanding the division, except when an immediate example is indispensably necessary, as in the case of plundering and violence on the part of soldiers in the line of march. In all cases the soldier who has been flogged must be dismissed.

A circular letter by the Commander-in-Chief, Sir E. Barnes, 2nd of November, 1832, dispenses with the duty of submitting the sentence of regimental, detachment, and brigade courts martial for confirmation to the general officer commanding the division; and authorizes the officer who assembles the court to carry the sentence into effect without reference to higher authority; and to mitigate the punishment awarded, or remit it altogether; and to order the dismissal of the soldier who has been sentenced to corporal punishment, though he should remit the flogging, 'for it may happen that a soldier may be found guilty of an offence which renders it improper that he should remain any longer in the service, although the general conduct of the man has been such that an example is unnecessary; or he may have relations in the regiment of excellent character, upon whom some part of the disgrace would fall if he were flogged.' Still no court martial but a general one could sentence a soldier to be simply dismissed. To secure his dismissal they must first sentence him to be flogged.

On the 24th of February, 1835, the Governor-General of India in Council, Lord William Bentinck, directed that the practice of punishing soldiers of the native army by the cat-o'-nine-tails, or rattan, be discontinued at all the presidencies; and that henceforth it shall be competent to any regimental, detachment, or brigade court martial to sentence a soldier of the native army to dismissal from the service for any offence for which such soldier might now be punished by flogging, provided such sentence of dismissal shall not be carried into effect unless confirmed by the general or other officer commanding the division.'

For crimes involving higher penalties, soldiers were, as heretofore, committed for trial before general courts martial.

By Act 23 of 1839, passed by the Legislative Council of India on the 23rd of September, it is made competent for courts martial to sentence soldiers of the native army in the service of the East India Company to the punishment of dismissal, and to be imprisoned, with or without hard labour, for any period not exceeding two years, if the sentence be pronounced by a general court martial; and not exceeding one year, if by a garrison or line court martial; and not exceeding six months, if by a regimental or district court martial. Imprisonment for any period with hard labour, or for a term exceeding six months without hard labour, to involve dismissal. Act

2 of 1840 provides for such sentences of imprisonment being carried into execution by magistrates or other officers in charge of the gaols. [W. H. S.]

This last paragraph has been brought up from the end of the volume where it is printed in the original edition.

The army has been completely reorganized since the author's time, and the regulations have been much modified.

In October, 1833, Lord William Bentinck had assumed the command of the army, on the retirement of Sir Edward Barnes, and thus combined the offices of Governor-General and Commander-in-Chief, as the Marquis Cornwallis and the Marquis of Hastings had done before him.

7. Batavia was occupied by Sir Samuel Auchmuty in August, and the whole island was taken possession of in September, 1811. But at the general peace which followed the great war the island of Java, with its dependencies, was restored to the Dutch.

8. The Isle of France, otherwise called the Mauritius, which is still British territory, was gallantly taken at the end of November, 1810, by Commodore Rowley and Major-General Abercrombie. Full details of the Java and Mauritius expeditions are given in Thornton's twenty- second chapter. The brilliant operations in both localities deserve more attention than they usually receive from students of Indian history.

9. The funeral obsequies which are everywhere offered up to the manes of parents by the surviving head of the family during the last fifteen days of the month Kuār (September) were never considered as acceptable from the hands of a soldier in our service who had been tied up and flogged, whatever might have been the nature of the offence for which he was punished; any head of a family so flogged lost by that punishment the most important of his civil rights — that, indeed, upon which all others hinged, for it is by presiding at the funeral ceremonies that the head of the family secures and maintains his recognition. [W. H. S.] I have invariably found that natives of India, enjoying a good social position, who happen to be interested in an offender, care nothing for the disgraceful nature of the offender's crime, while they dread the disgrace of the punishment, however just it may be.

10. The worst feature of this abolition measure is unquestionably the odious distinction which it leaves in the punishments to which our European and our native soldiers are liable, since the British legislation does not consider that it can be safely abolished in the British army. This odious distinction might be easily removed by an enactment declaring that European soldiers in India should be liable to corporal punishment for only two offences: first, mutiny, or gross insubordination; second, plunder or violence while the regiment or force to which the prisoner belongs is in the

field or marching. The same enactment might declare the soldiers of our native army liable to the same punishments for the same offences. Such an enactment would excite no discontent among our native soldiery; on the contrary, it would be applauded as just and proper. [W. H. S.] Subsequently, corporal punishment in the Indian or native army was again legalized. The present law is thus stated by Sir Edwin Collen: 'A "summary court martial"... may pass any sentence allowed by the articles of war, except . . . and may carry it out at once. Corporal punishment not exceeding fifty lashes may be given for certain offences, but is rarely awarded, and the amount of military crime is, on the whole, very small in the native army. The native officers have power to inflict minor punishments' [*I.G. (1908), vol. iv, p. 370*].

Flogging in the British army in time of peace was prohibited in April, 1868, by an amendment to the Mutiny Bill, and was completely abolished by the Army Discipline Act of 1881.

11. The author also gives the Hindustani word as 'kaelkur-hin', which seems to be intended for *qāil kareñ*, or in rustic form *karahiñ*, meaning 'confute'.

12. No wonder that the native army, pampered in this sentimental fashion, gradually became more and more inefficient, till it needed the fires of the Mutiny to purge away its humours. No army could be efficient when its subordinate officers on the active list were men of sixty or seventy years of age.

13. The sepoys were quite right; no other service in the world was managed on such principles. The illusion of the old Company's officers about the gratitude and affection of the men generally was rudely dispelled nineteen years after the conversations recorded in the text. But, even in 1857. a noble minority remained faithful and did devoted service.

14. The best troops now are the Sikhs, Gōrkhās, and frontier Muhammadans. Oudh men still enlist in large numbers, but do not enjoy their old prestige. The army known to the author comprised no Sikhs, Gōrkhās, or frontier Muhammadans. The recruitment of Gōrkhās only began in 1838, and the other two classes of troops were obtained by the annexation of the Panjāb in 1849.

15. Enlistment in the native army is absolutely voluntary, and does not even require to be stimulated by a bounty. A subsequent passage shows that the author refuses to describe the British army as an 'entirety voluntary' one, because a soldier when once enlisted is bound to serve for a definite term; whereas the sepoy could resign when he chose.

16. Desertions are frequent among the regiments recruited on the Afghan frontier. These regiments did not exist in the author's day.

17. An ordinance issued in France so late as 1778 required that a man should produce proof of four quarterings of nobility before he could get a commission in the army. [W. H. S.]

18. '*Est et alia causa, cur attenuatae sint legiones,*' says Vegetius. '*Magnus in illis labor est militandi, graviora arma, sera munera, severior disciplila. Quod vitantes plerique, in auxiliis festinant militiae sacramenta percipere, ubi et minor sudor, et maturiora sunt premia.' Lib.* II. *cap.* 3. [W. H. S.] Vegetius, according to Gibbon and his most recent editor (*recensuit Carolus Lang. Editio altera. Lipsiae, Teubner,* 1885), flourished during the reign of Valentinian III (A.D. 425-55). His 'Soldier's Pocket-book' is entitled 'Flavi Vegeti Renati Epitoma Rei Militaris'.

'Montesquieu thought that 'the Government had better have stuck to the old practice of slitting noses and cutting off ears, since the French soldiers, like the Roman dandies under Pompey, must necessarily have a greater dread of a disfigured face than of death. It did not occur to him that France could retain her soldiers by other and better motives. See *Spirit of Laws,* book vi, chap. 12. See *Necker on the Finances,* vol. ii, chap. 5; vol. iii, chap. 34. A day-labourer on the roads got fifteen sous a day; and a French soldier only six, at the very time that the mortality of an army of forty thousand men sent to the colonies was annually 13,333, or about one in three. In our native army the sepoy gets about double the wages of an ordinary day-labourer; and his duties, when well done, involve just enough of exercise to keep him in health. The casualties are perhaps about one in a hundred. [W. H. S.]

20. Just precisely what the French soldiers were after the revolution had purged France of all 'the perilous stuff that weighed upon the heart' of its people. Gibbon, in considering the chance of the civilized nations of Europe ever being again overrun by the barbarians from the North, as in the time of the Romans, says: 'If a savage conqueror should issue from the deserts of Tartary, he must repeatedly vanquish the robust peasantry of Russia, the numerous armies of Germany, the gallant nobles of France, and the intrepid free men of Britain.' Never was a more just, yet more unintended satire upon the state of a country. Russia was to depend upon her 'robust peasantry'; Germany upon her 'numerous armies'; England upon her 'intrepid free men'; and poor France upon her 'gallant nobles' alone; because, unhappily, no other part of her vast population was then ever thought of. When the hour of trial came, those pampered nobles who had no feeling in common with the people were shaken off' like dew-drops from the lion's mane'; and the hitherto spurned peasantry of France, under the guidance and auspices of men who understood and appreciated them, astonished the world with their powers. [W. H. S.]

21. The allusion is to the now half-forgotten war with the United States in the years 1812-14, during the course of which the English captured the city of Washington, and the Americans gained some unexpected naval victories.

22. The author has already denounced the practice of impressment, *ante*, chapter 26, note 27.

23. 'to' in the original edition.

24. See McCulloch, *Pol. Econ.*, p. 235, 1st ed., Edinburgh, 1825. [W. H. S.]

25. Many German princes adopted the discipline of Frederick in their little petty states, without exactly knowing why or wherefore. The Prince of Darmstadt conceived a great passion for the military art; and when the weather would not permit him to worry his little army of five thousand men in the open air, he had them worried for his amusement under sheds. But he was soon obliged to build a wall round the town in which he drilled his soldiers for the sole purpose of preventing their running away — round this wall he had a regular chain of sentries to fire at the deserters. Mr. Moore thought that the discontent in this little band was greater than in the Prussian army, inasmuch as the soldiers saw no object but the prince's amusement. A fight, or the prospect of a fight, would have been a feast to them. [W. H. S.] It is hardly necessary to observe that the modern system of drill is widely different.

26. Speaking of the question whether recruits drawn from the country or the towns are best, Vegetius says: '*De qua parte numquam credo potuisse dubitari, aptiorem armis rusticam plebem, quae sub divo et in labore nutritur; solis patiens; umbrae negligens; balnearum nescia; delictarurum ignara; simplicis animi; parvo contenta; duratis ad omnem laborem membris; cui gestara ferrum, fossam ducere, onus ferre, consuetudo de rare est.*' (*De Re Militari*, Lib. i, cap. 3.) [W. H. S.] The passage quoted is disfigured by many misprints in the original edition.

27. As the Madras sepoys do.

28. The writing of the bulk of this work was completed in 1839. These concluding supplementary chapters on the Bengal army seem to have been written a little later, perhaps in 1841, the year in which they were first printed. The publication of the complete work took place in 1844. The Mutiny broke out in 1857, and proved that the fidelity of the sepoys could not be so easily assured as the author supposed.

29. I believe the native army to be better now than it ever was — better in its disposition and in its organization. The men have now a better feeling of assurance than they formerly had that all their rights will be secured to them by their European officers that all those officers are men of honour, though they have not all of them the same fellow feeling that their officers

had with them in former days. This is because they have not the same opportunity of seeing their courage and fidelity tried in the same scenes of common danger. Go to Afghanistan and China, and you will find the feeling between officers and men as fine as ever it was in days of yore, whatever it may be at our large and gay stations, where they see so little of each other. [W. H. S.] The author's reputation for sagacity and discernment could not be made to rest upon the above remarks. His judgement was led astray by his lifelong association with and affection for the native troops. Lord William Bentinck took a far juster view of the situation, and understood far better the real nature of the ties which bind the native army to its masters. His admirable minute dated 13th March, 1835, published for the first time in Mr. D. Boulger's well-written little book (*Lord William Bentinck*, 'Rulers of India', pp. 177-201), is still worthy of study. As a corrective to the author's too effusive sentiment, some brief passages from the Governor-General's minute may be quoted. 'In considering the question of internal danger,' he observes, 'those officers most conversant with Indian affairs who were examined before the Parliamentary Committee apprehend no danger to our dominion as long as we are assured of the fidelity of our native troops. To this opinion I entirely subscribe. But others again view in the native army itself the source of our greatest peril. In all ages the military body has been often the prime cause, but generally the instrument, of all revolutions; and proverbial almost as is the fidelity of the native soldier to the chief whom he serves, more especially when he is justly and kindly treated, still we cannot be blind to the fact that many of those ties which bind other armies to their allegiance are totally wanting in this. Here is no patriotism, no community of feeling as to religion or birthplace, no influencing attachment from high considerations, or great honours and rewards. Our native army also is extremely ignorant, capable of the strongest religions excitement, and very sensitive to disrespect to their persona or infringement of their customs. . . . In the native army alone rests our internal danger, and this danger may involve our complete subversion. . . .

'All these facts and opinions seem to me to establish incontrovertibly that a large proportion of European troops is necessary for our security under all circumstances of peace and war. . . .

'I believe the sepoys have never been so good as they were in the earliest part of our career; none superior to those under De Boigne. . . I fearlessly pronounce the Indian army to be the least efficient and most expensive in the world.'

The events of 1857-9 proved the truth of Lord William Bentinck's wise words. The native army is no longer inefficient as a whole, though certain sections of it may still be so, but the less that is said about the supposed affection of mercenary troops for a foreign government, the better.

30. Of course, all the military forces, British and Indian, are now alike the King's. Each service has its own rules and regulations.

31. 'General Baird had started from Bombay in the end of December 1800, but only arrived at Kossir, on the coast of Upper Egypt, on the 8th of June. In nine days, with a force of 6,400 British and native troops, he traversed 140 miles of desert to the Nile, and reached Cairo on 10th August with hardly any loss. The united force then marched down on Alexandria, and on 31st August Menou capitulated, and the whole French army evacuated Egypt.' (Balfour, *Cyclopaedia*, 3rd ed., s.v. 'Egypt.') The Indian native army again did brilliant service in the Egyptian campaign of 1882.

32. Great progress has been made in the task of lightening the miseries of European soldiers in India by the provision of innocent amusements. Lord Roberts, during his long tenure of the office of Commander-in-Chief, pre-eminently showed himself to be the soldier's friend.

33. Their commanding officers say, as Pharaoh said to the Israelites, 'Let there be more work laid upon them, that they may labour therein, and not enter into vain discourses.' Life to such men becomes intolerable; and they either destroy themselves, or commit murder, that they may be taken to a distant court for trial. [W. H. S.] The quotation is from Exodus v. 9. The Authorized Version is, 'Let there be more work laid upon the men, that they may labour therein; and let them not regard vain words.'

34. See Livy, lib. ii, cap. 59. The infantry under Fabius had refused to conquer, that their general, whom they hated, might not triumph; but the whole army under Claudius, whom they had more cause to detest, not only refused to conquer, but determined to be conquered, that he might be involved in their disgrace. All the abilities of Lucullus, one of the ablest generals Rome ever had, were rendered almost useless by his disregard to the feelings of his soldiers. He could not perceive that the civil wars under Marius and Sylla had rendered a different treatment of Roman soldiers necessary to success in war. Pompey, his successor, a man of inferior military genius, succeeded much better because he had the sagacity to see that he now required not only the confidence but the affections of his soldiers. Caesar to abilities even greater than those of Lucullus united the conciliatory spirit of Pompey [W. H. S.]

35. This curious incident, which is not mentioned by Thornton in the detailed account of the Nepalese War given in his twenty-fourth chapter, may be the failure of the 53rd Regiment to support General Gllespie in the attack on Kalanga, in 1814, not 1815 (Mill, Bk. II, chap. 1; vol. viii, p. 19, ed.

1858). The war was notable for the number of blunders and failures which marked its earlier stages.

36. Vegetius, *De Re Militari*, Lib. iii, cap. 4, If corporal punishment be retained at all, it should be limited to the two offences I have already mentioned; [W. H. S.] namely, (1) mutiny or gross insubordination, (2) plunder or violence in the field or on the march. (*Ante*, chapter 76, note 6.)

37. Polybius says that 'as the human body is apt to get out of order under good feeding and little exercise, so are states and armies.' (Bk. II, chap. 6.)—Wherever food is cheap, and the air good, native regiments should be well exercised without being worried.

I must here take the liberty to give an extract from a letter from one of the best and most estimable officers now in the Bengal army: 'As connected with the discipline of the native army, I may here remark that I have for some years past observed on the part of many otherwise excellent commanding officers a great want of attention to the instruction of the young European officers on first joining their regiments. I have had ample opportunities of seeing the great value of a regular course of instruction drill for at least six months. When I joined my first regiment, which was about forty years ago, I had the good fortune to be under a commandant and adjutant who, happily for me and many others, attached great importance to this very necessary course of instruction, I then acquired a thorough knowledge of my duties, which led to my being appointed an adjutant very early in life. When I attained the rank of lieutenant-colonel I had, however, opportunities of observing how very much this essential duty had been neglected in certain regiments, and made it a rule in all that I commanded to keep all young officers on first joining at the instruction drill till thoroughly grounded in their duties. Since I ceased to command a regiment, I have taken advantage of every opportunity to express to those commanding officers with whom I have been in correspondence my conviction of the great advantages of this system to the rising generation. In going from one regiment to another I found many curious instances of ignorance on the part of young officers who had been many years with their corps. It was by no means an easy task to convince them that they really knew nothing, or at least had a great deal to learn; but when they were made sensible of it, they many of them turned out excellent officers, and now, I believe, bless the day they were first put under me.'

The advantages of the System here mentioned cannot be questioned; and it is much to be regretted that it is not strictly enforced in every regiment in the service. Young officers may find it irksome at first; but they soon become sensible of the advantages, and learn to applaud the commandant who has had the firmness to consult their permanent interests more than their present inclinations. [W. H. S.]

38. Among the many changes produced in India by the development of the railway system and by other causes one of the most striking is the abolition of small military stations. Almost all these have disappeared, and the troops are now massed in large cantonments, where they can be handled much more effectively than in out-stations. The discipline of small detached bodies of troops is generally liable to deterioration.

39. Many instances of semi-religious honour paid by natives to the tombs of Europeans have been noticed.

40. There are, I believe, many Jemadārs who still wear medals on their breasts for their service in the taking of Java and the Isle of France more than thirty years ago. Indeed, I suspect that some will be found who accompanied Sir David Baird to Egypt. [W. H. S.] Such old men must have been perfectly useless as officers. Sir David Baird' s operations took place in 1801.

41. The rate of pay of Jemadārs in the Bengal Native Infantry now is either forty or fifty rupees monthly. Half of the officers of this rank in each regiment receive the higher rate. The grievance complained of by the author has, therefore, been remedied. The pay of a Havīldār is still, or was recently, fourteen rupees a month.

CHAPTER 77

Invalid Establishment.

I have said nothing in the foregoing chapter of the invalid establishment, which is probably the greatest of all bonds between the Government and its native army, and consequently the greatest element in the 'spirit of discipline'. Bonaparte, who was, perhaps, with all his faults, 'the greatest man that ever floated on the tide of time', said at Elba, 'There is not even a village that has not brought forth a general, a colonel, a captain, or a prefect, who has raised himself by his especial merit, and illustrated at once his family and his country.' Now we know that the families and the village communities in which our invalid pensioners reside never read newspapers,[1] and feel but little interest in the victories in which these pensioners may have shared. They feel that they have no share in the *éclat* or glory which attend them; but they everywhere admire and respect the government which cherishes its faithful old servants, and enables them to spend the 'winter of their days' in the bosoms of their families; and they spurn the man who has failed in his duty towards that government in the hour of need.

No sepoy taken from the Rājpūt communities of Oudh or any other part of the country can hope to conceal from his family circle or village community any act of cowardice, or anything else which is considered disgraceful to a soldier, or to escape the odium which it merits in that circle and community.

In the year 1819 I was encamped near a village in marching through Oudh, when the landlord, a very cheerful old man, came up to me with his youngest son, a lad of eighteen years of age, and requested me to allow him (the son) to show me the best shooting grounds in the neighbourhood. I took my 'Joe Manton' and went out. The youth showed me some very good ground, and I found him an agreeable companion, and an excellent shot with his matchlock. On our return we found the old man waiting for us. He told me that he had four sons, all by God's blessing tall enough for the Company's service, in which one had attained the rank of 'havīldār' (sergeant), and two were still sepoys. Their wives and children lived with him; and they sent home every month two- thirds of their pay, which enabled him to pay all the rent of the estate and appropriate the whole of the annual returns to the subsistence and comfort of the numerous family. He was, he said, now growing old, and wished his eldest son, the sergeant, to resign the service and come home to take upon him the management of the estate; that as soon as he could be prevailed upon to do so, his old wife would permit my sporting companion, her youngest son, to enlist, but not before.

I was on my way to visit Fyzabad, the old metropolis of Oudh,[2] and on returning a month afterwards in the latter end of January, I found that the wheat, which was all then in ear, had been destroyed by a severe frost. The old man wept bitterly, and he and his old wife yielded to the wishes of their youngest son to accompany me and enlist in my regiment, which was then stationed at Partābgarh.[3]

We set out, but were overtaken at the third stage by the poor old man, who told me that his wife had not eaten or slept since the boy left her, and that he must go back and wait for the return of his eldest brother, or she certainly would not live. The lad obeyed the call of his parents, and I never saw or heard of the family again.

There is hardly a village in the kingdom of Oudh without families like this depending upon the good conduct and liberal pay of sepoys in our infantry regiments, and revering the name of the government they serve, or have served. Similar villages are to be found scattered over the provinces of Bihār and Benares, the districts between the Ganges and Jumna, and other parts where Rājpūts and the other classes from which we draw our recruits have been long established as proprietors and cultivators of the soil.

These are the feelings on which the spirit of discipline in our native army chiefly depends, and which we shall, I hope, continue to cultivate, as we have always hitherto done, with care; and a commander must take a great deal of pains to make his men miserable, before he can render them, like the soldiers of Frederick, 'the irreconcilable enemies of their officers and their government'.

In the year 1817 I was encamped in a grove on the right bank of the Ganges below Monghyr,[4] when the Marquis of Hastings was proceeding up the river in his fleet, to put himself at the head of the grand division of the army then about to take the field against the Pindhārīs and their patrons, the Marāthā, chiefs. Here I found an old native pensioner, above a hundred years of age. He had fought under Lord Clive at the battle of Plassey, A.D. 1757, and was still a very cheerful, talkative old gentleman, though he had long lost the use of his eyes. One of his sons, a grey-headed old man, and a Sūbadār (captain) in a regiment of native infantry, had been at the taking of Java,[5] and was now come home on leave to visit his father. Other sons had risen to the rank of commissioned officers, and their families formed the aristocracy of the neighbourhood. In the evening, as the fleet approached, the old gentleman, dressed in his full uniform of former days as a commissioned officer, had himself taken out close to the bank of the river, that he might be once more during his life within sight of a British Commander-in-Chief, though he could no longer see one. There the old patriarch sat listening with intense delight to the remarks of the host of his descendants around him, as the Governor-General's magnificent fleet passed along,[6] every one fancying that he had caught a glimpse of the great man, and trying to describe him to the old gentleman, who in return told them (no doubt for the thousandth time) what sort of a person the great Lord Clive was. His son, the old Sūbadār, now and then, with modest deference, venturing to imagine a resemblance between one or the other, and his *beau idéal* of a great man, Lord Lake. Few things in India have interested me more than scenes like these.

I have no means of ascertaining the number of military pensioners in England or in any other European nation, and cannot, therefore, state the proportion which they bear to the actual number of forces kept up. The military pensioners in our Bengal establishment on the 1st of May, 1841, were 22,381; and the family pensioners, or heirs of soldiers killed in action, 1,730; total 24,111, out of an army of 82,027 men. I question whether the number of retired soldiers maintained at the expense of government bears so large a proportion to the number actually serving in any other nation on earth.[7] Not one of the twenty-four thousand has been brought on, or retained upon, the list from political interest or court favour; every one receives his pension for long and faithful services, after he has been pronounced by a board of European surgeons as no longer fit for the active duties of his profession; or gets it for the death of a father, husband, or son, who has been killed in the service of government.

All are allowed to live with their families, and European officers are stationed at central points in the different parts of the country where they are most numerous to pay them their stipends every six months. These officers are at— 1st, Barrackpore; 2nd, Dinapore; 3rd, Allahabad; 4th, Lucknow; 5th, Meerut. From these central points they move twice a year to the several other points within their respective circles of payment where the pensioners can most conveniently attend to receive their money on certain days, so that none of them have to go far, or to employ any expensive means to get it—it is, in fact, brought home as near as possible to their doors by a considerate and liberal government.[8]

Every soldier is entitled to a pension when pronounced by a board of surgeons as no longer fit for the active duties of his profession, after fifteen years' active service; but to be entitled to the pension of his rank in the army, he must have served in such rank for three years. Till he has done so he is entitled only to the pension of that immediately below it. A sepoy gets four rupees a month, that is, about one-fourth more than the ordinary wages of common uninstructed labour throughout the country.[9] But it will be better to give the rate of pay of the native officers and men of our native infantry and that of their retired pensions in one table.

TABLE OF THE RATE OF PAY AND RETIRED PENSIONS OF THE NATIVE OFFICERS AND SOLDIERS OF OUR NATIVE INFANTRY.

Rank.	Rate of Pay per Mensum. Rupees.	Rate of Pension per Mensum. Rupees.
A Sepoy, or private soldier. (Note. — After sixteen years' service eight rupees a month, after twenty years he gets nine rupees a month)	7.0	4.0
A Nāik, or corporal	12.0	7.0
A Havīldār, or sergeant	14.0	7.0
A Jemadār, subaltern commissioned officer	24.8	13.0
Sūbadār, or Captain	67.0	25.0
Sūbadār Major	92.0	0.0[a]
A Sūbadār, after forty years service	0.0	50.0
A Sūbadār Bahādur of the Order of British India, First Class, two rupees a day extra; Second Class, one Rupee a day extra. This extra allowance they enjoy after they retire from the service during life.[b]		

a. I presume this means that no special rate of pension was fixed for the rank of Sūbadār Major.

b. The monthly rates of pay and pension now in force for native officers and men of the Bengal army are as follows:

	Pay.		Pension.	
Rank.	Ordinay.	Superior.	Ordinay.	Superior.
	Rs.	Rs.	Rs.	Rs.
Sūbadār	80	100[c]	30	50
Jemadār	40	50[c]	15	25
Havīldār	14	—	7	12
Naick (nāik)	12	—	7	12
Drummer or Bugler	7	—	4	7
Sepoy	7	—	4	7

c. Half of this rank in each regiment receive the higher rate of pay.

The circumstances which, in the estimation of the people, distinguish the British from all other rulers in India, and make it grow more and more upon their affections, are these: The security which public servants enjoy in the tenure of their office; the prospect they have of advancement by the gradation of rank; the regularity and liberal scale of their pay; and the provision for old age, when they have discharged the duties entrusted to them ably and faithfully.[l0] In a native state almost every public officer knows that he has no chance of retaining his office beyond the reign of the present minister or favourite; and that no present minister or favourite can calculate upon retaining his ascendancy over the mind of his chief for more than a few months or years. Under us they see secretaries to government, members of council, and Governors-General themselves going out and coming into office without causing any change in the position of their subordinates, or even the apprehension of any change, as long as they discharge their duties ably and faithfully.

In a native state the new minister or favourite brings with him a whole host of expectants who must be provided for as soon as he takes the helm; and if all the favourites of his predecessor do not voluntarily vacate their offices for them, he either turns them out without ceremony, or his favourites very soon concoct charges against them, which causes them to be tumed out in due form, and perhaps put into jail till they have 'paid the uttermost farthing'. Under us the Governors-General, members of council, the secretaries of state,[11] the members of the judicial and revenue boards, all come into office and take their seats unattended by a single expectant. No native officer of the revenue or judicial department, who is conscious of having done his duty ably and honestly, feels the slightest uneasiness at the change. The consequence is a degree of integrity in public officers never before known in India, and rarely to be found in any other country. In the province where I now write,[12] which consists of six districts, there are twenty-two native judicial officers, Munsifs, Sadr Amīns, and Principal Sadr Amīns;[13] and in the whole province I have never heard a suspicion breathed against one of them; nor do I believe that the integrity of one of them is at this time suspected. The only one suspected within the two and a half years that I have been in the province was, I grieve to say, a Christian; and he has been removed from office, to the great satisfaction of the people, and is never to be employed again.[14] The only department in which our native public servants do not enjoy the same advantages of security in the tenure of their office, prospect of rise in the gradation of rank, liberal scale of pay, and provision for old age, is the police; and it is admitted on all hands that there they are everywhere exceedingly corrupt. Not one of them, indeed, ever thinks it possible that he can be supposed honest; and those who really are so are looked upon as a kind of martyrs or penitents, who are determined by long suffering to atone for past crimes; and who, if they could not get into the police, would probably go long pilgrimages on all fours, or with unboiled peas in their shoes.[15]

He who can suppose that men so inadequately paid, who have no promotion to look forward to, and feel no security in their tenure of office, and consequently no hope of a provision for old age, will be zealous and honest in the discharge of their duties, must be very imperfectly acquainted with human nature — with the motives by which men are influenced all over the world. Indeed, no man does in reality suppose so; on the contrary, every man knows that the same motives actuate public servants in India as elsewhere. We have acted successfully upon this knowledge in all other branches of the public service, and shall, I trust, at no distant period act upon the same in that of the police; and then, and not till then, can it prove to the people what we must all wish it to be, a blessing.

The European magistrate of a district has, perhaps, a million of people to look after.[16] The native officers next under him are the Thānadārs of the different subdivisions of the district, containing each many towns and villages, with a population of perhaps one hundred thousand people. These officers have no grade to look forward to, and get a salary of *twenty-five rupees a month each*.[17]

They cannot possibly do their duties unless they keep each a couple of horses or ponies, with servants to attend to them; indeed, they are told so by every magistrate who cares about the peace of his district. The people, seeing how much we expect from the Thānadār, and how little we give him, submit to his demands for contribution without a murmur, and consider almost any demand venial from a man so employed and paid. They are confounded at our inconsistency, and say, where they dare to speak their minds, 'We see you giving high salaries and high prospects of advancement to men who have nothing on earth to do but to collect your revenues and to decide our disputes about pounds, shillings, and pence, which we used to decide much better among ourselves when we had no other court but that of our elders to appeal to; while those who are to protect life and property, to keep peace over the land, and enable the industrious to work in security, maintain their families and pay the government revenue, are left without any prospect of rising, and almost without any pay at all.'

There is really nothing in our rule in India which strikes the people so much as this glaring inconsistency, the evil effects of which are so great and so manifest. The only way to remedy the evil is to give the police what the other branches of the public service already enjoy — a feeling of security in the tenure of office, a higher rate of salary, and, above all, a gradation of rank which shall afford a prospect of rising to those who discharge their duties ably and honestly. For this purpose all that is required is the interposition of an officer between the Thānadār and the magistrate, in the same way as the Sadr Amīn is now interposed between the Munsif and the Judge.[18] On an average there are, perhaps, twelve Thānas, or police subdivisions, in each district, and one such officer to every four Thānas would be sufficient for all purposes. The Governor-General who shall confer this boon on the people of India will assuredly be hailed as one of their greatest benefactors. [19] I should, I believe, speak within bounds when I say that the Thānadārs throughout the country give at present more than all the money which they receive in avowed salaries from government as a share of indirect perquisites to the native officers of the magistrate's court, who have to send their reports to them, and communicate their orders, and prepare the cases of the prisoners they may send in for commitment to the Sessions courts.[20] The intermediate officers here proposed would obviate all this; they would be to the magistrate at once the *tapis* of Prince Husain and the telescope of Prince Ali — media that would enable them to be everywhere and see everything.

I may here seem to be 'travelling beyond the record', but it is not so. In treating on the spirit of military discipline in our native army I advocate, as much as in me lies, the great general principle upon which rests, I think, not only our *power* in India, but what is more, the *justification of that power*. It is our wish, as it is our interest, to give to the Hindoos and Muhammadans a liberal share in all the duties of administration, in all offices, civil and military, and to show the people in general the incalculable advantages of a strong and settled government, which can secure life, property, and character, and the free enjoyment of all their blessings throughout the land; and give to those who perform duties as public servants ably and honestly a sure prospect of rising by gradation, a feeling of security in their tenure of office, a liberal salary while they serve, and a respectable provision for old age.

It is by a steady adherence to these principles that the Indian Civil Service has been raised to its present high character for integrity and ability; and the native army made what it really is, faithful and devoted to its rulers, and ready to serve them in any quarter of the world.[21] I deprecate any innovation upon these principles in the branches of the public service to which they have already been applied with such eminent success; and I advocate their extension to all other branches as the surest means of making them what they ought and what we must all most fervently wish them to be.

The native officers of our judicial and revenue establishments, or of our native army, are everywhere a bond of union between the governing and the governed.[22] Discharging everywhere honestly and ably their duties to their employers, they tend everywhere to secure to them the respect and affection of the people. His Highness Muhammad S'aīd Khān, the reigning Nawāb of Rāmpur, still talks with pride of the days when he was one of our Deputy Collectors in the adjoining district of Badāon, and of the useful knowledge he acquired in that office.[23] He has still one brother a Sadr Amīn in the district of Mainpurī, and another a Deputy Collector in the Hamīrpur District; and neither would resign his situation under the Honourable Company to take office in Rāmpur at three times the rate of salary, when invited to do so on the accession of the eldest brother to the 'masnad'. What they now enjoy they owe to their own industry and integrity; and they are proud to serve a government which supplies them with so many motives for honest exertion, and leaves them nothing to fear, as long as they exert themselves honestly. To be in a situation which it is generally understood that none but honest and able men can fill[24] is of itself a source of pride, and the sons of native princes and men of rank, both Hindoo and Muhammadan, everywhere prefer taking office in our judicial and revenue establishments to serving under native rulers, where everything depends entirely upon the favour or frown of men in power, and ability, industry, and integrity can secure nothing.[25]

Notes:

1. This can no longer be safely assumed as true. Newspapers now penetrate to almost every village.

2. Fyzābād (Faizābād) was the capital for a short time of the Nawāb Wazīrs of Oudh. In 1775 Āsaf-ud-daula moved his court to Lucknow. The city of Ajodhya adjoining Fyzābād is of immense antiquity.

3. In. the south of Oudh. It is not now a military station.

4. Monghyr (Mungēr) is the chief town of the district of the same name, which lies to the east of Patna.

5. August, 1811.

6. Such a spectacle is no longer to be seen in India. Four or five inconspicuous railway carriages or motor-cars now take the place of the 'magnificent fleet'.

7. The percentage is 29½.

8. All these arrangements have been changed. Military pensioners are now paid through the civil authorities of each district.

9. Wages are now generally higher.

10. This sentence might misled readers unacquainted with the details of Indian administration. Every official who satisfies the formal rules of the Accounts department gets his pension, as a matter of course, in accordance with those rules, whether his service has been able and faithful or not. The pension list is often the last refuge of incompetent and dishonest officials, to which they are gladly consigned by code-bound superiors, who cannot otherwise get rid of them. Nor am I certain that British rule 'grows more and more upon the affections' of those subject to it.

11. The author means secretaries to the Government of India or provincial governments.

12. The Sāgar and Nerbudda (Narbadā) Territories, now included in the Central Provinces.

13. The designations Sadr Amīn and Principal Sadr Amīn have been superseded by the title of Subordinate Judge. The officers referred to have only civil jurisdiction, which does not include revenue and rent causes in the United Provinces.

14. Most experienced officers will, I think, agree with me that the author was exceptionally fortunate in his experience. So far as I can make

out, the standard of integrity among the higher Indian officials has risen considerably during the last century, but is still a long way from the perfection indicated by the author's remarks.

15. These observations on the police are merely a repetition of the remarks in Chapter 69, which have been discussed in the notes to that chapter.

16. The districts in the United Provinces of Agra and Oudh are usually much smaller than those in Bengal or Madras, but even in Northern India a district with only a million of inhabitants is considered to be rather a small one. Some districts have a population of more than three millions each.

17. All has been changed. Many comparatively well paid officials of Indian birth now intervene between the District Magistrate and the small people on twenty-five rupees a month. Sometimes the District Magistrate himself is an Indian.

18. The anthor's note to this passage repeats the quotation from Hobbes's *Leviathan*, Part II, sect. 30, which has been already cited in the text, chapter 69, following [12], and need not be repeated here. The note continues: 'Almost every Thānadār in our dominions is a little Tarquin in his way, exciting the indignation of the people against his master. When we give him the proper incentives to good, we shall be able with better conscience to punish him severely for bad conduct. The interposition of the officers I propose between him and the magistrate will give him the required incentive to good conduct, at the same time that it will deprive him of all hope of concealing his "evil ways", should he continue in them.' [W. H. S.] He still manages to continue in his evil ways, and generally to conceal them.

19. This statement seems almost like sarcasm to a reader who knows what manner of men well-paid Inspectors of Police commonly are, and how they are regarded by the non-official population. They are not usually reverenced as 'protectors of the poor'.

20. The reader who is not practically acquainted with the work of administration in India will probably think that the magistrate who allows such intrigues to go on must be very careless and inefficient. But that thought, though very natural, would be unjust. The author was one of the best possible district magistrates, and yet was unable to suppress the evils which he describes, nor have the remedies which he advocated, and which have been adopted, proved effectual. The Thānadār now has generally to

pay the Inspector and the people in the District Superintendent's office, in addition to 'the native officers of the magistrate's court'.

21. We have already seen how mistaken the author was concerning the army.

22. This statement requires to be guarded by many qualifications. The author's following remarks only illustrate the well-known fact that in India official rank is ardently desired by the classes eligible for it, and carries with it great social advantages.

23. Rāmpur is the small Rohilla state within the borders of the Bareilly District, United Provinces.

24. This description of the class of officials alluded to is somewhat idealized, though it applies to a considerable proportion of the class.

25. These propositions were, doubtless, literally correct in the author's time, but they are not at all fully applicable to the existing state of affairs.

APPENDIX

THUGGEE, AND THE PART TAKEN IN ITS SUPPRESSION BY GENERAL SIR W. H. SLEEMAN, K.C.B.

NOTE BY CAPTAIN J. L. SLEEMAN, ROYAL SUSSEX REGIMENT

The religion of murder known as 'Thuggee' was established in India some centuries before the British Government first became aware of its existence, It is remarkable that, after an intercourse with India of nearly two centuries, and the exercise of sovereignty over a large part of the country for no inconsiderable period, the English should have been so ignorant of the existence and habits of a body so dangerous to the public peace. The name 'Thug' signifies a 'Deceiver', and it will be generally admitted that this term was well earned.[1] There is reason to believe that between 1799 and 1808 the practice of 'Thuggee' (Thagī) reached its height and that thousands of persons were annually destroyed by its disciples. It is interesting to note the legendary origin of this strange and horrible religion: In remote ages a demon infested the earth and devoured mankind as soon as created. The world was thus left unpeopled, until the goddess of the Thugs (Dēvī or Kālī) came to the rescue. She attacked the demon, and cut him down; but from every drop of his blood another demon arose; and though the goddess continued to cut down these rising demons, fresh broods of demons sprang from their blood, as from that of their progenitors; and the diabolical race consequently multiplied with fearful rapidity. At length, fatigued and disheartened, the goddess found it necessary to change her tactics. Accordingly, relinquishing all personal efforts for their suppression, she formed two men from perspiration brushed from her arms. To each of these men she gave a handkerchief, and with these the two assistants of the goddess were commanded to put all the demons to death without shedding a drop of blood. Her commands were immediately obeyed; and the demons were all strangled. Having strangled all the demons, the two men offered to return the handkerchiefs; but the goddess desired that they should retain them, not merely as memorials of their heroism, but as the implements of a lucrative trade in which their descendants were to labour and thrive. They were in fact commanded to strangle men as they had strangled demons.

Several generations passed before Thuggee became practised as a profession — probably for the same reason that a sportsman allows game to accumulate — but in due time it was abundantly exercised. Thus, according to the creed of the Thug, did their order arise, and thus originated their mode of operation.

The profession of a Thug, like almost everything in India, became hereditary, the fraternity, however, receiving occasional reinforcements from strangers, but these were admitted with great caution, and seldom after they had attained mature age. The Thugs were usually men seemingly occupied in most respectable and often in most responsible positions. Annually these outwardly respectable citizens and tradesmen would take the road, and sacrifice a multitude of victims for the sake of their religion and pecuniary gain. The Thug bands would assemble at fixed places of rendezvous, and before commencing their expeditions much strange ceremony had to be gone through. A sacred pickaxe was the emblem of their faith: its fashioning was wrought with quaint rites and its custody was a matter of great moment. Its point was supposed to indicate the line of route propitious to the disciples of the goddess, and it was credited with other powers equally marvellous. The brute creation afforded a vast fund of instruction upon every proceeding. The ass, jackal, wolf, deer, hare, dog, cat, owl, kite, crow, partridge, jay, and lizard, all served to furnish good or bad omens to a Thug on the war-path. For the first week of the expedition fasting and general discomfort were insisted on, unless the first murder took place within that period. Women were never murdered unless their slaughter was unavoidable (i.e. when they were thought to suspect the cause of the disappearance of their men-folk). Children of the murdered were often adopted by the Thugs, and the boys were initiated in due course in the horrid rites of Thuggee. Men skilled in the practice of digging and concealing graves were always attached to each Thug gang. These were able to prepare graves in anticipation of a murder, and to effectually conceal all trace of the crime after they were occupied. To assist the grave-diggers in this duty all roads used by Thugs had selected places upon them at which murders were always carried out if possible. The Thugs would speak of such places with the same affection and enthusiasm as other men would of the most delightful scenes of their early life.

It was these people, versed in deceit and surrounded by a thousand obstacles to conviction, that General Sir W. H. Sleeman so nobly set out to exterminate. Within seven years of his first commencing the suppression of Thuggee it had practically ceased to exist as a religion; and he had the privilege of seeing it entirely suppressed as such before giving up this work for the Residentship at Lucknow.

He was described when taking over the latter appointment as follows: 'He had served in India nearly forty years. His work had been of the best. He had done more than any one to suppress 'Thuggee' finally, and had a knowledge of the Indian character and language possessed by very few. He was personally popular with all classes of Indians, and respected, feared, and trusted by all.'

SUPPLEMENTARY NOTES BY THE EDITOR

Captain J. L. Sleeman, who had intended to contribute an account in some detail of his grandfather's operations for the suppression of Thuggee, has been ordered on active service, and consequently has been unable to write more than the short note printed above.

The editor thinks it desirable to supplement Captain Sleeman's observations by certain additional remarks.

The earliest historical notice of Thuggee appears to be the statement in the History of Fīrōz Shāh Tughlak (1351-88) by a contemporary author that at some time or other in the reign of that sovereign about one thousand Thugs were arrested in Delhi, on the denunciation of an informer. The Sultan, with misplaced clemency, refused to sanction the execution of any of the prisoners, whom he shipped off to Lakhnauti or Gaur in Bengal, where they were let loose. (Elliot and Dowson, *Hist. of India*, iii. 141.) That absurd proceeding may well have been the origin of the system of river Thuggee in Bengal, which possibly may be still practised.

The next mention of Thugs refers to the reign of Akbar (1556-1605). Both Meadows Taylor and Balfour affirm that many Thugs were then executed, and according to Balfour, they numbered five hundred and belonged to the Etawah District, I have not succeeded in finding any mention of the fact in the histories of Akbar—the memory of the event may be preserved only by oral tradition. Etawah, between the Ganges and Jumna, in the province of Agra, has always been notorious for Thuggee and cognate crime.

In the year 1666, towards the close of Shahjahān's reign, the traveller de Thevenot noted that the road between Delhi and Agra was infested by Thugs. His words are:

'The cunningest Robbers in the World are in that Countrey. They use a certain slip with a running-noose, which they can cast with so much slight about a Man's Neck, when they are within reach of him, that they never fail; so that they strangle him in a trice.' (English transl., 1686, Part III, p. 41.)

After the capture of Seringapatam in 1799 the attention of the Company's government was drawn to the prevalence of Thuggee. In 1810 the bodies of thirty victims were found in wells between the Ganges and Jumna, and in

1816 Dr. Sherwood published a paper entitled 'On the Murderers called Phānsigars', *sc.* 'stranglers', in the *Madras Journal of Literature and Science,* which was reprinted in *Asiatic Researches,* vol. xiii (1820). Various officers then made unsystematic efforts to suppress the stranglers, but effectual operations were deferred until 1829. During the years 1881 and 1832 the existence of the Thug organization became generally known, and intense excitement was aroused throughout India. The Konkan, or narrow strip of lowlands between the Western Ghāts and the sea, was the only region in the empire not infested by the Thugs. (See H. H. Wilson in supplement to Mill, *Hist. of British India,* ed. 1858, vol. ix, p. 213; Balfour, *Cyclopaedia of India,* 3rd ed., 1885, *s.v.* Thug; and Crooke, *Things Indian,* Murray, 1906, *s.v.* Thuggee.)

The records summarized above prove that the Thug organization existed continuously on a large scale from the early part of the fourteenth century until Sir William Sleeman's time, that is to say, for more than five centuries. In all probability its origin was much more ancient, but records are lacking. It is said that a sculpture representing a Thug strangulation exists among the sculptures at Ellora executed in the eighth century. No such sculpture, however, is mentioned in the detailed account of the Ellora caves by Dr. Burgess.

The magnitude of the organization with which Sleeman grappled is indicated by the following figures.

During the years 1831-7 3,266 Thugs were disposed of one way or another, of whom 412 were hanged, and 483 were admitted as approvers. Amīr Alī, whose confessions are recorded in Meadows Taylor's fascinating book, *The Confessions of a Thug,* written in 1837 and first published in 1839, proudly admitted having taken part in the murders of 719 persons, and regretted that an interruption of his career by twelve years' imprisonment in Oudh had prevented him from completing a full thousand of victims. He regarded his profession as affording sport of the most exciting kind possible.

V. A. S.

Notes:

1. Pronounced 'T'ug', a hard cerebral *t*, with some aspiration.

INDEX

Bālā Bāi
Balban, Sultan
Baldēo (Bāladeva), (1) brother of Krishna, (2) Singh, defender of
Bharatpur
Bali Rājā, a demon
Ballabhgarh
Ballot Act
Bamboos
Bamhauri, in Orchhā State
Bāna-linga
Bānda, town
Baniyā, defined
Banjāra tribe
Bankers, Indian private
Banks, Presidency
Banyan tree
Bāolī, defined
Barber, as match-maker
Barlow, Sir George
Barnes, Sir B., C.-in-C-.
Baroda, Gaikwār of
Barrackpore, mutiny at
Barwā Sāgar
Basalt
Basant festival
Basrah (Bussorah)
Batavia, capture of
Bathing, religions merit of, l
Bāwarias of Muzaffarnagar
Beef, eating of
Bees, at Marble Rocks
Bēgam Sarāi at Delhi
Belemnites, fossil
Benares, city province
Bengal, permanent settlement of, Islam in, territories, defined,
river thuggee in
Bentinck, Lord William
Berār, kingdom
Bernier, (1) François, on suttee historical work of, (2) Major
Betel leaf
Betiyā (Bettia), Christian colony at.
Bhāgavata Purāna
Bhagvān = Vishnu = God
Bharat, brother of Rāma
Bharatpur (Bhurtpore), sieges of
Bherāghāt (-garh)
Bhīl tribes

Husain.
Hyderābād Contingent
Hyphasis (Biās) river .

Iblīs, the devil
Ibn Batuta, traveller
Ibrāhīm Lodi, Sultan
Id-ul-Bakr festival
Īltutmish, Sultan, buildings of tomb of
Imam Mashhadī, tomb of
Imām-ud-dīn Ghazzālī . Imperial Service Troops
Impressment
India, people of, vi population of
Indore State
Indra, god
Industries
Infanticide
Inheritance, law of
Invalid establishment
Iron mines pillar of Delhi
Islam in Lower Bengal
Isle of France (Mauritius)
Itimād-ud-daula.

Jabalpur, see Jubbulpore
Jack-tree
Jagannāth, shrine of
Jāgīrdārs
Jahānārā Bēgam, tomb of
Jahāngīr, (1) emperor mother of, birth of (2) Mirzā, tomb of
Jain statues at Gwālior
Jaipur State, xxxii
Jaitpur, Rāj of
Jalāl-ud-dīn, Fīrōz Shāh Khiljī
Jālaun State
Jamāldehī Thugs
Jang Bahādur, Sir
Jasmine
Jāts (Jats) outrages of, and Rājpūts
Java, conquest of
Jaxartes, river
Jesuit missionaries
Jesus, inscription quoting
Jeswant Rāo Holkar
Jhajjar, Nawāb of
Jhānsī State